TRANSACT-SQL DESK REFERENCE

This book is dedicated to my daughter,
Vicky (Torie) Sullivan,
my inspiration and my friend.

TRANSACT-SQL DESK REFERENCE

Deac Lancaster

PRENTICE HALL
PROFESSIONAL TECHNICAL REFERENCE
UPPER SADDLE RIVER, NJ 07458
WWW.PHPTR.COM

Library of Congress Cataloging-in-Publication Data

Lancaster, Deac.
Transact-SQL desk reference / Deac Lancaster
p. cm.
Includes bibliographical references and index.
ISBN 0-13-029339-3 (pbk.)
1. SQL server. 2. Database management. I. Title.

QA76.9.D3L348 2003
005.75'85—dc22

2003059668

Editorial/production supervision: *BooksCraft, Inc.*
Cover design director: *Jerry Votta*
Cover designer: *Nina Scuderi*
Art director: *Gail Cocker-Bogusz*
Manufacturing buyer: *Alexis Heydt-Long*
Publisher: *Jeff Pepper*
Editorial assistant: *Linda Ramagnano*
Marketing manager: *Debby Van Dijk*
Full-service production manager: *Anne R. Garcia*

Publishing as Prentice Hall Professional Technical Reference
Upper Saddle River, New Jersey 07458

Prentice Hall books are widely used by corporations and government agencies for training, marketing, and resale.

**Prentice Hall PTR offers excellent discounts on this book when ordered in quantity for bulk purchases or special sales. For more information,
please contact:
U.S. Corporate and Government Sales
1-800-382-3419
corpsales@pearsontechgroup.com**

For sales outside of the U.S., please contact:
International Sales
1-317-581-3793
international@pearsontechgroup.com

Printed in the United States of America
1st printing

ISBN 0-13-029339-3

Pearson Education LTD.
Pearson Education Australia PTY, Limited
Pearson Education Singapore, Pte. Ltd.
Pearson Education North Asia Ltd.
Pearson Education Canada, Ltd.
Pearson Educación de Mexico, S.A. de C.V.
Pearson Education—Japan
Pearson Education Malaysia, Pte. Ltd.

CONTENTS

PREFACE

For years I've wanted a single reference book that contained the Microsoft SQL Server SQL syntax for most of my common questions when writing SQL programs. I've needed one book that had not only the specific syntax for Microsoft SQL Server SQL, called Transact-SQL, with examples but also had some hints about the ANSI Standard SQL syntax. So when Mark Taub of Prentice Hall suggested that I write such a book, I was very receptive to the idea.

This book has a lot in common with Microsoft SQL Server on-line documentation called "Books Online," but it has both more than *and* less than what's in BOL. Wording is changed in places in a hope to add clarity. It was omitted when a feature is very infrequently used. Also, many different examples are added

This book is intended as a handy reference for SQL programmers needing to know how to construct correct SQL statements that will run on Microsoft SQL Server 2000 in a way to maximize portability. Syntax and examples are given using Microsoft SQL Server 2000 SQL with comments when the syntax varies from ANSI SQL.

This book concentrates on Microsoft SQL Server 2000 implementation of SQL features from the ANSI SQL-92 standard covering Data Definition Language and Data Manipulation Language. These features are commonly referred to as 4GL (fourth-generation language) constructs. The Microsoft SQL Server 2000 implementation of SQL is called Transact-SQL (T-SQL). It encompasses both these 4GL features plus 3GL programming features, which include IF-ELSE and looping and other constructs.

An introduction to these 3GL features is also included, but a more thorough coverage can be found in references listed in the bibliography, such the following:

Professional SQL Server 2000 Programming by Robert Vieira and
Advanced Transact-SQL for SQL Server 2000 by Itzik Ben-Gan and Tom Moreau.

There is also a section on Transaction Control and another on Backup, Restore and Recovery.

This book strives to be a handy reference covering the 4GL language and 3GL extensions available in Transact-SQL statements and constructs that one needs to do database work with Microsoft SQL Server.

The interested reader can find much more detail on the ANSI SQL-99 standard that updates the SQL-92 standard, in *SQL-99 Complete, Really* by Peter Gulutzan and Trudy Pelzer.

Throughout the book, I use the following terms:

SQL-92 refers to the 1992 ANSI/ISO SQL Standard, also known as SQL2.
SQL-99 refers to the 1999 ANSI/ISO SQL Standard, also known as SQL3.

Except for Chapter 1, which is provided in tutorial form as a quick RDBMS review, and Appendix B, which covers some Advanced Queries, this material is written as a reference, assuming previous exposure to SQL concepts. The book is intended to answer the question of “How exactly do I write a statement to do a certain job?” as well as “What is the full syntax with examples?”

It is also essential that the reader refer to the documentation on Web sites, such as *www. microsoft.com/sql* and the knowledge base there.

Clearly this book contains much information derived from Microsoft SQL Server Books Online, an excellent resource and one which should be used frequently. This book contains less of some detail than the 1000-plus page Books Online but has more explanation of what I consider to be core features and more examples of useful applications of these features. Together this book and Books Online make a powerful combination.

Additionally, this book gives information about standard ANSI SQL and will comment on which MSS SQL statements do not abide by the standard so that your SQL code may maximize portability to other relational database management systems (RDBMSs).

Sometimes SQL Server has two correct ways of doing a job, one that abides by the standard and is more portable and one that does not. For example, SQL Server has to declare column aliases and two forms of doing an inner join. In both cases the ANSI standard form is just as efficient but more portable.

There are occasions, however, where no ANSI standard approach exists in SQL Server, so it's useful to know that such code must be modified to transport it to another RDBMS. An example is the DATETIME data type in SQL Server that must be changed to DATE for use with other systems (except with Sybase, from which SQL Server was derived).

This is not intended to be an exhaustive treatise on all the nooks and crannies of either ANSI SQL or of Microsoft SQL Server 2000 Transact-SQL. It is intended to be a handy reference that covers the syntax of the SQL statements most of the time for most SQL users.

Happy databasing!

How to Use this Book

This book was written as a reference for experienced SQL programmers who will usually go directly to the Table of Contents or the Index and then to the section of interest. Except for the Chapter 1 tutorial review, topics are organized in chapters by purpose and function, for example, DDL, DML, SELECT, and so forth.

All examples were tested on Microsoft SQL Server 2000.

Chapter 1 is a tutorial summary of relational database management system background, terminology and concepts to serve as a refresher. The reader who is out of practice on these subjects may find it useful to read or skim this chapter before proceeding. Otherwise Chapter 1 may be skipped.

The remaining chapters contain the reference material intended for direct lookup of the subject sought.

Chapter 1—RDBMS Concepts: A Primer

Chapter 2—SQL Building Blocks and Server Settings

Chapter 3—Data Definition Language and Security

Chapter 4—Data Manipulation Language: INSERT, UPDATE, DELETE, SELECT

Chapter 5—Transaction Control, Backup and Restore and Transact-SQL Programming

Appendix A—Transact-SQL Keywords and System Stored Procedures

Appendix B— SELECT: Advanced Queries

Notation

The notation in this book includes a version of BNF (Backus-Nauer Form) to provide SQL syntax definitions. This notation is similar to that used in the Microsoft SQL Server 2000 Books Online.

`< >` A character string enclosed in angle brackets is the name of a syntactic element of the SQL language. The angle brackets are just delimiters; do not include them when constructing an SQL statement.

`: : =` The definition operator, used in a production rule to separate the element defined by the rule (on the left of ::=) from its definition on the right.

`[]` Enclose optional elements in a formula. The portion of the formula within the brackets may be explicitly specified or may be omitted. (Do not type the brackets.)

{ } Group required elements in a formula. Often used with "|" (see example). (Do not type the braces.)

| The alternative operator (OR) used to separate two or more alternatives. You may use any single choice among the alternatives.

Example: `[ itemA | itemB ]` - you may choose itemA or itemB or neither.

Example: `{ itemA | itemB }` - you must choose itemA or itemB.

[,...n] Indicates that the previous formula element may be repeated zero or more times with occurrences separated by commas.

[...n] Indicates that the previous formula element may be repeated zero or more times with occurrences separated by blanks (spaces).

`Code` Fixed-width font for code examples and for syntax where case is significant.

`CAPITALS` SQL keywords and SQL functions will be shown capitalized in fixed-width font in syntax and examples.

Bold Name of database objects including databases, tables, columns, indexes, stored procedures and text that must be typed exactly as shown.

italics Argument values, parameter values and options to be provided by the user. In text, italics are used for terms the first time they are defined as well as for filenames and directories.

underlined text Default value

Updated Books Online

To download the updated Microsoft SQL Server 2000 Books Online, go to

www.microsoft.com/SQL/techinfo/productdoc/2000/books.asp

This updated version may be installed either to replace an existing Books Online installation or as stand-alone, with or without a SQL Server installation.

Evaluation Copy of Microsoft SQL Server

You can download a free evaluation copy of some RDBMS software. All of the products listed here are copyrighted such that you can not distribute the product without permission. Carefully read the license and use agreement.

Microsoft SQL Server

www.microsoft.com/sql/
Click "Evaluation," or go directly to
www.microsoft.com/sql/evaluation/trial/2000/default.asp

At my last check, this free evaluation version only included the SQL Server 2000 Enterprise Edition which requires NT Server or higher operating system.

The SQL Server 2000 Personal Edition that runs on Windows ME series and Windows NT Workstation (Professional) series is not available for free download.

About Prentice Hall Professional Technical Reference

With origins reaching back to the industry's first computer science publishing program in the 1960s, and formally launched as its own imprint in 1986, Prentice Hall Professional Technical Reference (PH PTR) has developed into the leading provider of technical books in the world today. Our editors now publish over 200 books annually, authored by leaders in the fields of computing, engineering, and business.

Our roots are firmly planted in the soil that gave rise to the technical revolution. Our bookshelf contains many of the industry's computing and engineering classics: Kernighan and Ritchie's *C Programming Language*, Nemeth's *UNIX System Adminstration Handbook*, Horstmann's *Core Java*, and Johnson's *High-Speed Digital Design*.

PH PTR acknowledges its auspicious beginnings while it looks to the future for inspiration. We continue to evolve and break new ground in publishing by providing today's professionals with tomorrow's solutions.

PRENTICE HALL PTR

Acknowledgments

Many thanks to Mark Taub and Jeff Pepper, both of Prentice Hall; to Mark for getting me started and to Jeff for keeping it going and providing so much help about writing style.

My gratitude goes to Ellie Quigley, Queen of Perl and Shell books, for inspiring me to attempt to write a book and for her help in doing so. She's a true friend and scholar.

Shari Plummer did an excellent job of technical editing, noticing faults that completely missed my eyes and adding suggestions to enhance the usefulness of the book. Thank you very much, Shari.

Don MacLaren and Amy Jolin did the professional editing with great patience, teaching me how to compose ideas more effectively. You two are the best. Thanks so much.

I owe a big debt for all of the love and support from TTA—Torie, Tim and Amy Sullivan, my daughter, son-in-law and granddaughter. Talk about inspiration! They are the greatest.

I want to thank John and Kristine Wallack for helping me keep perspective by continuing to take me hiking and mountain climbing in places like Colorado, Utah, California, Grand Canyon, Nepal, Peru and the Alps.

Thanks to Boulder Bob Olson for acting as technical advisor on geographic and historic matters. Who would have thought that the continent with the highest average elevation would be Antarctica?

Chuck and Jean Carnell continue to be stalwarts in keeping me grounded in California.

Thanks lastly to Mary and Mike Trinkle, my kindred spirits who are with me always.

CHAPTER 1

RDBMS Concepts — A Primer

This chapter is introductory and tutorial in nature and should be bypassed if you are interested only in the reference material contained in the chapters that follow.

The chapter begins with a summary of relational database management system (RDBMS) terminology and concepts. If you are out of practice on these subjects, you may find it useful to read or at least skim this chapter before proceeding.

1.1 DATABASE MANAGEMENT SYSTEM BACKGROUND

A *Database Management System* (DBMS) is a software package whose purpose is to store, modify and retrieve large amounts of data.

A Relational Database Management System (RDBMS) can be thought of as a DBMS consisting of one or more *collections of tables*. Today's commercial RDBMS products

- are organized as collections of tables, and also
- use ANSI-standard SQL language
- use client-server architecture

1.1.1 Brief History of Relational DBMSs and SQL Language

Table 1-1 summarizes the history of RDBMSs and SQL language development.

Table 1-1 Summary of RDBMS History

1970	Dr. E. F. Codd of IBM Research Lab in San Jose published "A Relational Model of Data for Large Shared Data Banks." This paper is considered to be the definition and birth of the RDBMS.
1974	Research by Don Chamberlin and others at IBM San Jose Research Lab produced the origin of SQL called SEQUEL for Structured English Query Language. The name was soon changed from SEQUEL to SQL because the former was copyrighted. "SQL" is commonly pronounced both as the letters "S.Q.L." and as the word "sequel" from its original name.
1981	Oracle was the first to produce a commercial RDBMS. Recent releases of Oracle are Oracle 8.0 and 8i ("i" for "Internet") in late 1990's.
1982	IBM released its first RDBMS known as SQL/DS; in 1983 IBM changed the name of their product to DB2.
1980's	Other vendors, including Sybase, Informix and Ingres, released RDBMS products in the 1980's.
1988	Microsoft and Sybase rewrote the Sybase RDBMS to run on OS/2 and again in 1992 to Windows NT as Microsoft SQL Server 4.2. Later revisions include Microsoft SQL Server 7.0 in 1998 and Microsoft SQL Server 2000 (a k a 8.0) in the year 2000.
1990's	Progress on scalability and added capabilities of RDBMSs grew considerably, especially as hardware speed and capacity increased and prices decreased. Some object-oriented variations of RDBMS products came on the market in the late 1990's.

1.2 SQL LANGUAGE

SQL is the international standard database programming language and has been called the language for "Intergalactic Dataspeak." The current standard version of SQL used by commercial relational database management vendors is SQL–92, as in Table 1-2. The version of SQL used by Microsoft SQL Server is called Transact–SQL and it is SQL–92 compliant.

1.2.1 Where Does SQL Fit In?

SQL is the standard language used by a database client to communicate with the database management system to create, modify, delete and read both data and database objects such as table definitions.

Figure 1-1 depicts *client-server architecture*: the *client* program (running on the client machine) is one tier and the *server* program (on the server machine) is the second. The client provides a user interface, and the server responds to client requests by returning data from the repository. Business rules usually should be

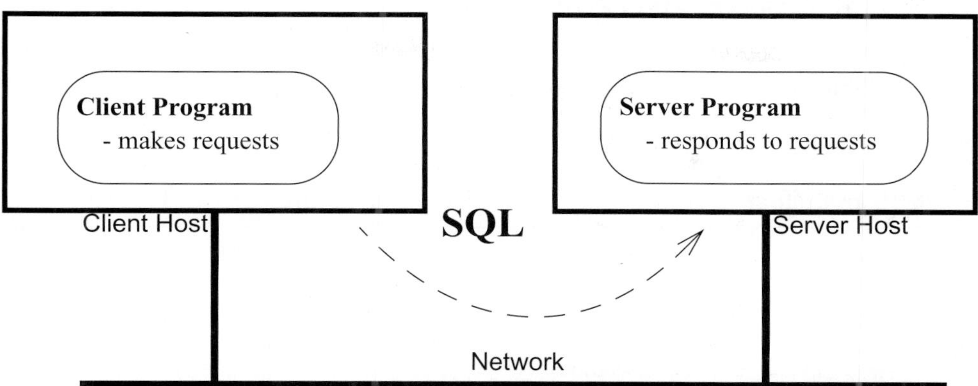

Figure 1-1 SQL and client-server architecture.

enforced at the server, though early checking at the client increases performance and is more convenient to the user.

1.2.2 Chronology of SQL Standards

The SQL language has been standardized and approved by the American National Standards Institute (ANSI), which has published the standards shown in Table 1-2.

Table 1-2 ANSI SQL Standards

1986	**SQL-86** was approved by ANSI, but no one really noticed. Needed immediate revision.
1989	**SQL-89** a k a **SQL1** was approved by ANSI.
1992	**SQL-92** a k a **SQL2** was approved by ANSI. SQL2 significantly expanded the functionality and became widely accepted by commercial RDBMS vendors. Many items in SQL2 are left as "implementation defined." SQL-92 has three levels: entry, intermediate and full.
1999	**SQL-99** was approved by ANSI in 1999, as standard 9075-2-1999, commonly called **SQL3**. It removed only arcane, unused features, so ANSI-92 compliant RDMBSs remain compliant with SQL-99. It also added some features such as triggers to the standard.

Each commercial RDBMS vendor has its own version of SQL, but most if not all comply with ANSI SQL-92 at the entry level.

Microsoft SQL Server 2000 supports ANSI SQL-92 at the entry level. The focus of this book is on Microsoft SQL Server 2000 "Transact-SQL" which includes the SQL-92 statements as well as procedural language extensions (see Introduction to Transact-SQL Programming, page 606).

1.2.3 SQL Server 2000 Product Line

Table 1-3 delineates the MSS 2K product line. Updated product information is available at *www.microsoft.com/sql/evaluation/overview/default.asp.*

Table 1-3 Editions of Microsoft SQL Server

MSS 2K Edition	Platforms
Personal	Windows 98/ME, Windows NT 4.0, Windows 2000, Windows Server 2003 all editions and Windows XP Professional. Windows 98/Millennium, Windows NT 4.0 (Service Pack 5+) or Windows 2000, Windows XP Professional, Windows Server 2003 all editions.
Standard	Windows NT 4.0 Server/Enterprise Edition (SP5) or Windows 2000 Server or higher, Windows Server 2003 all editions.
Enterprise	Same platforms as for Standard (an NT 4.0 installation is not full featured).
Developer	Same platforms as for Standard plus Windows NT 4.0 Workstation, Windows 2000 Professional and Windows XP Professional. Used by programmers developing applications that use SQL Server 2000 as their data store. Supports all of the Enterprise Edition features but is licensed for use only as a development and test system, not as a production server.
Windows CE	Windows SQL Server CE. Used as the data store on Windows CE devices. Capable of replicating data with any edition of SQL Server 2000 to keep Windows CE data synchronized with the primary database.
Enterprise Evaluation	Windows NT 4.0 Server (SP5), Windows 2000 Professions/Server (SP1), Windows XP Home/Professional. A full-featured version, downloadable free from the web at *www.microsoft.com/sql/evaluation/trial/default.asp.* It will stop running 120 days after downloading.
MSDE 2000	Same platforms as Personal edition. MSDE (Microsoft Data Engine) is a MSS 2K database engine (no clients) available as redistributable API engine with Visual Studio and MS Office. Limit of 2-GB database size and other restrictions. See link above.

Installing MSS 7.0 and MSS 2000 on the Same Host

An *instance* is a single installation of SQL Server on a host machine. Each instance has its own copy of the server engine program, sqlservr.exe, which runs as a single process managing all of the data and handling all incoming client requests for the instance.

A client makes a connection to an MSS instance to access the data on that instance. By default, the name of the first MSS instance is the same as the host name.

Only one instance of MSS 7.0 may be installed on a single host, but multiple instances of MSS 2000 may be installed on a single host. In addition, a single instance of MSS 7.0 plus one or more of MSS 2000 may be installed on one host. To avoid problems, install MSS 7.0 first and then MSS 2000. (One such problem is that installing MSS 2000 first and then MSS 7.0 causes the clients, most importantly Enterprise Manager, to be overwritten with the 7.0 version of EM. Since the 7.0 version cannot talk to MSS 2000, you need the MSS 2000 EM to talk to both. But you can't just install the MSS 2000 clients since the system thinks they've already been installed.)

Don't fight it, just install 7.0 first and then 2000.

It is worth noting that thus far I have only found it useful to install multiple instances of MSS on a single host for test and development purposes. For production it is usually desirable to put each instance on a separate machine to improve performance.

File locations (default)

```
MSS 7.0
C:\MSSQL7

MSS 2000
Common Files:  C:\Program Files\Microsoft SQL
  Server
Default Instance:C:\Program Files\Microsoft SQL
  Server\MSSQL
Second Instance CAT2:C:\Program Files\Microsoft SQL
  Server\MSSQL$CAT2
```

1.3 CLIENT-SERVER ARCHITECTURE

Client-Server, or two-tier, Architecture consists of a

- **client program—**makes requests, e.g., Enterprise Manager, Query Analyzer, VB or C Program
- **server program—**responds to those requests

The client program usually has a *graphical user interface* (*GUI*) and may run on the same computer, or machine or *host*, as the server program. The client may run on a different host than does the server as long as they have some network connection.

The server program often does not include a GUI as part of its program and is managed only by using a client. The MSS 2K database engine has no direct user interface and is managed through the Enterprise Manager GUI or an SQL client such as Query Analyzer, OSQL or ISQL. See Figure 1-2.

When one refers to a client or server without further qualification, it should be understood to mean the client or server program unless it's clear from the context that the machine is intended. If confusion might result, specify client program or client machine (host).

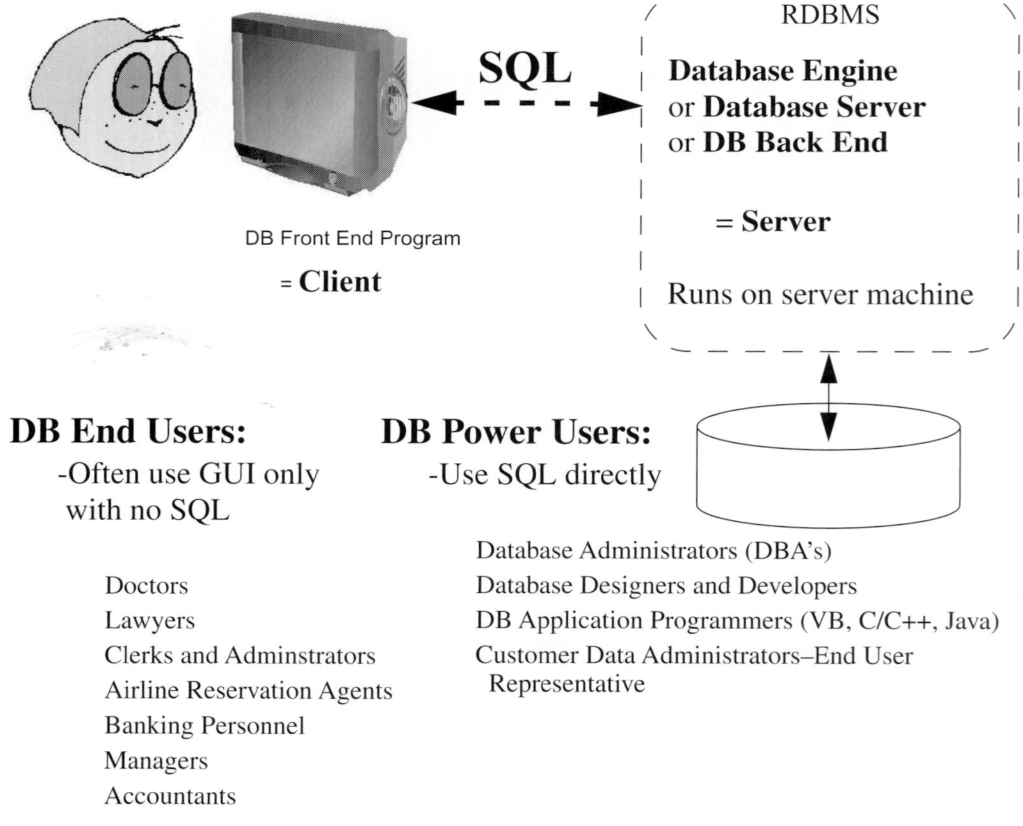

Figure 1-2 Two-tier client-server architecture.

Notice also that in doing its job, a server of one service may need to make a request of a second server. For example, a database server may make a request of a domain name server. In this case, the database server acts as a domain name client.

1.3.1 Three-Tier Client-Server Architecture

Three-tier architecture occurs frequently in database applications.

Three-tier architecture has an intermediate program, often called an application server, which repackages requests from the client to send to the ultimate server. See Figure 1-3. The application server frequently runs on the same machine as the database server.

Three-tier architecture features include:

- Client-to-application server program language is application dependent.
- Application server-to-database server communication is via SQL.
- Application server has primary responsibility for enforcing Business Rules.

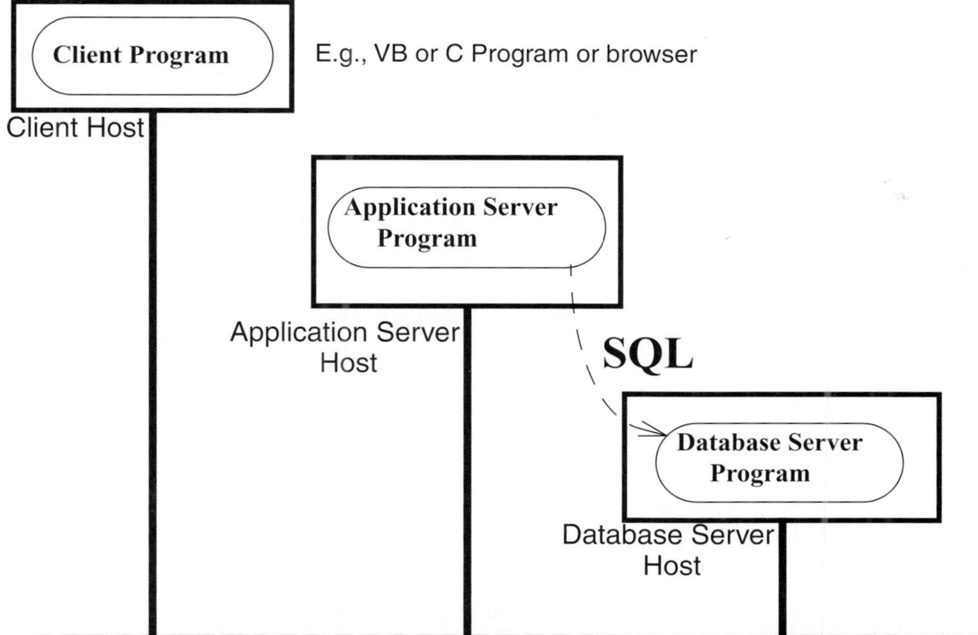

Figure 1-3 Three-tier client-server architecture.

Note that both client and database servers often redundantly enforce the same business rule for convenience and performance while maintaining reliability. Many Internet applications are three-tier client servers, the client being a browser, the ultimate thin client.

1.4 RDBMS: TABLES AND DATABASES

Officially, an RDBMS is a software package designed to manage large amounts of data organized as **collections of tables**. Commercial RDBMS characteristics include

- Being organized as collection(s) of tables
- Using client-server architecture
- Being ANSI SQL compliant, usually SQL-92 at the entry level

SQL Server specifies a single collection of related tables as a database, which contains the data tables, system tables and other objects, such as views, indexes, stored procedures and triggers used in operations on the data. Table 1-4 represents a collection of two tables: **emps** and **depts.**

Table 1-4 Collection of Two Tables

COMPANY ORGANIZATION				
emps				
ename	**empid**	**deptno**	**telnum**	**sales_amt**
Mary Smith	5555	100	5678	
Sammy Sosa	2222	102	2345	200
Bill Johnson	4444	101		
Mary Smith	7777	101	7890	400
Suzy Smith	1111	102		

depts			
dept_name	**deptno**	**mgr_emp_id**	**dept_telnum**
Accounting	100	1111	9100

Table 1-4 Collection of Two Tables (cont.)

depts			
Engineering	101	7777	9101
Sales	102	2222	9102

We will create these tables in exercises at the end of this chapter. Do not confuse this emps with the **employee** table of the pubs sample database provided with SQL Server.

There will be many *relationships* between data in different tables; for example, each employee in the **emps** table is assigned to a department that appears in the **depts** table. There will be many *relationships*.

1.4.1 Tables in a Database

A table is a named multiset of rows. A **set** is an unordered collection of objects with common properties that do not contain duplicates. A **multiset** is the same, but it allows duplicates. The table is the basic unit of an RDBMS.

A table consists of columns and rows. A **column** is a column name, unique within a table, and an associated *data type*. A **row** is a *list of values,* one value assigned for each column defined for the table. See Figure 1-4.

The minimum definition of a table includes its name and the definition of the columns that it contains. Each column is defined by its column name and the type of the data that it contains. The following SQL statement creates a new, empty table called **emps** as in Table 1-4.

```
CREATE TABLE emps (
    ename       VARCHAR(15) NOT NULL
,   empid       INT PRIMARY KEY
,   deptno      INT
,   telnum      CHAR(4)
,   hiredate    DATETIME
);
```

1.4.1.1 Table vs. Relation

There is an academic difference between the terms *relation* and *table*: A relation is a set, which means it contains no duplicates and no inherent order. In RDBMS implementations, a table may be allowed to have duplicates if it has no primary key (or other uniqueness constraint) and thus technically may be a multiset. We will use table.

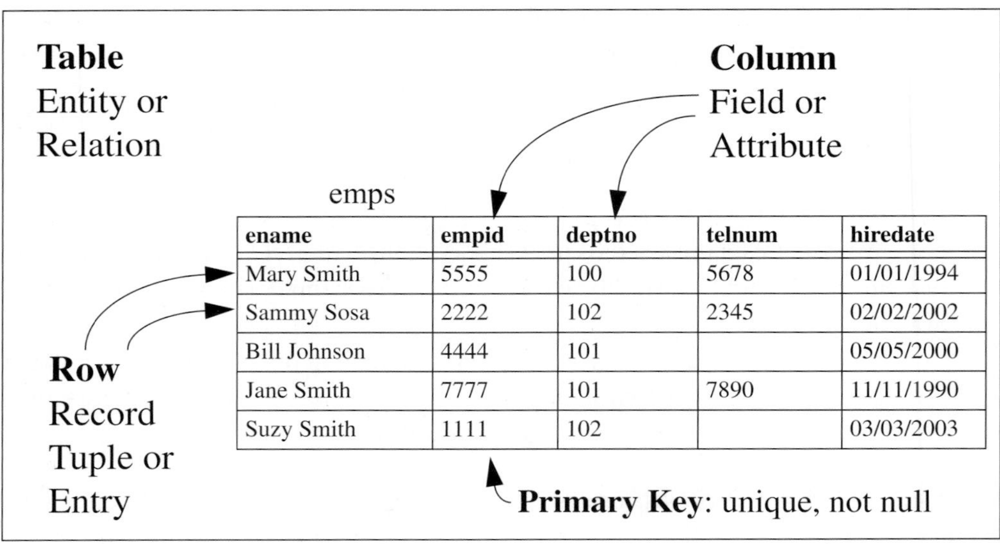

ename	empid	deptno	telnum	hiredate
Mary Smith	5555	100	5678	01/01/1994
Sammy Sosa	2222	102	2345	02/02/2002
Bill Johnson	4444	101		05/05/2000
Jane Smith	7777	101	7890	11/11/1990
Suzy Smith	1111	102		03/03/2003

Figure 1-4 Example table: **emps**.

A table may also be described as a named container for data consisting of the following.

- An ordered sequence of one or more columns, each made up of
  - –column name
  - –data type of the data allowed in the column
- A multiset of zero or more rows of data, where
  - –every column of each row contains a data value (possibly NULL)

The *degree* of a table is the number of columns defined for the table. The *cardinality* of a table is the number of rows currently in the table.

1.4.1.2 Columns

While *column* is the most common name used, the terms *field* and *attribute* are also used interchangeably. A column can be thought of as a name paired with a data type. The columns of a row are ordered.

1.4.1.3 Rows

The terms *row*, *record*, *tuple* and *entry* are interchangeable for our purposes. A row can be thought of as an ordered list of data values (possibly including NULL), with one value for each column defined for the table.

Commercial database users tend to use the terms *table*, *column* and *row* while academic and theory-based users tend to use the terms *relation*, *attribute* and *tuple*.

1.4.1.4 Primary Key

The *primary key* of a table is the set of columns specified by the table owner to uniquely identify each row in the table. Specifying a primary key for a table has three results: The database imposes both **UNIQUE** and **NOT NULL** constraints on the primary key column(s) and also creates an **INDEX** on them. A primary key is not required by the RDBMS for every table, but it is suggested for most tables.

1.4.1.5 Foreign Key

A *foreign key* is a column (or set of columns) of one table, often called the child table, which refers to the primary key of the parent table. A foreign key establishes a relationship between child and parent tables. As an example: In Figure 1-4, each employee row has a **deptno** to indicate which department that employee belongs to. The **deptno** column in the **emps** table, the child, is a foreign key referring to the primary key in **depts**, the parent. Department-specific information such as **dept_name** and **dept_telnum** is in the depts table.

***Question*:** What is the name of Sammy Sosa's department?

1.4.1.6 Identifiers

Identifiers are names a database user assigns to database objects such as tables and columns. An **identifier** must start with an upper or lower case alphabetic character, followed by any number of alphabetic, numeric or underscore ("_") characters.

Answer: The name of Sammy Sosa's department is Sales. In **emps** Sammy's **deptno** value is 102 and in **depts**, **deptno** 102 is the Sales department.

1.4.2 Databases in Microsoft SQL Server

A database in MSS is a named collection of tables with the data, views, indexes, stored procedures, triggers and any other related objects (including user-defined types) used with those tables.

Each successful installation of MSS creates one named *instance* of SQL Server. The default name of the first instance is the same as the host name. MSS

2K supports more than one instance on one host whose name is provided by the installer during installation. For example, I installed two instances of MSS 2K on host AMY; the first instance took the name AMY and I provided the name AMY2 for the second instance.

An instance of MSS has one database engine which is the process that runs when the instance is started (the server process is visible as **sqlservr.exe** in the Windows Task Manager). Also, an MSS instance contains several databases, collections of related tables and other objects. A default MSS installation has four system databases and two sample user databases.

The MSS System Databases include

- **Master:** Contains instance wide system tables, stored procedures, etc. Master database is essential for the server to start and run.
- **Model:** Template for new databases
- **Msdb:** Used by SQL agent to store jobs, etc.
- **Tempdb:** Scratch pad area used by all databases to hold temporary tables, etc.

The MSS Sample User Databases include:

- **Northwind:** Sample database based on sales of an import-export company
- **Pubs:** Sample database based on book publishing company

These sample user databases are used in many examples in this and other books and in Books Online and provide a good learning environment for all users. The sample databases are usually removed from a production MSS instance, though the system databases must remain.

You may list all databases of an instance by connecting an SQL client to it and executing:

SQL
`EXEC sp_databases`

SQL (cont.)		
Result		
DATABASE_NAME	DATABASE_SIZE	REMARKS
--------------------------	------------------------	-
master	17728	NULL
model	1152	NULL
msdb	13568	NULL
Northwind	4032	NULL
pubs	2368	NULL
tempdb	8704	NULL

See "Server, Database and Session Settings," page 174, for further discussion.

Figure 1-5 shows the relationships between the tables of Table 1-4 graphically. Primary key columns are identified by the key symbol.

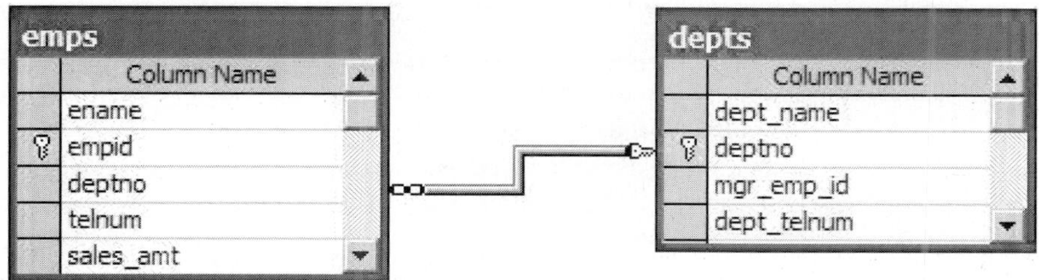

A Database Diagram may be created in the MSS Enterprise Manager under *ServerName* – **Databases** – *DatabaseName* – **Diagrams**
Right click on **Diagrams**, select "New Database Diagram" and follow the instructions.
Also see "Database Designer" in Books Online.

Figure 1-5 Database design.

1.5 THE SQL LANGUAGE AND MSS'S TRANSACT-SQL

The Microsoft SQL Server implementation of the SQL language is called *Transact-SQL*. Programming languages, such as Visual Basic (VB), Pascal, C, and COBOL, are 3GLs (third-generation languages), which means they are *procedural.* The programmer specifies each step that the program is to take. SQL is a 4GL and is a *declarative* language (also called a *nonprocedural* language): The programmer declares what he or she wants, but not how to get it. For example: "List all employee names and telephone numbers from the **emps** table who were hired on or after 1 January, 2003" would be accomplished by the following SQL (Transact-SQL).

SQL

```
SELECT ename, telnum
        FROM emps
        WHERE hiredate >= '1 Jan, 2003';
```

How to implement the job is left up to the RDBMS.

1.5.1 Comments

In an SQL statement, everything right of "--" (dash dash, or minus minus) is ignored by the database engine and may be used as a *comment.* A second form of comment is enclosed between "/*" and "*/" and may span lines.

SQL

```
SELECT ename, telnum   -- COMMENT to end of the line
        FROM emps     /* COMMENT which
                      may  SPAN MULTIPLE LINES   */
        WHERE hiredate >= '1 Jan, 2003';
```

Microsoft SQL Server 2000 uses the name *Transact-SQL* for its version of SQL, which includes both 4GL statements complying with ANSI SQL-92 at the entry level and some 3GL extensions.

1.5.2 Data Types — First Look

A data type specifies the way that data can be represented. Three often used data types are VARCHAR(n) , INT and DATETIME:

- **VARCHAR(n):** String data of variable length containing up to *n* characters.

  String literals are sequences of characters enclosed in single quotes: `'Mary'` is an example.
- **INT:** Positive or negative integer values.

  Integer literals are just numbers, such as `4444`, without any quotes.
- **DATETIME:** Date and time values such as `'4/01/2003 12:15 PM'`.

See the complete coverage of data types starting on page 67.

1.5.3 Domain and NULL Values

The *domain* of a column is the set of legal values for that column. The domain is determined by the data type assigned to the column, possibly further limited by a constraint. For example, a column called Age may have a data type of INT and a constraint that values must be between 0 and 200. Then the domain is the set of all integers between 0 and 200 inclusive. This book will use the term *column domain* value to refer to any value within the domain of the column.

NULL means "no domain value assigned." It can also be read as "not available," "not applicable" or "unknown." If you want to add an employee to the emps table who does not have a telephone number, NULL would be assigned to the telephone number value for the new row in the database. (Note that NULL is very different from a value of zero.)

A NOT NULL constraint may be placed on any column that you do not want to allow to have a NULL value. A NOT NULL constraint is appropriate for the **ename** column in Table 1-4, for example.

1.5.4 Metadata and Data

Metadata is often called "data about data." Metadata includes the definitions or structure of objects. For example, metadata associated with the definition of Table 1-5 tells us that it has a column called ename with data type of VARCHAR(15).

Table 1-5 emps Table

ename	empid	deptno	telnum	hiredate
Mary Smith	5555	100	5678	01/01/1994
Sammy Sosa	2222	102	2345	02/02/2002
Bill Johnson	4444	101		05/05/2000
Mary Smith	7777	101	7890	11/11/1990
Suzy Smith	1111	102		03/03/2003

The metadata are stored on disk in the **Data Dictionary**, also called the **database system catalog** or **system tables** area of the database.

Data consist of the actual values to be stored and retrieved from the database. In the emps table one row of data is

Sammy Sosa, 2222, 102, 2345, 200

The data are stored on disk in the data area of the database. See Table 1-6.

Table 1-6 Samples of Metadata and Data from the **emps** Table

Metadata	Table **emps** has a column **ename** with data type **VARCHAR(15)**
Data	**Sammy Sosa**, **2222, 102, 2345, 200**

So from these metadata we can see that the data **Sammy Sosa** can have a maximum of 15 characters and it can be accessed through the field named **ename**.

The RDBMS manages both data and metadata for users who issue DDL and DML statements.

1.5.5 Data Definition Language (DDL) and Data Manipulation Language (DML)

The SQL language has two main divisions: Data Definition Language (DDL), which is used to define and manage all the objects in an SQL database (discussed in Chapter 3), and Data Manipulation Language (DML), which is used to select, insert, update and delete data in the tables of an SQL database (discussed in Chapter 4).

1.5.5.1 DDL

DDL is the subset of SQL statements used for modeling the structure of a database. There are three fundamental DDL statements:

- **CREATE:** Creates a new database system object.

  Example: `CREATE TABLE table1 ( col1 INT, col2 INT);`

- **ALTER:** Modifies an existing object definition or structure, e.g., add a column to table1.

  Example: `ALTER TABLE table1 ADD col3 INT;`

- **DROP:** Removes the definition of the metadata *and* any underlying data!

  Example: `DROP TABLE table1 ;` This would eliminate all vestiges of metadata and data for table1, so be careful.

In addition to CREATE, ALTER and DROP, the following are sometimes considered to be part of DDL: **GRANT** and **REVOKE** privileges.

DDL is covered in detail in Chapter 3.

1.5.5.2 DML

DML consists of those SQL statements that manage database data, allowing the user to insert, access and change actual data values. There are four fundamental DML statements:

- **INSERT:** Adds a new row to a table, one row per insert statement.

  Example: `INSERT INTO table1 (col1, col2) VALUES (10, 20);`

- **UPDATE:** Modifies field(s) of existing row(s) in a table specified by WHERE clause.

  Example: `UPDATE table1 SET col1 = 12 WHERE col2 = 20;`

- **DELETE:** Removes the specified rows from a table.

  Example: `DELETE FROM table1 WHERE col2 = 20;`

- **SELECT:** Performs a query. Fetches data from the database and displays it.

  Example: `SELECT * FROM table1;`

In addition, the following are sometimes considered to be part of DML: **COMMIT** and **ROLLBACK**.

DML is covered in detail in Chapter 4.

1.5.6 DDL Examples—CREATE TABLE, ALTER TABLE, DROP TABLE

1.5.6.1 CREATE TABLE

WARNING Do not practice these statements on a production machine!

Do design and development of new tables and new database application software on a *test machine* until it's exhaustively tested and ready to deploy.

Deploy onto a *production machine* during off-production hours with time to back it out.

Practice performance tuning the test machine loaded with the same tables and same amount of data.

Do initial tuning of the production machine during off-peak hours, and then gather tuning data during peak production. Wait until off-peak hours before doing big jobs such as creating a new index.

We can create our emps table with the following statement.

ANSI SQL and Microsoft SQL Server:

```
CREATE  TABLE       emps (
        ename       VARCHAR(15)  NOT NULL,
        empid       INT       PRIMARY KEY,
        deptno      INT,
        telnum      CHAR(4) ,
        sales_amt   INT -- Comments: after -- to end of line.
        );
```

Notes: SQL is free form; lines may be combined or broken anywhere between words. The SQL statement terminator is a semicolon, though it is not always required.

1.5.6.2 ALTER TABLE

The ALTER TABLE statement changes the table definition such as to add or drop a column or change a column definition.

ANSI SQL and Microsoft SQL Server:

```
ALTER TABLE emps
  ADD [COLUMN] Office_Num   VARCHAR(10);
```

ANSI SQL permits but does not require the word *COLUMN*. Microsoft SQL Server does not allow it. ALTER TABLE varies considerably among RDBMS vendors.

ANSI SQL and Microsoft SQL Server:

```
ALTER TABLE emps
      ADD  Office_Num   VARCHAR(10);

ALTER TABLE emps
         DROP COLUMN Office_Num ;
```

1.5.6.3 DROP TABLE

The DROP TABLE statement removes both the definition of a table (its metadata) *and* all of its data contents; so be careful!

ANSI SQL and Microsoft SQL Server:

```
DROP TABLE emps;
```

1.5.7 DML Examples—INSERT, UPDATE, DELETE, SELECT

1.5.7.1 INSERT

The INSERT statement adds a new row to a table, one row per INSERT statement. There are two formats for INSERT.

Format 1: The user lists the column names (in any order) and the corresponding values in the same order as the names.

ANSI SQL and Microsoft SQL Server (listing column names is recommended):

```
INSERT INTO emps (ename, empid,  deptno, telnum)
    VALUES ( 'Newby Peoples', 9999, 100 , 9012  );
```

Format 2: The user does not list the column names, but there must be data values for every column and the values must be in same order as the table definition.

ANSI SQL and Microsoft SQL Server:

```
INSERT INTO emps
    VALUES ( 'Newby Peoples', 9999, 100 , 9012 , NULL
);
```

1.5.7.2 UPDATE

UPDATE modifies data in one or more fields of specified existing row(s).

ANSI SQL and Microsoft SQL Server:

```
UPDATE emps
  SET telnum = '9876',  deptno = 102
  WHERE empid = 9999;
```

Note: You need to be careful in specifying the WHERE clause to select exactly the rows desired. Notice that capitalization of the column names doesn't matter, e.g., either `OFFICE_NUM or Office_Num` is okay.

1.5.7.3 DELETE

The DELETE statement removes the specified rows from a table.

ANSI SQL and Microsoft SQL Server:

```
DELETE FROM emps WHERE empid = 9999;
```

1.5.7.4 SELECT

The SELECT statement performs a query. It etches data from the database and displays it. SELECT syntax is detailed in Chapter 4.

Every row in the FROM table has the WHERE predicate evaluated and if TRUE the row is selected. The final result is a set of rows where the values in each row correspond to the column_name(s) specified in the SELECT list. "SELECT * " means to include all columns in the result.

Microsoft SQL Server (and ANSI SQL): output shown from Microsoft SQL Server

SQL

```
SELECT   ename,   telnum,   empid   --   Show   values   of
                                    -- columns listed
  FROM emps;-- (No WHERE clause means ALL ROWS)
```

Result

ename	telnum	empid
---------------	---------	------
Suzy Smith	NULL	1111
Sammy Sosa	2345	2222
Bill Johnson	NULL	4444
Mary Smith	5678	5555
Mary Smith	7890	7777
(5 row(s) affected)		

Microsoft SQL Server (and ANSI SQL):

SQL

```
SELECT ename, telnum, empid    -- Show listed
                               -- columns, 1 row
  FROM emps       -- Words after "--" are ignored
  WHERE empid = 1111;
```

Result

ename	telnum	empid
-------- --------	------	--
Suzy Smith	NULL	1111
(1 row(s) affected)		

1.5.7.5 Query Processing

The goal of processing a query is create a virtual table called the *result set* which contains the columns and rows of data that match the query. This is how a query is processed to achieve this goal. When the query engine receives a query, it parses and compiles the entire statement. It then opens the target table, **emps,** and compares each row against the WHERE clause predicate and each row for which the WHERE predicate is true is put into an intermediate result set.

Finally, only the specified (requested) columns are retained in the final result set which is then displayed. This final result set is the answer to the query.

Microsoft SQL Server and ANSI SQL:

SQL

```
SELECT *              --     *     means   show   ALL   columns
                      --   (in table definition order)
  FROM emps
  WHERE empid = 1111;
```

Result

ename	empid	deptno	telnum	sales_amt
Suzy Smith	1111	102	NULL	NULL

An interesting variation of the statement above displays all of the data in the table.

```
SELECT *               --   *  means to display ALL columns
  FROM table_name;     -- No WHERE clause means display all rows
```

Microsoft SQL Server and ANSI SQL:

SQL

```
SELECT *
  FROM emps;
```

Result

ename	empid	deptno	telnum	sales_amt
Suzy Smith	1111	102	NULL	NULL
Sammy Sosa	2222	102	2345	200
Bill Johnson	4444	101	NULL	NULL
Mary Smith	5555	100	5678	NULL
Mary Smith	7777	101	7890	400

1.5.7.6 Base Tables and Derived Tables

A table whose data resides on disk is called a *base table* or *persistent base table.* A *derived table* is one obtained from one or more other tables through the evaluation of a query. It may also be called a *virtual table.* The data contained in the output of a specific SELECT statement is often called its *result set,* which is the derived table consisting of the data values for the selected columns and rows.

```
SELECT: Table(s) in,  Table out
```

It is useful to think of a SELECT statement operation as working on one or more tables as input and delivering a table structured result set as the output. Remember that a table is a set of rows with no inherent order. The output of a SELECT is a derived table in that the data only exists in memory and not on disk.

This discussion can also be extended to the other three DML statements, INSERT, UPDATE and DELETE, which are allowed to change data in the underlying base table. These statements may be thought of as having the old base table in and the changed base table out. See Figure 1-6.

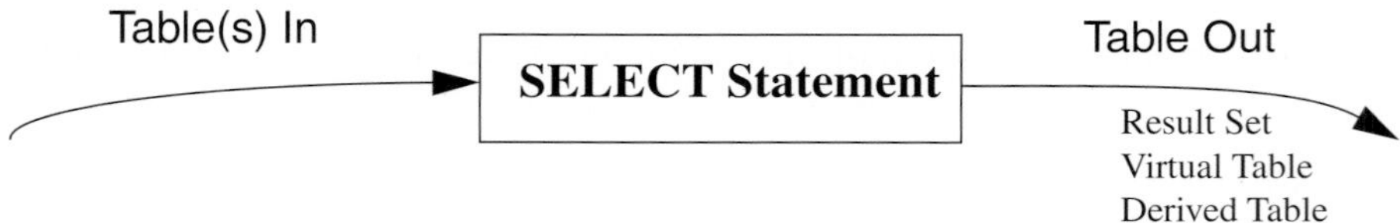

Figure 1-6 SELECT output.

1.5.8 Case Sensitivity in SQL Statements

Certain elements of SQL statements can be case sensitive.

1.5.8.1 Keywords

Keywords are not case sensitive. To enhance readability, many people use a convention of capitalizing all SQL keywords, such as CREATE TABLE. However, any mixture of upper- and lowercase will work, such as CreAtE TaBle.

1.5.8.2 Database Object Names (Table Names, Column Names)

These are mostly not case sensitive.

1.5.8.3 Regular Identifiers

Normal identifiers are called *regular identifiers* and may have up to 128 characters beginning with a letter (alphabetic character) followed by a letter, number or underscore ("_"). Such regular identifiers are user defined and are case insensitive.

In Microsoft SQL Server they are case insensitive if the instance is installed as case insensitive (the default) but are case sensitive if installed as case sensitive.

So either of the following statements would access the same data.

```
SELECT ename , empid FROM emps;
SELECT EnaME , empID FROM emps;
```

1.5.8.4 Delimited Identifiers

The SQL standard does allow for *delimited identifiers*, which are enclosed in double quotes when created. They cause the identifier to be case sensitive and allow it to contain embedded spaces.

Microsoft SQL Server requires executing SET QUOTED_IDENTIFIER ON before a CREATE TABLE statement which uses delimited identifiers.

Then the following statements may be executed.

```
SET QUOTED_IDENTIFIER ON
CREATE TABLE "AB cd" (
        "ENAme"   VARCHAR(15),
        Empid     INT
    );
```

When accessing the table, the double quotes are required:

```
SELECT  *  FROM "AB cd"
```

Using delimited identifiers does allow you to embed spaces in a table or column name, but they are neither portable nor convenient to use.

1.5.8.5 Storage of Identifiers in System Tables

If Microsoft SQL Server is installed as case insensitive, the default, then, both searching the data dictionary for an identifier and using the identifier in DML and DDL statements will be case insensitive. But if Microsoft SQL Server is installed as case sensitive then the correct case must be used for both searching the data dictionary and for use in DML and DDL statements.

1.5.8.6 Data

With Microsoft SQL Server, the default is case insensitive. Data values in a character format are stored in the case in which the data were entered. But most other RDBMS vendors support only case sensitive searches.

DDL and DML statement keywords may be mixed case, but object names (tables, columns, etc.) and data must all be the correct case unless the entire database is configured as case insensitive.

MSS configured as case insensitive (default):

SQL

```
seLECT dEPtno
-- column and table names and data are case-insensitive
  frOM dePTs
  WheRE  dept_name = 'engineering';
-- engineering or Engineering, etc, will return the correct row
```

MSS configured as case sensitive:

SQL

```
seLECT deptno
-- column and table names and data are case-sensitive
  frOM depts
  WheRE  dept_name = 'Engineering';
-- Capitalization of Engineering must match the stored data
```

A suggested SQL programming style is to capitalize all keywords to make it easier to read.

```
SELECT deptno
    FROM depts
    WHERE dept_name = 'Engineering';
```

1.5.8.7 Queries and Performance

Much database literature suggests that a **query** in SQL is synonymous with a **SELECT** statement. This idea is supported by the ANSI SQL-99 standard and Webster's Dictionary, which says that *query* is a "request for information." In most applications there are many more SELECT statements than any other kind of SQL statements, a fact that contributes to SELECT statement design having a large impact on performance of the application.

The part of a SELECT statement that has the biggest impact on performance is the WHERE clause because the WHERE clause determines which of the potentially very large number of rows on a disk are to be accessed, and disk access is the slowest part of any RDBMS operation. So, one often hears that the cause of most performance problems comes from poorly formed queries.

But one should keep in mind that the same amount of work is required to satisfy each WHERE clause, whether in a SELECT, UPDATE or DELETE statement. Perhaps the wording should be changed to read that the cause of most performance problems comes from poorly formed WHERE clauses and inadequate indexing. The performance of finding the rows to satisfy a given WHERE clause may often be improved by good index specification.

Database performance tuning is quite an involved subject and should be pursued separately.

1.5.9 RDBMS Utility to Show Table Structure

After creating a table as follows

```
SQL: CREATE TABLE emps (
          ename         VARCHAR(15)    NOT NULL
     ,    empid         INT            PRIMARY KEY
     ,    deptno        INT
     ,    telnum        VARCHAR(4)
     ,    sales_amt     INT
     );
```

it would be helpful to be able to display the definition of this or any table.

There is no ANSI SQL statement to do this, but each RDBMS has its own utilities for operations such as this. SQL Server has **sp_help** *table_name* as shown here.

sp_help reports the metadata of a specified database object.

EXEC[UTE] sp_help ***table-name***

As an example:

SQL

```
EXEC sp_help emps;
```

Result

```
Name            Owner                  Created_datetime
-------------   --------------------   --------------------------
                emps dbo user table    2002-07-12  14:08:20.723

Column_name     Type Computed          Length      Prec       Scale      Nullable ..
-------------   --------------------   ---------   --------   --------   -----
```

Result (cont.)

```
            empid        int      no   4   10   0    no
            deptno       int      no   4   10   0    yes
            telnum       varchar  no   4        yes
            sales_amt    int      no   4   10   0    yes

Identity                          Seed    Increment   Not For Replication
-------------------------------------------
No identity column defined.       NULL    NULL        NULL

RowGuidCol
----------------------------------------
No rowguidcol column defined.

Data_located_on_filegroup
----------------------------------
PRIMARY

index_name                        index_descriptionindex_keys
   ------------------------------------------------------------
   PK__emps__00DF2177             clustered, unique, primary key located on
   PRIMARY                                       empid

   constraint_type    constraint_name    delete_action   update_action ...
   ---------------------------------     -------------- ...
   PRIMARY KEY (clustered)        PK__emps__00DF2177 (n/a)      (n/a)          ...
No foreign keys reference this table.
No views with schema binding reference this table.
```

1.6 CHAPTER LAB EXERCISES

These lab exercises are optional but highly encouraged since working on the system is the only way to learn SQL. Lab Exercise 1 introduces using MSS. Lab Exercise 2 and beyond are RDBMS independent.

1.6.1 Lab Exercise 1: Introduction to Using Microsoft SQL Server

1.6.1.1 Microsoft SQL Server Enterprise Manager

Open a Microsoft SQL Server Enterprise Manager as follows.

Start – Programs – Microsoft SQL Server – Enterprise Manager

If prompted to log in, select "Use SQL Server authentication" and log in as sa with no password (unless you have changed the sa password during or after installation as you should on a production machine).

login:sa
password: <leave blank>

In the Console Root window open

Console Root – Microsoft SQL Servers – SQL Server Group

to see a list of server machines (there may be only one) that you have access to. You should see the host name of your current machine or (local) if you are working on the same machine where SQL Server is installed. If your target host has a green arrow beside it, that means it's running and you can connect to it. If it has a red square beside it, that means it's stopped, and you need to start it by right clicking on the host name and select Start. Soon it should return with the green arrow.

If the arrow is green with white background then you are not connected. Connect by right clicking on the host name and selecting Connect. Shortly the arrow should show in reverse colors (white arrow with dark green background) indicating that you are connected.

Expand the + sign next to your host name (AMY in the illustration)

to see the list items including Databases and Data Transformation Services.

Expand the + sign next to Databases

and notice the default databases installed with Microsoft SQL Server including

- System Databases: master, model, pubs and tempdb
- Sample User Databases: Northwind, pubs.

Click on the + sign just left of testdb, then click on Tables.

The Enterprise Manager should appear as it does in Figure 1-7.

Create your own new database that you can use to play with.

Right click on the word *Databases* and select New Database.

Enter the name *testdb* for your database and click OK.

After a few seconds the name *testdb* will appear in the list of database names.

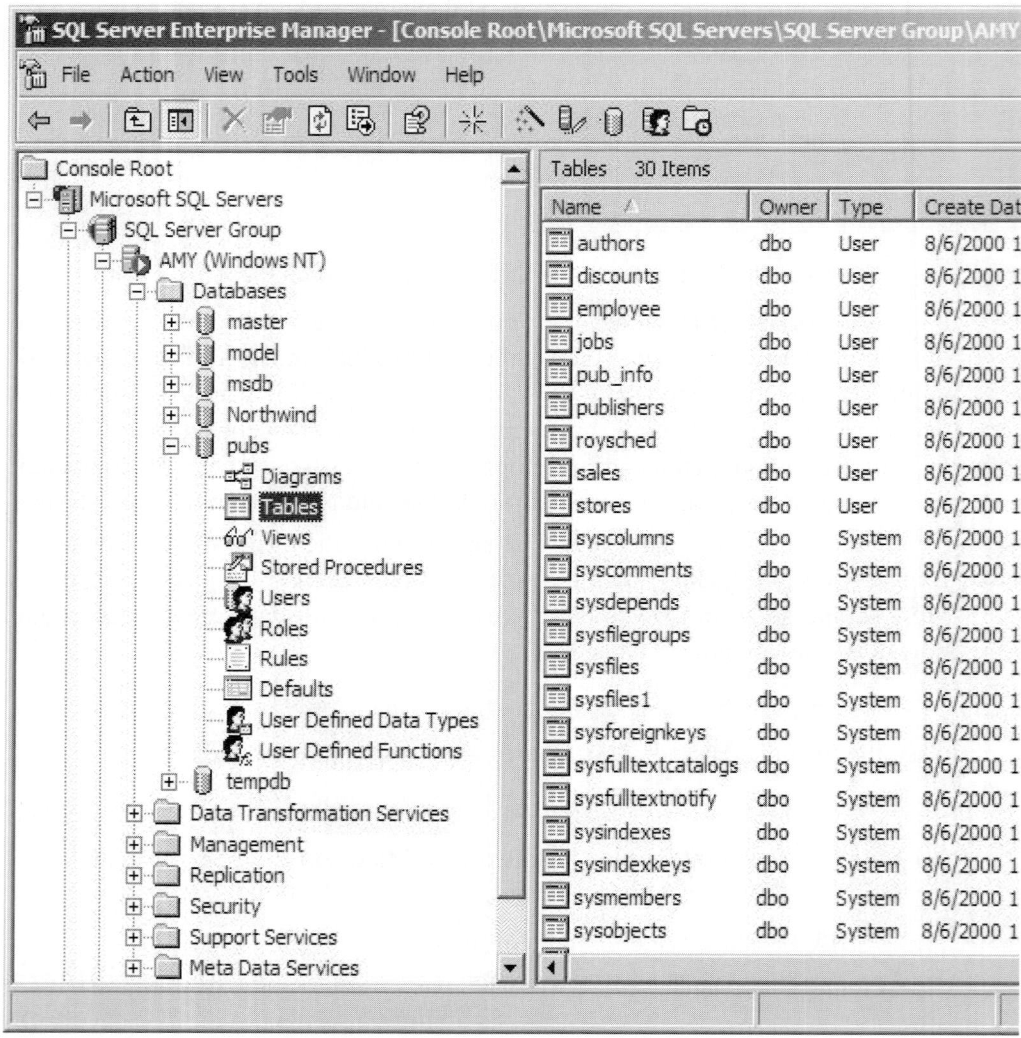

Figure 1-7 Enterprise manager.

Minimize or close your Enterprise Manager.

1.6.1.2 Microsoft SQL Server Query Analyzer

Open a Microsoft SQL Server Query Analyzer

Start – Programs – Microsoft SQL Server – Query Analyzer

To log in, select Use SQL Server Authentication and use the following default login information unless you changed it during or after installation.

```
login:sa
      password: <leave blank>
```

Maximize the Query Analyzer window or make it large enough to see the DB window, then in the DB window select "pubs" database. In the text edit area type in:

```
USE pubs
  go
```

and then execute this statement by any one of the following.

CONTROL-E
F5key
Query – Execute, or
right click on the green arrow

The USE pubs statement is the same as selecting *pubs* in the DB window.

You must remember each time you start the Query Analyzer to select the correct database.

The pubs database and Northwind database are sample databases used for learning Microsoft SQL Server. There is a table in the pubs database called publishers, whose column structure you can see by doing

```
SELECT * FROM publishers

EXEC sp_help authors
```

Notice that you may type statements into the Editor pane, the top section, of the Query Analyzer and see the output in the Results pane, the bottom section. The output in the bottom section can be changed to have resizable columns by choosing

Query – Results in Grid (Ctrl+D)

and reexecuting the command by any of the methods above. The results are shown in Figure 1-8.

You may have several statements in Query Analyzer at the same time. When you give the execute command in one of the five ways listed above, then all statements in the window will be executed in order if nothing is highlighted. But if you select only certain statements, then only those statements will be executed. This is a very convenient feature to use in debugging a certain portion of the program.

You may look at the column structure and at the properties of the authors table by doing

```
EXEC sp_help publishers
```

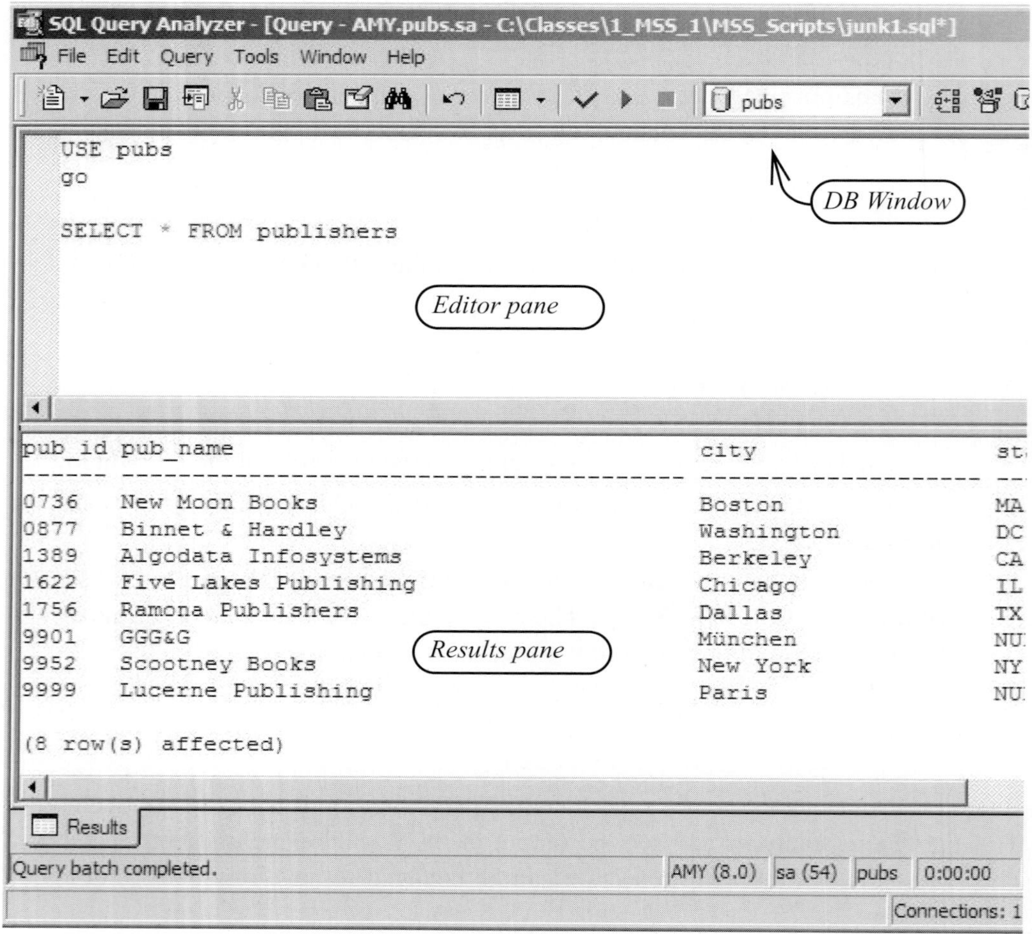

Figure 1-8 Query results.

Statements in Editor pane of the Query Analyzer may be saved to a file for later use from

File – Save As

and providing a file name. The extension .sql will be automatically appended.

Saving a sequence of commands in an SQL script in this way can be very useful for doing repeated tasks. The results may also be saved to a file; click the mouse in the Results pane and do

File – Save As

1.6.2 Lab Exercise 2: CREATE TABLE

Create an SQL Server database testdb where we'll create tables and other database objects. Enter the following statement in the Edit pane of the Query Analyzer and execute it.

```
CREATE DATABASE  testdb
```

See page 246 for the complete CREATE DATABASE syntax and examples.

Create an SQL Server database where you can create tables and other database objects. Type the following two lines before any other interactive SQL statements.

```
USE testdb
  go
```

To remove the database, including deleting the database files, execute:

```
USE master
  go


DROP DATABASE DeacDB
  go
```

Type the following SQL statements into a file, emps_0.sql, and run them on a RDBMS of your choice.

```
--  Comment to end of line
/*  Comments all enclosed text; may span lines */
/*
                    emps_0.sql
    */
DROP TABLE emps;
    DROP TABLE depts;

CREATE TABLE depts (
    dept_name             VARCHAR(15),
    deptno                INT,   -- PRIMARY KEY
    mgr_emp_id            INT,
    dept_telnum           VARCHAR(4),
       CONSTRAINT depts_pk PRIMARY KEY (deptno)
    );

CREATE TABLE emps (
    ename                 VARCHAR(15)NOT NULL,
```

```
    empid                   INT , -- PRIMARY KEY
    deptno                  INT,   -- FOREIGN KEY to depts
    telnum                  VARCHAR(4),
    sales_amt               INT,
       CONSTRAINT emps_pk PRIMARY KEY (empid),
       CONSTRAINT emps_dept_fk FOREIGN KEY (deptno)
    REFERENCES depts (deptno)
               );
```

The following is also in emps_0.sql to populate the tables with data:

```
INSERT INTO depts (dept_name, deptno , mgr_emp_id , dept_telnum )
  VALUES ( 'Accounting' ,  100 , 1111 , '9100' );
INSERT INTO depts (dept_name, deptno , mgr_emp_id , dept_telnum )
  VALUES ( 'Engineering' , 101 , 7777 , '9101' );
INSERT INTO depts (dept_name, deptno , mgr_emp_id , dept_telnum )
  VALUES ( 'Sales'        , 102 , 2222 , '9102'  );

INSERT INTO emps (ename, empid,  deptno, telnum, sales_amt)
  VALUES ( 'Mary Smith', 5555, 100 , '5678' , NULL );
INSERT INTO emps (ename, empid,  deptno, telnum, sales_amt)
  VALUES ( 'Sammy Sosa', 2222, 102 , '2345' , 200 );
INSERT INTO emps (ename, empid,  deptno, telnum, sales_amt)
  VALUES ('Bill Johnson', 4444, 101 , NULL  , NULL );
INSERT INTO emps (ename, empid,  deptno, telnum, sales_amt)
  VALUES ( 'Mary Smith', 7777, 101 , '7890' , 400 );
INSERT INTO emps (ename, empid,  deptno, telnum, sales_amt)
  VALUES ( 'Suzy Smith', 1111, 102 , NULL , NULL );

SELECT * FROM emps ;
SELECT * FROM depts ;

/*   -- Select and execute just these lines to test the DROP
TABLE statement.
DROP TABLE emps;
SELECT * FROM emps ;
*/
```

1.6.3 Lab Exercise 3

Type this in and run it. Save it as SQL script emps_1.sql.

```
/*
                     emps_1.sql
```

```
Run emps_0.sql before running this script.
*/

SELECT * FROM emps WHERE empid = 1111;

ALTER TABLE emps
ADD Office_Num   VARCHAR(10);

SELECT * FROM emps WHERE empid = 1111;

ALTER TABLE emps
DROP COLUMN Office_Num;

SELECT * FROM emps WHERE empid = 1111;

SELECT deptno
FROM depts
WHERE dept_name = 'Engineering';

exec sp_help emps;
```

Do as many of the examples from this chapter as you can. If you wish, save these in a script file labeled ch1_examples.sql.

```
CREATE TABLE table1 ( col1 INT, col2 INT);

INSERT INTO table1 (col1, col2 ) VALUES ( 10, 20 );
SELECT * FROM table1;

UPDATE table1 SET col2 = 29  WHERE col1 = 10;
SELECT * FROM table1;

ALTER TABLE table1 ADD  col3 INT;
SELECT * FROM table1;

INSERT INTO table1 (col1, col2, col3 ) VALUES ( 11, 21, 31 );
SELECT * FROM table1;

DELETE FROM table1 WHERE col1 = 10;
SELECT * FROM table1;

DROP TABLE table1 ;
SELECT * FROM table1;   -- error, there is not table1 now
```

CHAPTER 2

SQL Building Blocks and Server Settings

This chapter covers the building blocks available to the database designer and database user to create and modify database objects and data. The SQL Data Types will be covered along with data representation as literals (constants) and expressions. Also covered are methods to display and change server and database settings including using Enterprise Manager and the **sp_configure** and **sp_dboption** system stored procedures.

Throughout the book, the following terms will be used.

- *SQL-92* will refer to the 1992 ANSI/ISO SQL Standard, also called SQL2. *SQL-99* will refer to the 1999 ANSI/ISO SQL Standard,[1] also called SQL3 and ISO/IEC 9075.
- *SQL Server* will refer to Microsoft® SQL Server 2000 (version 8.0).
- *Books Online* will refer to Microsoft SQL Server 2000 Books Online.[2]

It is recommended that Books Online be used in conjunction with this book for coverage of some details not covered here and for different examples. Books Online is an excellent reference. This book, however, gathers related information

1. ANSI+ISO+IEC+9075-1-1999 through ANSI+ISO+IEC+9075-5-1999, American National Standards Institute.

2. Microsoft SQL Server 2000 Books Online, © 1988-2001 Microsoft Corporation. All Rights Reserved.

together and generally provides more examples per topic than does Books Online. Used together they provide quite strong reference material.

2.1 SQL SERVER INSTANCE

Each instance (or installation) of Microsoft SQL Server 2000 is composed of several databases, four system databases (**master**, **model**, **msdb** and **tempdb**) and as many user databases as specified by the database administrator. SQL Server 2000 supports installing more than one instance on the same host.

2.1.1 The SQL Server Database

Each database consists of a collection of system and user tables and related database objects such as views, indexes, stored procedures, triggers, etc. A database in a Microsoft SQL Server database maintains a list of its database objects in its `sysobjects` table in that database. Each object type and its `sysobjects` table symbol are listed in Table 2-1.

Table 2-1 Object Types

Object Type	Sysobjects Symbol
CHECK constraint	C
Default or DEFAULT constraint	D
FOREIGN KEY constraint	F
Scalar function	FN
Inlined table function	IF
PRIMARY KEY or UNIQUE constraint	K
Log	L
Stored procedure	P
Rule	R
Replication filter stored procedure	RF
System table	S
Table function	TF
Trigger	TR
User table	U

Table 2-1 Object Types (cont.)

Object Type	Sysobjects Symbol
View	V
Extended stored procedure	X

By default, two sample user databases, **Northwind** and **Pubs**, are installed with SQL Server. These databases will often be used in examples in this book.

Example: List all USER TABLE objects in the pubs database.

```
SQL SELECT * FROM pubs..sysobjects WHERE type = 'U';
```

Other database objects are recorded in a separate table such as **sysindexes** for indexes and **syscolumns** for details of table and view columns as well as stored procedure parameters.

2.1.1.1 System Stored Procedures

SQL Server provides some built-in system stored procedures to assist in determining information about databases and database objects and to assist in database administration. System stored procedures are covered as needed, and a complete listing starts on page 168. Two of the more useful are shown here: **sp_helpdb** and **sp_help**.

sp_helpdb This procedure reports information about a specified database or all databases.

Syntax

```
sp_helpdb [ [ @dbname= ] 'name' ]
```

Arguments

[@dbname=] 'name'

This is the name of the database for which to provide information. If a name is not specified, sp_helpdb reports on all databases in master.dbo.sysdatabases. (*dbo* stands for database owner, the predefined user name in each database that is able to perform all database operations. Any sysadmin server role member becomes **dbo** inside each database.)

Return Code Values

```
0 (success) or 1 (failure)
```

Example: Show information on database **pubs**.

```
SQL EXEC sp_helpdb pubs
```

Reports **db** size, owner, file locations and other information for the **pubs** database.

sp_help This procedure reports information about a database object, a user-defined data type or a system-supplied data type.

Syntax

```
sp_help [ [ @objname = ] name ]
```

Arguments

[@objname =] name

This is the name of any object in `sysobjects` or any user-defined data type in the `systypes` table. `name` has a default of `NULL`. (Database names are not acceptable.)

Return Code Values

```
0 (success) or 1 (failure)
```

Example: Show the structure of the titles table of the pubs database.

```
SQL
USE pubs -- must first move the context of SQL client to pubs database
go
```

```
SQL EXEC sp_help titles
```

lists all column names and data types, constraints, table owner, etc., of titles table.

2.2 DATA REPRESENTATION

2.2.1 General Data Type Information

Every data value belongs to some data type such as INTEGER, CHARACTER, etc. Microsoft SQL Server Transact-SQL has a number of native data types, which are described in the next section.

In addition to the built-in, native data types, Transact-SQL provides for the definition of user-defined types, covered later in this chapter.

2.2.2 Domain and NULL Value

2.2.2.1 Domain

The **domain** of a column is the set of legal data type values for that column as determined by the data type assigned to the column and applicable constraints.

A **domain value** is any value within the domain. For example, a column called Age may have a data type of INT and a CHECK constraint that values must be between 0 and 200. Then the domain is the set of all integers between 0 and 200 inclusive. In this case, 21 would be a valid domain value for the Age column.

2.2.2.2 NULL

NULL means "no domain value assigned." It indicates that the value is unknown. **NULL can also be read as "not available," "not applicable" or "unknown."** If you want to add an employee to the employees table who does not have a telephone number, NULL would be assigned to the field value in the database. Note that NULL is very different from a value of zero for INT or an empty string for VARCHAR, both of which are domain values.

A constraint of NOT NULL may be placed on any column that is not allowed to have a NULL value. This is true for a primary key, for example. Every row must have a valid domain value for each column specified as NOT NULL. The NULL value is represented by the keyword `NULL`.

The ANSI SQL-99 Standard says the following about `NULL`.[3]

null value: A special value that is used to indicate the absence of any data value. Every data type includes a special value, called the *null value*, sometimes denoted by the keyword NULL. This value differs from other values in the following respects: — Since the null value is in every data type, the data type of the null value implied by the keyword NULL cannot be inferred; hence NULL can be used to denote the null value only in certain contexts, rather than everywhere that a literal is permitted. —Although the null value is neither equal to any other value nor not equal to any other value— it is *unknown* whether or not it is equal to any given value—in some contexts, multiple null values are treated together; for example, the <group by clause> treats all null values together.

3. ANSI+ISO+IEC+9075-1-1999, American National Standards Institute, Inc. (1999), pp. 5, 13.

Every column of every row in a table must be assigned either a column domain value for that column or `NULL`. SQL Server Query Analyzer displays the word NULL when a query returns `NULL` for a column.

2.2.3 Constant (Literal) Defined

A constant or literal is a non-NULL specific data value of an indicated data type.

- **String Literal** is one or more characters enclosed in single quotes, e.g., 'Mary'.
- **Unicode String Literal** has capital N preceding the string, e.g., N'Mary'.
- **Date Literal** is a date contained in single quotes, '03-May-2000'.
- **Numeric Literal** is an integer (**int**) or floating point number (no quotation marks), e.g., 12 , 2.3.

The format for constants for each data type are given below.

2.2.4 Identifiers—Naming SQL Objects

An *identifier* is the name a database user assigns to a database object such as a table, column or view. This section describes the rules for creating identifier names. The next section describes how to use identifiers in one-, two-, three-, and four-part object names. The complete rules for forming legal Microsoft SQL Server identifiers are given below, but the safest and most portable subset of these rules is given here.

2.2.4.1 Identifier Format Rules, Short Form—Suggested Form

- The first character may be any alphabetic character in upper or lower case (a-z, A-Z).
- Subsequent characters may be any upper or lower case alphabetic or numeric or underscore character (a-z, A-Z, 0-9, _).
- It must contain between 1 and 128 characters (max of 116 for local temporary table).
- The identifier must not be a Transact-SQL reserved word (see Appendix A for list).

Examples: Table1, employees, hire_date

Every database object in SQL Server can have an identifier. Some objects, such as tables, are required to have an identifier; for other objects, such as constraints, identifiers are optional. Remember that identifiers are case-insensitive in SQL statements (unless installed case sensitive).

The maximum of 116 for a local temporary table name allows the system to add a unique suffix. This permits different users to concurrently call the same global stored procedure and each have a uniquely identified table.

2.2.4.2 Identifier Format Rules, Complete Form—Regular and Delimited

Microsoft SQL Server has two classes of identifiers: regular and delimited.

Regular Identifier Rules A regular identifier starts with a letter followed by an alphanumeric character or underscore, and it does not contain embedded spaces. A regular identifier is the most common and is the suggested form of name to give a database object.

Regular identifier characters must conform to the following rules.

- The first character must be
    a. an upper or lower case alphabetic character (a-z, A-Z), or
    b. a Unicode Latin character of another language, or
    c. underscore, "at" sign or number sign (_, @, #). See First Character below.
- Subsequent characters must be
    a. an upper or lower case alphabetic or numeric character (a-z, A-Z, 0-9), or
    b. a Unicode Latin character of another language, or
    c. underscore, "at" sign, number sign or dollar sign (_, @, #, $).

  (Note that embedded spaces are not allowed by these rules.)
- Identifiers must contain between 1 and 128 characters (max 116 for local temp table).
- The identifier must not be a Transact-SQL reserved word (see Appendix A for list).

First Character identifiers starting with some characters have special meaning as shown in Table 2-2.

Table 2-2 First Characters

First Character(s)	Meaning	Examples
@	local variable or parameter name	**@variablename**
@@	system function (do not start your own object names with @@)	**@@version**
#	temporary table (max of 116 characters) or a local temporary procedure (max of 128 characters)	**#localtable** **#localproc**
##	global temporary object	**##globaltable, ##globalproc**

Example: Typical use of regular identifiers

SQL

```
-- Regular Identifiers:  table1, column_av
CREATE TABLE  table1   (   column_a  VARCHAR(40)    )
```

SQL

```
INSERT INTO   table1   ( column_a )
VALUES ( 'String Data in single quotes' )
```

SQL

```
SELECT  *  FROM  table1
```

Result

```
column_a
----------------------------------------
String Data in single quotes
```

I recommend restricting your identifiers to regular identifiers such as **table1** and **column_a**.

2.2.4.3 Delimited Identifiers

A delimited identifier is an identifier enclosed in brackets ([ ]) or double quotes (" ") and may include special characters such as embedded spaces or tabs in the identifier name.

Remember the following comments about delimited identifiers.

- Many people, like me, don't recommend special characters such as spaces because they can cause problems.
- If you must use spaces or other special characters in an identifier, it is suggested that you use brackets instead of double quotes since the latter require the session setting QUOTED_IDENTIFIER be set to ON, but brackets are always valid.
- A regular identifier enclosed in brackets refers to the same object. E.g., **[table1]** and **table1** are the same object.

Note: When SQL Server generates scripts, it puts all identifiers in brackets, so don't be concerned that pubs.dbo.jobs looks a little funny when it appears as **[pubs.[dbo].[jobs]**.

2.2.4.4 Delimited Identifier Rules

First and subsequent characters may be any alphanumeric, punctuation or special character (including space or tab) except for the delimiter characters themselves. Delimited identifiers may include basically any character on the keyboard (except the delimiters) including spaces, tabs and punctuation marks.

Identifier must contain between 1 and 128 characters not counting the delimiters (max of 116 for local temporary table, see page 302). Also, Transact-SQL keywords may be used as identifiers if delimited.

`CREATE TABLE [table] ( column_a INT ) --` Keyword as table name is a bad idea!

Example: Using a delimited identifier using [ ] to delimit the identifier

SQL

```
CREATE TABLE  [three word table]
( column_a  VARCHAR(40) )
```

SQL

```
INSERT [three word table]  ( column_a )
VALUES ( 'String Data in single quotes' )
```

SQL

```
SELECT  *  FROM  [three word table]
```

Result

```
column_a
------------------------------------
String Data in single quotes
```

Underscore or capital letters can be used to avoid embedded spaces: three_word_table or ThreeWordTable.

I recommend adhering to ANSI SQL and good form as follows.

- Use the ON setting for QUOTED_IDENTIFIER.
- Use regular identifiers (no embedded spaces, see Identifier Format Rules, Short Form—Suggested Form above).
- If you must delimit an identifier use brackets as they are always valid.
- Use single quotes to delimit all string literals.

If you follow these suggestions then you may skip Section 2.2.4.5.

2.2.4.5 QUOTED_IDENTIFIER

This section is applicable if you have identifiers, which are delimited by double quotes.

A **QUOTED_IDENTIFIER** is a database option that, when ON, causes adherence to ANSI SQL rules regarding quotation mark delimiting identifiers and literal strings. When the option **QUOTED_IDENTIFIER** is set to ON (usual and recommended) follow these recommendations.

- Either brackets ([ ]) or double quotes (" ") may be used to delimit identifiers.
- All strings delimited by double quotes are interpreted as object identifiers.
- String literals must be delimited by single quotes and NOT by double quotes.

When database option QUOTED_IDENTIFIER is set to OFF follow these guidelines.

- Only brackets ([ ]) may be used to delimit identifiers.
- String literals may be delimited by either single or double quotes, though double quotes do not conform to the ANSI SQL and so single quotes are always recommended to enclose string literals.

The default setting for the QUOTED_IDENTIFIER is technically OFF, effectively ON. Although the default database setting for QUOTED_IDENTIFIER is OFF , both the ODBC driver and the OLE DB Provider for SQL Server automatically set QUOTED_IDENTIFIER to ON when connecting which overrides the default database setting.

This ON setting for QUOTED_IDENTIFIER is in effect unless the user explicitly executes

SET QUOTED_IDENTIFIER OFF

as is done in the following example. So clients using ODBC or OLE DB (almost all SQL Server clients today including Query Analyzer) see an ON setting for QUOTED_IDENTIFIER. (ON is good.)

See a complete discussion in Server, Database and Session Settings on p.174 and also see Which Session Setting Is in Effect? on p. 219.

Example: QUOTED_IDENTIFIER is ON, so either [ ] or " " may be used to delimit identifier.

SQL

```
CREATE TABLE  [three word table] (  a  VARCHAR(40)   )
```

SQL

```
INSERT INTO   "three word table"  ( a )
VALUES ( 'String Data in single quotes' )
```

SQL

```
SELECT  *  FROM  [three word table]
```

Result

```
a
----------------------------------------
String Data in single quotes
```

Example: Setting QUOTED_IDENTIFIER is OFF allows only [ ] to delimit identifier.

```
SQL SET  QUOTED_IDENTIFIER  OFF
```

```
SQL
```

```
CREATE TABLE  [multi word table name in brackets]   (   a  VARCHAR(40)   )
```

```
SQL
```

```
INSERT INTO "multi word table name in dbl quotes"   ( a )
VALUES ( 'String Data in single quotes' )
```

Result

```
Server: Msg 170, Level 15, State 1, Line 1
Line 1: Incorrect syntax near 'three word table'.
```

2.2.5 Using Identifiers as Qualified Object Names

Names of objects used in examples in this book usually use a one-part name, the object name itself. This section describes SQL Server one-, two-, three- and four-part names.

The complete name of an object consists of four identifiers: the server name, database name, owner name, and object name. They appear in the following format:

[[[*server*.] [*database*] **.**] [*owner_name*] **.**] *object_name*

server defaults to the server of the current connection.

database defaults to the current database.

owner_name defaults to current login.

Qualifiers may be omitted as follows.

- Leading default qualifiers may be omitted resulting in three-, two- or one-part names.
- Intermediate default qualifier(s) may be replaced by a period. owner_name marked by a period defaults first to the current login if the object owned by that owner can be found and, if not, then to dbo.

Valid forms of object names are as follows.

- *server.database.owner_name.object_name*: Fully Qualified Object Name
- *database.owner_name.object_name*: Current server
- *database..object_name*: Current server and current login or dbo
- *owner_name.object_name*: Current server and current database
- *object_name*: Current server and database and current login or dbo

Example: The local server is named amy.

Create a link to SQL Server instance CAT2 on host CAT and do a query to it.

SQL

```
EXEC  sp_addlinkedserver @server = 'CAT2_Link'        --
Specify Server Link Name
,     @srvproduct = ' '
,     @provider = 'SQLOLEDB'
,    @datasrc = 'CAT\CAT2'
-- hostname\SQLServerInstanceName

USE pubs
        go
SELECT *   FROM  authors              -- OR:  .authors
SELECT *   FROM  dbo.authors          -- OR:  ..authors
SELECT *   FROM  pubs.dbo.authors     -- OR:  pubs..authors
SELECT *   FROM  .pubs.dbo.authors
-- OR:  ...authors OR:  .pubs..authors
SELECT *   FROM  amy.pubs.dbo.authors
SELECT *   FROM  northwind.dbo.orders
-- Etc. for any database on the current server
SELECT *   FROM  CAT2_Link.pubs.dbo.authors
-- OR:  CAT2_Link.northwind.dbo.orders
```

The following forms do not work.

SQL

```
SELECT *   FROM  amy.pubs..authors
-- OR: amy..dbo.authors    OR:  amy...authors
SELECT *   FROM  CAT2_Link.pubs..authors
-- OR: CAT2_Link..dbo.authors OR:  CAT2_Link...authors
```

2.2.5.1 Qualified Column Names

Column names of a table or view may be qualified using the form:

table_name.column_name, view_name.column_name, or **table_alias.column_name**

where **table_name** or **view_name** may be a one-, two-, three- or four-part name as described above.

Example: Create a link to SQL Server instance CAT2 on host CAT and do a query to it.

Run a distributed query from the local host to the linked server using tables from both.

SQL

```
USE pubs
go
```

SQL

```
SELECT  TOP 2   p.pub_name , e.lname + ', ' + e.fname EmpName
   FROM       publishers p , CAT2_Link.pubs.dbo.employee e
   WHERE       p.pub_id  =  e.pub_id
```

Result

```
pub_name                   EmpName
--------------------------  ----------------------------
Algodata Infosystems       Afonso, Pedro
Binnet & Hardley           Accorti, Paolo
```

Notice that pub_id column names p.pub_id and e.pub_id must be qualified by table alias (or table name if no table alias had been declared) to avoid ambiguity.

The SELECT list uses the form *table_alias.column_name*. The FROM clause uses the fully qualified four-part name for the employee table on CAT2.

2.3 EXPRESSIONS IN AN SQL STATEMENT

An expression is a combination of operands and operators, which evaluates to a scalar:

- **Scalar:** a single data value such as number 13, date '1 Jan 2003' or string 'Jim Doe'

- **Operand:** a constant (literal), column name, variable, scalar function subquery whose result set is a scalar value
- **Operator:** any legal operator symbol allowed by the data type of the operand(s)

An expression generally assumes the data type of its component operands except that operands combined using comparison or logical operators result in a value of Boolean data type.

String, numeric and date expressions may usually be used anywhere a scalar value of their data type is required in INSERT, UPDATE, DELETE and SELECT statements. (See the SELECT example below.)

Boolean (logical) expressions may appear where a <search_condition> is specified as in a WHERE clause of UPDATE, DELETE or SELECT statements. They may evaluate to TRUE, FALSE or NULL (unknown). A Boolean expression may also be used in an IF or WHILE construct.

Syntax:

```
expression ::= operand | ( expression ) | unary_operator expression
             | expression binary_operator expression
operand ::= constant | [table_alias.]column_name | variable | scalar_function
             | ( scalar_subquery )
unary_operator ::= operator that operates on one expression: operator expression
             E.g.,  unary minus, -, as with ( - 6 ).
binary_operator ::= operator that operates on two expressions: expr operator expr.
             E.g.,  binary minus, -, as with ( 12 - 6 ).
```

For complete syntax see Books Online, Index: expressions, overview.

Example: Examples of string expressions:

```
ename
'Mary Smith'
first_name || ' ' || last_name
```

Examples of numeric expressions:

```
salary
123.45
22 + 33
(salary + 22) * 1.2
AVG(salary)
1.5 * AVG(salary)
```

Example of Boolean (logical) expressions:

qty > 45 -- evaluates to TRUE, FALSE or NULL (unknown, as if **qty** is NULL)

Example of subquery expression:

A subquery is a SELECT statement enclosed in parenthesis used inside another DML statement. See page 702 for more detail on subqueries.

The bold text in the following statement is a subquery expression

```
SELECT *  FROM titles
    WHERE  price >=
    ( SELECT AVG(price) FROM titles WHERE type = 'business')
```

Example of numeric, string and date expressions in SELECT list

SQL

```
SELECT   'Hello', 1 ,   (SELECT 1) + 2 ,    GETDATE()
```

Result

```
-------          -----------     -----------     -----------------------------------
Hello            1               3               2001-05-11 16:28:27.140
```

Example of Boolean expression in WHERE clause <search condition>

SQL

```
SELECT ord_num, qty  FROM sales WHERE qty > 45
```

Result

```
ord_num          qty
---------------  ------
A2976            50
QA7442.3         75
```

2.3.1 Operators

An operator is a symbol specifying an action that is performed on one or more expressions. Microsoft SQL Server 2000 uses the following operator categories.

- Arithmetic operators: all numeric data types
- Assignment operators: all data types
- Bitwise operators: all integer data types plus binary and varbinary data types
- Comparison operators: all data types except text, ntext or image
- Logical operators: operand data type depends on operator

- String concatenation operators: character or binary string data types
- Unary operators: all numeric data types

When two expressions of different compatible data types are combined by a binary operator the expression of lower precedence is implicitly converted to the data type of higher precedence, the operation is performed and the resulting value is of the higher precedence data type. See Data Type Precedence List on page 73.

2.3.1.1 Arithmetic Operators

The arithmetic operators, as shown in Table 2-3, may be used with any of the numeric types. Addition and subtraction also work with datetime and smalldatetime for adding or subtracting a number of days.

Table 2-3 Arithmetic Operators

Operator	Description
+	Addition
–	Subtraction and unary negation
*	Multiplication
/	Division
%	Module (Remainder)
( )	Grouping

Notes:

Both symbols + and – are unary and binary operators.

The symbol / returns the data type with the higher precedence as usual. So if both dividend (top) and divisor are integer types, the result is truncated (not rounded) to an integer.

The symbol % is *modulo* or *remainder* and returns the integer remainder of the division. Both operands must be integer data types. So 1%3 is 1 and 4%3 is also 1 as is 7%3.

Examples:

1 + 2

4 / 2

(2.5 + 3) * 2

2.3.1.2 Relational Operators

These relational operators, shown in Table 2-4, may be used with string, numeric or date values.

Table 2-4 Relational Operators

=	equal to
<>	not equal to
<	less than
<=	less than or equal to
>	greater than
>=	greater than or equal to

2.3.1.3 Assignment Operator: =

There is one assignment operator, equal sign (=), used primarily with local variables.

Example:

SQL

```
DECLARE    @MyInt    INT
SET  @MyInt = 123   -- Assignment Operation
PRINT @MyInt
```

Result

```
123
```

2.3.1.4 Bitwise Operators

Bitwise operators work on all integer data types and bit data types. (See Transact-SQL Data Type Hierarchy, page 73.)

Binary and varbinary data types may be one operand if an integer type is the other operand. Table 2-5 shows the necessary symbols for this use.

Table 2-5 Bitwise Operators

Bitwise AND	Bitwise OR	Bitwise EOR
&	|	^

Example:

SQL

```
PRINT 1 | 2
```

SQL (cont.)
Result
3

2.3.1.5 Comparison Operators

Comparison operators, shown in Table 2-6, also called relational operators, work on all data types except text, ntext or image.

Table 2-6 Comparison Operators

Equal To	Greater Than	Less Than	Greater or Equal To	Less Than or Equal To	Not Equal To	Not Less Than	Not Greater Than
=	>	<	>=	<=	<>	!<	!>

The result of a comparison is of Boolean type with three possible values: TRUE, FALSE or NULL (unknown). Boolean type may not be used as column or variable data types.

Comparisons are most often used in a WHERE clause or an IF statement.

Example:

SQL

```
SELECT price FROM titles WHERE price > 21
```

Result

```
price
---------------------
22.95
21.59
```

2.3.1.6 Logical Operators and Boolean Predicates

Logical operations test the truth of some condition and return a Boolean value: TRUE, FALSE or NULL (unknown). Acceptable operand data types of logical operations depend on the operator.

Books Online lists all of the entries in Table 2-7 as logical operators. They can all appear in a WHERE clause as a Boolean <search condition>.

Table 2-7 Logical Operators

AND	OR	NOT	ANY/ SOME	ALL	BETWEEN	IN	EXISTS	LIKE

2.3.1.7 AND, OR, NOT with NULL

The first three are the well-known logical operators from classical Boolean algebra. A significant difference of SQL Boolean logic from classical Boolean logic is the effect that NULL has in creating three-way logic (TRUE, FALSE, NULL).

Using NULL in SQL Boolean Logic The ANSI SQL-99 Standard[4] says the following about NULL.

> Although the null value is neither equal to any other value nor not equal to any other value — it is *unknown* whether or not it is equal to any given value

So NULL can be read as UNKNOWN in SQL Boolean logic expressions.

In evaluating a WHERE clause as in a SELECT, UPDATE or DELETE statement,

WHERE <search_condition>

the <search_condition> is a Boolean predicate which evaluates to TRUE, FALSE or NULL. Only those rows that are *known to be true* are selected to be in the result set. So any row for which the WHERE predicate evaluates to FALSE (known to be FALSE) or `NULL` (unknown) will not be retained. See WHERE clause syntax page 478. The same is true when applied to the HAVING clause of a SELECT statement.

Example: Consider the rows in Table 2-8 of the `titles` table in the `pubs` database.

Table 2-8 Rows from Titles Table

title_id	price
PC1035	22.95
MC3021	2.99
PC9999	NULL
...	...

4. ANSI+ISO+IEC+9075-1-1999, American National Standards Institute, Inc. (1999), pp. 5, 13.

Which of these rows will be returned by the following SELECT statement on that table?

SQL

```
SELECT  title_id, price
FROM   pubs.dbo.titles
WHERE price > 22
```

Of these rows only the first row is returned since, for the other two rows, the predicate evaluates to FALSE and NULL (unknown) respectively.

Result

```
title_id        price
--------        ---------------------
PC1035          22.9500
```

IS NULL The correct way to find all rows for which a column value is NULL is to use the IS NULL predicate.

SQL

```
SELECT  title_id, price
FROM    pubs.dbo.titles
WHERE   price IS NULL
```

This returns only PC9999 from the previous table.

Result

```
title_id        price
--------        ---------------------
PC9999          NULL
```

IS NOT NULL or NOT IS NULL The correct way to find all rows for which a column value is not NULL is to use the IS NOT NULL predicate or to negate the IS NULL predicate by preceding it with NOT.

SQL

```
SELECT  title_id, price
FROM     pubs.dbo.titles
WHERE  price IS NOT NULL   -- Or: WHERE  NOT price  IS NULL
```

Either form returns both of the first two rows from the previous table.

Caution: Never use "columnname = NULL" or "columnname <> NULL" to find rows with NULL or non-NULL values. These forms are syntactically correct but logically of no value since they always return zero rows. Always use **IS NULL**.

Despite this caution, the = as an assignment operator is used in UPDATE to change a column value to NULL.

Updating a Value to NULL A value may be set to NULL using the form

UPDATE *tablename* SET *columnname* = NULL

Example: Change the price to NULL for title_id MC3021.

SQL

```
UPDATE   pubs.dbo.titles
SET price = NULL
WHERE title_id = 'MC3021'
```

Compound Predicates using AND, OR and NOT with NULL The WHERE or HAVING predicate of a SELECT statement may include compound conditions using AND and OR operators.

Example: Consider the SELECT statement in Figure 2-1.

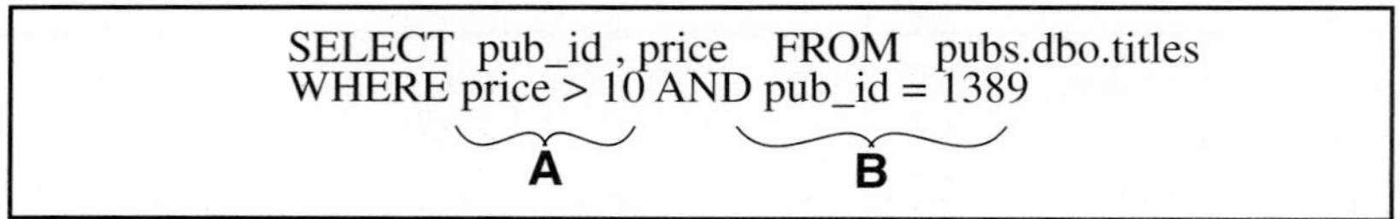

Figure 2-1 Selected statement.

When executed, the WHERE predicate is evaluated on each row in the table and only if both A and B are known to be TRUE then the row is included in the result set. So any row where price or pub_id is NULL will not appear in the final result set.

Tables 2-9, 2-10 and 2-11 are truth tables for AND, OR and NOT.

Table 2-9 Truth Table for A AND B

		B		
		TRUE	**FALSE**	**NULL**
A	**TRUE**	TRUE	FALSE	NULL
	FALSE	FALSE	FALSE	FALSE
	NULL	NULL	FALSE	NULL

Hint: Read NULL as UNKNOWN

Table 2-10 Truth Table for A OR B

		B		
		TRUE	**FALSE**	**NULL**
A	**TRUE**	TRUE	TRUE	TRUE
	FALSE	TRUE	FALSE	NULL
	NULL	TRUE	NULL	NULL

Table 2-11 Truth Table for NOT A

A	TRUE	FALSE	NULL
NOT A	FALSE	TRUE	NULL

2.3.1.8 ANY/SOME

ANY and SOME are equivalent and may be used interchangeably.

Syntax:

```
scalar_expression { = | < > | ! = | > | > = | ! > | < | < = | ! < }
        { ANY | SOME } ( subquery )
```

Arguments

```
scalar_expression
```

This is any valid Microsoft SQL Server expression.

```
{ = | <> | != | > | >= | !> | < | <= | !< }
```

This is any valid comparison operator.

```
subquery
```

This is a SELECT statement that has a result set of one column. The data type of the column returned must be the same data type as scalar_expression.

Return

Type: Boolean

ANY/SOME returns TRUE if the comparison specified is TRUE for ANY pair (scalar_expression, x) where x is a value in the single-column set. Otherwise, ANY/SOME returns FALSE.

Example: List all publishers' names that have a `title` in the `titles` table.

SQL

```
USE  pubs        --  Move to the pubs database
go

SELECT pub_id, pub_name FROM publishers
WHERE pub_id = ANY ( SELECT pub_id FROM titles )
```

Result

```
pub_id          pub_name
------          ------------------------------
0736            New Moon Books
0877            Binnet & Hardley
1389            Algodata Infosystems
```

This same result can be obtained by using the IN and EXISTS operators (explained on the following pages) or by doing an INNER JOIN of **publishers** and **titles**.

SQL

```
SELECT DISTINCT p.pub_id, p.pub_name -- Same result as previous query
FROM publishers p , titles t
WHERE p.pub_id = t.pub_id
```

2.3.1.9 ALL

ALL compares a scalar value with a single-column set of values.

Syntax:

```
scalar_expression { = | <> | != | > | >= | !> | < |
<= | !< } ALL ( subquery )
```

Arguments

scalar_expression

This is any valid SQL Server (scalar) expression.

```
{ = | <> | != | > | >= | !> | < | <= | !< }
```

This is a comparison operator.

subquery

This is a subquery that returns a result set of one column. The data type of the returned column must be the same data type as the data type of *scalar_expression*. It may not contain an ORDER BY clause, COMPUTE clause or INTO keyword.

Result

Type: Boolean

ALL returns TRUE if the specified comparison is TRUE for *scalar_expression* and every value in the single-column set returned from the subquery, otherwise ALL returns FALSE.

`ALL` can often be used to find the complement of an `ANY/SOME` query.

Example: List all publishers' names that have NO `title` in the `titles` table.

SQL

```
SELECT pub_id, pub_name FROM publishers
WHERE pub_id <>  ALL ( SELECT pub_id FROM titles )
```

Result

pub_id	pub_name
------	------------------------------
1622	Five Lakes Publishing
1756	Ramona Publishers
9901	GGG&G
9952	Scootney Books
9999	Lucerne Publishing

2.3.1.10 BETWEEN

BETWEEN specifies inclusion in a specified range.

Syntax

```
test_expr [ NOT ] BETWEEN begin_expr AND end_expr
```

Arguments

test_expr

This is the expression to test for in the range defined by *begin_expr* and *end_expr*.

NOT

Not specifies that the result of the predicate be negated.

begin_expr

This is any valid expression.

end_expr

This too is any valid expression.

Result

Type: Boolean

BETWEEN returns TRUE if the value of test_expr is greater than or equal to the value of begin_expr and less than or equal to the value of end_expr.

NOT BETWEEN returns TRUE if the value of test_expr is less than the value of begin_expr or greater than the value of end_expr.

Remarks

test_expr, *begin_expr* and *end_expr* must be the same data type.

If any input to the BETWEEN or NOT BETWEEN predicate is NULL, the result is UNKNOWN.

The BETWEEN operator is a shorthand equivalent to

```
( test_expr >= begin_expr AND test_expr <= end_expr )
```

Example: Find all publishers with pub_id values between 500 and 900 — use both forms.

SQL

```
SELECT pub_id, pub_name FROM publishers
WHERE pub_id BETWEEN 500 AND 900

SELECT pub_id, pub_name FROM publishers  -- equivalent result
WHERE pub_id >= 500 AND pub_id <= 900
```

Result

```
pub_id      pub_name
------      ------------------------------------
0736        New Moon Books
0877        Binnet & Hardley
```

Example: Find all publishers with pub_id values outside of 500 and 900—use both forms.

SQL

```
SELECT pub_id, pub_name FROM publishers
WHERE pub_id NOT BETWEEN 500 AND 900
SELECT pub_id, pub_name FROM publishers -- equivalent result
WHERE NOT (pub_id >= 500 AND pub_id <= 900)
```

Result

```
pub_id        pub_name
------        ------------------------------------
1389          Algodata Infosystems
1622          Five Lakes Publishing
...           ...
```

2.3.1.11 IN

IN determines if a given value matches any value in a subquery or a list.

Syntax

```
test_expression [ NOT ] IN
    (      subquery    | expression [ ,...n ]      )
```

Arguments

test_expression

This is any valid Microsoft SQL Server expression.

subquery

A subquery has a result set of one column. This column must have the same data type as *test_expression*.

expression [,...n]

This is a list of expressions to test for a match. All expressions must be of the same type as *test_expression*.

Result

Type: Boolean

If the value of *test_expression* is equal to any value returned by *subquery* or is equal to any expression from the comma-separated list, the result value is TRUE. Otherwise, the result value is FALSE.

Using NOT IN negates the returned value.

Example with *subquery*: List all publishers' names with a **title** in the **titles** table.

SQL

```
SELECT pub_id, pub_name FROM publishers
WHERE pub_id IN ( SELECT pub_id FROM titles )
```

Result

Same as shown above using ANY.

Example: With *expression* list, list all publishers' names with a **pub_id** of 0736 or 0877.

SQL

```
SELECT pub_id, pub_name FROM publishers
WHERE pub_id IN ( 0736 , 0877 )
```

Result

```
pub_id        pub_name
------        ----------------------
0736          New Moon Books
0877          Binnet & Hardley
```

2.3.1.12 EXISTS

EXISTS is used only with a subquery (a SELECT statement enclosed in parentheses used inside another DML statement). It is TRUE if the subquery result set is nonempty.

See page 702 for more detail on subqueries.

Syntax

```
EXISTS subquery
```

Result

Type: Boolean

EXISTS returns TRUE if the subquery returns any rows at all (nonempty result set).

Example: List all publishers' names that have a `title` in the `titles` table.

SQL

```
SELECT pub_id, pub_name FROM publishers p
WHERE EXISTS
( SELECT pub_id FROM titles WHERE pub_id = p.pub_id)
```

Result

The result of this is the same as that shown above using ANY.

2.3.1.13 LIKE

LIKE provides pattern matching searching of character strings. LIKE determines whether or not a given character string matches a specified pattern. A pattern can include regular characters and wildcard characters. During pattern matching, regular characters must exactly match the characters specified in the character string. Wildcard characters, however, can be matched with arbitrary fragments of the character string. If any of the arguments are not of character string data type, SQL Server converts them to character string data type, if possible.

Syntax

```
match_expression [ NOT ] LIKE pattern [ ESCAPE
escape_character ]
```

Arguments

match_expression

This is any valid SQL Server expression of character string data type.

pattern

This syntax is the pattern to search for in match_expression, and can include the valid SQL Server wildcard characters shown in Table 2-12.

Table 2-12 Valid Wildcard Characters

LIKE Wildcard	Matches
% (percent)	Any string of zero or more characters
_ (underscore)	Exactly one of any character
[ ]	Any single among those listed inside the [ ]. E.g., a, b, c or d will match [abcd] or its shortcut form [a-d].
[^]	Any single character NOT listed in the [ ]. E.g., any character other than a, b, c or d will match [^abcd] or [^a-d].
Note: The [ ] and [^] notations are not included in the ANSI SQL standard and are thus not guaranteed to be portable. The rest of the LIKE notation does comply with SQL-92 and 99.	

escape_character

This is any valid SQL Server expression of any of the character string data types. The escape_character has no default and may consist of only one character.

For example, if you want to search for a literal percent sign (%) embedded in text, you could declare an escape character that does not occur in the text, e.g., \, and use it to escape the %. A sample search might be as follows.

```
SELECT * FROM titles
        WHERE notes LIKE '% 30\% discount %'
        ESCAPE '\'
```

The first and last % are wildcards, the \% causes the search for a literal %.

Some people prefer to use % as the escape character so that %% becomes a literal percent sign and a single % is a wildcard.

Result

Type: Boolean

LIKE returns TRUE if the match_expression (usually a column name) matches the specified pattern.

Example: List all authors whose last names begin with Gr.

SQL
`SELECT au_lname FROM authors WHERE au_lname LIKE 'Gr%'`

SQL (cont.)
Result
au_lname ------------------- Green Greene Gringlesby

Remarks

When you perform string comparisons with LIKE, all characters in the pattern string are significant, including leading or trailing spaces.

For example, using LIKE 'abc ' (abc followed by one space), a row with the value abc (without a space) is not returned. However, trailing blanks, in the expression to which the pattern is matched, are ignored. For example, using LIKE'abc'(abc without a space), all rows that start with abc followed by zero or more trailing blanks are returned.

2.3.1.14 Performance Note: Anywhere Search

A LIKE query which begins with a wildcard, either % or _, is called an Anywhere Search and is usually not recommended if it can be avoided.

```
WHERE  au_lname  LIKE '%st%'
```

, or

```
WHERE  au_lname  LIKE '%st'
```

, or

```
WHERE  au_lname  LIKE '_st'
```

The reason to avoid anywhere searches is the impact on performance, especially if the table being searched is large. This is because an index, if one exists on the au_lname column, can not be used in an anywhere search. Queries on large tables will take a very, very, very long time if no index is used.

To see why an anywhere search disables the use of an index, think of an index being similar to a telephone book and imagine the usefulness of the telephone book if looking for each of the queries above.

On the other hand, the following query does NOT disable the use of an index on au_lname if one exists since the match string does not BEGIN with a wildcard: WHERE au_lname LIKE 'st%'

2.3.1.15 String Concatenation Operator: +

There is one concatenation operator, plus sign (+), and it may be used with character or binary string data types.

Example:

SQL

```
SELECT lname, fname, lname + ', ' + fname FROM employee
```

Result

```
lname       fname
-------     -------     ----------------
Cruz        Aria        Cruz, Aria
```

Note: The ANSI SQL concatenation operator is "||" used in Oracle, DB2 and others. The + string concatenation operator in SQL Server is not portable to other RDBMSs.

2.3.1.16 Unary Operators

Unary operators work on a single numeric operand expression.

Bitwise NOT only works with integer data types, the other two take any numeric data type. See Table 2-13.

Table 2-13 Unary Operators

Positive	Negative	Bitwise NOT
+	—	~

Notes:
Positive (+) means the numeric value is positive.
Negative (–) means the numeric value is negative.
Bitwise NOT returns the ones complement of the number.

Example:

SQL

```
print  1  +  -3     -- + is binary operator, - is unary
```

Result

```
-2
```

2.3.1.17 Operator Precedence

When a complex expression has multiple operators, operator precedence determines the sequence in which the operations are performed. Operators have the precedence levels shown in Table 2-14. An operator on higher levels is evaluated before an operator on a lower level. In case of two operators of equal precedence evaluation proceeds from left to right.

Table 2-14 Operator Precedence

Operator
+ (Positive), – (Negative), ~ (Bitwise NOT)
* (Multiply), / (Division), % (Modulo)
+ (Add), (+ Concatenate), – (Subtract)
=, >, <, >=, <=, <>, !=, !>, !< (Comparison operators)
^ (Bitwise Exclusive OR), & (Bitwise AND),	(Bitwise OR)
NOT
AND
ALL, ANY, BETWEEN, IN, LIKE, OR, SOME
= (Assignment)

2.4 SQL SERVER 2K DATA TYPES

SQL Server supports a wide variety of native data types which may be used for column data type in a CREATE TABLE statement and for local variables and function return types. Virtually all SQL-92 data types are supported as well as a few additional ones as shown in Table 2-15.

Table 2-15 Data Types

T-SQL Data Type Name	SQL-92	General Comments Each type is described individually in the following sections.
BIGINT		
BINARY		SQL-92 has **BLOB** (binary large object)
BIT	Yes	SQL-92 has a different **BIT** data type.
CHAR	Yes	

Table 2-15 Data Types (cont.)

T-SQL Data Type Name	SQL-92	General Comments Each type is described individually in the following sections.
DATETIME		SQL-92 has **DATE** and **TIME**
DECIMAL	Yes	
FLOAT	Yes	
IMAGE		SQL-92 has **BLOB** (binary large object)
INT	Yes	
MONEY		
NCHAR	Yes	
NTEXT		
NVARCHAR	Yes	
NUMERIC	Yes	
REAL	Yes	
SMALLDATETIME		
SMALLINT	Yes	
SMALLMONEY		
SQL_VARIANT		
SYSNAME		NVARCHAR(128) — predefined by SQL Server
TEXT		
TIMESTAMP		SQL-92 has a different **TIMESTAMP** type.
TINYINT		
VARBINARY		SQL-92 has **BLOB** (binary large object)
VARCHAR	Yes	
UNIQUEIDENTIFIER		

SQL Server data types are divided into three major categories: Numeric, String and Other as shown in the following tables.

2.4.1 Numeric Data Type Overview

Table 2-16 broadly describes the numeric data types. The last column gives the page where each is described in detail with examples given.

Table 2-16 Numeric Data Types

SQL Server 2000 Numeric Data Types	Description	Details and Examples
BIGINT	Integer values from -2^{63} through $+(2^{63}-1)$ or $-9.22\text{x}10^{18}$ through $9.22\text{x}10^{18}$	page 76
INT INTEGER	Integer values from -2^{31} through $+(2^{31}-1)$ or –2 billion through + 2 billion INTEGER is a synonym for data type INT.	page 76
SMALLINT	Integer values from -2^{15} through $+(2^{15}-1)$ or (–32,768) through +32,767)	page 76
TINYINT	Integer values from 0 through +255	page 76
BIT	Integer data with value either 0 or 1 (or NULL)	page 82
DECIMAL(p,s) **DEC(p,s)** **NUMERIC (p,s)**	Numeric data , fixed precision (*p*) and scale (*s*) from -10^{38} through $+(10^{38}-1)$. $p <= 38$, $s <= p$ DEC is a synonym for DECIMAL. DECIMAL and NUMERIC are functionally equivalent. See DECIMAL and NUMERIC details below.	page 83
MONEY	Monetary data values from -2^{63} through $+(2^{63}-1)$ with accuracy to a ten-thousandth of a monetary unit. ($-9.22\text{x}10^{18}$ through $9.22\text{x}10^{18}$)	page 86
SMALLMONEY	Monetary data values from –214,748.3648 through +214,748.3647, with accuracy to a ten-thousandth of a monetary unit.	page 86
FLOAT(n) DOUBLE PRECISION	Floating point number data from –1.79E + 308 through 1.79E + 308. FLOAT(*n*) causes *n* bits to be used to store the mantissa, *n* = 1–53 If *n* = 1–24, storage size is 4 Bytes and precision is 7 digits If *n* = 25–53, storage size is 8 Bytes and precision is 15 digits If (*n*) is missing as in FLOAT, then *n* defaults to 53. DOUBLE PRECISION is a synonym for FLOAT(53)	page 87

Table 2-16 Numeric Data Types (cont.)

SQL Server 2000 Numeric Data Types	Description	Details and Examples
REAL FLOAT(24)	Floating point number data from –3.40E + 38 through 3.40E + 38. FLOAT(24) is a synonym for REAL	page 87
DATETIME	Date and time data from January 1, 1753, through December 31, 9999, with an accuracy of three-hundredths of a second, or 3.33 milliseconds.	page 90
SMALLDATETIME	Date and time data from January 1, 1900, through June 6, 2079, with an accuracy of one minute.	page 90
The words in bold are the SQL Server 2K base data type name. The other word appearing in the same cell is a synonym, which may be used interchangeably with the base data type name in Transact-SQL statements. It is the base data type and not the synonym that is stored and will be seen from operations such as **sp_help**.		

2.4.2 String Data Type Overview

Table 2-17 broadly describes the parameters of string, or character, data types. In Sections 2.4.12 through 2.4.16, the string data types listed here are described in detail.

Table 2-17 String Data Types

SQL Server 2000 String Data Types	Description	Details and Examples
CHAR (*n*) CHARACTER (*n*)	Fixed-length non-Unicode character data with a length of *n* bytes where n = 1 to 8,000. Default length with DDL is 1, with CAST function is 30. Always stores *n* bytes, with blanks appended for strings less than *n* char. Example non-Unicode literal: 'Sue'	page 97
VARCHAR (*n*) CHAR VARYING (*n*) CHARACTER VARYING (*n*)	Variable-length non-Unicode character data with maximum length of *n* bytes. *n* = 1 to 8,000. Default length with DDL is 1, with CAST function is 30. Stores the actual number of bytes in the string up to the maximum of *n*.	page 97

Table 2-17 String Data Types (cont.)

SQL Server 2000 String Data Types	Description	Details and Examples
NCHAR (*n*) NATIONAL CHAR NATIONAL CHARACTER	Fixed-length Unicode data with a maximum length of 4,000 characters. Always stores 2x*n* bytes, with blanks appended as needed as for CHAR. Unicode is the ISO standard 16-bit (2 byte) character set capable of representing every language in the world. Example Unicode literal: N'Sue'	page 102
NVARCHAR (*n*) NATIONAL CHAR VARYING NATIONAL CHARACTER VARYING	Variable-length Unicode character data with maximum length of *n* characters. *n* must be a value from 1 through 4,000. Storage size, in bytes, is two times the number of characters entered. The data entered can be 0 characters in length.	page 102
TEXT	Variable-length non-Unicode data and with a maximum length of $2^{31}-1$ (2 billion) characters.	page 107
NTEXT NATIONAL TEXT	Variable-length Unicode data with a maximum length of $2^{30}-1$ (1 billion) characters. Storage size, in bytes, is two times the number of characters entered.	page 107
IMAGE	Variable-length binary data from 0 through $2^{31}-1$ or 0 through 2 GB.	page 107
SYSNAME	System supplied user-defined data type defined as NVARCHAR(128).	page 107
BINARY (*n*)	Fixed-length binary data with a length of *n* bytes. *n* = 1 to 8,000. Default length with DDL is 1, with CAST function is 30. Stores (*n* + 4 bytes).	page 110
VARBINARY (*n*) BINARY VARYING (*n*)	Variable-length binary data with a maximum length of 8,000 bytes. Default length with DDL is 1, with CAST function is 30. Stores (actual length + 4 bytes).	page 110

The words in bold are the SQL Server 2K base data type name. The other word or words appearing in the same cell are synonyms, which may be used interchangeably with the data type name in Transact-SQL statements.

2.4.3 Other Data Type Overview

Table 2-18 broadly describes the characteristics of several other data types. The last column gives the page where each is described in detail with examples given. We should note that cursor and table data types may not be used as column data types but they may be used for local variables and function return types.

Table 2-18 Other Data Types

SQL Server 2000 Other Data Types	Description	Details and Examples
CURSOR	A data type for cursor variables or stored procedure OUTPUT parameters that contain a reference to a cursor variable. A cursor variable is a Transact-SQL variable capable of containing the result set of a query; it may be updatable. See Cursors, p. 498. Cursors cannot be used as the column data type of a table.	page 111
SQL_VARIANT	A data type that can store values of any SQL Server–supported data types, except TEXT, NTEXT, TIMESTAMP and SQL_VARIANT.	page 112
TABLE	A special data type to store table structured data such as a result set. **Table** data type cannot be used as the column data type of a table. It is somewhat similar to cursors: a table variable is for temporary storage of data whereas cursors have more programmatic control including the ability to cause updates back to the original base table.	page 120
TIMESTAMP ROWVERSION	A data type that exposes automatically generated binary numbers, which are guaranteed to be unique within a database. Timestamp is used typically as a mechanism for version-stamping table rows. The storage size is 8 bytes. ROWVERSION should be used in place of TIMESTAMP data type as the latter is slated to change behavior in a future release of SQL Server to correspond to ANSI SQL behavior.	page 123
UNIQUEIDENTIFIER	A globally unique identifier (GUID). The only operations that are allowed against a uniqueidentifier value are comparisons (=, <>, <, >, <=, >=) and checking for NULL (IS NULL and IS NOT NULL).	page 127

The words in bold are the SQL Server 2K base data type name. The other word appearing in the same cell is a synonym which may be used interchangeably with the data type name in Transact-SQL statements. It is the base data type and not the synonym that is stored and will be seen from operations such as **sp_help**.

2.4.4 Transact-SQL Data Type Precedence

2.4.4.1 Implicit Data Type Conversions

Implicit data type conversions are those conversions that are done by SQL Server when neither the CAST or CONVERT function is specified. Implicit data type conversions use the Data Type Precedence List shown and are done to complete either of the following tasks.

- **comparing two expressions of different data types:** When comparing two expressions of different data types supported by implicit conversion, the expression of the lower precedence data type is implicitly converted to the data type of the higher precedence, and then the comparison is made. If implicit conversion is not supported, an error is returned. For a table containing all implicit data type conversions and which conversions are supported, see Books Online index: "CAST and CONVERT" and scroll to the table shown under "Remarks."
- **evaluating two operand expressions of different types joined by a binary operator:** When two expressions of different compatible data types are combined by a binary operator, the expression of lower precedence is implicitly converted to the data type of higher precedence, the operator's operation is performed and the resulting value is of the higher precedence data type. If implicit conversion is not supported, an error is returned.

Data Type Precedence List	
sql_variant (highest)	**bit**
datetime	**ntext**
smalldatetime	**text**
float	**image**
real	**timestamp**
decimal	**uniqueidentifier**
money	**nvarchar**
smallmoney	**nchar**
bigint	**varchar**
int	**char**
smallint	**varbinary**
tinyint	**binary** (lowest)

2.4.5 Transact-SQL Data Type Hierarchy

SQL Server documentation divides similar data types into three major categories.

- Numeric Data Types
- Character and Binary String Data Types
- Other Data Types

It further arranges them in the hierarchy shown in Figure 2-2.

Numeric Data Types

- exact numeric
  - integer
    - **bigint**
    - **int**
    - **smallint**
    - **tinyint**
  - **bit**
  - decimal and numeric
    - **decimal**
    - **numeric**
  - money and smallmoney
    - **money**
    - **smallmoney**
- approximate numeric
  - **float**
  - **real**
- datetime and smalldatetime
  - **datetime**
  - **smalldatetime**

Bold words are
Data Type names

Non-bold words are
category names

Character and Binary String Data Types

- character string
  - char, varchar, and text
    - char and varchar
      - **char**
      - **varchar**
    - **text**
  - Unicode character string
    - nchar and nvarchar
      - **nchar**
      - **nvarchar (and sysname**[1]**)**
    - **ntext**
- binary strings
  - binary and varbinary
    - **binary**
    - **varbinary**
  - **image**

Other Data Types

- **cursor**
- **sql_variant**
- **table**
- **timestamp**
- **uniqueidentifier**

Note:
Books Online is not consistent in using the term "data type hierarchy".

The one here is "Transact-SQL Syntax Conventions."

It disagrees with the term shown with "sql_variant data type" for comparing values shown with SQL_VARIANT below.

1. **sysname** is predefined as nvarchar(128), used for object names

Figure 2-2 Data Type hierarchy.

The three major categories of data type are described in the following sections.

2.4.5.1 sp_datatype_info

The **sp_datatype_info** system-stored procedure in Microsoft SQL Server returns information about the data types supported by the current environment. Table 2-19 gives a partial listing of output from **sp_datatype_info** run on SQL Server 2K. See Books Online for more details.

Table 2-19 sp_datatype_info

SQL `EXEC sp_datatype_info`

Result

```
TYPE_NAME          ...  PRECISION     LITERAL_PREFIX    LITERAL_SUFFIX
------------------ ...  ------------  ----------------  ----------------
sql_variant        ...  8000          NULL              NULL
uniqueidentifier   ...  36            '                 '
ntext              ...  1073741823    N'                '
nvarchar           ...  4000          N'                '
sysname            ...  128           N'                '
nchar              ...  4000          N'                '
bit                ...  1             NULL              NULL
tinyint            ...  3             NULL              NULL
bigint             ...  19            NULL              NULL
image              ...  2147483647    0x                NULL
varbinary          ...  8000          0x                NULL
binary             ...  8000          0x                NULL
timestamp          ...  8             0x                NULL
text               ...  2147483647    '                 '
char               ...  8000          '                 '
numeric            ...  38            NULL              NULL
decimal            ...  38            NULL              NULL
money              ...  19            $                 NULL
smallmoney         ...  10            $                 NULL
int                ...  10            NULL              NULL
smallint           ...  5             NULL              NULL
float              ...  15            NULL              NULL
real               ...  7             NULL              NULL
datetime           ...  23            '                 '
smalldatetime      ...  16            '                 '
varchar            ...  8000          '                 '
```

2.4.6 `BIGINT`, `INT`, `SMALLINT` and `TINYINT` Details

Table 2-20 provides a recap of the first four data types. Details and examples of these types follow.

Table 2-20 Recapping Data Types

Data Type	Description	Storage Size
`BIGINT`	Integer values from -2^{63} through $+(2^{63}-1)$ or $-9.22x10^{18}$ through $9.22x10^{18}$	8 Bytes
`INT` `INTEGER`	Integer values from -2^{31} through $+(2^{31}-1)$ or –2 billion through + 2 billion `INTEGER` is a synonym for data type INT.	4 Bytes
`SMALLINT`	Integer values from -2^{15} through $+(2^{15}-1)$ or (–32,768) through (+32,767)	2 Bytes
`TINYINT`	Integer values from 0 through +255	1 Byte

2.4.6.1 Integer Data Type Constants (Literals)

A constant (literal) is a representation of a specific, fixed scalar data value.The format of a constant depends on the data type of the value it represents. Integer literals consist of a sequence of numeric characters not enclosed in quotation marks, containing neither decimal point nor comma and optionally preceded by plus or minus prefix.

Example:

–13, 13, +13

13.89 is truncated to 13, not rounded. So a decimal point is permitted, but not used.

Any fractions generated by arithmetic operations on these four integer data types are truncated, not rounded.

Example:

3 / 4 evaluates to 0.

2.4.6.2 `BIGINT` — Special Considerations

The **bigint** data type is new with SQL Server 2K. It is intended for cases where the integer values may exceed the range supported by the **int** data type. The **int** data type remains the primary integer data type in SQL Server.

BIGINT with Expressions SQL Server will not automatically promote **tinyint**, **smallint** or **int** values to bigint, although it sometimes does automatically promote **tinyint** or **smallint** to int.

BIGINT with Functions Functions will return bigint only if the input parameter expression is a **bigint** data type.

Example:

SQL

```
CREATE TABLE a ( x int)
INSERT INTO a VALUES (2000000000)  -- 2 x 10^9, almost the max int value
INSERT INTO a VALUES (2000000000) -- the sum of exceeds int range

SELECT SUM(x)  FROM a -- Error, Input parameter is int, sum returns int
```

Result

Server: Msg 8115, Level 16, State 2, Line 1
Arithmetic overflow error converting expression to data type **int**.

SQL

```
SELECT CAST(SUM(x) AS bigint) FROM a  -- Error happens
        -- before the cast
```

Result

Server: Msg 8115, Level 16, State 2, Line 1
Arithmetic overflow error converting expression to data type **int**.

The solution is to CAST the column value to **bigint** before doing the SUM.

SQL

```
SELECT SUM( CAST(x AS bigint) ) FROM a  -- Correct result
```

Result

```
--------------------
4000000000
```

Unless explicitly stated in the documentation, functions and system-stored procedures with **int** expressions for their parameters have not been changed to support implicit conversion of **bigint** expressions to those parameters. For this reason, SQL Server implicitly converts **bigint** to **int** only when the **bigint** value is within the range supported by the **int** data type. A conversion error occurs at run time if the **bigint** expression contains a value outside the range supported by the **int** data type.

When you provide **bigint** as input parameters and the return values are of type **bigint**, you may use the Transact-SQL functions shown in Table 2-21. See details under Functions, page 137.

Table 2-21 Functions

ABS	FLOOR	POWER
AVG	IDENTITY	RADIANS
CEILING	MAX	ROUND
COALESCE	MIN	SIGN
DEGREES	NULLIF	SUM

According to Books Online, certain aggregate functions will not return a **bigint** unless the input parameter expression is of type **bigint**.

Example:

SQL

```
CREATE TABLE b ( y bigint)
INSERT INTO b VALUES (2000000000) -- 2 x 109, almost the max int value
INSERT INTO b VALUES (2000000000)


SELECT AVG(y) FROM b  -- Input parameter y is bigint, returns in int
range
```

Result

```
--------------------
2000000000
```

SQL
`SELECT SUM(y) FROM b -- Input parameter y is bigint, sum returns bigint`

Result
--------------------   4000000000

Recall previous example, x is **int** so it must be CAST to **bigint** as input parameter to SUM so that result will be bigint to accommodate the large result value.

Example:

SQL
`SELECT SUM( CAST(x AS bigint) ) FROM a -- Correct result`

Result
--------------------   4000000000

The functions shown in Table 2-22 may be used to reference **bigint** columns or variables though they do not return **bigint** values. See details under Functions, page 137.

Table 2-22 **bigint** References

@@IDENTITY	ISNULL	VARP
COL_LENGTH	ISNUMERIC	
DATALENGTH	STDEV[P]	

SQL Server provides two functions just for **bigint** values, COUNT_BIG and ROWCOUNT_BIG.

COUNT_BIG Function This function is used when counting the number of items in a very large group if the value might exceed the range supported by the **int** data type. It returns a **bigint** type.

Example:

SQL

```
SELECT COUNT_BIG( a_column )  FROM  verybigtable
  -- Works like count() but returns bigint
  -- The data type of column doesn't matter,
     the number of rows does
```

Result

```
--------------------
4000000000
```

Note: If the number of rows is within the **int** range then either COUNT_BIG() or COUNT() may be used though the return type differs.

ROWCOUNT_BIG Function Use this function when counting the number of rows affected in the last statement executed and when the value exceeds the range supported by the **int** data type. This function is similar to the @@ROWCOUNT function, except that ROWCOUNT_BIG() returns a **bigint** data type.

Example:

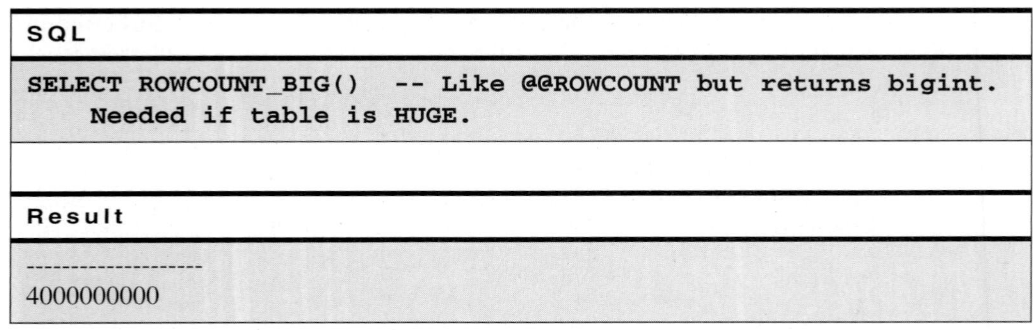

SQL

```
SELECT ROWCOUNT_BIG()   -- Like @@ROWCOUNT but returns bigint.
    Needed if table is HUGE.
```

Result

```
--------------------
4000000000
```

Note: If the number of rows returned by the last statement is within the **int** range, then either ROWCOUNT_BIG() or @@ROWCOUNT may be used though the return type differs.

BIGINT with Stored Procedures and Other Transact-SQL Elements

SQL Server will not automatically promote tinyint, smallint or int values to **bigint**, although sometimes it automatically promotes tinyint or smallint to int.

CAST and CONVERT support **bigint**, applying similar conversion rules for **bigint** as for the other integer data types. The **bigint** data type fits above **int** and below **smallmoney** in the data type precedence chart. For more information about **bigint** conversions, see CAST and CONVERT page 166.

When using the CASE expression, you will get a result of type **bigint** if either the *result_expression* or the *else_result_expression* if present evaluates to **bigint**. See CASE page 164.

You may use **bigint** for exact numeric data type in these Transact-SQL statements.

- CREATE TABLE
  ALTER TABLE
  Example:

```
CREATE TABLE c ( x int, y bigint)
INSERT INTO c  VALUES ( 20 , 3000000000 )
```

- CREATE PROC[EDURE]
  ALTER PROC[EDURE]
  Example:

```
CREATE PROC pr ( @parm bigint ) AS print @parm + 4
EXEC pr 3000000000
```

- DECLARE variable
  Example:

```
DECLARE  @var1   bigint
SET  @var1 = 3000000000 ;   print @var1
```

2.4.6.3 Specifying BIGINT Constants

Whole number constants outside the range supported by the **int** data type continue to be interpreted as **numeric**, with a scale of 0 and a precision sufficient for the value specified.

Example: The constant 3000000000 is interpreted by SQL Server as `NUMERIC(10,0)`.

These constants are implicitly convertible to **bigint** and can be assigned to **bigint** columns and variables. So in the examples from the previous section, the constant 3000000000 is seen by SQL Server as `NUMERIC(10,0)` and implicitly cast to **bigint**.

```
INSERT INTO c  VALUES ( 20 , 3000000000 )
```

and

```
EXEC pr 3000000000
```

To explicitly create a **bigint** constant use the CAST function,

```
CAST( 3000000000 AS BIGINT).
```

Example:

SQL
`print CAST( 3000000000 AS BIGINT)`

Result
3000000000

2.4.7 BIT Data Type Details

The **bit** data type is described in Table 2-23.

Table 2-23 BIT Data Type

Data Type	Description	Storage Size
BIT	Integer data with value either 0 or 1 (or NULL) Columns of type **bit** cannot have indexes on them.	1 Byte for bits 1 to 8 2 Bytes if NULLABLE

2.4.7.1 BIT Data Type Constants (Literals)

The numbers zero and one represent **bit** constants.. If a number larger than one is used, it is converted to one. (Empirically, any number other than 0 is stored as 1.)

No quote marks are used.

Example **bit** constants:

0 1

Example:

SQL

```
CREATE TABLE d ( x BIT )

INSERT INTO d VALUES (0);
INSERT INTO d VALUES (1);
INSERT INTO d VALUES (12);

SELECT * FROM d;
```

SQL (cont.)
Result

```
x
----
0
1
1
```

2.4.8 DECIMAL and NUMERIC Data Type Details

Table 2-24 offers an overview of the DECIMAL and NUMERIC data types.

Table 2-24 DECIMAL and NUMERIC Data Type

Data Type	Description
DECIMAL(*p*, *s*)	Numeric data , fixed precision (*p*) and scale (*s*) from -10^{38} through $+(10^{38} - 1)$. $p <= 38$, $s <= p$
DEC(*p*, *s*)	DEC is a synonym for DECIMAL.
NUMERIC (*p*, *s*)	DECIMAL and NUMERIC are functionally equivalent.
	Storage size depends on precision; see Table 2-25.

DECIMAL and NUMERIC are exact numeric data types with fixed precision (*p*) and scale (*s*) containing numbers from $(-10^{38} + 1)$ through $(+10^{38} - 1)$. That is, they store an exact representation of any number up to 38 digits which may all be to the left or right of the decimal point (or some on the left and the rest on the right). FLOAT and REAL may store larger and smaller numbers, but they are approximate. The number for *p* (precision) specifies the maximum total number of decimal digits that can be stored, both to the left and to the right of the decimal point. The precision must be a value from 1 through the maximum precision which is 38. If not specified *p* defaults to 18. In SQL Server 7.0 the maximum value for *p* is 28 unless the server is started with the /p option, **sqlserver /p**, in which case the maximum precision is 38.

The number for *s* (scale) specifies the maximum number of decimal digits that can be stored to the right of the decimal point. Scale must be a value from 0 through *p*, so, $0 <= s <= p$. The default scale is 0.

Legal declarations are as follows:

- DECIMAL(*p*,*s*) where 0 <= *p* <= 38 and 0 <= *s* <= p.
- DECIMAL(*p*) where 0 <= *p* <= 38 and *s* defaults to 0.
- DECIMAL where *p* defaults to 18 and *s* defaults to 0.

Note: DECIMAL may be replaced by either DEC or NUMERIC with equivalent results.

For DECIMAL(*p*,*s*) and NUMERIC(*p*,*s*), the **integer part may not exceed (p – s) digits**. The result will be an error. If more than *s* digits are specified for the **fractional part the value stored is rounded to *s* digits**. Table 2-25 below shows how the storage sizes vary based on the precision.

Table 2-25 Varying Storage Size

Precision	Storage bytes
1–9	5
10–19	9
20–28	13
29–38	17

2.4.8.1 Numeric Data Type Constants (Literals)

Table 2-26 summarizes the constant (literal) format for the numeric and decimal data types. Examples of these types follow.

Table 2-26 Numeric Data Type Constants

Data Type	Constant (Literal) Format
DECIMAL (*p*, *s*) DEC (*p*, *s*) **NUMERIC** (*p*, *s*)	A sequence of numbers not enclosed in quotation marks that may include decimal point but not a comma. Value must be within the range for the data type. Examples: For DEC(4,2): –13 or –13.24 or 13 or 13.24

Constants for numeric data types are represented by a sequence of numeric digits optionally preceded by a plus symbol or a minus symbol and are optionally followed by a decimal point and another sequence of numeric digits. No quote marks are used.

Example:

SQL

```
CREATE TABLE e ( x DEC(5,2) , y DEC(5) , z DEC)
EXEC SP_HELP e
```

Result

Column_name	Type	Length	Prec	Scale
x	decimal	... 5	5	2
y	decimal	... 5	5	0
z	decimal	... 9	18	0

Length represents the number of bytes of storage as given in Table 2-26.

This **sp_help** output shows that	is stored as
DEC(5,2)	DEC(5,2)
DEC(5)	DEC(5,0)
DEC	DEC(18,0)

Example: DEC(5,2) can store from –999.99 to +999.99.

```
SQL INSERT INTO e (x) VALUES (123.45)     -- Okay
```

Entering a number with more than ($p - s$) digits to the left of the decimal point, or $(5 - 2) = 3$ in this example, is an error.

```
SQL INSERT INTO e (x) VALUES(1234.00)-- Error - overflow
```

Any number of digits may be entered to the right of the decimal point. If more than s digits are entered, the number is rounded to have exactly s digits to the right of the decimal.

Example:

SQL

```
INSERT INTO e (x) VALUES (-999)        -- Okay
INSERT INTO e (x) VALUES (12.89)       -- Okay
INSERT INTO e (x) VALUES (123.899)     -- Okay
INSERT INTO e (x) VALUES (-123.899)    -- Okay

SELECT  x  FROM e
```

SQL (cont.)

Result

```
x
-------
123.45
-999.00
12.89
123.90
-123.90
```

2.4.9 MONEY and SMALLMONEY Data Type Details

The data types **money** and **smallmoney** are distinguished by their range, as shown in Table 2-27.

Table 2-27 MONEY and SMALLMONEY Data Type

Data Type	Range	Accuracy	Storage Size
MONEY	From –922,337,203,685,477.5808 through +922,337,203,685,477.5807	4 Decimal Places	8 Bytes
SMALLMONEY	From -214,748.3648 through 214,748.3647	4 Decimal Places	4 Bytes

The monetary data types, **money** and **smallmoney**, can store positive or negative amounts of money. However, if more than four decimal places are required, use the decimal data type instead.

The data type is versatile enough to accept many national currency symbols including the British pound, the Euro, the Yen and many others. See details in Books Online, search for "Using Monetary Data."

2.4.9.1 Monetary Data Type Constants (Literals)

The acceptable constant (literal) format for monetary data types is summarized in Table 2-28.

Table 2-28 Monetary Data Type

MS SQL Server 2K Data Type	Constant (Literal) Format
MONEY	A sequence of numbers not enclosed in quotation marks with one optional decimal point and one optional currency symbol as a prefix within the range from -2^{63} through $+(2^{63}-1)$ i.e., -9.22×10^{18} through 9.22×10^{18}. Ex: –13 or –13.24 or 13.24 or –$13.24 or –$922337203685477.5808
SMALLMONEY	Same as for MONEY with range from –214,748.3648 through +214,748.3647. Examples: -$13 or 13.24 or -214748.3648 or $214748.3647

Example:

SQL

```
CREATE TABLE f ( m MONEY, s SMALLMONEY )

INSERT INTO f VALUES ( 12, 12);                 -- Okay
INSERT INTO f VALUES ( $12345678, 12);          -- Okay
INSERT INTO f VALUES ( 12, $12345678 );         -- Error --  s too large
INSERT INTO f VALUES ( $12,345,678, 12);        -- Error --  no commas
INSERT INTO f VALUES
   ( CAST('$12,345,678' AS MONEY), 12);          -- Okay

SELECT * FROM f;
```

Result

```
m                     s
-------------------   ------------
12.0000               12.0000
12345678.0000         12.0000
12345678.0000         12.0000
```

2.4.10 FLOAT and REAL Data Type Details

The data types FLOAT and REAL allow numerical approximations. They are summarized in Table 2-29.

DECIMAL and NUMERIC contain an exact representation of any number up to 38 digits. MONEY and SMALLMONEY also store an exact representation of numbers with a smaller range than DECIMAL and NUMERIC. However,

Table 2-29 FLOAT and REAL Data Type

Data Type	Description	Storage Size and Precision
FLOAT(*n*) DOUBLE PRE-CISION	Floating point number data in [–1.79E + 308, 1.79E + 308] FLOAT(*n*) causes *n* bits to be used to store the mantissa, *n* in [1,53] *n* defaults to 53 so FLOAT is the same as FLOAT(53) DOUBLE PRECISION is a synonym for FLOAT(53)	If *n* in [1,24] then storage = 4 bytes, precision = 7 digits If *n* in [25,53] then storage = 8 bytes, precision = 15 digits
REAL FLOAT(24)	Floating point number data in [–3.40E + 38, 3.40E + 38] FLOAT(24) is a synonym for REAL	storage = 4 bytes, precision = 7 digits

FLOAT and REAL contain an approximate representation with a range of much larger and smaller fractional numbers and take less storage space than the other data types for the same number.

2.4.10.1 FLOAT and REAL Data Type Constants (Literals)

Constants for approximate numeric data types are represented by a sequence of numeric digits with an optional decimal point and optionally preceded by a plus symbol or a minus symbol and optionally suffixed with the letter *E* and an integer representing an exponent of 10. No quote marks are used. See Table 2-30.

Table 2-30 FLOAT and REAL Data Types

MS SQL Server 2K Data Type	Constant (Literal) Format
Floating Point Format	[+|–]<nums>[.<nums>][E[+|–]<nums>] where <nums> is sequence of one or more numeric characters and the value following E, if present, represents the exponent of 10. Example Format: [+|–]12[.34][E[+|–]5] Examples: –12 or 12 or 12E–1 (which is 1.2) or 12E1 (which is 120)
FLOAT [(*n*)] DOUBLE PRECISION	Floating Point Format in the range [–1.79E + 308, 1.79E + 308]
REAL	Floating Point Format in the range [–3.40E + 38, 3.40E + 38].

Example: Create a table with a REAL and a FLOAT and enter exactly the same value for each though using different notation

SQL

```
CREATE TABLE g ( r REAL , f FLOAT )

INSERT INTO g VALUES ( 123, 1.23E2 );            -- Okay
INSERT INTO g VALUES ( .0123 , 1.23E-2 );        -- Okay
INSERT INTO g VALUES ( .00123 , 1.23E-3 );       -- Okay

SELECT * FROM g;
```

Result

r	f
123.0	123.0
0.0123	0.0123
1.2300001E-3	0.00123

Because the stored values of FLOAT and REAL, all other values are approximate. WHERE clause comparisons with FLOAT and REAL columns should use >, <, >= and <= relational operators and should avoid = and <> operators.

Example:

SQL

```
SELECT * FROM g -- For each row the same value was entered for r and f
WHERE  r = f; -- But "=" only finds the first row as the same
```

Result

r	f
123.0	123.0

SQL

```
SELECT * FROM g
WHERE NOT ( r < f  AND r > f ); -- This finds all three rows
```

Result

```
r                       f
----------------------- -----------------------------------------------------
123.0                   123.0
0.0123                  0.0123
1.2300001E-3            0.00123
```

2.4.11 DATETIME and SMALLDATETIME Data Type Details

Microsoft SQL Server 2000 has only **datetime** and **smalldatetime** data types (Table 2-31) to store both date and time data.

Table 2-31 DATETIME and SMALLDATETIME Data Type

Data Type	Description	Storage Size
DATETIME	Date and time data from Jan 1, 1753, through Dec 31, 9999, accurate to three-hundredths of a second, or 3.33 milliseconds.	8 Bytes
SMALLDATETIME	Date and time data from Jan 1, 1900, through Jun 6, 2079, accurate to one minute.	4 Bytes

There is no separate data type for just date or just time. A date with no time changes to the default time of midnight (12:00 AM). A time with no date changes to the default date of Jan 1, 1900.

Guidelines for searching for dates and/or times are as follows:

- To search for an exact match on both date and time, use an equal sign (=).
- The relational operators <, <=, >, >=, <> may be used to search for dates and times before or after a specified value.
- To search for a partial date or time value (year, day, hour), use the LIKE operator.

WHERE hiredate LIKE 'Jan 200%'

However, because the standard display formats do not include seconds or milliseconds, you cannot search for them with LIKE and a matching pattern, unless you use the CONVERT function with the *style* parameter set to 9 or 109. (See details under Functions, page 136.) For more information about searching for partial dates or times, see LIKE on page 63.

- To search for an exact match on both date and time, use an equal sign (=).
- SQL Server evaluates **datetime** constants at run time.
- A date string that works for the date formats expected by one language may not work if the query is executed by a connection using a different language and date format setting. For more information see Books Online. Search for "Writing International Transact-SQL Statements."

2.4.11.1 DATETIME Data Type Constants (Literals) Formats—for INPUT

SQL Server recognizes date and time literals enclosed in single quotation marks (') in the formats shown in Tables 2-32 and 2-33 for DATE and TIME data. A DATETIME value may be specified as either DATE [TIME] or [DATE] TIME where DATE and TIME follow the formats below.

Table 2-32 DATE Formats

DATE only Format Names (no time defaults to 12:00 AM)	Formats - put inside single quotes ' '
Alphabetic date format Month may be any case, e.g., April or april or APRIL or any other mixed case	Apr[il] [22] [,] 2001 Apr[il] 22 [,] [20]01 Apr[il] 2001 [22] Apr[il] 01 22 [22] Apr[il] [,] 2001 22 Apr[il] [,] [20]01 22 [20]01 Apr[il] [22] 2001 Apr[il] 2001 Apr[il] [22] 2001 [22] Apr[il]

Table 2-32 DATE Formats **(cont.)**

DATE only Format Names (no time defaults to 12:00 AM)	Formats - put inside single quotes ' '
Numeric date format	[0]4/22/[20]01 -- (mdy) [0]4-22-[20]01 -- (mdy) [0]4.22.[20]01 -- (mdy) [04]/[20]01/22 -- (myd) 22/[0]4/[20]01 -- (dmy) 22/[20]01/[0]4 -- (dym) [20]01/22/[0]4 -- (ydm) [20]01/[04]/22 -- (ymd) 2001-22-04
Unseparated string format	[20]010422

DATETIME values may be subtracted to give the number of days between, but test it carefully to make sure it gives what you want.

Example:

SQL

```
SELECT CAST (
CAST( '1/3/2003' AS DATETIME ) - CAST( '1/1/2003'AS DATETIME )
  AS INT )
```

Result

```
-------
```

Table 2-33 TIME Formats

TIME only Format Names (no date defaults to 1 Jan, 1900)	Formats - put inside single quotes ' '
Time format AM and PM may be any case	17:44 17:44[:20:999] 17:44[:20.9] 5am 5 PM [0]5[:44:20:500]AM
Note: Milliseconds can be preceded by either a colon (:) or a period (.). If preceded by a colon, the number means thousandths-of-a-second. If preceded by a period, a single digit means tenths-of-a-second, two digits mean hundredths-of-a-second, and three digits mean thousandths-of-a-second. For example, 12:30:20:1 indicates twenty and one-thousandth seconds past 12:30; 12:30:20.1 indicates twenty and one-tenth seconds past 12:30.	

Table 2-34 shows several examples of DATETIME Constants.

Table 2-34 DATETIME Constants

	Examples - Represent same date and/or time
Alphabetic date format	'April 22, 2001' or '22 April, 2001'
Numeric date format	'04/22/2001' or '4/22/2001' or '4/22/01'
Unseparated string format	'20010422' or '010422'
Time only format	'5:44PM' or '17:44' or '17:44:20.999'
Date and Time - any combination of the above forms 'DATE TIME' 'TIME DATE'	'April 22, 2001 5:44PM' '20010422 17:44' '5:44PM April 22, 2001' '17:44 20010422'

SET DATEFORMAT SET DATEFORMAT sets the order of the dateparts (month/day/year) for entering datetime or smalldatetime data values as a string of 3 numbers separated by slash, /. See the example below which changes the order from the default mdy to the European format of dmy.

Syntax

SET DATEFORMAT { *mdy* | *dmy* | *ymd* | *ydm* | *myd* | *dym* }

See Server, Database and Session Settings, page 174.

Remarks

In the U.S. English, the default is mdy. Remember that this setting is **used for input only**, that is, only in the interpretation of character strings as they are converted to date values. It has no effect on the display of date values. All users may use SET DATEFORMAT without special permission.

Examples:

SQL

```
DECLARE   @v_date   DATETIME
SET @v_date = '04/22/03'
PRINT @v_date
```

Result

```
Apr 22 2003 12:00AM
```

SQL

```
SET DATEFORMAT dmy

DECLARE   @v_date   DATETIME
SET @v_date = '22/04/03'

PRINT @v_date

SET DATEFORMAT mdy --  Set input date format back to the default
```

Result

```
Apr 22 2003 12:00AM
```

Notice that PRINT and SELECT use a different output format for datetime objects.

SQL

```
DECLARE   @v_date   DATETIME
SET @v_date = '04/22/03'

SELECT @v_date
```

Result

```
------------------------------------------------------
2003-04-22 00:00:00.000
```

2.4.11.2 Formatting DATETIME Data Type Constants (Literals) for OUTPUT

The default display format for DATETIME in SQL Server is arguably ugly: 2001-04-22 17:44:20.999. Table 2-35 gives some alternatives to obtain a more presentable output for a datetime column, variable or function.

Perhaps the easiest are CONVERT(VARCHAR[(19)] , *datetimevariable*) and CAST(*datetimevariable* AS VARCHAR[(19)]).

Table 2-35 Formatting DATETIME

Format String	Output
SELECT CONVERT(VARCHAR(19), GETDATE())	Apr 22 2001 5:44PM
SELECT CAST(GETDATE() AS VARCHAR(19))	Apr 22 2001 5:44PM
SELECT CONVERT(VARCHAR, GETDATE())	Apr 22 2001 5:44PM
SELECT CAST(GETDATE() AS VARCHAR)	Apr 22 2001 5:44PM
SELECT CONVERT(VARCHAR(10), GETDATE(), 101) (see CONVERT for more options)	04/22/2001
MONTH(GETDATE())	4
DAY(GETDATE())	22
YEAR(GETDATE())	2001

Example:

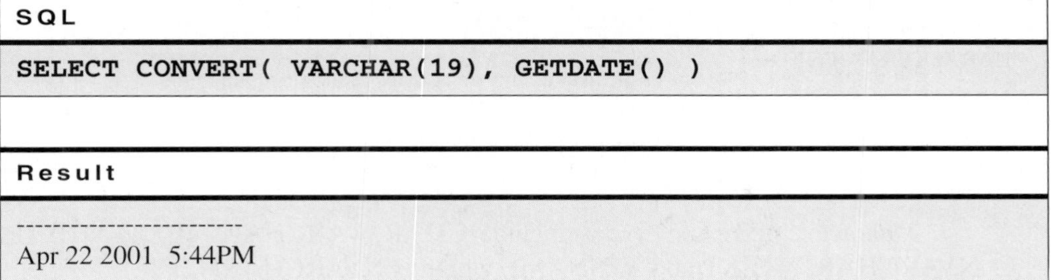

SQL

```
SELECT CONVERT( VARCHAR(19), GETDATE() )
```

Result

```
-------------------------
Apr 22 2001  5:44PM
```

2.4.11.3 Avoiding the Problems of Y2K

The primary way to avoid problems such as that caused by Y2K is to always enter datetime values with four digits for the year. This should be standard procedure by now. Nonetheless, SQL Server does provide a two-digit year cutoff option which tells how two-digit years should be interpreted. A two-digit year that is less than or equal to the last two digits of the cutoff year is in the same century as the cutoff year. A two-digit year that is greater than the last two digits of the cutoff year is in the century that precedes the cutoff year.

The default **two-digit year cutoff** for SQL Server is 2049. That means that a two-digit year of 40 is interpreted as 2040.A two-digit year of 60 is interpreted as 1960.

See Books Online and search for "cutoff" to learn how to change the **two-digit year cutoff** value for the entire server.

2.4.12 CHAR and VARCHAR Data Type Details

An overview of char and varchar is contained in Table 2-36.

Table 2-36 CHAR and VARCHAR Data Type

Data Type	Description	Storage Size
CHAR(*n*) CHARACTER(*n*)	Fixed-length, non-Unicode character data of *n* characters with a fixed length of *n* bytes. Default length *n* with DDL is 1. (See page 106) Default length *n* with CAST function is 30. (See page 107) Always stores *n* bytes, padding the right with blanks for strings less that *n* characters. Example non-Unicode literal: 'Sue'	*n* Bytes *n* = 1 to 8,000.
VARCHAR(*n*) CHAR VARYING(*n*) CHARACTER VARYING(*n*)	Variable-length, non-Unicode character up to *n* characters data with maximum length of *n* bytes. Default length *n* with DDL is 1. (See page 106) Default length *n* with CAST function is 30. (See page 107) Stores the actual number of bytes in the string up to the maximum of *n*. Example non-Unicode literal: 'Sue'	length of the data entered <= *n* Bytes *n* = 1 to 8,000.

Character string data types include CHAR, VARCHAR, TEXT, NCHAR, NVARCHAR, NTEXT and SYSNAME which is NVARCHAR(128).

String data types are for storing sequences of zero or more characters. Essentially any character on the keyboard may be stored in a string data type, including the following characters.

- Upper and lower case alphabetic characters such as a, b, c, ..., z, A, B, C, ..., Z
- Numeric characters such as 0, 1, ..., 9
- Punctuation and special characters such as ., ,, ;, [,], @, #, &, !, ...

2.4.12.1 CHAR and VARCHAR Data Type Constants (Literals)

Character string constants consist of a sequence of characters enclosed in single quotes in accordance with ANSI SQL standard. Essentially any alphabetic, numeric or punctuation character on the keyboard may be stored in a string data type.

A literal single quote (apostrophe) in a string is represented by two consecutive single quote characters, as in 'O''Reilly' for O'Reilly.

Example string constants:

'Mary Smith'

'O''Reilly'

2.4.12.2 Storage of CHAR and VARCHAR Data Types

CHAR(*n*) and VARCHAR(*n*) are data types for storing string data in one byte per character, non-Unicode. The main difference between the two is as follows.

- CHAR(*n*) always stores *n* bytes to contain a string up to *n* characters long, filling in by right padding with blanks if the data is less than n characters.
- VARCHAR(*n*) stores one byte for each of the actual number of characters up to *n*.
- Both CHAR(*n*) and VARCHAR(*n*) truncate data longer than *n* bytes to exactly *n* bytes for a local variable but return an error on INSERT or UPDATE into a table column. See "Truncation Examples" below.

Storage Size Examples

'Sue' inserted into CHAR(6) will be stored as "Sue   " with three blanks on the right. 'Sue' inserted into VARCHAR(6) will be stored as "Sue" plus number 3 for the length.

An explicit trailing space inserted into a VARCHAR will be retained, space permitting.

'Sue ' will correctly insert all four characters into VARCHAR(6) as "Sue". 'Sue ' will store six characters as usual in CHAR(6) as 'Sue   ".

An empty string of zero characters may be stored by entering '' (<single quote><single quote>). Such an empty string is very different from NULL, which is "no domain value entered" (see NULL, page 39).

Truncation Examples for a Local Variable

'Sammy' inserted into CHAR(3) or VARCHAR(3) variable will be truncated to "Sam."

Example:

SQL

```
DECLARE  @name   VARCHAR(3)          -- or CHAR(3)

SET @name  =   'Sammy'

PRINT   @name
```

Result

Sam

Truncation Examples for a Table Column

If the string 'Sammy' is inserted into CHAR(3) or VARCHAR(3) column it returns an error and fails.

Example:

SQL

```
CREATE  TABLE   t ( name  VARCHAR(3) )-- or CHAR(3)

INSERT INTO   t   VALUES   ( 'Sammy'   )
go
```

Result

Server: Msg 8152, Level 16, State 9, Line 1
String or binary data would be truncated.
The statement has been terminated.

SQL

```
SELECT  *   FROM  t
```

Result

name

(0 row(s) affected)

Concatenation Operator

The concatenation operator is the plus sign (+). It may be used with string concatenation types.

Example:

SQL
`PRINT 'Mary' + ' ' + 'Smith'` `-- The middle term is <single quote><space><single quote>`
Result
Mary Smith

Relational Operators

These relational operators, shown in Table 2-37 may be used with string values as well as numeric or date values. They behave the same as if one is alphabetizing a list, "Al" is before "Alan."

Table 2-37 Relational Operators

=	equal to
<>	not equal to
<	less than
<=	less than or equal to
>	greater than
>=	greater than or equal to

Strings are compared according to the collation, and they generally behave according to dictionary order. So 'Mary Smith' > 'Ma' is TRUE and 'Mary Smith' < 'N' is TRUE.

2.4.12.3 Comparing CHAR() and VARCHAR() Values

If a value of CHAR() data type value is compared to a VARCHAR() value, then SQL Server trims trailing blanks, if any, from the CHAR() value to allow them to be compared as equal values if the leading strings of both are the same.

Note that Oracle will not compare the two as equal, so this behavior is RDBMS dependent.

This behavior is true whether the values are local variables or table column values. The following example demonstrates it using local variables.

Example: In this example, `@charname` will contain five characters, abc followed by two spaces, as can be seen from the first SELECT output where it is concatenated with `@vchrname` since there are spaces between the two, that is **abc abc**. But `@vchrname` contains only the three visible characters as shown by the second SELECT output with the two reversed, **abcabc**. Last, the IF statement comparison shows that the values do compare as equal.

SQL

```
DECLARE @charname CHAR(5) '@vchrname VARCHAR(5)
SET @charname = 'abc'     -- Declared as CHAR(5) so it
  will store 5 characters 'abc'
SET @vchrname = 'abc'     -- Declared as VARCHAR(5) so it
  will store 3 characters 'abc'

SELECT 'Char-HELLO:    ' + @charname   + 'HELLO'
SELECT 'Varchar- HELLO:    ' + @vchrname   + 'HELLO'

IF @charname = @vchrname
  PRINT 'Same'
ELSE
  PRINT 'Different' >
```

Result

```
-------------------------
Char-HELLO:  abc  HELLO

---------------------------
Varchar- HELLO:  abcHELLO

Same
```

This last behavior of comparing the two showing equality is caused by implicit data type conversion from CHAR() to VARCHAR() before doing the comparison. See the discussion of implicit data type conversion and precedence on pages 73 and 74.

2.4.12.4 String Functions

The scalar functions, shown in Table 2-38, perform an operation on a string input value and return a string or numeric value. See details under Functions, page 137.

Table 2-38 Scalar Functions

ASCII	NCHAR	SOUNDEX
CHAR	PATINDEX	SPACE
CHARINDEX	REPLACE	STR
DIFFERENCE	QUOTENAME	STUFF
LEFT	REPLICATE	SUBSTRING
LEN	REVERSE	UNICODE
LOWER	RIGHT	UPPER
LTRIM	RTRIM	

ANSI_PADDING ON I suggest heeding the following good advice from Books Online—**Warning: It is recommended that ANSI_PADDING always be set to ON.**

- `VARCHAR(n)` — not trimmed, not padded
    - data inserted or updated retain and store trailing blanks provided (not trimmed).
    - only the characters provided are stored (not padded to the length of the column).
    - The four character string 'Sue ' inserted or updated into a VARCHAR(6) will retain the trailing blank explicitly inserted.
- `CHAR(n)` — padded (never trimmed)

ANSI_PADDING OFF

- `VARCHAR(n)` — trimmed, not padded.
    - The four-character string 'Sue ' inserted (or updated) into a VARCHAR(6) would be truncated storing only three characters, 'Sue'.
- `CHAR(n)` — NULLable not padded, NOT NULLable always padded, (neither ever trimmed)
    - CREATE TABLE t (a CHAR(3) , b VARCHAR(3)):a and b behave the same.

You can display the current setting of the ANSI_PADDING option as follows.

SQL

```
SELECT SESSIONPROPERTY ( 'ANSI_PADDING' )   ANSI_PADDING
```

Result

```
ANSI_PADDING
------------------------
1
```

The OLE DB and ODBC libraries always set ANSI_PADDING option to ON when making a connection. For more on OLE DB and ODBC automatic settings, see page 215.

Collation A COLLATE clause (new in SQL Server 2K) may be applied to a string expression, column definition, or database definition to determine comparison (search) and sorting characteristics. See Collation on page 233. Objects using **CHAR** or **VARCHAR** are assigned the default collation of the database, unless a specific collation is assigned using the COLLATE clause. (The same is true for **NCHAR** or **NVARCHAR**.)

2.4.13 NCHAR and NVARCHAR Data Type Details

The data types of nchar and nvarchar can be summarized as shown in Table 2-39.

Table 2-39 NCHAR and NVARCHAR Data Types

Data Type	Description	Storage Size
NCHAR(*n*) NATIONAL CHAR(*n*) NATIONAL CHARACTER(*n*)	Fixed-length Unicode character data of *n* characters with a fixed length of 2*n* bytes. Default length *n* with DDL is 1. (See p. 106) Default length *n* with CAST function is 30. (See p. 107) Always stores two times *n* bytes, padding the right with blanks for strings less that *n* characters. The ANSI SQL synonyms for **nchar** are **national char** and **national character**. Example Unicode literal: N'Sue'	2*n* Bytes *n* = 1 to 4,000.

Table 2-39 NCHAR and NVARCHAR Data Types (cont.)

NVARCHAR(*n*) NATIONAL CHAR VARYING(*n*) NATIONAL CHARACTER VARYING(*n*)	Variable-length Unicode character data of *n* characters. Default length *n* with DDL is 1. (See p. 105) Default length *n* with CAST function is 30. (See p. 106) Storage size, in bytes, is two times the number of characters entered. The data entered can be zero characters in length. The ANSI SQL synonyms for **nvarchar** are **national char varying** and **national character varying**. Example Unicode literal: N'Sue'	2 x length of the data entered <= 2*n* Bytes n = 1 to 4,000.

2.4.13.1 UNICODE

UNICODE Data Types use two bytes per character to enable handling of international character sets. UNICODE Data Types were introduced with SQL Server 7.0.

Single-byte ASCII is able to accommodate European languages (Latin1) including English and German (with umlauts), but UNICODE is required for languages such as those of Asian and Middle Eastern countries. See Books Online: "Collations, overview."

UNICODE string literals have N prefixed to the string enclosed in single quotes.

Example UNICODE Literal

```
N'This specifies a UNICODE string literal'
```

The server will still have a default character set determined during installation. But you may now specify a column of a table to be of NCHAR, NVARCHAR or NTEXT data type able to contain any character set defined by the Unicode Standard (that is, any of the National Character data types in the ANSI SQL standard).

NCHAR(*n*) behaves similarly to CHAR(*n*) in that (*n*) characters are always stored, but the storage size for CHAR is one byte per character whereas NCHAR is two bytes per character. See the discussion of CHAR above.

NVARCHAR(*n*) behaves similarly to VARCHAR(*n*) in that only the number of characters in the string up to a maximum of (*n*) characters are stored. See the discussion of VARCHAR in section 2.4.12 above.

UNICODE Data Type FUNCTIONS Two of the string functions listed in the previous section specifically support Unicode data types.

NCHAR (*integer_expression*) returns the Unicode character with the given integer code.

UNICODE (*'ncharacter_expression'*) returns the integer value for the first character of the input expression.

Example:

SQL
`PRINT NCHAR(252)`
Result
ü

SQL
`PRINT UNICODE( 'ü' )`
Result
252

Books Online provides other examples of the use of NCHAR, NVARCHAR and the functions NCHAR() and UNICODE().

2.4.13.2 NCHAR and NVARCHAR Data Type Constants (Literals)

Unicode character string constants consist of a capital **N** followed by a sequence of characters enclosed in single quotes in accordance with ANSI SQL standard. The capital N stands for the National Language support in the SQL-92 standard. The N prefix must be uppercase.

Example Unicode (NCHAR and NVARCHAR) String Constants

N'Mary Smith'

N'O''Reilly'

2.4.13.3 Storage of NCHAR and NVARCHAR Data Types

NCHAR(*n*) always stores *n* characters, right padding with blanks if the data is less than *n* characters long. Storage space for these *n* characters is 2*n* bytes.

Example: If a column declared as NCHAR(5) has 'abc' inserted, then 'abc ' is stored, five characters occupying ten bytes.

NVARCHAR(*n*) stores the actual number of characters up to *n*, using two bytes per character.

Example: If a column declared as NVARCHAR(5) has 'abc' inserted, then those three characters are stored, occupying six bytes (plus the number 3 indicating the number of characters).

Collation A COLLATE clause (new in SQL Server 2K) may be applied to a string expression, column definition or database definition to determine comparison (search) and sorting characteristics. See Collation on page 233.

Objects using **NCHAR** or **NVARCHAR** are assigned the default collation of the database, unless a specific collation is assigned using the COLLATE clause. The same is true for **CHAR** or **VARCHAR**.

2.4.13.4 Default Length for CHAR, VARCHAR, NCHAR, NVARCHAR with DDL

The default length of CHAR, VARCHAR, NCHAR and NVARCHAR with DDL is 1. This means that a DDL declaration of CHAR defaults to CHAR(1).

Example 1: CHAR with DDL

SQL

```
CREATE TABLE  t  (
  a  CHAR                      -- Defaults to  CHAR(1)
)

INSERT INTO  t  ( a ) VALUES ( 'A' ) -- Succeeds
INSERT INTO  t  ( a ) VALUES ( 'AAA' ) --  Fails.   A column
input too long fails
SELECT * FROM  t

CREATE TABLE  t  (
  a  CHAR                      -- Defaults to  CHAR(1)
)

INSERT INTO  t  ( a ) VALUES ( 'A' ) -- Succeeds
INSERT INTO  t  ( a ) VALUES ( 'AAA' ) --  Fails, column
                                            input too long
SELECT * FROM  t
```

Result

```
Server: Msg 8152, Level 16, State 9, Line 1
String or binary data would be truncated.
The statement has been terminated.
a        b
----     ----
A        B
```

Example 2: CHAR with DDL

SQL

```
DECLARE  @variable CHAR -- Defaults to  CHAR(1)

SET  @variable = 'V'     -- Succeeds
PRINT @variable

SET  @variable = 'WWW'   -- Succeeds. A string variable input
                            that is too long is truncated.
PRINT @variable
```

Result

```
V
W
```

2.4.13.5 Default Length for CHAR, VARCHAR, NCHAR, NVARCHAR with CAST

The Default length of CHAR, VARCHAR, NCHAR and NVARCHAR with CAST is 30. This means that CAST (object AS CHAR) is the same as CAST (object AS CHAR(30))

Example: CHAR with CAST

SQL

```
PRINT CAST(  GETDATE()   AS  CHAR ) -- Defaults to CHAR(30)
```

Result

```
Jul 22 2002  3:36PM
```

SQL

```
PRINT  CAST(  GETDATE()   AS  CHAR(30) )
```

Result

```
Jul 22 2002  3:36PM
```

2.4.14 `SYSNAME` Data Type Details

SYSNAME is a system-supplied user-defined data type as NVARCHAR(128). SYSNAME is used to reference database object names.

2.4.15 `TEXT`, `NTEXT` and `IMAGE` Data Type

TEXT, NTEXT and IMAGE data types, as summarized in Table 2-40, are fixed and variable-length data types for storing large non-Unicode and Unicode character and binary data. They are generally for large data values up to 2 GB in size, which are more efficiently stored on their own pages than on the same page as the other columns of the row. They serve the function of BLOBs (Binary Large OBjects) in some systems.

Restrictions on their use include the inability to refer to them directly in a WHERE clause. But they may be used in WHERE clauses as input parameter to functions such as ISNULL(), SUBSTRING(), PATINDEX() as well as in IS NULL, IS NOT NULL and LIKE expressions. They may not be used as variables, although they may be parameters to stored procedures.

Table 2-40 TEXT, NTEXT and IMAGE Data Types

Data Type	Description	Storage Size
TEXT	Variable-length non-Unicode data with a maximum length of 231-1 (2,147,483,647) characters.	Multiples of 8KB Pages Max storage is 2GB
NTEXT	Variable-length Unicode data with a maximum length of 2^{30} - 1 (1,073,741,823) characters. Storage size, in bytes, is two times the number of characters entered. The ANSI SQL synonym for **ntext** is **national text**.	
IMAGE	Variable-length binary data from 0 through 2^{31}-1 (2,147,483,647) bytes.	

2.4.15.1 Text and Image Functions and Statements

Text and image functions, summarized in Table 2-41, perform an operation on a text or image value or column and return information about the value. All are nondeterministic (see page 162).

Table 2-41 Text and Image Functions and Statements

Statement Name	Description and Syntax
DATALENGTH	Returns the number of bytes used to represent any expression. Syntax: DATALENGTH (expression)
PATINDEX	Returns the starting position of the first occurrence of a pattern in a specified expression or zero if the pattern is not found. All text and character data types. Syntax: PATINDEX ('%pattern%' , expression)
SUBSTRING	Returns part of a character, binary, text, or image expression. Syntax: SUBSTRING (expression , start , length)
TEXTPTR	Returns the text-pointer value that corresponds to a text, ntext, or image column as a varbinary value. The retrieved text pointer value can be used in READTEXT, WRITETEXT, and UPDATETEXT statements. Syntax: TEXTPTR (column)
TEXTVALID	Returns 1 if a given text, ntext, or image pointer is valid, 0 if not. Syntax: TEXTVALID ('table.column' , text_ ptr)
READTEXT	Reads text, ntext, or image values from a text, ntext, or image column, starting from a specified offset and reading the specified number of bytes. Syntax: READTEXT { table.column text_ptr offset size } [HOLDLOCK]
SET TEXTSIZE	Specifies the size of text and ntext data returned with a SELECT statement. Syntax: SET TEXTSIZE { number }
UPDATETEXT	Updates an existing text, ntext, or image field. Use UPDATETEXT to change only a portion of a text, ntext, or image column in place. Logging depends on recovery model in effect for the database. Syntax: UPDATETEXT { *table_name.dest_column_name dest_text_ptr* } { NULL | *insert_offset* } { NULL | *delete_length* } [WITH LOG] [*inserted_data* | *table_name.src_column_name src_text_ptr*]
WRITETEXT	Permits nonlogged, interactive updating of an existing text, ntext, or image column. This statement overwrites any existing data in the column it affects. (WRITETEXT cannot be used on text, ntext, and image columns in views.) Syntax: WRITETEXT { table.column text_ptr } [WITH LOG] { data }

Example: This example shows the use of TXTPTR and WRITETEXT.

SQL

```
CREATE TABLE t (  id    INT , txtcol TEXT )
INSERT INTO t ( id , txtcol ) VALUES ( 1 , 'txtcol initial data' )
SELECT  *  FROM  t
```

SQL (cont.)

Result

```
id        txtcol
---       --------------------
1         txtcol initial data
```

SQL

```
DECLARE   @b_ptr   VARBINARY(16)

SELECT   @b_ptr = TEXTPTR( txtcol ) FROM   t WHERE   id = 1

WRITETEXT t.txtcol @b_ptr  'This represents a very long text message.'

SELECT   *   FROM   t
```

Result

```
id        txtcol
---       ------------------------------------------------
1         This represents a very long text message.
```

Arguments

Text in Row

If your data is 7000 bytes or less, you may set the "Text in Row" feature that lets you store the large object on the same page as the other columns. This feature is enabled for an entire table with **sp_tableoption**.

The next statement turns the feature on and sets an upper limit on data size to the default maximum size of 256 bytes. Objects larger than the maximum value are stored on separate pages, not in rows.

```
sp_tableoption  tablename , 'text in row', 'ON'
-- ON must be enclosed in single quotes.
```

The next statement both turns the feature on and sets an upper limit on data size. The value specified must be between 24 and 7000.

```
sp_tableoption  tablename , 'text in row', 2000
```

2.4.16 BINARY(n) and VARBINARY(n) Data Type Details

BINARY and VARBINARY data types, summarized in Table 2-42, store strings of bits up to a maximum of 8000 bytes. From Books Online:

> Use binary data when storing hexadecimal values such as a security identification number (SID), a GUID (using the **uniqueidentifier** data type), or using a complex number that can be stored using hexadecimal shorthand.

Table 2-42 BINARY(n) and VARBINARY (n) Data Type

Data Type	Description	Storage Size
BINARY(*n*)	Fixed-length binary data of *n* bytes. *n* must be a value from 1 through 8,000. Storage size is *n*+4 bytes. Default length n with DDL is 1. Default length n with CAST function is 30.	*n*+4 bytes
VARBINARY(*n*) BINARY VARY-ING(*n*)	Variable-length binary data of *n* bytes. *n* must be a value from 1 through 8,000. Default length *n* with DDL is 1. Default length *n* with CAST function is 30. The data entered can be zero bytes in length. The ANSI SQL synonym for VARBINARY is BINARY VARYING.	length of the data entered + 4 bytes <= *n*+4 Bytes

2.4.16.1 BINARY and VARBINARY Data Type Constants (Literals)

Binary constants have a leading 0x (a zero and the lowercase letter x) followed by the hexadecimal representation of the bit pattern, each hex digit representing four bits.

So 0x3A (or 0x3a) represents the hexadecimal value of 3A or both four-bit "nibbles".

	3 represents the four bits	0011
and	A represents the four bits	1010

Therefore 0x3A represents the eight-bit Byte 00111010 which is equal to decimal 58.

Examples:

SQL
`PRINT CAST( 0x3A AS INT)`

SQL (cont.)

Result

```
58
```

SQL

```
PRINT CAST( 58 AS BINARY(2) )
```

Result

```
0x003A
```

SQL

```
PRINT CAST( 58 AS BINARY ) -- Default length n with CAST is 30
```

Result

```
0x000000000000000000000000000000000000000000000000000000000000003A
```

2.4.17 CURSOR Data Type Details

As summarized in Table 2-43, a cursor data type contains a pointer to a cursor object, which is required for writing code that accesses a result set including more than one row of data. The cursor object in a sense contains the entire result set but only allows access to one result set row at a time.

Table 2-43 CURSOR Data Type

Data Type	Description	Storage Size
CURSOR	Pointer to a cursor	1 byte for cursor pointer, variable size for the result set

CURSOR data type is for variables or stored procedure OUTPUT parameters that contain a reference to a cursor. Any variables created with the cursor data type are nullable.

Operations that can reference variables and parameters having a **cursor** data type are as follows. Remember that the **cursor** data type cannot be used for a column in a CREATE TABLE statement.

- DECLARE @local_variable and SET @local_variable statements.
- OPEN, FETCH, CLOSE, and DEALLOCATE cursor statements as well as UPDATE and DELETE.
- Stored procedure output parameters.
- The CURSOR_STATUS function.
- The **sp_cursor_list**, **sp_describe_cursor**, **sp_describe_cursor_tables**, and **sp_describe_cursor_columns** system stored procedures.

For more in-depth treatment of cursors, see Cursors, page 638.

For a thorough coverage of using cursors see *Professional SQL Server 2000 Programming* by Robert Vieira and *Advanced Transact-SQL for SQL Server 2000* by Itzik Ben-Gan and Tom Moreau.

2.4.18 `SQL_VARIANT` Data Type Details

SQL_VARIANT data type can be assigned to a column or variable into which you can put data with different base data types. (See Table 2-44.) Each SQL_VARIANT object stores both the data value and the data type (metadata) for the SQL_VARIANT value assigned, so extra space is required for using SQL_VARIANT. ODBC does not fully support SQL_VARIANT. See Books Online under SQL_VARIANT.

Table 2-44 SQL_VARIANT Data Type

Data Type	Description	Storage Size
SQL_VARIANT	A data type that stores values of any data type except TEXT, NTEXT, IMAGE, TIMESTAMP and SQL_VARIANT.	<= 8016 bytes

2.4.18.1 Using `SQL_VARIANT`

General Value Assignment

- SQL_VARIANT objects can hold data of any SQL Server data type except TEXT, NTEXT, IMAGE, TIMESTAMP and SQL_VARIANT.
- Predicates or assignments referencing SQL_VARIANT columns can include constants of any data type.
- An SQL_VARIANT object assigned a value of NULL does not have an underlying base data type.

- When assigning the value of an SQL_VARIANT object to a non-SQL_VARIANT data object, the SQL_VARIANT value must be explicitly cast to the data type of the destination.

  ```
  SET @intvar = CAST( @variantvar AS INT )
  ```

  There are no implicit conversions from SQL_VARIANT to non-SQL_VARIANT.
- When doing arithmetic operations with an SQL_VARIANT object, the SQL_VARIANT value must be explicitly cast to the appropriate numeric data type.
- Catalog objects such as the DATALENGTH function that report the length of SQL_VARIANT objects report the length of the data only (not including the length of the meta data contained in a SQL_VARIANT object).
- SQL_VARIANT columns always operate with ANSI_PADDING ON. If CHAR, NCHAR, VARCHAR, NVARCHAR or VARBINARY values are assigned from a source that has ANSI_PADDING OFF, the values are not padded.

SQL_VARIANT in Tables

- SQL_VARIANT columns can be used in indexes and with unique keys, as long as the length of the data in the key columns does not exceed 900 bytes.
- SQL_VARIANT columns do not support the IDENTITY property, but SQL_VARIANT columns are allowed as part of primary or foreign keys.
- SQL_VARIANT columns cannot be used in a computed column.
- Use ALTER TABLE to change a column to SQL_VARIANT. All existing values (of the prior data type) are converted to SQL_VARIANT values.
- ALTER TABLE cannot be used to change the data type of an SQL_VARIANT column to any other data type.

Collation

- The COLLATE clause cannot be used to assign a column collation to an SQL_VARIANT column.
- When a value is assigned to an SQL_VARIANT instance, both the data value and base data type of the source are assigned. If the source value has a collation, the collation is also assigned. If the source value has a user-defined data type, the *base data type* of the user-defined data type is assigned (not the user-defined data type itself).

The new function SQL_VARIANT_PROPERTY(): is used to obtain property information about SQL_VARIANT values, such as data type, precision or scale.

The following example shows how to use and assign SQL_VARIANT.

Example:

SQL

```
DECLARE @intvar INT, @chvar CHAR(4)
DECLARE @vrntvar SQL_VARIANT

SET @chvar = '123'
SET @intvar = @chvar  -- implicit conversion okay
PRINT @intvar

SET @vrntvar = @chvar
PRINT CAST( @vrntvar AS CHAR )-- must cast SQL_VARIANT

-- SET @intvar = @vrntvar -- Fails, no implicit conversion

SET @intvar = CAST( @vrntvar AS INT ) -- explicit
                                        conversion- ok
PRINT @intvar
```

Result

```
123
123
123
```

2.4.18.2 Comparisons with SQL_VARIANT Objects

Since an SQL_VARIANT object may contain any of various data types, it is always best to explicitly cast the SQL_VARIANT object to the data type you wish to compare against when doing your own comparisons, as in a WHERE search of in an IF statement.

For situations in which you can not cast each item, such as those on the following list, special comparison rules will apply.

- Using ORDER BY, GROUP BY
- Creating Indexes
- Using MAX and MIN aggregate functions
- Using UNION (without ALL)
- Evaluating CASE expressions and using comparison operators

For SQL_VARIANT comparisons, the SQL Server data type hierarchy order is grouped into data type families from highest (top of Table 2-45) to lowest.

Table 2-45 Data Type Families

Data type	Data type family
sql_variant	sql_variant
datetime	Datetime
smalldatetime	Datetime
float	approximate number
real	approximate number
decimal	exact number
money	exact number
smallmoney	exact number
bigint	exact number
int	exact number
smallint	exact number
tinyint	exact number
bit	exact number
nvarchar	Unicode
nchar	Unicode
varchar	Unicode
char	Unicode
varbinary	Binary
binary	Binary
uniqueidentifier	Uniqueidentifier

For comparing SQL_VARIANT objects, the data type hierarchy shown in Table 2-45 is used.When comparing two SQL_VARIANT objects of *different* data type families, the object with the family higher in the table is deemed greater (regardless of data value). When comparing two SQL_VARIANT objects of the *same* data type family, both objects are implicitly converted to the higher data type and are compared based on value.

When comparing two SQL_VARIANT objects with data type of CHAR, VARCHAR, NCHAR or NVARCHAR, the comparison is based on integer comparison of the following four values in this order: LCID (locale ID), LCID version, comparison flags and sort ID.

LCID has to do with regional language settings and both LCID and LCID versions will usually be the same for all string objects in a given database. In these cases the comparison seems to behave the same as for non-SQL_VARIANT comparisons of the underlying data type values. If you can, however, it is always safer to explicitly cast and do testing of sample cases.

Examples Comparing `SQL_VARIANT` Objects Since number families are a higher family than string families, the INT value 222 would evaluate as greater than CHAR value 444.

SQL

```
DECLARE @intvariant SQL_VARIANT,@charvariant SQL_VARIANT
SET @intvariant = 222
SET @charvariant = '444'

if @intvariant > @charvariant
  PRINT '@intvariant is greater'
else
  PRINT '@charvariant is greater'
```

Result

```
@intvariant is greater
```

An explicit cast of both to INT would, of course, reverse this result.

SQL

```
DECLARE @intvariant SQL_VARIANT,@charvariant SQL_VARIANT
SET @intvariant = 222
SET @charvariant = '444'

if CAST(@intvariant AS INT) > CAST(@charvariant AS INT)
  PRINT '@intvariant is greater'
else
  PRINT '@charvariant is greater'
```

SQL (cont.)

Result

```
@charvariant is greater
```

String comparison examples. Explicit casting is suggested.

SQL

```
DECLARE @chvariant1 SQL_VARIANT
DECLARE @chvariant2 SQL_VARIANT
SET @chvariant1 = 'AAA'
SET @chvariant2 = 'MMM'

if @chvariant1  > @chvariant2
  PRINT '@chvariant1 is greater'
else
  PRINT '@chvariant2 is greater'
```

Result

```
@chvariant2 is greater
```

This example was run on a server installed as case-insensitive and behaves as hoped.

SQL

```
DECLARE @chvariant1 SQL_VARIANT
DECLARE @chvariant2 SQL_VARIANT
SET @chvariant1 = 'AAA'
SET @chvariant2 = N'aaa'        -- UNICODE

if @chvariant1 = @chvariant2
  PRINT 'They''re Equal'
else
PRINT 'They''re Not Equal'
```

Result

```
They're Equal
```

2.4.18.3 New Function `SQL_VARIANT_PROPERTY()`

The new function for an SQL VARIANT PROPERTY is used to obtain data type and other properties about an SQL_VARIANT value.

Syntax

```
SQL_VARIANT_PROPERTY ( expression, property )
```

Arguments

expression

Expression is the input expression of type SQL_VARIANT.

property

Property is the name from the Table 2-46 of the SQL_VARIANT property for which information is requested. *property* is VARCHAR(128)

Return Type

Return Type sql_variant—see base type in Table 2-46.

Table 2-46 SQL VARIANT Properties

Value	Description	Base type of sql_variant Returned
BaseType	The SQL Server data type CHARINTMONEY NCHARNTEXTNUMERIC NVARCHARREALSMALLDATETIME SMALLINT-SMALLMONEYTEXT TIMESTAMPTINYINTVARBI-NARY UNIQUEIDENTIFIERVARCHAR	**SYSNAME** Invalid input = NULL
Precision	Precision of the numeric base data type: DATETIME = 23 SMALLDATETIME = 16 FLOAT = 53 REAL = 24 DECIMAL (p,s) and NUMERIC (p,s) = p MONEY = 19 SMALLMONEY = 10 INT = 10 SMALLINT = 5 TINYINT = 3 BIT = 1 all other types = 0	**INT** Invalid input = NULL
Scale	Scale of the numeric base data type: DECIMAL (p,s) and NUMERIC (p,s) = s MONEY and SMALLMONEY = 4 DATETIME = 3 all other types = 0	**INT** Invalid input = NULL
TotalBytes	The number of bytes required to hold both the meta data and data of the value. If the value is greater than 900, index creation will fail.	**INT** Invalid input = NULL
Collation	Represents the collation of the particular SQL_VARIANT value.	**SYSNAME** Invalid input = NULL
MaxLength	The maximum data type length, in bytes. For example, **MaxLength** of NVARCHAR(**50**) is 100, **MaxLength** of INT is 4.	**INT** Invalid input = NULL

Examples Using SQL_VARIANT_PROPERTY() Function Since number families are a higher family than string families,the INT value 222 would evaluate as greater than CHAR value 444.

SQL

```
DECLARE @chvariant1 SQL_VARIANT
DECLARE @chvariant2 SQL_VARIANT
SET @chvariant1 = 'AAA'
SET @chvariant2 = N'aaa'

SELECT SQL_VARIANT_PROPERTY( @chvariant1 , 'BaseType' )
SELECT SQL_VARIANT_PROPERTY( @chvariant2 , 'BaseType' )
```

Result

```
------------------------------------------------
varchar

------------------------------------------------
nvarchar
```

It should be noted that the PRINT operation requires an explicit CAST if used in place of SELECT in the code segment above.

SQL

```
PRINT CAST ( SQL_VARIANT_PROPERTY( @chvariant1 , 'BaseType' ) AS SYSNAME)
```

Result

```
varchar
```

2.4.18.4 SQL_VARIANT Data with Functions

These Transact-SQL functions accept SQL_VARIANT parameters and return a SQL_VARIANT value when a SQL_VARIANT parameter is input.

COALESCE	MAX	MIN	NULLIF

These functions support references to SQL_VARIANT columns or variables but do not use SQL_VARIANT as the data type of their return values.

COL_LENGTH	DATALENGTH	TYPEPROPERTY
COLUMNPROPERTY	ISNULL	

These Transact-SQL functions do not support SQL_VARIANT input parameters.

AVG	RADIANS	STDEV[P]
IDENTITY	ROUND	SUM
ISNUMERIC	SIGN	VAR[P]
POWER		

The CAST and CONVERT functions support SQL_VARIANT.

2.4.19 TABLE Data Type Details

The TABLE data type, new inMSS 2000, allows the user to declare a local variable capable of storing any table-structured data, such as a query result, set in any code and especially contain the return value from a table-valued function.

Table 2-47 TABLE Data Type

Data Type	Description
TABLE	A special data type that can be used to store a result set for later processing in the current sequence of SQL statements. It's primarily used to hold the result set of a table-valued function.

Syntax:

```
DECLARE  @local_variable    table_type_definition

table_type_definition ::=
 TABLE ( { column_definition | table_constraint } [ ,...n ] )

column_definition ::=
 column_name scalar_data_type
 [ COLLATE collation_definition ]
 [ [ DEFAULT constant_expression ] | IDENTITY [ ( seed , increment ) ] ]
 [ ROWGUIDCOL ]
 [ column_constraint ] [ ...n ]
```

```
column_constraint ::=
  { [ NULL | NOT NULL ]
  | [ PRIMARY KEY | UNIQUE ]
  | CHECK ( logical_expression )
  }

table_constraint ::=
  { { PRIMARY KEY | UNIQUE } ( column_name [ ,...n ] )
  | CHECK ( search_condition )
  }
```

Arguments

table_type_definition

table_type_definition is the same subset of information used to define a table in CREATE TABLE. The table declaration includes column definitions, names, data types and constraints. The only constraint types allowed are PRIMARY KEY, UNIQUE KEY and NULL.
See also CREATE TABLE, CREATE FUNCTION, and DECLARE. @local_variable

collation_definition

collation_definition is the collation of the column consisting of a Microsoft Windowslocale and a comparison style, a Windows locale and the binary notation or a Microsoft SQL Server collation.

Comments

- Functions and variables can be declared to be of type TABLE.
- TABLE variables can be used in functions, stored procedures and batches.
- Use TABLE variables instead of temporary TABLEs, whenever possible.

TABLE variable benefits (over temporary tables)

- A TABLE variable behaves like a local variable in that it has a well-defined scope, which is the function, stored procedure or batch in which it is declared.
- Within its scope, a TABLE variable may be used like a regular TABLE. It may be applied anywhere a TABLE or TABLE expression may be used in SELECT, INSERT, UPDATE and DELETE statements.

- TABLE variables are automatically dropped at the end of the function, stored procedure or batch in which they are defined.
- TABLE variables used in stored procedures result in fewer recompilations of the stored procedures than when temporary tables are used.
- Table variables require fewer locking and logging resources because transactions involving table variables last only for the duration of the table variable update.

TABLE variable limitations

- TABLE may not be used in the following statements:
  - INSERT INTO *table_variable* EXEC stored_procedure
  - SELECT *select_list* INTO *table_variable* *statements*
- Assignment operation between table variables is not supported.
- Table variables are not impacted by transaction rollbacks because they have limited scope and are not part of the persistent database.

2.4.19.1 TABLE Data Type Examples

Example:

SQL

```
DECLARE @tablevar TABLE (
   id     INT               PRIMARY KEY,
   name   VARCHAR(10)       NOT NULL,
   age    TINYINT
     CHECK( age > 0 and age < 180 ) --    Table variables may even have
                                          Check constraints
INSERT INTO @tablevar VALUES ( 1 , 'Sue' , 35)
INSERT INTO @tablevar VALUES ( 2 , 'Sam' , 25)

SELECT * FROM @tablevar
```

Result

```
id        nam        age
----      -------    ------
1         Sue        35
2         Sam        25
```

2.4.20 `TIMESTAMP` (`ROWVERSION`) Data Type Details

Table 2-48 TIMESTAMP Data Type

Data Type	Description	Storage Size
`TIMESTAMP` `ROWVERSION`	A database-wide unique number that gets updated every time a row gets updated. Automatically generated binary numbers, which are guaranteed to be unique within a database. TIMESTAMP is used typically as a mechanism for version-stamping table rows.	8 bytes
Note: ROWVERSION should always be in place of TIMESTAMP.		

Although ROWVERSION (Table 2-48) is now a data type synonym for TIMESTAMP, it should always be used in place of TIMESTAMP as the latter may completely change definition and usage in a future release of Microsoft SQL Server. Books Online says the following.

> The Transact-SQL **timestamp** data type is not the same as the **timestamp** data type defined in the ANSI SQL standard. The ANSI SQL **timestamp** data type is equivalent to the Transact-SQL **datetime** data type.
>
> A future release of Microsoft SQL Server may modify the behavior of the Transact-SQL **timestamp** data type to align it with the behavior defined in the standard. At that time, the current **timestamp** data type will be replaced with a **rowversion** data type.
>
> Microsoft SQL Server 2000 introduces a **rowversion** synonym for the **timestamp** data type. Use **rowversion** instead of **timestamp** wherever possible in DDL statements.

TIMESTAMP is as of now the SQL Server 2K base data type name. ROWVERSION is a synonym, which may be used interchangeably with the TIMESTAMP in Transact-SQL statements. It is the base data type TIMESTAMP and not the synonym that is stored and will be seen from operations such as **sp_help**. Nonetheless, in this case it is recommended to always use ROWVERSION and avoid TIMESTAMP as its definition is likely to change.

This book will use the term ROWVERSION exclusively except to note when the word TIMESTAMP has a different behavior.

2.4.20.1 Using ROWVERSION (TIMESTAMP) Data Type

A ROWVERSION (TIMESTAMP) data type column contains a database-wide unique number that gets updated every time a row gets updated. This column can act as a version number for the row, which gives some control over optimistic locking.

Example using ROWVERSION (TIMESTAMP):

SQL

```
CREATE TABLE table1 (
       data     INT,
       rowver   ROWVERSION
    )

    INSERT INTO table1 (data) VALUES (1)
    INSERT INTO table1 (data) VALUES (2)
    INSERT INTO table1 (data) VALUES (3)

    SELECT * FROM table1
```

Result

```
data          rowver
-----------   ------------------
1             0x00000000000003F3
2             0x00000000000003F4
3             0x00000000000003F5
```

Notice that the ROWEVERSION (TIMESTAMP) values under the `rowver` column have nothing to do with dates or time values but are unique integer values in the current database. When any updateable column for a row is updated, the ROWVERSION column is updated by the system to a new value as shown in the next code segment. The new value is not necessarily sequential within the table depending on what else is going on within the database. What's important is the fact that any update on a row causes the system to change its ROWVERSION value. Its use is discussed next under Optimistic Locking.

Example:

SQL

```
UPDATE table1 SET data = 20 WHERE data = 2
SELECT * FROM table1
```

SQL (cont.)

Result

```
data            rowver
-----------     ------------------
1               0x00000000000003F3
20              0x00000000000003F7
3               0x00000000000003F5
```

2.4.20.2 Optimistic Locking

Generally speaking "pessimistic locking" (pessimistic concurrency) is the scheme in which exclusive locks are obtained as they are required when data is to be changed. This ensures consistency within the database, but it introduces the possibility of deadlock and has overhead due to doing the locking. It also decreases concurrency by holding exclusive (write) locks for a relatively long time.

Under optimistic locking (optimistic concurrency) schemes locking is deferred or omitted, and a check is made to see if a data value has been changed by another process between the time it was read and the time a new value is to be written. If not changed by another process, the writing may proceed. If changed by another process, the programmer can choose to abort the current attempt, try again or even offer the user the choice to overwrite the data value, abort or start over. Optimistic locking is useful in high transaction environments in which the chance of conflict on the same piece of data is small. Savings by less locking overhead and increase in concurrency can make up for the very rare conflicts that do occur.

One optimistic locking scheme is for a program to use a ROWVERSION column. The program reads the target row and releases the shared read lock immediately allowing other processes to access the row. The data value read may be used in doing some work and then calculating the new value. When the new value is ready for update, the row is again read and then, if the ROWVERSION column has not changed, the data value is updated to the new value.

This scheme is often used with cursors where the client program may obtain several rows into a cursor (read operation) releasing the lock. The user may then take several minutes to study the data and decide to change a value on one row.

Having a ROWVERSION column and declaring the cursor as OPTIMISTIC, when a row has been changed between read time and update time the system generates a 16934 error, which reads as follows: "Optimistic concurrency check failed. The row was modified outside of this cursor." Your program then refetches the row in question and may either abort, start over or overwrite the value with your new value or present the changed data to the user for a decision.

For a further discussion of the subjects of ROWVERSION (TIMESTAMP) data type, using cursors and optimistic locking, see *Advanced Transact-SQL for SQL Server 2K* by Itzik Ben-Gan and Tom Moreau. Also see Books Online under DECLARE CURSOR and Cursor Concurrency.

Comments

- In a CREATE TABLE or ALTER TABLE statement, you do not have to supply a column name for the TIMESTAMP data type:

```
CREATE TABLE ExampleTable (
  PriKey      INT    PRIMARY KEY,
    TIMESTAMP   -- column name defaults to "timestamp"
)
```

- If you do not supply a column name, SQL Server generates a column name of TIMESTAMP. The ROWVERSION data type synonym does not follow this behavior. You must supply a column name when you specify ROWVERSION.

```
CREATE TABLE ExampleTable (
  PriKey          INT    PRIMARY KEY,
  timestamp_col   ROWVERSION   -- column name must be entered
)
```

- A table can have only one ROWVERSION column.
- The value in a ROWVERSION (TIMESTAMP) column, like an IDENTITY column, is set by the system and cannot be updated by the user via the UPDATE statement. However, the value in the ROWVERSION column is updated every time a row containing a ROWVERSION column is inserted or updated. Do not use a ROWVERSION column as a primary key and do not put an index on it because the continual changes of ROWVERSION column value cause many problems.
- The only comparison operators allowed with ROWVERSION data types are the relational operators for equality or inequality. Usually the programmer doesn't do the comparison but lets the system raise an exception if the row has had a data change.

A nonnullable ROWVERSION column is semantically equivalent to a BINARY(8) column.A nullable ROWVERSION column is semantically equivalent to a VARBINARY(8) column.

2.4.21 **UNIQUEIDENTIFIER** Data Type Details

The UNIQUEIDENTIFIER data type (Table 2-49) lets you manage globally unique identifiers (GUID). It is used with the NEWID() function.

Table 2-49 UNIQUEIDENTIFIER Data Type

Data Type	Description	Storage Size
UNIQUEIDENTIFIER	A globally unique identifier (GUID), which is a 16-byte binary number unique on any computer in the world. Used to hold such an identifier that must be unique throughout the entire corporate network and beyond. Used in conjunction with the NEWID() function which generates such a UNIQUEIDENTIFIER value.	16 bytes

The UNIQUEIDENTIFIER data type used with the NEWID() function is similar to an integer data type with the IDENTITY property, although the latter just guarantees uniqueness within the table.

2.4.21.1 Using **UNIQUEIDENTIFIER**

- UNIQUEIDENTIFIER objects
  - may be compared using the relational operators (=, <>, <, >, <=, >=)
  - may be checked for NULL (IS NULL and IS NOT NULL)
  - allow no other arithmetic operators
- All column constraints and properties except IDENTITY are allowed on the UNIQUEIDENTIFIER data type.
- Multiple columns within a table may be assigned as UNIQUEIDENTIFIER data type.
- Declaring a column as UNIQUEIDENTIFIER data type does not preclude manually inserting the same value again.
- To make the values unique, it is suggested that the column also be specified as PRIMARY KEY and always be given a new value using the NEWID() function.

Suggested usage of UNIQUEIDENTIFIER To have a column unique within the table and worldwide, declare the column as *columnname* UNIQUEIDENTIFIER PRIMARY KEY DEFAULT NEWID()

The NEWID() Function The function generates a unique value of type UNIQUEIDENTIFIER each time it's called.

SQL

```
DECLARE @uid UNIQUEIDENTIFIER
SET @uid = NEWID()
PRINT '@uid is:  '+ CONVERT(varchar(255), @uid)
```

Result

```
@uid is:  C24922A8-51B6-40DA-B53B-E40A81516C60
```

The values generated by NEWID() are not sequential from one call to the next but instead have a random appearance.

Example of a table using UNIQUEIDENTIFIER as Primary Key To generate a new UNIQUEIDENTIFIER for each new row, give a DEFAULT as the NEWID() function.

Example:

SQL

```
CREATE TABLE table1 (
  uid    UNIQUEIDENTIFIER  PRIMARY KEY  DEFAULT NEWID(),
  data   INT
)

INSERT INTO table1 (data) VALUES (1)
INSERT INTO table1 (data) VALUES (2)
INSERT INTO table1 (data) VALUES (3)

SELECT * FROM table1
```

Result

```
uid                                     data
------------------------------------    -----------
00516380-0291-4B90-A113-C10B92F2622B    1
64A88B51-1BCC-4FE0-81E4-69BC65A3E957    2
FF8BD9CB-8793-4E87-80F0-1AF46036C288    3
```

The UNIQUEIDENTIFIER value is certainly bulky and awkward to work with, but when you need a world-wide globally unique identifier, it fills the bill.

Example:

SQL
`SELECT * FROM table1` `WHERE uid = '64A88B51-1BCC-4FE0-81E4-69BC65A3E957'`

Result

```
uid                                     data
------------------------------------    -----------
64A88B51-1BCC-4FE0-81E4-69BC65A3E957    2
```

2.4.21.2 The ROWGUIDCOL Property

The ROWGUIDCOL column property is primarily used by SQL Server replication, but otherwise it does not seem to add much value.

- ROWGUIDCOL property can be assigned to only one column in a table, and that must be a UNIQUEIDENTIFIER data type.
- The table may contain other UNIQUEIDENTIFIER columns.
- ROWGUIDCOL property can only be assigned to a UNIQUEIDENTIFIER column, but neither ROWGUIDCOL property nor the UNIQUEIDENTIFIER data type ensures uniqueness within the table. So either a UNIQUE or PRIMARY KEY constraint (recommended) is still required to get that result.
- The OBJECTPROPERTY function can be used to determine if a table has a ROWGUIDCOL column, and the COLUMNPROPERTY function can be used to determine the name of the column.
- A column declared with the ROWGUIDCOL property can be referenced in a SELECT list either by the word ROWGUIDCOL or by the column name itself. This is similar to using the IDENTITYCOL keyword to reference an IDENTITY column.

Examples with UNIQUEIDENTIFIER and ROWGUIDCOL Property

SQL

```
CREATE TABLE table2 (
uid1    UNIQUEIDENTIFIER  ROWGUIDCOL ,
uid2    UNIQUEIDENTIFIER
)

INSERT INTO table2 (uid1,uid2) VALUES ( NEWID() , NEWID() )

SELECT * FROM table2
```

Result

```
B63E88-1B19-42E9-BADF-814CE00656A0        5E30BAC7-FEF6-4217-BEA9-ED78C247E273
```

Re-insert the same values to demonstrate that neither column has a uniqueness constraint.

SQL

```
INSERT INTO table2 (uid1,uid2) VALUES
      ( 'A7B63E88-1B19-42E9-BADF-814CE00656A0' ,
        '5E30BAC7-FEF6-4217-BEA9-ED78C247E273'
      )

SELECT uid1, uid2 FROM table2
```

Result

```
uid1                                    uid2
------------------------------------    ------------------------------------
A7B63E88-1B19-42E9-BADF-814CE00656A0    5E30BAC7-FEF6-4217-BEA9-ED78C247E273
A7B63E88-1B19-42E9-BADF-814CE00656A0    5E30BAC7-FEF6-4217-BEA9-ED78C247E273
```

SQL

```
SELECT ROWGUIDCOL FROM table2
```

SQL (cont.)

```
SELECT ROWGUIDCOL FROM table2
```

Result

```
uid1
------------------------------------
A7B63E88-1B19-42E9-BADF-814CE00656A0
A7B63E88-1B19-42E9-BADF-814CE00656A0
```

2.4.21.3 `UNIQUEIDENTIFIER` Data Type Constants (Literals)

For completeness, the two ways to specify a `UNIQUEIDENTIFIER` constant are shown here, although typically the `NEWID()` function is always used to generate a new `UNIQUEIDENTIFIER` value.

- Character string format

  'FF8BD9CB-8793-4E87-80F0-1AF46036C288'

  '6F9619FF-8B86-D011-B42D-00C04FC964FF'

- Binary format

  0xff19966f868b11d0b42d00c04fc964ff

  0x46463842443943422D383739332D 344538372D383046302D314146343630

You almost never enter your own `UNIQUEIDENTIFIER` value as a constant because the `UNIQUEIDENTIFIER` column even with `ROWGUIDCOL` property does impose a uniqueness constraint; therefore, entering a duplicate value would not be detected. But if you use the `NEWID()` function, then uniqueness of the new value is guaranteed.

2.5 USER-DEFINED DATA TYPES

User-defined data types are data types based on intrinsic system types given a name by the user, which may then be used in future DDL statements within the database where they were created.

It is particularly useful to create a user-defined data type for a unique key that has foreign key columns (usually in another table) that refer to it. Creating a user-defined type and using it for the unique key and foreign key column definitions ensures that they are the same data type.

The following parts of user-defined data types must be provided when created.

- **Name.**
- **Underlying System Data Type**—see Table 2-50.
- **Nullability**—'NULL', 'NOT NULL', 'NONULL' in single quotes, see below. For a discussion of default nullability see page 230.

2.5.1 Enterprise Manager—Create and Manage a User-Defined Data Type

- **Create**
  1. Expand the console tree to the database in which you want the new type.
  2. Right click on **User-Defined Types** and select **New User-Defined Data Type**.
  3. Enter the desired values.
- **Drop, Copy, Rename, Properties or Generate Script**
  4. Expand the console tree to the database and **User Defined Types**.
  5. Right click on the user-defined data type and select the operation desired.

2.5.2 Transact-SQL—Create and Manage a User-Defined Data Type

Four phrases can be used to create and manage a user-defined data type:

- **sp_addtype:** Creates a user-defined data type in the current database.
- **sp_droptype:** Deletes a user-defined data type from the current database.
- **sp_rename:** Changes the name of the user-created object.
- **sp_help** *<typename>*: Displays the definition of the user-defined data type (or system data type).

sp_addtype The addtype phrase creates a user-defined data type in the current database.

Syntax

```
sp_addtype [ @typename = ] type,
[ @phystype = ] system_data_type
[ , [ @nulltype = ]{ 'NULL' | 'NOT NULL' | 'NONULL' }  ]
[ , [ @owner = ] 'owner_name' ] -- defaults to current user
```

Arguments

[@typename =] type

This is the name of the user-defined data type to be created; it must be unique in the database.

[@phystype =] system_data_type

This is the physical SQL Server data type being defined as the underlying or base data type. It has no default and must be one of the values given in Table 2-50.

Table 2-50 Base Data Type Values

'BINARY(*n*)'	IMAGE	SMALLDATETIME
BIT	INT	SMALLINT
'CHAR(*n*)'	'NCHAR(*n*)'	TEXT
DATETIME	NTEXT	TINYINT
DECIMAL	NUMERIC	UNIQUEIDENTIFIER
'DECIMAL[(*p* [, *s*])]'	'NUMERIC[(*p* [, *s*])]'	'VARBINARY(*n*)'
FLOAT	'NVARCHAR(*n*)'	'VARCHAR(*n*)'
'FLOAT(*n*)'	REAL	
Quotation marks are required if there are embedded blank spaces or punctuation marks including parenthesis, (), or square brackets, [].		

```
[ , [ @nulltype = ]  { 'NULL' | 'NOT NULL' | 'NONULL' }  ]
```

If not specified in **sp_addtype** the nullability is set to the current default nullability for the database as can be seen with the GETANSINULL() system function and which can be changed using SET or ALTER DATABASE.

I suggest that nullability be explicitly specified in **sp_addtype**. If specified in **sp_addtype,** the setting becomes the default nullability for the user-defined data type but can be set to a different value as with CREATE TABLE or ALTER TABLE.

For a discussion of nullability see page 230.

[@owner =] '*owner_name*'

This specifies the owner or creator of the new data type. When not specified, *owner_name* is the current user.

Return Code Values

0 (success) or 1 (failure)

Comments

Note that the main features that can be set in a user-defined data type are the

- base data type
- size
- nullability
- owner

Constraints to limit permissible values cannot be assigned as in the ANSI SQL notion of domain. Nonetheless, user-defined data type is a useful concept to improve readability and consistency among related tables using foreign keys.

Permissions

Execute permissions default to the public role.

sp_droptype The droptype phrase deletes a user-defined data type from the current database.

Syntax

```
sp_droptype [ @typename = ] 'type'
```

Arguments

```
[@typename =] type
```

This is the name of the user-defined data type to be dropped.

sp_rename The rename function changes the name of the user-created object.

Syntax

```
sp_rename [ @objname = ] 'object_name' -- Current name of the type to be renamed
, [ @newname = ] 'new_name' -- New name of the type
[ , [ @objtype = ] 'object_type' ]  -- USERDATATYPE for a user-defined data
                                       type

sp_rename [ @objname = ] 'object_name' ,
[ @newname = ] 'new_name'
[ , [ @objtype = ] 'object_type' ]  -- USERDATATYPE for a user-defined data
                                       type
```

Example:

SQL

```
EXEC sp_addtype empidtype , 'DEC(4)' , 'NULL'

  CREATE TABLE emps2 (
    empid empidtype  PRIMARY KEY, -- makes it NOT NULL
    ename     VARCHAR(20)
  )

  INSERT INTO emps2 VALUES ( 1111 , 'James Bond' )

EXEC  sp_help  empidtype
```

Result

```
Type_name     Storage_type     Length    Prec    Scale    Nullable    ...
------------  ---------------- --------  -----   ------   ----------- ...
empidtype     decimal          5         4       0        yes         ...
```

SQL

```
EXEC  sp_help  emps2
-- Partial listing to show the new data type for empid column
```

Result

```
Column_name          Type            ...
-------------------- -------------   ...
empid                empidtype       ...
ename                varchar         ...
```

2.6 TRANSACT-SQL FUNCTIONS

Microsoft SQL Server 2000 has a large number of built-in functions available for SQL programming, database administration and other purposes. The major categories are listed in Table 2-51.

The following sections contain detailed explanations for each of the categories from Table 2-51, categorizing the functions and describing their general pur-

Table 2-51 Built-in Functions

Function Category	Description
Aggregate Functions	Perform a calculation on a set of values and return a single summarizing value, e.g., COUNT(), SUM(), AVG()
Cursor Functions	Returns information about cursors.
Configuration Functions	Returns information about the current configuration.
Date and Time Functions	Performs an operation on a date and time input value and returns either a string, numeric or date and time value.
Mathematical Functions	Performs a calculation based on input values provided as parameters to the function, and returns a numeric value.
Metadata Functions	Returns information about the database and database objects.
Rowset Functions	Returns an object that can be used in an SQL statement like a table.
Security Functions	Returns information about users and roles.
String Functions	Performs an operation on a string (CHAR or VARCHAR) input value and returns a string or numeric value.
System Functions	Performs operations and returns information about values, objects and settings in Microsoft SQL Server.
System Statistical Functions	Returns statistical information about the system.
Text and Image Functions	Performs an operation on a text or image input values or column and returns information about the value.

pose. Some of the commonly used functions are covered in greater detail, with examples. All functions can be found in Books Online.

See also Deterministic and Nondeterministic Functions, page 162.

2.6.1 Aggregate Functions

Aggregate functions perform a calculation on a set of values and return a single summarizing value. Table 2-52 lists the function names and their details.COUNT(), AVG(), MIN(), MAX() and SUM() are ANSI SQL-92 and 99 standard. All are deterministic (see page 162).

Aggregate functions are only allowed as expressions in the following cases.

- The select list of a SELECT statement (either a subquery or an outer query).
- A COMPUTE or COMPUTE BY clause.
- A HAVING clause.

Table 2-52 Aggregate Functions

Aggregate Function Name	Description and Syntax
AVG	Returns the average of the values in a group. Null values are ignored.
BINARY_CHECKSUM	Returns the binary checksum value computed over a row of a table or over a list of expressions. It can be used to detect changes to a row of a table. *Syntax:* `BINARY_CHECKSUM ( * | expression [ ,...n ] )`
CHECKSUM	Returns the checksum value computed over a row of a table, or over a list of expressions. CHECKSUM is intended for use in building hash indices. *Syntax:* `CHECKSUM ( * | expression [ ,...n ] )`
CHECKSUM_AGG	Returns the checksum of the values in a group. Null values are ignored. *Syntax:* `CHECKSUM_AGG ( [ ALL | DISTINCT ] expression )`
COUNT	Returns the number of items in a group as an INT data type value. *Syntax:* `COUNT ( { [ ALL | DISTINCT ] expression ] | * } )`
COUNT_BIG	Returns the number of items in a group as a BIGINT data type value. *Syntax:* `COUNT_BIG ( { [ ALL | DISTINCT ] expression } | * )`
GROUPING	Works only in SELECT statement with GROUP BY plus either ROLLUP or CUBE to determine whether a NULL in the result set was generated by ROLLUP/CUBE or comes from NULL value(s) in the underlying data. *Syntax:* `GROUPING` (*column_name*) returns 1 if a NULL under *column_name* is from ROLLUP or CUBE returns 0 if a NULL under *column_name* is from the data See examples with ROLLUP and CUBE.
MAX	Returns the maximum value in the expression. *Syntax:* `MAX ( [ ALL | DISTINCT ] expression )`
MIN	Returns the minimum value in the expression. *Syntax:* `MIN ( [ ALL | DISTINCT ] expression )`
SUM	Returns the sum of the values in the expression. SUM can be used with numeric columns only. Null values are ignored. *Syntax:* `SUM ( [ ALL | DISTINCT ] expression )`
STDEV	Returns the sample statistical standard deviation of all values in the given expression. For sample statistics the divisor is (n-1). *Syntax:* `STDEV ( expression ) )`
STDEVP	Returns the population statistical standard deviation for all values in the given expression. For population statistics the divisor is (n). *Syntax:* `STDEVP ( expression ) )`

Table 2-52 Aggregate Functions (cont.)

VAR	Returns sample statistical variance of all values in the given expression. For sample statistics the divisor is (n-1). *Syntax:* `VAR ( expression )`
VARP	Returns the population statistical variance for all values in the given expression. For population statistics the divisor is (n). *Syntax:* `VARP ( expression ) )`

2.6.2 Cursor Functions

Cursor Functions, listed in Table 2-53, return cursor status information. All are nondeterministic (see page 162).

Table 2-53 Cursor Functions

Function Name	Description and Syntax
@@CURSOR_ROWS	Returns the number of rows in the last cursor opened on the connection.
@@FETCH_STATUS	Returns the status of the last cursor FETCH statement issued against any cursor currently opened by the connection. Global function to all cursors in the connection, so use it immediately after the FETCH whose status you're interested in.
CURSOR_STATUS	A scalar function that allows the caller of a stored procedure to determine whether or not the procedure has returned a cursor and result set.

These functions are discussed in more detail in Cursors, page 638.

2.6.3 Configuration Functions

Configuration functions, listed in Table 2-54, return information about the current server and database configuration settings. All are nondeterministic (see page 162).

Table 2-54 Configuration Functions

Configuration Function Name	Description (Syntax is just the Function Name since all are read-only and none take parameters.)
@@DATEFIRST	Returns the current value of the SET DATEFIRST parameter, which indicates the specified first day of each week: 1 for Monday, 2 for Wednesday, and so on through 7 for Sunday. The U.S. English default is 7, Sunday.

Table 2-54 Configuration Functions (cont.)

Configuration Function Name	Description (Syntax is just the Function Name since all are read-only and none take parameters.)
	Syntax: **--** Syntax for all functions in this table is just the function name @@DATEFIRST **Example:** **SQL:** `SET DATEFIRST 1 -- Sets session value, See Books Online` `SELECT @@DATEFIRST As'Beginning of Week'` **Result:** Beginning of Week ----------------- 1
@@DBTS	Returns the value of the current **timestamp** data type for the current database. This **timestamp** is guaranteed to be unique in the database. *Syntax:* **@@DBTS**
@@LANGID	Returns local language identifier (ID) of the language currently in use.
@@LANGUAGE	Returns the name of the language currently in use.
@@LOCK_TIMEOUT	Returns the current lock time-out setting, in milliseconds, for the current session.
@@MAX_CONNECTIONS	Returns the maximum number of simultaneous user connections allowed on a Microsoft SQL Server. The number returned is not necessarily the number currently configured.
@@MAX_PRECISION	Returns the precision level used by **decimal** and **numeric** data types as currently set in the server.
@@NESTLEVEL	Returns the nesting level of the current stored procedure execution (initially 0).
@@OPTIONS	Returns information about current SET options. See description page 204.
@@REMSERVER	Returns the name of the remote Microsoft SQL Server database server as it appears in the login record. It enables a stored procedure to check the name of the database server from which the procedure is run.
@@SERVERNAME	Returns the name of the local server running Microsoft SQL Server.
@@SERVICENAME	Returns the name of the registry key under which Microsoft SQL Server is running. @@SERVICENAME returns MSSQLServer if the current instance is the default instance; this function returns the instance name if the current instance is a named instance.

Table 2-54 Configuration Functions (cont.)

Configuration Function Name	Description (Syntax is just the Function Name since all are read-only and none take parameters.)
@@SPID	Returns the server process identifier (ID) of the current user process.
@@TEXTSIZE	Returns the current value of the TEXTSIZE option of the SET statement, which specifies the maximum length, in bytes, of **text** or **image** data that a SELECT statement returns.
@@VERSION	Returns the date, version and processor type for the current installation of Microsoft SQL Server.

Example:

SQL

```
SELECT @@SERVERNAME As Server , @@SERVICENAME Service
```

Result

```
Server          Service
--------------- ----------------------
AMY             MSSQLServer
```

2.6.4 Date and Time Functions

Date and time functions perform an operation on a date and time input value and return either a string, numeric or date and time value. See Table 2-55.

These functions are deterministic and nondeterministic. See details page 163. DATENAME, GETDATE and GETUTCDATE are nondeterministic. DATEPART is deterministic unless used with dw datepart. The rest are deterministic.

Table 2-55 Date and Time Functions

Date Function Name	Description and Syntax
DATEADD	Returns a new **datetime** value after adding an interval (number argument) to the specified date argument. The interval is an integer whose date/time units are specified by the datepart argument as in DATEDIFF below. *Syntax:* `DATEADD ( datepart , number, date )`

Table 2-55 Date and Time Functions (cont.)

Date Function Name	Description and Syntax
	Example: **SQL:** `SELECT DATEADD(week, 1, '1 Jan, 2002' ) As '2d week in 2002'` **Result:** 2d week in 2002 -------------------------------- 2002-01-08 00:00:00.000
DATEDIFF	Returns the integer difference between two DATETIME arguments in the date or time increments specified by the datepart argument (year, quarter, ..., minute, ...). *Syntax:* `( datepart , startdate , enddate )` **Example:** **SQL:** `SELECT DATEDIFF (week, '1 Jan, 2002', '19 Jan, 2002' ) As NumWeeks` **Result:** NumWeeks ----------- 2
DATENAME	Returns a character string representing the specified datepart of the specified date. *Syntax:* `DATENAME ( datepart , date )` **Example:** **SQL:** `SELECT DATENAME (month, '1 Jan, 2002' ) As '1st Month in 2002'` **Result:** 1st Month in 2002 ------------------------------ January
DATEPART	Returns an integer representing the specified datepart of the specified date. *Syntax:* `DATEPART ( datepart , date )` **Example:** **SQL:** `SELECT DATEPART ( month, '1 Jan, 2002' ) As '1st Month in 2002'` **Result:** 1st Month in 2002 ----------------- 1

Table 2-55 Date and Time Functions (cont.)

Date Function Name	Description and Syntax
DAY	Returns an integer representing the day datepart of the specified date. *Syntax:* `DAY ( date )` **Example:** **SQL:** `SELECT DAY( '1 Jan, 2002' )  As 'Day of Month'` **Result:** Day of Month ------------ 1 Note: DAY(date) is equivalent to: DATEPART(dd, date)
MONTH	Returns an integer that represents the month part of a specified date. *Syntax:* `MONTH ( date )` **Example:** **SQL:** `SELECT MONTH( '1 Jan, 2002' )  As 'Month Number'` **Result:** Month Number ------------ 1 Note: MONTH(date) is equivalent to: DATEPART(mm, date)
YEAR	Returns an integer that represents the year part of a specified date. *Syntax:* `YEAR ( date )` **Example:** **SQL:** `SELECT YEAR( '1 Jan, 2002' )  As Year` **Result:** Year ----------- 2002 Note: YEAR(date) is equivalent to: DATEPART(yy, date)
GETDATE	Returns the current system date and time in the Microsoft SQL Server standard internal format for datetime values. *Syntax:* `GETDATE ( )` **Example:** **SQL:** `SELECT GETDATE() As Today` **Result:** Today ------------------------------ 2002-03-27 17:26:14.723

Table 2-55 Date and Time Functions (cont.)

Date Function Name	Description and Syntax
GETUTC-DATE	Returns the datetime value representing the current UTC time (Universal Time Coordinate or Greenwich Mean Time). The current UTC time is derived from the current local time and the time zone setting in the operating system of the computer on which SQL Server is running. *Syntax:* `GETUTCDATE()` **Example:** **SQL:** `SELECT GETDATE() As Now , GETUTCDATE() As NowUTC -- From PST` **Result:** Now NowUTC ------------------------------ ------------------------------- 2002-03-27 16:29:13.250 2002-03-27 23:29:13.250

2.6.5 Mathematical Functions

A mathematical function performs a calculation based on input values provided as parameters to the function and returns a numeric value (Table 2-56). All are deterministic except RAND. See listing page 162.

Table 2-56 Mathematical Functions

Math Function Name	Description and Syntax
ABS	Returns the absolute, positive value of the given numeric expression. *Syntax:* `( numeric_expression )`
ACOS	Returns the angle, in radians, (arccosine) whose cosine is the given float expression. *Syntax:* `ACOS ( float_expression )`
ASIN	Returns the angle, in radians, (arcsine) whose sine is the given float expression. *Syntax:* `ASIN ( float_expression )`
ATAN	Returns the angle in radians (arctangent) whose tangent is the given float expression. *Syntax:* `ATAN ( float_expression )`
ATN2	Returns the angle, in radians, whose tangent is between the two given float expressions. *Syntax:* `ATN2 ( float_expression , float_expression )`
CEILING	Returns the smallest integer greater than, or equal to, the given numeric expression. E.g., CEILING(2.67) is 3. *Syntax:* `CEILING ( numeric_expression )`

Table 2-56 Mathematical Functions (cont.)

Math Function Name	Description and Syntax
COS	A mathematical function that returns the trigonometric cosine of the given angle (in radians) in the given expression. *Syntax:* `COS ( float_expression )`
COT	A mathematic function that returns the trigonometric cotangent of the specified angle (in radians) in the given float expression. *Syntax:* `COT ( float_expression )`
DEGREES	Returns the angle in degrees for an input angle in radians. E.g., DEGREES(PI()/2) is 90.0. *Syntax:* `DEGREES ( numeric_expression )`
EXP	Returns the exponential value of the given float expression. That is, the natural logarithm base (approx. 2.71) raised to the exponent passed as argument. E.g., EXP(1) is 2.71. *Syntax:* `EXP ( float_expression )`
FLOOR	Returns the largest integer less than or equal to the given numeric expression. E.g., FLOOR(2.67) is 2. *Syntax:* `FLOOR ( numeric_expression )`
LOG	Returns the natural logarithm of the given float expression. *Syntax:* `LOG ( float_expression )`
LOG10	Returns the base-10 logarithm of the given float expression. *Syntax:* `LOG10 ( float_expression )`
PI	Returns the constant value of PI. I.e., PI() is 3.14159. *Syntax:* `PI ( )`
POWER	Returns the value of the given expression to the specified power. *Syntax:* `POWER ( numeric_expression , y )`
RADIANS	Returns radians when a numeric expression, in degrees, is entered. *Syntax:* `RADIANS ( numeric_expression )`
RAND	Returns a random float value from 0 through 1. *Syntax:* `RAND ( [ seed ] )`
ROUND	Returns a numeric expression, rounded to the specified length or precision. *Syntax:* `ROUND ( numeric_expression , length [ , function ] )`
SIGN	Returns the positive (+1), zero (0), or negative (–1) sign of the given expression. *Syntax:* `SIGN ( numeric_expression )`

Table 2-56 Mathematical Functions (cont.)

Math Function Name	Description and Syntax
SIN	Returns the trigonometric sine of the given angle (in radians) in an approximate numeric (float) expression. *Syntax:* `SIN ( float_expression )`
SQRT	Returns the square root of the given expression. *Syntax:* `SQRT ( float_expression )`
SQUARE	Returns the square of the given expression. *Syntax:* `SQUARE ( float_expression )`
TAN	Returns the tangent of the input expression which is an angle in radians. *Syntax:* `TAN ( float_expression )`

Example:

SQL

```
SELECT  CEILING(2.13) Ceil , LOG(10) Log , LOG10(10) Log10 ,
  PI() Pi , SIN(1) Sine
```

Result

```
Ceil   Log                  Log10   Pi                   Sine
-----  -------------------  ------  -------------------  ------------------
3      2.3025850929940459   1.0     3.1415926535897931   0.8414709848078965
```

2.6.6 Metadata Functions

A metadata function returns information about the database and database objects (Table 2-57). All are nondeterministic (see page 163).

Table 2-57 Metadata Functions

Function	Description and Syntax
@@PROCID	Returns the current stored procedure identifier (ID).
COL_LENGTH	Returns the defined length (in bytes) of a column. *Syntax:* `COL_LENGTH ( 'table' , 'column' )`

Table 2-57 Metadata Functions (cont.)

Function	Description and Syntax
COL_NAME	Returns the name of a database column given the corresponding table identification number and column identification number. *Syntax:* `COL_NAME ( table_id , column_id )`
COLUMNPROP-ERTY	Returns information about a column or procedure parameter. *Syntax:* `COLUMNPROPERTY ( id , column , property )`
DATABASE-PROP-ERTY	Returns named database property value for the given database and property name for SQL Server 7.0 and before. *Syntax:* `DATABASEPROPERTY( database , property )`
DATABASE-PROPERTYEX	Returns named database property value for the given database and property name for SQL Server 2K and later. *Syntax:* `DATABASEPROPERTYEX( database , property )`
DB_ID	Returns the database identification (ID) number. *Syntax:* `DB_ID ( [ 'database_name' ] )`
DB_NAME	Returns the database name. *Syntax:* `DB_NAME ( database_id )`
FILE_ID	Returns the file identification (ID) number for the given logical file name in the current database. *Syntax:* `FILE_ID ( 'file_name' )`
FILE_NAME	Returns the logical file name for the given file identification (ID) number. *Syntax:* `FILE_NAME ( file_id )`
FILEGROUP_ID	Returns the filegroup identification (ID) number for the given filegroup name. *Syntax:* `FILEGROUP_ID ( 'filegroup_name' )`
FILEGROUP_NA ME	Returns the filegroup name for the given filegroup identification (ID) number. *Syntax:* `FILEGROUP_NAME ( filegroup_id )`
FILEGROUP-PROPERTY	Returns the specified filegroup property value when given a filegroup and property name. *Syntax:* `FILEGROUPPROPERTY ( filegroup_name , property )`
FILEPROPERTY	Returns the specified file name property value when given a file name and property name. *Syntax:* `FILEPROPERTY ( file_name , property )`

Table 2-57 Metadata Functions (cont.)

<table>
<tr><th>Function</th><th>Description and Syntax</th></tr>
<tr><td>fn_listextended-property</td><td>Returns extended property values of database objects.
Syntax:
<code>fn_listextendedproperty (</code>
<code>{ default | [@name =] 'property_name' | NULL }</code>
<code>, { default | [@level0type =] 'level0_object_type' | NULL }</code>
<code>, { default | [@level0name =] 'level0_object_name' | NULL }</code>
<code>, { default | [@level1type =] 'level1_object_type' | NULL }</code>
<code>, { default | [@level1name =] 'level1_object_name' | NULL }</code>
<code>, { default | [@level2type =] 'level2_object_type' | NULL }</code>
<code>, { default | [@level2name =] 'level2_object_name' | NULL }</code>
<code>)</code></td></tr>
<tr><td>FULLTEXTCATA-LOGPROPERTY</td><td>Returns information about full-text catalog properties.
Syntax:
<code>FULLTEXTCATALOGPROPERTY (catalog_name , property)</code></td></tr>
<tr><td>FULLTEXTSERVI-CEPROPERTY</td><td>Returns information about full-text service-level properties.
Syntax: <code>FULLTEXTSERVICEPROPERTY (property)</code></td></tr>
<tr><td>INDEX_COL</td><td>Returns the indexed column name.
Syntax: <code>INDEX_COL ('table' , index_id , key_id)</code></td></tr>
<tr><td>INDEXKEY_ PROPERTY</td><td>Returns information about the index key.
Syntax:
<code>INDEXKEY_PROPERTY (tableID, indexID, keyID, property)</code></td></tr>
<tr><td>INDEXPROPERTY</td><td>Returns the named index property value given a table identification number, index name and property name.
Syntax: <code>INDEXPROPERTY (table_ID , index , property)</code></td></tr>
<tr><td>OBJECT_ID</td><td>Returns the database object identification number.
Syntax: <code>OBJECT_ID ('object')</code></td></tr>
<tr><td>OBJECT_NAME</td><td>Returns the database object name.
Syntax: <code>OBJECT_NAME (object_id)</code></td></tr>
<tr><td>OBJECT-PROPERTY</td><td>Returns information about objects in the current database.
Syntax: <code>OBJECTPROPERTY (id , property)</code></td></tr>
<tr><td>SQL_VARIANT_ PROPERTY</td><td>Returns the base data type and other information about an sql_variant value.
Syntax: <code>SQL_VARIANT_PROPERTY (expression, property)</code></td></tr>
<tr><td>TYPEPROPERTY</td><td>Returns information about a data type.
Syntax: <code>TYPEPROPERTY (type , property)</code></td></tr>
</table>

2.6.7 Rowset Functions

A rowset is a set of rows that contain columns of data and can be used like a table in SQL. Rowsets are central objects that enable all OLE DB data providers to expose result set data in tabular form. Rowset Functions return rowsets (Table 2-58). All are nondeterministic (see page 163).

A rowset is a set of rows that contain columns of data. Rowsets are central objects that enable all OLE DB data providers to expose result set data in tabular form.

Table 2-58 Rowset Functions

<table>
<tr><th>Rowset Function Name</th><th>Description and Syntax</th></tr>
<tr><td>CONTAINSTABLE</td><td>Returns a table of zero or more rows after doing a full-text type query based on precise or near (fuzzy) match criteria.
CONTAINSTABLE can be referenced in the FROM clause of a SELECT statement as if it were a regular table name.
Syntax:
<code>CONTAINSTABLE (table , { column | * } , ' <</code>
<code>   contains_search_condition > '</code>
<code>   [, top_n_by_rank])</code></td></tr>
<tr><td>FREETEXTTABLE</td><td>Returns a table of zero or more rows after doing a full-text type query based on meaning of the text.
FREETEXTTABLE can be referenced in the FROM clause of a SELECT statement as if it were a regular table name.
Syntax:
<code>FREETEXTTABLE (table , { column | * } ,</code>
<code>   'freetext_string' [, top_n_by_rank])</code></td></tr>
<tr><td>OPENDATASOURCE</td><td>Provides ad hoc connection information as part of a four-part object name without using a linked server name. See Books Online.
Syntax: <code>OPENDATASOURCE (provider_name, init_string)</code></td></tr>
<tr><td>OPENQUERY</td><td>Executes the specified pass-through query on the given linked server, which is an OLE DB data source.
The OPENQUERY function can be referenced in the FROM clause of a query as though it is a table name or as the target table of an INSERT, UPDATE or DELETE statement, subject to the OLE DB provider.
Syntax: <code>OPENQUERY (linked_server , 'query')</code></td></tr>
</table>

Table 2-58 Rowset Functions (cont.)

<table>
<tr><th>Rowset Function Name</th><th>Description and Syntax</th></tr>
<tr><td>OPENROWSET</td><td>This is an ad hoc method of connecting and accessing remote data using OLE DB and is an alternative to accessing tables in a linked server.
The OPENROWSET function can be referenced in the FROM clause of a query like a table or as the target table of an INSERT, UPDATE or DELETE statement, subject to the OLE DB provider.
Syntax:
<pre>OPENROWSET ('provider_name'
     , { 'datasource' ; 'user_id' ; 'password'
         | 'provider_string' }
     , { [catalog.] [schema.] object
         | 'query' }
)</pre></td></tr>
<tr><td>OPENXML</td><td>Opens an XML document and returns the data as a rowset which may be used as a table in a read-only SQL statement.
Often used with sp_xml_preparedocument as in the example below.
Syntax:
<pre>OPENXML (
  idoc int [in], -- the document handle created by
    sp_xml_preparedocument
  rowpattern nvarchar[in] -- XPATH pattern to identify XML
    document nodes to be used as rows
       [, flags byte[in]] -- XML mapping:
    0 (default) attribute-centric,
    1 - attribute-centric then can use XML_ELEMENTS,
    2 - element-centric then can use XML_ATTRIBUTES,
    8 - combine XML_ELEMENTS and XML_ATTRIBUTES
)[WITH (SchemaDeclaration | TableName)] -- may specify
    nodes to display in result set</pre></td></tr>
</table>

Example: Use OPENQUERY — requires a link be made to remote server. See Section 2.2.5, page 46.

SQL

```
SELECT  TOP 2   *
FROM  OPENQUERY( CAT2_Link , 'SELECT *   FROM pubs.dbo.authors')
```

Result

au_id	au_lname	au_fname	phone	address	city	state
172-32-1176	White	Johnson	408 496-7223	10932 Bigge Rd.	Menlo Park	CA
213-46-8915	Green	Marjorie	415 986-7020	309 63rd St. #411	Oakland	CA

This example uses the link `CAT2_Link` created on page 47. That version is repeated below as it seems more direct than the OPENQUERY method above.

SQL
`SELECT TOP 2 * FROM CAT2_Link.pubs.dbo.authors`

Result
Same result as previous.

Example: Use OPENROWSET — Does not require that a link be created first.

```
SQL
SELECT a.*
FROM    OPENROWSET('SQLOLEDB','cat\cat2';'sa';'',
```

```
SQL
'SELECT  TOP 2 * FROM pubs.dbo.authors ') AS a
```

Result
Same result as previous.

Example: Use OPENXML Create an xml document with **sp_xml_preparedocument**, then read it with OPENXML.

Create an internal representation of an XML data document and assign the document handle value to the idoc handle variable so it can be passed in to OPENXML to read.

```
DECLARE @idoc int -- Declare an int variable for the xml document handle

        EXEC sp_xml_preparedocument @idoc OUTPUT,
        '<ROOT>
        <Customer >
            <CustomerID>12</CustomerID>
            <Name>Amy Darling</Name>
            <Telephone>111-2222</Telephone>
        </Customer>
```

```
<Customer >
    <CustomerID>36</CustomerID>
    <Name> Torie Dearest </Name>
    <Telephone>333-4444</Telephone>
</Customer>
</ROOT>'
```

Do a query using OPENXML to read the desired parts of the XML data document.

SQL

```
SELECT    *
FROM OPENXML (@idoc, '/ROOT/Customer', 2)
  WITH (CustomerID  varchar(10), Name varchar(20))
```

Result

```
CustomerID          Name
----------          --------------------
2                   Amy Darling
36                  Torie Dearest

(2 row(s) affected)
```

With the XML data thus available at a virtual table in SQL, it may be inserted into a database table as in this example run in the same batch as the previous statements.

SQL

```
SELECT    *
INTO table1
FROM       OPENXML (@idoc, '/ROOT/Customer', 2)
  WITH (CustomerID  varchar(10), Name varchar(20))
go

SELECT *  FROM table1
```

SQL (cont.)

Result

```
CustomerID    Name
----------    --------------------
12            Amy Darling
36            Torie Dearest

(2 row(s) affected)
```

2.6.8 Security Functions

A security function returns information about users and roles. All are nondeterministic (see Table 2-59 and page 162).

Table 2-59 Security Functions

Security Function Name	Description and Syntax
fn_trace_geteventinfo	Returns information about the events traced. *Syntax:* `fn_trace_geteventinfo ( [ @traceid = ] trace_id )`
fn_trace_getfilterinfo	Returns information about the filters applied to a specified trace. *Syntax:* `fn_trace_getfilterinfo( [ @traceid = ] trace_id )`
fn_trace_getinfo	Returns information about a specified trace or existing traces. *Syntax:* `fn_trace_getinfo( [ @traceid = ] trace_id )`
fn_trace_gettable	Returns trace file information in a table format. *Syntax:* `fn_trace_gettable( [ @filename = ] filename , [ @numfiles = ] number_files )`
HAS_DBACCESS	Indicates whether the user has access to the specified database. Returns int 0 if no, 1 if yes, NULL if database name is invalid. *Syntax:* `HAS_DBACCESS ( 'database_name' )`
IS_MEMBER	Indicates whether the current user is a member of the specified Microsoft Windows NT group or Microsoft SQL Server role. Returns int 0 if no, 1 if yes, NULL if group or role is invalid. *Syntax:* `IS_MEMBER ( { 'group' | 'role' } )`
IS_SRVROLEMEMBER	Indicates whether the current or specified user login is a member of the specified server role. Returns int 0 if no, 1 if yes, NULL if role or login is invalid. *Syntax:* `IS_SRVROLEMEMBER ( 'role' [ , 'login' ] )`

Table 2-59 Security Functions (cont.)

SUSER_SID	Returns the security identification number (SID) for the user's login name. *Syntax:* `SUSER_SID ( [ 'login' ] )` **Example:** **SQL:** `SELECT SUSER_SID( 'sa')` **Result:** ------------- 0x01
SUSER_SNAME	Returns the login identification name for the current user or from the user's security identification number (SID) if specified. *Syntax:* `SUSER_SNAME ( [ server_user_sid ] )` **Example:** **SQL:** `SELECT  SUSER_SNAME ( 0x1 )` **Result:** ----------- sa
USER	Allows a system-supplied value for the current user's database username to be inserted into a table when no default value is specified. *Syntax:* `USER` **Example:** **SQL:** `SELECT USER` **Result:** ------ dbo
USER_ID	Returns a user's database identification number. *Syntax:* `USER_ID ( [ 'user' ] )` **Example:** **SQL:** `SELECT USER_ID()` **Result:** ------ 1

2.6.9 String Functions — for CHAR or VARCHAR expressions

A string function for CHAR or VARCHAR expressions performs an operation on a string input value and returns a string or numeric value (Table 2-60). All are deterministic except CHARINDEX and PATINDEX (see page 162).

Table 2-60 String Functions

String Fcn	Description and Syntax
ASCII	Returns the ASCII code value of the leftmost character of a char expression. *Syntax:* `ASCII ( character_expression )` **SQL:** `PRINT ASCII('abc') -- The ASCII value of the letter "a" is 97` **Result:** 97

Table 2-60 String Functions (cont.)

String Fcn	Description and Syntax
CHAR	A string function that converts an int ASCII code to a character. Inverse of ASCII. *Syntax:* `CHAR ( integer_expression )` **SQL:** `PRINT CHAR(97) -- 97 is the ASCII value of the letter "a"` **Result:** a
CHARINDEX	Returns the starting position of expr1 in a character string expr2. Search begins with 1st character unless start_location is given and is > 1. *Syntax:* `CHARINDEX ( expr1 , expr2 [ , start_location ] )`
DIFFERENCE	Returns the difference between the SOUNDEX values of two character expressions as an integer. See Books Online. *Syntax:* `DIFFERENCE ( character_expression , character_expression )`
LEFT	Returns the leftmost *integer_expression characters* of *character_expr*. *Syntax:* `LEFT ( character_expr , integer_expression )` **SQL:** `PRINT LEFT('abcd' , 2)` **Result:** ab
LEN	Returns the number of characters (may not be the number of bytes) of the given string expression, excluding trailing blanks. *Syntax:* `LEN ( string_expression )` **SQL:** `PRINT LEN('abc')` **Result:** 3
LOWER	Returns the character_expression string in all lower case. *Syntax:* `LOWER ( character_expression )` **SQL:** `PRINT LOWER('AbCd')` **Result:** abcd
LTRIM	Returns a character expression after removing leading blanks. *Syntax:* `LTRIM ( character_expression )`
NCHAR	Returns the Unicode character with the given integer code. *Syntax:*`NCHAR ( integer_expression )`
PATINDEX	Returns the starting position of the first occurrence of a pattern in the char_expr or zero if the pattern is not found (text or character data types). *Syntax:*`PATINDEX ( '%pattern%' , char_expr )` **Example:** **SQL:** `SELECT PATINDEX( '%cd%' , 'abcde' )` **Result:** 3

Table 2-60 String Functions (cont.)

String Fcn	Description and Syntax
QUOTENAME	Returns a Unicode string with the delimiters added to make the input string a valid Microsoft SQL Server delimited identifier. *Syntax:* `QUOTENAME ( 'character_string' [ , 'quote_character' ] )`
REPLACE	Replaces all occurrences of the second given string expression in the first string expression with a third expression. *Syntax:* `REPLACE ( 'string_expr1' , 'string_expr2' , 'string_expr3' )` **Example:** **SQL:** `SELECT REPLACE ('aaaXXXbbbXXXccc' , 'XXX' , 'YYY')` **Result:** ----------------------- aaaYYYbbbYYYccc
REPLICATE	Repeats a character expression for a specified number of times. *Syntax:* `REPLICATE ( character_expression , integer_expression )`
REVERSE	Returns the reverse of a character expression. *Syntax:* `REVERSE ( character_expression )`
RIGHT	Returns the rightmost <integer_expr> characters of <character_expr>. *Syntax:*`RIGHT ( character_expr , integer_expr )`
RTRIM	Returns a character expression after removing trailing blanks. *Syntax:* `RTRIM ( character_expression )`
SOUNDEX	Returns a four-character (SOUNDEX) code to evaluate the similarity of two strings. *Syntax:* `SOUNDEX ( character_expression )`
SPACE	Returns a string of repeated spaces. *Syntax:* `SPACE ( integer_expression )`
STR	Returns character data converted from numeric data. *Syntax:* `STR ( float_expression [ , length [ , decimal ] ] )`
STUFF	Replaces characters in char_expr1 from start to start plus length with char_expr2. *Syntax:* `STUFF ( char_expr1 , start , length , char_expr2 )`
SUBSTRING	Returns part of a character, binary, text, or image expression. *Syntax:* `SUBSTRING ( expression , start , length )`
UNICODE	Returns the integer Unicode value for the first character of the expression. *Syntax:* `UNICODE ( 'ncharacter_expression' )`
UPPER	Returns the character_expression string in all upper case. *Syntax:* `UPPER ( character_expression )`

2.6.10 System Functions

System functions, listed in Table 2-61, perform operations and return information about values, objects and settings in Microsoft SQL Server. Some are deterministic and some are not. See list page 162.

Table 2-61 System Functions

System Function Name	Description and Syntax
@@ERROR	Returns the error number for the last Transact-SQL statement executed. *Syntax:* `@@ERROR`
@@IDENTITY	Returns the last-inserted identity value. *Syntax:* `@@IDENTITY`
@@ROWCOUNT	Returns the number of rows affected by the last statement. *Syntax:* `@@ROWCOUNT`
@@TRANCOUNT	Returns the number of active transactions for the current connection. *Syntax:* `@@TRANCOUNT`
APP_NAME	Returns the application name for the current session if set. *Syntax:* `APP_NAME ( )`
CASE expression	Evaluates a list of conditions and returns one of multiple possible result expressions. See explanation and examples, page 165.

CAST and CONVERT	Explicitly converts an expression of one data type to another. CAST and CONVERT provide similar functionality. See explanation and examples, page 167.
	Syntax:
	`CAST ( expression AS data_type )`
	`CONVERT ( data_type [ ( length ) ] , expression [ , style ] )`

COALESCE	Returns the first nonnull expression among its arguments. *Syntax:* `COALESCE ( expression [ ,...n ] )`
COLLATIONPROPERTY	Returns the property of a given collation. *Syntax:* `COLLATIONPROPERTY( collation_name, property)`
CURRENT_TIMESTAMP	Returns the current date and time. Equivalent to GETDATE(). *Syntax:* `CURRENT_TIMESTAMP`
CURRENT_USER	Returns the current user. This function is equivalent to USER_NAME(). *Syntax:* `CURRENT_USER`

Table 2-61 System Functions (cont.)

System Function Name	Description and Syntax
DATALENGTH	Returns the number of bytes used to represent an expression. *Syntax:* `DATALENGTH ( expression )`
fn_helpcollations	Returns a list of all the collations supported by SQL Server 2K. *Syntax:* `fn_helpcollations ()`
fn_servershareddrives	Returns the names of shared drives used by the clustered server. *Syntax:* `fn_servershareddrives()`
fn_virtualfilestats	Returns I/O statistics for database files, including log files. *Syntax:* `fn_virtualfilestats ( [@DatabaseID=] database_id , [ @FileID = ] file_id )`
FORMATMESSAGE	Constructs a message from an existing message in sysmessages. The functionality of FORMATMESSAGE resembles that of the RAISERROR statement; however, RAISERROR prints the message immediately. FORMATMESSAGE returns the edited message for further processing. *Syntax:* `FORMATMESSAGE ( msg_number , param_value [ ,...n ] )`
GETANSINULL	Returns the effective default nullability for the database for this session. *Syntax:* `GETANSINULL ( [ 'database' ] )`
HOST_ID	Books Online says this returns the client workstation identification number. This value appears to be the process id for each client program from the client host. Thus the value differs for each client program. *Syntax:* `HOST_ID ( )`
HOST_NAME	Returns the client workstation name. This name is the same for each connection from the client host. *Syntax:* `HOST_NAME ( )`
IDENT_CURRENT	Returns the last identity value generated for a specified table in any session and any scope. *Syntax:* `IDENT_CURRENT('table_name')`
IDENT_INCR	Returns the numeric increment value specified during the creation of an identity column in a table or view that has an identity column. *Syntax:* `IDENT_INCR ( 'table_or_view' )`
IDENT_SEED	Returns the numeric seed value specified during the creation of an identity column in a table or a view that has an identity column. *Syntax:* `IDENT_SEED ( 'table_or_view' )`

Table 2-61 System Functions (cont.)

System Function Name	Description and Syntax
IDENTITY (Function)	Is used only in a SELECT statement with an INTO table clause to insert an identity column into a new table. The IDENTITY function is similar to the IDENTITY property used with CREATE TABLE. *Syntax:* `IDENTITY ( data_type [ , seed , increment ] ) AS column_name` **Example:** **SQL:** `SELECT  IDENTITY(INT) As id , name INTO newemp FROM emp`
ISDATE	Returns 1 if the expression is a valid date, 0 if not. *Syntax:* `ISDATE ( expression )`
ISNULL	If *expr1* is NULL, it is replaced with *expr2*. That is, IF *expr1* IS NOT NULL returns *expr1* ELSE returns *expr2* *Syntax:* `ISNULL ( expr1 , expr2 )` **Example:** **SQL:** `SELECT  ISNULL( 'Hello', 'Null') ,  ISNULL (NULL, 'Null word')` **Result:** ----------- ------------- Hello Null word
ISNUMERIC	Returns 1 if the expression is a valid numeric type, 0 if not. *Syntax:* `ISNUMERIC ( expression )`
NEWID	Creates a unique value of type uniqueidentifier. *Syntax:* `NEWID ( )`
NULLIF	Returns NULL if the two expressions are equivalent. If not equivalent, returns the first expression. See Books Online for meaningful example. *Syntax:* `NULLIF ( expression , expression )`
PARSENAME	Returns the specified part of an object name. Parts of an object that can be retrieved are the object name, owner name, database name, and server name. Note: This function does not indicate whether or not the specified *object* exists. It just returns the specified piece of the given *object name*. *Syntax:* `PARSENAME ( 'object_name' , object_piece )` object_piece (integer) Meaning 1 Object name 2 Owner name 3 Database name 4 Server name

Table 2-61 System Functions (cont.)

PERMISSIONS	Returns a value containing a bitmap that indicates the statement, object or column permissions for the current user. *Syntax:* `PERMISSIONS ( [ objectid [ , 'column' ] ] )`
ROWCOUNT_BIG	Returns the number of rows affected by the last statement executed. This function operates like @@ROWCOUNT, except that the return type of ROWCOUNT_BIG is bigint. *Syntax:* `ROWCOUNT_BIG ( )`
SCOPE_IDENTITY	Returns the last IDENTITY value inserted into an IDENTITY column in the same scope. A scope is a module — a stored procedure, trigger, function or batch. Thus, two statements are in the same scope if they are in the same stored procedure, function or batch. *Syntax:* `SCOPE_IDENTITY( )`
SERVERPROPERTY	Returns property information about the server instance. *Syntax:* `SERVERPROPERTY ( propertyname )`
SESSIONPROPERTY	Returns the SET options settings of a session. *Syntax:* `SESSIONPROPERTY ( option )`
SESSION_USER	Returns the username of the current user. May be used as a column DEFAULT in CREATE TABLE to insert the name of the user executing an INSERT statement. See example below under SYSTEM_USER. *Syntax:* `SESSION_USER`
STATS_DATE	Returns the date and time that the statistics for the specified index were last updated. See example page 297. *Syntax:* `STATS_DATE ( table_id , index_id )`
SYSTEM_USER	Returns the system username of the current user. May be used as a column DEFAULT in CREATE TABLE to insert the name of the user executing an INSERT statement. *Syntax:* `SYSTEM_USER` **Example:** **SQL:** `SELECT SESSION_USER As Sess , SYSTEM_USER As Sys` **Result:** Sess Sys ----- ------- dbo sa
USER_NAME	Returns a user database username from a given identification number. *Syntax:* `USER_NAME ( [ id ] )`

2.6.11 System Statistical Functions

A system statistical function, returns statistical information about the system. See Table 2-62 for details. All are nondeterministic (see page 162).

Table 2-62 System Statistical Functions

Function Name	Description and Syntax
@@CONNECTIONS	Returns the number of connections, or attempted connections, since Microsoft SQL Server was last started.
@@CPU_BUSY	Returns the time in milliseconds (based on the resolution of the system timer) that the CPU has spent working since Microsoft SQL Server was last started.
@@IDLE	Returns the time in milliseconds (based on the resolution of the system timer) that Microsoft SQL Server has been idle since last started.
@@IO_BUSY	Returns the time in milliseconds (based on the resolution of the system timer) that Microsoft SQL Server has spent performing input and output operations since it was last started.
@@PACK_RECEIVED	Returns the number of input packets read from the network by Microsoft SQL Server since last started.
@@PACK_SENT	Returns the number of output packets written to the network by Microsoft-SQL Server since last started.
@@PACKET_ERRORS	Returns the number of network packet errors that have occurred on Microsoft SQL Server connections since SQL Server was last started.
@@TIMETICKS	Returns the number of microseconds per tick.
@@TOTAL_ERRORS	Returns the number of disk read/write errors encountered by Microsoft SQL Server since last started.
@@TOTAL_READ	Returns the number of disk reads (not cache reads) by Microsoft SQL Server since last started.
@@TOTAL_WRITE	Returns the number of disk writes by Microsoft SQL Server since last started.
fn_virtualfilestats	Returns I/O statistics for database files, including log files. *Syntax:* `fn_virtualfilestats ( [@DatabaseID=]database_id , [ @FileID = ] file_id )`

2.6.12 Text and Image Functions and Statements

Text and image functions, listed in Table 2-63, perform an operation on a text or image input value or column and return information about the value. All are nondeterministic (see page 162).

Table 2-63 Text and Image Functions

Function Name	Description and Syntax
DATALENGTH	Returns the number of bytes used to represent any expression. *Syntax:* `DATALENGTH ( expression )`
PATINDEX	Returns the starting position of the first occurrence of a pattern in a specified expression or zero if the pattern is not found. All text and character data types. *Syntax:* `PATINDEX ( '%pattern%' , expression )`
SUBSTRING	Returns part of a character, binary, text, or image expression. See Books Online. *Syntax:* `SUBSTRING ( expression , start , length )`
TEXTPTR	Returns the text-pointer value that corresponds to a text, ntext, or image column in varbinary format. The retrieved text pointer value can be used in READTEXT, WRITETEXT, and UPDATETEXT statements. *Syntax:* `TEXTPTR ( column )`
TEXTVALID	Returns 1 if a given text, ntext, or image pointer is valid, 0 if not. *Syntax:* `TEXTVALID ( 'table.column' , text_ ptr )`

See Text examples on page 109.

Text and image statements are summarized in Table 2-64.

Table 2-64 Text and Image Statements

Statement Name	Description and Syntax
READTEXT	Reads text, ntext, or image values from a text, ntext, or image column, starting from a specified offset and reading the specified number of bytes. *Syntax:* `READTEXT { table.column text_ptr offset size } [ HOLDLOCK ]`
SET TEXTSIZE	Specifies the size of text and ntext data returned with a SELECT statement. *Syntax:* `SET TEXTSIZE { number }`
UPDATETEXT	Updates an existing text, ntext, or image field. Use UPDATETEXT to change only a portion of a text, ntext or image column in place.

Table 2-64 Text and Image Statements (cont.)

Statement Name	Description and Syntax
WRITETEXT	Permits nonlogged, interactive updating of an existing text, ntext or image column. This statement completely overwrites any existing data in the column it affects. WRITETEXT cannot be used on text, ntext and image columns in views. *Syntax:* `WRITETEXT { table.column text_ptr } [ WITH LOG ] { data }`

2.6.13 Deterministic and Nondeterministic Functions

All functions are either deterministic or nondeterministic. Deterministic functions always return the same result any time they are called with the same input values. For example, ABS(-2) always returns 2. Nondeterministic functions may return different results each time they are called even though input values are the same. For example, GETDATE() returns a different result each time it's called.

Indexed views or indexes on computed columns cannot include nondeterministic functions. An index cannot be created on a view which references any nondeterministic functions. An index cannot be created on a computed column if the *computed_column_expression* references any nondeterministic functions.

2.6.13.1 Listing of Deterministic and Nondeterministic Functions

Aggregate built-in functions (page 139) are all deterministic. String built-in functions (page 154) are all deterministic except CHARINDEX and PATINDEX. Tables 2-65 thorugh 2-68 identify characteristics of many functions.

Always Deterministic The functions in Table 2-65 are always deterministic.

Table 2-65 Deterministic Functions

ABS	COS	EXP	NULLIF	SIN
ACOS	COT	FLOOR	PARSENAME	SQUARE
ASIN	DATALENGTH	ISNULL	PI	SQRT
ATAN	DATEADD	ISNUMERIC	POWER	TAN
ATN2	DATEDIFF	LOG	RADIANS	YEAR
CEILING	DAY	LOG10	ROUND	
COALESCE	DEGREES	MONTH	SIGN	

The System Functions listed in Table 2-66 are deterministic.

Table 2-66 Deterministic System Functions

CASE expression	COALESCE	DATALENGTH	fn_helpcollations	ISNULL
ISNUMERIC	NULLIF	PARSENAME		

Sometimes Deterministic These functions, listed in Table 2-67, are not always deterministic but can be used in indexed views or indexes on computed columns when they are specified in a deterministic manner.

Table 2-67 Sometimes Deterministic Functions

Function	Comments
CAST	Deterministic unless used with **datetime**, **smalldatetime** or **sql_variant**.
CONVERT	Deterministic unless used with **datetime**, **smalldatetime** or **sql_variant**. The **datetime** and **smalldatetime** data types are deterministic if style parameter is given.
CHECKSUM	Deterministic, with the exception of CHECKSUM(*).
DATEPART	Deterministic except when used as DATEPART (dw, *date*). The value returned by **dw**, weekday, depends on the value set by SET DATEFIRST.
ISDATE	Deterministic only if used with the CONVERT function, the CONVERT style param- e ter is specified and style is not equal to 0, 100, 9 or 109.
RAND	RAND is deterministic only when a *seed* parameter is specified.

Never Deterministic The System and Built-in Functions in Table 2-68 are always nondeterministic.

Table 2-68 Nondeterministic Functions

@@ERROR	fn_servershareddrives	IDENT_INCR	SESSIONPROPERTY
@@IDENTITY	fn_virtualfilestats	IDENT_SEED	STATS_DATE
@@ROWCOUNT	FORMATMESSAGE	IDENTITY	SYSTEM_USER
@@TRANCOUNT	GETANSINULL	NEWID	TEXTPTR
APP_NAME	GETDATE	PERMISSIONS	TEXTVALID
COLLATIONPROPERTY	GETUTCDATE	ROWCOUNT_BIG	USER_NAME
CURRENT_TIMESTAMP	HOST_ID	SCOPE_IDENTITY	

Table 2-68 Nondeterministic Functions (cont.)

CURRENT_USER	HOST_NAME	SERVERPROPERTY	
DATENAME	IDENT_CURRENT	SESSION_USER	

As discussed earlier, all configuration, cursor, meta data, rowset, security, and system statistical functions are nondeterministic. Functions that call extended stored procedures are nondeterministic because the extended stored procedures can cause side effects on the database.

2.6.14 CASE Expression

CASE can be considered an expression or a function because it evaluates to a single scalar value of the same data type as the input expression. CASE has two formats: simple CASE and searched CASE.

Simple CASE compares the input expression to a series of simple expressions.

```
CASE input-expression WHEN match-expression THEN result
                      [ WHEN match-expression THEN result ]
                      . . .
                      [ELSE result]
END
```

Searched CASE evaluates a series of Boolean expressions to determine the result.

```
CASE                WHEN Boolean-condition THEN result
                    [ WHEN Boolean-condition THEN result ]
                    . . .
                    [ELSE result2]
END
```

2.6.14.1 Example of Simple CASE

Consider Table 2-69, which has a column containing a car manufacturer abbreviation.

Table 2-69 Autos

Make	Manufacturer	...	...
Buick	GM		
Quattro	Au		

Table 2-69 Autos (cont.)

Jeep	DC		
Sebring	DC		

The following query uses CASE to convert the manufacturer abbreviation to the full name.

SQL

```
SELECT Make, CASE Manufacturer
  WHEN 'GM' THEN 'General Motors'
  WHEN 'Au'THEN 'Audi'
  WHEN 'DC'THEN 'Daimler-Chrysler'
  ELSE 'Manufacturer not found'
END   As Manufacturer
FROM Autos;
```

Result

```
Make          Manufacturer
----------    --------------------
Buick         General Motors
Quattro       Audi
Jeep          Daimler-Chrysler
Sebring       Daimler-Chrysler
```

2.6.14.2 Example of Searched CASE

This form of CASE can be used for inequalities, as in the example, as well as equalities. Consider Table 2-70, for which we want to do a query that assigns letter grades.

Table 2-70 Grades

Student	Grade	Major	...
Torie	87	Counselling	
James	76	Dog Husbandry	
Amy	93	Tae Kwon Do	

Table 2-70 Grades (cont.)

Student	Grade	Major	...
Tim	82	Jet Skiing	
Ina	98	Flower Gardening	

SQL

```
SELECT Student, CASE  WHEN Grade > 90 THEN 'A'
                      WHEN Grade > 80 THEN 'B'
                      WHEN Grade > 70 THEN 'C'
                      WHEN Grade > 60 THEN 'D'
                      ELSE 'F'
END    As   LetterGrade
FROM Grades
ORDER BY Student;
```

Result

```
Student       LetterGrade
----------    --------------
Amy           A
Ina           A
James         C
Tim           B
Torie         B
```

2.6.15 CAST and CONVERT

Both CAST and CONVERT functions are used to explicitly convert a value from one data type to another data type. CAST and CONVERT provide similar functionality but only CAST complies with ANSI SQL-92 and -99. CAST and CONVERT may be used anywhere a scalar valued expression may occur in an SQL statement.

CAST Syntax

```
CAST ( expression AS datatype )
```

CONVERT Syntax

```
CONVERT (data_type[(length)], expression [, style])
```

Example: Error

SQL

```
SELECT Make, CASE Manufacturer
    WHEN 'GM' THEN 'General Motors'
    WHEN 'Au'THEN 'Audi'
    WHEN 'DC'THEN 'Daimler-Chrysler'
    ELSE 'Manufacturer not found'
   END   As Manufacturer
FROM Autos;
```

Result

Server: Msg 241, Level 16, State 1, Line 2
Syntax error converting datetime from character string.

SQL

```
SELECT  'Today is ' + GETDATE()   -- Error, incompatible data types
```

CAST Example: CAST is ANSI standard which makes it more portable than CONVERT.

SQL

```
SELECT  'Today is ' + CAST( GETDATE() AS CHAR ) -- Okay
```

Result

```
--------------------------------------------------
Today is Sep  2 2001  2:14PM.
```

CONVERT Example:

SQL

```
SELECT  'Today is ' + CONVERT( CHAR , GETDATE() )  -- Okay
```

Result

```
--------------------------------------------------
Today is Sep  2 2001  2:14PM.
```

2.7 SYSTEM STORED PROCEDURES AND DBCC

System stored procedures and extended procedures are built-in commands that perform a variety of tasks to do database administration and to provide information.

2.7.1 System Stored Procedures

There are hundreds of system stored procedures and extended procedures. Some individual stored procedures will be described as needed throughout the book. You may check the index to see if a given stored procedure is described in the book. A complete list of system stored procedures may be found in Appendix A. Metadata stored procedures are discussed on p. 376. Additional details may be found by looking each up by name in Books Online.

In general, system stored procedure names start with sp_ and return results within SQL Server. Extended stored procedure names start with xp_ and require doing work outside of SQL Server such as making calls to the operating system or an external process.

Some useful system stored procedures and extended procedures are summarized in Table 2-71.

Table 2-71 System Stored Procedures

sp_configure [*settingname* [, *settingvalue*]]	No arguments—lists all current server settings in five columns name minimum maximum config_value run_value where config_value is value configured but may not yet be effective until server restarts or "reconfigure" command is executed. 1 argument—shows its value; 2 arguments—sets its value See page 177 for discussion and examples.
sp_dboption	Included for backward compatibility. Use ALTER DATABASE.
sp_help [*objname*]	No arguments—lists all objects in the current database. 1 argument—reports information about the database object in the current database.
sp_helpdb *dbname*	Reports information about a specified database or all databases.
sp_helpindex *tablename*	Reports indexes on the table or view.
sp_helptext *objname*	Prints the code text of a rule, a default or an unencrypted stored procedure, user-defined function, trigger or view.
sp_lock [*spid*]	Reports locks held by all processes or by spid (page 140).

Table 2-71 System Stored Procedures (cont.)

sp_who	Reports all current users and processes connected to SQL Server.
xp_cmdshell	Executes a given command string as an operating system command shell and returns any output as rows of text.
xp_grantlogin	Grants a Microsoft Windows NT group or user access to Microsoft SQL Server.
xp_revokelogin	Revokes access from a Microsoft Windows NT group or user to Microsoft SQL Server.

Stored procedures are executed using the following syntax.

Syntax

```
[EXEC[UTE]]    sp_stored_procedure_name
```

EXEC or EXECUTE keyword is optional if this is the first statement in a batch.

2.7.1.1 The sp_ Procedures

The stored procedures provided by SQL server that begin with sp_ are predefined to provide administrative functions for managing SQL Server and displaying information about databases and users. Examples include the following: **sp_helpdb**, **sp_help**, **sp_configure**. See a complete list in Appendix A.

Example: Use **sp_helpdb** to display size and file information about pubs database.

SQL

```
EXEC  sp_helpdb  pubs
```

Result

```
name      db_size     owner      dbid     created        ...
-------   ----------  --------   ------   ----------     ...
pubs      2.00 MB     sa         5        Aug  6 2000    ...

name      fileid      filename                                                    ...
-------   ------      -----------                                                 ...
pubs      1           C:\Program Files\Microsoft SQL Server\MSSQL\data\pubs.mdf      ...
pubs_log  2           C:\Program Files\Microsoft SQL Server\MSSQL\data\pubs_log.ldf  ...
```

2.7.1.2 The xp_ Procedures—Provided

The procedures that begin with xp_, called extended stored procedures, allow creation of external routines in a programming language such as C.

They are used to do work outside of SQL Server, such as accessing the registry, etc. A competent user may create his or her own extended stored procedures with **sp_addextendedproc**. Some examples include the following: **xp_cmdshell**, **xp_grantlogin**, **xp_revokelogin**. For more details, see Books Online Index: xp_ .

Example: Use **xp_cmdshell** to show contents of C:\ directory on server machine.

SQL

```
EXEC master..xp_cmdshell   'dir/w  C:\'
```

Result

```
output
---------------------------------------------------------------------
Volume in drive C is AMY_C
Volume Serial Number is 2CA0-6A55
Directory of C:\
boot.ini    [Documents and Settings]     [HySnap]     [Inetpub]    [WINNT]
1 File(s)           189 bytes
4 Dir(s)   9,494,585,344 bytes free
```

Example: Display the names of database objects in the **pubs** database.

SQL

```
USE pubs
go

EXEC sp_help       -- List all database objects in pubs database
```

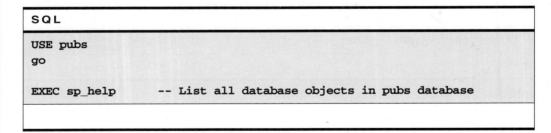

SQL (cont.)

Result

```
Name                            Owner           Object_type
------------------------------  ------------    --------------
titlevie                        dbo             view
authors                         dbo             user table
discounts                       dbo             user table
employee                        dbo             user table
...
titleauthor                     dbo             user table
titles                          dbo             user table
syscolumns                      dbo             system table
syscomments                     dbo             system table
...
PK__jobs__117F9D94              dbo             primary key cns
PK_emp_id                       dbo             primary key cns
UPK_storeid                     dbo             primary key cns
UPKCL_auidind                   dbo             primary key cns
...
FK__discounts__stor___0F975522  dbo             foreign key cns
...
DF__authors__phone__78B3EFCA    dbo             default (maybe cns)
...
CK__authors__au_id__77BFCB91    dbo             check cns
...

User_type  Storage_type  Length  Prec  Scale  Nullable  Default_name  Collation
---------- ------------- ------- ----- ----   -----     -------       -----------------------------------
empid      char          9       9     NULL   no        none          SQL_Latin1_General_CP1_CI_AS
id         varchar       11      11    NULL   no        none          SQL_Latin1_General_CP1_CI_AS
tid        varchar       6       6     NULL   no        none          SQL_Latin1_General_CP1_CI_AS
```

Example: Display the metadata for the authors table of the **pubs** database including column names.

SQL

```
EXEC sp_help  authors      -- Show structure and
  properties of "authors" table in pubs database
```

SQL (cont.)

Result

```
Name          Owner    Type         Created_datetime
------------  -------  ----------   -----------------------
authors       dbo      user table   2000-08-06 01:33:52.123

Column_name   Type     Computed     Length   Prec   Scale   Nullable
------------  -------  -----------  -------  -----  ------  ---------
au_id         id       no           11                      no
au_lname      varchar  no           40                      no
au_fname      varchar  no           20                      no
...
```

2.7.2 DBCC

The initials DBCC stand for Database Console Command (a k a Database Consistency Checker before SQL Server 2K). DBCC statements check the physical and logical consistency of a database. Many DBCC statements can fix detected problems.

The four categories of DBCC statements and descriptions are shown in Tables 2-72 through 2-75 below. See Books Online for details.

2.7.2.1 DBCC Maintenance Statements

The commands listed in Table 2-72 will help you perform maintenance tasks on a database, index or filegroup.

Table 2-72 DBCC Maintenance Statements

DBCC DBREINDEX	Rebuilds one or more indexes for a table in the specified database.
DBCC DBREPAIR	Drops a damaged database. NOTE: DBCC DBREPAIR is included in Microsoft SQL Server 2000 for backward compatibility only and may not appear in future versions. DROP DATABASE is recommended to drop damaged databases.
DBCC INDEXDEFRAG	Defragments indexes of the specified table or view.
DBCC SHRINKDATABASE	Shrinks the size of the data files in the specified database.
DBCC SHRINKFILE	Shrinks the size of the specified data file or log file for the related database.
DBCC UPDATEUSAGE	Reports and corrects inaccuracies in the **sysindexes** table. This may result in incorrect space usage reports by **sp_spaceused**.

2.7.2.2 DBCC Miscellaneous Statements

The commands in Table 2-73 will help you do miscellaneous tasks such as enabling row-level locking or removing a DLL from memory.

Table 2-73 DBCC Miscellaneous Statements

DBCC dllname (FREE)	Unloads the specified extended stored procedure dynamic-link library (DLL) from memory.
DBCC HELP	Returns syntax information for the specified DBCC statement.
DBCC PINTABLE	Marks a table to be pinned, which means Microsoft SQL Server does not flush the pages for the table from memory.
DBCC ROWLOCK	Does not affect the locking behavior of SQL Server 2K. It is included for backward compatibility for SS 6.5 scripts and may not appear in future versions.
DBCC TRACEOFF	Disables the specified trace flag(s).
DBCC TRACEON	Turns on (enables) the specified trace flag.
DBCC UNPINTABLE	Marks a table as unpinned. After a table is marked as unpinned, the table pages in the buffer cache can be flushed.

2.7.2.3 DBCC Status Statements

The commands listed in Table 2-74 allow you to perform status checks.

Table 2-74 DBCC Status Statements

DBCC INPUTBUFFER	Displays the last statement sent from a client to Microsoft SQL Server.
DBCC OPENTRAN	Displays information about the oldest active transaction and the oldest distributed and nondistributed replicated transactions, if any, within the specified database. Results are displayed only if there is an active transaction or if the database contains replication information. An informational message is displayed if there are no active transactions.
DBCC OUTPUTBUFFER	Returns the current output buffer in hexadecimal and ASCII format for the specified system process ID (SPID).
DBCC PROCCACHE	Displays information in a table format about the procedure cache.
DBCC SHOWCONTIG	Displays fragmentation information for the data and indexes of the specified table.
DBCC SHOW_STATISTICS	Displays the current distribution statistics for the specified target on the specified table.

Table 2-74 DBCC Status Statements (cont.)

DBCC SQLPERF	Provides statistics about the use of transaction-log space in all databases.
DBCC TRACESTATUS	Displays the status of trace flags.
DBCC USEROPTIONS	Returns the SET options active (set) for the current connection.

2.7.2.4 DBCC Validation Statements

The commands shown in Table 2-75 allow you to perform validation operations on a database, table, index, catalog, filegroup, system tables or allocation of database pages.

Table 2-75 DBCC Validation Statements

DBCC CHECKALLOC	Checks consistency of disk space allocation structures of specified database.
DBCC CHECKCATALOG	Checks for consistency in and between system tables in specified database.
DBCC CHECKCONSTRAINTS	Checks integrity of a specified constraint or all constraints on the specified table.
DBCC CHECKDB	Checks the allocation and structural integrity of all the objects in the specified database.
DBCC CHECKFILEGROUP	Checks the allocation and structural integrity of all tables in the current database in the specified filegroup.
DBCC CHECKIDENT	Checks the current identity value for the specified table and, if needed, corrects the identity value.
DBCC CHECKTABLE	Checks the integrity of the data, index, **text**, **ntext** and **image** pages for the specified table or indexed view.
DBCC NEWALLOC	DBCC NEWALLOC is identical to DBCC CHECKALLOC which is recommended. DBCC NEWALLOC is included in SS 2000 for backward compatibility and may not appear in future versions.

2.8 SERVER, DATABASE AND SESSION SETTINGS

Server configuration settings, database configuration settings and session (or connection) property settings in some cases interact and in some cases are disjointed. Because some settings interact, I have found it less confusing to consider them all together.

2.8.1 Settings Overview

Most people can live a long and happy life without delving into the morass of these settings. Microsoft has done an excellent job of designing the database engine to set appropriate default values and of self-tuning to keep performance at a peak for most applications. Nonetheless, I think they need to clean up the interfaces for setting and reading the settings (see Author's Opinion below).

Generally speaking, server settings are of interest mainly to database administrators and most should be used only by experienced users and then on a test machine first. I'm not likely to change the number of "max worker threads" or "nested triggers," but if you have a reason and know what you're doing, we'll show you how. The rest of us will defer. ;-)

For database settings, one is likely to occasionally need to a change a database from MULTI_USER to RESTRICTED_USER in order to do maintenance. One may also want to set a specific database to READ_ONLY if its use does not require making data changes.Most database settings are best left as the default unless there is a specific reason to do otherwise.

Most session (connection) settings are also best left as the default values unless one has a specific reason to make a change. Exceptions include the occasional guidance given for using OLE DB or ODBC library call to set a specific option to a certain value. In these cases, I just follow the guidance without asking questions.

Session settings that can be quite useful for debugging or performance testing include NOEXEC, NOCOUNT, PARSEONLY, SHOWPLAN_*xxx*, STATISTICS *xxx*, etc. These options are well worth studying and testing to see the information they provide.

Having an understanding of the differences between server, database and session configuration settings will facilitate your programming. The major differences are listed below.

2.8.1.1 Server Configuration

Server settings affect server-wide settings and some database settings. Methods to see and assign server settings are (see details page 178):

- **sp_configure** system stored procedure (sets all options)
- **Enterprise Manager** (sets only the most commonly used options)

2.8.1.2 Database Configuration

Database settings affect database and default settings for connections to the database. Methods to see and assign database settings are (see details page 187):

- **ALTER DATABASE** with a **SET** clause — Set all db settings. See page 188.
- **DATABASEPROPERTYEX(** *'dbname'* **,** *'propertykeyword'*) — Read db settings. See page 195.
- **Enterprise Manager** — Set primary settings only
- **EXEC sp_dboption** — obsolete (may not be in new versions). Use ALTER DATABASE.

2.8.1.3 Session (Connection) Configuration

New sessions inherit server and database settings and the user may change some. Methods to see and assign session settings are (see details page 202):

- **SET** — Set all session options. See page 204.
- **SELECT @@OPTIONS** — Read all session options. See page 208.
- **DBCC USEROPTIONS** — Read all session options. See page 210.
- **SELECT SESSIONPROPERTY (** ***'option'***) — Read all session options. See page 211.

Session settings for Query Analyzer can also be read and set from its "Query" menu: "Query — Current Connection Properties."

Author's Opinion The subject of Server, Database and Session settings on SQL Server is overly confusing and needs cleanup work by Microsoft to make it easier to understand and manage. For example, why must one use ALTER DATABASE pubs SET READ_ONLY, or READ_WRITE to change whether a database is updateable, but have to use SELECT DATABASEPROPERTYEX ('pubs' , 'Updateability') to read the current setting?

And notice that **pubs** in the first statement must have no quotation marks and in the second statement it must have them. The now-out-of-favor **sp_dboption** at least had a very consistent interface for changing and reading settings.

Utilities to read current session settings also need cleanup work. @@OPTION is relatively complete but a bit awkward to use. SESSIONPROPERTY uses consistent keywords with SET, but only covers seven of them. DBCC USEROPTIONS only shows the ON settings, which is fine, but it doesn't report on all of the SET options. Oh, well!

2.8.1.4 Server Configuration Settings

Figure 2-3 shows a brief summary of the settings for server configuration. The details of these settings are in the sections that follow.

2.8.1.5 sp_configure

Use **sp_configure** to display or change global configuration settings for the current server. Table 2-76 summarizes the accessible settings.

Syntax

```
sp_configure [ [ @configname = ] 'name'        [ , [
@configvalue = ] 'value' ] ]
```

sp_configure may be executed with 0, 1 or 2 arguments:

- 0 arguments: Lists all configuration setting names addressable with **sp_configure**
- 1 argument: Displays the current setting for the configuration name specified
- 2 arguments: Sets the specified configuration name to the specified value

Configuration settings for a SQL Server instance are **observed and assigned** with

- **sp_configure** system stored procedure (all options are available)
  (must then run **reconfigure** command to effect the changes. See **reconfigure** below.)

  See Exercise 1 at the end of Chapter 1 for using Enterprise Manager and Query Analyzer.

Configuration settings for a SQL Server instance are also **observed and assigned** with

- **Enterprise Manager** (primary settings only) — Right click on Server name and select **Properties**. When the dialog appears, explore each tab in turn.

Figure 2-3 Summary of server configuration statements.

Table 2-76 Server Configuration Settings Accessible with **sp_configure**

sp_configure Configuration Option	Minimum	Maximum	Default	Requires 'show advanced options'	Requires Server Stop and Restart
affinity mask	0	2147483647	0	Yes	Yes
allow updates	0	1	0		
awe enabled	0	1	0	Yes	Yes

Table 2-76 Server Configuration Settings Accessible with **sp_configure** (cont.)

sp_configure Configuration option	Minimum	Maximum	Default	Requires 'show advanced options'	Requires Server Stop and Restart
c2 audit mode	0	1	0	Yes	Yes start audit, No stop audit
cost threshold for parallelism	0	32767	5	Yes	
cursor threshold	1	2147483647	–1	Yes	
default full-text language	0	2147483647	1033	Yes	
default language	0	9999	0		
fill factor (%)	0	100	0	Yes	Yes
index create memory (KB)	704	2147483647	0	Yes	
lightweightpooling	0	1	0	Yes	Yes
locks	5000	2147483647	0	Yes	Yes
max degree of parallelism	0	32	0	Yes	
max server memory (MB)	4	2147483647	2147483647	Yes	
max text repl size (B)	0	2147483647	65536		
max worker threads	32	32767	255	Yes	
media retention	0	365	0	Yes	Yes
min memory per query (KB)	512	2147483647	1024	Yes	
min server memory (MB)	0	2147483647	0	Yes	
nested triggers	0	1	1		
network packet size (B)	512	65536	4096	Yes	

Table 2-76 Server Configuration Settings Accessible with **sp_configure** (cont.)

sp_configure Configuration option	Minimum	Maximum	Default	Requires 'show advanced options'	Requires Server Stop and Restart
open objects	0	2147483647	0	Yes	Yes
priority boost	0	1	0	Yes	Yes
query governor cost limit	0	2147483647	0	Yes	
query wait (s)	–1	2147483647	–1	Yes	
recovery interval (min)	0	32767	0	Yes	
remote access	0	1	1		Yes
remote login timeout (s)	0	2147483647	20		
remote proc trans	0	1	0		
remote query timeout (s)	0	2147483647	600		
scan for startup procs	0	1	0	Yes	Yes
set working set size	0	1	0	Yes	Yes
show advanced options	0	1	0		
two digit year cutoff	1753	9999	2049	Yes	
user connections	0	32767	0	Yes	Yes
user options (See page 202)	0	32767	0		

To see the listing and current settings, execute **sp_configure** with no arguments. By default only a partial listing is given unless show advanced options is enabled.

SQL

```
EXEC sp_configure  -- Lists common configuration options.
  Enable 'advanced options' to see all.
```

SQL (cont.)

Result

name	minimum	maximum	config_value	run_value
allow updates	0	1	0	0
default language	0	9999	0	0
max text repl size (B)	0	2147483647	65536	65536
nested triggers	0	1	1	1
remote access	0	1	1	1
remote login timeout (s)	0	2147483647	20	20
remote proc trans	0	1	0	
remote query timeout (s)	0	2147483647	600	600
show advanced options	0	1	0	0
user options	0	32767	0	0

For a description of each item see Books Online: Setting Configuration Options.

2.8.1.6 `sp_configure` SHOW ADVANCED OPTIONS

To see all **sp_configure** options, not just the basic ones, enable show advanced options as shown here.

Example:

SQL

```
EXEC sp_configure 'show advanced options' , 1
RECONFIGURE  -- Must run this to make the change effective .
```

2.8.1.7 `sp_configure` USER OPTIONS

The **sp_configure USER OPTIONS** value is a single integer which is a bit-set specifying global defaults for 15 settings that affect each user's session (connection). A user may override each setting using the SET statement.

See discussion and examples of **sp_configure user options** on page 202.

Example:

SQL

```
EXEC sp_configure  -- Now lists ALL 36 configuration options.
```

SQL (cont.)

Result

name	minimum	maximum	config_value	run_value
affinity mask	0	2147483647	1	1
...				
user options	0	32767	0	0

2.8.1.8 When Do `sp_configure` Changes Become Effective?

Here is the short answer to this question: They become effective when **run_value** matches **config_value**, which depends on the option.

- All **sp_configure** changes need **RECONFIGURE** to be run to become effective.
    - Two options ('allow updates' and 'recovery interval') sometimes require RECONFIGURE WITH OVERRIDE to be run (see RECONFIGURE below).
- Some options also **require server stop and restart** as indicated in Table 2-76. The following do not need server stop and restart.

allow updates cost threshold for parallelism
cursor threshold
index create memory (KB)
max degree of parallelism
max server memory (MB)
max text repl size (B)
max worker threads
min memory per query (KB)
min server memory (MB)
network packet size (B)
query governor cost limit
query wait (s)
recovery interval (min)
remote login timeout (s)
remote proc trans
remote query timeout (s)
show advanced options
user options
default full-text language?
default language?
nested triggers?
two digit year cutoff?

When using **sp_configure,** you must always run either RECONFIGURE (or RECONFIGURE WITH OVERRIDE for the two indicated above) after setting a configuration option.

Example 1: The allow updates option requires RECONFIGURE WITH OVERRIDE.

SQL

```
EXEC sp_configure   'allow updates'
```

Result

```
name             minimum      maximum      config_value     run_value
---------------- ------------ ------- ---- ------- -------- --- --------
allow updates    0            1            0                0
```

SQL

```
EXEC sp_configure   'allow updates'    ,  1
EXEC sp_configure   'allow updates'
```

Result

```
name             minimum      maximum      config_value     run_value
---------------- ------------ ------- ---- ------- -------- --- --------
allow updates    0            1            1                0
```

SQL

```
RECONFIGURE WITH OVERRIDE
EXEC sp_configure   'allow updates'
```

Result

```
name             minimum      maximum      config_value     run_value
---------------- ------------ ------- ---- ------- -------- --- --------
allow updates    0            1            1                1
```

Example 2: The 'fill factor' option also requires server stop and restart

SQL

```
EXEC sp_configure   'fill factor'
```

Result

```
name              minimum     maximum       config_value    run_value
----------------  ----------  ------------  --------------  ----------
fill factor (%)   0           100           0               0
```

SQL

```
EXEC sp_configure   'fill factor' , 80

EXEC sp_configure   'fill factor'
```

Result

```
name              minimum     maximum       config_value    run_value
----------------  ----------  ------------  --------------  -----------
fill factor (%)   0           100           80              0
```

Option fill factor requires reconfigure then server stop and restart so the config_value is shown as changed but not the run_value.

SQL

```
reconfigure
EXEC sp_configure   'fill factor'
```

Result

```
name              minimum     maximum       config_value    run_value
----------------  ----------  ------------  --------------  -----------
fill factor (%)   0           100           80              0
```

Still no change until we stop and restart the server, which we do now.

SQL

```
EXEC sp_configure   'fill factor' -- After server stop and restart
```

Result

name	minimum	maximum	config_value	run_value
fill factor (%)	0	100	80	80

2.8.1.9 RECONFIGURE

The reconfigure command updates the currently configured value of a configuration option changed with the **sp_configure** system stored procedure (the **config_value** column in the **sp_configure** result set). Some configuration options require a server stop and restart to update the currently running value. Therefore, **RECONFIGURE** does not always update the currently running value (the **run_value** column in the **sp_configure** result set) for a changed configuration value.

Syntax

```
RECONFIGURE [ WITH OVERRIDE ]
```

2.8.1.10 RECONFIGURE—Without the WITH OVERRIDE Option

The reconfigure command without the override option specifies that, if the configuration setting does not require a server stop and restart, the currently running value should be updated. Afterward the **config_value** and **run_value** should be the same for those options not requiring server stop and restart.

RECONFIGURE also checks the new configuration value for either invalid values or nonrecommended values.

2.8.1.11 RECONFIGURE WITH OVERRIDE

Without OVERRIDE, RECONFIGURE is for allow updates and recovery interval only. This allows invalid or nonrecommended values to be to be set for:

allow updates—default of 0 does not allow updates to system tables using DML (INSERT, UPDATE, DELETE). System procedures must be used. Setting to 1 is not recommended and requires WITH OVERRIDE.

recovery interval—default is 0 (self-configuring), recommended is 0 or 1 to 60. The value is the maximum number of minutes to recover each database. Over 60 minutes is not recommended and requires WITH OVERRIDE.

Books Online says the following.

Keep **recovery interval** set at 0 (self-configuring) unless you notice that checkpoints are impairing performance because they are occurring too frequently. If this is the case, try increasing the value in small increments.[5]

Example:

SQL

```
EXEC sp_configure   'recovery interval'
```

Result

name	minimum	maximum	config_value	run_value
recovery interval (min)	0	32767	0	0

SQL

```
EXEC sp_configure   'recovery interval' , 120 -- 120 minutes = 2 hours
```

Result

DBCC execution completed. If DBCC printed error messages, contact your system administrator.
Configuration option 'recovery interval (min)' changed from 0 to 120.
Run the RECONFIGURE statement to install.

SQL

```
EXEC sp_configure   'recovery interval'
```

Result

name	minimum	maximum	config_value	run_value
recovery interval (min)	0	32767	0	0

5. Microsoft SQL Server 2K Books Online

SQL

```
PRINT 'RECONFIGURE'
RECONFIGURE
```

Result

RECONFIGURE
Server: Msg 5807, Level 16, State 1, Line 2
Recovery intervals above 60 minutes not recommended.
Use the RECONFIGURE WITH OVERRIDE statement to force this configuration.

SQL

```
EXEC sp_configure   'recovery interval' -- No change, RECONFIGURE is
                                           not strong enough
```

Result

name	minimum	maximum	config_value	run_value
recovery interval (min)	0	32767	120	0

SQL

```
PRINT  'RECONFIGURE WITH OVERRIDE'
RECONFIGURE WITH OVERRIDE
```

Result

RECONFIGURE WITH OVERRIDE

SQL

```
EXEC sp_configure   'recovery interval'
```

Result

name	minimum	maximum	config_value	run_value
recovery interval (min)	0	32767	120	120

2.8.1.12 SQL Server Settings in Enterprise Manager

Primary configuration settings for SQL Server are accessible in Enterprise Manager from the server properties dialog for a selected server as shown in the figure. In EM, right click on the server name and select "Properties" (see Figure 2-4).

Examine the settings available on these tabs and see Books Online for further details.

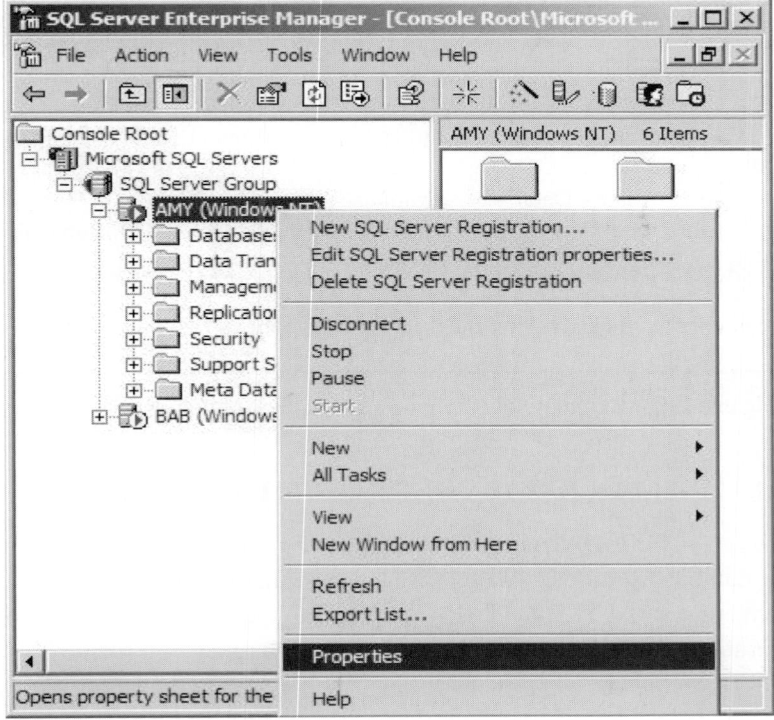

Figure 2-4 The Server Properties Dialog box for the AMY server.

2.8.2 Database Configuration (Database Properties)

Most database settings are best left as the default unless there is a specific reason to change. Database settings that you may need to a change occasionally are MULTI_USER and RESTRICTED_USER or SINGLE_USER in order to do maintenance. One may also want to set a specific database to READ_ONLY if its users do not need to change the data. A summary of database configuration statements is given in Figure 2-5. For more detail see Books Online, Index: database options.

Configuration settings for each database are assigned with

- **ALTER DATABASE** with a **SET** clause (all settings)

Configuration settings for each database are observed using

- **SELECT DATABASEPROPERTYEX(** ***'dbname'*** **,** ***'propertykeyword'***)
  - The propertykeyword is not the same as the ALTER DATABASE keyword.
  - A complete list of **propertykeywords** is provided below in Table 2-78 (and in Books Online).
  - The **propertykeyword**, if there is one, is repeated in Table 2-77 in the "Description" column on a separate line and in parentheses.

Configuration settings for each database are **observed and assigned** with

- **Enterprise Manager** (primary settings only) - Right click on database name in EM
  - *ServerName* - Databases - *Databasename*

  and select **Properties**. When the dialog appears, click on the **Options** tab.
- **EXEC sp_dboption -obsolete**. Use ALTER DATABASE instead.

For more detail see Books Online, Index: database options.

Figure 2-5 Summary of database configuration statements.

2.8.2.1 ALTER DATABASE dbname SET option

Only ALTER DATABASE with the SET clause, which may be used to change database settings, will be discussed in this section. See page 250 for the main coverage of ALTER DATABASE. See Table 2-77 for a summary of database configuration option keywords.

SQL Server 2K database options are set using ALTER DATABASE with a SET clause. In previous versions of SQL Server, database options were set with the **sp_dboption** system stored procedure. SQL Server 2K continues to support **sp_dboption**, which has been rewritten to call ALTER DATABASE, but it may not do so in the future.

DATABASEPROPERTYEX() may be used to show current settings for database options.

Partial Syntax

```
ALTER DATABASE  databasename  SET <optionspec>  [WITH
<termination>]
```

```
< optionspec >   See table

< termination > ::=
            ROLLBACK AFTER integer [ SECONDS ]
          | ROLLBACK IMMEDIATE
          | NO_WAIT
```

Table 2-77 ALTER Database Configuration Option Keywords

<optionspec> Keyword for both ALTER DATABASE and SET	Has Session Setting	Database Default	Description (DATABASEPROPERTYEX keyword)
Database State Options [abc]	[d]		See also Books Online: DATABASEPROPERTYEX and Setting Database Options
SINGLE_USER | RESTRICTED_USER | MULTI_USER	No	MULTI_ USER	Determines who may connect to the specified database. Example below. **(UserAccess)**
OFFLINE | ONLINE	No	ONLINE	When put OFFLINE the database is shutdown and can not be accessed. **(Status)**
READ_ONLY | READ_WRITE	No	READ_ WRITE	When put READ_ONLY users can not modify the database. **(Updateability)**
Cursor Options			
CURSOR_CLOSE_ON_COMMIT { ON | OFF }	Yes	OFF[b]	ON: (SQL-92) All open cursors are closed when a transaction is committed. OFF: Cursors must be closed explicitly and may cross transaction boundaries. **(IsCloseCursorsOnCommitEnabled)**
CURSOR_DEFAULT { LOCAL | GLOBAL }	No	GLOBAL	GLOBAL—cursors default to GLOBAL LOCAL—cursors default to LOCAL. Cursors may always be explicitly defined as LOCAL or GLOBAL. See Cursors page 638. **(IsLocalCursorsDefault)**

Table 2-77 ALTER Database Configuration Option Keywords (cont.)

<optionspec> Keyword for both ALTER DATABASE and SET	Has Session Setting	Database Default	Description (DATABASEPROPERTYEX keyword)
Automatic Options			
AUTO_CLOSE { ON | OFF } Comment from Books Online The AUTO_CLOSE option is useful for desktop databases because it allows database files to be managed as normal files. They can be moved, copied to make backups, or even e-mailed to other users. The AUTO_CLOSE option should not be used for databases accessed by an application that repeatedly makes and breaks connections to SQL Server. The overhead of closing and reopening the database between each connection will impair performance.	No	ON for SS 2000 Desktop Engine (MSDE 2000) OFF for all other SS 2000 editions	ON: the database is closed and shut down cleanly when the last user of the database exits and when all processes in the database are complete, thereby freeing any resources. The database reopens automatically when a user tries to use the database again. OFF: the database remains open even if no users are currently using it. **(IsAutoClose)**
AUTO_CREATE_STATISTICS { ON | OFF }	No	ON	ON: statistics are automatically created on columns without an index used in a predicate so as to speed the query. OFF: statistics not automatically created; but they can be manually created. **(IsAutoCreateStatistics)**
AUTO_UPDATE_STATISTICS { ON | OFF }	No	ON	ON: existing statistics are automatically updated when they become out-of-date. OFF: statistics are not automatically updated but can be manually updated. **(IsAutoUpdateStatistics)**
AUTO_SHRINK { ON | OFF } Default: ON for SS 2000 Desktop Engine (MSDE 2000) OFF for all other SS 2000 editions	No	See first column	ON: the database data and log files are periodically checked for unused space. OFF: files are not periodically checked for unused space. It is not possible to shrink a read-only database. **(IsAutoShrink)**

Table 2-77 ALTER Database Configuration Option Keywords (cont.)

<optionspec> Keyword for both ALTER DATABASE and SET	Has Session Setting	Database Default	Description (DATABASEPROPERTYEX keyword)
ANSI SQL-92 Compliance Options			
ANSI_NULL_DEFAULT { ON | OFF} This keyword applies to ALTER DATABASE only. The corresponding session SET keywords are ANSI_NULL_DFLT_ON and ANSI_NULL_DFLT_OFF	No	OFF but effectively ON[a]	Sets **Default Nullability** of a column—If ON is specified, CREATE TABLE follows SQL-92 rules to determine whether a column allows null values. OLE DB and ODBC set this to ON. **(IsAnsiNullDefault)**
ANSI_NULLS { ON | OFF }	Yes	OFF but effectively ON[a]	ON: SQL-92 behavior, comparing to NULL with = and <> returns NULL. OFF: NULL = NULL returns TRUE. **(IsAnsiNullsEnabled)**
ANSI_PADDING { ON | OFF }	Yes	OFF but effectively ON[a]	ON: Does NOT trim explicit trailing blanks in varchar and trailing zeros in varbinary columns. OFF: Does trim them. Books Online Recommendation: Leave t ON. **(IsAnsiPaddingEnabled)**
ANSI_WARNINGS { ON | OFF }	Yes	OFF but effectively ON[a]	ON means SQL-92 standard behavior of raising error messages or warnings for conditions like divide-by-zero and arithmetic overflow. **(IsAnsiWarningsEnabled)**
ARITHABORT { ON | OFF } Default: Query Analyzer sets ARITHABORT to ON for each session	Yes	OFF[c]	ON: Terminates a query if overflow or divide-by-zero occurs during query. OFF: Warning message displayed and processing continues. **(IsArithmeticAbortEnabled)**
Miscellaneous SET Options			
CONCAT_NULL_YIELDS_NULL	Yes	OFF but effectively ON[a]	ON: Concatenating NULL yields NULL (ON) versus empty string (OFF) **(IsNullConcat)**

Table 2-77 ALTER Database Configuration Option Keywords (cont.)

<optionspec> Keyword for both ALTER DATABASE and SET	Has Session Setting	Database Default	Description (DATABASEPROPERTYEX keyword)
NUMERIC_ROUNDABORT { ON | OFF }	Yes	OFF	ON: an error is generated when loss of precision occurs in an expression. OFF: the result is rounded to the precision of the destination with no error. **(IsNumericRoundAbortEnabled)**
QUOTED_IDENTIFIER { ON | OFF }	Yes	OFF but effectively ON[a]	See QUOTED_IDENTIFIER discussion with examples page 44. **(IsQuotedIdentifiersEnabled)**
RECURSIVE_TRIGGERS { ON | OFF }	No	OFF	ON allows triggers to fire recursively. **(IsRecursiveTriggersEnabled)**
Recovery Mode Statements			
RECOVERY { FULL | BULK_LOGGED | SIMPLE }	No	FULL -- except MSDE 2000 is SIMPLE	See Recovery Models page 559. **(Recovery)**
TORN_PAGE_DETECTION { ON | OFF } A torn page occurs when not all 16 sectors (512 bytes) of the 8 KB database page can be written to disk, as in power loss.	No	ON	ON causes the database to be marked as suspect if a torn page is found during recovery. If a torn page is found the database should be restored. This option should be left ON. **(IsTornPageDetectionEnabled)**

a. OLE DB and ODBC explicitly set this to ON for each client connection overriding database setting. See p. 215.

b. OLE DB and ODBC explicitly set this to OFF for each client connection overriding database setting. See p. 215.

c. Query Analyzer sets ARITHABORT to ON for each of its connections overriding database setting. See p. 216.

d. Database Options marked with "Yes" in the Session Setting column have corresponding session (connection) options which, if SET at the session level, take precedence over the database setting. See page 204.

2.8.2.2 Examples—ALTER DATABASE to Change UserAccess of a Database

Database Access Modes determines who may connect to the specified database as follows.

- MULTI_USER: Allows all users with database access privilege to connect
- RESTRICTED_USER: Allows only members of db_owner, dbcreator and sysadmin
- SINGLE_USER: Allows only the user issuing the ALTER DATABASE statement

Examples: You may read current access mode of the **pubs** database as shown.

SQL

```
SELECT DATABASEPROPERTYEX( 'pubs' , 'UserAccess' )
```

Result

```
--------------------------
MULTI_USER
```

Now set the access mode to any of the three values using ALTER DATABASE.

SQL

```
ALTER DATABASE pubs  SET MULTI_USER
```

Setting to Either RESTRICTED_USER or SINGLE_USER Database Access

The following form waits indefinitely if unqualified users are connected to the database.

SQL

```
ALTER DATABASE pubs  SET SINGLE_USER  -- may wait indefinitely
```

WITH NO_WAIT causes the ALTER DATABASE to fail immediately if unqualified users are connected to the specified database.

SQL

```
ALTER DATABASE pubs  SET RESTRICTED_USER  WITH NO_WAIT
ALTER DATABASE pubs  SET SINGLE_USER  WITH NO_WAIT
```

This command returns immediately. The new access can be seen with the following.

SQL

```
SELECT DATABASEPROPERTYEX( 'pubs' , 'UserAccess' )
```

Result

```
--------------------------
SINGLE_USER
```

WITH ROLLBACK IMMEDIATE forces immediate rollback of open transactions and terminates the connections of all unqualified users of the database.

SQL

```
ALTER DATABASE pubs SET RESTRICTED_USER  WITH ROLLBACK IMMEDIATE
ALTER DATABASE pubs SET SINGLE_USER  WITH ROLLBACK IMMEDIATE
```

WITH ROLLBACK AFTER *integer* **[SECONDS]** rolls back transactions and breaks the connections of all unqualified database users after the specified number of seconds.

SQL

```
ALTER DATABASE pubs
  SET RESTRICTED_USER  WITH ROLLBACK AFTER 60
ALTER DATABASE pubs
  SET SINGLE_USER  WITH ROLLBACK AFTER 60 SECONDS
```

Example: Set Recovery model for database mydb1 to FULL.

SQL

```
ALTER DATABASE mydb1 SET RECOVERY FULL
```

Example: Set database mydb1 access to RESTRICTED_USER (allowing only members of **sysadmin** and **dbcreator** fixed server roles and **db_owner** fixed database roles). Unauthorized users currently connected will be unceremoniously disconnected and open transactions rolled back 60 seconds from the time the statement is executed.

SQL

```
ALTER DATABASE mydb1 SET RESTRICTED_USER
  WITH ROLLBACK AFTER 60 SECONDS
```

Change access for database mydb1 back to MULTI_USER.

SQL

```
ALTER DATABASE mydb1 SET MULTI_USER
  SELECT DATABASEPROPERTYEX( 'pubs' , 'UserAccess' )
```

SQL (cont.)
Result
-------------------------- MULTI_USER

The code **dbo** stands for database owner, the predefined user name in each database who is able to perform all database operations. Any **sysadmin** server role member becomes **dbo** inside each database.

2.8.2.3 DATABASEPROPERTYEX—Displays Database Settings

This function returns the current setting of the specified property in the specified database.

Syntax

```
SELECT DATABASEPROPERTYEX( 'dbname' , 'propertykeyword' )
```

Table 2-78 below lists all of the DATABASEPROPERTYEX property keywords, and some examples appear below the table. Most of these keywords were also listed above in the ALTER DATABASE keyword table (Table 2-77). A few examples were given there.

Additional database options are listed in Table 2-78.

Table 2-78 Keywords for DATABASEPROPERTYEX

DATABASE PROPERTYEX keyword	Description	Value Returned
Collation	Default collation name for the database.	Collation name
IsAnsiNullDefault	Database follows SQL-92 rules for allowing null values.	1=TRUE, 0=FALSE, NULL=Bad input
IsAnsiNullsEnabled	All comparisons to a null evaluate to null.	1=TRUE, 0=FALSE, NULL=Bad input
IsAnsiPaddingEnabled	Strings are padded to the same length before comparison or insert.	1=TRUE, 0=FALSE, NULL=Bad input
IsAnsiWarningsEnabled	Error or warning messages are issued when standard error conditions occur.	1=TRUE, 0=FALSE, NULL=Bad input
IsArithmeticAbortEnabled	Queries are terminated when an overflow or divide-by-zero error occurs.	1=TRUE, 0=FALSE, NULL=Bad input
IsAutoClose	Database shuts down cleanly and frees resources after the last user exits.	1=TRUE, 0=FALSE, NULL=Bad input

Table 2-78 Keywords for DATABASEPROPERTYEX (cont.)

DATABASE PROPERTYEX keyword	Description	Value Returned
IsAutoCreateStatistics	Existing statistics are automatically updated when they become out-of-date.	1=TRUE, 0=FALSE, NULL=Bad input
IsAutoShrink	Database files are candidates for automatic periodic shrinking.	1=TRUE, 0=FALSE, NULL=Bad input
IsAutoUpdateStatistics	Auto update statistics database option is enabled.	1=TRUE, 0=FALSE, NULL=Bad input
IsCloseCursorsOn-CommitEnabled	Cursors that are open when a transaction is committed are closed.	1=TRUE, 0=FALSE, NULL=Bad input
IsFulltextEnabled	Database is full-text enabled.	1=TRUE, 0=FALSE, NULL=Bad input
IsInStandBy	Database is online as read-only, with restore log allowed.	1=TRUE, 0=FALSE, NULL=Bad input
IsLocalCursorsDefault	Cursor declarations default to LOCAL.	1=TRUE, 0=FALSE, NULL=Bad input
IsMergePublished	The tables of a database can be published for replication, if replication is installed.	1=TRUE, 0=FALSE, NULL=Bad input
IsNullConcat	Null concatenation operand yields NULL.	1=TRUE, 0=FALSE, NULL=Bad input
IsNumericRoundAbortEnabled	Errors are generated when loss of precision occurs in expressions.	1=TRUE, 0=FALSE, NULL=Bad input
IsQuotedIdentifiersEnabled	Double quotation marks can be used on identifiers.	1=TRUE, 0=FALSE, NULL=Bad input
IsRecursiveTriggersEnabled	Recursive firing of triggers is enabled.	1=TRUE, 0=FALSE, NULL=Bad input
IsSubscribed	Database can be subscribed for publication.	1=TRUE, 0=FALSE, NULL=Bad input
IsTornPageDetectionEnabled	SQL Server detects incomplete I/O operations caused by power failures, etc.	1=TRUE, 0=FALSE, NULL=Bad input
Recovery	Recovery model for the database.	FULL = full recovery model BULK_LOGGED = bulk logged model SIMPLE = simple recovery model
SQLSortOrder	SQL Server sort order ID supported in previous versions of SQL Server.	0 = Database uses Windows collation >0 = SQL Server sort order ID

Table 2-78 Keywords for DATABASEPROPERTYEX (cont.)

DATABASE PROPERTYEX keyword	Description	Value Returned
Status	Database status.	ONLINE = database is available OFFLINE = db was taken offline RESTORING = db is being restored RECOVERING = db is recovering and not yet ready for queries SUSPECT = db cannot be recovered
Updateability	Indicates whether data can be modified.	READ_ONLY READ_WRITE
UserAccess	Which users can access the database.	SINGLE_USER = only one user of **db_owner**, **dbcreator**, **sysadmin** RESTRICTED_USER = any of **db_owner**, **dbcreator**, **sysadmin** MULTI_USER = all users
Version	Database Version number for internal use only by SQL Server tools.	Integer = Database is open NULL = Database is closed

Example:

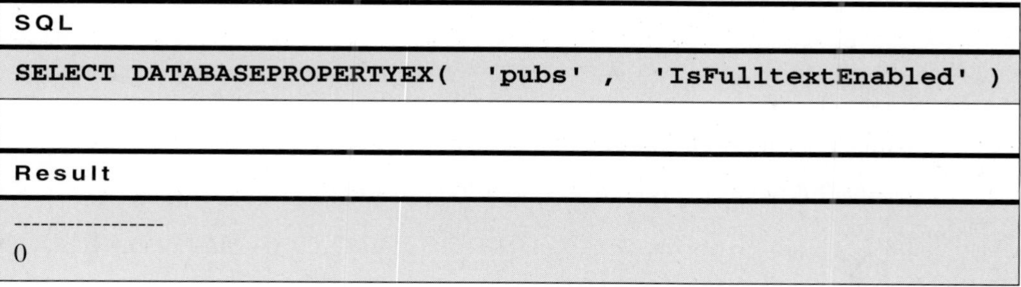

SQL

```
SELECT DATABASEPROPERTYEX( 'pubs' , 'IsFulltextEnabled' )
```

Result

```
-----------------
0
```

This says that full text searches are not presently enabled on the pubs database.

Many DATABASEPROPERTYEX keywords are also listed in the ALTER DATABASE table in the preceding section.

SQL

```
SELECT DATABASEPROPERTYEX( 'pubs' , 'UserAccess' )
```

SQL (cont.)
Result
---------------- MULTI_USER

2.8.2.4 Database Level Settings in Enterprise Manager

Primary configuration settings for SQL Server databases are accessible in Enterprise Manager from the server properties dialog for a selected server and database.

Expand the Console Tree in Enterprise Manager under the desired server.

Select your Server Name – Databases – <database name>

Right click on the <database name> and select Properties.

The tabs available for the database Properties dialog are:
General Data Files Transaction Log Filegroups Options Permissions

Options tab—The options tab, shown in Figure 2-6, has some settings that can be set from this tab or from the command line using ALTER DATABASE (see page 188).

Access

Restrict Access: db_owner, dbcreator, sysadmin only or Single user

Read-only

Recovery Model: Simple or Bulk-Logged or Full

Settings to allow or disallow features such as ANSI NULL default.

Compatibility Level: 60 or 65 or 70 or 80

2.8.2.5 `sp_dboption`—Brief Description Only (It Has Been Replaced by ALTER DATABASE)

The stored procedure **sp_dboption** displays or changes database options. It is provided only for backward compatibility and might not appear in future releases of SQL Server. ALTER DATABASE is now recommended.

sp_dboption should not be used on either the master or tempdb databases.

Syntax

```
sp_dboption     [   [ @dbname = ] 'database' ]
                [ , [ @optname = ] 'option_name' ]
                [ , [ @optvalue = ] 'value' ]
```

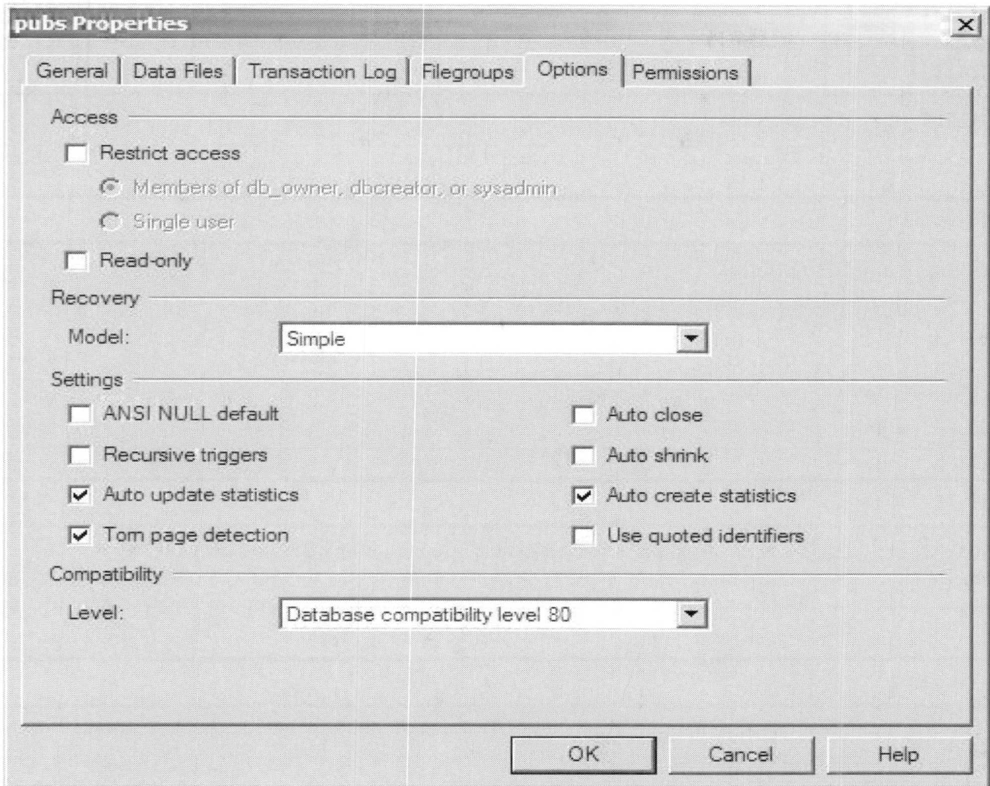

Figure 2-6 The Options Tab of the Properties Dialog Box.

These settings display or change global configuration settings for the current server.

sp_dboption may be executed with 0, 1, 2, or 3 arguments as follows.

- 0 arguments: Lists all configuration setting names addressable with sp_dboption
- 1 argument: Displays the current settings that are set for the database specified
- 2 arguments: Displays the current setting of the specified option in the named database
- 3 arguments: Sets the specified option in the named database to the specified value

Examples:

SQL

```
EXEC sp_dboption
```

Result

```
Settable database options:
-----------------------------------
ANSI null default
...
dbo use only
...
```

SQL

```
EXEC sp_dboption  pubs  -- shows pubs settings which are
"set"
```

Result

```
The following options are set:
-----------------------------------
trunc. log on chkpt.
torn page detection
auto create statistics
auto update statistics
```

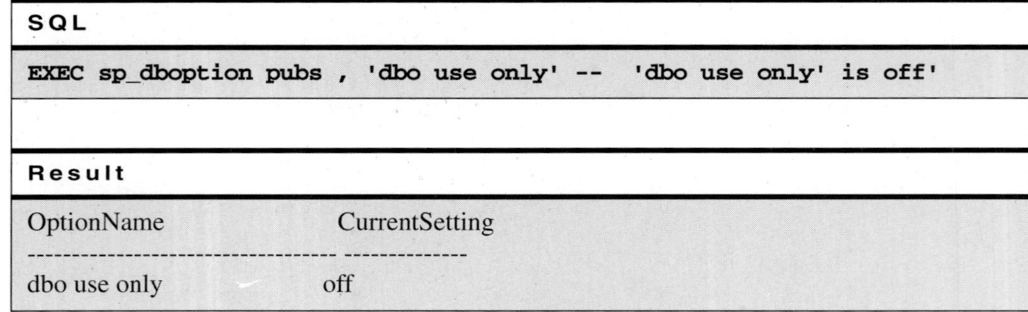

SQL

```
EXEC sp_dboption pubs , 'dbo use only' --  'dbo use only' is off'
```

Result

```
OptionName                          CurrentSetting
----------------------------------- --------------
dbo use only                        off
```

SQL
`EXEC sp_dboption pubs , 'dbo use only', TRUE --  turn in on'`
Result
The command(s) completed successfully.

2.8.2.6 Database Compatibility Level —`sp_dbcmptlevel`

MSS 2000 (version 8.0) implements SQL-92 more thoroughly than earlier versions, and it also adds new keywords. When upgrading a database from an earlier version of MSS, especially MSS 6.0 or 6.5, some of these changes may conflict with your existing application code.

Though running on SQL Server 2K, you may set a database to behave like an earlier version of SQL by using **sp_dbcmptlevel** system stored procedure. This will keep your production database operational while giving you a chance to rewrite your code. See Table 2-79.

Table 2-79 Compatibility Levels

Compatibility Level	Version
80	SQL Server 2K (version 8.0)
70	SQL Server 7.0
65	SQL Server 6.5
60	SQL Server 6.0

`sp_dbcmptlevel` sets the specified database to behave according to the specified version of SQL Server.

Syntax

```
sp_dbcmptlevel    [ [ @dbname = ] name ]     [ , [ @new_cmptlevel = ] version ]
```

Argument

version

The version of SQL Server with which the database is to be made compatible. The value must be 80, 70, 65 or 60.

References

Books Online: **sp_dbcmptlevel;** compatibility issues, overview

2.8.3 Session (Connection) Configuration Settings

Session or connection settings are values that apply to the current connection of a client program for the SQL Server database engine. They will remain in effect until the end of the session (when the connection is closed) or a SET statement is issued as described below.

Session settings that can be quite useful for debugging or performance testing include NOEXEC, NOCOUNT, PARSEONLY, SHOWPLAN_xxx, STATISTICS xxx, etc. These options are well worth studying and testing to see the information they provide.

To determine how your current session settings are determined, I suggest starting with the OLE DB and ODBC driver connection settings (see page 215) and Query Analyzer connection settings (see page 216) and then reading the section on Which Session Setting Is in Effect? (see page 219).

Some session settings will be changed by the client libraries (OLE DB and ODBC) and by Query Analyzer, if that is the client program. And all session option settings may be changed by the user using the SET command.

Figure 2-7 is a summary of session configuration statements. The pages that follow contain detailed information about the information in the box.

2.8.3.1 sp_configure user options

sp_configure is a server setting that affects future sessions. The options allow a user to set all 15 default session query processing options applicable ONLY FOR NEW LOGIN SESSIONS (CONNECTIONS). Anyone currently logged in is not affected until the next time they log in.

The **sp_configure** USER OPTIONS value is a single integer representing a bitset specifying global defaults for 15 settings that affect each user's session (connection). A user may override any setting by changing it with the SET statement.

Executing **sp_configure 'user options'**, *value* assigns default settings for new logins.

Any user may use SET to override any setting for the current session.

If a user has SET an option then that setting is used for the current session Recall ODBC and OLE DB set some options when connecting or if the current database has a setting for the option then it will be used or if **sp_configure 'user options'** for the option is in effect it will be used or the default setting for the option will be used.

The options settable by **sp_configure 'user options'** and the setting value are the same as those visible with **@@OPTIONS** (page 208) and are listed in Table 2-80.

New sessions inherit server or database options and may change some of them. Configuration settings for the current session or connection are changed using

- **sp_configure 'user options'**

  Assigns default session settings, which are in effect unless overridden by a SET command. See full description page 204.

  Client libraries often issue SET statements for each connection. See OLE DB and ODBC driver connection settings, page 215.

  Query Analyzer additionally assigns SET options, which may be configured by the user. See Query Analyzer connection settings, page 216.
- **SET** (page 204)

Configuration settings for each session or connection are observed using

- **@@OPTIONS** — Displays integer bitset of set options (page 209)
- **DBCC USEROPTIONS**—Displays all options currently set (page 210)
- **SELECT SESSIONPROPERTY (*'option'*)** —Displays an option setting (page 211)
- **Session Configuration Functions** —Each displays an option setting (page 214)

Primary settings for each Query Analyzer connection are observed and changed using

- Query Analyzer primary session settings.

See also Books Online: SET Options That Affect Results.

Figure 2-7 Session configuration statements summary.

Syntax

```
sp_configure 'user options'     [ , [ @configvalue = ]  value ]
```

value = The sum of the values of all options desired to be set for future new logins.

Remember to run **RECONFIGURE** to make the change effective.

Table 2-80 sp_configure USER OPTIONS

Value	Option	Description — Behavior when ON
1	DISABLE_DEF_CNST_CHK	Controls interim or deferred constraint checking.
2	IMPLICIT_TRANSACTIONS	Controls whether a transaction is committed automatically (OFF) when a statement is executed or the transaction requires explicit commit (ON).
4	CURSOR_CLOSE_ON_COMMIT	Controls behavior of cursors after a commit operation has been performed.
8	ANSI_WARNINGS	Controls truncation and NULL in aggregate warnings.

Table 2-80 sp_configure USER OPTIONS (cont.)

Value	Option	Description — Behavior when ON
16	ANSI_PADDING	Controls padding of character variables. See page 102.
32	ANSI_NULLS	Controls NULL handling when using equality operators.
64	ARITHABORT	Terminates a query when an overflow or divide-by-zero error occurs.
128	ARITHIGNORE	Returns NULL when overflow or divide-by-zero error occurs during a query.
256	QUOTED_IDENTIFIER	Differentiates between single and double quotation marks when evaluating an expression.
512	NOCOUNT	Turns off the "how many rows affected" message at the end of each statement.
1024	ANSI_NULL_DFLT_ON	Alters the session's behavior to use ANSI compatibility for nullability. New columns defined without explicit nullability are defined to allow nulls.
2048	ANSI_NULL_DFLT_OFF	Alters the session to not use ANSI compatibility for nullability. New columns defined without explicit nullability will not allow nulls.
4096	CONCAT_NULL_YIELDS_NULL	Returns NULL when concatenating a NULL value with a string.
8192	NUMERIC_ROUNDABORT	Generates an error when a loss of precision occurs in an expression.
16384	XACT_ABORT	Rolls back a transaction if a Transact- SQL statement raises a run-time error.

For an example of the use of **sp_configure 'user options'**, see page 219.

2.8.3.2 SET

The SET statement assigns current session (connection) option settings. These settings are listed in Table 2-81.

Table 2-81 SET Statement Options

SET Command Option Keyword	Default Setting	@@ OPTIONS value[d] See p. 209	Description
Date and Time Options	a,b		
DATEFIRST { 1|2|3|4|5|6|7 } 1=Monday, 7=Sunday	7 (Sunday)		Sets first day of week. **Ex:** SET DATEFIRST 7

Table 2-81 SET Statement Options (cont.)

SET Command Option Keyword	Default Setting	@@ OPTIONS value[d] See p. 209	Description
DATEFORMAT { mdy|dmy|ymd|ydm|myd|dym }	mdy		Sets the order of (month/day/year) for entering datetime or smalldatetime data. **Ex:** SET DATEFORMAT mdy
Locking Options			
DEADLOCK_PRIORITY { LOW | NORMAL | *@deadlock_var }*	NORMAL		Controls how session reacts if in deadlock. LOW — Current session is victim NORMAL — Let SQL Server decide *@deadlock_var* - 3=LOW, 6=NORMAL
LOCK_TIMEOUT *millisec_til_timeout*	1		Specifies the number of milliseconds a statement waits for a lock to be released.
Miscellaneous SET Options			See also Books Online: "SET Options"
CONCAT_NULL_YIELDS_NULL	OFFa	4096	ON means concatenating with NULL yields NULL versus empty string (OFF) OLE DB and ODBC set this to ON when making a new connection.
DISABLE_DEF_CNST_CHK	OFF	1	For backward compatibility only
FIPS_FLAGGER { ENTRY|FULL | INTERMEDIATE | OFF }			Specifies checking for compliance with the FIPS 127-2 standard, and specifies SQL-92 Entry, Full or Intermediate Level or None.
IDENTITY_INSERT	OFF		ON allows explicit values to be inserted into an identity column.

LANGUAGE { [N] '*language*' | *@language_var* }	us_english See p. 177.		Specifies the session language including **datetime** formats and system messages.
			EXEC sp_helplanguage — list languages
			
			Example:
			`SET LANGUAGE Deutsch PRINT CAST ( '2003-05-10 14:35' As DATETIME )`
			Okt 5 2003 2:35PM
			`SET LANGUAGE us_english PRINT CAST ( '2003-05-10 14:35' As DATETIME )`
			May 10 2003 2:35PM

OFFSETS *keyword_list*			Use only in DB-Library applications. See Books Online.

Table 2-81 SET Statement Options (cont.)

SET Command Option Keyword	Default Setting	@@ OPTIONS value[d] See p. 209	Description
Query Execution Statements			
ARITHABORT Note on Default: See footnote c.	OFF[c]	64	Terminates a query if overflow or divide-by-zero occurs during query.
ARITHIGNORE	OFF	128	ON means Error Message is returned from overflow or divide-by-zero.
FMTONLY	OFF		Returns only meta data, no data
NOCOUNT	OFF	512	Stops the message with number of rows affected from being returned.
NOEXEC	OFF		Parse and compile but do not execute.
NUMERIC_ROUNDABORT	OFF	8192	Sets level of error reporting when rounding causes a loss of precision.
PARSEONLY	OFF		Parse but do not execute from now on.
QUERY_GOVERNOR_COST_LIMIT *integervalue*	0 (unlim ited)		**sysadmin** setting to disallow queries whose estimated run time exceeds the spec ified number of seconds. Default is 0, unlimited time, so all queries run.
ROWCOUNT *integervalue*	0 (unlim)		Stops processing the query after the specified number of rows.
TEXTSIZE *integervalue*	4 KB		Specifies the size in bytes of **text** and **ntext** data returned from a SELECT Either 0 or 4096 sets to default of 4 KB.
SQL-92 Settings Statements			
ANSI_DEFAULTS	n/a		ON sets all options in this section to ON except ANSI_NULL_DFLT_OFF to OFF. OFF leaves ANSI_NULL_DFLT_OFF unchanged and sets rest to OFF
ANSI_NULLS	OFF[a]	32	Sets ANSI SQL-92 compliant behavior in effect when comparing to NULL with equals (=) and not equal to (<>) .
ANSI_NULL_DFLT_ON	OFF[a]	1024	Only one of these two can be ON at a time. So setting one ON sets the other OFF. Both may be set to OFF at the same time.

Table 2-81 SET Statement Options (cont.)

SET Command Option Keyword	Default Setting	@@ OPTIONS value[d] See p. 209	Description
ANSI_NULL_DFLT_OFF	OFF	2048	
ANSI_PADDING	ON[a]	16	Set blank padding for values shorter than the defined size of the column and for values that have trailing blanks in char and binary data.
ANSI_WARNINGS	OFF[a]	8	ON means SQL-92 standard behavior of raising error messages or warnings for conditions like divide-by-zero and arithmetic overflow.
CURSOR_CLOSE_ON_COMMIT	OFF[b]		As described by the name when ON
QUOTED_IDENTIFIER	OFF[a]	256	See QUOTED_IDENTIFIER discussion with examples page 44.
IMPLICIT_TRANSACTIONS	OFF[b]	2	See details with **Transactions** below.
Statistics Statements			
FORCEPLAN	OFF		Makes the query optimizer process a join in the same order as tables appear in the FROM clause of a SELECT statement.
SHOWPLAN_ALL	OFF		ON: does not execute SQL statements but instead returns the detailed execution plan and estimates of the resource requirements to execute the statements.
SHOWPLAN_TEXT	OFF		ON: does not execute SQL statements but instead returns the execution plan for the statements.
STATISTICS IO	OFF		ON: displays the disk activity generated by Transact-SQL statements when executed.
STATISTICS PROFILE	OFF		ON: Displays profile information for a statement including number of rows produced and number of times the query ran.
STATISTICS TIME	OFF		Displays the time in milliseconds to parse, compile and execute each statement.

Table 2-81 SET Statement Options (cont.)

SET Command Option Keyword	Default Setting	@@ OPTIONS value[d] See p. 209	Description
Transaction Statements		d	See "Transaction Control," page 529.
IMPLICIT_TRANSACTIONS	OFFb	2	IMPLICIT_TRANSACTION mode ON requires an explicit COMMIT/ROLL BACK for each transaction. OLE DB and ODBC set this to OFF when making a new connection. When OFF, AUTOCOMMIT MODE is in effect. See "Transaction Control," page 529.
REMOTE_PROC_TRANSACTIONS	OFF		Specifies that when a local transaction is active, executing a remote stored procedure starts a Transact-SQL distributed transac tion managed by the Microsoft Distributed Transaction Manager (MS DTC).
TRANSACTION ISOLATION LEVEL { READ UNCOMMITTED I READ COMMITTED I REPEATABLE READ I SERIALIZABLE }	READ COMMITTED		Controls the default locking behavior for the session (connection). See "Transaction Control," p. 529.
XACT_ABORT	OFF	16384	ON: rolls back the entire transaction if a statement raises a run-time error OFF: rolls back just the statement and the transaction continues.

a. OLE DB and ODBC explicitly set this to ON for each client connection overriding database setting. See p. 215.

b. OLE DB and ODBC explicitly set this to OFF for each client connection overriding database setting. See p. 215.

c. Query Analyzer sets ARITHABORT to ON for each of its connections overriding database setting. See p. 216.

d. See @@OPTIONS, p. 208.

2.8.3.3 @@OPTIONS

The value @@OPTIONS returns a bitmask of session options from Table 2-82 SET for the current connection. The value includes all options currently SET by virtue of server settings including **sp_configure 'user options'** and SET operations including those set by OLE DB and ODBC drivers (see page 215).

Bit positions in @@OPTIONS are identical to those in sp_configure 'user options' but the @@OPTIONS value represents current session settings of the options.

@@OPTIONS reports on the following 15 settings which includes the 7 options that SESSIONPROPERTY() reports. So @@OPTIONS is more complete.

Table 2-82 @@OPTIONS Settings

Option	Default [a,b]	@@OPTIONS Value
DISABLE_DEF_CNST_CHK	OFF	1
IMPLICIT_TRANSACTIONS	OFF[b]	2
CURSOR_CLOSE_ON_COMMIT	OFF[b]	4
ANSI_WARNINGS	OFF[a]	8
ANSI_PADDING	ON[a]	16
ANSI_NULLS	OFF[a]	32
ARITHABORT	OFF[c]	64
ARITHIGNORE	OFF	128
QUOTED_IDENTIFIER	OFF[a]	256
NOCOUNT	OFF	512
ANSI_NULL_DFLT_ON	OFF[a]	1024
ANSI_NULL_DFLT_OFF	OFF	2048
CONCAT_NULL_YIELDS_NULL	ON[a]	4096
NUMERIC_ROUNDABORT	OFF	8192
XACT_ABORT	OFF	16384

a. OLE DB and ODBC explicitly set this to ON for each client connection overriding database setting. See p. 215.

b. OLE DB and ODBC explicitly set this to OFF for each client connection overriding database setting. See p. 215.

c. Query Analyzer sets ARITHABORT to ON for each of its connections overriding database setting.. See p. 216.

See more examples displaying current session (connection) settings on page 220.

SQL

```
SELECT @@OPTIONS & 4096 -- Shows that CONCAT_NULL_YIELDS_NULL is currently ON
```

Result

```
4096
```

SQL

```
SELECT @@OPTIONS -- Shows the integer bitmask which
  includes all @@OPTIONS currently ON
```

Result

```
5496
```

SQL

```
SET CONCAT_NULL_YIELDS_NULL    OFF
SELECT @@OPTIONS & 4096       -- Shows that
CONCAT_NULL_YIELDS_NULL is currently OFF
```

Result

```
0
```

SQL

```
SELECT @@OPTIONS -- Shows the integer bitmask which
  includes all @@OPTIONS currently ON
```

Result

```
1400
```

2.8.3.4 DBCC USEROPTIONS

DBCC USEROPTIONS returns all SET options which are active (set) for the current session (connection).

Syntax

```
DBCC USEROPTIONS
```

Example: Example of ways to display current session (connection) settings.

SQL

```
DBCC USEROPTIONS
```

SQL (cont.)

Result

```
Set Option                          Value
----------------------------------- ---------------------------
textsize                            64512
language
us_english
dateformat                          mdy
datefirst                           7
quoted_identifier                   SET
ansi_null_dflt_on                   SET
ansi_defaults                       SET
ansi_warnings                       SET
ansi_padding                        SET
ansi_nulls                          SET
concat_null_yields_null             SET
DBCC execution completed. If DBCC printed error messages, contact your system administrator.
```

2.8.3.5 SESSIONPROPERTY

SESSIONPROPERTY returns the current setting of one of the seven session options listed in Table 2-83. Returns on the setting are listed in Table 2-84.

Returns 1 if SET, 0 if NOT SET and NULL if the input *option* name was invalid.

Syntax

```
SESSIONPROPERTY ( 'option' )
```

Arugment

option

The SESSIONPROPERTY *option* names are the same as for ALTER DATABASE.

Table 2-83 SESSIONPROPERTY Options

Option Name	Option Name
ANSI_NULLS	CONCAT_NULL_YIELDS_NULL
ANSI_PADDING	NUMERIC_ROUNDABORT
ANSI_WARNINGS	QUOTED_IDENTIFIER
ARITHABORT	

For the meaning of each option see ANSI SQL-92 Compliance Options, see page 191.

Table 2-84 Returns

Return Value	Option Is Currently
1	ON
O	OFF
NULL	Invalid Option name

Examples using SESSIONPROPERTY()

SQL

```
SELECT   SESSIONPROPERTY( 'QUOTED_IDENTIFIER' )    -- Option ON returns 1
```

Result

```
--------
1
```

SQL

```
SELECT   SESSIONPROPERTY( 'NUMERIC_ROUNDABORT' )    -- Option OFF returns 0
```

Result

```
--------
0
```

SQL

```
SELECT   SESSIONPROPERTY( 'Foo_Foo' ) -- Invalid input option name, returns
  NULL
```

Result

```
--------
NULL
```

2.8.3.6 Comparing @@OPTIONS, DBCC USEROPTIONS and SESSIONPROPERTY()

The following methods show current session settings as indicated:

@@OPTIONS enables you to determine the setting of a specific option but it requires looking up the option number of interest and doing a bitwise AND to determine if a specific setting is on or off. Only the settings that have a value in the @@OPTIONS column of Table 2-81, page 204, may be read with this function.

DBCC USEROPTIONS is convenient since it reports all options that are currently set. It is silent on options not currently set.

SESSIONPROPERTY() returns the one option setting specified, as does @@OPTIONS, and it uses the same option keyword as SET, so it's more consistent in its use. But it is less complete than @@OPTIONS because it only reports on the seven options listed in Table 2-83.

Examples Comparing the Three:

SQL

```
SELECT @@OPTIONS & 1024 -- Shows that ANSI_NULL_DFLT_ON  is currently ON
```

Result

```
--------
1024
```

SQL

```
SELECT @@OPTIONS & 4096 -- Shows that CONCAT_NULL_YIELDS_NULL
   is currently ON
```

Result

```
--------
4096
```

SQL

```
SELECT  SESSIONPROPERTY( 'ANSI_NULL_DFLT_ON' ) -- Can't check this one
```

Result

```
--------
NULL
```

SQL

```
SELECT  SESSIONPROPERTY( 'CONCAT_NULL_YIELDS_NULL' )   -- Option ON returns 1
```

Result

```
--------
1
```

SQL

```
DBCC USEROPTIONS
```

Result

```
Set Option                            Value
------------------------------------  ---------------------------
ansi_null_dflt_on                     SET
...
concat_null_yields_null               SET
DBCC execution completed. If DBCC printed error messages, contact your system
administrator.
```

2.8.3.7 Session Configuration Functions

These built-in scalar functions return the current session setting indicated by the name. Table 2-85 provides a description.

Table 2-85 Session Configuration Functions

Function Name	Description
@@DATEFIRST	Returns the current value of the SET DATEFIRST parameter, which indicates the specified first day of each week: 1 for Monday, 2 for Wednesday, and so on through 7 for Sunday.
@@DBTS	Returns the value of the current **timestamp** data type for the current database. This **timestamp** is guaranteed to be unique in the database.
@@LANGID	Returns the local language identifier (ID) of the language currently in use.
@@LANGUAGE	Returns the name of the language currently in use.
@@LOCK_TIMEOUT	Returns the current lock time-out setting, in milliseconds, for the current session.

Table 2-85 Session Configuration Functions (cont.)

Function Name	Description
@@MAX_CONNECTIONS	Returns the maximum number of simultaneous user connections allowed on a Microsoft SQL Server. The number returned is not necessarily the number currently configured.
@@MAX_PRECISION	Returns the precision level used by **decimal** and **numeric** data types as currently set in the server.
@@NESTLEVEL	Returns the nesting level of the current stored procedure execution (initially 0).
@@OPTIONS	Returns information about current SET options.
@@REMSERVER	Returns the name of the remote Microsoft SQL Server database server as it appears in the login record.
@@SERVERNAME	Returns the name of the local server running Microsoft SQL Server.
@@SERVICENAME	Returns the name of the registry key under which Microsoft SQL Server is running. @@SERVICENAME returns MSSQLServer if the current instance is the default instance; this function returns the instance name if the current instance is a named instance.
@@SPID	Returns the server process identifier (ID) of the current user session.
@@TEXTSIZE	Returns the current value of the TEXTSIZE option of the SET statement, which specifies the maximum length, in bytes, of **text** or **image** data that a SELECT statement returns.
@@VERSION	Returns the date, version and processor type for the current installation of Microsoft SQL Server.

Example:

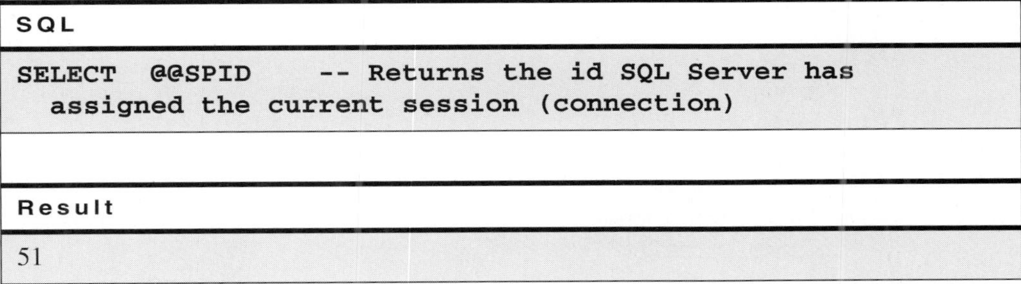

SQL
`SELECT @@SPID -- Returns the id SQL Server has assigned the current session (connection)`

Result
51

2.8.3.8 OLE DB and ODBC Driver Connection Settings

OLE DB and ODBC drivers make the following settings for every new connection.

ON

```
CONCAT_NULL_YIELDS_NULL
ANSI_NULL_DEFAULT
ANSI_DEFAULTS  -- which set all of the following to ON
  ANSI_NULLS BOL -- 'SET Options' for ANSI_DEFAULTS

  ANSI_NULL_DFLT_ON -- sets ANSI_NULL_DFLT_OFF to OFF
  ANSI_PADDING       -- See page 112.
  ANSI_WARNINGS
  QUOTED_IDENTIFIER
```

OFF

```
CURSOR_CLOSE_ON_COMMIT
  IMPLICIT_TRANSACTIONS
```

See each item under "SETTING DATABASE OPTIONS" "SET CONCAT_NULL_YIELDS_NULL" for ODBC/OLE DB sessions settings.

ODBC and OLE DB first turn on the above settings identified as ON. Then they turn off the two items identified as OFF (they were set to ON when ANSI_DEFAULTS was set ON). See "SET ANSI_DEFAULTS" for ODBC/OLE DB sessions settings. These settings will be in effect for every ODBC and OLE DB client unless you change them with an explicit SET statement. See Query Analyzer additions next.

2.8.3.9 Query Analyzer Connection Settings

Query Analyzer uses ODBC, so it starts with the ODBC settings listed above in effect, then it sets the following additional options as shown.

ON

```
ARITHABORT
```

OFF

```
NOCOUNT
  NOEXEC
  PARSEONLY
  SHOWPLAN_TEXT
  STATISTICS TIME
  STATISTICS IO
```

0 `ROWCOUNT (0 or NULL means unlimited rows in result sets)`

The net result of these default actions can be confirmed by executing this statement in Query Analyzer.

SQL

```
-- In a Query Analyzer with default settings
  DBCC USEROPTIONS
```

Result

```
Set Option                        Value
-------------------------------   -------------
textsize                          64512
language                          us_english
dateformat                        mdy
datefirst                         7
quoted_identifier                 SET
arithabort                        SET
ansi_null_dflt_on                 SET
ansi_defaults                     SET
ansi_warnings                     SET
ansi_padding                      SET
ansi_nulls                        SET
concat_null_yields_null           SET
```

These settings, except the first four, are set explicitly by ODBC and Query Analyzer as just described. The first four were inherited from the defaults as summarized in the next section. See also Books Online: Using SET Options in SQL Query Analyzer.

2.8.3.10 Changing Query Analyzer Default Connection Settings

You may change the default connection settings for your own Query Analyzer from Query—Current Connection Properties, which opens the dialog shown in Figure 2-8. Check a box for ON or uncheck for OFF and click Apply. Table 2-86 lists the default SET session settings made by Query Analyzer.

Table 2-86 Summary of All Default SET Session Settings Made by Query Analyzer

Option	Setting
Set nocount	OFF
Set noexec	OFF
Set parseonly	OFF

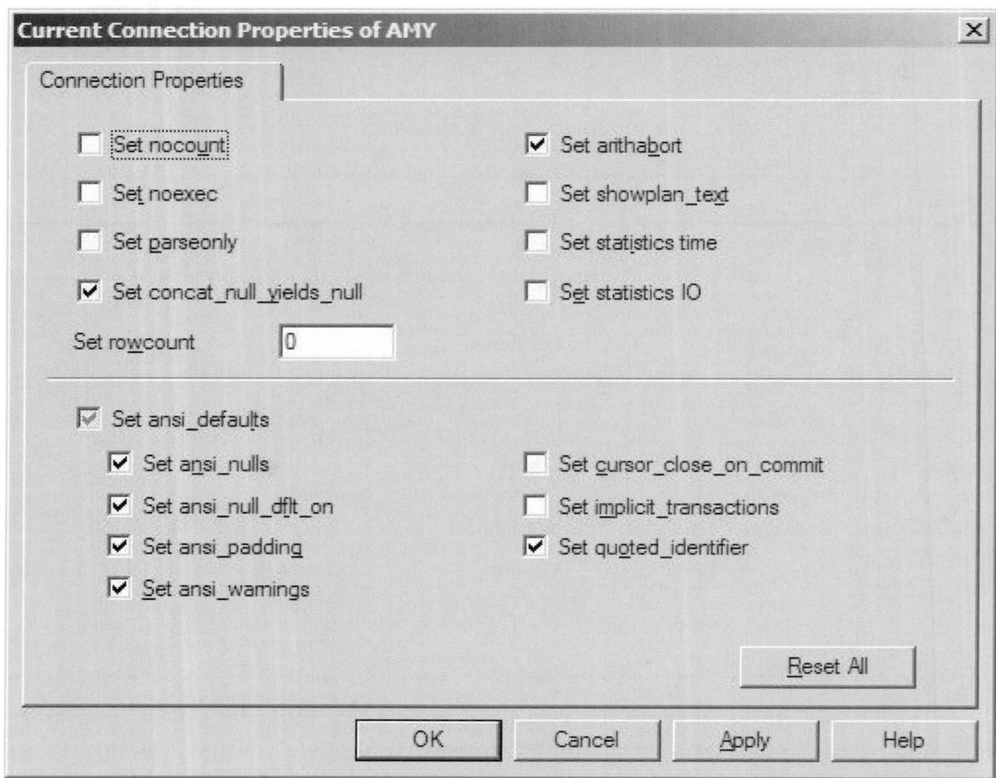

Figure 2-8 The Connection Properties Dialog Box in Query Analyzer.

Table 2-86 Summary of All Default SET Session Settings Made by Query Analyzer (cont.)

Option	Setting
Set concat_null_yields_null	ON
Set rowcount	0
Set ansi_defaults	ON
Set arithabort	ON
Set showplan_text	OFF
Set statistics time	OFF
Set statistics 10	OFF

Table 2-86 Summary of All Default SET Session Settings Made by Query Analyzer (cont.)

Option	Setting
Set ansi_nulls	ON
Set ansi_null_dflt_on	ON
Set ansi_padding	ON
Set ansi_warnings	ON
Set cursor_close_on_commit	OFF
Set implicit_transactions	OFF
Set quoted_identifier	ON

2.8.3.11 Which Session Setting Is in Effect?

What follows is my version of SQL Server's algorithm to decide which setting to use.

If a user has SET an option then that setting is used for the current session else if it is an option set by ODBC, OLE DB or Query Analyzer then it will be used (page 215) else if **sp_configure 'user options'** for the option is in effect it will be used (page 202) else if the current database has a setting for the option then it will be used (page 187) else the SQL Server default setting for the option will be used (page 203).

The case numbers are given below to identify what is happening in the following examples.

1. An explicit session SET statement takes precedence and lasts until changed by a new SET statement or the end of the session (connection).

2a. OLE DB and ODBC drivers make the following settings for each new connection.

ON

```
CONCAT_NULL_YIELDS_NULL
  ANSI_NULL_DEFAULT
  ANSI_DEFAULTS (which set esach of the following to ON)
    ANSI_NULLS
    ANSI_NULL_DFLT_ON (which sets ANSI_NULL_DFLT_OFF to OFF)
    ANSI_PADDING (see page 102)
    ANSI_WARNINGS
    CURSOR_CLOSE_ON_COMMIT
    IMPLICIT_TRANSACTIONS
    QUOTED_IDENTIFIER
```

OFF

```
CURSOR_CLOSE_ON_COMMIT
                    IMPLICIT_TRANSACTIONS
```

So these settings will be in effect for every ODBC and OLE DB client until you change them with an explicit SET statement. This is true regardless of **sp_configure 'user options'** or database options assigned with **ALTER DATABASE**.

2b. Query Analyzer sets ARITHABORT to ON (see page 216).

3. In the absence of 1 or 2, any option set with **sp_configure 'user options'** will be used.

4. **Database default** is next (can be set with **ALTER DATABASE**, pages 189 and 250).

5. Lastly, the **SQL Server default** will be used, page 202.

Examples Showing which Session Setting Is in Effect Examples are given here to demonstrate Case 1, 2a, 2b, 3 and 4. Each example starts with a new connection and shows user actions, if any, to change a setting and the result.

Example: CASE 1—Explicit SET CONCAT_NULL_YIELDS_NULL to OFF

Open a new database connection to the pubs database.

SQL

```
SELECT SESSIONPROPERTY( 'CONCAT_NULL_YIELDS_NULL' ) -- Show it's ON
```

Result

```
-------
0
```

SQL

```
SET  COmAT_NULL_YIELDS_NULL  OFF              -- changes OLE DB setting

SELECT SESSIONPROPERTY( 'CONCAT_NULL_YIELDS_NULL' ) -- Show it's now OFF
```

Result

SQL

```
SELECT DATABASEPROPERTYEX( 'pubs' , 'IsNullConcat' )
  -- Show DB default is OFF
```

Result

```
-------
0
```

Table 2-87 contains a summary of actions in order of precedence. The first "Yes" from the left takes precedence.

Table 2-87 Case 1 Explicit SET of CONCAT_NULL_YIELDS_NULL Option

Explicit SET	Set by OLE DB/ODBC	User Option	Database Default
Yes—**SET to OFF**	Yes—ON but overridden	Would be overridden even if set	OFF but overridden

Example: **CASE 2a**—OLE DB sets CONCAT_NULL_YIELDS_NULL to ON. Open a new database connection to the pubs database.

SQL

```
SELECT SESSIONPROPERTY( 'CONCAT_NULL_YIELDS_NULL' )
  -- Session setting is ON
-- (I'm using Query Analyzer and OLE DB set it ON)
```

Result

```
-------
1
```

SQL

```
SELECT  @@OPTIONS & 4096   -- Same result, this is an
  alternative to SESSIONPROPERTY
```

SQ (cont.)

Result

```
-------
4096
```

SQL

```
SELECT DATABASEPROPERTYEX( 'pubs' , 'IsNullConcat' )
  -- Show DB default is OFF
```

Result

```
-------
0
```

Table 2-88 contains a summary of actions in order of precedence. The first "Yes" from the left takes precedence.

Table 2-88 Case 2a—ODBC Set of CONCAT_NULL_YIELDS_NULL option

Explicit SET	Set by OLE DB/ ODBC	User Option	Database Default
No	Yes — ON	Would be overridden even if set	OFF but overridden

Example: **CASE 2b**—Query Analyzer sets ARITHABORT to ON.

See "Query Analyzer Connection Settings" on page 216.

Example: **CASE 3**—NUMERIC_ROUNDABORT, we'll change User Option to ON.

NUMERIC_ROUNDABORT is one of the few options not set by OLE DB or ODBC, so setting the default user option will have a visible effect. In Session 1 below we first demonstrate that no user options settings are in effect and that NUMERIC_ROUNDABORT defaults to OFF. Then we use sp_configure to set the new user default to ON. Session 1 won't be affected, so we open a new connection as Session 2 and see the new setting is ON.

Session 1 This session observes and changes the sp_configure 'user options', but only new login sessions will see the effect. Open a new database connection to the pubs database.

SQL

```
EXEC sp_configure  'user options' -- Show that no 'user
                                     options' are currently set

-- (run value is 0)
```

Result

name	minimum	maximum	config_value	run_value
user options	0	32767	0	0

SQL

```
-- For fun, show that the setting in this session is off before and after
the 'user option' is changed
SELECT SESSIONPROPERTY( 'NUMERIC_ROUNDABORT' ) -- Session setting is OFF
```

Result

```
-------
0
```

Change the 'user option':

SQL

```
-- Set option for NUMERIC_ROUNDABORT to ON
EXEC sp_configure 'user options' , 8192

RECONFIGURE -- Don't forget that reconfigure is required
  to make the change effective

EXEC sp_configure 'user options'
  -- NUMERIC_ROUNDABORT 'user options is set' (8192)
```

Result

name	minimum	maximum	config_value	run_value
user options	0	32767	8192	8192

SQL

```
-- The setting is on for new sessions, but our
  NUMERIC_ROUNDABORT option setting is still OFF.
SELECT SESSIONPROPERTY( 'NUMERIC_ROUNDABORT' )
```

Result

```
-------
0
```

Session 2 New Login Sessions (Connections) will see the Change Open NEW Query Analyzer CONNECTION. The session setting is now ON.

SQL

```
Again show that the Database default for IsNumericRoundAbortEnabled = OFF
SELECT DATABASEPROPERTYEX( 'pubs' , 'IsNumericRoundAbortEnabled')
```

Result

```
-------
1
```

SQL

```
SELECT  @@OPTIONS & 8192 -- Same result as SESSIONPROPERTY
```

Result

```
-------
8192
```

SQL

```
-- Show that the Database default for IsNumericRoundAbortEnabled = OFF
SELECT DATABASEPROPERTYEX( 'pubs' , 'IsNumericRoundAbortEnabled')
```

Result

```
-------
0
```

```
-- Clean up by returning User Options to 0 for future
sessions
EXEC sp_configure  'user options' , 0
RECONFIGURE                               -- Don't forget
that reconfigure is required to make the change
effective
```

Summary of actions in order of precedence: The first "Yes" from the left takes precedence.

Table 2-89 Case 3—NUMERIC_ROUNDABORT Option— Recall 'user option' Affects Only New Sessions

Explicit SET	Set by OLE DB/ ODBC	User Option	Database Default
No	No	ON	OFF

Example: CASE 4—NUMERIC_ROUNDABORT option, uses the Database default. Open a new database connection to the pubs database.

SQL

```
SELECT DATABASEPROPERTYEX( 'pubs' ,
  'IsNumericRoundAbortEnabled') -- Default OFF
```

Result

```
-------
0
```

SQL

```
SELECT SESSIONPROPERTY( 'NUMERIC_ROUNDABORT' )
  --Show session setting is also off
```

Result

```
-------
0
```

SQL

```
SELECT   @@OPTIONS & 8192                  -- Same result as SESSIONPROPERTY
```

Result

```
-------
0
```

Summary of actions in order of precedence: The first "Yes" from the left takes precedence.

Table 2-90 Case 4—NUMERIC_ROUNDABORT Option Uses Database Option Unless Explicitly Set

Explicit SET	Set by OLE DB/ ODBC	User Option	Database Default
No	No	Not set	OFF

2.8.3.12 Examples of Displaying Session Properties in Different Clients

Example: This example starts with a new SQL Server instance with all default settings.

No Options Set: Use isql to connect to the new SQL Server instance using (old) DB-Lib

```
C:>    isql   -Usa  -P
1> SELECT @@OPTIONS  As  OptionSettings
2> go
OptionSettings
------ ------------
                        0

1> DBCC USEROPTIONS
2> go
 Set Option          Value
 --------------------------
 textsize          4096
 language          us_english
 dateformat          mdy
```

```
 datefirst        7
(4  row(s) affected)
DBCC execution completed. If DBCC printed error
messages, contact your system administrator.
```

Add ODBC initial settings: The osql utility uses ODBC to connect to SQL Server. This shows the added options set by ODBC (and OLE DB).

```
C:>    osql   -Usa  -P

1> SELECT @@OPTIONS  As  OptionSettings
2> go
OptionSettings
-------------------
                  5176


1> DBCC USEROPTIONS
2> go
 Set OptionValue
 ------------------------------------
 textsize                    2147483647
 language                    us_english
 dateformatmdy
 datefirst                    7
 ansi_null_dflt_onSET
 ansi_warningsSET
 ansi_paddingSET
 ansi_nullsSET
 concat_null_yields_nullSET
(9  row(s) affected)
DBCC execution completed. If DBCC printed error
messages, contact your system administrator.
```

Other examples of SET, DBCC USEROPTIONS, @@OPTIONS, SESSIONPROPERTY()

SQL
PRINT @@OPTIONS
Result
5496

SQL

```
PRINT @@OPTIONS & 64 -- arithabort bitmask
```

Result

```
64
```

SQL

```
SELECT SESSIONPROPERTY( 'arithabort' )
```

Result

```
-------
1
```

Now turn one option off and re-run the display statements.

SQL

```
 SET arithabort OFF

DBCC USEROPTIONS
```

Result

```
Set Option                     Value
-----------------------------  ------------
textsize                       64512
language                       us_english
dateformat                     mdy
datefirst                      7
quoted_identifier              SET
ansi_null_dflt_on              SET -- arithabort is missing now
ansi_defaults                  SET
ansi_warnings                  SET
ansi_padding                   SET
ansi_nulls                     SET
concat_null_yields_null        SET
(11 row(s) affected)
```

SQL

```
PRINT @@OPTIONS
```

Result

5432

SQL

```
PRINT @@OPTIONS & 64 -- arithabort bitmask
```

Result

0

SQL

```
SELECT SESSIONPROPERTY( 'arithabort' )
```

Result

0

SQL

```
SELECT SESSIONPROPERTY( 'CONCAT_NULL_YIELDS_NULL' ) -- Show it's ON
```

Result

0

Here's a nice way to show arithabort setting which uses @@OPTIONS.

SQL

```
PRINT 'ARITHABORT: ' + CASE WHEN @@OPTIONS & 64 > 0 THEN 'ON' ELSE  'OFF' END
```

SQL (cont.)

Result

```
ARITHABORT: OFF
```

SQL

```
SET ARITHABORT ON

PRINT 'ARITHABORT: ' + CASE WHEN @@OPTIONS & 64 > 0 THEN 'ON' ELSE  'OFF' END
```

Result

```
ARITHABORT: ON
```

2.8.4 Default Nullability of New Columns in a Table

This subject seems unduly complex. Leaving everything default as it comes out of the box seems most useful and is certainly easiest, as in the example CREATE TABLE t below. But here are the details for those who enjoy confusing topics.

What I call the *default nullability* setting means that if a user executes CREATE TABLE or ALTER TABLE to add a new column to a table and does not specify either NULL or NOT NULL explicitly, the default nullability setting determines the nullability of the new column, that is, whether it will be created as NULL or NOT NULL.

ANSI SQL-92 standard specifies default nullability to be nullable, that is, default is NULL.

Default nullability is determined by database and session settings. Session setting for ANSI_NULL_DFLT_ON or ANSI_NULL_DFLT_OFF determines the default nullability if either is ON. (Setting one ON sets the other OFF.) Database setting ANSI_NULL_DEFAULT will rule if both session settings are OFF.

Bottom line: ODBC drivers and OLE DB providers set ANSI_NULL_DFLT_ON to ON for each connection, so the Query Analyzer and other clients using these libraries behave with new columns defaulting to nullable.

ANSI_NULL_DFLT_ON will thus be ON unless you explicitly issue either

SET ANSI_NULL_DFLT_ON OFF

or SET ANSI_NULL_DFLT_OFF ON

This setting will remain in effect for the rest of your connection unless you change it.

It is suggested that you do not issue either of these statements and so leave the out-of-the-box defaults intact. In this case, use the following CREATE TABLE statement.

```
CREATE TABLE  t (
   col1   INT   NOT NULL,-- col1 will NOT allow NULL and
   col2   INT   NULL     ,-- col2 will allow NULL regardless of settings
   col3   INT            )-- col3 heeds the settings
```

This would result in **col3** being nullable as if it had been created just like col2.

If you do issue either of the two SET statements above, then col3 would be non-nullable as if it had been created like **col1**.

The only way for the ANSI_NULL_DEFAULT database setting to have an effect is if SET ANSI_NULL_DFLT_ON   OFF is executed, so this database option seems pretty much useless unless you want to issue that statement, or if you can find a way to connect without using either OLE DB or ODBC.

It should be noted for the record that, according to Books Online, "Microsoft SQL Server 2000 defaults to NOT NULL." So the database option ANSI_NULL_DEFAULT will be found to be OFF, but again, this is overridden by the OLE DB and ODBC drivers turning ON the ANSI_NULL_DFLT_ON option.

2.8.4.1 How to Set and Determine the Current Nullability Settings

The remaining discussion in this section is for completeness and could easily be skipped.

Three levels have a hand in determining the ultimate default nullability of a new column.

Server Configuration This affects session options of logins created after the change.

```
sp_configure  'user options'  ,  1024    – Turns on ANSI_NULL_DFLT_ON
sp_configure  'user options'  ,  2048    – Turns on ANSI_NULL_DFLT_OFF
```

Only one may be ON or both OFF: Setting one ON sets the other OFF.

These seem to have no effect since they assign the SET options of the session, but both ODBC and ODE DB set ANSI_NULL_DFLT_ON to true for each session.

Database Configuration

```
ALTER DATABASE dbname SET  ANSI_NULL_DEFAULT {ON|OFF}
```

Default setting is OFF.
Current database setting is visible with:

```
SELECT  DATABASEPROPERTYEX( 'dbname' ,
'IsAnsiNullDefault'  )
```

Session (Connection) Settings These take precedence if either is ON.

```
SET   ANSI_NULL_DFLT_ON      {ON | OFF}
```

```
SET   ANSI_NULL_DFLT_OFF   {ON | OFF}
```

Only one may be ON or both OFF: Setting one ON sets the other OFF.

Also, SET ANSI_DEFAULTS ON includes SET ANSI_NULL_DFLT_ON ON.

Settings of the current session in the current database are visible with:

```
DBCC USEROPTIONS
```

Shows if ANSI_NULL_DFLT_ON or ANSI_NULL_DFLT_OFF is SET.

Show effective nullability settings in specified database in current session.

```
SELECT  GETANSINULL ( [ 'dbname' ] )
```

Returns 1 if NULL, 0 if NOT NULL is the effective nullability. This is what is used.

Example:

SQL
SELECT GETANSINULL ('pubs') --Shows the default nullability is NULL in pubs db in this session
Result
------- 1

GETANSINULL() result shows what will be used in a CREATE TABLE. Table 2-91 shows how.

Table 2-91 Default Nullability

Session ANSI_NULL_DFLT_ON	Session ANSI_NULL_DFLT_OFF	Default Nullability of New Columns
ON	ON	Impossible (either ON turns other OFF)
ON	OFF	New columns default to **nullable** DATABASE setting is IGNORED
OFF	ON	New columns default to **not nullable** DATA-BASE setting is IGNORED
OFF	OFF	DATABASE ANSI_NULL_DEFAULT **SETTING RULES**

2.8.5 Collation

A collation determines how sort order, case sensitivity and related issues are handled for columns of string data types, that is **char**, **varchar**, **text**, **nchar**, **nvarchar** and **ntext**.

SQL Server is installed with a default server level collation. SS 2000 default is, "=Dictionary order, case-insensitive, for use with 1252 Character Set.

SQL Server 2K supports different collations for each database down to the level of columns within a table. SQL Server 7.0 allows only a single collation for an instance.

The server level default collation will usually be the collation of every database, and the database default will be the default collation of each table column of string data type.

The COLLATE clause may specify collation for a database or for a column in a table.

A COLLATE clause may be applied at several levels including to a

- database definition,
- column definition in a table or
- string expression

These determine comparison and sorting characteristics. See examples of each below.

New in SQL Server 2K is the capability to create a new database using the COLLATE clause to specify a different collation.

```
CREATE DATABASE  databasename COLLATE  <collation_name>

ALTER DATABASE   databasename COLLATE  <collation_name>
```

See Books Online for restrictions on changing an existing database collation.

Also new with SQL Server 2K is the ability to set a collation for a single column of a table or table variable.

```
CREATE TABLE tablename (
  columnname   columndefinition   COLLATE <collation_name>
... )
```

The code *collation_name* can be a Windows collation name or SQL collation name, and is applicable only for columns of **char, varchar, text, nchar, nvarchar** and **ntext** data types.

For a list of all Windows and SQL collations, execute the following sequence.

SQL

```
SELECT * FROM ::fn_helpcollations()
```

Result

```
name                      description
------------------------  ----------------------------------------------------------------------------------
Albanian_BIN              Albanian, binary sort
Albanian_CS_AS            Albanian, case-sensitive, accent-sensitive, kanatype-insensitive, width-ins...
...
Latin1_General_CI_AS      Latin1-General, case-insensitive, accent-sensitive, kanatype-insensitive, ...
Latin1_General_CS_AS      Latin1-General, case-sensitive, accent-sensitive, kanatype-insensitive, ...
....
```

Note: Unicode was designed to eliminate the code page conversion difficulties of the non-Unicode **char**, **varchar** and **text** data types. When you support multiple languages, use the Unicode data types **nchar, nvarchar** and **ntext** for all character data.

Two example collations follow.

Latin1_General_CI_ASCI means case insensitive

Latin1_General_CS_ASCS means case sensitive

Latin1_General is the Latin alphabet used by western European languages. It is also referred to as the **1252 character set**.

Example: Create a **Database** with a specified collation (Case Sensitive).

SQL

```
CREATE DATABASE  mydb COLLATE Latin1_General_CS_AS

USE mydb
go

CREATE TABLE Table1 ( a  INT  ,  A INT )

INSERT INTO Table1   VALUES ( 1 , 2 )

SELECT * FROM Table1  WHERE  a = 1
```

SQL (cont.)

Result

```
a        A
------   ------
1        2
(1 row(s) affected)
```

SQL

```
SELECT * FROM Table1  WHERE  a = 2
```

Result

```
a        A
------   ------

(0 row(s) affected)
```

SQL

```
SELECT * FROM Table1  WHERE  A = 1
```

Result

```
a        A
------   ------

(0 row(s) affected)
```

SQL

```
SELECT * FROM table1
```

Result

```
Server: Msg 208, Level 16, State 1, Line 1
Invalid object name 'table1'.
```

Example: Specify the collation of a string using CASTNotice that CI is for case insensitive and CS is for case sensitive. Without the CAST statement, the database collation is used for comparison.

SQL

```
USE pubs     -- pubs has default case insensitive collation
go
IF 'abc' = 'ABC'    -- We expect TRUE if case insensitive,
  FALSE if case sensitive
             PRINT 'TRUE.  Yes, they compare'
ELSE
             PRINT 'FALSE.  Nope, not the same'
```

Result

TRUE. Yes, they compare

SQL

```
USE mydb     -- mydb was created above with case sensitive
  collation, so it should be FALSE
go
IF 'abc' = 'ABC'    -- We expect TRUE if case insensitive,
  FALSE if case sensitive
             PRINT 'TRUE.  Yes, they compare'
ELSE
             PRINT 'FALSE.  Nope, not the same'
```

Result

FALSE. Nope, not the same

But, the string can be CAST to case insensitive.

SQL

```
IF 'abc' = CAST( 'ABC' as VARCHAR(10) ) COLLATE  Latin1_General_CI_AS
   PRINT 'Yes, they compare'
ELSE
   PRINT 'Nope, not the same'
```

Result

TRUE. Yes, they compare

Example: Create table columns with a specified collation. Overrides database default.

```
CREATE  TABLE t (
    ci VARCHAR(10) COLLATE  Latin1_General_CI_AS
  , cs VARCHAR(10) COLLATE Latin1_General_CS_AS
    )

    INSERT INTO t VALUES ( 'aaa', 'aaa' );
    INSERT INTO t VALUES ( 'AAA', 'AAA' );
```

Column ci is case insensitive for searches, column cs is case sensitive.

SQL

```
SELECT * FROM t WHERE ci = 'aaa'
```

Result

```
ci          cs
----------  ----------
aaa         aaa
AAA         AAA
```

SQL

```
SELECT * FROM t WHERE cs = 'aaa'
```

Result

```
ci          cs
----------  ----------
aaa         aaa
```

Use the string CAST on the column to get case insensitive search.

SQL

```
SELECT * FROM t
WHERE   'aaa'  =  CAST( cs  AS   VARCHAR(10) ) COLLATE  Latin1_General_CI_AS
```

SQL (cont.)

Result

```
ci          cs
----------  ----------
aaa         aaa
AAA         AAA
```

CHAPTER 3

Data Definition Language and Security

This chapter covers methods available to the database designer and database user to create and modify database objects. It starts with the Data Definition Language (DDL) statements CREATE, ALTER and DROP.

The SQL language has two main divisions:

- **DDL**—Data Definition Language, which is used to define and manage all the objects in an SQL database (discussed starting page 240), and
- **DML**—Data Manipulation Language, which is used to select, insert, update and delete data in the tables contained in an SQL database (discussed starting page 423).

Microsoft SQL Server Books Online describes DDL nicely:

> The Transact-SQL DDL used to manage objects such as databases, tables, and views is based on SQL-92 DDL statements, with extensions. For each object class, there are usually CREATE, ALTER, and DROP statements, such as CREATE TABLE, ALTER TABLE, and DROP TABLE. Permissions are controlled using the SQL-92 GRANT and REVOKE statements, and the Transact-SQL DENY statement.

This chapter contains a Data Definition Language overview including the DDL statements CREATE, ALTER, DROP, GRANT and REVOKE. It also covers Server Settings, which are additional features not part of the SQL language.

3.1 DATA DEFINITION LANGUAGE (DDL)

Data Definition Language consists of those SQL statements used to define and manage all the objects or components in an SQL database. DDL is the subset of SQL statements used for modeling the structure (rather than the data contents) of a database. DDL consists of three primary statements for each type of database object.

- **CREATE** creates a new database system object in the current database.

Example: Create a new table with two columns.

```
CREATE TABLE table1 ( col1   INT, col2 INT);
```

- **ALTER** modifies an existing object definition or structure.

Example: **Add a column to table1.**

```
ALTER TABLE table1 ADD  col3   INT;
```

- **DROP** removes the definition of the metadata AND any underlying data.

Example: Remove **table1** and all of its data.

```
DROP TABLE table1
```

Caution: This eliminates all vestiges of metadata and data for table1. So be careful!

In addition to CREATE, ALTER and DROP, the following statements are sometimes considered to be part of DDL:

- GRANT and REVOKE privileges

Example: Give login2 these permissions to access the titles table.

```
GRANT INSERT, UPDATE, DELETE, SELECT ON titles TO login2
```

Example: Remove UPDATE and DELETE permissions just granted.

```
REVOKE UPDATE, DELETE ON titles FROM login2
```

3.1.1 Metadata and Data

3.1.1.1 Metadata

Metadata, often called data about data, includes the structure definitions of database objects such as tables, views, etc.

Metadata includes information such as the table definitions, including name, column names, data types and constraints as well as definitions of views, stored procedures and triggers. Microsoft SQL Server 2000 provides two methods for obtaining metadata: system stored procedures, like **sp_help**, or information schema views.

3.1.1.2 Data

Data consists of the actual values to be stored and retrieved from the database: **Mary Smith**, **7777, 101, 7890, 400**. Every database in SQL Server contains data tables and metadata. The difference between data and metadata is outlined in Table 3-1.

Table 3-1 Comparing Metadata to Data

	Description	Example	Is Stored on Disk in	Is Managed Using
Metadata	Information about definition of database objects	**persons** table name **name** column name & **CHAR(20)** data type	**System Tables**, also called **Data Dictionary**, also called **System Catalog**	**Data Definition Language (DDL)**
Data	Information values for which the database was created	'Mary Smith' 5555	Data tables	**Data Manipulation Language (DML)**

3.1.2 Types of Objects Managed by DDL

Table 3-2 identifies the Microsoft SQL Server objects that are managed by DDL statements.

Table 3-2 Objects Managed by DDL

Object Type	Description	DDL Statements
DATABASE	A database in Microsoft SQL Server 2000 consists of a collection of tables that contain data and other objects, such as views, indexes, stored procedures and triggers, defined to support activities performed with the data.	CREATE, ALTER, DROP

Table 3-2 Objects Managed by DDL (cont.)

Object Type	Description	DDL Statements
DEFAULT	When bound to a column or a user-defined data type, a default specifies a value to be inserted into the column to which the object is bound (or into all columns, in the case of a user-defined data type) when no value is explicitly supplied during an insert. Defaults, a backward compatibility feature, perform some of the same functions as default definitions created using the DEFAULT keyword of ALTER TABLE or CREATE TABLE statements. Default definitions are the preferred, standard way to restrict column data because the definition is stored with the table and is automatically dropped when the table is dropped. A default is beneficial, however, when the default is used multiple times for multiple columns.	CREATE, DROP
FUNCTION,CREATE, ALTER, DROPFUNCTION	Functions are subroutines made up of one or more Transact-SQL statements that can be used to encapsulate code for reuse. Microsoft SQL Server 2000 allows users to create their own user-defined functions with CREATE FUNCTION.	CREATE, ALTER, DROP
INDEX	Indexes are provided to allow the database program to find data in a table usually more quickly than by scanning the entire table.	CREATE, DROP
PROCEDURE	A stored procedure is a group of Transact-SQL statements compiled into a single execution plan and executed by name.	CREATE, ALTER, DROP
RULE	Rule is a backward compatibility feature that performs some of the same functions as CHECK constraints. CHECK constraints are the preferred, standard way to restrict the values in a column.	CREATE, DROP
SCHEMA	A conceptual object containing definitions of tables, views and permissions.	CREATE
STATISTICS	CREATE STATISTICS creates a named histogram and associated density groups (collections) over the supplied column or set of columns of a table. These statistics are used by the SQL Server 2000 query optimizer to choose the most efficient plan for performing DML operations. For more information see: http://msdn.microsoft.com/library/default.asp?URL=/library/techart/statquery.htm	CREATE, UPDATE, DROP STATS_DATE
TABLE	A two-dimensional object, consisting of rows and columns, used to store data in a relational database. Each table stores information about one of the types of objects modeled by the database.	CREATE, ALTER, DROP

Table 3-2 Objects Managed by DDL (cont.)

Object Type	Description	DDL Statements
TRIGGER	A trigger is a special type of stored procedure defined to be automatically executed whenever data in a specified table is modified (Insert, Update or Delete).	CREATE, ALTER, DROP
UNIQUE CLUSTERED INDEX	A unique clustered index is an index constrained to not allow duplicate values in which the logical order of the key values determines the physical order of the corresponding rows in a table. Microsoft SQL Server 2000 Enterprise or Developer edition also supports defining a unique clustered index on views. Such an index can permit significant query performance improvement especially on views that join many rows or aggregate large amounts of data.	CREATE
VIEW	A view is a named stored SELECT statement. A view is a database object that can be referenced the same way as a table in SQL statements. Views are defined using a SELECT statement and are analogous to an object that contains the result set of this statement.	CREATE, ALTER, DROP

Although the following information is not discussed in detail in this book, Table 3-3 lists Analysis Services objects that are managed by DDL statements.

Table 3-3 Analysis Services Managed by DDL

Object Type	CREATE	DDL Statements
ACTION	An action is an end user initiated operation upon a selected cube or portion of a cube. The operation can launch an application with the selected item as a parameter or retrieve information about the selected item.	CREATE, DROP
CACHE	A cache is a slice of cube data defined by sets of members.	CREATE
CELL CALCULATION	Calculated cells are cells whose value is calculated at run time using a Multidimensional Expressions (MDX) expression defined by the user with either CREATE CELL CALCULATION or using Enterprise Manager or Analysis Manager.	CREATE, DROP
CUBE	A cube is a set of data that is organized and summarized into a multidimensional structure defined by a set of dimensions and measures.	CREATE, ALTER, DROP

Table 3-3 Analysis Services Managed by DDL (cont.)

Object Type	CREATE	DDL Statements
MEMBER	A member is an item in a dimension representing one or more occurrences of data. A member can be either unique or nonunique. For example, 2002 and 2003 represent unique members in the year level of a time dimension. But January represents nonunique members in the month level because there can be more than one January in the time dimension if it contains data for more than one year.	CREATE, DROP
MINING MODEL	A mining model is an object that contains the definition of a data mining process and the results of the training activity. For example, a data mining model may specify the input, output, algorithm and other properties of the process and hold the information gathered during the training activity, such as a decision tree.	CREATE, DROP
SET	A named set is a set of dimension members (or an expression that defines a set) that is created to be used again. For example, by using a named set it is possible to define a set of dimension members that consists of the set of top ten stores by sales. This named set can then be used wherever the set of top ten stores is needed.	CREATE, DROP

3.1.3 sp_detach_db and sp_attach_db

These system-stored procedures allow you to detach a working database from a server, copy or move the files to a new server where you can attach the database for use.

These system stored procedures are introduced here as they relate to a CREATE DATABASE option of ATTACH. The two procedures given here are suggested if the database consists of less than 16 files.

3.1.3.1 sp_detach_db

The **sp_detach_db** procedure detaches a database from a server. It can optionally run UPDATE STATISTICS before detaching.

Syntax

```
sp_detach_db [ @dbname = ] 'dbname'
[ , [ @skipchecks = ] 'skipchecks' ]
```

Arguments

[@dbname =]

'*dbname*' is the name of the database to be detached.

[@skipchecks =] '*skipchecks*';

If *skipchecks* is **true**, UPDATE STATISTICS is skipped, if **false**, it's run. This is useful for databases that are to be moved to read-only media.

3.1.3.2 sp_attach_db

The **sp_attach_db** statement attaches a database to a server.

sp_attach_db should only be executed on databases that were previously detached from the database server using an explicit **sp_detach_db** operation. If more than 16 files must be specified, use CREATE DATABASE with the FOR ATTACH clause.

Syntax

```
sp_attach_db [ @dbname = ] 'dbname'
, [ @filename1 = ] 'filename_n' [ ,...16 ]
```

Arguments

[@dbname =]

'*dbname*' is the name of the database to be attached to the server.

[@filename1 =]

'*filename_n*' is the physical name, including path, of a database file.

There can be up to 16 file names specified. The parameter names start at **@filename1** and increments to **@filename16**. The file name list must include at least the primary file, which contains the system tables that point to other files in the database. The list must also include any files that were moved after the database was detached.

Example: Detach and reattach the pubs database.

SQL

```
EXEC  sp_detach_db   @dbname = N'pubs'

EXEC  sp_attach_db   @dbname = N'pubs'
,  @filename1   =   N'c:\Program   Files\Microsoft   SQL
Server\MSSQL\Data\pubs.mdf'
   -- put the string on single line
,  @filename2   =   N'c:\Program   Files\Microsoft   SQL
Server\MSSQL\Data\pubs_log.ldf' --put on single line
```

3.1.4 CREATE, ALTER, DROP DATABASE

A database in SQL Server 2000 consists of a collection of tables that contain data and other objects, such as views, indexes, stored procedures and triggers defined to support activities performed with the data.

3.1.4.1 CREATE DATABASE

The CREATE DATABASE command creates a new database and the files used to store the database.

Syntax

```
CREATE DATABASE database_name
[ ON
[ < filespec > [ ,...n ] ]
[ , < filegroup > [ ,...n ] ]
]
[ LOG ON { < filespec > [ ,...n ] } ]
[ COLLATE collation_name ]
[ FOR LOAD | FOR ATTACH ]


  < filespec > ::=
  [ PRIMARY ]
  ( [ NAME = logical_file_name , ]
  FILENAME = 'os_file_name'
  [ , SIZE = size ]
  [ , MAXSIZE = { max_size | UNLIMITED } ]
  [ , FILEGROWTH = growth_increment ] ) [ ,...n ]


  < filegroup > ::=
  FILEGROUP filegroup_name < filespec > [ ,...n ]
```

See CREATE DATABASE examples in "Database Layout for Performance and Restorability," page 588.

Arguments

database_name

database_name is the name of the new database. Database names must be unique within a server and conform to the rules for identifiers.

database_name can be a maximum of 128 characters, unless no logical name is specified for the log in which case the maximum is 123. If no logical log file name is specified, SQL Server generates a logical name by appending a suffix to *database_name*.

ON

The ON statement specifies that the disk files used to store the data portions of the database (data files) are defined explicitly. The keyword is followed by a comma-separated list of <filespec> items defining the data files for the primary filegroup. The list of files in the primary filegroup can be followed by an optional, comma-separated list of <filegroup> items defining user filegroups and their files.

n

The letter *n* indicates that multiple files can be specified for the new database.

LOG ON

The LOG ON statement specifies that the disk files used to store the database log (log files) are explicitly defined. The keyword is followed by a comma-separated list of <filespec> items defining the log files. If LOG ON is not specified, a single log file is automatically created with a system-generated name and a size that is 25 percent of the sum of the sizes of all the data files for the database.

FOR LOAD

This FOR LOAD clause is supported for compatibility with earlier versions of Microsoft SQL Server. The database is created with the **dbo use only** database option turned on, and the status is set to loading. This is not required in SQL Server version 7.0 because the RESTORE statement can recreate a database as part of the restore operation.

FOR ATTACH

FOR ATTACH specifies that a database is attached from an existing set of operating system files. There must be a <filespec> entry specifying the first primary file. The only other <filespec> entries needed are those for any files that have a different path from when the database was first created or last attached. A <filespec> entry must be specified for these files. The database attached must have been created using the same code page and sort order as SQL Server.

Use the **sp_attach_db** system-stored procedure (page 245) instead of using CREATE DATABASE FOR ATTACH directly. Use CREATE DATABASE FOR ATTACH only when you must specify more than 16 <filespec> items.

collation_name

collation_name specifies the default collation for the database. collation_name can be either a Windows collation name or an SQL collation name. If not specified, the database is assigned the default collation of the SQL Server instance.

For more information about the Windows and SQL collation names, see COLLATE.

PRIMARY

PRIMARY specifies that the associated <filespec> list defines the primary file. The primary filegroup contains all of the database system tables. It also contains all objects not assigned to user filegroups. The first <filespec> entry in the primary filegroup becomes the primary file, which is the file containing the logical start of the database and its system tables. A database can have only one primary file. If PRIMARY is not specified, the first file listed in the CREATE DATABASE statement becomes the primary file.

NAME

NAME specifies the logical name for the file defined by the <filespec>. The NAME parameter is not required when FOR ATTACH is specified.

logical_file_name

logical_file_name is used to reference the file in any Transact-SQL statements executed after the database is created.

FILENAME

FILENAME specifies the operating system file name for the file defined by the <filespec>.

'os_file_name'

'*os_file_name*' is the path and file name used by the operating system when it creates the physical file defined by the <filespec>. The path in *os_file_name* must specify a directory on an instance of SQL Server. *os_file_name* cannot specify a directory in a compressed file system. Files in a directory permit *autogrow* wherein the database engine increases the allocated space for the database when needed. See the FILEGROWTH specification below on this page.

If the file is created on a raw partition, *os_file_name* must specify only the drive letter of an existing raw partition. Only one file can be created on each raw partition. Files on raw partitions do not autogrow; therefore, the MAXSIZE and FILEGROWTH parameters are not needed when *os_file_name* specifies a raw partition.

SIZE

SIZE specifies the size of the file defined in the <filespec>. When a SIZE parameter is not supplied in the <filespec> for a primary file, SQL Server uses the size of the primary file in the **model** database. When a SIZE parameter is not specified in the <filespec> for a secondary or log file, SQL Server makes the file 1 MB.

size

In the lowercase, size is the initial size of the file, default in MB, defined in the <filespec>.

The kilobyte (KB), megabyte (MB), gigabyte (GB) or terabyte (TB) suffixes can be used. The default is MB. Specify a whole number with no decimal.

The minimum value for *size* is 512 KB.

If *size* is not specified, the default is 1 MB.

The size specified for the primary file must be at least as large as the primary file of the **model** database.

MAXSIZE

MAXSIZE specifies the maximum size to which the file defined in the <filespec> can grow.

max_size

In the lowercase, max_size is the maximum size to which the file defined in the <filespec> can grow. The kilobyte (KB), megabyte (MB), gigabyte (GB) or terabyte (TB) suffix can be used. The default is MB. Specify a whole number; do not include a decimal. If *max_size* is not specified, the file grows until the disk is full.

Note The Microsoft Windows NT S/B system log warns the SQL Server system administrator if a disk is almost full.

UNLIMITED

UNLIMITED specifies that the file defined in the <filespec> grows until the disk is full.

FILEGROWTH

FILEGROWTH specifies the growth increment of the file defined in the <filespec>. The FILEGROWTH setting for a file cannot exceed the MAXSIZE setting.

growth_increment

The amount of space added to the file each time new space is needed is indicated by growth_increment. The amount must be specified by a whole number with no decimal. A value of 0 indicates no growth. The value can be specified in MB, KB, GB, TB or percent (%). If a number is specified without an MB, KB or % suffix, the default is MB. If FILEGROWTH is not specified, the default value is 10 percent and the minimum value is 64 KB. The size specified is rounded to the nearest 64 KB.

3.1.4.2 ALTER DATABASE

ALTER DATABASE can be used to accomplish the following tasks.

- Add or remove files and filegroups from a database.
- Modify the attributes of files and filegroups, such as changing the name or size of a file. Change the database name, filegroup names and logical names of data and log files.
- Set database options (examples at "Server, Database and Session Settings," page 175). Database options were set in previous versions of Microsoft SQL Server with the **sp_dboption** stored procedure. SQL Server continues to support **sp_dboption** in this release but may not do so in the future. Use the **DATABASEPROPERTYEX** function to retrieve current settings for database options.

Syntax

```
ALTER DATABASE database
{ ADD FILE < filespec > [ ,...n ] [ TO FILEGROUP
filegroup_name ]
| ADD LOG FILE < filespec > [ ,...n ]
| REMOVE FILE logical_file_name
| ADD FILEGROUP filegroup_name
| REMOVE FILEGROUP filegroup_name
| MODIFY FILE < filespec >
| MODIFY NAME = new_dbname
| MODIFY FILEGROUP filegroup_name
{filegroup_property | NAME = new_filegroup_name }
/ SET < optionspec > [ ,...n ] [ WITH < termination > ]
| COLLATE < collation_name >
}


< filespec > ::=
    ( NAME = logical_file_name
        [ , NEWNAME = new_logical_name ]
        [ , FILENAME = 'os_file_name' ]
        [ , SIZE = size ]
        [ , MAXSIZE = { max_size | UNLIMITED } ]
        [ , FILEGROWTH = growth_increment ] )
```

```
< filegroup_property > ::= READONLY | READWRITE | DEFAULT

< optionspec > ::=
    < state_option >
    | < cursor_option >
    | < auto_option >
    | < sql_option >
    | < recovery_option >

< state_option > ::=
    { SINGLE_USER | RESTRICTED_USER | MULTI_USER }
    | { OFFLINE | ONLINE }
    | { READ_ONLY | READ_WRITE }

< cursor_option > ::=
     CURSOR_CLOSE_ON_COMMIT { ON | OFF }
     | CURSOR_DEFAULT { LOCAL | GLOBAL }

< auto_option > ::=
     AUTO_CLOSE { ON | OFF }
     | AUTO_CREATE_STATISTICS { ON | OFF }
     | AUTO_SHRINK { ON | OFF }
     | AUTO_UPDATE_STATISTICS { ON | OFF }

< sql_option > ::=
     ANSI_NULL_DEFAULT { ON | OFF }
     | ANSI_NULLS { ON | OFF }
     | ANSI_PADDING { ON | OFF }
     | ANSI_WARNINGS { ON | OFF }
     | ARITHABORT { ON | OFF }
     | CONCAT_NULL_YIELDS_NULL { ON | OFF }
     | NUMERIC_ROUNDABORT { ON | OFF }
     | QUOTED_IDENTIFIER { ON | OFF }
     | RECURSIVE_TRIGGERS { ON | OFF }

< recovery_option > ::=
     RECOVERY { FULL | BULK_LOGGED | SIMPLE }
     | TORN_PAGE_DETECTION { ON | OFF }

< termination > ::=
     ROLLBACK AFTER integer [ SECONDS ]
     | ROLLBACK IMMEDIATE
     | NO_WAIT
```

See ALTER DATABASE settings examples at "Server, Database and Session Settings," page 174.

See Books Online (Index: ALTER DATABASE) for examples that add and remove data and log files to/from a database, add a new filegroup to a database and make the primary filegroup the default.

Examples that change database access settings (formerly used **sp_dboption**) are included in the next section.

3.1.4.3 DROP DATABASE

DROP DATABASE removes all database objects and data within the specified database.

Syntax

DROP DATABASE *database_name* [,...*n*]

CREATE, ALTER, DROP DATABASE Examples

Example: Simplest form to create a database "mydb1" taking all default values.

```
SQL CREATE DATABASE mydb1
```

The defaults include creating data file and log file on the same disk, which is not good for either performance or restorability.

Example:

```
SQL DROP DATABASE mydb1
```

3.1.5 sp_bindefault and sp_unbindefault

These system-stored procedures are closely associated with CREATE DEFAULT. They allow you to bind (and remove) a default value to a user-defined data type or a table column (DEFAULT constraint is preferred for a table column).

3.1.5.1 sp_bindefault

sp_bindefault binds a default to a column or to a user-defined data type.

Syntax

```
sp_bindefault [ @defname = ] 'default' , [ @objname = ] 'object_name'
[ , [ @futureonly = ] { 'futureonly' | NULL } ]
```

Arguments

[@defname =] 'default'

This is the name of the default created by the CREATE DEFAULT statement. The term *default* is **nvarchar(776)**, with no default.

[@objname =] 'object_name'

[**@objname** =] '*object_name*' is the name of table and column or the user-defined data type to which the default is to be bound. If *object_name* is not of the form *table.column*, it is assumed to be a user-defined data type.

Existing columns of the user-defined data type inherit *default* unless a default has been bound directly to the column.

A default cannot be bound to a **timestamp** or IDENTITY column or to a column that already has a DEFAULT constraint.

Note: *object_name* can contain the [and] characters as delimited identifier characters.

[@futureonly =] { 'futureonly' | NULL }

[**@futureonly** =] { 'futureonly' | NULL } is used only with a user-defined data type. When set to 'futureonly' it prevents existing columns of that data type from inheriting the new default.

If NULL or missing, the new default is bound to any columns of the user-defined data type that currently have no default bound directly to the column.

3.1.5.2 sp_unbindefault

sp_unbindefault removes a default from a column or user-defined data type in the current database.

```
sp_unbindefault [@objname =] 'object_name' [, [@futureonly =]
  {'futureonly' | NULL}]
```

Arguments

[**@objname** =] '*object_name*'

[**@objname** =] '*object_name*' is the name of the table.column or user-defined data type from which to unbind the default.

When unbinding a default from a user-defined data type, any columns of that data type that have the same default are also unbound. Columns of that data type with defaults bound directly to them are unaffected.

[**@futureonly** =] { 'futureonly' | NULL }

When 'futureonly', existing columns of the user-defined data type don't lose the default. If NULL or missing, columns of the user-defined data type do lose the default.

3.1.6 CREATE, DROP DEFAULT

A *default* object is a constant expression that can be created by a user in a database. When bound to a column or user-defined data type, the default object specifies the default value for that column on INSERT statements. Use sp_bindefault to bind a default object to a column or to a user-defined data type.

CREATE DEFAULT statements must appear alone in a TRANSACT-SQL batch.

Remember that the default object discussed in this section is for backward compatibility; using the DEFAULT keyword in CREATE TABLE or ALTER TABLE is preferred.

3.1.6.1 CREATE DEFAULT

Syntax

```
CREATE DEFAULT default
    AS constant_expression
```

Arguments

constant_expression

This is an expression that contains only constant, built-in function, or mathematical expressions.

3.1.6.2 DROP DEFAULT Syntax

Syntax

```
DROP DEFAULT { default } [ ,...n ]
```

CREATE, DROP DEFAULT Examples

Create two default objects in the **pubs** database, one for a VARCHAR and one for an INT column and bind them to the **dept** and **telnum** columns of the **titles** table.

Example:

SQL

```
CREATE TABLE table1 ( dept VARCHAR(20), telnum INT )
go
CREATE DEFAULT deptdft  AS  'Unassigned'
go
EXEC sp_bindefault   deptdft , 'table1.dept'
go
CREATE DEFAULT telnumdft  AS  4000
                   -- Receptionist telnum
go

EXEC sp_bindefault   telnumdft , 'table1.telnum'

INSERT INTO table1 DEFAULT VALUES
SELECT  * FROM table1
```

SQL (cont.)

Result

```
dept            telnum
----------      ----------
Unassigned      4000
```

Example: Attempt to DROP DEFAULT before sp_unbindefault and then do it right.

SQL
```
DROP DEFAULT deptdft
```

Result

```
Server: Msg 3716, Level 16, State 3, Line 1
The default 'deptdft' cannot be dropped because it is bound to one or more column.
```

SQL
```
EXEC sp_unbindefault   'table1.dept'
```

Result

```
(1 row(s) affected)
Default unbound from table column.
```

SQL
```
DROP DEFAULT deptdft
```

3.1.7 CREATE, ALTER, DROP FUNCTION

Functions are subroutines that return a value. They are ruled by the following parameters.

- SQL Server 2000 allows users to create their own user-defined functions with CREATE FUNCTION.
- Functions are objects that belong to the database in which they were created.
- Scalar-valued functions may be invoked where scalar expressions are used.
- Invocation of a scalar-valued function requires at minimum the two-part name.
- Users other than the owner and dbo do not have EXECUTE permissions unless explicitly granted EXECUTE permissions on the specific function.

By convention, functions should change nothing in the database (they should have no side effects), they just look data up and perform calculations as needed and return a value. A stored procedure, on the other hand, may change something in the database and may pass out one or more values. The procedure writer is obliged to document its exact effect.

3.1.7.1 CREATE Function Syntax

Scalar Functions return a single object of any scalar database data type.

Syntax

```
CREATE FUNCTION [ owner_name. ] function_name
( [ { @parameter_name [AS] scalar_parameter_data_type [ = default ] }
  [ ,...n ] ] )
RETURNS scalar_return_data_type
[ WITH { ENCRYPTION | SCHEMABINDING }   [ [,] ...n] ]
[ AS ]
BEGIN
   function_body
   RETURN scalar_expression
END
```

Inline Table-Valued Functions contain only a single SELECT statement whose result set is the return table value. It is similar to a view but the function can have input parameters.

Syntax

```
CREATE FUNCTION [ owner_name. ] function_name
( [ { @parameter_name [AS] scalar_parameter_data_type [ = default ] }
  [ ,...n ] ] )
RETURNS TABLE
[ WITH { ENCRYPTION | SCHEMABINDING }   [ [,] ...n ] ]
[ AS ]
RETURN [ ( ] select-stmt [ ) ]
```

Multi-Statement Table-Valued Functions contain any number of statements including a RETURN statement returning a single table variable.

Syntax

```
CREATE FUNCTION [ owner_name. ] function_name
( [ { @parameter_name [AS] scalar_parameter_data_type [ = default ] }
  [ ,...n ] ] )


RETURNS @return_variable TABLE   ( { column_definition
  | table_constraint } [ ,...n ] )
  -- Define TABLE var
```

```
[ WITH { ENCRYPTION | SCHEMABINDING }   [ [,] ...n ] ]
[ AS ]
BEGIN
  function_body
  RETURN
END
```

Arguments

ENCRYPTION

ENCRYPTION indicates that SQL Server encrypts the definition of the CREATE FUNCTION statement in the system tables. Using ENCRYPTION prevents the function from being published in SQL Server replication.

SCHEMABINDING

SCHEMABINDING specifies that the function is bound to the database objects that it references. If a function is created with the SCHEMABINDING option, then the database objects that the function references cannot be altered or dropped. These objects can be altered or dropped only if the function declaring SCHEMABINDING is dropped or is altered to remove SCHEMABINDING.

3.1.7.2 ALTER FUNCTION Syntax

Scalar Functions

Syntax

```
ALTER FUNCTION [ owner_name. ] function_name
( [ { @parameter_name scalar_parameter_data_type [ = default ] } [ ,...n ] ] )
RETURNS scalar_return_data_type
[ WITH < function_option> [,...n] ]
[ AS ]
BEGIN
function_body
RETURN scalar_expression
END
```

Inline Table-Valued Functions

Syntax

```
ALTER FUNCTION [ owner_name. ] function_name
( [ { @parameter_name scalar_parameter_data_type [ = default ] } [ ,...n ] ] )
RETURNS TABLE
[ WITH  { ENCRYPTION | SCHEMABINDING } [ ,...n ] ]
[ AS ]
RETURN [ ( ] select-stmt [ ) ]
```

Multi-Statement Table-Valued Functions

Syntax

```
ALTER FUNCTION [ owner_name. ] function_name
( [ { @parameter_name scalar_parameter_data_type [ = default ] } [ ,...n ] ] )
RETURNS @return_variable TABLE   ( { column_definition | table_constraint } [
,...n ] )
[ WITH  { ENCRYPTION | SCHEMABINDING } [ ,...n ] ]
[ AS ]
BEGIN
function_body
RETURN
END
```

3.1.7.3 DROP FUNCTION Syntax

Syntax

```
DROP FUNCTION { [ owner_name . ] function_name } [ ,...n ]
```

CREATE, ALTER, DROP FUNCTION Examples

Example: CREATE FUNCTION for ScalarFunction

Write a function in the pubs database which returns the average price of all books in the titles table for a given pub_id.

SQL

```
USE pubs
go

  -- Find avg price of all titles for publisher
  -- identified by pub_id parameter
CREATE FUNCTION avgpriceForPubid
     (   @pub_id          INT  )
RETURNS INTEGER
AS
BEGIN
  DECLARE @avg INT
  SELECT @avg = AVG(price)  FROM titles  WHERE
pub_id =  @pub_id
  IF ( @avg IS NULL )
    SET @avg = -99
  RETURN @avg
END
```

Example: Invoking a User-Defined Function

Scalar-valued functions may be invoked where scalar expressions are used. Invocation of a scalar-valued function requires the two-part name at minimum.

SQL

```
PRINT  dbo.avgpriceForPubid( 0736 )
```

Result 10

SQL

```
CREATE FUNCTION hello ()  RETURNS VARCHAR(10) AS BEGIN RETURN 'Hi' END
PRINT  dbo.hello()
```

Result Hi

Example: CREATE FUNCTION—A More Involved User Scalar Function

The **kids** table in Figure 3-1 forms a tree structure with 0 as the root.

Problem: For each `kid` in the **kids** table, list the highest level ancestor below 0 (root) unless 0 is the direct parent of the `kid` in which case we are to return 0.

An ancestor of node is a node higher in the tree in the same lineage from root. The root is the highest ancestor for all nodes, but we want the highest ancestor below root, which in this tree is either 1 or 7. If the given node has root (0) as its direct parent, then the returned highest ancestor should be 0.

kids

kid	dad
1	0
2	1
3	1
4	1
5	3
6	3
7	0
8	7
9	8

Kids Family Tree

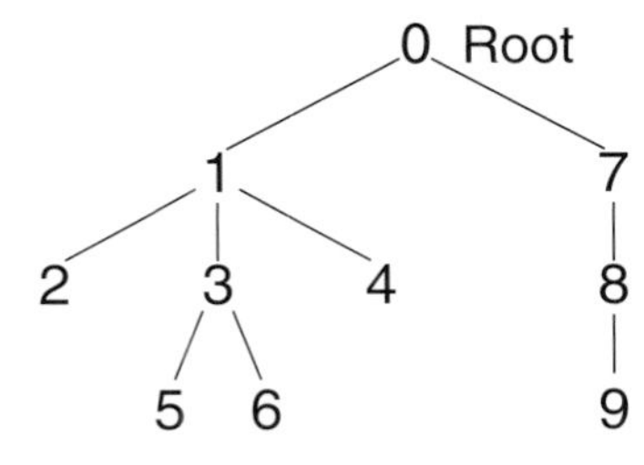

Desired Result:

Kid	Highest_Ancestor
1	0
2	1
3	1
4	1
5	1
6	1
7	0
8	7
9	7

Figure 3-1 A user scalar function.

Solution: We'll write a function called `fn_highestancestor`, which for each kid

returns 0 if 0 is the direct parent and otherwise

returns the highest ancestor below 0, that is, a direct kid of 0. For our data this is 1 or 7. This is a recursive function in that there are times where it calls itself.

SQL

```
CREATE FUNCTION fn_highestancestor
  ( @kid INT )
RETURNS INT
AS
BEGIN
    -- DECLARE @kid INT; -- Uncomment to debug
    -- SET  @kid = 5;    -- Uncomment to debug
    DECLARE @anc INT;
    SET @anc = (SELECT dad FROM kids WHERE kid = @kid);
    -- PRINT @anc          -- Uncomment to debug
    IF @anc <> 0
    WHILE @anc NOT IN ( SELECT kid FROM kids WHERE dad = 0 )
    BEGIN
      SET @anc =
      (SELECT dad FROM kids WHERE kid = @anc );
    END
    -- PRINT @anc          -- Uncomment to debug
    RETURN @anc;
END
go
SELECT       Kid,               dbo.fn_highestancestor(kid)
Highest_Ancestor
FROM kids;
```

Result

Kid	Highest_Ancestor
--------	----------------
1	0
2	1
3	1
4	1
5	1
6	1
7	0
8	7
9	7

Example: CREATE FUNCTION for Inline Table-Valued Function—An inline table-valued function has similar functionality to a view except that the function can take a parameter as in this example.

We want to list the number of books in the titles table for each pub_id.

SQL

```
USE pubs
go

CREATE FUNCTION TitleCountByType (
    @type char(12)   )
RETURNS TABLE
AS
RETURN (SELECT pub_id , count(*) count
       FROM titles  WHERE type = @type GROUP BY pub_id )
```

Invoking the example Inline table-valued defined function

SQL `SELECT * FROM dbo.TitleCountByType( 'business' )`

Result

pub_id	count
------	----------
0736	1
1389	3

SQL

```
SELECT * FROM dbo.TitleCountByType( 'business' )
WHERE count > 2
```

Result

```
pub_id          count
------          ----------
1389            3
```

Example: CREATE FUNCTION for Multi-Statement Table-Valued Function—This example is an embellished version of one in Books Online. The requirement is to list every empname who reports to a given person (by staffid) either directly or indirectly.

We are given Table 3-4 that represents a hierarchical relationship:

Table 3-4 Staff

StaffId	empname	mgrid	title
0	CEO	0	CEO
1	Boss1	0	Boss1
2	Boss2	0	Boss2
3	Mgr	1	Mgr
4	Bob	3	Worker
5	Chuck	3	Worker

SQL

```
CREATE TABLE staff (
    StaffId                         DEC(5) PRIMARY KEY
,    empname       NVARCHAR(50)
,    mgrid         DEC(5)           REFERENCES staff(StaffId)
,    title         NVARCHAR(30)
);
```

Problem: Given an ID (StaffId), return a table containing all StaffId's who report to this person either directly or indirectly.

Solution: Since this logic is not expressible in a single query it is a good candidate for implementing as a user-defined function.

Example: Create sample Multi-Statement Table-Valued User Function

SQL

```
CREATE FUNCTION fn_FindReports ( @InStaffId nchar(5))
RETURNS @retFindReports TABLE (
   StaffId          NCHAR(5)            PRIMARY KEY,
   empname          NVARCHAR(50)        NOT NULL,
   mgrid            NCHAR(5),
   title            NVARCHAR(30))
    /* Returns result set with all the staff who report to
        given employee directly or indirectly.   */
AS
BEGIN
    DECLARE @RowsAdded int
    DECLARE @reports TABLE ( -- table variable to hold
                                accumulated results
    StaffId          DEC(5)              PRIMARY KEY,
    empname          NVARCHAR(50)        NOT NULL,
    mgrid            DEC(5),
    title            NVARCHAR(30),
    processed        TINYINT             DEFAULT 0
      -- "processed" is an added status column
   )
     /* fill @reports table variable with direct
        reports of the given employee */
INSERT INTO @reports
      SELECT StaffId, empname, mgrid, title, 0
      FROM staff
      WHERE mgrid = @InStaffId;
    SET @RowsAdded = @@rowcount
    WHILE @RowsAdded > 0 -- Iterate until no entry in @reports
          has any reporting emp in staff table
    BEGIN
     /* Mark processed=1 for emp records whose direct reports
        are to be found in this iteration.    */
      UPDATE @report  SET processed = 1  WHERE processed = 0
-- Insert staff who report to staff marked 1.
```

SQL (cont.)

```
      INSERT INTO @reports
         SELECT e.StaffId, e.empname, e.mgrid, e.title, 0
         FROM staff e, @reports r
         WHERE e.mgrid=r.StaffId
            and e.mgrid <> e.StaffId    and r.processed = 1
            -- Increment @RowsAdded by number inserted
SET @RowsAdded = @@rowcount
         /*Mark processed = 2 for staff records whose direct reports were
          found in this iteration.*/
         UPDATE @reports       SET processed = 2 WHERE processed = 1
      END  -- WHILE

      INSERT INTO @retFindReports -- copy the required columns to the
                                    function result
         SELECT StaffId, empname, mgrid, title
         FROM @reports
   RETURN
END
GO
```

SQL

```
SELECT *
FROM fn_FindReports(1)
```

Result

StaffId	empname	mgrid	title
-----	---------------	-----	------------
3	Mgr	1	Mgr
4	Bob	3	Worker
5	Chuck	3	Worker

Invoking the Example User Function:

SQL

```
SELECT *
FROM fn_FindReports(1)
WHERE  title  =  'Worker'
```

Result

StaffId	empname	mgrid	title
-----	---------------	-----	------------
4	Bob	3	Worker
5	Chuck	3	Worker

3.1.8 Query Analyzer Debugger Functions (UDF)

The Query Analyzer Debugger in SQL Server 2000 was designed to work with stored procedures. So to debug User Defined Functions (UDF), you need to create at least a simple stored procedure that calls the function, and then all of the function code becomes accessible, even in recursive function calls. See page 283 for complete discussion of the Query Analyzer Stored Procedure Debugger. It is mentioned here only as it pertains to the special measures needed to debug functions.

Do not run the Query Analyzer on production machines; critical resources may become locked.

3.1.8.1 No Debugger for UDFs

The Query Analyzer cannot directly debug a User Defined Function. But you may create a Stored Procedure (SP) to call the UDF as shown in the following code. Then you can call up the Query Analyzer Stored Procedure Debugger on uspTest to debug the UDF.

```
CREATE PROC uspTest
   ( @p_kid INT )
AS
BEGIN
    PRINT
dbo.fn_highestancestor(
@p_kid )
END
```

See Figure 3-2.

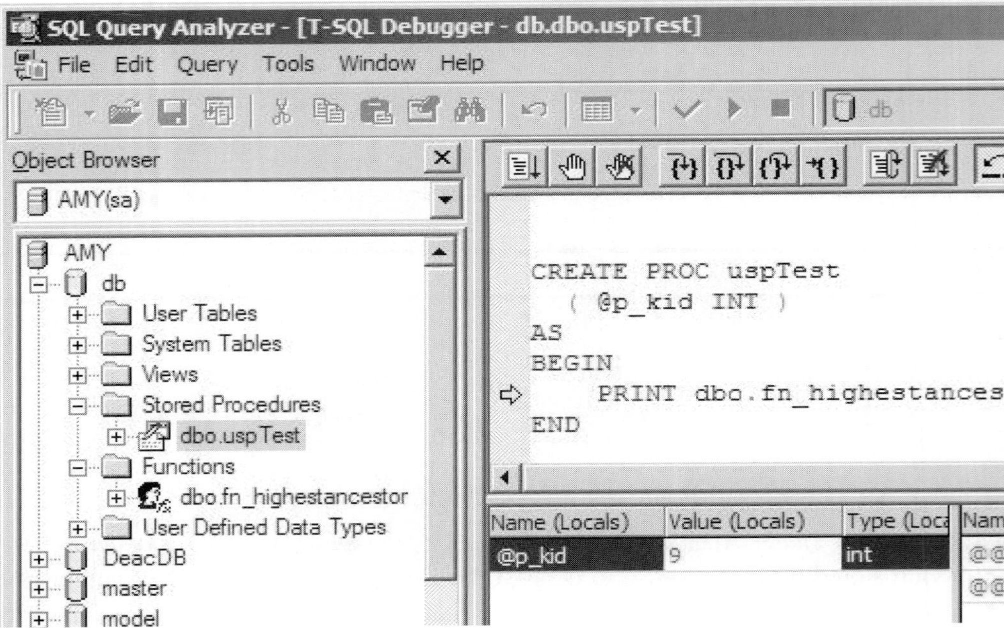

Figure 3-2 The Debugger window in Query Analyzer.

Give the parameter **@p_kid** a value of 9.
The dad of 9 is 8 whose dad is 7, which is the answer.

Click on "Step Into (F11)" once.

The Callstack on the right side now lists

fn_highestancestor -- at the top of stack (current context), and below that uspTest -- which was the outer call

On the left side notice the local variable @ancestor has a value of NULL.

The yellow arrow points to the next line which will be executed,
SET @ancestor = (SELECT dad FROM kids WHERE kid = @kid);

Click on "Step Into (F11)" once which will execute that line and move to the next.

On the left side notice the local variable @ancestor now has a value of 8.

The yellow arrow points to: IF @ancestor <> 0 as shown in Figure 3-3.

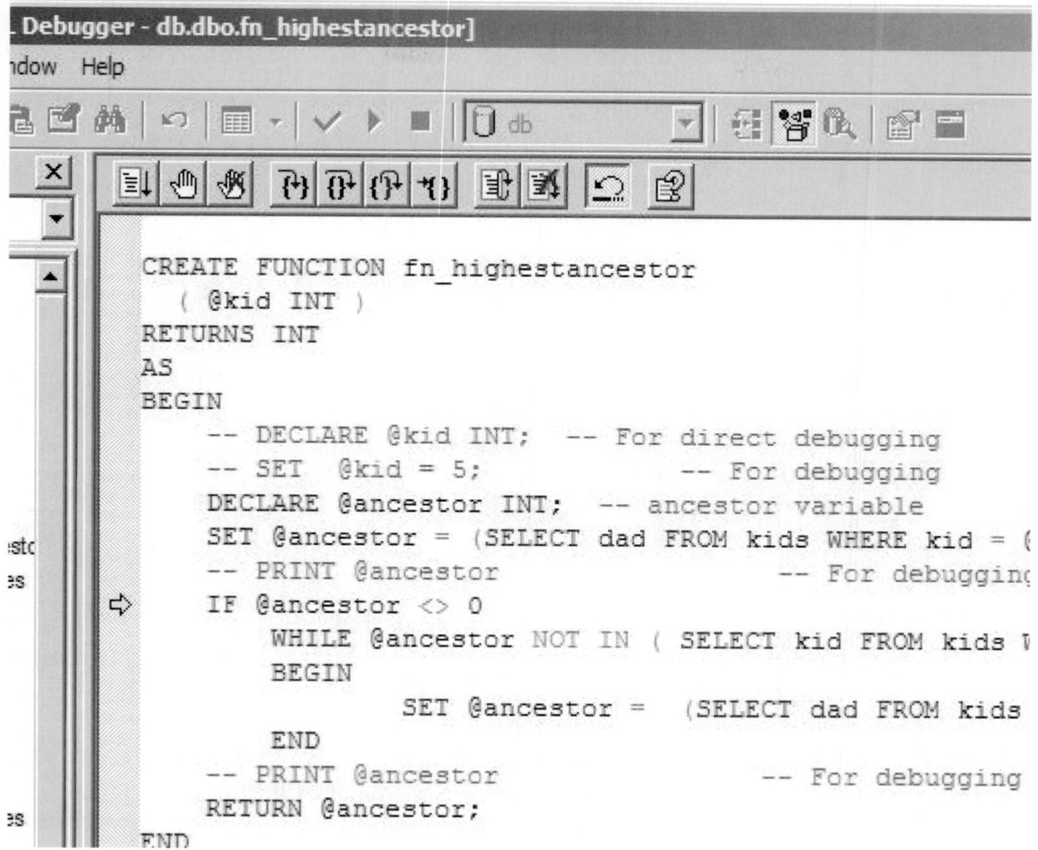

Figure 3-3 The yellow arrow points to the next statement to be executed.

Click on "Step Into (F11)" several more times or "Go (F5)" to run to completion.

3.1.9 CREATE, DROP INDEX

Indexes may allow the database program to find data in a table more quickly than by scanning the entire table. An index is an ordered list of values of specified columns (often called the "index keyindex key") of a data table and the row location in that table where the index key value is found.

A database index is like a book index that contains pairs of values, such as the index key value and the location of the value in the book or table, for example, apple, 234.

The primary key of a table is automatically indexed, by default with a clustered index (see definition below by keyword CLUSTERED). A UNIQUE constraint also automatically causes an index to be created. All other columns (or sets of columns) are only indexed by a CREATE INDEX statement. SQL Server 2000 Enterprise and Developer Editions permit Indexes on Views. See page 364.

3.1.9.1 CREATE INDEX Syntax

Syntax

```
CREATE [ UNIQUE ] [ CLUSTERED | NONCLUSTERED ] INDEX index_name
ON { table | view } ( column [ ASC | DESC ] [ ,...n ] )
[ WITH < index_option > [ ,...n] ]
[ ON filegroup ]

  < index_option > :: =
  {
      PAD_INDEX | FILLFACTOR = fillfactor | DROP_EXISTING |
      STATISTICS_NORECOMPUTE | SORT_IN_TEMPDB
  }
```

Arguments

UNIQUE

The UNIQUE parameter creates a unique index, one in which no two rows are permitted to have the same index key value, on a table or view. A clustered index on a view must be UNIQUE.

By default, when a UNIQUE constraint on a set of columns is a part of a CREATE TABLE or ALTER TABLE statement, SQL Server automatically creates a unique index on that set of columns.

CLUSTERED

CLUSTERED specifies the index to be a clustered index, with a maximum of one per data table.

A clustered index causes the data table itself to be sorted by the index key. The data table actually becomes part of the index for a clustered index.

When a CREATE TABLE or ALTER TABLE is executed, specifying a PRIMARY KEY, SQL Server by default automatically creates a clustered index on the PRIMARY KEY unless NONCLUSTERED is specified (see example below).

NONCLUSTERED

NONCLUSTERED specifies the index to be a nonclustered index, up to 249 per data table.

FILLFACTOR

FILLFACTOR is used by SQL Server to determine what percentage to fill leaf pages when it creates an index.

This value is used only at index creation and only for leaf pages of the index as follows:

- 1 to 100 specifies the percentage the leaf page is to be filled. E.g., 70 leaves 30% of the leaf empty for new inserts before the leaf page must be split.
- 0 (default) means that the leaf pages are completely filled. So 0 and 100 have the same effect.

Unless PAD_INDEX is specified (see below), SQL Server ignores FILLFACTOR for intermediate pages and almost fills them up, leaving space for one more entry.

After the index is created, all pages are allowed to fill to 100% such that the next new row will cause a page split. A page split occurs when a new entry is to be inserted into a full page. The procedure is that the existing full page of entries plus the one new entry are placed in memory, sorted and then split into two groups with one half put back into the original page and the other half put into a new page. A page split takes some time to execute and many of them will degrade performance. Adjusting FILLFACTOR to a value smaller than 100 allows you to postpone page splits.

FILLFACTOR Trade-Offs—A small FILLFACTOR causes some more disk space to be used and some more time to access the index, but it can accommodate more inserts before requiring a more costly page split.
Suggestions:

- 100 or 0 (or no FILLFACTOR, which defaults to 0) causes leaf pages to be 100% filled and is appropriate if no new index rows are expected, as in a read-only table.
- 60–80 works well with typical OLTP tables expecting moderate number of inserts.
- 10–30 or so would be appropriate if the table is expected to grow considerably.

PAD_INDEX

PAD_INDEX specifies that the FILLFACTOR value will not only be used for the leaf pages but also for intermediate (internal) pages of the index. By default, internal pages all have enough space left for one more row unless this option is specified. PAD_INDEX is only considered if FILLFACTOR is specified.

DROP_EXISTING

DROP_EXISTING specifies that the existing index of the specified name should be dropped and rebuilt. An index must exist.

STATISTICS_NORECOMPUTE

STATISTICS_NORECOMPUTE specifies that out-of-date index statistics are not to be automatically recomputed by SQL Server. This should be used only by experienced administrators as it can degrade performance.

SORT_IN_TEMPDB

SORT_IN_TEMPDB specifies that the intermediate sort results used to build the index will be stored in the tempdb database. This increases the amount of disk space used but may speed up index creation if tempdb is on a separate disk.

3.1.9.2 DROP INDEX Syntax

Syntax

```
DROP INDEX 'table.index | view.index' [ ,...n ]
```

CREATE INDEX, DROP INDEX Examples

Example: Create a **customers** table with a PRIMARY KEY whose clustered index has fillfactor given.Then create an index on the name column with a fillfactor and put it on a separate disk to improve performance.

SQL

```
/* On page 512 is the CREATE DATABASE bankdb
   statements that creates a filegroup for indexes
   called fg_bankdb_indexes which is used here. */
USE bankdb
go
```

We will first create a **customers** table.

SQL

```
CREATE TABLE customers ( -- The table goes onto the default disk
  id            DEC(4) ,
  name          VARCHAR(10) ,
  CONSTRAINT pk_customers PRIMARY KEY   -- We put the Primary Key clustered
                                           index
   CLUSTERED ( id ) -- on the Primary (default) disk since it's the data table
   WITH FILLFACTOR = 70 -- If NONCLUSTERED, we could specify
                           "ON fg_bankdb_indexes"
);
```

Now create an index on the **name** column of the **customers** table and put it on the specified **fg_bankdb_indexes** filegroup. Fill the leaf pages to only 70% at index creation.

SQL

```
CREATE INDEX ind_customers_name
ON customers ( name )   -- Add separate index
WITH FILLFACTOR = 70
ON fg_bankdb_indexes;
```

That was fun. If we want to get rid of the index, we can drop it.

SQL

```
DROP INDEX customers.ind_customers_name
-- table name and index name are required
-- for DROP INDEX
DROP TABLE customers
-- DROP TABLE also drops all indexes on the table
```

Example: Same, but this time fill the **name** column index leaf pages *and* intermediate pages to 70%.

SQL

```
CREATE TABLE customers ( -- The table goes onto the
default disk
id                  DEC(4) ,
name                VARCHAR(10) ,
/* Next we put the Primary Key clustered index on the
    Primary (default) disk since it is the data table. */
CONSTRAINT pk_customers PRIMARY KEY
  CLUSTERED ( id )      WITH FILLFACTOR = 70
    /* If NONCLUSTERED, we would specify
       "ON fg_bankdb_indexes" to improve performance. */
);
```

Again create an index on the **name** column of **customers** table, but fill the leaf pages and intermediate pages to only 70% at index creation.

SQL

```
CREATE INDEX ind_customers_name
ON customers ( name )    -- Add separate index
WITH PAD_INDEX,  FILLFACTOR =  70
ON fg_bankdb_indexes;
```

Note: The PAD_INDEX keyword used in the CREATE INDEX statement is what caused both leaf and intermediate pages to be only 70% filled on index creation. But SQL Server does not allow the PAD_INDEX keyword to be used in the CREATE TABLE statement to pad the PRIMARY KEY clustered index.

SQL

```
DROP TABLE customers
  -- DROP TABLE also drops all indexes on the table
```

Example: See CREATE INDEX and DROP INDEX examples in Section 5.6, page 588.

3.1.10 CREATE, ALTER, DROP PROCEDURE

A stored procedure is a group of Transact-SQL statements compiled into a single execution plan and executed by name. Authorized users may create and manage their own stored procedures using the CREATE, ALTER and DROP PROCEDURE.

A stored procedure may have input parameters, may change something in the database and may pass out one or more values. The writer is obliged to document its exact effect.

3.1.10.1 Stored Procedures

A stored procedure is a named precompiled collection of Transact-SQL statements stored under its name and processed as a unit by calling it by name.

A stored procedure is a single unit of Transact-SQL code that is

- A parsed, optimized and compiled image stored in the database where created
- Executed on demand by invoking its name
- Recompiled when underlying statistics change

A stored procedure is much like a utility program written in Transact-SQL. Since a stored procedure has already been parsed, optimized and compiled, it is ready to execute. This makes it faster and particularly useful for a set of code that is executed many times during high production activity.

3.1.10.2 Stored Procedure Types

Stored procedures may be provided by SQL Server (p. 168) or written by the user. The four you should know about are as follows.

User Stored Procedures Users may create their own stored procedures with "Create Procedure" statement. They may be named as any legal identifier, but it is best to avoid starting with sp_ or xp_. Some prefer to use start names with "usp_" standing for user stored procedure.

User stored procedures are associated with a single database and may be either permanent (most common), local temporary or global temporary.

Permanent Stored Procedures Permanent stored procedures are persistent within the database and may be accessed by anyone with requisite privilege.

Local Temporary Stored Procedures Local temporary stored procedures are visible only in the current session. Names of local temporary stored procedures must start with a single number sign (#localproc) and cannot exceed 128 characters.

Global Temporary Stored Procedures Global temporary stored procedures are visible to all sessions.

Global temporary stored procedures' names must start with a double number sign (##globalproc) and cannot exceed 128 characters.

Stored procedure complete names, including # or ##, cannot exceed 128 characters.

Temporary stored procedures are automatically dropped when they go out of scope, unless explicitly dropped using DROP PROCEDURE.

3.1.10.3 CREATE PROCEDURE

Syntax

```
CREATE PROC [ EDURE ] procedure_name [ ; number ]
    [ { @parameter   data_type  }   [ VARYING ] [ =
default ] [ OUTPUT ]   ] [ ,...n ]

[ WITH
{ RECOMPILE | ENCRYPTION | RECOMPILE , ENCRYPTION } ]
```

```
[ FOR REPLICATION ]

AS
    sql_statement [ ...n ]
```

Arguments

procedure_name

procedure_name user-defined identifier must be unique within the database. Permanent stored procedure names follow the rules for identifiers (but must not start with a number sign, #). Local temporary procedures can be created by preceding the name with a number sign (#procedure_name). Global temporary procedures are created using a double number sign (##procedure_name). The complete name, including # or ##, cannot exceed 128 characters.

;number

An optional integer is used to group procedures of the same name so they can be dropped together with a single DROP PROCEDURE statement. So procedures named **myproc**;1, **myproc**;2, ... may all be dropped with the single statement DROP PROCEDURE **myproc**. This practice can cause confusion and should be used with caution.

@parameter

The name of the parameter is @ symbol followed by a user-defined identifier. A stored procedure can have a maximum of 2,100 parameters. The parameter list may optionally be placed inside parentheses: (*@param datatype* **etc. [, ...*n*]**)

data_type

Both input and output parameters may be any SQL datatype including **text, ntext** or **image**, though **cursor** datatype may be output only and must have the VARYING keyword specified.

Both input and output parameters may be any SQL datatype including **text**, **ntext** or **image**.

The **cursor** datatype may be output only and must have the VARYING keyword specified. A procedure with **cursor** datatype can be called only from Transact-SQL batches, stored procedures, or triggers with the **cursor** OUTPUT variable assigned to a Transact-SQL local **cursor** variable.

Such a procedure can not be called from a database API (such as OLE DB and ODBC).

VARYING

VARYING applies only to cursor OUTPUT parameters. It specifies that the result set is constructed dynamically by the stored procedure and its contents can vary.

default

This is a default value for the parameter.

The default must be a constant or it can be NULL. It can include wildcard characters (%, _, [], and [^]) if the procedure uses the parameter with the LIKE keyword.

If a default is specified, the procedure can be executed without passing a value for that parameter.

OUTPUT

OUTPUT indicates that the parameter is an output or return parameter of the specified datatype.

Output parameters and return codes must return their values into a variable (see examples for syntax). If the OUTPUT keyword is missing the parameter defaults to being an input parameter. An input parameter may be given a value in the invocation and may be provided a *default* value for use when the invocation does not specify a value.

RECOMPILE

RECOMPILE tells SQL Server to recompile each time its run rather than storing a compiled version.

According to Books Online, "Use the RECOMPILE option when using atypical or temporary values without overriding the execution plan cached in memory." This option cannot be used in the same statement as FOR REPLICATION.

ENCRYPTION

This option encrypts the syscomments table entry which contains the text (source code) of the procedure. This precludes the procedure from being published in replication. This option is usually used only by software vendors.

FOR REPLICATION

A stored procedure created with FOR REPLICATION is used as a stored procedure filter and is only executed during replication. It cannot be executed on the subscriber.

This option cannot be used with the WITH RECOMPILE option.

sql_statement

sql_statement is any number and type of Transact-SQL statements to be included in the procedure terminated by the end of the batch such as keyword "go." The list of statements may include one or more RETURN statements (if missing, the return value is 0).

RETURN [integer_expression]

The return value is often used as a status value, usually 0 for success and non-zero for failure.

3.1.10.4 ALTER PROCEDURE

Syntax

```
ALTER PROC [ EDURE ] procedure_name [ ; number ]
[ { @parameter   data_type   }
[ VARYING ] [ =  default ] [ OUTPUT ]
] [ ,...n ]
[ WITH    RECOMPILE | ENCRYPTION | RECOMPILE , ENCRYPTION
}
]
[ FOR REPLICATION ]
AS
    sql_statement [ ...n ]
```

3.1.10.5 DROP PROCEDURE

Syntax

```
DROP PROCEDURE { procedure } [ ,...n ]
```

CREATE, ALTER, DROP PROCEDURE Examples

Example: Stored Procedures belong to a database, so remember: USE <database>.

SQL

```
USE mydb
go

CREATE PROCEDURE usp_DeacProc1
    -- Create User Stored Procedure
AS
BEGIN
     /* BEGIN and END block delimiters are
     suggested but not required */
  PRINT 'World''s simplest stored procedure'
END
go
```

SQL

```
EXEC usp_DeacProc1
```

SQL (cont.)

Result

This is world's simplest stored procedure.

SQL

```
ALTER PROCEDURE usp_DeacProc1
AS
BEGIN
  PRINT 'Modified stored procedure'
END
go

EXEC usp_DeacProc1
```

Result

This is a modified stored procedure.

SQL

```
DROP PROCEDURE usp_DeacProc1

EXEC usp_DeacProc1
```

Result

Server: Msg 2812, Level 16, State 62, Line 1
Could not find stored procedure 'usp_DeacProc1'.

Example: Create a Stored Procedure that uses RETURN

SQL

```
CREATE PROCEDURE usp_DeacProc2
AS
BEGIN
  PRINT 'This stored proc returns this value:'
  RETURN 2
END
go
```

SQL (cont.)

Result

The command(s) completed successfully.

Call the Stored Procedure capturing its return value in a variable.

SQL

```
DECLARE  @v_Status int

EXEC     @v_Status = usp_DeacProc2 -- 1st output line

PRINT    @v_Status              --  2d output line
```

Result

This stored procedure has the following RETURN value
2

Example: Create a Stored Procedure with INPUT Parameter.

SQL

```
CREATE PROCEDURE usp_DeacProc3 -- sp with input parm
    @p_str    VARCHAR(50)    -- The input parm
AS
BEGIN
-- Optional, but I usually prefer to use BEGIN here
  DECLARE @v_length INT
  SET @v_length = LEN( @p_str )
  RETURN @v_length
END
-- and END here to help readability
go

DECLARE  @v_size  INT
EXEC  @v_size   = usp_DeacProc3  'hello'
     -- Passing input parm by position
PRINT   'The size of the word ''hello'' is: '  +
     CAST(@v_size AS CHAR)
```

SQL (cont.)

Result

The size of the word 'hello' is: 5

SQL

```
/* On page 419 we create database mydb and
  table emps3 used in the next example. */
USE mydb
go

-- Show contents of emps3 for reference
SELECT  *   FROM  emps3
```

Result

ename	empid	deptno	telnum	salary	hiredate	sales_amt
Suzy Smith	1111	102	NULL	20	2003-01-01	NULL
Sammy Sosa	2222	102	2345	30	1992-01-01	200
Bill Johnson	4444	101	NULL	40	1994-01-01	NULL
Mary Smith	5555	100	5678	50	1990-01-01	NULL
Mary Smith	7777	101	7890	60	1996-01-01	400

Example: Create a Stored Procedure with INPUT and OUTPUT Parameters.

We want to pass in a department number and get back two pieces of information: the amount of the maximum salary in that department and the name of one person in that department making the maximum salary.

SQL

```
CREATE PROCEDURE usp_BigSalary
 -- sp with input & output parms
  @p_deptno  DEC(4), -- Input parm = Dept number to be searched
  @p_max_sal DEC(4)             OUTPUT
  @p_ename   VARCHAR(15)        OUTPUT
```

SQL (cont.)

```
AS
   SELECT  @p_max_sal  =  MAX(salary)
     FROM  emps3   WHERE  deptno  =  @p_deptno
   SELECT  @p_ename  =  ename
     FROM  emps3
     WHERE  deptno  =  @p_deptno AND salary = @p_max_sal
go
```

Result

The command(s) completed successfully.

Invoke (Call) the Stored Procedure Passing Parameters by Position
Parameters passed in must be in the same order and of the same type as in the definition.

SQL

```
DECLARE   @v_max_sal    DEC(4)
DECLARE   @v_ename      VARCHAR(15)

EXEC  usp_BigSalary 101 , @v_max_sal  OUTPUT ,  @_ename OUTPUT

PRINT 'Dept 101 has max salary of ' + CAST(@v_max_sal AS  CHAR)
PRINT  'Employee is:  '  +  @v_ename
```

Result

Dept 101 has max salary of 60
Employee is: Mary Smith

Invoke (Call) the Stored Procedure Passing Parameters by Name Parameters are passed in by name in any order.

SQL

```
DECLARE   @v_max_sal    DEC(4)
DECLARE   @v_ename      VARCHAR(15)

EXEC  usp_BigSalary  @p_deptno  =  101 ,
   @p_max_sal  =  @v_max_sal    OUTPUT ,
   @p_ename    =   @v_ename   OUTPUT

PRINT  'Dept 101 has max salary of ' + CAST(@v_max_sal  AS  CHAR)
PRINT  'Employee is:  '  +  @v_ename
```

Result

Dept 101 has max salary of 60
Employee is: Mary Smith

Input Parameters Defined with a Default Value Input parameters defined with a default value may be left out of the list in a call.

Example: Specify a default for @p_deptno.

SQL

```
ALTER PROCEDURE usp_BigSalary
    -- Input parm with default of 101
  @p_deptno       DEC(4)    = 101 ,
  @p_max_sal      DEC(4)              OUTPUT,
  @p_ename        VARCHAR(15)         OUTPUT
AS
  SELECT  @p_max_sal   =   MAX(salary)
    FROM  emps3   WHERE  deptno   =  @p_deptno

  SELECT @p_ename   =   ename
    FROM  emps3
    WHERE  deptno   =   @p_deptno AND  salary   =   @p_max_sal
go
```

Result

The command(s) completed successfully.

Call the stored procedure omitting deptno and thus using the default.To get the default we Pass By NAME and omit the input parameter whose default is desired.

SQL

```
DECLARE    @v_max_sal     DEC(4)
DECLARE    @v_ename       VARCHAR(15)

EXEC  usp_BigSalary
    @p_max_sal  =  @v_max_sal  OUTPUT ,
    @p_ename  =  @v_ename OUTPUT

PRINT  'Dept 101 has max salary of ' +
           CAST(@v_max_sal  AS  CHAR)
PRINT  'Employee is:  '  +  @v_ename
```

Result

Dept 101 has max salary of 60
Employee is: Mary Smith

Calling the stored procedure providing deptno of 102 is done as before.

SQL

```
DECLARE    @v_max_sal     DEC(4)
DECLARE    @v_ename       VARCHAR(15)

EXEC  usp_BigSalary  @p_deptno  =  102 ,
  @p_max_sal  =  @v_max_sal  OUTPUT ,
  @p_ename  =  @v_ename OUTPUT

PRINT 'Dept 102 has max salary of ' + CAST(@v_max_sal  AS  CHAR)
PRINT  'Employee is:  '  +  @v_ename
```

Result

Dept 102 has max salary of 30
Employee is: Sammy Sosa

Example: A stored procedure example using Transact-SQL is given on page 625.

3.1.11 Query Analyzer Stored Procedure Debugger

SQL Server 2000 has introduced a debugger for stored procedures. Be aware that this debugger should not run on a production machine because critical resources may become locked.

The debugger works only on an existing stored procedure in a SQL Server database. See "Transact-SQL Debugger Window" in Books Online.

There are two ways to start the debugger.

1. In Query Analyzer open the **Object Browser** (F8 or Tools-Object Browser-Show). Open the *database*-Stored Procedures and the stored procedure of interest. Right click on the stored procedure, select **Debug**.
2. In Query Analyzer open **Tools-Object Search-New**. Enter search information: Procedure name, database. Click Stored Procedure box and click **Find Now**. After the search, right click on the name, select **Debug**.

The following examples show details of using the debugger.

1. Type the following into a Query Analyzer and execute.

SQL

```
CREATE PROCEDURE  uspLooper
  (  @p_num    INT  )
AS
BEGIN
    DECLARE  @v_cnt    INT

    PRINT 'A'
    SET  @v_cnt   =  1
    WHILE  @v_cnt   <=   @p_num
      BEGIN
      PRINT   'Count is:   ' + CAST( @v_cnt  AS CHAR )
      SET  @v_cnt   =   @v_cnt   +   1
      END
    PRINT 'B'
    RETURN 1
END
```

Result

The command(s) completed successfully.

Execute to test.

SQL

```
EXEC   uspLooper  3
```

Result

```
A
Count is:  1
Count is:  2
Count is:  3
B
```

2. In the same or new Query Analyzer open **Object Browser**
   Object Browser (F8) or
   Tools - Object Browser - Show/Hide

Open the Object Browser to the same database and stored procedure, right click on the stored procedure name and select **Debug**. (See Figure 3-4.)

Selecting **Debug** opens the **Debug Procedure dialog** (Figure 3-5) where you are able to enter a value for each input parameter.

Note: You must provide a value for each input parameter before you click on **Execute**.

1. Select each parameter on the left of the dialog.
2. Enter its value in the lower right. You can change the parameters at any time during procedure execution. However, if you fail to give a value for each parameter before clicking Execute, the Parameters window may be disabled (greyed out). To enable it, right click on the stored procedure name and select Debug. This time give each parameter some value.
3. When all input parameters have been given a value, click Execute to run the debugger. As soon as you click Execute, the Debugger window opens (a new connection window to the database, you may see your previous connection window with CTRL-TAB).

   The Debugger Window contains the following items as shown in Figure 3-6: the Transact-SQL code of the stored procedure you have selected to debug and a Debugger Toolbar.

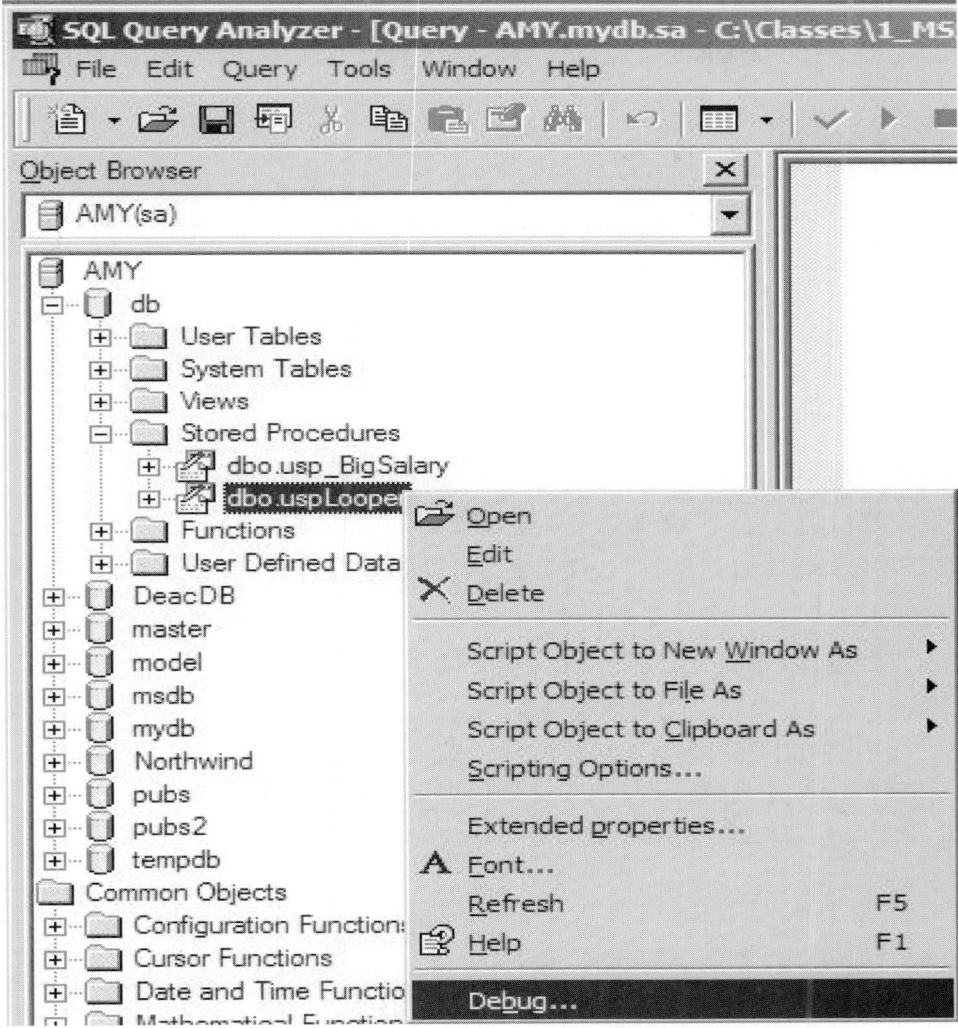

Figure 3-4 Select Debug while in the Object Browser.

4. The Debugger window contains the Debugger Toolbar and the procedure Transact-SQL code, as shown in Figures 3-6 and 3-7.

The yellow arrow indicates the next line of code that will execute whenever you give an execution command such as Go (F5), Step Into (F11), etc., from the debugging icon toolbar.

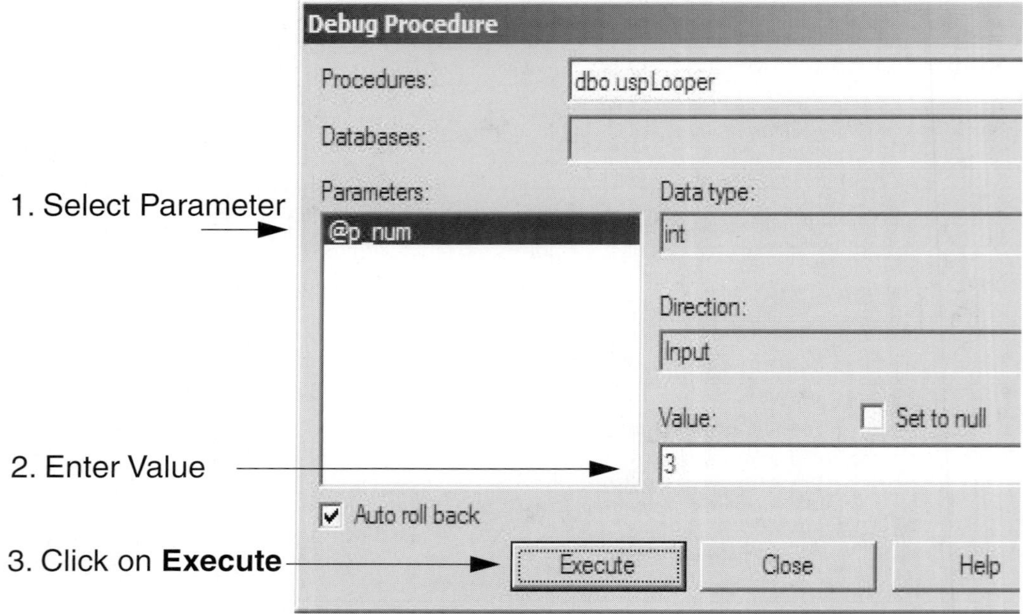

Figure 3-5 Debug Procedure Dialog Box.

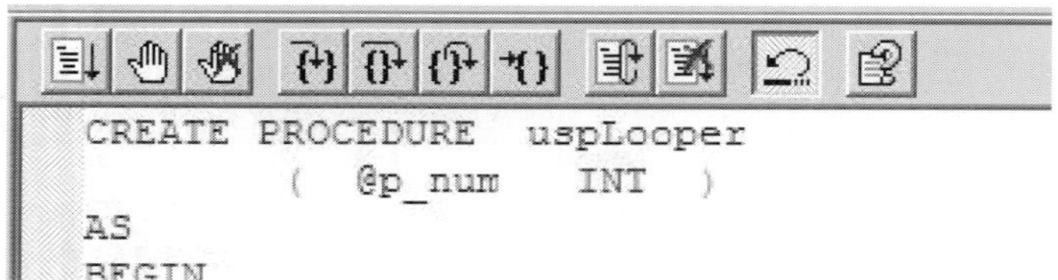

Figure 3-6 A **Debugger Toolbar** appears along the top of the code window.

When you first open the debugging window, the yellow execution arrow rests on the first executable line of the procedure. The debugger is an excellent tool for controlling statement by statement execution of the procedure or function and for observing the values of the variables as they change.

If you haven't used a debugger before, first study the definitions of the debugger icons in Table 3-5, and then play with the debugger to see what it can do for you. Some sample steps are provided below to assist you.

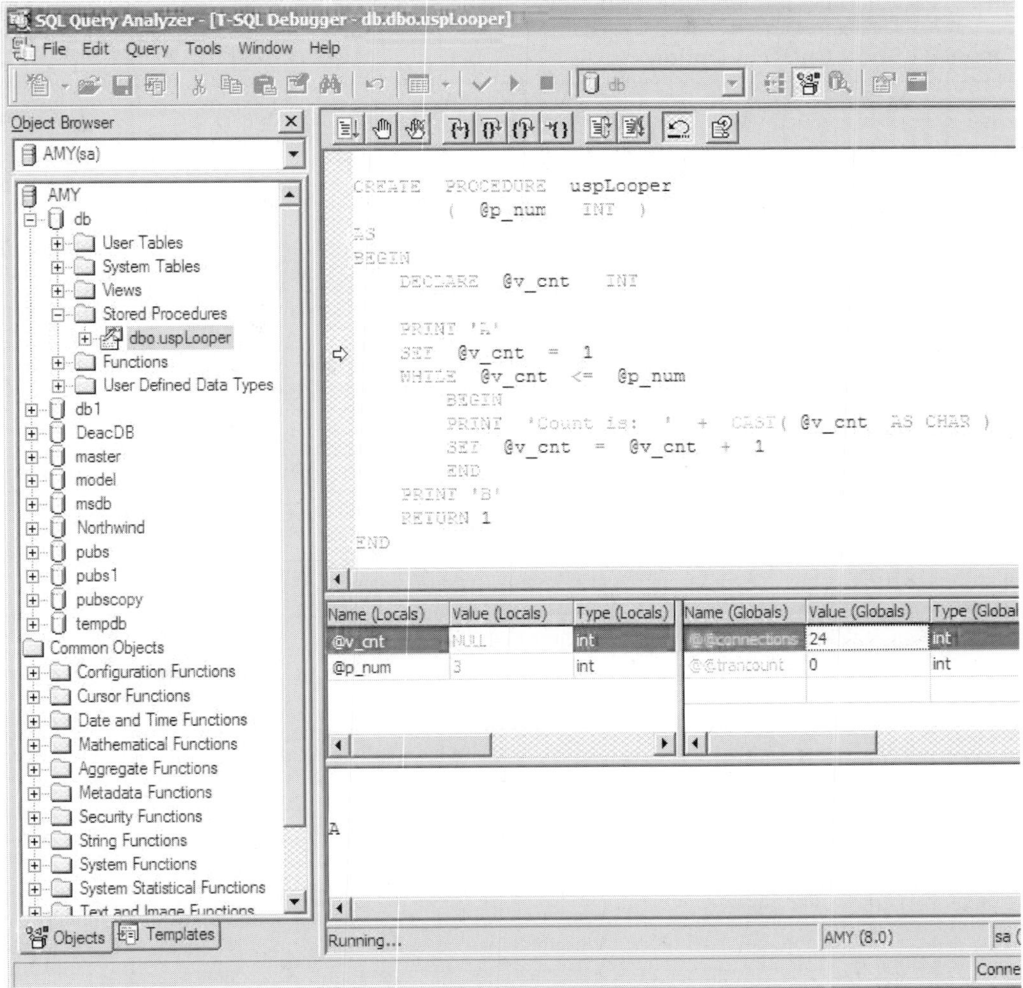

Figure 3-7 The Debugger window.

3.1.11.1 Debugging Icons

The icons listed in Table 3-5 can be used by clicking on the Toolbar icon / right clicking on SQL line and then selecting the option listed.

Table 3-5 Icons Used in the Debugging Process

Icon	Short Cut	Option	Description
	F5	Go	Runs the stored procedure in debugging mode.
	F9	Toggle Breakpoint	Sets or removes a breakpoint at the current line. A breakpoint marks the line before which execution will stop when run in free execution mode (Go or Restart). A breakpoint can =not be set on lines containing nonexecutable code.
	CTL SHIFT F9	Remove All Breakpoints	Clears all breakpoints in your code.
	F11	Step Into	Executes one code statement; if the next statement is a call to a procedure or function then Step Into enters that procedure or function and sets the execution point to its first statement.
	F10	Step Over	Executes one code statement; if the next statement is a call to a procedure then Step Over executes the entire procedure and returns to the next statement in the current procedure. If the next statement is not a procedure or function call, then Step Over and Step Into behave the same.
	SHIFT F11	Step Out	Executes the remaining lines of a function in which the current execution point lies. The next statement displayed is the statement following the procedure call. All of the code is executed between the current and the final execution points.
	CTL F10	Run to Cursor	Specifies a statement further down in your code where you want execution to stop. Use this option to avoid stepping through large loops.
	CTL SHIFT F5	Restart	Restarts execution from the beginning of the stored procedure.
	SHIFT F5	Stop Debugging	Halts debugging.

Table 3-5 Icons Used in the Debugging Process (cont.)

Icon	Short Cut	Option	Description
		Auto Roll-back	Automatically rolls back all work performed during execution of the procedure during debugging.
		Help	

3.1.11.2 Sample Debugging Session 1

Just click on the Go icon or press F5 to execute the entire procedure in free run mode. In the bottom pane you will see the same output as when we ran it previously on page 284.

```
A
Count is:  1
Count is:  2
Count is:  3
B

@RETURN_VALUE = 1
```

Notice that there is an additional line with @RETURN_VALUE, and the lines are much more spread out. Resize the three panes to taste.

After executing the procedure, you need to click Go or F5 one more time to have the procedure finish execution before it will run again. Or click Restart, CTL-SH-F5.

3.1.11.3 Sample Debugging Session 2

Set a "breakpoint" at the start of the WHILE loop. What is a breakpoint? A breakpoint marks the line before which execution will stop when it is run in free execution mode (Go or Restart).

Click on the word WHILE and click on the hand icon or press F9
Or
Right click on the word WHILE and select the hand icon from the menu.

a. Click on Restart (CTL-SHIFT-F5) to make sure we're ready to start.

Look at the local variables pane (middle up and down, far left).

```
@v_cnt    NULL  -- Hasn't been set yet since we haven't started execution
@p_num    3     -- Input parameter passed in to the procedure as 3
```

b. Click on the Go icon or press F5 to run in free execution mode to the first (and only, for us) breakpoint. Look at the local variables pane now.

```
@v_cnt    1    -- Assigned to 1 by the SET statement we just executed.
@p_num    3    -- Input parameter passed in to the procedure as 3
```

In the bottom pane you will see the following output.

```
A
```

c. Click on Go (F5) to execute the entire loop the first time back to our only breakpoint. Look at the variables pane now

```
@v_cnt    2    -- Incremented by 1 by the SET statement inside the loop.
@p_num    3    -- Input parameter passed in to the procedure as 3.
```

In the bottom pane you will see the following output.

```
A
Count is:  1
```

d. Click on Go (F5) to execute the entire loop the second time back to our breakpoint. Look at the local variables pane.

```
@v_cnt    3    -- Incremented by 1 by the SET statement inside the loop.
@p_num    3    -- Input parameter passed in to the procedure as 3.
```

In the bottom pane you will see the following output.

```
A
Count is:  1
Count is:  2
```

e. Experiment with single stepping (Step Into, Step Over) and observe the changes. When you're ready, remove the breakpoint (click on WHILE and click on the hand or F9). Click on Go (F5) to execute the remainder of the program. Look at the local variables pane.

```
@v_cnt    3    -- Incremented by 1 by the SET statement inside the loop.
@p_num    3    -- Input parameter passed in to the procedure as 3.
```

In the bottom pane you will see the following output.

```
A
Count is:  1
Count is:  2
Count is:  3
B

@RETURN_VALUE = 1
```

Notes

The middle-middle pane labelled "Globals" really refers to system functions starting with @@. Global variable is a legacy term for built-in functions having names that start with @@.

The Callstack window, middle-right, shows the sequence of a procedure or function calling a procedure or function (even calling itself as in recursion). When you click on a particular occurrence on the callstack, the variables for that occurrence are displayed. You may play with this using the recursive function example in the section on debugging functions, page 265.

If you find a bug in the program that you want to fix, you can open an edit window. In Object Browser window, right click on the stored procedure name and select **Edit**. An editable window opens with ALTER PROCEDURE and your code. Make your desired edits and execute the ALTER PROCEDURE statement.

After editing and executing you may re-open the debugger as you did before to test it. In Object Browser, again right click on the stored procedure name and select **Debug**.

3.1.12 CREATE RULE, DROP RULE, sp_bindrule

Rules are a backward-compatibility feature that perform some of the same functions as CHECK constraints. Rules are not recommended for new designs. Use CHECK constraints instead.

CHECK constraints are the preferred, ANSI standard way to restrict the values in a column and are more concise than rules. There can only be one rule applied to a column, but multiple CHECK constraints can be applied. CHECK constraints are specified as part of the CREATE TABLE (or ALTER TABLE) statement, while rules are created as separate objects and then bound to the column. If you want the same restriction on multiple tables, a rule might be easier than a CHECK constraint.

3.1.12.1 CREATE RULE Syntax

Syntax

```
CREATE RULE rule
    AS condition_expression
```

Comments

The CREATE RULE statement must appear alone in a single batch. Rules do not apply to data already existing in the database at the time the rules are created, and rules cannot be bound to system data types.

A rule can be created only in the current database. After creating a rule, execute **sp_bindrule** to bind the rule to a column or to a user-defined data type. The rule must be compatible with the column data type. A rule cannot be bound to a **text, image** or **timestamp** column. If the rule is not compatible with the column to which it is bound, Microsoft SQL Server returns an error message when inserting a value, but not when the rule is bound.

A rule bound to a user-defined data type is activated only when you attempt to insert a value into, or to update, a database column of the user-defined data type. Because rules do not test variables, do not assign a value to a user-defined data type variable that would be rejected by a rule bound to a column of the same data type unless you manually check that the variable value complies with the rule.

To get a report on a rule, use **sp_help**. To display the text of a rule, execute **sp_helptext** with the rule name as the parameter. To rename a rule, use **sp_rename**.

3.1.12.2 DROP RULE Syntax

Syntax

```
DROP RULE { rule } [ ,...n ]
```

3.1.12.3 sp_bindrule, sp_unbindrule

To become useful, rules must be bound to the column of a table using **sp_bindrule** as in the next example. See Books Online for complete details of **sp_bindrule**.

Syntax

```
System Stored Procedures sp_bindrulesp_bindrule [ @rulename = ] 'rule' ,
         [ @objname = ] 'object_name'
         [ , [ @futureonly = ]  { futureonly | NULL } ]
```

Syntax

```
System Stored Procedures sp_unbindrulesp_unbindrule [@objname =]
   'object_name'
     [, [ @futureonly = ]  { futureonly | NULL } ]
```

Examples: CREATE, ALTER, DROP RULE

Example 1a: Use a RULE to ensure a non-negative balance.

SQL

```
CREATE RULE  non_negative_value AS  @value >= 0
go

CREATE TABLE accounts (
    acctnum    INT       PRIMARY KEY,
    balance    DEC(38,2)
)
go
```

SQL

```
EXEC sp_bindrule
    non_negative_value ,  'accounts.balance'
go
```

Result

Rule bound to table column.

SQL

```
INSERT INTO  accounts (acctnum , balance )
VALUES ( 1 , 100 )
```

Result

(1 row(s) affected)

SQL

```
INSERT INTO  accounts (acctnum , balance )
VALUES ( 2 , -100 )
```

SQL (cont.)

Result

```
Server: Msg 513, Level 16, State 1, Line 1
A column insert or update conflicts with a rule imposed by a previous CREATE RULE statement. The statement was terminated. The conflict occurred in database 'playdb', table 'accounts', column 'balance'.
The statement has been terminated.
```

SQL

```
EXEC sp_unbindrule    'accounts.balance'
go
```

Result

```
Rule unbound from table column.
```

Now the second INSERT into accounts would succeed.

SQL `DROP RULE  non_negative_value`

Example 1b: Use a CHECK CONSTRAINT to ensure a non-negative balance.

SQL

```
CREATE TABLE accounts2 (
    acctnum    INT      PRIMARY KEY,
    balance    DEC(38,2),
    CONSTRAINT chk_pos_bal
        CHECK  ( balance >= 0 )
)
go

INSERT INTO  accounts2 (acctnum , balance )
VALUES ( 1 , 100 )
```

Result

```
(1 row(s) affected).
```

SQL

```
INSERT INTO  accounts2 (acctnum , balance )
VALUES ( 2 , -100 )
```

Result

Server: Msg 547, Level 16, State 1, Line 1
INSERT statement conflicted with COLUMN CHECK constraint 'chk_pos_bal'. The conflict occurred in database 'playdb', table 'accounts2', column 'balance'.
The statement has been terminated.

SQL

```
ALTER TABLE  accounts2
    DROP CONSTRAINT  chk_pos_bal
```

Now the second INSERT into accounts2 would succeed.

3.1.13 CREATE SCHEMA

A *schema* is a conceptual object containing definitions of tables, views and permissions. CREATE SCHEMA provides a way to create tables and views and to grant permissions for objects with a single statement.

Inclusion of SCHEMA in Microsoft SQL Server provides compliance with ANSI SQL. The preferred way to collect related objects such as tables and views is to use separate databases, not schemas.

3.1.13.1 CREATE SCHEMA Syntax

Syntax

```
CREATE SCHEMA AUTHORIZATION owner
  [ < schema_element > [ ...n ] ]

< schema_element > ::=
    { table_definition | view_definition | grant_statement }
```

Arguments

Omit the comma when separating one <schema_element> from another, i.e., [...n] instead of [, ...n].

AUTHORIZATION owner

AUTHORIZATION *owner* specifies the ID of the schema object owner. It must be a valid security account in the database.

table_definition
: table_definition specifies a CREATE TABLE statement that creates a table within the schema.

view_definition
: view_definition specifies a CREATE VIEW statement that creates a view within the schema.

grant_statement
: grant_statement specifies a GRANT statement that grants permissions for a user or a group of users.

If errors occur when creating any objects or granting any permissions specified in a CREATE SCHEMA statement, none of the objects are created.

The created objects do not have to appear in logical order, except for views that reference other views. For example, a GRANT statement can grant permission for an object before the object itself is created, or a CREATE VIEW statement can appear before the CREATE TABLE statements, creating the tables referenced by the view. Also, CREATE TABLE statements can declare foreign keys to tables specified later. The exception is that if the selection from one view references another view, the referenced view must be specified before the view that references it.

Notice that CREATE SCHEMA does not create a named schema, so there is no DROP SCHEMA. It just allows executing several steps in a single statement.

Permissions

CREATE SCHEMA permissions default to all users, but each user must have permission to create the objects contained in the schema.

CREATE SCHEMA Examples

Example 1: Use CREATE SCHEMA to create a new table, create a view on that table and grant permissions on that view all in one statement and in reverse order.

SQL

```
CREATE SCHEMA AUTHORIZATION dbo
    GRANT SELECT on v1 TO public
    CREATE VIEW v1(empid) AS    SELECT c1 from t
    CREATE TABLE t  (c1 int)
```

Example 2a: Create two tables each with FOREIGN KEY constraint referencing the other.

Using CREATE SCHEMA here, this task can be done in a single statement. Without CREATE SCHEMA it requires three statements (see Example 2b).

```
SQL

CREATE SCHEMA AUTHORIZATION tim
    CREATE TABLE t1 ( empid INT PRIMARY KEY,
         deptno INT CONSTRAINT
fk_emp_memberof_dept  REFERENCES t2 (deptno)    )
    CREATE TABLE t2 (deptno INT PRIMARY KEY,  mgrem-
pid INT REFERENCES t1(empid))
```

Example 2b: Perform the same task as Example 2a but without using CREATE SCHEMA.

Without CREATE SCHEMA it requires three separate statements.

```
SQL

CREATE TABLE t1 (
  empid INT PRIMARY KEY,
  deptno INT
)
CREATE TABLE t2 (
  deptno INT PRIMARY KEY,
  mgrempid INT REFERENCES t1(empid)
)

ALTER TABLE t1
  ADD CONSTRAINT  fk_emp_memberof_dept
  FOREIGN KEY (deptno) REFERENCES t2 (deptno)
```

Whether the tables and constraints are created as in Example 2a or 2b, dropping the tables must be done in three steps.

Example 2c: Remove one FOREIGN KEY constraint and drop both tables from 2a or 2b.

This requires three separate statements.

```
SQL

ALTER TABLE t1    DROP CONSTRAINT fk_emp_memberof_dept

DROP TABLE t2

DROP TABLE t1
```

3.1.14 CREATE, UPDATE, DROP STATISTICS

CREATE STATISTICS creates a named histogram and associated density groups (collections) over the supplied column or set of columns of a table or view. To create statistics on a view requires that the view have a clustered index. These statistics are used by the SQL Server 2000 query optimizer to choose the most efficient plan for performing DML operations. For more information see: *http://msdn.microsoft.com/library/default.asp?URL=/library/techart/statquery.htm.*

3.1.14.1 CREATE STATISTICS Syntax

Syntax

```
CREATE STATISTICS  statistics_name
  ON { table | view } ( column [ ,...n ] )
  [ WITH
      { FULLSCAN | SAMPLE number { PERCENT | ROWS }  [ , NORECOMPUTE ] }
    | NORECOMPUTE
  ]
```

Arguments

{ table | view } (column [,...n])

This parameter determines the table or view and set of columns on which the statistics will be created.

FULLSCAN

This is the same as SAMPLE 100 PERCENT.

SAMPLE number { PERCENT | ROWS }

SAMPLE number { PERCENT | ROWS } specifies a percentage of rows in the table, or a specified number of rows, that should be read using random sampling to gather the statistics. *number* can be only an integer. If neither FULLSCAN nor SAMPLE phrase is used, SQL Server determines sample size.

NORECOMPUTE

NORECOMPUTE specifies that statistics that become out of date are not automatically recomputed. (It is not recommended except for experienced administrators.)

3.1.14.2 UPDATE STATISTICS Syntax

The UPDATE STATISTICS statement updates information about the distribution of key values for one or more statistics groups (collections) in the specified table or indexed view.

Distribution statistics can be updated manually using the UPDATE STATISTICS statement. SQL Server 2000 can also detect when distribution statistics are out of date, and it can update the statistics automatically.

Manually running UPDATE STATISTICS should be considered whenever the following conditions apply.

- There is significant change in the key values in the index.
- A large amount of data in an indexed column has been added, changed or removed, or if the table has been truncated using TRUNCATE TABLE and UPDATE STATISTICSTRUNCATE TABLE and then repopulated.
- To see when the statistics were last updated, use the STATS_DATESTATS_DATE function, described in the next section.

Syntax

```
UPDATE STATISTICS table | view
   [ index | ( statistics_name [ ,...n ] ) ]
   [ WITH
      {
        FULLSCAN   [ , { ALL | COLUMNS | INDEX } ]   [ , NORECOMPUTE ]
        | SAMPLE number { PERCENT | ROWS }   [ , { ALL | COLUMNS | INDEX } ]
            [ , NORECOMPUTE ]
        | RESAMPLE  [ , { ALL | COLUMNS | INDEX } ]   [ , NORECOMPUTE ]
        | { ALL | COLUMNS | INDEX }
        |  NORECOMPUTE
        | { ALL | COLUMNS | INDEX } ,  NORECOMPUTE
      }
]
```

Arguments

{ALL | COLUMNS | INDEX}

{ALL | COLUMNS | INDEX} specifies whether the UPDATE STATISTICS statement affects column statistics, index statistics or all existing statistics (both categories).

RESAMPLE

RESAMPLE specifies that statistics will be gathered using an inherited sampling ratio for all existing statistics including indexes.

3.1.14.3 DROP STATISTICS Syntax

The DROP STATISTICS statement is used to drop statistics for multiple collections within the specified tables (in the current database).

Notice that DROP STATISTICS requires the two-part name, table.statistics_name.

Syntax

```
DROP STATISTICS  table.statistics_name  |  view.statistics_name  [ ,...n ]
```

CREATE, ALTER, DROP STATISTICS and STATS_DATE Examples

Example:

SQL

```
CREATE TABLE table1 ( dept VARCHAR(10) , telnum INT )
```

Choose any of the these forms.

SQL (cont.)

```
CREATE STATISTICS  stat_table1_dept ON table1 ( dept )

CREATE STATISTICS  stat_table1_dept ON table1 ( dept )
  WITH FULLSCAN

CREATE STATISTICS  stat_table1_dept ON table1 ( dept )
  WITH SAMPLE 10 PERCENT

CREATE STATISTICS  stat_table1_dept ON table1 ( dept )
  WITH FULLSCAN, NORECOMPUTE
```

SQL

```
UPDATE STATISTICS  table1 -- Update all statistics on table1

UPDATE STATISTICS  table1 stat_table1_dept -- Update named statistics

UPDATE STATISTICS  table1 WITH FULLSCAN -- Use 100% sample to update

UPDATE STATISTICS  table1 WITH SAMPLE 10 PERCENT -- Use 10% sample

UPDATE STATISTICS  table1 WITH FULLSCAN, NORECOMPUTE

DROP STATISTICS  table1.stat_table1_dept
```

3.1.15 STATS_DATE

3.1.15.1 STATS_DATE Function Syntax

The STATS_DATE function is able to return the date that the statistics for the specified index were last updated.

Syntax

STATS_DATE (*table_id* , *index_id*)

Example:

SQL

```
USE pubs
go
```

SQL

```
SELECT i.name  As Index_Name ,
   CAST(STATS_DATE(i.id, i.indid) AS CHAR) As Stats_Date
FROM sysobjects o, sysindexes i
WHERE o.id = i.id  AND  o.name = 'employee'
```

Result

```
Index_Name              Stats_Date
---------------------   ------------------------------
employee_ind            Aug  6 2000  1:33AM
PK_emp_id               Aug  6 2000  1:33AM
```

SQL

```
UPDATE STATISTICS  employee employee_ind
      -- Update only one of the two indexes
```

SQL

```
SELECT i.name  As Index_Name ,
   CAST(STATS_DATE(i.id, i.indid) AS CHAR) As Stats_Date
FROM sysobjects o, sysindexes i
WHERE o.id = i.id  AND  o.name = 'employee'
```

Result

```
Index_Name              Stats_Date
---------------------   ------------------------------
employee_ind            Nov 30 2002  4:04PM
PK_emp_id               Aug  6 2000  1:33AM
```

Example:

```
SQL
DROP STATISTICS  table1.stat_table1_dept
  -- table or view name is required
```

3.1.16 CREATE, ALTER, DROP TABLE

A table is a two-dimensional object, consisting of rows and columns, used to store data in a relational database. Each table stores information about one of the types of objects modeled by the database.

Tables are associated with a single database and may be either permanent (most common), local temporary or global temporary.

- *Permanent* or *base tables* are persistent within the database and may be accessed by anyone with requisite privilege. Names have a maximum of 128 characters.
- *Local temporary tables* are visible only in the current session. Names of local temporary tables must start with a single number sign (*#table_name*) and have a maximum of 116 characters including the #.
- *Global temporary tables* are visible to all sessions. Global temporary table names must start with a double number sign (##table_name) and have a maximum of 128 characters including the ##.

Temporary tables are automatically dropped when they go out of scope, unless explicitly dropped using DROP TABLE. Otherwise, temporary tables are used in SQL statements much like base tables.

3.1.16.1 CREATE TABLE Syntax

Syntax

```
CREATE TABLE [ database_name.[ owner ] . | owner. ] table_name
(
   { < column_definition > | column_name AS computed_column_expression }
                             [ ,...n ]
   [ , < table_constraint > ] ] [ ...n ]
)
[ ON { filegroup | DEFAULT } ]
[ TEXTIMAGE_ON { filegroup | DEFAULT } ]
```

```
< column_definition > ::= column_name     data_type
   [
     DEFAULT constant_expression
     | IDENTITY [ ( seed , increment ) [ NOT FOR REPLICATION ] ]
   ]
   [ ROWGUIDCOL]
   [ COLLATE < collation_name > ]
   [ < column_constraint > ] [ ...n ]

< column_constraint > ::= [ CONSTRAINT constraint_name ]
   {  [ NULL | NOT NULL ]
     [ { PRIMARY KEY | UNIQUE }   [ CLUSTERED | NONCLUSTERED ]
       [ WITH FILLFACTOR = fillfactor ]     [ON {filegroup | DEFAULT} ] ]
     ]
    | [ [ FOREIGN KEY ]    REFERENCES ref_table [ ( ref_column ) ]
       [ ON DELETE { CASCADE | NO ACTION } ]
       [ ON UPDATE { CASCADE | NO ACTION } ]
       [ NOT FOR REPLICATION ]
     ]
   | CHECK [ NOT FOR REPLICATION ]  ( logical_expression )
   }

< table_constraint > ::= [ CONSTRAINT constraint_name ]
   {  [ { PRIMARY KEY | UNIQUE }  [ CLUSTERED | NONCLUSTERED]  { ( column [
ASC | DESC ] [ ,...n ] ) }
     [ WITH FILLFACTOR = fillfactor ]     [ ON { filegroup | DEFAULT } ]
   ]
   | FOREIGN KEY  [ ( column [ ,...n ] ) ]  REFERENCES ref_table [ (
ref_column [ ,...n ] ) ]
       [ ON DELETE { CASCADE | NO ACTION } ]
       [ ON UPDATE { CASCADE | NO ACTION } ]
       [ NOT FOR REPLICATION ]
   | CHECK [ NOT FOR REPLICATION ]   ( logical_expression )
   }
```

Arguments

database_name

database_name names an existing database in which the table is created; it defaults to current database if no name is specified.

The login for the current connection must be an existing user ID in the specified database, and that user ID must have create table permissions.

owner

The owner is the name of the user ID that owns the new table. *owner* must be an existing user ID in the specified database. *owner* defaults to the user ID associated with the login for the current connection.

If the CREATE TABLE statement is executed by a member of the **sysadmin** fixed server role, or by a member of the **db_dbowner** or **db_ddladmin** fixed database roles in the specified database, *owner* can specify a user ID other than the one associated with the login of the current connection.

If the CREATE TABLE statement is executed by a login associated with a user, ID that has only create table permissions, *owner*, if specified, must be the user ID associated with the current login.

Members of the **sysadmin** fixed server role, or logins aliased to the **dbo** user are associated with the user ID **dbo**; therefore, tables created by these users default to having **dbo** as the owner.

table_name

The name of the new table is table_name. Table names must conform to the rules for identifiers. The combination of *owner.table_name* must be unique within the database. *table_name* can contain a maximum of 128 characters, except for local temporary table names (names prefixed with a single number sign (#)) that cannot exceed 116 characters.

```
#    temporary tabletemporary table (max of 116 characters)  e.g., #tablename
       or a local temporary procedure                        e.g., #procname

##   global temporary objectglobal temporary object          e.g., ##globaltable,
                                                                   ##globalproc
```

column_name

The name of a column in the table is column_name. Column names must conform to the rules for identifiers and must be unique in the table.

column_name can be omitted for columns created with a **timestamp** data type. The name of a **timestamp** column defaults to **timestamp** if *column_name* is not specified.

computed_column_expression

The computed_column_expression is an expression defining the value of a computed column. A computed column is a virtual column not physically stored in the table. It is computed from an expression using other columns in the same table. For example, a computed column can have the definition: **cost** AS **price * qty**.

The expression can be any expression using noncomputed column names, constants, functions or variables. The expression cannot be a subquery.

Computed columns can be used in select lists, WHERE clauses, ORDER BY clauses or any other locations in which regular expressions can be used, with the following exceptions:

- A computed column cannot be used as a DEFAULT or FOREIGN KEY constraint definition or with a NOT NULL constraint definition.
- A computed column can be used as a key column in an index or as part of any PRIMARY KEY or UNIQUE constraint, if the computed column value is defined by a deterministic expression and the data type of the result is allowed in index columns.

  For example, if the table has integer columns **a** and **b**, the computed column **a+b** may be indexed. But computed column **a+DATEPART(dd, GETDATE())** cannot be indexed because the value may change in subsequent invocations.
- A computed column cannot be the target of an INSERT or UPDATE statement.

Note: Each row in a table can have different values for columns involved in a computed column; therefore the computed column may not have the same value for each row.

The nullability of computed columns is determined automatically by SQL Server based on the expressions used. The result of most expressions is considered nullable even if only non-nullable columns are present because possible underflows or overflows will produce NULL results as well. Use the COLUMNPROPERTY function (AllowsNull property) to investigate the nullability of any computed column in a table. An expression *expr* that is nullable can be turned into a non-nullable one by specifying ISNULL(*check_expression*, constant) where the constant is a non-NULL value substituted for any NULL result.

ON { *filegroup* | DEFAULT}

ON { filegroup | DEFAULT}specifies the filegroup on which the table is stored. If *filegroup* is specified, the table is stored in the named filegroup. The filegroup must exist within the database. If "ON filegroup" is not specified or if "DEFAULT" is specified, the table is stored on the default filegroup.

ON {*filegroup* | DEFAULT} can also be specified in a PRIMARY KEY or UNIQUE constraint to indicate where the index resulting from the constraint is to be created. If no filegroup is specified in the constraint, the index is stored on the same filegroup as the table. If the PRIMARY KEY or UNIQUE constraint creates a clustered index, the data pages for the table are stored in the same filegroup as the index.

Note: DEFAULT, in the context of ON {filegroup | DEFAULT} and TEXTIMAGE_ON {filegroup | DEFAULT}, is not a keyword. DEFAULT is an identifier for the default filegroup and must be delimited, as in ON

"DEFAULT" or ON [DEFAULT] and TEXTIMAGE_ON "DEFAULT" or TEXTIMAGE_ON [DEFAULT].

TEXTIMAGE_ON { *filegroup* | DEFAULT}

TEXTIMAGE_ON { filegroup | DEFAULT}indicates where to store the **text**, **ntext** and **image** columns in the table. TEXTIMAGE ON is not allowed if there are no **text**, **ntext** or **image** columns in the table. If not specified, the **text**, **ntext** and **image** columns are stored in the same filegroup as the table.

data_type

data_type specifies the data type for the column. System or user-defined data types are acceptable. User-defined data types are created with **sp_addtype** before they can be used in a table definition. The NULL/NOT NULL assignment for a user-defined data type can be overridden in the CREATE TABLE statement. However, the length specification cannot be changed for a user-defined data type in a CREATE TABLE statement.

DEFAULT

DEFAULT specifies the value provided for the column when a value is not explicitly supplied during an INSERT.

DEFAULT definitions can be applied to any columns except IDENTITY or **timestamp** columns. Only a constant value, such as a character string, a system function such as GETDATE() or NULL, can be used as a default. To maintain compatibility with earlier versions of SQL Server, a constraint name can be used as a DEFAULT.

constant_expression

constant_expression is the constant, NULL or a system function used as the default value for the column.

IDENTITY

IDENTITY indicates that the new column is an identity column. When a new row is added to the table, SQL Server provides a unique, incremental value for the column.

Identity columns are commonly used in conjunction with PRIMARY KEY constraints to serve as the unique row identifier for the table. The IDENTITY property can be assigned to **tinyint**, **smallint**, **int**, **bigint**, **decimal(p,0)** or **numeric(p,0)** columns. Only one identity column can be created per table. Bound defaults and DEFAULT constraints cannot be used with an identity column. You must specify both the seed and increment or neither. If neither is specified, the default is (1,1).

seed

The seed parameter is the value used for the very first row loaded into the table. The default is 1.

increment

increment is the incremental value added to the identity value to generate the next identity value. The default is 1.

NOT FOR REPLICATION

NOT FOR REPLICATION indicates that the IDENTITY property should not be enforced when a replication login such as **sqlrepl** inserts data into the table. Replicated rows must retain the key values assigned in the publishing database; the NOT FOR REPLICATION clause ensures that rows inserted by a replication process are not given new identity values. Rows inserted by other logins continue to have new identity values created in the usual way.

It is suggested that a CHECK constraint with NOT FOR REPLICATION also be defined to ensure that the identity values assigned are within the range wanted for the current database.

ROWGUIDCOL

ROWGUIDCOL indicates that the new column is a row global unique identifier column. Only one **uniqueidentifier** column per table can be designated as the ROWGUIDCOL column. The ROWGUIDCOL property can be assigned only to a **uniqueidentifier** column. See examples page 127.

The ROWGUIDCOL property does not enforce uniqueness of the values stored in the column nor does it automatically generate values for new rows inserted into the table.

To generate unique values for each column, either use the NEWID function on INSERT statements or use the NEWID function as the default for the column. The ROWGUIDCOL keyword is not valid if the database compatibility level is 65 or lower.

collation_name

The parameter *collation_name* specifies the collation for the column. Collation name can be either a Windows collation name or a SQL collation name. The *collation_name* is applicable only for columns of the **char**, **varchar**, **text**, **nchar**, **nvarchar** and **ntext** data types. See COLLATE.

If not specified, the column is assigned the collation of the user-defined data type if applicable or the default collation of the database.

CONSTRAINT

CONSTRAINT is an optional keyword indicating the beginning of a PRIMARY KEY, NOT NULL, UNIQUE, FOREIGN KEY or CHECK constraint definition.

constraint_name

constraint_name is the name of a constraint. Constraint names must be unique within a database.

NULL | NOT NULL

NULL | NOT NULL are keywords that determine if null values are allowed in the column.

PRIMARY KEY

PRIMARY KEY is a constraint that enforces uniqueness and NOT NULL for a given column or columns. Only one PRIMARY KEY constraint can be created per table.

UNIQUE

UNIQUE is a constraint that enforces uniqueness for a given column or columns through a unique index. A table can have multiple UNIQUE constraints.

CLUSTERED | NONCLUSTERED

CLUSTERED | NONCLUSTERED are keywords used to indicate that a clustered or a nonclustered index is to be created for the PRIMARY KEY or UNIQUE constraint. PRIMARY KEY constraints default to CLUSTERED and UNIQUE constraints default to NONCLUSTERED.

You can specify CLUSTERED for only one constraint in a CREATE TABLE statement. If you specify CLUSTERED for a UNIQUE constraint and also specify a PRIMARY KEY constraint, the PRIMARY KEY will be NONCLUSTERED.

[WITH FILLFACTOR = fillfactor]

[WITH FILLFACTOR = fillfactor] specifies percentage of fill SQL Server should use to create each index leaf page. See discussion of FILLFACTOR with the CREATE INDEX statement, page 267.

FOREIGN KEY...REFERENCES

FOREIGN KEY...REFERENCES is a constraint that provides referential integrity for the data in the column or columns. FOREIGN KEY constraints require that each value in the column(s) of the foreign key table (child table) exists in the corresponding referenced column(s) in the referenced table (parent table).

FOREIGN KEY constraints can reference only columns in the referenced table that are PRIMARY KEY or UNIQUE constraints or columns referenced in a UNIQUE INDEX on the referenced table.

ref_table

ref_table is the name of the table referenced by the FOREIGN KEY constraint, also called the "parent" table.

(ref_column[,...n])

A column or list of columns of the parent table (the table referenced by the FOREIGN KEY constraint) can be referenced with (ref_column[,...n]).

ON DELETE {CASCADE | NO ACTION}

This is a characteristic of a FOREIGN KEY constraint. It specifies what action takes place to a row in the child table if the referenced row is deleted from the parent table. The default is NO ACTION. See REFERENTIAL INTEGRITY below.

If CASCADE is specified and a delete statement is issued on a row of the parent table, then every row in the child table will be deleted whose foreign key value is the same as the parent key value being deleted.

If NO ACTION is specified and a delete statement is issued on a row of the parent table, and if there are any rows in the child table whose foreign key value matches the parent key value of the row being deleted, then SQL Server raises an error and the delete action on the row in the parent table is rolled back.

For example, in the **Northwind** database, the **Orders** table **CustomerID** column references the primary key **CustomerID** column of the **Customers** table.

If ON DELETE CASCADE is specified on this foreign key and DELETE FROM Customers WHERE CustomerId = ANTON is issued, then every row in **Orders** whose **CustomerID** value is ANTON is also deleted.

If NO ACTION is specified, SQL Server raises an error and rolls back the delete action on the **Customers** row if there is at least one row in the **Orders** table whose **CustomerID** value is ANTON.

ON UPDATE {CASCADE | NO ACTION}

This is a characteristic of a FOREIGN KEY constraint. It specifies what action takes place to a row in the child table if the referenced row is updated in the parent table. The default is NO ACTION. See REFERENTIAL INTEGRITY below.

If CASCADE is specified and an update statement is issued on a parent key value in the parent table, then every row in the child table whose foreign key value is the same as the parent key value will be updated to the same value as the new parent key.

If NO ACTION is specified and an update statement is issued to change a parent key value in the parent table, and if there are any rows in the child table whose foreign key value matches the original parent key value, then SQL Server raises an error and the update action on the row in the parent table is rolled back.

For example, in the **Northwind** database, the **Orders** table **CustomerID** column references the primary key **CustomerID** column of the **Customers** table.

If ON UPDATE CASCADE is specified on this foreign key and **CustomerID** ANTON is changed to FOO in **Customers**, then every occurrence of **CustomerID** ANTON in **Orders** is also changed to FOO.

If NO ACTION is specified, SQL Server raises an error and rolls back the update action on the **Customers** row if there is at least one row in the **Orders** table whose **CustomerID** value is ANTON.

CHECK

CHECK is a constraint that enforces domain integrity by limiting the possible values that can be entered into a column or columns to those for which the (logical_expression) evaluates to TRUE. An example CHECK constraint is CHECK (age > 0 AND age < 150).

NOT FOR REPLICATION

This clause means the constraint is enforced on user modifications but not on the replication process.

A CHECK constraint can be defined on the subscription table to prevent users from modifying it or to limit the range of user modifications from encroaching on a range set aside for replication. By specifying NOT FOR REPLICATION, the replication process is allowed to distribute modifications from the publishing table to the subscribing table without the CHECK constraint being enforced.

The NOT FOR REPLICATION CHECK constraint is applied to both the before and the after image of an updated record to prevent records from being added to or deleted from the specified range. All deletes and inserts are checked; if they fall within the specified range, they are rejected.

For example, CHECK NOT FOR REPLICATION (partnum < 30000) allows users to insert, update and delete values under 30000 but preserves values over that for the replication process.

When this constraint is used with an identity column, SQL Server allows the table not to have its identity column values reseeded when a replication user updates the identity column.

logical_expression

logical_expression is a logical expression that returns TRUE or FALSE.

column

column is a column or list of columns, in parentheses, to indicate the columns used in a table constraint definition.

[ASC | DESC]

[ASC | DESC]specifies the order in which the column or columns participating in table constraints are sorted. The default is ASC.

n

The letter *n* is a placeholder indicating that the preceding item can be repeated *n* number of times.

Comments

SQL Server can have as many as two billion tables per database and 1,024 columns per table. The number of rows and total size of the table are limited only by available storage.

The maximum number of bytes per row is 8,060. If you create tables with **varchar**, **nvarchar** or **varbinary** columns in which the total defined width exceeds 8,060 bytes, the table is created, but a warning message appears. Trying to insert more than 8,060 bytes into such a row or to update a row so that its total row size exceeds 8,060 produces an error message, and the statement fails.

Each table can contain one clustered index and a maximum of 249 nonclustered indexes. These include the indexes generated to support any PRIMARY KEY and UNIQUE constraints defined for the table.

SQL Server does not enforce an order in which DEFAULT, IDENTITY, ROWGUIDCOL or column constraints are specified in a column definition.

3.1.16.2 Temporary Tables

You can create local and global temporary tables. Local temporary tables are visible only in the current session; global temporary tables are visible to all sessions. Local temporary table names must be prefixed with single number sign (#*table_name*), and global temporary table names with a double number sign (##*table_name*).

temporary tabletemporary table (maximum of 116 characters) e.g., #tablename
or a local temporary procedure e.g., #procname

global temporary object e.g., ##globaltable, ##globalproc

SQL statements reference the temporary table using the value specified for *table_name* in the CREATE TABLE statement:

```
CREATE TABLE #MyTempTable (cola INT PRIMARY KEY)

INSERT INTO #MyTempTable VALUES (1)
```

If a local temporary table is created in a stored procedure or application that can be executed at the same time by several users, SQL Server distinguishes the tables created by the different users by internally appending a numeric suffix to each local temporary table name. To allow for the suffix, *table_name* specified for a local temporary name cannot exceed 116 characters.

Temporary tables are automatically dropped when they go out of scope, unless they are explicitly dropped using DROP TABLE:

- A local temporary table created in a stored procedure is dropped automatically when the stored procedure completes. The table can be referenced by any nested stored procedures that had been executed by the stored procedure that created the table. The table cannot be referenced by the stored-procedure process that created the table.
- All other local temporary tables are dropped automatically at the end of the current session.
- Global temporary tables are automatically dropped when the session that created the table ends and all other tasks have stopped referencing them. The association between a task and a table is maintained only for the life of a single Transact-SQL statement. This means that a global temporary table is dropped at the completion of the last Transact- SQL statement, which was actively referencing the table when the creating session ended.

Nested stored procedures can create temporary tables with the same name as a temporary table created by the stored procedure that called it. All references to the table name in the nested stored procedure are resolved to the table created in the nested procedure.

Example: Nested Temporary Tables (based on Books Online example)

SQL

```
CREATE PROCEDURE Test2
AS
CREATE TABLE #t(x INT PRIMARY KEY)

INSERT INTO #t VALUES (2)

SELECT Test2Col = x FROM #t
GO
```

SQL

```
CREATE PROCEDURE Test1
AS
CREATE TABLE #t(x INT PRIMARY KEY)
INSERT INTO #t VALUES (1)
SELECT Test1Col = x FROM #t
EXEC Test2
GO
```

SQL

```
CREATE TABLE #t(x INT PRIMARY KEY)
INSERT INTO #t VALUES (99)
GO
```

SQL

```
EXEC Test1
GO
```

Result

```
(1 row(s) affected)

Test1Col
-----------
1

(1 row(s) affected)

Test2Col
-----------
2
```

SQL

```
SELECT MainSession = x FROM #t
```

SQL (cont.)

Result

```
MainSession
-----------
99

(1 row(s) affected)
```

When you create local or global temporary tables, the CREATE TABLE syntax supports constraint definitions with the exception of FOREIGN KEY constraints. Temporary tables cannot participate in FOREIGN KEY constraints as either child or parent table.

Consider using table variables instead of temporary tables. Temporary tables are useful in cases when indexes need to be created explicitly on them, or when the table values need to be visible across multiple stored procedures or functions. In general, table variables contribute to more efficient query processing. See page 121 for table variables.

3.1.16.3 PRIMARY KEY Constraints

- A table can contain only one PRIMARY KEY constraint.
- Each UNIQUE constraint, including PRIMARY KEY constraint, generates an index.
- If CLUSTERED or NONCLUSTERED is not specified for a PRIMARY KEY constraint, CLUSTERED is used if no clustered index is otherwise specified.
- All columns defined within a PRIMARY KEY constraint must be defined as NOT NULL. If nullability is not specified, their nullability is set to NOT NULL.

3.1.16.4 UNIQUE Constraints

- If CLUSTERED or NONCLUSTERED is not specified for a UNIQUE constraint, NONCLUSTERED is used by default.
- Each UNIQUE constraint generates an index. The number of UNIQUE constraints cannot cause the number of indexes on the table to exceed 249 nonclustered indexes and 1 clustered index.

3.1.16.5 FOREIGN KEY Constraints

- REFERENTIAL INTEGRITY
  Creation of a FOREIGN KEY constraint causes REFERENTIAL INTEGRITY (RI) to be enforced. RI can be summarized as allowing "no orphans." RI means that SQL Server allows no foreign key column(s) value to exist in the child table unless that same value exists in the referenced key column(s) of the parent table.
  RI enforces checks of INSERT and UPDATE statements on the child and DELETE and UPDATE on the parent.
  When a value other than NULL is entered into the (child table) columns of a FOREIGN KEY constraint, the value must exist in the referenced columns (of parent table); otherwise, a foreign key violation error message is returned and the statement is rolled back.
  Likewise, when a DELETE or UPDATE statement on the parent table attempts to delete or change a referenced column value for which one or more rows are present in the child table, the statement will not be allowed and will be rolled back. An exception is if there is a DELETE CASCADE or UPDATE CASCADE clause in the FOREIGN KEY constraint (see above).
  RI implemented by FOREIGN KEY constraints as described here is also called DECLARATIVE REFERENTIAL INTEGRITY or DRIDRI. When implemented by triggers and other program code, it is called PROCEDURAL REFERENTIAL INTEGRITY or PRIPRI. If not otherwise indicated, RI can be assumed to mean DRI.

- FOREIGN KEY constraints can reference only tables within the same database. Cross-database referential integrity must be implemented through triggers. See CREATE TRIGGER.

- FOREIGN KEY constraints can reference another column in the same table (a self-reference).

- The REFERENCES clause of a column-level FOREIGN KEY constraint can list only one reference column, which must have the same data type as the column on which the constraint is defined.

- The REFERENCES clause of a table-level FOREIGN KEY constraint must have the same number of reference columns as the number of columns in the constraint column list. The data type of each reference column must also be the same as the corresponding column in the constraint column list.

- CASCADE may not be specified if a column of type, **timestamp**, is part of either the foreign key or the referenced key.
- It is possible to combine CASCADE and NO ACTION on tables that have referential relationships with each other. If SQL Server encounters NO ACTION, it terminates and rolls back related CASCADE actions. When a DELETE statement causes a combination of CASCADE and NO ACTION actions, all the CASCADE actions are applied before SQL Server checks for any NO ACTION.
- A table can contain a maximum of 253 FOREIGN KEY constraints.
- FOREIGN KEY constraints are not enforced on temporary tables.
- A table can reference a maximum of 253 different tables in its FOREIGN KEY constraints.
- FOREIGN KEY constraints can reference only columns in PRIMARY KEY or UNIQUE constraints in the referenced table or in a UNIQUE INDEX on the referenced table.

3.1.16.6 DEFAULT Definitions

- A column can have only one DEFAULT definition.
- A DEFAULT definition can contain constant values, functions, the SQL-92 niladic functions (take no arguments and use no parentheses), or NULL. Table 3-6 shows the niladic functions and the values they return for the default during an INSERT statement.

Table 3-6 The Values of the niladic Function

SQL-92 niladic function	Value returned
CURRENT_TIMESTAMP	Current date and time.
CURRENT_USER	Name of user performing insert.
SESSION_USER	Name of user performing insert.
SYSTEM_USER	Name of user performing insert.
USER	Name of user performing insert.

- *constant_expression* in a DEFAULT definition cannot refer to another column in the table, or to other tables, views or stored procedures.

- DEFAULT definitions cannot be created on columns with a **timestamp** data type or columns with an IDENTITY property.
- DEFAULT definitions cannot be created for columns with user-defined data types if the user-defined data type is bound to a default object.

3.1.16.7 CHECK Constraints

- A column can have any number of CHECK constraints, and the condition can include multiple logical expressions combined with AND and OR. Multiple CHECK constraints for a column are validated in the order created.
- The search condition must evaluate to a Boolean expression and cannot reference another table.
- A column-level CHECK constraint can reference only the constrained column, and a table-level CHECK constraint can reference only columns in the same table.
- CHECK CONSTRAINTS and rules serve the same function of validating the data during INSERT, UPDATE and DELETE statements.

Example: Check Constraint

SQL

```
CREATE TABLE  t (
  id            INT ,
  age           TINYINT
    CHECK( age > 0 and age < 180 )
   -- Every DML operation must meet this constraint
)

INSERT INTO t VALUES ( 1 , 35)

SELECT * FROM t
```

Result

```
id              age
-----------     ----
1               35
```

SQL

```
INSERT INTO t  VALUES ( 2 , 225)
```

Result

Server: Msg 547, Level 16, State 1, Line 1
INSERT statement conflicted with COLUMN CHECK constraint 'CK__t__age__2610A626'.
The conflict occurred in database 'db', table 't', column 'age'.
The statement has been terminated.

3.1.16.8 Additional Constraint Information

- An index created for a constraint cannot be dropped with the DROP INDEX statement; the constraint must be dropped with the ALTER TABLE statement. An index created for and used by a constraint can be rebuilt with the DBCC DBREINDEX statement.
- Constraint names must follow the rules for identifiers, except that the name cannot begin with a number sign (#). If constraint_name is not supplied, a system-generated name is assigned to the constraint, which may be seen using **System Stored Procedures sp_help** tablename. The constraint name appears in any error message about constraint violations.
- When a constraint is violated in an INSERT, UPDATE or DELETE statement, the statement is terminated but the transaction continues to be processed.
- You can check the @@ERROR system function and use the ROLLBACK TRANSACTION statement if desired.
- If a table has FOREIGN KEY or CHECK CONSTRAINTS along with triggers, the constraint conditions are evaluated before the trigger is executed.
- For a report on a table and its columns, use **sp_help** or **System Stored Procedures sp_helpconstraint**. To rename a table, use **System Stored Procedures sp_rename**. For a report on the views and stored procedures that depend on a table, use **System Stored Procedures sp_depends**.

3.1.16.9 Nullability Rules Within a Table Definition

The *nullability* of a column determines whether or not that column can allow a NULL as the data value in that column. NULL means "no domain value assigned" (see Chapter 1) and may be read as "not available," "not applicable" or "unknown." It means that no entry was made or an explicit NULL was supplied.

The possible nullability values for a column are NULL (this column may have NULL values) or NOT NULL (this column is not permitted to have NULL entered for any row). The current nullability of each column in a table may be displayed using "sp_help table_name."

When you create or alter a table with the CREATE TABLE or ALTER TABLE statements, database and session settings influence the nullability of the data type used in a column definition (see "ANSI_NULL_DEFAULT," page 195, and "Which Session Setting Is in Effect?" on page 219). Microsoft recommends that you always explicitly define a column as NULL or NOT NULL for noncomputed columns or, for a user-defined data type, that you allow the column to use the default nullability of the data type.

See further discussion of this topic in Books Online under "CREATE TABLE."

Note: The SQL Server ODBC driver and Microsoft OLE DB Provider for SQL Server both default to having ANSI_NULL_DFLT_ON set to ON.

This means that clients such as Query Analyzer have nullability as the default in CREATE TABLE unless the user changes it as described above. ODBC and OLE DB users can configure this in ODBC data sources, or with connection attributes or properties set by the application.

Permissions

CREATE TABLE permission defaults to the members of the **db_owner** and **db_ddladmin** fixed database roles. Members of the **db_owner** fixed database role and members of the **sysadmin** fixed server role can grant CREATE TABLE permission to other users.

Example: Simplest table with PRIMARY KEY

SQL

```
CREATE DATABASE  mydb
     --  Create mydb to play with
     -- if you already haven't done so
go
USE mydb
go
```

SQL

```
CREATE TABLE mydepts ( --  A new table created just for the
                           current example
   deptno      INT            PRIMARY KEY ,
   deptname    VARCHAR(30)
)
```

SQL

```
INSERT INTO mydepts VALUES ( 222 , 'dept1' )

SELECT * FROM mydepts
```

Result

```
deptno          deptname
-----------     --------
222             dept1
```

Example: Add IDENTITY and a FOREIGN KEY CONSTRAINT.

SQL

```
CREATE TABLE myemps ( -- A new table created just for the
                         current example
  empid        INT        IDENTITY(1000, 1    PRIMARY KEY
  ename        VARCHAR(30),
  deptno       INT,
  CONSTRAINT   fk_emp_memberof_dept FOREIGN KEY (deptno)
    REFERENCES   mydepts (deptno)
)
```

SQL

```
INSERT INTO myemps VALUES ( 'sam' , 222 )

SELECT * FROM myemps
```

SQL (cont.)

Result

empid	ename	deptno
1000	sam	222

Example: Use a CREATE TABLE statement to create a **customers** table with the index on the primary key specified to be initially 70% filled. See Section 3.1.9, page 267, for a discussion of fill factor and Section 5.6, page 588, for more examples.

SQL

```
CREATE TABLE customers ( --

      id        DEC(4) ,

      name      VARCHAR(10) ,
        CONSTRAINT pk_customers PRIMARY KEY
           CLUSTERED ( id ) WITH FILLFACTOR = 70
);
```

3.1.16.10 ALTER TABLE Syntax

Syntax

```
ALTER TABLE table
   {
     ALTER COLUMN column_name
     {
      new_data_type [ ( precision [ , scale ] ) ] [ COLLATE
  < collation_name > ]    [ NULL | NOT NULL ]
       | {ADD | DROP } ROWGUIDCOL
     }
   | ADD { [ < column_definition > ] | column_name AS
  computed_column_expression } [ ,...n ]
   | [ WITH CHECK | WITH NOCHECK ] ADD   { < table_constraint > } [ ,...n ]
   | DROP   { [ CONSTRAINT ] constraint_name   | COLUMN column } [ ,...n ]
   | { CHECK | NOCHECK } CONSTRAINT   { ALL | constraint_name [ ,...n ] }
   | { ENABLE | DISABLE } TRIGGER   { ALL | trigger_name [ ,...n ] }
}

< column_definition > ::=  See definition with CREATE TABLE

< column_constraint > ::=  See definition with CREATE TABLE

< table_constraint > ::=  See definition with CREATE TABLE
```

Comments

The parameter definitions and rules for ALTER TABLE are the same as for CREATE TABLE except as noted below.

ALTER COLUMN

Arguments

column_name

For new columns, *column_name* may be omitted for columns created with a **timestamp** data type. The name **timestamp** is used if no *column_name* is specified for a **timestamp** data type column.

The altered column cannot be:

- A column with a **text**, **image**, **ntext** or **timestamp** data type.
- The ROWGUIDCOL for the table.
- A computed column or be used in a computed column.
- A replicated column.
- Used in an index, unless the column is a **varchar**, **nvarchar** or **varbinary** data type, the data type is not changed and the new size is equal to or larger than the old size.
- Used in statistics generated by the CREATE STATISTICS statement. First remove the statistics using DROP STATISTICS. Afterward recreate using CREATE STATISTICS if desired.
- Used in a PRIMARY KEY or [FOREIGN KEY] REFERENCES constraint.
- Used in a CHECK or UNIQUE constraint (but altering the length of a column is allowed).
- Associated with a default but changing the length, precision or scale of a column is allowed if the data type is not changed.

In addition, some data type changes may result in a change in the data. For example, changing an **nchar** or **nvarchar** column to **char** or **varchar** can result in the conversion of extended characters. See CAST and CONVERT. Also, reducing the precision and scale of a column may result in data truncation.

new_data_type

This statement is the new data type for the altered column. Criteria for the *new_data_type* of an altered column are as follows:

- The previous data type must be implicitly convertible to the new data type.
- *new_data_type* cannot be **timestamp**.

- ANSI null defaults are always on for ALTER COLUMN; if not specified, the column is nullable.
- ANSI padding is always on for ALTER COLUMN.
- If an identity column, *new_data_type* must be a data type that supports the identity property.
- ALTER TABLE operates as if the ARITHABORT option is ON.

COLLATE < collation_name >

The COLLATE clause can be used to alter the collations only of columns of the **char**, **varchar**, **text**, **nchar**, **nvarchar** and **ntext** data types. If not specified, the column is assigned the default collation of the database.

ALTER COLUMN cannot have a collation change if any of the following conditions apply:

- If a check constraint, foreign key constraint or computed columns reference the column changed.
- If any index, statistics or full-text index are created on the column. Statistics created automatically on the column changed will be dropped if the column collation is altered.
- If a SCHEMABOUND view or function references the column.

See Collation, page 233.

DEFAULT

DEFAULT specifies the value provided for the column when a value is not explicitly supplied during an INSERT.

See discussion under CREATE TABLE above.

DEFAULT definitions cannot be added to columns that have a **timestamp** data type, an IDENTITY property, an existing DEFAULT definition or a bound default. If the column has an existing default, the default must be dropped before the new default can be added. The default is stored as a constraint and is given a name. To drop it, use sp_help to determine the default name. See the example below.

NULL | NOT NULL

If either NULL or NOT NULL is specified with ALTER COLUMN, *new_data_type* [(*precision* [, *scale*])] must also be specified even if not changed. Even if they are not changed, specify the current column values:

- **NULL with an existing column:** NULL can be specified in ALTER COLUMN to make an existing NOT NULL column changed to allow null values, except for any column in a PRIMARY KEY constraint. Existing rows are not changed by this action.

- **NULL and NO DEFAULT with a new column:** If a new column is added with NULL and NO DEFAULT, then every existing row in the table is loaded with NULL for the new column.
- **NULL and a DEFAULT with a new column:** If a new column is added with NULL and a DEFAULT, then every existing row in the table is loaded with NULL for the new column unless the WITH VALUES option is used, in which case the DEFAULT value is loaded.
- **NOT NULL with an existing column:** NOT NULL can be specified in ALTER COLUMN to change an existing NULL column to NOT NULL only if no existing row of the table contains a null value in the column. Existing rows are not changed by this action.
- **NOT NULL with a new column:** Columns can be added with ALTER TABLE with NOT NULL only if they have a default specified. If a new column is added with NOT NULL and a DEFAULT, every existing row in the table is loaded with that DEFAULT value for the new column.

WITH VALUES

In an ALTER TABLE statement adding a new column with a DEFAULT value, a WITH VALUES clause specifies that this default value be stored in that column for each existing row in the table.

If the new column is NOT NULL and has a DEFAULT, then the default will be stored in each existing table row with or without the WITH VALUES clause.

NOT NULL and WITH VALUES Examples

Example: ALTER TABLE

Change NULL to NOT NULL and add new NULL and NOT NULL columns.

SQL

```
CREATE TABLE  t (   col1      INT )
    -- Create simple table t and give it a row

INSERT INTO   t   VALUES ( -1 )
```

SQL

```
SELECT  *  FROM t
```

Result

```
col1
-----------
-1
```

SQL

```
ALTER TABLE t
    ALTER COLUMN  col1     INT     NOT NULL
                  -- Change col1 to NOT NULL
```

SQL

```
ALTER TABLE t      -- Add col2, col3, col4, col5
  ADD     col2 INT    NOT NULL  DEFAULT -9   ,
          col3 INT    NULL ,
          col4 INT    NULL    DEFAULT -9   ,
          col5 INT    NULL    DEFAULT -9 WITH VALUES
```

SQL

```
   -- Show effect on existing data of adding columns
SELECT  *  FROM t
```

Result

col1	col2	col3	col4	col5
–1	–9	NULL	NULL	–9

To Change DEFAULT **is** more involved than you might think.

Example: ALTER TABLE—Change DEFAULT on col2 from –9 to –2.

SQL (cont.)

```
EXEC sp_help  t      -- Determine name of col2 default (constraint name)
```

Result

```
...
constraint_type              constraint_name          ....   constraint_keys
---------------------------- ------------------       ....   ------------------
DEFAULT on column col2       DF__t__col2__3D2915A8    ....   –9
```

SQL

```
ALTER TABLE  t
  DROP CONSTRAINT  DF__t__col2__3D2915A8

ALTER TABLE t        ADD DEFAULT  -2  FOR col2

INSERT INTO  t  ( col1  ,  col2  )
    VALUES  ( 2 , DEFAULT )

SELECT  *  FROM t
```

Result

col1	col2	col3	col4	col5
–1	–9	NULL	NULL	–9
2	–2	NULL	-9	–9

[{ADD | DROP} ROWGUIDCOL]

The ROWGUIDCOL property is added to or dropped from the specified column.

See ROWGUIDCOL and **uniqueidentifier** discussion under CREATE TABLE and on page 129.

ADD

ADD specifies that one or more column definitions, computed column definitions or table constraints are added.

computed_column_expression

computed_column_expression is an expression that defines the value of a computed column.

See discussion under CREATE TABLE above.

WITH CHECK | WITH NOCHECK

Use WITH CHECK | WITH NOCHECK clauses to specify whether the data in the table is or is not validated against a newly added or re-enabled FOREIGN KEY or CHECK constraint.

If not specified, WITH CHECK is assumed for new constraints, and WITH NOCHECK is assumed for re-enabled constraints.

The WITH CHECK and WITH NOCHECK clauses cannot be used for PRIMARY KEY and UNIQUE constraints.

If you do not want to verify new CHECK or FOREIGN KEY constraints against existing data, use WITH NOCHECK. This is not recommended except in rare cases. The new constraint will be evaluated in all future updates. Any constraint violations suppressed by WITH NOCHECK when the constraint is added may cause future updates to fail if the user updates rows with data that does not comply with the constraint.

Constraints defined WITH NOCHECK are not considered by the query optimizer. These constraints are ignored until all such constraints are re-enabled using ALTER TABLE *table* CHECK CONSTRAINT ALL.

DROP { [CONSTRAINT] *constraint_name* | COLUMN *column_name* }

This clause specifies that *constraint_name* or *column_name* is removed from the table. Multiple columns and constraints can be listed.

A column cannot be dropped if it is:

- A replicated column.
- Used in an index.
- Used in a CHECK, FOREIGN KEY, UNIQUE or PRIMARY KEY constraint.
- Associated with a default defined with the DEFAULT keyword, or bound to a default object.
- Bound to a rule.

DROP COLUMN is not allowed if the compatibility level is 65 or earlier.

{ CHECK | NOCHECK} CONSTRAINT

This constraint specifies that *constraint_name* is enabled or disabled. When disabled, future inserts or updates to the column are not validated against the constraint conditions. This option can only be used with FOREIGN KEY and CHECK constraints. ALL specifies that all constraints are disabled with the NOCHECK option, or enabled with the CHECK option.

{ENABLE | DISABLE} TRIGGER

This trigger specifies that trigger_name is enabled or disabled. When a trigger is disabled it is still defined for the table; however, when INSERT,

UPDATE or DELETE statements are executed against the table, the actions in the trigger are not performed until the trigger is re-enabled. ALL specifies that all triggers in the table are enabled or disabled. trigger_name specifies the name of the trigger to be disabled or enabled.

column_name data_type

The data type for the new column is specified with column_name or data_type. The name used for *data_type* can be any Microsoft SQL Server or user-defined data type.

IDENTITY

IDENTITY specifies that the new column is an identity column. When a new row is added to the table, SQL Server provides a unique, incremental value for the column. Identity columns are commonly used in conjunction with PRIMARY KEY constraints to serve as the unique row identifier for the table. The IDENTITY property can be assigned to a **tinyint**, **smallint**, **int**, **bigint**, **decimal(p,0)** or **numeric(p,0)** column. Only one identity column can be created per table. The DEFAULT keyword and bound defaults cannot be used with an identity column. Either both the seed and increment must be specified, or neither. If neither is specified, the default is (1,1). *Seed* is the value used for the first row loaded into the table. *Increment* is the incremental value added to the identity value of the previous row loaded.

NOT FOR REPLICATION

NOT FOR REPLICATION specifies that the IDENTITY property should not be enforced when a replication login, such as **sqlrepl**, inserts data into the table. NOT FOR REPLICATION can also be specified on constraints. The constraint is not checked when a replication login inserts data into the table.

CONSTRAINT

CONSTRAINT specifies the beginning of a PRIMARY KEY, UNIQUE, FOREIGN KEY or CHECK constraint, or a DEFAULT definition.

constraint_name

This is the name of the new constraint. Constraint names must follow the rules for identifiers, except that the name cannot begin with a number sign (#). If *constraint_name* is not supplied, a system-generated name is assigned to the constraint.

PRIMARY KEY

PRIMARY KEY is a constraint that enforces entity integrity for a given column or columns through a unique index. Only one PRIMARY KEY constraint can be created for each table.

UNIQUE

UNIQUE is a constraint that provides entity integrity for a given column or columns through a unique index.

CLUSTERED | NONCLUSTERED

CLUSTERED | NONCLUSTERED specifies that a clustered or nonclustered index is created for the PRIMARY KEY or UNIQUE constraint. PRIMARY KEY constraints default to CLUSTERED; UNIQUE constraints default to NONCLUSTERED.

If a clustered constraint or index already exists on a table, CLUSTERED cannot be specified in ALTER TABLE. If a clustered constraint or index already exists on a table, PRIMARY KEY constraints default to NONCLUSTERED.

This specifies the percentage of fill SQL Server should use to create each index leaf page. `WITH FILLFACTOR =` *`fillfactor`*

See discussion of FILLFACTOR with the CREATE INDEX statement, page 264.

ON {*filegroup* | DEFAULT}

This phrase specifies the storage location of the index created for the constraint. If *filegroup* is specified, the index is created in the named filegroup. If DEFAULT is specified, the index is created in the default filegroup. If ON is not specified, the index is created in the filegroup that contains the table. If ON is specified when adding a clustered index for a PRIMARY KEY or UNIQUE constraint, the entire table is moved to the specified filegroup when the clustered index is created.

DEFAULT, in this context, is not a keyword. DEFAULT is an identifier for the default filegroup and must be delimited, as in ON "DEFAULT" or ON [DEFAULT].

FOREIGN KEY...REFERENCES

FOREIGN KEY. . . REFERENCES is a constraint that provides referential integrity for the data in the column. FOREIGN KEY constraints require that each value in the column exists in the specified column in the referenced table.

ref_table

ref_table refers to the table referenced by the FOREIGN KEY constraint.

ref_column

ref_column is a column or list of columns in parentheses referenced by the new FOREIGN KEY constraint.

ON DELETE {CASCADE | NO ACTION}

See discussion under CREATE TABLE above.

ON UPDATE {CASCADE | NO ACTION}

See discussion under CREATE TABLE above.

[ASC | DESC]

[ASC | DESC] specifies the order in which the column or columns participating in table constraints are sorted. The default is ASC.

FOR *column*

FOR column specifies the column associated with a table-level DEFAULT definition.

CHECK

CHECK is a constraint that enforces domain integrity by limiting the possible values that can be entered into a column or columns.

logical_expression

logical_expression is a logical expression used in a CHECK constraint. It returns TRUE or FALSE. *Logical_expression* used with CHECK constraints cannot reference another table but can reference other columns in the same table for the same row.

3.1.16.11 DROP TABLE Syntax

Syntax

```
DROP TABLE   table_name
```

CREATE, ALTER, DROP TABLE Examples

SQL
DROP TABLE t
Result
The command(s) completed successfully.

3.1.16.12 IDENTITY Property

The IDENTITY property automatically generates integer values usually for Primary Key.

- IDENTITY is a property applied in CREATE TABLE or ALTER TABLE to a column of decimal, int, numeric, smallint, bigint or tinyint data type to have SQL Server automatically generate a sequence of numbers upon INSERT of a new row.

```
IDENTITY [ ( initial , increment ) ]
```

- First INSERT uses the *initial* value, each subsequent INSERT adds *increment*. Either both values (*initial* , *increment*) are given or neither (uses default (1,1)).
- Maximum of one IDENTITY property column is allowed per table.
- By default, the column name of the IDENTITY column cannot be listed in an INSERT statement. See below: SET IDENTITY_INSERT tablename ON.
- SQL Server only, not portable to other RDBMSs.

Example: In Query Analyzer or isql or osql execute the following:

SQL

```
CREATE TABLE table2 (
          a     DEC          IDENTITY     PRIMARY  KEY,
          b     VARCHAR(10)     NOT NULL,
          c     DATETIME   DEFAULT GETDATE()
         -- GETDATE() is the SQL Server
         -- function that returns system time
);
```

- Row 1: Correct. We do *not* provide a value for column a, the IDENTITY column.

SQL

```
INSERT              table2  (b,c)
VALUES (  'Bab', NULL );                -- OK
```

- Row 2: Incorrect. It fails because we provide a value for column a, the IDENTITY column.

SQL

```
INSERT INTO table2 (b) VALUES ( 'Amy' );     -- OK INSERT
INTO table2 (a,b)
VALUES ( DEFAULT, 'Amy' );
        -- FAILS, can't mention column a
```

SQL (cont.)

Result

```
Server: Msg 544, Level 16, State 1, Line 1
Cannot insert explicit value for identity column in table 'table2' when IDENTITY_INSERT is set to OFF.
```

SQL

```
INSERT INTO table2 (b) VALUES ( 'Amy' );     -- OK
```

- Row 3

SQL

```
INSERT INTO table2            VALUES ( 'Carl' );
     -- Fails, must give value for "c"
     -- Value for "c" must be a legal domain
     -- value of DATETIME, DEFAULT or NULL
```

SQL

```
INSERT INTO table2     VALUES ( 'Carl', DEFAULT ); -- OK
```

SQL

```
SELECT * FROM table2
```

Result

```
a            b            c
----------   ---------    --------------------------
1            Bab          NULL
2            Amy          2002-11-01 15:49:09.543
3            Carl         2002-11-01 15:53:08.077.
```

3.1.16.13 The @@IDENTITY Function

The @@IDENTITY function returns the last identity value generated by the most recent successful INSERT, SELECT INTO or bulk copy statement. If the statement did not affect any tables with identity columns, @@IDENTITY returns NULL.

If the statement fires one or more triggers that perform inserts generating identity values, calling @@IDENTITY immediately after the statement returns the last identity value generated by the triggers.

Example:

SQL

```
INSERT INTO table2
VALUES ( 'Dave', DEFAULT );   -- OK
```

SQL

```
SELECT @@IDENTITY
```

Result

```
----------------------------------------
4
```

3.1.16.14 `IDENT_CURRENT` (*table*) Function

IDENT_CURRENT (*table*) returns the last identity value generated for the specified table in any session and scope.

SQL

```
SELECT IDENT_CURRENT('table2')
-- Must enclose table name in single quotes 'table'
```

Result

```
----------------------------------------
4
```

SQL

```
USE pubs
go

SELECT IDENT_CURRENT('table2')
```

SQL (cont.)

Result

```
--------------------------------------
NULL
```

SQL

```
SELECT IDENT_CURRENT('mydb..table2')
```

Result

```
--------------------------------------
4
```

3.1.16.15 Allow Inserting a Value into an IDENTITY Column

You may allow inserting into an IDENTITY column for a table by executing SET IDENTITY_INSERT table_name ON.

Example: Using the same table "table2"

- Row 4

SQL

```
SET IDENTITY_INSERT table2 ON

INSERT INTO table2  (a,b,c) VALUES (8, 'Edna', ' March 22,
2003' );  -- OK

SET IDENTITY_INSERT table2 OFF
```

- Row 5

SQL

```
INSERT INTO table2 (b) VALUES ( 'Frank' );      -- OK
```

SQL

```
SELECT * FROM table2
```

SQL (cont.)

Result

a	b	c
1	Bab	NULL
2	Amy	2002-11-01 15:49:09.543
3	Carl	2002-11-01 15:53:08.077
4	Dave	2002-11-01 15:53:08.077
8	Edna	2003-03-22 00:00:00.000
9	Frank	2002-11-01 15:57:31.653

Enabling **IDENTITY_INSERT** can cause some confusion and should not be done unless carefully tested on a nonproduction server. When **IDENTITY_INSERT** is **ON**, each INSERT must give a value for the identity column. When **IDENTITY_INSERT** is later set to **OFF**, the next identity value will be one more than the higher of the highest value explicitly inserted. It will also be the last value automatically used.

Example: Using IDENTITY property

Create two tables, one called **ipaddrs** to store IP Addresses and one called **traps** to store information about each SNMP trap event on that IP address.

```
CREATE TABLE ipaddrs (
   id        INT IDENTITY    PRIMARY KEY
,  ipaddr    VARCHAR(15)     UNIQUE
);

INSERT INTO ipaddrs VALUES
  ('111.111.1.1')
```

```
CREATE TABLE traps (
   id          INT
,  trapinfo    VARCHAR(15)
,   CONSTRAINT fk_trap_addr FOREIGN KEY (id)
   REFERENCES ipaddrs (id)
);

INSERT INTO traps VALUES ( 1 , 'Info11')
INSERT INTO traps VALUES ( 1 , 'Info12')
```

We now want to write the code to add new trap events given the **ipaddr.**

For the new trap event we have the ipaddr and trap info, so we must do two things:

1. Look up the given **ipaddr** in the **ipaddrs** table to find its **id**; if not in **ipaddrs** we must insert it and remember the new **id**.
2. Insert the trapinfo into **traps** table with the correct **id**.

SQL

```
SELECT * FROM table2
```

Result

```
id          ipaddr
-------     --------------
1           111.111.1.1
2           222.222.2.2

id          trapinfo
-------     --------------
1           Info11
1           Info12
2           Info21
```

3.1.16.16 A Table with a UNIQUEIDENTIFIER Column

UNIQUEIDENTIFIER Data Type The UNIQUEIDENTIFIER data type is a globally unique identifier (GUID). According to Books Online:

> If an application must generate an identifier column that is unique across the entire database, or every database on every networked computer in the world, use the ROWGUIDCOL property, the **uniqueidentifier** data type, and the NEWID function.

The following rules apply to UNIQUEIDENTIFIER data type.

- The only operations that are allowed against a **uniqueidentifier** value are comparisons (=, <>, <, >, <=, >=) and checking for NULL (IS NULL and IS NOT NULL). No other arithmetic operators are allowed.
- All column constraints and properties except IDENTITY are allowed on the **uniqueidentifier** data type.
- To generate unique values for each column use the **NEWID( )** function.

Syntax

```
NEWID()
```

Returns a unique value of type **UNIQUIDENTIFIER**.

ROWGUIDCOL Property This property indicates that the new column is a Row Global Unique Identifier Column.

The ROWGUIDCOL property

- can be assigned only to a **uniqueidentifier** column.
- can be assigned to only one **uniqueidentifier** column per table.
- does not enforce uniqueness of the values in the column.
- does not automatically generate values for new rows inserted into the table.

Examples with UNIQUEIDENTIFIER: CREATE table 3 with UNIQUIDENTIFIER column.

SQL

```
CREATE TABLE table3 (
    a    UNIQUEIDENTIFIER      PRIMARY  KEY
         -- DEFAULT NEWID()    -- could be used here
,   b    VARCHAR(10)     NOT NULL
);
```

SQL

```
INSERT INTO table3 (a,b) VALUES ( NEWID() , 'Amy' );
INSERT INTO table3 (a,b) VALUES ( NEWID() , 'Bab' );
SELECT * FROM table3
ORDER BY a DESC    -- is okay since comparison operators
are defined on UID
```

Result

```
a                                                    b
---------------------------------------------------- ----------
79439DA8-2B36-4E28-AE55-98EA53355CE7                 Amy
5AC15E51-AE28-40EF-B85E-E5B95D5586AA                 Bab
```

CREATE table 4 with UNIQUIDENTIFIER column having NEWID() as default.

SQL

```
CREATE TABLE table4 (
    a            uniqueidentifier
CONSTRAINT t4_Guid_Default   DEFAULT NEWID()
    b            varchar(10)
CONSTRAINT  t4_Guid_PK   PRIMARY KEY (a)
)
```

SQL

```
INSERT INTO table4 (a,b) VALUES ( DEFAULT, 'Amy' );
INSERT INTO table4 (a,b) VALUES ( DEFAULT, 'Bab' );
SELECT * FROM table4;
```

Result

```
a                                                      b
------------------------------------------------------ ----------
10C83C70-E337-4E4A-873B-5C7010AF1BD9                   Amy
8E9D090F-8250-4ED7-848A-C3ABF723A1F2                   Bab
```

There is no equivalent of @@IDENTITY for UNIQUEIDENTIFIER. If you need the last UNIQUEIDENTIFIER value used, do the following.

SQL

```
SELECT * FROM table2
```

Result

```
9CEB4FFB-28DB-4395-A3A7-CA707EB0F55A

a                                                      b
------------------------------------------------------ ----------
10C83C70-E337-4E4A-873B-5C7010AF1BD9                   Amy
8E9D090F-8250-4ED7-848A-C3ABF723A1F2                   Bab
9CEB4FFB-28DB-4395-A3A7-CA707EB0F55A                   Carl
```

3.1.17 CREATE, ALTER, DROP TRIGGER

A trigger is a type of stored procedure defined on a specified table; the trigger code is automatically executed upon an INSERT, UPDATE and/or DELETE on that table.

The trigger and the statement that fires it are placed in a single transaction which can be rolled back from within the trigger. Note the following terms:

- *triggering action*—the INSERT, UPDATE or DELETE statement that fires the trigger
- *trigger code*—the trigger Transact-SQL statement(s) that execute when the trigger fires

3.1.17.1 CREATE TRIGGER Syntax

Syntax

```
CREATE TRIGGER     [ owner_name. ] trigger_name
ON {  [ owner_name. ] table |   [ owner_name. ] view } [ WITH ENCRYPTION ]
{
    {  { { FOR | AFTER } | INSTEAD OF }    { [ INSERT ] [ , ] [ UPDATE ] [ , ]
  [ DELETE ] }
   [ WITH APPEND ]       [ NOT FOR REPLICATION ]
   AS
   sql_statement [ ...n ]
    }
}
```

Arguments

trigger_name

This is the name of the trigger to be created.

Table | view

Table | *view* is the table or view on which the trigger is executed, and it is sometimes called the trigger table or trigger view. A view can be referenced only by an INSTEAD OF trigger.

WITH ENCRYPTION

WITH ENCRYPTION encrypts the **syscomments** entries that contain the text of CREATE TRIGGER. It prevents the trigger from being published as part of SQL Server replication.

{ AFTER | FOR } | INSTEAD OF

The choice of AFTER, FOR or INSTEAD OF keyword specifies the relationship of executing the trigger code (`sql_statement`) with respect to executing the triggering action INSERT, UPDATE and/or DELETE. (Unlike

Oracle, SQL Server has no *BEFORE trigger* where the trigger code executes before the triggering action.)

AFTER and FOR have the same effect. AFTER is suggested for new code. FOR is kept for backward compatibility. AFTER or FOR specify that the trigger code will execute *after the triggering action* AND all referential cascade actions and constraint checks have executed successfully. If any fails, the trigger code is not executed.

AFTER triggers can only be defined on tables (not on views).

INSTEAD OF specifies that the trigger is executed instead of the triggering action INSERT, UPDATE and/or DELETE. At most, one INSTEAD OF trigger per INSERT, UPDATE or DELETE statement can be defined on a table or view. But it is possible to define views where each view has its own INSTEAD OF trigger.

INSTEAD OF triggers can be quite useful when defined on a view to do the INSERT/UPDATE/DELETE on one or more base tables. INSTEAD OF triggers may update text, ntext, or image columns.

INSTEAD OF triggers are not allowed on:

- updatable views WITH CHECK OPTION
- DELETE on tables with a FOREIGN KEY with cascade ON DELETE
- UPDATE on tables with a FOREIGN KEY with cascade ON UPDATE

{ [INSERT] [,] [UPDATE] [,] [DELETE] }

This is the *triggering action* that causes the trigger to fire.

One, two or all three keywords may be specified in any order. Occurrence of any specified action fires the trigger.

NOT FOR REPLICATION

NOT FOR REPLICATION specifies that the trigger will not fire on a triggering action (INSERT,UPDATE,DELETE) due to replication.

AS sql_statement

This section of the CREATE TRIGGER statement is the trigger body or trigger code consisting of the Transact-SQL statements executed when the trigger is activated. The trigger body may do things like checking data values in the current operation and, if unsatisfactory, execute ROLLBACK to abort the operation. These statements may also modify data in the database but **should not return data to the user**. For example, the PRINT statements shown in examples below are used for test and demonstration only and should be removed from production code.

In addition to the usual Transact-SQL constructs, there are three special capabilities available only in trigger code:

- **deleted** and **inserted** logical tables providing old and new data values
- **UPDATE** (*column_name*) Boolean predicate telling whether a specified column is being changed
- **COLUMNS_UPDATED()** function telling all columns being changed as a bitmask

These three constructs are described here.

Deleted and Inserted Logical Tables The **deleted** and **inserted** keywords represent logical (conceptual) tables with either 1 row or 0 rows containing the previous and new data values of the row being changed by the action which fired the trigger. These tables are structurally the same as the table on which the trigger is defined. The contents of **deleted** and **inserted** are summarized in Table 3-7.

Table 3-7 Capabilities of Triggering Action

	TRIGGERING ACTION		
	INSERT	**UPDATE**	**DELETE**
deleted	empty table	before row image	before row image
inserted	after row image	after row image	empty table

For UPDATE and DELETE operations the **deleted** table ("before" or "old" table) consists of 1 row containing the old data values of the current row before doing the UPDATE or DELETE. For an INSERT operation the **deleted** table is empty (0 rows).

For UPDATE and INSERT operations the **inserted** table ("after" or "new" table) consists consists of 1 row containing the new data values for the current row after doing the UPDATE or INSERT. For a DELETE operation the **inserted** table is empty (0 rows).

Example: Trigger using "deleted"—show that when a new row is inserted the deleted table is empty.

SQL

```
CREATE TABLE  t  (   a   INT  ,   b   INT )

CREATE TRIGGER trg_t_insert
ON  t
AFTER INSERT
AS
BEGIN                  -- BEGIN/END are not required
  PRINT 'Deleted row follows: '
        -- PRINT and SELECT in the trigger are
        -- for testing only
  SELECT * FROM deleted
    -- Should not have output on a production trigger
  PRINT 'Inserted row follows: '
  SELECT * FROM inserted
END
```

SQL

```
INSERT INTO t VALUES ( 1 , 2 )
  -- This INSERT will fire the trigger trg_t_insert
```

Result

```
Deleted row follows:
a               b
--------        --------
(0 row(s) affected)

Inserted row follows:
a               b
--------        --------
1               2
(1 row(s) affected)
```

UPDATE (column) UPDATE (*column_name*) allows you to check whether a certain column is being changed by the current INSERT or UPDATE operation. UPDATE (*column_name*) is a Boolean predicate available in INSERT and UPDATE triggers which may be used anywhere in the trigger's *sql_statement*, usually in an IF construct. The *column* parameter is the column name to be tested.

UPDATE (*column_name*) returns

TRUE if the specified column name is changed by an UPDATE triggering action

TRUE for every column in INSERT actions

FALSE for every column in DELETE actions

UPDATE (*column_name*) may be used like any other predicate in IF, IF ... ELSE or WHILE constructs including the ability to use BEGIN...END blocks if desired. Either simple or compound predicates can be specified such as

IF UPDATE (col1)
IF UPDATE (col1) AND UPDATE (col2)
IF UPDATE (col1) OR UPDATE (col2)

Example: Demonstrate UPDATE (column_name)

SQL

```
CREATE TABLE t ( a INT , b CHAR(10) );
```

The following trigger will fire (activate) every time there is either an INSERT or UPDATE statement executed on table t. The "DID update" print statement will execute for every INSERT on table **t** and for each UPDATE that changes the value of column **b**.

Example:

SQL

```
CREATE  TRIGGER trg_t_ins_upd
ON t
AFTER INSERT , UPDATE
AS
IF UPDATE (b)
   print 'IN TRIGGER trg_t_ins_upd: DID update b'
      -- PRINT in the trigger is for testing only
ELSE
   print 'IN TRIGGER trg_t_ins_upd: NO update b'
      -- PRINT in the trigger is for testing only
```

Compound predicates can be specified.

- `IF UPDATE (col1 )`
- `IF UPDATE (col1 )  AND  UPDATE (col2 )`
- `IF UPDATE (col1 )  OR  UPDATE (col2 )`

COLUMNS_UPDATED ( ) COLUMNS_UPDATED() provides an alternative to UPDATE (*column_name*) by giving you a single bitmask containing 1 for each column in the table that is being changed by the current INSERT or UPDATE operation. The least significant bit is leftmost and represents column 1. The returned value is a **varbinary** bit pattern containing enough 8-bit bytes to account for all columns in the table. Each bit of COLUMNS_UPDATED() returns

- 1 if the specified column is changed by an UPDATE triggering action
- 1 for every column in INSERT actions
- 0 for every column in DELETE actions

COLUMNS_UPDATED() can be used anywhere inside the body of the trigger, but it often appears in an IF statement like the following:

IF (COLUMNS_UPDATED() *bitwise_operator updated_bitmask*) *comparison_operator column_bitmask*

Bitwise operators are used to compare two bitmasks in the form of **int**, **smallint** or **tinyint** data on a bit-by-bit basis and return a resulting bitmask depending on the operator used. The bitwise operators are shown in Table 3-8.

Table 3-8 Bitwise Operators

Bitwise Operator	Meaning
&	Bitwise AND
|	Bitwise OR
~	Bitwise NOT
^	Bitwise Exclusive OR

An *updated_bitmask* is the decimal representation of your bitmask created to check the columns in which you are interested.

To check column *n* calculate the decimal value of 2^{n-1} (e.g., for column 2 use 2^1 or 2. For column 4 use 2^3 or 8.

To check multiple columns, add the decimal values for each column (e.g., for columns 2 and 4 use $2^1 + 2^3$ or 2 + 8 or 10. See Tables 3-9 and 3-10.

For the comparison_operator, use the greater than symbol (>) to check if ANY OF THE COLUMNS specified in updated_bitmask are updated. Or use the equal sign (=) to check whether ALL COLUMNS specified in updated_bitmask are updated.

A column_bitmask is the integer bitmask (as a decimal number) of those columns to check whether they are being updated or inserted. This is usually 0 with > (> 0) to see if any of the columns were changed and it is usually the same as updated_bitmask for = (= updated_bitmask) to see if all of these columns were changed.

SQL

```
CREATE TABLE  t
  (   a   INT   ,    b    INT   ,    c    INT   ,    d    INT )

INSERT INTO  t
      ( a , b , c , d )  VALUES  ( 1 , 2 , 3 , 4 )
```

SQL

```
SELECT  *  FROM  t
   -- table t has 4 columns and only 1 row
```

Result

```
a       b       c       d
-----   -----   -----   -----
1       2       3       4
```

Table 3-9 Bitmask Value

	a	b	c	d
bit position, n	0	1	2	3
2^n	1	2	4	8

If these columns are updated, then COLUMNS_UPDATED( ) value is as shown in Table 3-10.

Table 3-10 Updated Column Results

Columns that were updated	COLUMNS_UPDATED( ) Returns
a	1
b	2
c	4
d	8
a and b	3
b and c	6
b and d	**10**
c and d	12
b and c and d	14

Examples of the entire clause to check if columns 2 (b) and 4 (d) were updated is as follows.

To check if *EITHER* column 2 *OR* 4 was updated use

```
IF (COLUMNS_UPDATED() & 10) > 0
```

To check if *BOTH* column 2 *AND* 4 was updated use

```
IF (COLUMNS_UPDATED() & 10) = 10
```

Example Trigger to Use COLUMNS_UPDATED()

When a new row is inserted into table t, display both columns. The **deleted** table is empty.

```
SQL
CREATE TABLE  t
  (   a  INT  ,   b   INT  ,   c   INT  ,   d   INT )

INSERT INTO  t
  ( a , b , c , d )  VALUES  ( 1 , 2 , 3 , 4 )
```

```
SQL
  SELECT  *  FROM  t
     -- table t has 4 columns and only 1 row
```

SQL (cont.)

Result

```
a       b       c       d
-----   -----   -----   -----
1       2       3       4
```

SQL

```
CREATE TRIGGER  trg_t_update
ON   t
AFTER UPDATE
AS
    IF (COLUMNS_UPDATED() & 10) = 10
       -- TRUE if BOTH columns 2 and 4 are updated
      PRINT 'Both 2 and 4 updated'
    ELSE
      PRINT 'Not Both 2 and 4 updated'
    PRINT  CAST( COLUMNS_UPDATED() AS INT )
```

SQL

```
UPDATE t SET a = a          -- Update only column 1
```

Result

```
Not Both 2 and 4 updated
(1 row(s) affected)
1
```

SQL

```
UPDATE t SET d = d -- Update only column 4
```

Result

```
Not Both 2 and 4 updated
(1 row(s) affected)
8
```

SQL

```
UPDATE t SET b = b , d = d  -- Update columns 2 and 4
```

Result

Both 2 and 4 updated
(1 row(s) affected)
10

Additional Comments

CREATE TRIGGER must be the first statement in the batch and can apply to only one table.

A trigger is created in the current database, but it can reference objects outside the current database.

If the trigger owner name is specified to qualify the trigger, qualify the table name in the same way.

A trigger may specify any SET statement. The SET option is in effect only during trigger execution.

When a trigger fires, results are returned to the calling application as with stored procedures.

I suggest that SELECT statements and variable assignment statement be avoided in triggers as they require special handling in every application which might activate the trigger.

- TRUNCATE TABLE statements do not fire a DELETE trigger.
- The WRITETEXT statement, whether logged or unlogged, does not activate a trigger.
- These Transact-SQL statements are not allowed in a trigger:

ALTER DATABASE	CREATE DATABASE	DISK INIT
DISK RESIZE	DROP DATABASE	LOAD DATABASE
LOAD LOG	RECONFIGURE	RESTORE DATABASE
RESTORE LOG		

- SQL Server does not support user-defined triggers on system tables.

3.1.17.2 Multiple AFTER Triggers

SQL Server 7.0 and 2000 allow multiple AFTER triggers (with different trigger names) to be created for each data modification event (INSERT, UPDATE, or DELETE).

sp_settriggerorder If you have multiple AFTER triggers on the same trigger action on the same table you may use the procedure sp_settriggerorder to set one trigger set to fire First and one trigger to fire Last.

Syntax

```
sp_settriggerorder   [@triggername = ] 'triggername'
         , [@order = ] { 'First ' | 'Last' | 'None' }
         , [@stmttype = ]  { 'INSERT ' | 'UPDATE' | 'DELETE'
}
```

Using ALTER TRIGGER drops the first (or last) attribute, so sp_settriggerorder must be re-executed to again assign it as First (or Last).

Other triggers on the same trigger action and table fire in random order between First and Last.

Nested Triggers —Enabled by Default for Server Triggers can be nested to a maximum of 32 levels. If a trigger changes a table on which there is another trigger, the second trigger is activated and can then call a third trigger, and so on.

If a trigger in the chain sets off an infinite loop, the nesting level is exceeded and the trigger aborts.

If nested triggers is disabled, direct recursive triggers (below) is also disabled, regardless of the **RECURSIVE_TRIGGERS** setting of **ALTER DATABASE**.

Nested triggers and indirect recursion are enabled (default) and disabled for the server with

```
EXEC sp_configure   'nested triggers' ,   {0|1}   - 0 disables, 1 enables

RECONFIGURE    -- run to make the sp_configure change effective now
```

Recursive Triggers—Disabled by Default for Database SQL Server allows recursive invocation of triggers when the **RECURSIVE_TRIGGERS** is enabled.

SQL
SELECT DATABASEPROPERTYEX ('pubs' , 'IsRecursiveTriggersEnabled')

SQL (cont.)

Result

```
------------------------------------------
0
```

SQL

```
ALTER DATABASE pubs   SET RECURSIVE_TRIGGERS   ON
    -- ON enables, OFF disables
```

SQL

```
SELECT DATABASEPROPERTYEX
   ( 'pubs' , 'IsRecursiveTriggersEnabled' )
```

Result

```
------------------------------------------
1
```

Recursive triggers allow two types of recursion to occur:

1. *Direct recursion*

A table **T1** update fires trigger **TR1** which updates table **T1** and again fires trigger **TR1**, etc.

Direct recursion is enabled and disabled (default) for the database with
ALTER DATABASE pubs SET RECURSIVE_TRIGGERS {ON|OFF}

This also requires the server nested triggers setting to be enabled (default is enabled).

2. *Indirect recursion* — circular nested triggers

An update on table **T1** fires trigger **TR1** which updates table **T2** firing trigger **TR2** which updates table **T1** and again fires trigger **TR1**, etc.

Nested triggers and indirect recursion are enabled (default) and disabled for the server with

```
EXEC sp_configure   'nested triggers' ,   {0|1}   - 0
disables, 1 enables

RECONFIGURE   -- run to make the sp_configure change
effective now
```

3.1.17.3 ALTER TRIGGER Syntax

```
ALTER TRIGGER trigger_name
   ON ( table | view )
   [ WITH ENCRYPTION ]
   {
       { ( FOR | AFTER | INSTEAD OF ) { [ DELETE ] [ , ] [ INSERT ] [ , ]
   [ UPDATE ] }
                      [ NOT FOR REPLICATION ]
      AS
      sql_statement [ ...n ]
        }
      |
        { ( FOR | AFTER | INSTEAD OF ) { [ INSERT ] [ , ] [ UPDATE ] }
                      [ NOT FOR REPLICATION ]
      AS
       {
          IF UPDATE ( column )      [ { AND | OR } UPDATE ( column ) ] [ ...n ]
          | IF ( COLUMNS_UPDATED ( ) { bitwise_operator } updated_bitmask )
                          { comparison_operator } column_bitmask [ ...n ]
          }
      sql_statement [ ...n ]
      }
   }
```

3.1.17.4 DROP TRIGGER Syntax

```
DROP TRIGGER { trigger } [ ,...n ]
```

3.1.17.5 Trigger Example—Maintain Data Consistency of Denormalized Tables

We have intentionally denormalized the itemsuppliers table, Table 3-11, to hold a copy of the supplier telephone number (supptelnum) column from the suppliers table, Table 3-12.

Table 3-11 itemsuppliers Table

itemnum	supplierid	supptelnum
33	500	2222
34	500	5555
35	500	5555

Table 3-12 suppliers Table

supplierid	suppname	supptelnum
500	BB Inc.	2222
502	EE Inc.	5555

We must create two triggers to keep the data consistent.

- **Trigger 1:** INSERT new row into **itemsuppliers** => copy **suppltelnum** from **suppliers**
- **Trigger 2:** UPDATE suppltelnum in **suppliers** => update **suppltelnum** in **itemsuppliers**

Implement the Triggers:

Trigger 1: INSERT a new row into itemsuppliers => copy suppltelnum from suppliers.

SQL

```
CREATE TRIGGER   trg_supptelnum_to_itemsupp
ON   itemsuppliers
AFTER INSERT
AS
BEGIN
  UPDATE  itemsuppliers SET  supptelnum   =
    ( SELECT supptelnum  FROM suppliers
    WHERE supplierid = (SELECT supplierid FROM inserted)    )
  WHERE supplierid   =
    (SELECT supplierid FROM inserted );
END ;
go
```

Trigger 2: UPDATE a suppltelnum in suppliers => update suppltelnum in itemsuppliers.

SQL

```
CREATE TRIGGER   trg_update_supptelnum
ON  suppliers
AFTER UPDATE
AS
--  No option, all are FOR EACH ROW
IF UPDATE (supptelnum)
BEGIN
    UPDATE  itemsuppliers   SET  supptelnum  =
      (SELECT supptelnum FROM inserted)
        -- can't use "inserted.supptelnum"
    WHERE    supplierid =
      (SELECT supplierid FROM inserted)
END ;
go
```

3.1.17.6 Test the Triggers

We'll use the previous Initial Values.

SQL

```
SELECT * FROM suppliers ;
```

Result

supplierid	suppname	suppteln\um
500	BB Inc	2222
502	EE Inc	5555

SQL

```
SELECT * FROM itemsuppliers ;
```

Result

itemnum	supplierid	supptelnum
33	500	2222
34	500	2222
35	500	2222

Test Trigger 1—INSERT new row into itemsuppliers

SQL

```
INSERT INTO itemsuppliers  (itemnum , supplierid )  VALUES ( 44 , 502 ) ;
```

Result

1 row affected.

SQL

```
SELECT * FROM suppliers ;
```

Result

upplierid	suppname	supptelnum
500	BB Inc	2222
502	EE Inc	5555

SQL

```
SELECT * FROM itemsuppliers ;
```

Result

```
itemnum        supplierid      supptelnum
---------      ----------      ----------
33             500             2222
34             500             2222
35             500             2222
44             502             5555
```

Test Trigger 2—UPDATE supptelnum in suppliers

SQL

```
UPDATE suppliers  SET  supptelnum  =  9999
WHERE supplierid = 500 ;
```

Result

1 row updated

SQL

```
SELECT * FROM suppliers ;
```

Result

```
supplierid     supplierid      supptelnum
---------      ----------      ----------
500            BB Inc.         9999
502            EE Inc.         5555
```

SQL

```
SELECT * FROM itemsuppliers ;
```

Result

```
itemnum        supplierid      supptelnum
---------      ----------      ----------
33             500             9999
34             500             9999
35             500             9999
44             502             5555
```

3.1.18 CREATE, ALTER, DROP VIEW

A view is a named stored SELECT statement. It can be used in SQL statements like a table.

Note: When discussing views, we need to recall that a base table is the result of a CREATE TABLE. A base table contains persistent data on disk.

3.1.18.1 View Properties

Views share these characteristics:

- A view is a "virtual table" returning the result set of its SELECT statement.
- A view contains no persistent data in the database (except for indexed views, new in SQL Server 2K).
- A view name may be used in any DML statement (almost) anywhere a table name may be used.
- SQL Server dynamically merges the logic needed to build the view result set into the logic needed to build the complete final query result set from the data in the base tables.
- Essentially any legal *select-statement* may be used in a view except for the restrictions given below.

There are similarities between a view and an inline table-valued function, but only the view is standard ANSI SQL, and only the function can take parameters.

3.1.18.2 Views' Advantages

Views offer:

- Ease of use: Views are often more convenient for users, as when giving a simplified look at complex tables.
- Security: The administrator can grant permission on the view which restricts access to data.
- Access to obsolete tables: An obsolete table that has been restructured into two new tables can be given a view with the former table name. This allows legacy programs to continue to run without error.

3.1.18.3 CREATE VIEW Syntax

```
CREATE VIEW   [ < owner > . ] view_name [ ( column [ ,...n ] ) ]
[ WITH  { ENCRYPTION | SCHEMABINDING | VIEW_METADATA }  [ ,...n ] ]
AS
```

```
    select_statement
[ WITH CHECK OPTION ]
```

Arguments

WITH ENCRYPTION

WITH ENCRYPTION encrypts the **syscomments** entries that contain the text of CREATE VIEW. It prevents the view from being published as part of SQL Server replication.

WITH SCHEMABINDING

WITH SCHEMABINDING binds the view to the schema which means that views or tables named in the definition cannot be altered in a way as to invalidate this definition, and cannot be dropped until this view is either dropped or altered to remove SCHEMABINDING.

When SCHEMABINDING is specified, the SELECT statement must include the two-part names (owner.object) of tables, views or user-defined functions referenced.

WITH VIEW_METADATA

WITH VIEW_METADATA causes the server to return view metadata information to DBLIB, ODBC and OLE DB APIs.

select_statement

A select_statement is one SELECT (or multiple SELECT statements connected by UNION or UNION ALL) that defines the view. It may reference one or more tables or views and may contain subqueries. A view's SELECT statement may *not* include the following:

- COMPUTE or COMPUTE BY clause
- ORDER BY clause unless it has a TOP phrase in the select list
- INTO keyword
- a reference to a temporary table nor table variable

WITH CHECK OPTION

WITH CHECK OPTION causes all data modifications executed through the view to be checked for adherence to defining SELECT statement criteria so that rows changed through the view remain visible through the view after the modification. For example, a column value not included in the view definition cannot be changed through the view. Also a column in the view cannot be changed to a value no longer satisfying the WHERE clause.

3.1.18.4 ALTER VIEW Syntax

```
ALTER VIEW [ < database_name > . ] [ < owner > . ] view_name [ ( co
  [ ,...n ] ) ]
[ WITH  { ENCRYPTION | SCHEMABINDING | VIEW_METADATA }  [ ,...n ] ]
AS
     select_statement
[ WITH CHECK OPTION ]
```

3.1.18.5 DROP VIEW Syntax

```
DROP VIEW { view } [ ,...n ]
```

3.1.18.6 Comments on CREATE VIEW and ALTER VIEW

Updatable Views: A view of a single table may accommodate INSERT statements if care is taken to include all NON-NULL columns without specified defaults. UPDATE and DELETE work on a single table view with fewer restrictions, but they should be carefully planned and tested. See examples below.

Multiple table views usually require the use of INSTEAD OF triggers (new in SQL Server 2K) to permit INSERT or DELETE. UPDATE of a multiple table view may be done with an INSTEAD OF trigger or, in some cases, without one if well planned.

Partitioned Views (new with SS 2000): According to Books Online, "A partitioned view joins horizontally partitioned data from a set of member tables across one or more servers, making the data appear as if from one table." See Section 3.1.20 for details on partitioned views.

ALTER VIEW causes complete replacement of the view without changing permissions, so desired keywords such as WITH ENCRYPTION must be included or their effect will be lost.

Examples: CREATE, DROP VIEW

SQL

```
     /*  On page 371 we created database mydb and
     table emps3 used in the next example. */
USE mydb
go
```

SQL

```
SELECT  *   FROM  emps3
        -- Show contents of emps3 for reference
```

SQL (cont.)

Result

```
ename           empid   deptno  telnum  salary  hiredate        sales_amt
--------------- ------  ------  ------  ------  --------------- ---------
Suzy Smith      1111    102     NULL    20      2003-01-01      NULL
Sammy Sosa      2222    102     2345    30      1992-01-01      200
zill Johnson    4444    101     NULL    40      1994-01-01      NULL
Mary Smith      5555    100     5678    50      1990-01-01      NULL
Mary Smith      7777    101     7890    60      1996-01-01      400
```

Example: Create a view as a horizontal slice, all columns but certain rows (empid > 4000).

SQL

```
CREATE VIEW   emps_over_4000
AS
      SELECT   *
      FROM     emps3
      WHERE empid > 4000
go
```

A view is a database object that is a virtual table used like a table in queries.

SQL

```
SELECT  ename, empid
FROM emps_over_4000
   -- VIEW  emps_over_4000 can be used like a table
```

Result

```
ename                empid
-------------------- ------
Bill Johnson         4444
Mary Smith           5555
Mary Smith           7777
```

SQL

```
SELECT ename
FROM emps_over_4000
WHERE empid = 4444;
```

Result

ename
Bill Johnson

Example: A view as a vertical slice of emps3 **for security**. Hides salary, etc.

SQL

```
CREATE VIEW  public_emps
      -- Might call this "staff" instead of public_emps
AS
      SELECT ename, empid , deptno , telnum
      FROM    emps3

GRANT  SELECT ON  public_emps TO public
```

SQL

```
SELECT  *   FROM   public_emps
```

Result

ename	empid	deptno	telnum
Suzy Smith	1111	102	NULL
Sammy Sosa	2222	102	2345
Bill Johnson	4444	101	NULL
Mary Smith	5555	100	5678
Mary Smith	7777	101	7890

Question: What metadata and data are stored for a view?

Answer: View name and the SELECT statement are the metadata stored for a view. No data are stored for a view.

```
SQL
DROP VIEW   emps_over_4000
```

3.1.18.7 Updatable Views

Any view may always be used in the FROM clause of a SELECT statement. A view that may appear in INSERT, UPDATE or DELETE is called "updatable." Views that meet the following conditions are updatable

- The select list does not contain an aggregate function, TOP, DISTINCT, GROUP BY or UNION.
- The select list contains only simple column names and no complex expressions.
- The FROM clause references at least one base table.
- The select list must contain enough columns to permit the DML statement to succeed without violating constraints. For example, an INSERT requires the view select list to contain each column having a NOT NULL constraint and no DEFAULT value specified.

An INSERT, UPDATE or DELETE will succeed only if the view is updatable and the statement modifies only one base table referenced in the FROM clause of the view.

Views are also updatable by means of "INSTEAD OF" triggers or by being a partitioned view. See Books Online.

Example:

```
SQL
USE pubs
go

CREATE VIEW   cheap_books
AS
      SELECT title_id , title , price
      FROM   titles
      WHERE price < 20
```

SQL

```
SELECT   TOP 3   *   FROM cheap_books
```

Result

```
title_id   title                                                   price
--------   -----------------------------------------------------   ----------
BU1032     The Busy Executive's Database Guide                     19.9900
BU1111     Cooking with Computers: Surreptitious Balance Sheets    11.9500
BU2075     You Can Combat Computer Stress!                          2.9900
```

SQL

```
UPDATE   cheap_books   SET price = 15
WHERE title_id = 'BU1032'
```

SQL

```
SELECT   *   FROM cheap_books
WHERE title_id = 'BU1032'
```

Result

```
title_id   title                                                   price
--------   -----------------------------------------------------   ----------
BU1032     The Busy Executive's Database Guide                     15.0000
```

3.1.18.8 CHECK Option

Partial Syntax

```
CREATE VIEW  view-name
AS
    select-statement
[WITH CHECK OPTION]
```

WITH CHECK OPTION

WITH CHECK OPTIONS forces all data modification statements executed against the view to adhere to the criteria set within select_statement of the view definition.

When a row is modified through a view, the WITH CHECK OPTION ensures that the data remains visible through the view after the modification is committed.

SUCCEEDS—no CHECK OPTION so UPDATE beyond range of the view succeeds

SQL

```
UPDATE cheap_books SET price = 35
WHERE title_id = 'BU1032'        -- No CHECK OPTION
```

Result

(1 row(s) affected)

SQL

```
SELECT  * FROM cheap_books
WHERE title_id = 'BU1032'
   -- Can't see 35 price from the view
```

Result

(0 row(s) affected)

SQL

```
SELECT  title_id , title , price  FROM titles
WHERE title_id = 'BU1032' -- Can see 35 from table
```

Result

```
title_id   title                                                            price
--------   ---------------------------------------------------------------- ----------
BU1032     The Busy Executive's Database Guide                              35.0000
```

SQL

```
ALTER VIEW cheap_books
-- Change View to include CHECK OPTION
AS
       SELECT title_id , title , price
       FROM   titles
       WHERE price < 20
WITH  CHECK OPTION
```

FAILS—CHECK OPTION causes UPDATE beyond range of the view to fail

SQL

```
UPDATE   cheap_books   SET price = 35
WHERE title_id = 'BU1111'  --  FAILS
```

Result

Server: Msg 550, Level 16, State 1, Line 1
The attempted insert or update failed because the target view either specifies WITH CHECK OPTION or spans a view that specifies WITH CHECK OPTION and one or more rows resulting from the operation did not qualify under the CHECK OPTION constraint.
The statement has been terminated.

SQL

```
SELECT  title_id , title , price   FROM titles
WHERE title_id = 'BU1111'  --  No change BU1111
```

Result

title_id	title	price
BU1111	Cooking with Computers: Surreptitious Balance Sheets	11.9500

SQL

```
UPDATE   titles   SET price = 35
WHERE title_id = 'BU1111'
     -- UPDATE base table still Okay
```

3.1.19 Indexed View

An indexed view is a view with a unique clustered index created on the view. Non-clustered indexes may be created on the same view after the unique clustered index is created.

A view without an index has no persistent data in the database. But when a unique clustered index is created on a view, the view SELECT is executed to obtain its result set in memory, it is sorted by the index key column(s), uniqueness is checked and the final result set is stored on disk.

This stored index on the view is updated when data in underlying base tables is modified (as are the usual base table indexes).

3.1.19.1 When to Use an Indexed View

There is a performance advantage when a view is used in SELECT operations so that the view query does not have to be executed (expanded). But there is an index maintenance cost involved to update the index whenever the base table data is changed, usually more cost than on base table indexes.

So an indexed view is most helpful when the view is used frequently in SELECT operations and the underlying base table data is not changed often.

This behavior strongly favors using indexed views on read only and read mostly tables.

Note: Indexed views can be created in any edition of SQL Server 2K. In SQL Server 2K Enterprise Edition, the query optimizer will automatically consider the indexed view. To use an indexed view in all other editions, the NOEXPAND hint must be used.[1]

Indexed views were reported to be available only in SQL Server 2K Enterprise and Developer editions. But indexes may be created on views for all SQL Server 2K editions, though the optimizer on only Enterprise will consider using these indexes. See examples below for using the NOEXPAND hint on other editions.

Steps to Create an Indexed View

```
CREATE VIEW view1
WITH SCHEMABINDING
AS
    select-statement -- See properties and restrictions below
go

SET ARITHABORT ON -- See below for options required to be set
```

1. Updated SQL Server 2000 Books Online, Sept., 2001, ©1988-2001 Microsoft Corporation. All Rights Reserved.

```
CREATE UNIQUE CLUSTERED INDEX ivView1
     ON view1 ( col1 , col2 )
go
```

Properties of Indexed Views

- Indexed views are available starting with SQL Server 2K Enterprise or Developer Edition.
- Configuration options must be set as indicated below.
- The view must be created with the SCHEMABINDING option, and any user-defined functions used in the view must have been created with SCHEMABINDING option.
- All tables and user-defined functions used in the view must use two-part names.
- The view may not contain a subquery or any of these keywords: TOP, DISTINCT, COMPUTE, HAVING or UNION.
- All functions used in the view must be deterministic. That is, statements of the following form must return 1:
  SELECT OBJECTPROPERTY(OBJECTID('*functionname*'), 'IsDeterministic')
- Every column of the view must be deterministic. That is, statements of the following form must return 1:
  SELECT COLUMNPROPERTY(OBJECTID('*tablename*'), *columnname*, 'IsDeterministic')
- Table column names in the view's select-list must be explicitly stated (no *) and must appear alone in only one view column. For example,
  SELECT salary , AVG(salary)
  is okay, but
  SELECT salary , salary
  is not.
- The view select-list may not include DISTINCT, aggregates or base table computed columns.
- An indexed view may not include a **text**, **ntext** or **image** column.
- The view FROM clause must reference only base tables, not other views. These base tables must be in the same database and have the same owner as the indexed view.
- Indexed Views may also be used in queries on the base tables if the Query Optimizer so decides. See example below.

Indexed Views (new with SS 2K) — Enterprise Edition or Developer Edition Only

To create an indexed view the following configuration options must be set as shown in Table 3-13.

Table 3-13 Configuration Options

Option	Required Setting	Default Setting	@@OPTION value
ARITHABORT	ON	OFF[a]	64
CONCAT_NULL_YIELDS_NULL	ON	ON	4096
QUOTED_IDENTIFIER	ON	ON	256
ANSI_NULLS	ON	ON	32
ANSI_PADDING	ON	ON	16
ANSI_WARNINGS	ON	ON	8
NUMERIC_ROUNDABORT	OFF	OFF	8192

a. Query Analyzer sets ARITHABORT to ON automatically. (Open Query Analyzer to Query-Current Connection Properties...and click on Options tab.)

ARITHABORT is the only one in the list that needs to be changed from its default setting. Its current setting may be displayed and changed as shown.

ARITHABORT should be explicitly set to ON when creating indexed views.

SQL

```
SET ARITHABORT ON
```

SQL

```
PRINT 'ARITHABORT: ' + CASE
  WHEN @@OPTIONS & 64 > 0
  THEN 'ON' ELSE  'OFF'
END
```

Result

```
ARITHABORT: ON
```

See "Server, Database and Session Settings," page 174.

Examples: CREATE CLUSTERED INDEX on a View (SQL Server 2K Enterprise Edition or Developer Edition)

Use Query Analyzer with CTL-L to show Estimated Execution Plan or CTL-K for actual.

SQL

```
USE pubs
go

--Set the options to support indexed views.
SET NUMERIC_ROUNDABORT OFF
go

SET ANSI_PADDING,ANSI_WARNINGS,CONCAT_NULL_YIELDS_NULL,
ARITHABORT,QUOTED_IDENTIFIER,ANSI_NULLS ON
go
--Create view.
CREATE VIEW   store_sales_view
WITH   SCHEMABINDING
AS
    SELECT st.stor_id , st.stor_name , sa.ord_num , sa.title_id
    FROM dbo.stores st , dbo.sales sa
    WHERE st.stor_id = sa.stor_id
go

--Create index on the view.
CREATE UNIQUE CLUSTERED INDEX store_sales_view_ind
  ON store_sales_view ( ord_num , stor_id , title_id )
go
```

On Enterprise and Developer Editions the query optimizer will consider using, or not using, the view index whether or not the view name is explicitly referenced.

The next query will use the above indexed view.

SQL

```
SELECT * FROM store_sales_view
WHERE ord_num = 'P3087a'
```

The next query will ALSO USE THE INDEXED VIEW, though only base tables are referenced.

SQL

```
SELECT  st.stor_id , st.stor_name ,
       sa.ord_num , sa.title_id
FROM  stores st , sales sa
WHERE st.stor_id  =   sa.stor_id
   AND  ord_num = 'P3087a'
```

The next query DOES NOT USE THE INDEXED VIEW, though the view is referenced by name. It uses index on sales (title_id) to get stor_id and then index on stores (stor_id) to get the rest.

SQL

```
SELECT * FROM store_sales_view
WHERE title_id = 'BU1032'
```

Note that this last query does not use the view index because the order of its index key is (ord_num , stor_id , title_id) and it's better to use the base table indexes. But if the view index key is rearranged to (title_id , stor_id , ord_num) then the view index will be used for this query. Of course other queries will also be affected.

The query optimizer looks at the content of each query and the facilities (such as indexes) available to execute the query most efficiently. Designing these indexes takes skill and a lot of experimentation to see what the optimizer actually uses.

3.1.19.2 Query Hints with Indexed Views

Syntax

```
SELECT  select-list
FROM   table-or-view-list
...    [  ( optional WHERE clause, GROUP BY clause, etc. ) ]


table-or-view-list  may include 1 or more instances of:
   indexed-view [ WITH { NOEXPAND [ , INDEX( index_value [ , ...n ] ) ] }
```

Arguments

NOEXPAND

NOEXPAND specifies that the view is not to be expanded, and it forces the optimizer to use an index for the indexed view.

INDEX(*index_value*)

INDEX specifies the name or ID of the indexes to be used by SQL Server when it processes the statement. Only one index hint per view can be specified.

Examples: CREATE CLUSTERED INDEX on a View (SQL Server 2K Personal Edition or Standard Edition)

Use Query Analyzer with CTL-L to show Estimated Execution Plan or CTL-K for actual.

Use the same view and index on the view from the previous example, but the results here are also valid for SS 2K Personal and Standard Editions.

Note: This query DOES USE THE INDEXED VIEW because of the NOEXPAND hint.

```
SQL
SELECT *
FROM store_sales_view  WITH (NOEXPAND)
WHERE title_id = 'BU1032'
```

Since there's only one index on the view, store_sales_view_ind, this query has the same result.

```
SQL
SELECT *
FROM store_sales_view
     WITH (NOEXPAND , INDEX(store_sales_view_ind) )
WHERE title_id = 'BU1032'
```

3.1.20 PARTITIONED VIEWS

According to the updated SQL Server 2000 Books Online,"a partitioned view joins horizontally partitioned data from a set of member tables across one or more servers, making the data appear as if from one table."

For a **Local Partitioned View**, all tables are on one instance of SQL Server. For a **Distributed Partitioned View or Federation**, at least two tables are on separate linked instances. This is also called *federated views.*

Partitioning of data is more often done over different servers than on the same server to take advantage of the processing power and possible geographical dispersion of a second host.

3.1.20.1 Federation of Servers

You can create a federation of servers by mutually linking a collection of autonomous servers to each other. You then partition a table horizontally by placing certain rows on each server in the federation. Then partitioned views may be used to access the entire logical table; this provides the key to SQL Server 2K's ability to scale out.

Data may be most easily partitioned over two servers by executing the same CREATE TABLE statement on both servers, perhaps in databases of the same name.

Example: A read-only partition on servers AMY and BAB.

We will copy the **Northwind** database to **nwind_fed** database on both AMY and BAB but such that the original **orders** and **[order details]** tables are split about half onto each server. We then create a partitioned view combining AMY **orders** and BAB **orders** tables.

1. **Mutually link AMY and BAB** (in both directions).

   On AMY, execute

SQL

```
EXEC  sp_addlinkedserver @server = 'BAB',
  @srvproduct = '', @provider = 'SQLOLEDB', @datasrc = 'BAB'
```

On BAB, execute (not required to use the partitioned view on AMY to BAB)

SQL

```
EXEC  sp_addlinkedserver @server = 'AMY',
  @srvproduct = '', @provider = 'SQLOLEDB', @datasrc = 'AMY'ROP
  VIEW   emps_over_4000
```

To drop a link, use

SQL

```
EXEC  sp_dropserver  BAB
```

2. **Split the data between the servers.**

   Put identical table structures on AMY and BAB with about half of the total data in each. For the example, I used DTS to copy **Northwind** database on AMY to **nwind_fed** on AMY and then to **nwind_fed** on BAB.

Using the **orders** table, I ran the following statements on AMY to split the data. Foreign key constraints referencing the **orders** table must be revised to allow for splitting the data. This will require careful thought.

On AMY:

SQL

```
USE nwind_fed
```

Create a temporary reference table orderids_half with the first half of orders table orderid's.

SQL

```
SELECT top 50 PERCENT   orderid
INTO orderids_half
FROM orders
```

Table **[order details]** has a foreign key referencing **orders(orderid)**, so we need to remove AMY's **[order details]** rows not remaining on AMY and then the same for BAB.

SQL

```
DELETE FROM  [order details]
  -- Delete top half of orderid's
WHERE orderid  NOT IN (SELECT orderid FROM orderids_half)
  -- from AMY [order details]
```

Now remove these high rows from AMY's orders table as they will be on BAB.

SQL

```
DELETE FROM  orders
  -- Delete top half of orderid's
WHERE orderid  NOT IN (SELECT orderid FROM orderids_half)
  -- from AMY orders
```

On BAB: BAB's [order details] and orders tables will keep the top half of orderid's. (These statements may be executed from AMY using the link.)

SQL

```
DELETE FROM  BAB.nwind_fed.dbo.[order details]
  -- Delete bottom half of orderid's
WHERE orderid   IN (SELECT orderid FROM orderids_half)
  -- from BAB [order details]
```

Now remove these low rows from Bab's orders table as they will remain only on AMY.

SQL

```
DELETE FROM  BAB.nwind_fed.dbo.orders
  -- Delete bottom half of orderid's
WHERE orderid   IN (SELECT orderid FROM orderids_half)
  -- from BAB orders
```

3. **Create and Use the Partitioned View to Read (SELECT)**

This example uses read-only partitioned views.

SQL

```
CREATE VIEW  allorders AS
  SELECT *  FROM  AMY.nwind_fed.dbo.orders
    UNION ALL
  SELECT *  FROM  BAB.nwind_fed.dbo.orders
```

To demonstrate the partitioned view, we'll read the row count and minimum and maximum of orderid from AMY and BAB separately and combined through the view.

SQL

```
SELECT count(*) AS AMY , MIN(orderid) MIN , MAX(orderid) MAX
FROM AMY.nwind_fed.dbo.orders
```

Result

```
AMY           MIN           MAX
-----------   -----------   -----------
415           10248         10662
```

SQL

```
SELECT count(*) AS BAB , MIN(orderid) MIN , MAX(orderid) MAX
FROM BAB.nwind_fed.dbo.orders
```

Result

```
BAB          MIN          MAX
-----------  -----------  -----------
415          10663        11077
```

SQL

```
SELECT count(*) AS BOTH , MIN(orderid) MIN , MAX(orderid) MAX
FROM  allorders
```

Result

```
BOTH         MIN          MAX
-----------  ----------   -----------
830          10248        11077
```

The following view definition may be executed on both servers.

SQL

```
CREATE VIEW  allorders AS
  SELECT *  FROM  AMY.nwind_fed.dbo.orders
    UNION ALL
  SELECT *  FROM  BAB.nwind_fed.dbo.orders
```

SQL

```
SELECT count(*) AS AMY , MAX(orderid) MAX
FROM AMY.nwind_fed.dbo.orders
```

Result

```
AMY
---------------------
415
```

SQL

```
SELECT count(*) AS BOTH , MIN(orderid) MIN , MAX(orderid) MAX
FROM  allorders
```

Result

```
BAB
---------------------
415
```

SQL

```
SELECT count(*)  AS ALL , MAX(orderid) MAX
FROM allorders
```

Result

```
ALL
---------------------
830
```

3.1.20.2 Updatable Partitioned Views—Enterprise and Developer Editions only

A partitioned view may be used to update data only on SQL Server 2K Enterprise Edition or Developer Edition.

A view is considered an updatable partitioned view if

- the view is a set of SELECT statements whose individual result sets are combined into one using the UNION ALL statement,
- each SELECT statement references one base table, either local or linked, and
- the view does contain any table which has a trigger or cascading update defined on it.

Partitioning Column and INSERT An updatable partitioned view will allow INSERT operations if the partitioned view

- has no member table with an IDENTITY or TIMESTAMP column
- does not contain a self-join
- has a Partitioning Column

A partitioning column is a column of each member table having a CHECK constraint that disjointly identifies the data in that table.

Partitioning columns must do the following:

- be part of the primary key of the member tables
- appear in the same ordinal position in each member table (all first, all second, etc.)
- be NOT NULL
- have a single CHECK constraint that specifies disjoint ranges of values on each member table.

The partitioning column often represents the only difference between member tables.

Server1.

```
SQL
CREATE TABLE  ptable (
     a     INT       PRIMARY KEY       CHECK ( a <= 1000 )
,    b     ....
)
```

Server2.

```
SQL
CREATE TABLE  ptable (
    a        INT      PRIMARY KEY CHECK ( a > 1000 AND a <= 2000 )
,   b        ....
)
```

Server3.

```
SQL
CREATE TABLE  ptable (
     a     INT       PRIMARY KEY       CHECK ( a > 2000 )
,    b     ....
)
```

3.2 DISPLAYING METADATA

The two primary ways to programmatically display metadata for a database are to use system stored procedures and the SQL-92 compliant INFORMATION_SCHEMA. There are also Metadata Functions, and one may, if absolutely necessary, query directly on the system tables. The following ways to access metadata programmatically are discussed in this section.

- **System Stored Procedures**—These procedures return information about database and database objects.
- **ANSI Information Schema Views**—These views are based on system tables in each database.
- **Metadata Functions**–Such functions return information about a database and database objects.
- SELECT statements on the system tables (often not desirable)

Metadata may also be displayed from the Enterprise Manager GUI.

3.2.1 System Stored Procedures to Display Metadata

There are hundreds of system stored procedures and extended procedures. Individual stored procedures will be described throughout the book as a need for them arises. You may check the index to find the location of a given stored procedure. See a complete list of system stored procedures in Appendix A. Details may be found by looking each up in Books Online. Several are summarized in Table 3-14.

Table 3-14 Some Stored Procedures that Display Metadata

sp_dboption	Included for backward compatibility. Use ALTER DATABASE.
sp_help [*objname*]	No arguments — lists all objects in the current database 1 argument — Reports information about the database object in the current database
sp_helpdb *dbname*	Reports information about a specified database or all databases
sp_helpindex *tablename*	Reports indexes on the table or view
sp_helptext *objname*	Prints the code text of a rule, a default, or an unencrypted stored procedure, user-defined function, trigger or view

SQL Server provides some built-in system stored procedures to assist in determining information about databases and database objects. Two are shown here.

3.2.1.1 sp_helpdb

sp_helpdb reports information about a specified database or all databases.

Syntax

```
sp_helpdb [ [ @dbname= ] 'name' ]
```

Arguments

[@dbname=] 'name'

@dbname is the name of the database for which to provide information. If name is not specified, sp_helpdb reports on all databases in master.dbo.sysdatabases. (**dbo** means database owner, the predefined user name in each database who is able to perform all database operations. Any **sysadmin** server role member becomes B inside each database.)

Return Code Values:

0 (success) or 1 (failure)

Example: Show information on database `pubs`.

SQL
EXEC sp_helpdb pubs

This reports database size, owner, file locations and other information for the **pubs** database.

3.2.1.2 sp_help

sp_help reports information about a database object, a user-defined data type or a system-supplied data type.

Syntax

```
sp_help [ [ @objname = ] name ]
```

Arguments

[@objname =] name

`@objname` is the name of any object in sysobjects or any user-defined data type in the `systypes` table. name has a default of `NULL`. (Database names are not acceptable.)

Return Code Values

0 (success) or 1 (failure)

Example: Show the structure of the "titles" table of the `pubs` database.

SQL

```
/* must first move the context of SQL client
  to pubs database */
USE pubs
go

EXEC sp_help titles
```

This sequence lists all column names and data types, constraints, table owner, etc., of titles table.

Example: List all User Tables in the pubs database.

SQL

```
USE pubs
go
```

SQL

```
sp_help
```

Result

Name	Owner	Object_type
defs	dbo	view
sysconstraints	dbo	view... -- more views
authors	dbo	user table
discounts	dbo	user table
dtproperties	dbo	user table
...	...	...
sales	dbo	user table
store	dbo	user table
titleauthor	dbo	user table
titles	dbo	user table
employee_insupd	dbo	trigger
syscolumns	dbo	system table... system tables
byroyalty	dbo	stored procedure... stored procedures
UPKCL_titleidind	dbo	primary key cns... primary key cns's

Result (cont.)

FK__discounts__stor___0F975522	dbo	foreign key cns... foreign key cns's
DF__authors__phone__78B3EFCA	dbo	default (maybe cns)... defaults
CK__authors__au_id__77BFCB91	dbo	check cns... check cns's

User_type	Storage_type	Length	Prec	Scale	Nullable
empid	char	9	9	NULL	no
id	varchar	11	11	NULL	no
tid	varchar	6	6	NULL	no

SQL

```
sp_help  authors
```

Result

Name	Owner	Type	Created_datetime
authors	dbo	user table	2000-08-06 01:33:52.123

Result (cont.)

Column_name	Type	Computed	Length	Prec	Scale	Nullable
au_id	id	no	11			no
au_lname	varchar	no	40			no
au_fname	varchar	no	20			no
phone	char	no	12			no
address	varchar	no	40			yes
city	varchar	no	20			yes
state	char	no	2			yes
zip	char	no	5			yes
contract	bit	no	1			no

3.2.2 ANSI Information Schema Views

Information Schema views are SQL-92 standard. They allow access to metadata within a database. SQL Server and the other RDBMS vendors implement INFORMATION_SCHEMA to provide similar output that is independent of the internal implementation.The information schema views return information about the objects to which the current user has permissions. For more detail see "Information Schema Views" in Books Online.

Table 3-15 lists the name of each Information Schema view available in SQL Server 2K. The names in first column will be referred to as *ISView_name* in the discussion below.

Table 3-15 Information Schema Views in SQL Server 2K

Information Schema View Name - *ISview_name*	Description
CHECK_CONSTRAINTS	Contains one row for each CHECK constraint in the current database.
COLUMN_DOMAIN_USAGE	Contains one row for each column in the current database that has a user-defined data type.
COLUMN_PRIVILEGES	Contains one row for each column with a privilege either granted to or by the current user in the current database.
COLUMNS	Contains one row for each column accessible to the current user in the current database.
CONSTRAINT_COLUMN_USAGE	Contains one row for each column that has a constraint defined on itin the current database.
CONSTRAINT_TABLE_USAGE	Contains one row for each table that has a constraint defined on it in the current database.
DOMAIN_CONSTRAINTS	Contains one row for each user-defined data type, accessible to the current user in the current database, with a rule bound to it.
DOMAINS	Contains one row for each user-defined data type accessible to the current user in the current database.
KEY_COLUMN_USAGE	Contains one row for each column that is constrained as a key in the current database.
PARAMETERS	Contains one row for each parameter of a user-defined function or stored procedure accessible to the current user in the current database.
REFERENTIAL_CONSTRAINTS	Contains one row for each foreign constraint in the current database. This information schema view returns information about the objects to which the current user has permissions.
ROUTINE_COLUMNS	Contains one row for each column returned by the table-valued functions accessible to the current user in the current database.

Table 3-15 Information Schema Views in SQL Server 2K (cont.)

Information Schema View Name - *ISview_name*	Description
ROUTINES	Contains one row for each stored procedure and function accessible to the current user in the current database. The columns that describe the return value apply only to functions. For stored procedures, these columns will be NULL.
SCHEMATA	Contains one row for each database that has permissions for the current user.
TABLE_CONSTRAINTS	Contains one row for each table constraint in the current database.
TABLE_PRIVILEGES	Contains one row for each table privilege granted to or by the current user in the current database.
TABLES	Contains one row for each table in the current database for which the current user has permissions.
VIEW_COLUMN_USAGE	Contains one row for each column, in the current database, used in a view definition. This information schema view returns information about the objects to which the current user has permissions.
VIEW_TABLE_USAGE	Contains one row for each table in the current database used in a view. This information schema view returns only information about the objects to which the current user has permissions.
VIEWS	Contains one row for views accessible to the current user in the current database.

In order to display metadata, do a SELECT from INFORMATION_SCHEMA.*ISview_name* in the database of interest where *ISview_name* comes from the above table.

Example: Use Information Schema TABLES to list the tables in the pubs database.

SQL

```
USE pubs
go
```

SQL

```
SELECT *  FROM INFORMATION_SCHEMA.TABLES
-- Or:   SELECT *  FROM
--                 pubs.INFORMATION_SCHEMA.TABLES
```

SQL (cont.)

Result

```
TABLE_CATALOG  TABLE_SCHEMA  TABLE_NAME                     TABLE_TYPE
-------------  ------------  -----------------------------  -----------
pubs           dbo           author_title_view              VIEW
pubs           dbo           authors                        BASE TABLE
pubs           dbo           discounts                      BASE TABLE
pubs           dbo           dtproperties                   BASE TABLE
pubs           dbo           employee                       BASE TABLE
pubs           dbo           jobs                           BASE TABLE
pubs           dbo           pub_info                       BASE TABLE
pubs           dbo           publishers                     BASE TABLE
pubs           dbo           roysched                       BASE TABLE
pubs           dbo           sales                          BASE TABLE
pubs           dbo           stores                         BASE TABLE
pubs           dbo           sysalternates                  VIEW
pubs           dbo           sysconstraints                 VIEW
pubs           dbo           syssegments                    VIEW
pubs           dbo           titleauthor                    BASE TABLE
pubs           dbo           titles                         BASE TABLE
pubs           dbo           titles_by_author_view          VIEW
pubs           dbo           titleview                      VIEW
```

3.2.3 Metadata Functions

You can use a number of functions in your Transact-SQL to determine the properties of tables, columns and other objects in the database.

3.2.3.1 Database Objects Metadata Functions

Table 3-16 Scalar Functions

COL_LENGTH	fn_listextendedproperty
COL_NAME	FULLTEXTCATALOGPROPERTY
COLUMNPROPERTY	FULLTEXTSERVICEPROPERTY
DATABASEPROPERTY	INDEX_COL
DATABASEPROPERTYEX	INDEXKEY_PROPERTY
DB_ID	INDEXPROPERTY

Table 3-16 Scalar Functions (cont.)

DB_NAME	OBJECT_ID
FILE_ID	OBJECT_NAME
FILE_NAME	OBJECTPROPERTY
FILEGROUP_ID	@@PROCID
FILEGROUP_NAME	SQL_VARIANT_PROPERTY
FILEGROUPPROPERTY	TYPEPROPERTY
FILEPROPERTY	

Every object in a database is given both a name and an object ID. Both are stored in the sysobjects system table, but the object name is only stored once. All the other references to the object in other system tables are made to the object ID. That's why it's so easy to rename an object: Only the name need be changed in sysobjects.

Examples: If you know the name of an object, you can get its ID using the `OBJECT_ID()` function.

SQL

```
SELECT OBJECT_ID('Authors')
```

Conversely, if you know the object ID, you can get the name with the `OBJECT_NAME` function.

SQL

```
SELECT OBJECT_NAME(453576654)
```

One use of these functions is to find out if an object exists before trying to drop it.

SQL

```
IF NULLIF(OBJECT_ID('dbo.junk'),0) > 0
                    -- TRUE if 'dbo.junk' exists
  DROP TABLE dbo.junk

CREATE TABLE dbo.junk(id int)
```

Note: NULLIF(expr1 , expr2) returns NULL if expr1 = expr2 else returns expr1.

SQL

```
SELECT NULLIF( 2 , 2 ) , NULLIF( 2 , 3 )
```

Result

```
NULL        2
```

A more sophisticated object function is the OBJECTPROPERTY() function. It is extremely extensive, and with it you can find out any property of any object. For more information, see the Books Online, OBJECTPROPERTY and DATABASEPROPERTYEX().

3.2.3.2 Column Metadata Functions

There are also some column functions. The `COL_LENGTH()` function returns the length of a column, as shown in the following code.

SQL
```
SELECT COL_LENGTH('Authors', 'au_id')
```

The `COL_NAME()` function returns the name of a column, based on its order.

SQL
```
SELECT COL_NAME(OBJECT_ID('Authors'), 2).
```

With the COLUMNPROPERTY() function, you can determine the property of any column, provided you supply the ID of the table, the column name and the property in question.

```
SQL SELECT OBJECT_NAME(453576654)
```

A return value of zero means false and one means true.

Finally, the TYPEPROPERTY() function returns properties of any datatype.

```
SQL SELECT TYPEPROPERTY('int', 'precision')
```

This returns a ten, indicating that the integer data type can handle ten decimal digits.

3.2.3.3 Index Metadata Functions

There are two index metadata functions. The first, INDEX_COL(), determines whether there is an index on a column.

```
SQL
SELECT INDEX_COL('Authors', OBJECT_ID('UPKCL_auidind'), 1)
```

Finally, the INDEXPROPERTY() function lets you determine the properties of an index.

```
SQL
SELECT INDEXPROPERTY(
  OBJECT_ID('Authors'),'UPKCL_auidind' , 'IsUnique')
```

The INDEXPROPERTY() function also returns a one if true, zero if false.

3.2.4 SELECT statements on the system tables

System tables were designed to enhance SQL Server performance, not ease of user access, which is why the system stored procedures and INFORMATION_SCHEMA are made available. You may access the system tables directly, but they are often difficult to read and there is risk that their structure may change in the future.

SQL Server keeps this metadata information in

- **The System Catalog**—serverwide system tables in master and msdb databases (e.g., sysdatabases, syslogins [a view in master])
- **The Database Catalogs**—in each database (e.g., sysobjects, sysusers)

DO NOT make any data change (INSERT, UPDATE, DELETE) directly on a system table at the risk of making the database or entire server unusable. These tables should only be changed through the higher level DDL statements. SELECT statements on system tables are acceptable, though usually awkward.

Example: Do some queries on system tables master..sysdatabases and syslogins.

SQL

```
USE master
go
```

SQL

```
SELECT * FROM sysdatabases
  -- This lists all system and user databases
  -- on the instance
```

Result

name	dbid	...	crdate	...	filename
-------	----	...	---------	...	--------------------
DeacDb	10	...	2002-05-10 14:56	...	C:\Program Files\...\DATA\deacdb.mdf
master	1	...	1998-11-13 03:00	...	C:\Program Files\...\DATA\master.MDF
model	3	...	2000-05-02 11:04	...	C:\Program Files\...\DATA\model.mdf
msdb	4	...	2000-05-02 11:04	...	C:\Program Files\...\DATA\msdbdata.mdf
Northwind	6	...	2000-05-02 11:04	...	C:\Program Files\...\DATA\northwnd.mdf
pubs	5	...	2000-05-02 11:04	...	C:\Program Files\...\DATA\pubs.mdf
pubs2	10	...	2002-07-10 14:56	...	C:\Program Files\...\DATA\pubs2.mdf
tempdb	2	...	2000-05-04 20:05	...	C:\Program Files\...\DATA\tempdb.MDF

In SQL Server 2K, the default directory for data files is in (the very long path)

C:\Program Files\Microsoft SQL Server\MSSQL\Data\

syslogins is a View in master database on the sysxlogins system table which contains information on every login account for the system. In EM, look in the master database Views to find syslogins view, open view – all rows. Or, do the same in QA with this code.

SQL

```
SELECT * FROM master.dbo.syslogins
```

You should recognize the login names (you may have to scroll to the right to see them).

You may view the definition of the syslogins view in EM by looking in the master database under Views. Right click on syslogins and open Design View. To facilitate viewing you may copy the entire SELECT statement and paste it to Notepad.

Using System Tables to Explore Metadata We can explore metadata of tables and other objects in a user database also by doing SELECT on system tables, though this is usually more awkward than other means described previously.

Example: List all User Tables in the **pubs** database.

SQL

```
USE pubs
go
```

SQL

```
select name , id , xtype , uid , crdate
  -- Use * to list all column names, then use
  -- ones of interest
FROM sysobjects
where type = 'u'
order by name
```

SQL

Result

```
name             id            type    uid   crdate
---------------  ------------  ------- ----  ----------------------------
authors          1977058079    U       1     2000-08-06 01:33:52.123
discounts        245575913     U       1     2000-08-06 01:33:52.873
dtproperties     645577338     U       1     2002-04-29 08:39:54.530
employee         277576027     U       1     2000-08-06 01:33:52.983
jobs             277576027     U       1     2000-08-06 01:33:52.983
pub_info         357576312     U       1     2000-08-06 01:33:53.093
publishers       2057058364    U       1     2000-08-06 01:33:52.217
roysched         213575799     U       1     2000-08-06 01:33:52.763
sales            149575571     U       1     2000-08-06 01:33:52.653
stores           117575457     U       1     2000-08-06 01:33:52.547
titleauthor      53575229      U       1     2000-08-06 01:33:52.437
titles           2121058592    U       1     2000-08-06 01:33:52.327
```

Example: List all columns of the authors table (id = 1977058079).

SQL

```
SELECT id , colid , name  FROM syscolumns
where id = 1977058079
order by id , colid, name
```

Result

```
id              colid    name
--------------- ------   ------------------
1977058079      1        au_id
1977058079      2        au_lname
1977058079      3        au_fname
1977058079      4        phone
1977058079      5        address
1977058079      6        city
1977058079      7        state
1977058079      8        zip
1977058079      9        contract
```

3.2.5 Using Enterprise Manager to Observe Metadata

Use the following instructions to show databases using Enterprise Manager.

Open the Enterprise Manager, EM, to show the databases on the SQL Server instance.

In EM, open the console tree to the name of server you're interested in.

Open the "Databases" node to see a list of databases on that instance. See the screen capture in Figure 3-8.

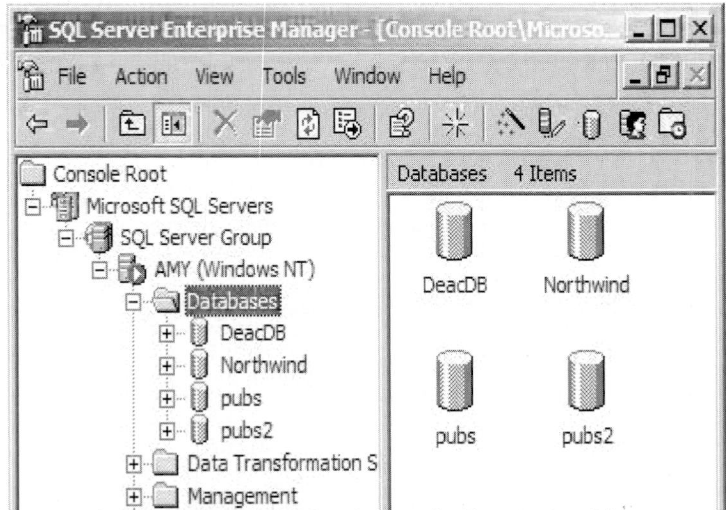

Figure 3-8 Screenshot of databases in Enterprise Manager.

Figure 3-9 Right click on the authors table and select "Design Table."

You may observe the system databases also by configuring your Enterprise Manager to show system databases and system objects.

In Enterprise Manager, EM, right click on the server name and select
Edit SQL Server Registration Properties ...

Check the middle of the three checkboxes at the bottom of the dialog; it is labelled
"Show system databases and system objects"

Click OK.

Use the instructions in Figures 3-9 and 3-10 to show table metadata using Enterprise Manager. In Figure 3-10, the design table shows column definitions.

We want to show the table metadata of the authors table of the pubs database.

In EM open the console tree for your server to
ServerName - Databases - pubs - Tables

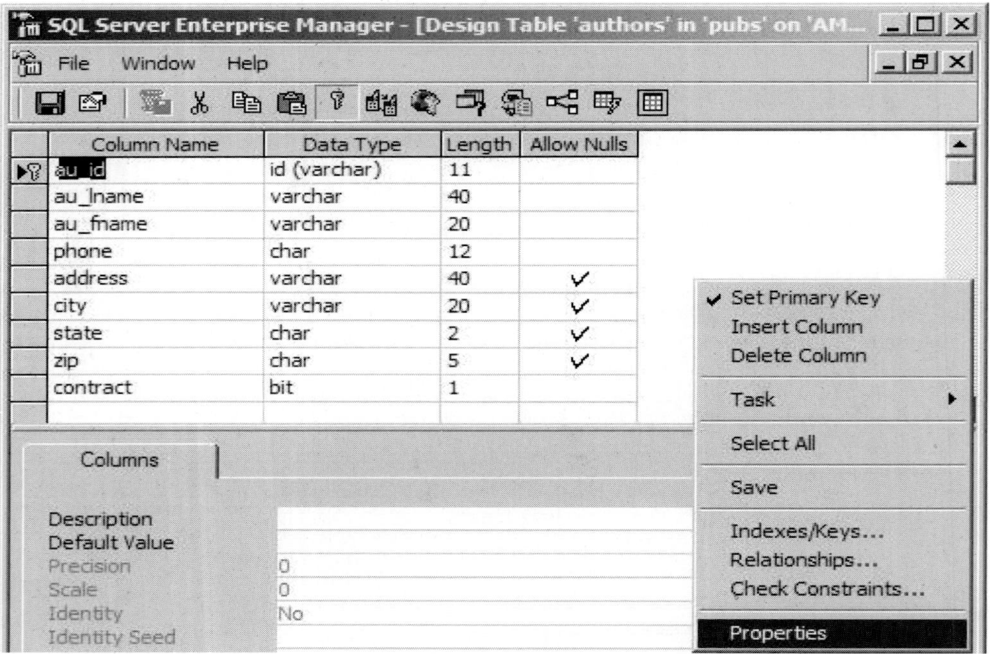

Figure 3-10 To see other table properties including indexes, foreign keys and check constraints, right click and select Properties.

3.3 SECURITY

The security model used by Microsoft SQL Server is described in this section.

3.3.1 Client Program Login to SQL Server

The SQL Server Database Engine does not have a GUI as part of the database server. As shown in Figure 3-11, the only way to communicate with the server process is via a "Client Application" program, or a "client," such as Query Analyzer, an interactive SQL interface program; Enterprise Manager, a DBA GUI; or any other program written using any of the interfaces previously discussed.

For a client application to connect to SQL Server it must use a **login and password** that SQL Server can authenticate.That login may be an SQL Server login or a Windows NT login.

MSS encompasses these layers of security (see Figure 3-12):

- **Windows:** Individual needs a Windows NT Users or Group to log in to machine
- **SQL Server:** To log in to SQL Server, a user must have an SQL Server login.
    - SQL Server (Instance) Logins: SQL Server recognizes three types of logins: Windows NT User, Windows NT Group or SQL Server (SS type)
      Note: Do not confuse this with Authentication Modes described below.

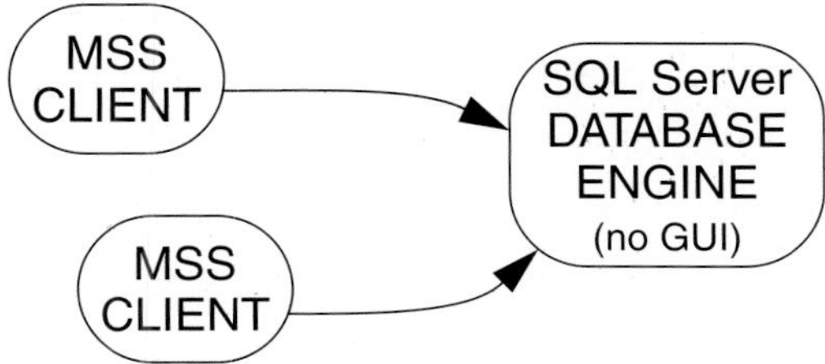

Figure 3-11 Microsoft SQL Server (MSS) client-server.

- **Database:** SQL Server login is assigned to Database Users and Roles.
- **DB Object (data):** Permission is given to User or Role by database object owner.

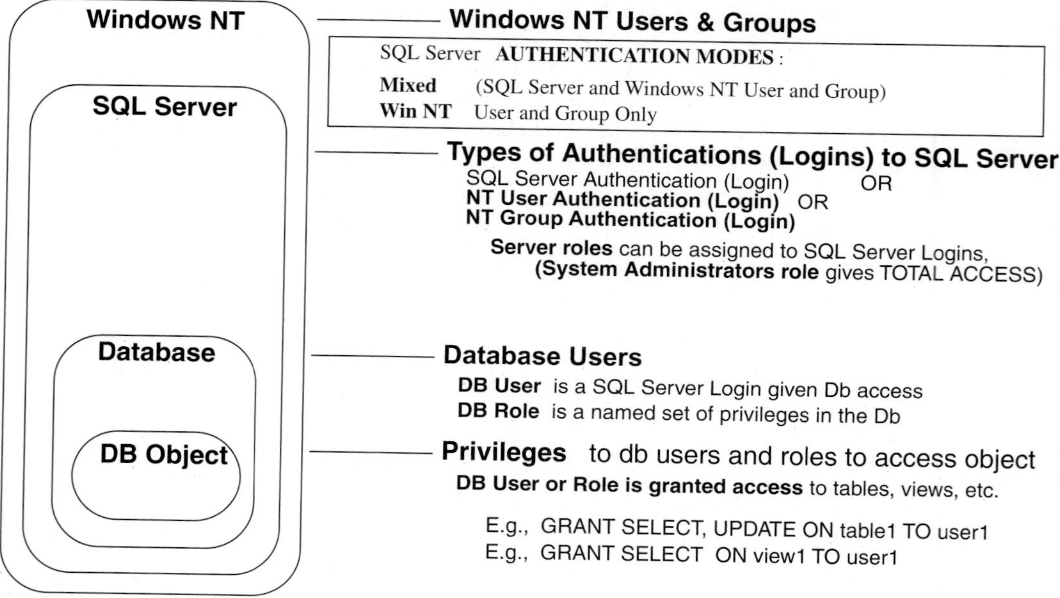

Figure 3-12 Layers of security.

The three steps to granting access to database data (for user logged on to computer) are:

1. SA Creates a SQL Server Login, one of the three types listed above. The user can do nothing yet.
2. DBO Grants the SQL Server Login access to a specific database.
3. DBO Grants the Login privilege (INSERT, UPDATE, DELETE, SELECT) on object and/or grants a role to the Login.

3.3.2 SQL Server Authentication Mode Options

The Authentication Mode is a setting on a SQL Server instance that determines which kinds of authentications (logins) are permitted on that server.

SQL Server on Windows NT has two authentication modes, Mixed and Win NT only. Mixed authentication mode is sometimes referred to as "SQL Server and Windows NT," which is very descriptive. Win NT only authentication mode allows Windows NT user or group logins but not SQL Server logins (which means that "sa" login is disabled).

SQL Server on Windows 98/ME has only one authentication mode: SQL Server logins only are allowed.

To set authentication mode in Enterprise Manager:

Server Properties Dialog

Security Tab

Right Click on *ServerName*: **Properties**

Security Tab: Click desired authentication mode, shown in Figure 3-13.

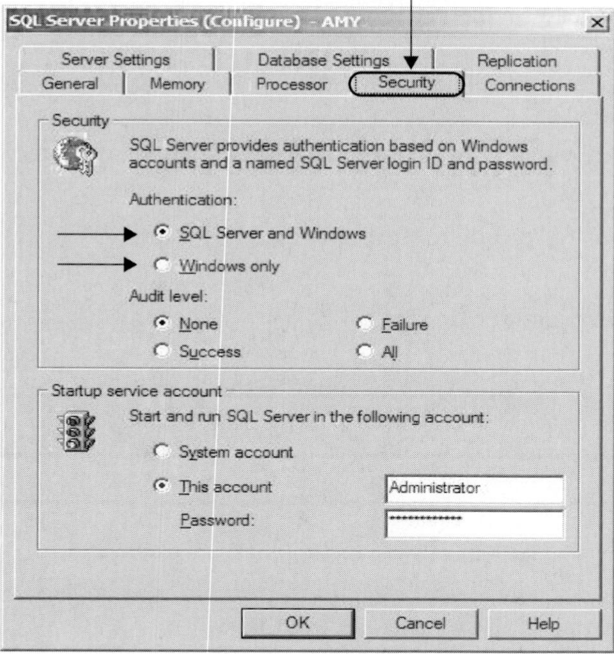

Figure 3-13 The Security Tab of the SQL Server Properties Dialog.

3.3.3 Database Level Access

Once a SQL Server Login is created, it can log in to the server but it can only do activities of guest user (if present) and public role in each database.

A user is a guest if the following conditions apply.

- an individual has a SQL Server instance login (any of the three types)
- a database has a user account named *guest*
- the login does not have access to the database by the login name

If these conditions apply, then the individual may log in to the SQL Server instance and enter the database automatically assuming the identity of the **guest** user.

Guest user privileges may be assigned as desired by the dbo. By default, a **guest** user account does not exist in a newly created database, but the dbo may add one and specify whatever permissions are desired. The **guest** user account may be added and deleted from any database except master and tempdb, where it must always exist. If a **guest** user account does not exist in a database then a login must have explicit access to the database in order to enter it (that is, to do **USE** *dbname*).

The **public** role exists in every database (including system databases).

- Every login with access to the database is automatically a member of **public** role.
- Permissions for **public** role seem to default to SELECT on system tables (only).
- **Public** role cannot be dropped.

Example: To add a **guest** user account to the **Accounts** database, execute the following:

SQL

```
USE Accounts
GO

EXECUTE sp_grantdbaccess guest, guest
```

Except for guest user in a database, a new SQL Server (instance) login must be given either a server role or access to a specific database in order to access any data The same SQL Server Login could be given both a server role and specific database access.

3.3.3.1 Manage Database Permissions—GRANT, REVOKE, DENY

Three permission responses are possible:

- **GRANT**—Permissions granted to a login are cumulative to permissions for that login's roles. Any single GRANT provides access (Figure 3-14).
- **REVOKE**—A REVOKE removes a previously GRANTed privilege, but it does not prevent access to the login via another role.
- **DENY**—A single DENY removes the privilege regardless of how many GRANTs the login may have. This is true whether the DENY is applied to the login or to a role of which the login is a member.

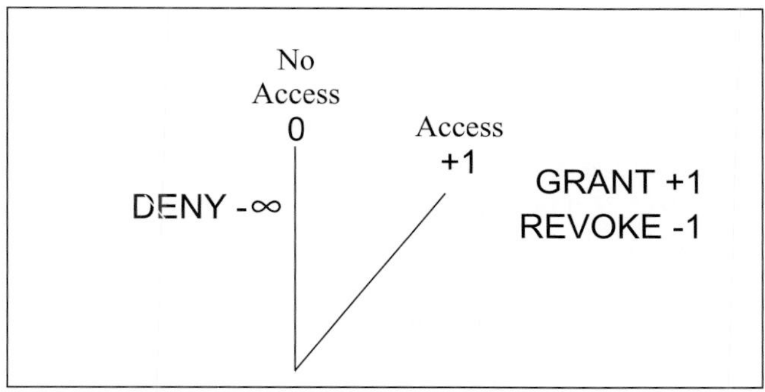

Figure 3-14 GRANT, REVOKE and DENY allow varying degrees of privilege.

GRANT GRANT creates an entry in the security system that allows a user to work with data in the current database or to execute specific Transact-SQL statements.

Syntax: GRANT form 1—Statement permissions

```
GRANT { ALL | statement [ ,...n ] }  TO  security_account [ ,...n ]
```

Syntax: GRANT form 2—Object permissions

```
GRANT  { ALL [ PRIVILEGES ] | permission [ ,...n ] }
{
[  (  column [ ,...n ]  )  ] ON { table | view }
| ON { table | view } [ ( column [ ,...n ] ) ]
| ON { stored_procedure | extended_procedure }
```

```
  | ON { user_defined_function }
  }
  TO security_account [ ,...n ]
  [ WITH GRANT OPTION ]
  [ AS { group | role } ]
```

SQL

```
GRANT INSERT, UPDATE, DELETE, SELECT
ON titles TO Login2
```

Arguments

ALL

ALL specifies that all applicable permissions are being granted. For statement permissions, ALL can be used only by members of the **sysadmin** role. For object permissions, ALL can be used by members of the **sysadmin** and **db_owner** roles and by database object owners.

statement

This is the statement for which permission is being granted. The statement list can include the following.

CREATE DATABASE
CREATE DEFAULT
CREATE FUNCTION
CREATE PROCEDURE
CREATE RULE
CREATE TABLE
CREATE VIEW
BACKUP DATABASE
BACKUP LOG

n

The letter *n* is a placeholder indicating that the item can be repeated in a comma-separated list.

TO

TO specifies the security account list.

security_account

The security account to which the permissions are applied can be one of the following:

- SQL Server user
- SQL Server role

- Microsoft Windows NT user
- Windows NT group

When a permission is granted to a SQL Server user or Windows NT user account, the specified *security_account* is the only account affected by the permission. If a permission is granted to a SQL Server role or a Windows NT group, the permission affects all users in the current database who are members of the group or role. If there are permission conflicts between the members of a group or role, the most restrictive permission (DENY) takes precedence. *security_account* must exist in the current database; permissions cannot be granted to a user, role or group in another database, unless the user has already been created or has been given access to the current database.

Two special security accounts can be used with GRANT. Permissions granted to the **public** role are applied to all users in the database. Permissions granted to the **guest** user are used by all users who do not have a user account in the database.

When granting permissions to a Windows NT local or global group, specify the domain or computer name the group is defined on, followed by a backslash, then the group name. However, to grant permissions to a Windows NT built-in local group, specify BUILTIN instead of the domain or computer name.

PRIVILEGES

PRIVILEGES is an optional keyword that can be included for SQL-92 compliance.

permission

Permission is an object permission that is being granted. When object permissions are granted on a table, a table-valued function, or a view, the permission list can include one or more of these permissions: SELECT, INSERT, DELETE, REFERENCES, or UPDATE. A column list can be supplied along with SELECT and UPDATE permissions. If a column list is not supplied with SELECT and UPDATE permissions, then the permission applies to all the columns in the table, view or table-valued function.

Object permissions granted on a stored procedure can include only EXECUTE. Object permissions granted on a scalar-valued function can include EXECUTE and REFERENCES.

SELECT permission is needed on a column in order to access that column in a SELECT statement. UPDATE permission is needed on a column in order to update that column using an UPDATE statement.

The REFERENCES permission on a table is needed in order to create a FOREIGN KEY constraint that references that table.

The REFERENCES permission is needed on an object in order to create a FUNCTION or VIEW with the WITH SCHEMABINDING clause that references that object.

column

Column is the name of a column in the current database for which permissions are being granted.

table

Table is the name of the table in the current database for which permissions are being granted.

view

View is the name of the view in the current database for which permissions are being granted.

stored_procedure

stored_procedure is the name of the stored procedure in the current database for which permissions are being granted.

extended_procedure

extended_procedure is the name of the extended stored procedure for which permissions are being granted.

user_defined_function

user_defined_function is the name of the user-defined function for which permissions are being granted.

WITH GRANT OPTION

WITH GRANT OPTION specifies that the *security_account* is given the ability to grant the specified object permission to the other security accounts. The WITH GRANT OPTION clause is valid only with object permissions.

AS {*group* | *role*}

AS specifies the optional name of the security account in the current database that has the authority to execute the GRANT statement. AS is used when permissions on an object are granted to a group or role, and the object permissions need to be further granted to users who are not members of the group or role. Because only a user, rather than a group or role, can execute a GRANT statement, a specific member of the group or role grants permissions on the object under the authority of the group or role.

REVOKE REVOKE removes a previously granted or denied permission from a user in the current database.

Syntax: REVOKE form 1—Statement permissions

```
REVOKE { ALL | statement [ ,...n ] } FROM security_account [ ,...n ]
```

Syntax: REVOKE form 2—Object permissions

```
REVOKE [ GRANT OPTION FOR ]  { ALL [ PRIVILEGES ] | permission [ ,...n ] }
   {
        [ ( column [ ,...n ] ) ] ON { table | view }
      | ON { table | view } [ ( column [ ,...n ] ) ]
      | ON { stored_procedure | extended_procedure }
      | ON { user_defined_function }
   }
   { TO | FROM } security_account [ ,...n ]  [ CASCADE ] [ AS { group | role } ]
```

DENY DENY creates an entry in the security system that denies a permission from a security account in the current database and prevents the security account from inheriting the permission through its group or role memberships. **One DENY overrides all GRANTs on an object.**

Syntax: DENY form 1—Statement permissions

```
DENY { ALL | statement [ ,...n ] } TO security_account [ ,...n ]
```

Syntax: DENY form 2—Object permissions

```
DENY { ALL [ PRIVILEGES ] | permission [ ,...n ] }
{
[ ( column [ ,...n ] ) ] ON { table | view }
| ON { table | view } [ ( column [ ,...n ] ) ]
| ON { stored_procedure | extended_procedure }
| ON { user_defined_function }
}
TO security_account [ ,...n ]
[ CASCADE ]
```

3.3.3.2 Examples for Database Roles and GRANT / DENY Database access

Example: Database Roles

/* sa */ Log in as sa

SQL

```
USE pubs
go

EXEC sp_addrole  'AccountantsRole'

GRANT ALL ON titles TO AccountantsRole;

EXEC sp_addrolemember  'AccountantsRole' , Login2

EXEC sp_droprolemember  'AccountantsRole' , Login2

EXEC sp_droprole  'AccountantsRole'
```

Example: Database Permissions

/* sa */ Log in as sa

SQL

```
USE pubs
go

GRANT CREATE TABLE TO Login2

GRANT INSERT, UPDATE, DELETE, SELECT ON titles TO Login2

      -- Let's take back titles table
      -- UPDATE and DELETE permissions
REVOKE UPDATE, DELETE ON titles FROM Login2

DENY ALL ON authors TO Login2
```

/* Login2 */ Log in as Login2 with password pwd

SQL

```
USE pubs
go
```

SQL

```
SELECT TOP 1 * FROM titles
           -- succeeds since does have privilege
```

Result

title_id	title	type	...
--------	--	------	...
BU1032	The Busy Executive's Database Guide	business	...

SQL

```
SELECT TOP 1 * FROM authors
   -- fails since does not have privilege
```

Result

SELECT permission denied on object 'authors', database 'pubs', owner 'dbo'.

Granted permissions are cumulative. Users can perform all of the actions that they have been granted individually or as a result of Windows NT group membership, as well as all of the actions granted to any roles to which they belong.

One DENY overrides all GRANTs on an object. Whether assigned by user or role, one DENY overrides any GRANT, whether assigned by user or role. That is, users have permission to perform an action only if both of the following are true:

- Permission has been granted directly to the users or they belong to a role that has directly or indirectly been granted the permission, and
- Permission has not been denied to the user directly or to any of the roles of which the user is a member.

NOTE: there is no GUI way to specify column permissions. You must use the SQL commands: GRANT, REVOKE and DENY.

3.3.4 Roles

A Role is a named collection of privileges. A user who is made a member of a role is granted the privileges of that role. Roles in SQL Server can be categorized into four types: *Fixed Server Roles*, *Fixed Database Roles*, *User-Defined Database Roles* and *Application Roles*. The first two are "fixed" which means they are predefined and available upon installation of SQL Server. Roles of the latter two types only exist if created by a user. The types of roles are as follows.

3.3.4.1 Fixed Server Roles

Server roles allow server operations specified for the role. All server roles are predefined and are listed in Table 3-17. Some server roles also give access to user database data, others do not.

Table 3-17 Fixed Server Roles

Server Role	Operation(s) Allowed
sysadmin	**Can perform any activity in SQL Server**
serveradmin	Can configure server-wide settings
setupadmin	Can manage linked servers and extended stored procedures

Table 3-17 Fixed Server Roles

Server Role	Operation(s) Allowed
securityadmin	Can manage server logins
processadmin	Can manage processes running in an instance of SQL Server
dbcreator	Can create and alter databases
diskadmin	Can manage disk files
bulkadmin	Can execute the BULK INSERT statement

3.3.4.2 Fixed Database Roles

Fixed database roles are the same in every database. They are shown in Table 3-18.

Table 3-18 Fixed Database Roles

Database Role	Operation(s) Allowed
db_owner	**Can perform any activity within the database**
db_accessadmin	Can manage NT groups and users and SQL Server users in the db
db_datareader	Can see all data from all user tables in the database
db_datawriter	Can do any DML on data from all user tables in the database
db_ddladmin	Can do any DDL on all objects in the database
db_securityadmin	Can manage roles, role members and permissions in the db
db_backupoperator	Can back up the database
db_denydatareader	Can deny permission to select data in the database
db_denydatawriter	Can deny permission to change data in the database

In addition to the roles in Table 3-18, there is the **public** role, which is a special database role to which every database user belongs. The **public** role:

- Captures all default permissions for users in a database
- Cannot have users, groups or roles assigned to it because they belong to the role by default

- Is contained in every database, including **master**, **msdb**, **tempdb**, **model** and all user databases
- Cannot be dropped

The **dbo** (database owner) is not a role but is the designation for the database user who created the db and has full access to every activity and object within the database. The dbo may want to specify others as members of the db_owner role to assist in management duties. The server sa login assumes dbo user in every database.

3.3.4.3 User-Defined Database Roles

The dbo (and some others) may also create their own database role in **EM** or with **sp_addrole, sp_addrolemember** and **sp_droprole**. See the next section for syntax and examples.

3.3.4.4 Application Roles—SQL Server 7.0 and later

Application roles were created to be used by programmers writing application programs that access the database, as with Visual Basic, C++, etc. Like server and database roles, they have a name and are given a collection of privileges to database objects, but they have some differences as listed here.

Application roles share the following characteristics:

- Application roles contain no members. They are instead activated at run time.
- Application roles are inactive by default and require a password to be activated.
- A connection with an activated application role loses all privileges normally granted to the user (except public role) and the connection has only privileges explicitly granted to the application role and the database's public role. Once activated, an application role is in effect for the remainder of the connection.
- The original user's login name is still available via SUSER_SNAME.
- An application role is associated with a single database, but it does not allow USE databasename.
- An application role is associated with a single database, and access to another database is available only through the guest account in the other database.

Roles and Privileges

The administrator grants privileges to a role and then makes users members of that role. A user who is made a member of a role is granted the privileges of that role subject to the following provisions:

- Privileges gained by being a member of a Server or Database role are cumulative to any other privileges the user is granted. However, any DENY of a specific privilege supercedes all grants. See "Manage Database Permissions—GRANT, REVOKE, DENY," page 395.
- Privileges gained by activating an Application role replace all other privileges the user has. Other privileges are lost and only the application role privileges are in effect while the application role is activated.
- Role permissions are transitive. That is, users can get permissions by being a member of a role that is in turn a member of another role to which permissions have been granted.

3.3.5 Creating Logins and Roles

3.3.5.1 Creating New Logins to SQL Server—Using EM

In this section we'll use EM to create each of the three types of login to SQL Server:

SQL Server login
Windows User account
Windows Group account

3.3.5.2 Creating a SQL Server Login Account to SQL Server—Using EM

Follow the steps below to create a SQL Server type of login using Enterprise Manager.

1. Open EM to the Security tab, right click on "Logins" and select "New Login...". The "SQL Server Login Properties - New Login" dialog opens containing three tabs: General, Server Roles and Database Access (see Figure 3-15). Enter the data below for each tab.
   Note: Selecting a database name here does NOT grant access to it.
   Must do Step 3 to grant database access (or grant access in the specific database).
2. **General tab:**
   Name: Enter **msslogin1** (or choose your own login name).

Authentication: Click "SQL Server Authentication" radio button.

Password: Enter the password for the new login.

Defaults: Database—Select **pubs** (or choose your default database).

The default database is the database this user will automatically be in when connecting. Do *not* leave it as **master**. This step does not give this user permission to enter the database; we do that two steps from here.

3. **Server Roles tab:** Look at the Server Roles tab. You may click any of these server roles desired. Our new user only needs to access certain data in **pubs**, so we'll pass by this tab.

4. **Database Access tab:** In the top window, specify which database can be accessed by this login, scroll down and check "Permit" box next to **pubs**. Check Permit for all databases you wish to allow this login to enter. This step gives the login membership to the public role in the specified database. We will shortly grant access for other database objects in **pubs**.

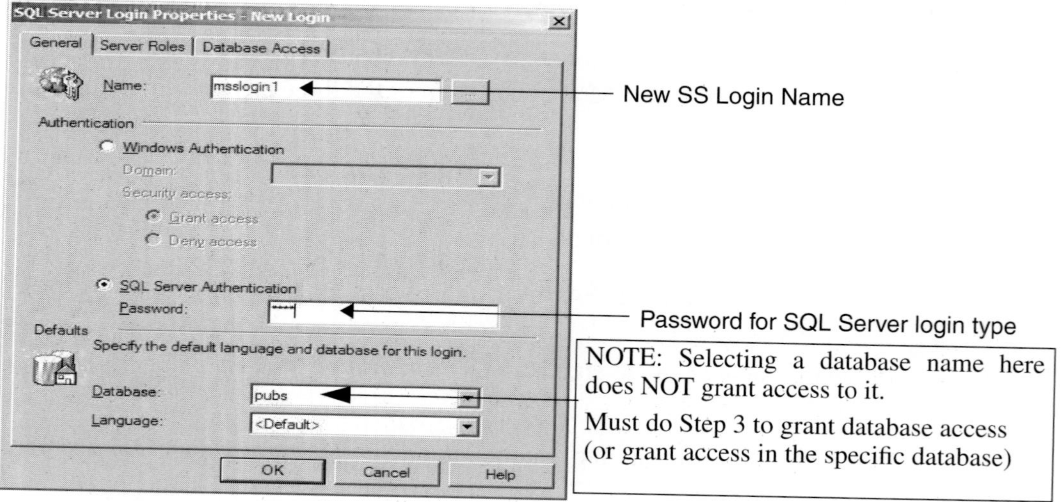

Figure 3-15 New Login Dialog.

5. Click "OK."

6. You have created the login to SQL Server and granted access to the **pubs** database. But the new login has only **public** role access to database objects in the **pubs** database. To grant access to other database objects, see Section 3.3.3.1, page 395.

3.3.5.3 Creating a Windows User or Group Account Login to SQL Server—Using EM

Follow the steps below to create a Windows User Account login to SQL Server using Enterprise Manager. Such a login allows that user to log in to his or her machine and then log in to SQL Server without further authentication.

1. Follow step 1 from the previous section to open the "New Login..." dialog. See Figure 3-16.
2. **General tab:**
   Name: Click on the ellipses "..." to the right of the Name box and select an existing user or group name on your machine. It will enter the correct format.
   Authentication: Click "Windows Authentication" radio button.
   Domain: Select the domain or current host from the menu.
   Defaults: Database: Select **pubs** (or choose your default database).

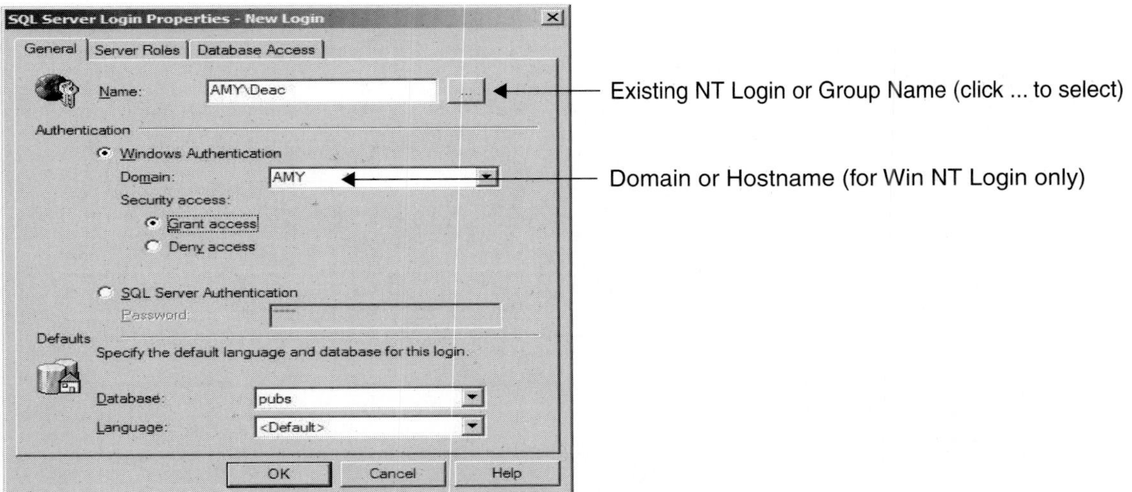

Figure 3-16 New Login Dialog (Windows Users/Groups).

3. Finish steps 3 and beyond from the preceding section to complete creating the login.

3.3.5.4 Creating New Logins to SQL Server—Using SQL

In this section we'll use SQL to create each of the three types of login to SQL Server:

SQL Server login

Windows User account

Windows Group account

3.3.5.5 Creating a SQL Server login account to SQL Server—Using SQL

SQL Server login accounts are managed in SQL using sp_addlogin and sp_droplogin system stored procedures.

sp_addlogin This creates a new SQL Server login.

Syntax

```
sp_addlogin [ @loginame = ] 'login'
[ , [ @passwd = ] 'password' ]
[ , [ @defdb = ] 'database' ]
[ , [ @deflanguage = ] 'language' ]
[ , [ @sid = ] sid ]
[ , [ @encryptopt = ] 'encryption_option' ]
```

The parameters are generally self-evident; see Books Online for detailed definition.

sp_droplogin This removes a SQL Server login.

Syntax

```
sp_droplogin [@loginame =] 'login'
```

Example: Create NEW login “amy” as SQL Server Authentication.

SQL

```
EXEC sp_addlogin
    'amy'
  , @passwd = 'amypassword'
  , @defdb = 'pubs'

EXEC sp_droplogin  'amy'
```

3.3.5.6 Creating a Windows User or Group Account login to SQL Server—Using SQL

Windows NT User and Group login accounts allow an existing Windows NT User or Group account to log in to SQL Server using Windows Authentication ("trusted" connection). They are managed in SQL using **sp_grantlogin and sp_revokelogin.**

sp_grantlogin This creates a new Win NT User or Group login to SS 2K.

Syntax

```
sp_grantlogin [@loginame =] 'login'
```

sp_revokelogin This removes login entries for Win NT User or Group login to SS 2K.

Syntax

```
sp_revokelogin [@loginame =] 'login'
```

Example: Create Win NT user (or group) "torie" a login to SQL Server.

```
SQL
-- torie must already be Win NT user or group name
EXEC sp_grantlogin  'torie'

EXEC sp_revokelogin  'torie'
```

Note: sp_addlogin and **sp_grantlogin** allow access to SQL Server but not to a user database.

3.3.5.7 Managing Server Roles—Using SQL

Server Roles in MSS are fixed, which means that all are predefined, so the only operations available are adding a login to a role membership using **sp_addsrvrolemember** or removing a login from a role membership using **sp_dropsrvrolemember**.

sp_addsrvrolemember This adds a login to a role membership.

Syntax

```
sp_addsrvrolemember [@loginame =] 'login', [@rolename
=] 'role'
```

sp_dropsrvrolemember This removes a login from a role membership.

Syntax

```
sp_dropsrvrolemember [@loginame = ] 'login',
[@rolename =] 'role'
```

3.3.5.8 Managing Database Access and Database Roles Using SQL

Database Roles in MSS may be either fixed (predefined) or user defined. The operations for managing database access and database roles are:

- sp_grantdbaccess
- sp_revokedbaccess
- sp_addrole
- sp_droprole
- sp_addrolemember
- sp_droprolemember

sp_grantdbaccess This allows a login to SS 2K to access the current database.

Syntax

```
sp_grantdbaccess [@loginame =] 'login'
    [,[@name_in_db =] 'name_in_db' [OUTPUT]]
```

The second parameter, @name_in_db, is the name of the account within the database; if not provided it's the same as @loginame. This second parameter is both an input and output parameter of type SYSNAME (though the keyword OUTPUT is optional), which returns the name just created in the database. If NULL on input, the first parameter is used as the account name in the database and that value is returned in the second parameter.

sp_revokedbaccess This removes a login to SS 2K from access to the current database.

Syntax

```
sp_revokedbaccess [ @name_in_db = ] 'name'
```

sp_addrole This adds a new user defined database role in the current database.

Syntax

```
sp_addrole [ @rolename = ] 'role'   [ , [ @ownername
= ] 'owner' ]
```

```
[@rolename =] 'role'
```

The name of the new role.

```
[@ownername =] 'owner'
```

The owner of the new role, with a default of **dbo** (recommended). *owner* must be a user or role in the current database.

sp_droprole This removes a user-defined database role from the current database. The role must be empty (no members) before it can be dropped.

Syntax

```
sp_droprole [ @rolename = ] 'role'
```

sp_addrolemember This adds a login to a fixed or user-defined role membership in the current database

Syntax

```
sp_addrolemember [ @rolename = ] 'role'
                , [ @membername = ] 'security_account'
```

'*security_account*' is any valid login or role.

sp_droprolemember This removes a login from a role membership in the current database.

Syntax

```
sp_droprolemember [ @rolename = ] 'role'
                 , [ @membername = ]
'security_account'
```

Examples:

```
SQL
USE pubs

/* Grant login2 access to pubs database.
  See OUTPUT example below. */
EXEC sp_grantdbaccess 'login2'

/* Create user defined role "MyRole" in pubs
      database */
EXEC sp_addrole  'MyRole' , 'dbo'
```

SQL (cont.)

```
/* Give MyRole SELECT privilege on authors table */
GRANT SELECT ON authors TO MyRole

/* Add login2 to MyRole granting login2 all
     of MyRole's privileges */
EXEC sp_addrolemember  'MyRole' , 'login2'

/* Add login2 to fixed database role "db_owner" */
EXEC sp_addrolemember   db_owner  ,  login2

/* Remove login2 from MyRole */
EXEC sp_droprolemember  'MyRole' , 'login2'

/* Remove login2 from db_owner */
EXEC sp_droprolemember  'db_owner' , 'login2'

-- Remove role MyRole from pubs database. We first removed
all members.
EXEC sp_droprole 'MyRole'

/* Remove login2's access to pubs database */
EXEC sp_revokedbaccess 'login2'
```

Example: Using **sp_grantdbaccess** OUTPUT parameter

This example uses **sp_grantdbaccess** returning the **name_in_db** value as an output parameter. I see no use for this because you just gave it that value. I also don't recommend making the name in the database different from the login name unless there's a compelling reason. So, your life may be happier if you skip this example.

SQL

```
DECLARE @v_name SYSNAME
SET @v_name = 'pubs2_login2'
     -- If NULL then the login name is used
PRINT 'Name before is:       ' + @v_name
EXEC sp_grantdbaccess 'login2' , @v_name  -- OUTPUT
PRINT 'Name in pubs DB is:   ' + @v_name
```

SQL (cont.)	
Result	
Name before is:	pubs2_login2
Granted database access to 'login2'.	
Name in pubs DB is:	pubs2_login2

3.3.5.9 Managing Application Roles

Application roles, included in SQL Server 7.0 and later, were created to be used by programmers writing application programs which access the database, as with Visual Basic, C++, etc. Like server and database roles they have a name and are given a collection of privileges to database objects but they have some differences as listed here.

Characteristics of application roles:

- Application roles contain no members.
- Application roles are inactive by default and require a password to be activated.
- A connection with an activated application role loses all privileges normally granted to the user (except public role) and the connection has only privileges explicitly granted to the application role and the database's **public** role.
- Once activated, an application role is in effect for the remainder of the connection.
- The original user's login name is still available via SUSER_SNAME.
- An application role is associated with a single database but does not allow USE databasename.
- An application role is associated with a single database and access to another database is available only through the **guest** account in the other database.

3.3.5.10 Creating and Using an Application Role

There are three operations for managing application roles: **sp_addapprole**, **sp_setapprole** and **sp_dropapprole.**

sp_addapprole This adds a new application role to the current database.

Syntax

```
sp_addapprole [ @rolename = ] 'role' , [ @password =
] 'password'
```

Arguments

[@rolename =] '*role*'

Is the name of the new role, with no default. *role* must be a valid identifier and cannot already exist in the current database.

[@password =] '*password*'

Is the password required to activate the role. *password* is **sysname**, with no default. *password* is stored in encrypted form.

sp_setapprole This activates a current database application role permissions for the current session.

Syntax

```
sp_setapprole [@rolename =] 'role' ,
    [@password =] {Encrypt N 'password'} | 'password'
    [,[@encrypt =] 'encrypt_style']
```

Arguments

[@rolename =] '*role*'

The application role being activated. *role* must exist in the current database.

[@password =] {Encrypt **N** '*password*'} | '*password*'

The password required to activate the application role; there is no default. *password* can be encrypted using the ODBC **Encrypt** function. When using the **Encrypt** function, the password must be converted to Unicode by preceding the password with **N**.

[@encrypt =] '*encrypt_style*'

This specifies the encryption style used by *password*. *encrypt_style* is **varchar(10)**, and can be either "None," not encrypted or "ODBC" as described here.

- None The password is not encrypted and is passed to Microsoft SQL Server as plaintext. This is the default.
- Odbc The password is encrypted by either an ODBC client or the OLE DB Provider for SQL Server using the ODBC canonical **Encrypt** function before being sent to SQL Server.

sp_dropapprole This removes an application role from the current database.

Syntax

```
sp_dropapprole [@rolename =] 'role'
```

Note: An application program can prompt the user for their usual login and password which is used to connect. Then the program activates the application role to ensure that the correct privileges are in effect. The SUSER_SNAME() system function will produce the original user name which can be used by the application for logging.

3.3.5.11 Example Using an Application Role

Assume we have a **Login2** with access to pubs database and ALL access to the **titles** table, and DENY access to **authors** table. Create **Login3** with default database as northwind (no access to northwind or pubs).

SQL

```
EXEC sp_addlogin
    'Login3'
  , @passwd = 'Login3password'
  , @defdb = 'northwind'
```

Example: Create **approle1** in **pubs** database and grant the role ALL access to **authors** table.

/*sa */ Log in as **sa**

SQL

```
USE pubs
go

EXEC sp_addapprole   'approle1'  , 'approle1pwd'

GRANT ALL ON authors TO approle1
```

An application role would normally be used in an application program, not interactively. But this example shows the flow of privileges and the response to SUSER_SNAME().

/* Login2 */ Log in as **Login2** with password **pwd**

SQL

```
SELECT SUSER_SNAME() LOGIN , USER_NAME() DB_USERNAME
```

Result

```
LOGIN              DB_USERNAME
-----------------  -------------------
Login2             Login2
```

SQL

```
SELECT TOP 1 * FROM authors
   -- FAILS  - Login2 is DENY'd access to authors
```

Result

SELECT permission denied on object 'authors', database 'pubs', owner 'dbo'.

SQL

```
SELECT TOP 1 * FROM titles
   -- SUCCEEDS  - Login2 has ALL access to titles
```

Result

```
title_id   title                                          type        ...
--------   ---------------------------------------------  ----------  ...
BU1032     The Busy Executive's Database Guide            business    ...
```

SQL

```
EXEC sp_setapprole   'approle1'  , 'approle1pwd'
  -- Activate App Role
```

SQL (cont.)

Result

The application role 'approle1' is now active.

SQL

```
SELECT TOP 1 * FROM authors
   -- Now this SUCCEEDS
```

Result

au_id	au_lname	au_fname	phone	address	city
172-32-1176	White	Johnson	408 496-7223	10932 Bigge Rd.	Menlo Park

SQL

```
SELECT TOP 1 * FROM titles
   -- Now this FAILS
```

Result

SELECT permission denied on object 'titles', database 'pubs', owner 'dbo'.

SQL

```
SELECT SUSER_SNAME() LOGIN , USER_NAME() DB_USERNAME
```

Result

LOGIN	DB_USERNAME
Login2	approle1

/* Login3 */ Log in as **Login3** with password **Login3password**

SQL

```
USE pubs
go
```

Result

The command(s) completed successfully.

SQL

```
SELECT SUSER_SNAME() LOGIN , USER_NAME() DB_USERNAME
```

Result

```
LOGIN              DB_USERNAME
------------------ -------------------
Login3             guest
```

SQL

```
EXEC sp_setapprole   'approle1'   , 'approle1pwd'
  -- Activate App Role
```

Result

The application role 'approle1' is now active.

SQL

```
SELECT SUSER_SNAME() LOGIN , USER_NAME() DB_USERNAME
```

SQL (cont.)

Result

```
LOGIN              DB_USERNAME
-----------------  -------------------
Login3             approlel
```

So anyone who has a login to any database on the server can, by default, activate the application role if he or she has the password. So an application program (VB, C, etc.) needs to prompt the user for loginname, password and application role password.

An alternative approach is create a normal database role with the appropriate privileges that just accumulate to the user's individual privileges. This approach is shown in the next section.

Server roles and database roles, however, are cumulative to a user's privileges. So when no application role is activated (the normal condition) any DENY in any user or role privilege completely overrides any other number of GRANTs for an object.

Demo: Use EM to create application role "**approle1**" in **pubs** db, password "**pwd**," grant SELECT privilege on **authors** table.

Login is sa and create database **db1**. Activate approle1 with

SQL

```
EXEC sp_setapprole approle1 ,  pwd
```

We have privileges of **approle1** and **guest** in the **pubs** database but have lost **Login1** privileges.

3.4 CHAPTER LAB EXERCISES

3.4.1 Lab Exercise 1: CREATE TABLE emps3, depts3

Create a test database playdb with some sample data to work with.

(Execute each "SQL:" section separately or add "go" after each to make it a separate batch.)

SQL

```
/*  Create a test database to play in.
  Omit if you already have one. */
CREATE DATABASE mydb
go

USE mydb
go
```

Type the following SQL statements into a file, Ch3_emps3_0.sql. .

SQL

```
/* -- ####################################################
                  Ch3_emps3_0.sql
*/  -------------------####################------------------
ALTER TABLE emps3
  DROP CONSTRAINT fk_emps3_member_of_dept;
go

DROP TABLE depts3;
DROP TABLE emps3;
go

CREATE TABLE emps3 (  ------------------------------
  ename          VARCHAR(15)        NOT NULL
, empid          INT                PRIMARY KEY
, deptno         INT                -- FOREIGN KEY to depts3
, telnum         VARCHAR(4)
, salary         INT
, hiredate       DATETIME
, sales_amt      INT
);

CREATE TABLE depts3 (  ------------------------------
  deptnoINT      PRIMARY KEY
, dnameVARCHAR(15) UNIQUE
, mgrempidINT    -- FOREIGN KEY to emps3
, dept_telnumVARCHAR(4)

,   CONSTRAINT fk_depts3_managed_by_emp FOREIGN KEY (mgrempid)
      REFERENCES emps3 (empid)
);
```

SQL (cont.)

```
ALTER TABLE emps3       ----------------------------------
  ADD CONSTRAINT fk_emps3_member_of_dept FOREIGN KEY (deptno)
  REFERENCES depts3 (deptno)
;
```

INSERT all **dept3** columns except **mgrempid** since it requires an **empid** value in the **emps3** table.

SQL

```
INSERT INTO depts3 (dname, deptno , dept_telnum )
  VALUES ( 'Accounting' ,  100 , 9100 );
INSERT INTO depts3 (dname, deptno , dept_telnum )
  VALUES ( 'Engineering' , 101 , 9101 );
INSERT INTO depts3 (dname, deptno , dept_telnum )
  VALUES ( 'Sales'       , 102 , 9102  );


INSERT INTO emps3 (ename,empid,deptno,telnum,salary,hiredate,sales_amt)
  VALUES ( 'Mary Smith', 5555, 100 , 5678 , 50, '01-Jan-1990', NULL);
INSERT INTO emps3 (ename,empid,deptno,telnum,salary,hiredate,sales_amt)
  VALUES ( 'Sammy Sosa', 2222, 102 , 2345 , 30, '01-Jan-1992'  , 200);
INSERT INTO emps3 (ename,empid,deptno,telnum,salary,hiredate,sales_amt)
  VALUES ('Bill Johnson', 4444, 101 , NULL  , 40, '01-Jan-1994',NULL);
INSERT INTO emps3 (ename,empid,deptno,telnum,salary,hiredate,sales_amt)
  VALUES ( 'Mary Smith', 7777, 101 , 7890 , 60, '01-Jan-1996'  , 400);
INSERT INTO emps3 (ename,empid,deptno,telnum,salary,hiredate,sales_amt)
  VALUES ( 'Suzy Smith', 1111, 102 , NULL , 20, '01-Jan-2003' , NULL);
```

Now we can add the **mgrempid** values since the **emps3** table has been populated.

SQL

```
UPDATE  depts3   SET mgrempid = 1111   WHERE  deptno = 100;
UPDATE  depts3   SET mgrempid = 7777   WHERE  deptno = 101;
UPDATE  depts3   SET mgrempid = 2222   WHERE  deptno = 102;


PRINT 'SELECT * FROM emps3   ******'   SELECT * FROM emps3;
PRINT 'SELECT * FROM depts3 ******'    SELECT * FROM depts3
;
```

Result

```
SELECT * FROM emps3; ******
ename           empid       deptno    telnum     salary   hiredate        sales_amt
--------------- ----------  --------  ---------  -------  --------------  -------------
Suzy Smith      1111        102       NULL       20       2003-01-01      NULL
Sammy Sosa      2222        102       2345       30       1992-01-01      200
Bill Johnson    4444        101       NULL       40       1994-01-01      NULL
Mary Smith      5555        100       5678       50       1990-01-01      NULL
Mary Smith      7777        101       7890       60       1996-01-01      400

(5 row(s) affected)

SELECT * FROM depts3 ; ******
deptno      dname            mgrempid      dept_telnum
-------     --------------   -----------   -----------
100         Accounting       1111          9100
101         Engineering      7777          9101
102         Sales            2222          9102
```

To remove the database, including deleting the database files, execute:

SQL

```
USE master
go

DROP DATABASE playdb
go
```

CHAPTER 4

Data Manipulation Language—INSERT, UPDATE, DELETE, SELECT

This chapter covers Data Manipulation Language (DML) statements for Microsoft SQL Server.

Data Manipulation Language consists of those SQL statements that manage database data values.

The four fundamental DML statements are as follows:

- INSERT—adds a new row to a table. See page 424.

Example:
```
INSERT INTO table1  (col1, col2) VALUES (10, 20);
```

- UPDATE—modifies data in one or more fields of specified existing row(s) in a table. See page 448.

Example:
```
UPDATE table1 SET col1 = 12 WHERE col2 = 20;
```

- DELETE—removes the specified rows from a table. See page 456.

Example:
```
DELETE FROM table1 WHERE col2 = 20;
```

- SELECT—performs a Query. It fetches data from the database and displays it. See page 466.

Example: `SELECT * FROM table1;`

In addition, the following are sometimes considered to be part of DML:

- COMMIT and ROLLBACK

4.1 INSERT

INSERT adds a new row to a table or a view.

4.1.1 INSERT Syntax

Syntax

```
INSERT [ INTO]
{
     table_name  [ WITH ( < table_hint_limited > [ ...n ] ) ]
   | view_name
   | OPENQUERY ( linked_server , 'query' )
   | OPENROWSET ( 'provider_name'
, { 'datasource' ; 'user_id' ; 'password'  | 'provider_string' }
, { [ catalog. ] [ schema. ] object  | 'query' }
       )
}
{
   { [ ( column_list ) ]
    {
        VALUES  ( { DEFAULT | NULL | expression } [ ,...n] )
      | SELECT-statement -- any valid SELECT statement that returns rows of data
                            to be inserted .
           -- Sometimes referred to as an INSERT INTO ... SELECT statement
      | execute_statement   -- any valid EXECUTE stmt that returns data with
                              SELECT or READTEXT
   }
   }
| DEFAULT VALUES
}
```

Arguments

INSERT [INTO]

INSERT [INTO] begins the INSERT statement. The INTO keyword is optional, but many people prefer to include it.

table_name | view_name

table_name | view_name is the name of the target table, table variable or (updatable) view to receive the inserted data.

- The name may also be the four-part table or view name using the OPENDATASOURCE function as the server name. See OPENDATA-SOURCE in Books Online.
- If a view name is used, the view must be updatable and must affect only one base table in the view.

If the table or view exists in another database or has an owner other than the current user, use a four-part qualified name in the format *server_name***.***data-base***.**[*owner*]**.***object_name*.

WITH < table_hint_limited > See "Table Hints," page 528.

OPENQUERY | OPENROWSET

This position specifies either the OPENQUERY or OPENROWSET function. See page 148 and Books Online.

(*column_list*)

(*column_list*) is a comma-separated list of one or more columns in which to insert data. Columns not in the list are given either the column's default value or the next value if an IDENTITY column.

VALUES

VALUES specifies the list of data values to be inserted. There must be one data value for each column and in the same order as in *column_list* if specified, or in the table definition if *column_list* is not specified.

DEFAULT

DEFAULT forces SQL Server to load the default value defined for a column. If a default does not exist for the column and the column allows NULLs, NULL is inserted. (If no non-NULL value has been specified as the default, then the default value is NULL. In my experience, though, documentation often says there is no default.) For a column defined with the **timestamp** data type, the next timestamp value is inserted. DEFAULT is not valid for an identity column.

expression

expression is a constant, a variable or an expression. The expression cannot contain a SELECT or EXECUTE statement.

DEFAULT VALUES

DEFAULT VALUES forces the new row to contain the default values defined for each column.

Comments

INSERT INTO *table* SELECT ... form may be used to **populate an existing table** via a query from another table. This statement is akin to the SELECT INTO newtable FROM ... in which newtable must NOT already exist as it is created by the statement and populated with data from the query on another table.

With either the **INSERT INTO table SELECT** or **SELECT INTO table FROM** statements, multiple rows may be inserted.

A **table** variable, in its scope, may be accessed like a regular table. Thus, **table** variable may be used as the table to which rows are to be added in an INSERT statement.

A four-part name constructed with the OPENDATASOURCE function as the server-name part may be used as a table source in all places a table name can appear in INSERT statements.

When you insert rows, these rules apply:

- If INSERT is loading multiple rows with SELECT or EXECUTE, any violation of a rule or constraint that occurs from the values being loaded causes the entire statement to abort and no rows are loaded.
- When inserting values into remote SQL Server tables and not all values for all columns are specified, the user must identify the columns to which the specified values are to be inserted.
- When an INSTEAD-OF trigger is defined on INSERT actions against a table or view, the trigger executes *instead of* the INSERT statement. INSTEAD-OF triggers are new with SQL Server 2000.
- When an INSERT statement encounters an arithmetic error (overflow, divide by zero, or a domain error) occurring during expression evaluation, SQL Server handles these errors as if SET ARITHABORT is ON. The remainder of the batch is halted, and an error message is returned.

There are two significant variations of the INSERT statement.

Form 1. List inserted column names.

```
INSERT INTO table (columnlist) VALUES (....)
```

- Column number and order must agree between the two lists but may be in any order. They do not have to contain all columns in the table.
- NOT NULL columns without a non-NULL default must be listed.

Example:

```
INSERT INTO table1 (a,b) VALUES (1, 'Amy' );
-- equivalent to next line
INSERT INTO table1 (b,a) VALUES ('Amy', 1 );
```

Form 2. Don't list inserted column names.

```
INSERT INTO table VALUES (....)
```

- VALUES list must contain all columns (except Identity, see page 436) in table DDL order.

Example: `INSERT INTO table1  VALUES (2, 'Bob' );`

```
SQL
CREATE TABLE t ( a INT , b CHAR(10) );

USE junkdb
go

CREATE TABLE table1 (
    a    DEC          PRIMARY  KEY,
    b    VARCHAR(10)     NOT NULL,
    c    DATETIME    DEFAULT GETDATE()
  --GETDATE() is the MSS function that returns time
);
```

Row 1: Insert using Form 1.

```
SQL
INSERT INTO table1 (a,b) VALUES (1, 'Amy' );  -- OK
```

Row 2: Insert using Form 2.

```
SQL
INSERT INTO table1  VALUES (2, 'Bob' );  -- FAILS,
-- must provide "c" a value because did not list
-- column names list

INSERT INTO table1  VALUES (2, 'Bob', DEFAULT );
  --  Using DEFAULT is OK
```

Row 3: Insert using Form 2 including NULL value.

```
SQL
INSERT INTO table1  VALUES (3, 'Carl', NULL );   -- OK
```

Although "INTO" is optional, I prefer to show it for clearer readability.

```
SQL
INSERT  table1  VALUES (3, 'Carl', NULL );   -- Works
```

If all columns have DEFAULT values, with one column possibly being an IDENTITY column, then a new row can be inserted with just the keywords DEFAULT VALUES. First alter the table to add default values.

```
SQL
ALTER TABLE table1
  ADD DEFAULT 999 FOR a, DEFAULT 'Default b' FOR b
```

Row 4: Insert with all defaults.

```
SQL INSERT INTO  table1  DEFAULT VALUES ;    -- OK
```

```
SQL
SELECT * FROM table1
```

Result

a	b	c
1	Amy	2003-05-12 13:21:58.223
2	Bob	2003-05-12 13:23:09.527
3	Carl	NULL
999	Default b	2003-05-12 15:55:19.913

Setting a DEFAULT and using DEFAULT VALUES for the PRIMARY KEY column here doesn't make much sense since it can only be used once. But

DEFAULT VALUES can be useful for a PRIMARY KEY column with IDENTITY as in the next section.

4.1.2 INSERT and SELECT with an IDENTITY Column

A table created with IDENTITY keyword on a column specifies that the column is an IDENTITY column. When a new row is added to the table, SQL Server generates a unique, incremental value for the IDENTITY column.

Using the INSERT and SELECT statements with a table containing an IDENTITY column requires some special considerations, which are discussed in this section.

IDENTITY Property automatically generates integer values, usually for the Primary Key.

- IDENTITY is a property applied in CREATE TABLE or ALTER TABLE to a column of **decimal, int, numeric, smallint, bigint,** or **tinyint** data type. It has SQL Server automatically generate a sequence of numbers upon INSERT of a new row. (See "CREATE TABLE," page 302.)
- The first INSERT uses the *seed* value; each subsequent INSERT adds *increment*. It gives both values (*seed*, *increment*) or neither (uses default of [1,1]).
- The IDENTITY property allows a maximum of one IDENTITY column per table.
- By default, the column name of the IDENTITY column cannot be listed in an INSERT statement. See below: SET IDENTITY_INSERT tablename ON.
- IDENTITY runs on SQL Server only. It is not portable to other RDBMSs.

Example: In Query Analyzer or isql or osql execute the following.

SQL

```
CREATE TABLE table2 (
    a   DEC          IDENTITY      PRIMARY  KEY,
    b   VARCHAR(10)     NOT NULL,
    c   DATETIME    DEFAULT GETDATE()
  -- GETDATE() is the MSS function that returns time
);
```

INSERT must NOT mention IDENTITY column.

A. ***INSERT*** *with* **(column name list)** — NO IDENTITY column in *column list* nor *VALUES list*

Row 1: Correct, we do NOT provide a value for column a, the IDENTITY column.

SQL

```
INSERT  table2  (b,c)  VALUES (  'Bob', NULL );
 -- OK
```

Row 2: Incorrect, this fails because we provide a value for a, which is IDENTITY column

SQL

```
INSERT INTO table2 (a,b) VALUES (DEFAULT,'Amy')
 -- FAILS, can't mention a

INSERT INTO table2 (b) VALUES ( 'Amy' );   -- OK
```

B. ***INSERT*** *without* **(column name list)** — *VALUES list* must include *all columns except IDENTITY*

Row 3

SQL

```
INSERT INTO table2        VALUES ( 'Carl' ) -- FAILS,
       -- must give value for  c
       -- Value for c must be a legal domain
       -- value: (DATETIME), DEFAULT or NULL

INSERT INTO table2     VALUES ( 'Carl', DEFAULT );
```

SQL

```
SELECT * FROM table1
```

Result

```
a            b            c
----------   ---------    --------------------------
1            Bob          NULL
2            Amy          2003-11-01 15:49:09.543
3            Carl         2003-11-01 15:53:08.077
```

4.1.2.1 Functions Returning Most Recent IDENTITY Values

The functions listed in Table 4-1 return the identity value generated by the most recent successful INSERT, SELECT INTO or bulk copy statement for the table, session (connection) and scope as indicated.

Table 4-1 Functions Returning Most Recent IDENTITY Values

Function Name	Table, Session and Scope Affected
SCOPE_IDENTITY () (This is usually my choice.)	any table, current session, current scope
@@IDENTITY	any table, current session, any scope
IDENT_CURRENT ('table-name')	specified table, any session, any scope

It is very common to write an external client in a 3 GL (such as Perl, C, VB, etc.) which inserts data from a GUI to create a new row such as a new book order and then needs to retrieve the newly created order id which is implemented as an identity column. These functions allow retrieving the most recent identity value. The three functions differ in the scope and session of the new identity value they return.

Scope refers to a *module*, the visible body of code in a stored procedure, trigger, function or batch. If one module calls another, such as a batch calling a stored procedure, the batch statements are in one scope and the stored procedure statements are in another. Likewise, if a batch contains an INSERT statement which fires a trigger, the batch code and trigger code are in different scopes.

If a user opens a Query Analyzer window, a session (connection) I established, and then opens a second window (File- >Connect...) using the same or different login, the new window represents a separate session or connection. Each session is identified by a different spid (server process identifier) which may be displayed using SELECT @@SPID.

IDENT_CURRENT This is the only one of the three functions that can observe a new identity value generated in different sessions and the only one which specifies a particular table.

SCOPE_IDENTITY() This returns the most recently generated new identity value in any table in the current session directly in the same body of code (scope) in which the SCOPE_IDENTITY() is called. See the example in the next section.

Suppose you do an insert into table1, which has an IDENTITY column. This column fires a trigger that does an insert into table2 also having an IDENTITY column. Then @@IDENTITY will return the new identity value from the trigger, table2, and SCOPE_IDENTITY() will return the new identity value from the original insert, table1.

@@IDENTITY This returns the most recently generated new identity value in any table in the current session in any scope.

Comparison of SCOPE_IDENTITY() and @@IDENTITY

Although most books use @@IDENTITY in their examples to find the newest identity value, I find SCOPE_IDENTITY() to be the function I most often need unless there is a specific reason for using one of the others. For example, suppose you have a batch that does an insert into **table2** which has an IDENTITY column that generates an identity value of 4, and this INSERT fires a trigger whose code does an insert into **table3** also having an IDENTITY column and it generates a value of 33. Then @@IDENTITY will return 33, the new identity value from the trigger, **table3**, and SCOPE_IDENTITY() will return 4, the new identity value from the original insert, **table2**. If there is no trigger on **table3**, then both functions return 4.

Example: Use SCOPE_IDENTITY() and @@IDENTITY on a table with no trigger.

Row 4: Add fourth row to example two pages prior.

SQL

```
INSERT INTO table2 VALUES ( 'Dave', DEFAULT ); -- OK
```

SQL

```
-- Notice that this SELECT statement needs no FROM clause.
SELECT SCOPE_IDENTITY() AS ScopeIdent
     ,  @@IDENTITY AS AtAtIdent
```

Result

```
ScopeIdent      AtAtIdent
---------------  --------------
4               4
```

They return the same value unless there is an underlying trigger, but SCOPE_IDENTITY() is safer unless you specifically want the value from the trigger.

See another example using IDENTITY property and SCOPE_IDENTITY() on page 335.

IDENT_CURRENT The IDENT_CURRENT(table) function returns the last identity value generated for the specified table in any session and scope.

Example: For this example you may open a new connection and log in as any user with access to **table2**.

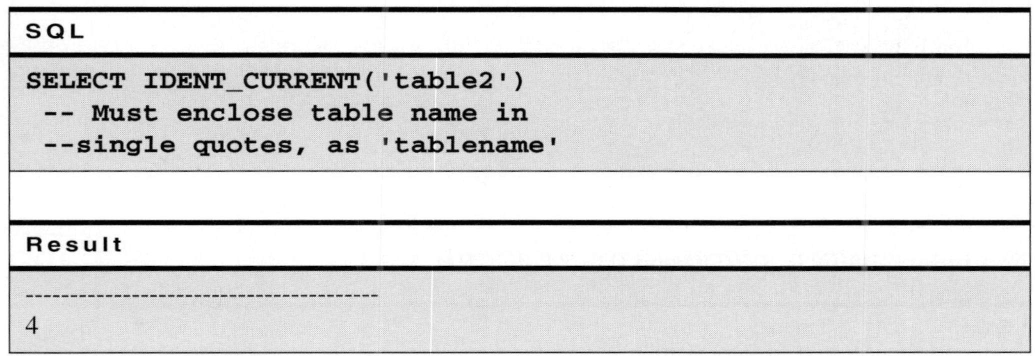

SQL

```
SELECT IDENT_CURRENT('table2')
 -- Must enclose table name in
 --single quotes, as 'tablename'
```

Result

```
----------------------------------------
4
```

IDENTITY Column Keywords and Functions Used with SELECT The key-word functions listed in Table 4-2 are used in SELECT. They return the values indicated.

Table 4-2 Functions Returning Most Recent IDENTITY Values

Function Name	Returns
IDENTITYCOL Keyword	In SELECT, returns identity column data values
IDENT_SEED ('table or view')	Returns the seed value of an identity column
IDENT_INCR ('table or view')	Returns the increment value of an identity column
IDENTITY (data_type [, seed , increment])	Is used only in a SELECT .. INTO statement to insert an identity column into a new table.

Example: IDENTITYCOL

If a table has an identity column, the IDENTITYCOL keyword may be used in a select list in place of the column name to reference the identity column. This feature is useful if the user knows the table has an identity column but doesn't know the column name.

SQL

```
SELECT IDENTITYCOL , b FROM table2
```

Result

```
a           b
---------   --------
1           Bob
2           Amy
3           Carl
--------------------------------------
4
```

Example: IDENT_SEED() and IDENT_INCR()

SQL

```
SELECT IDENT_SEED('table2') 'Seed'
     , IDENT_INCR('table2') 'Incr'
```

Result

```
Seed           Incr
-------------  ----------
1              1
```

Example: IDENTITY()

This example shows the use of SELECT ... INTO statement (see page 443) to create a new table, **newtable**, with a new IDENTITY column having seed and increment as specified and to populate it with data from an existing table. The source table may or may not have an identity column.

Changing the recovery model is not required, but it lets the SELECT ... INTO run faster. See "MSS 2000 Recovery Models," page 559.

SQL

```
DROP TABLE newtable    -- SELECT list INTO creates destina-
tion table which must not already exist.

ALTER DATABASE mydb SET RECOVERY BULK_LOGGED
```

The next statement creates a new table, **newtable**, with columns **id** and **bb**. Table **newtable**'s column **id** is automatically generated starting at 10 with increment of 1; column **bb** is filled from column **b** of **table2**.

SQL

```
SELECT IDENTITY(INT, 10, 1) INTO newtable
FROM table2
```

Result

```
---------------------------------------
(4 row(s) affected)
```

SQL

```
ALTER DATABASE mydb SET RECOVERY FULL
  -- A good idea to do database backup now.
```

SQL

```
SELECT * FROM newtable
```

Result

```
id          bb
-------     ------
10          Bob
11          Amy
12          Carl
13          Dave1
```

4.1.2.2 Allow Inserting a Value into an `IDENTITY` Column

You may allow inserting into an IDENTITY column for a table by executing SET IDENTITY_INSERT *table_name* ON.

Example: Using the same table table2

Row 5

SQL

```
SET IDENTITY_INSERT table2 ON

INSERT INTO table2  (a,b,c)
VALUES (8, 'Edna', ' March 22, 1998' );   -- OK

SET IDENTITY_INSERT table2 OFF
```

Row 6

SQL

```
INSERT INTO table2 (b) VALUES ( 'Frank' );      -- OK
```

SQL

```
SELECT * FROM table2
```

Result

```
a           b           c
----------  ---------   ---------------------------
1           Bob         NULL
2           Amy         2003-11-01 15:49:09.543
3           Carl        2003-11-01 15:53:08.077
4           Dave        2003-11-01 15:53:08.077
8           Edna        1998-03-22 00:00:00.000
9           Frank       2003-11-01 15:57:31.653
```

Comments

Enabling **IDENTITY_INSERT** can cause some confusion and should not be done unless it is carefully tested on a nonproduction server.

When **IDENTITY_INSERT** is **ON**, each INSERT must give a value for the identity column.

When **IDENTITY_INSERT** is later set to **OFF**, the next identity value will be one more than the higher of the highest value explicitly inserted and the last value automatically used.

DEFAULT VALUES If a table has an IDENTITY column and every other NOT NULL column has specified non-null default value, then INSERT using DEFAULT VALUES may be used.

Example: Using IDENTITY property

SQL

```
CREATE TABLE  table3
 (  a   INT IDENTITY , b VARCHAR(10) DEFAULT 'Hello' )

INSERT INTO  table3  DEFAULT VALUES ;

INSERT INTO  table3  DEFAULT VALUES ;

INSERT INTO  table3  DEFAULT VALUES ;
```

SQL

```
SELECT * FROM table2
```

Result

```
a           b
----------- ----------
1           Hello
2           Hello
3           Hello
```

4.1.2.3 A Table with a `UNIQUEIDENTIFIER` Column

`UNIQUEIDENTIFIER` Data Type is a globally unique identifier (GUID). According to MSS Books Online (Index ROWGUIDCOL):

> If an application must generate an identifier column that is unique across the entire database, or every database on every networked computer in the world, use the ROWGUIDCOL property, the **uniqueidentifier** data type, and the NEWID function.

- The only operations that are allowed against a **uniqueidentifier** value are comparisons (=, <>, <, >, <=, >=) and checking for NULL (IS NULL and IS NOT NULL). No other arithmetic operators are allowed.
- All column constraints and properties except IDENTITY are allowed on the **uniqueidentifier** data type.
- To generate unique values for each column use the **NEWID( )** function.

Syntax

```
NEWID()
```

Returns a unique value of type **UNIQUIDENTIFIER.**

`ROWGUIDCOL` Property The ROWGUIDCOL Property indicates that the new column is a **Row Global Unique Identifier Column**. The ROWGUIDCOL property has the following attributes.

- It can be assigned only to a **uniqueidentifier** column.
- It can be assigned to only one **uniqueidentifier** column per table.
- It does not enforce uniqueness of the values in the column.
- It does not automatically generate values for new rows inserted into the table.

Example: CREATE table 3 with UNIQUIDENTIFIER column.

SQL

```
CREATE TABLE table4 (
     a   UNIQUEIDENTIFIER      PRIMARY  KEY
              -- DEFAULT NEWID()    -- could be used here
,    b   VARCHAR(10)     NOT NULL
);
```

SQL

```
INSERT INTO table4 (a,b) VALUES ( NEWID() , 'Amy' );
INSERT INTO table4 (a,b) VALUES ( NEWID() , 'Bob' );
SELECT * FROM table4;    -- ORDER BY a
 -- is okay since comparison operators are
 -- defined on UID
```

SQL

Result

```
a                                                    b
---------------------------------------------------- ----------
79439DA8-2B36-4E28-AE55-98EA53355CE7                 Amy
5AC15E51-AE28-40EF-B85E-E5B95D5586AA                 Bob
```

CREATE table5 with UNIQUIDENTIFIER column having NEWID() as default.

SQL

```
CREATE TABLE table5 (
     a   uniqueidentifier CONSTRAINT t4_Guid_Default
         DEFAULT NEWID()
,    b   varchar(10)
,   CONSTRAINT  t4_Guid_PK   PRIMARY KEY (a)
)
```

SQL

```
INSERT INTO table5 (a,b) VALUES ( DEFAULT, 'Amy' );
INSERT INTO table5 (a,b) VALUES ( DEFAULT, 'Bob' );
SELECT * FROM table5;
```

Result

```
a                                                    b
---------------------------------------------------- ----------
10C83C70-E337-4E4A-873B-5C7010AF1BD9                 Amy
8E9D090F-8250-4ED7-848A-C3ABF723A1F2                 Bob
```

There is no equivalent of @@IDENTITY for UNIQUEIDENTIFIER.
If you need the last UNIQUEIDENTIFIER value used, do the following.

SQL

```
DECLARE  @v_newuid     UNIQUEIDENTIFIER
SET @v_newuid   = NEWID()
INSERT INTO  table5 ( a , b )
VALUES ( @v_newuid , 'Carl' )

PRINT @v_newuid -- Or  SELECT @v_newuid
SELECT * FROM table5;
```

Result

```
9CEB4FFB-28DB-4395-A3A7-CA707EB0F55A

a                                                      b
------------------------------------------------------ ----------
10C83C70-E337-4E4A-873B-5C7010AF1BD9                   Amy
8E9D090F-8250-4ED7-848A-C3ABF723A1F2                   Bob
9CEB4FFB-28DB-4395-A3A7-CA707EB0F55A                   Carl
```

4.1.2.4 Inserting from a `SELECT` Statement

There are two forms of Transact-SQL statement which allow inserting multiple rows of data into one table (target table) using a SELECT statement to provide the data. Virtually any legal SELECT statement may be used which fetches data from one or more source tables.

The main difference between the two is that in the first form the target table must already exist (it may be empty or not) and in the second form the target table must not exist as it is created by the statement.

1. **INSERT INTO** *table* SELECT ... -- *target table must exist*
2. **SELECT** *list* **INTO** *table* FROM ... -- *target table must NOT exist*

The syntax and examples of each are provided below.

INSERT INTO ***table*** SELECT -- target table must exist

Syntax

```
INSERT [INTO] table-or-view [ ( columnname_list ) ]
        select-statement
```

Example: From Query Analyzer or isql or osql

Let's create a couple of tables to play with.

SQL

```
CREATE TABLE t1 ( a  INT , b  CHAR(10)   )
INSERT INTO  t1  ( a , b ) VALUES ( 1 , 'aaa' )
INSERT INTO  t1  ( a , b ) VALUES ( 2 , 'bbb' )
```

SQL

```
CREATE TABLE t2 ( d  INT , e  VARCHAR(20)
                         , f  DATETIME   )
INSERT INTO  t2  ( d , e , f ) VALUES ( 1 , 'dd'
                         , GETDATE() )
INSERT INTO  t2  ( d , e , f ) VALUES ( 2 , 'ee'
                         , GETDATE() )
```

SQL

```
SELECT * FROM t1
   -- t1 before
```

Result

```
a          b
-----      -----
1          aaa
2          bbb
```

SQL

```
SELECT * FROM t2
   -- t2 before
```

Result

```
d          e          f
----       ----       -------------------- -----------
1          dd         2003-07-27 22:49:35.760
2          ee         2003-07-27 22:49:35.760
```

Now use INSERT INTO table SELECT.

SQL

```
INSERT INTO t1 ( a , b )
  -- The ( a, b) is optional here since all
  -- columns are used in DDL order
     SELECT d , e
     FROM t2
```

Check the result.

SQL

```
SELECT * FROM t1        -- t1 after
```

Result

```
a        b
-----    -----
1        aaa
2        bbb
1        dd
2        ee
```

Here's an easy way to update a reference table when the new version arrives.

SQL

```
TRUNCATE TABLE  t1
-- This empties all rows of t1 leaving
-- an empty table

INSERT INTO  t1      SELECT * FROM t1_update
```

4.1.2.5 SELECT ... INTO table -- target table must NOT exist

This method is used when the target table does *not* exist. The SELECT INTO statement creates a new table and populates it with the result set of the SELECT. The columns in the new table are specified by the select list and may even contain an identity column (see example, page 436).

Syntax

```
SELECT select_list

INTO new_table

FROM { table_source } [ , ...n ]

[ WHERE search_condition ]
    [ GROUP BY group_by_expression ]
    [ HAVING search_condition ]
    [ ORDER BY order_expression [ ASC | DESC ] ]
```

Example: We use the SELECT ... INTO statement to create a new table **table1_copy** and populate it with data from table **table1**.

Changing recovery model is not required, but it lets SELECT INTO run faster. See "MSS 2000 Recovery Models," page 559.

SQL

```
DROP TABLE newtable
  -- SELECT list INTO creates the destination table
  -- which must not already exist.

ALTER DATABASE mydb SET RECOVERY BULK_LOGGED
```

The next statement creates a new table **table1_copy** as a copy of **table1** with the same column names and data but not having any of **table1**'s constraints.

SQL

```
SELECT *
 -- table1_copy must not exist, will be created
INTO table1_copy
FROM table1

ALTER DATABASE mydb SET RECOVERY FULL
  -- Good idea to do database backup now.
```

SQL

```
SELECT * FROM t1          -- t1 after
```

SQL (cont.)

Result

```
a          b          c
--------   -------    -------------------------
3          Carl       2003-11-01 16:17:01.153
999        Dave       2003-11-01 16:17:01.153e
```

Since we just created **table1_copy**, trying the same SELECT ... INTO will now fail.

SQL

```
SELECT *
INTO table1_copy
FROM table1
```

Result

```
Server: Msg 2714, Level 16, State 6, Line 1
There is already an object named 'table1_copy' in the database.
```

4.2 UPDATE

The UPDATE command changes existing data in a table.

4.2.1 UPDATE—Basic Syntax

The complete syntax and the arguments of UPDATE can be found on page 448, in section 4.2.2. The following code shows the basics of the UPDATE syntax and some examples of its use.

Syntax

```
UPDATE { table_name | view_name | rowset_function_limited }
  SET     column_name = { expression | DEFAULT | NULL } [ ,...n ]
  [ WHERE < search_condition > ]
```

4.2.1.1 Examples of UPDATE

Example: Let's first create a sample database with some sample data to play with. (Execute each "SQL:" section separately or add "go" after each to make it a separate batch.)

SQL

```
CREATE DATABASE mydb

USE mydb

SELECT  *  INTO shippers
FROM northwind.dbo.shippers
```

Display the data before making changes.

SQL

```
SELECT  *  FROM shippers
```

Result

```
ShipperID    CompanyName          Phone
-----------  -------------------- --------------------
1            Speedy Express       (503) 555-9831
2            United Package       (503) 555-3199
3            Federal Shipping     (503) 555-9931
```

Example: Simple Updates

Update one or more columns of specified rows.

Change the first row company name.

SQL

```
UPDATE shippers
SET CompanyName =  'NewCompanyName'
WHERE ShipperID =  '1'
```

Change the second row company name and phone.

SQL

```
UPDATE shippers
SET CompanyName =  'AAA' ,  Phone = '(101) 111-1111'
WHERE ShipperID =  '2'
```

Display the data after making changes.

SQL

```
SELECT  *  FROM shippers
```

Result

```
ShipperID      CompanyName           Phone
-----------    --------------------  --------------------
1              NewCompanyName        (503) 555-9831
2              AAA                   (101) 111-1111
3              Federal Shipping      (503) 555-9931
```

Example: Give everyone in the **employees** table a 10% **salary** increase.

SQL

```
UPDATE employees
  -- Omitting the WHERE clause updates
  -- every row in the table
SET   salary = salary * 1.1
```

Example: Give a 10% **salary** increase to employees whose **sales** meet their branch **target**.

SQL

```
UPDATE employees
  -- Omitting the WHERE clause updates
  -- every row in the table
SET   salary = salary * 1.1
WHERE  sales >=
  (SELECT target FROM branches
    WHERE branchid = employee.branchid)
```

Example: Update a table using a correlated subquery.

Copy the **titles** and **sales** tables from the **pubs** database into our **mydb** database so we can change the data without changing data in **pubs**.

SQL

```
USE mydb
go

SELECT  *  INTO titles  FROM pubs.dbo.titles
SELECT  *  INTO sales   FROM pubs.dbo.sales
```

The **titles** table has a **ytd_sales** column for each book (**title_id**), which we will consider to be the quantity of that title sold year to date up to the beginning of the current quarter.

The sales table has each book sale including quantity, **qty**, which we assume is for the current quarter.

At the end of each quarter, we want to update the **titles** table **ytd_sales** column for each title from sales table **qty** column. (For the first solution we assume both ytd_sales and qty are number of books.)

Show the before values of **qty** from **sales** and **ytd_sales** from titles for **title_id** BU1032.

SQL

```
SELECT  title_id , qty , ord_num
FROM sales
WHERE title_id   = 'BU1032'
```

Result

```
title_id        qty        ord_num
--------        -----      -------------
BU1032          5          6871
BU1032          10         423LL930
```

SQL

```
SELECT  title_id , ytd_sales  FROM titles
WHERE title_id = 'BU1032'
```

Result

```
title_id ytd_sales
-------- -----------
BU1032   4095
```

So **title_id** BU1032 has **ytd_sales** value of 4095 in the **titles** table and two sales of five and ten books each. So we need to update the **ytd_sales** to 4095 + 15 = 4110.

Do the update for all rows.

SQL

```
UPDATE titles    SET ytd_sales = titles.ytd_sales +
    ( SELECT SUM((s.qty) FROM sales s WHERE s.title_id = titles.title_id )
```

If **ytd_sales** in **titles** represents total dollar sales and **qty** in **sales** is the number of books for the current quarter, we would need to multiply the latter by price to get its dollar amount.

SQL

```
UPDATE titles    SET ytd_sales = titles.ytd_sales +
    titles.price * ( SELECT SUM(s.qty) FROM sales s WHERE s.title_id =
titles.title_id )
```

4.2.2 UPDATE—Complete Syntax

The following syntax and arguments outline the precise details of the UPDATE code.

Syntax

```
{
    table_name [WITH ( < table_hint_limited > [ ...n ] ) ]
    | view_name                          -- view must be updatable, update
  may affect only one base table in the view
    | rowset_function_limited
}
SET
{
    column_name = { expression | DEFAULT | NULL }
    | @variable = expression
    | @variable = column = expression
} [ ,...n ]

{
    { [ FROM { < table_source > } [ ,...n ] ]
      [ WHERE < search_condition > ]
    }
    | [ WHERE CURRENT OF { { [ GLOBAL ] cursor_name } | cursor_variable_name } ]
  }

[ OPTION ( < query_hint > [ ,...n ] ) ]
```

```
< table_source > ::=
      table_name [ [ AS ] table_alias ] [ WITH ( < table_hint > [ ,...n ] ) ]
   |  view_name [ [ AS ] table_alias ]
   |  rowset_function [ [ AS ] table_alias ]
   |  derived_table [ AS ] table_alias [ ( column_alias [ ,...n ] ) ]
   | < joined_table >


< joined_table > ::=
      < table_source > < join_type > < table_source > ON < search_condition >
    | < table_source > CROSS JOIN < table_source >
    | < joined_table >


< join_type > ::=  [ INNER | { { LEFT | RIGHT | FULL } [ OUTER ] } ]
  [ < join_hint > ] JOIN


< join_hint > ::=  { LOOP | HASH | MERGE | REMOTE }   -- See join_hint
  descriptions page 421


< table_hint_limited >   See page 528.


< table_hint >   See page 528.


< query_hint > ::=      -- See query_hint descriptions page 527.
  {
      { HASH | ORDER } GROUP
   | { CONCAT | HASH | MERGE } UNION
   | {LOOP | MERGE | HASH } JOIN
   | FAST number_rows
   | FORCE ORDER
   | MAXDOP
   | ROBUST PLAN
   | KEEP PLAN
}
```

Arguments

table_name | view_name

The name of the target table or view to be updated is table_name | view_name. A view must be updatable and must affect only one base table in the view. A view with an INSTEAD OF UPDATE trigger cannot be a target of an UPDATE with a FROM clause.

WITH < table_hint_limited >   See page 528.

rowset_function_limited

The rowset_function_limited position specifies either the OPENQUERY or OPENROWSET function. See page 149 and Books Online.

SET

The SET keyword marks the start of the list of one or more columns to be updated.

column_name

column_name is the column to be updated. It must be a column name in the table or view specified in the UPDATE clause. Identity columns cannot be updated.

DEFAULT

DEFAULT is the keyword to specify that the default value defined for the column is to replace the existing value in the column. This can also be used to change the column to NULL if the column has no default and is defined to allow null values.

@variable

@variable is a declared variable that is being set to the value returned by *expression.*

```
SET @variable = column = expression
```

sets the variable to the same value as the column, the value of *expression*.

```
SET @variable = column, column = expression
```

sets the variable to the pre-update value of the column and then updates the column to *expression*.

FROM <table_source>

The FROM clause allows other tables to be used to determine the rows and values of the target table to be updated. It is not ANSI SQL compliant.

- The target table may or may not appear in the FROM clause.
- Table aliases may be used in the FROM clause.
- A view with INSTEAD OF UPDATE trigger cannot be in both UPDATE and FROM clauses.

See an example following the Permissions section below.

WHERE <search_condition>

The WHERE clause specifies a Boolean predicate to determine the rows of the target table to be updated. It is ANSI SQL compliant.

See page 54 for a discussion and examples of Boolean predicates and logic in SQL. See WHERE clause syntax, page 479.The rows for which the predicate evaluates to TRUE will be updated. This is called a **SEARCHED UPDATE** and may modify multiple rows depending on the search condition.

WHERE CURRENT OF

WHERE CURRENT OF specifies that the update or delete is performed at the current position of the specified cursor. It is ANSI SQL compliant. This is a **POSITIONED UPDATE** using a WHERE CURRENT OF *cursor* clause to update the single row at the current cursor position. The positioned update is contrasted with a **searched update** described above.

[GLOBAL] *cursor_name* | *cursor_variable_name*

This is the name of an open, updatable cursor or cursor variable. See Cursors page 638.

Simplified UPDATE and DELETE Syntax using "WHERE CURRENT OF" clause: This syntax applies where the cursor specifies a single row in the base table to update or delete.

See UPDATE/DELETE Using a Cursor (positioned update), page 648.

```
UPDATE table
    SET column_name =  expression  [ ,...n ]
    WHERE CURRENT OF cursor
```

```
DELETE [FROM] table
    WHERE CURRENT OF cursor
```

OPTION (<query_hint> [**,**...*n*])

These keywords indicate that optimizer hints are used to customize SQL Server's processing of the statement. See query_hint descriptions page 526.

Comments

An UPDATE statement will return an error with no records updated in the following conditions:

- If a constraint or rule would be violated on any row
- If column nullability would be violated on any row
- If the update value is an incompatible data type
- If an arithmetic error occurs (overflow, divide by zero or a domain error)
- If an update to a clustered index column causes the size of the row to exceed 8,060 bytes
- If an update query could alter more than one row while updating both the clustering key and one or more **text**, **image** or Unicode columns

When an INSTEAD-OF trigger on UPDATE is defined for a table or view, the trigger executes *instead of* the UPDATE statement.

Modifying a **text**, **ntext** or **image** column with UPDATE initializes the column, assigns a valid text pointer to it, and allocates at least one data page unless you are updating the column with NULL. Remember that the UPDATE statement is logged. If you are replacing or modifying large blocks of **text**, **ntext** or **image** data, use the WRITETEXT or UPDATETEXT statement instead of the UPDATE statement. The WRITETEXT and UPDATETEXT statements (by default) are not logged.

Explicit trailing spaces for VARCHAR and CHAR columns are handled according to the ANSI_PADDING session setting (recommended setting is ON). See page 102.

A **table** variable may be accessed like a regular table including being updated in an UPDATE statement. UPDATE statements are only allowed in user-defined functions if the table being modified is a **table** variable.

A four-part name constructed with the OPENDATASOURCE function as the server-name part may be used as a table source in all the places a table name can appear in UPDATE statements.

Permissions

UPDATE permissions default to members of the **sysadmin** fixed server role, the **db_owner** and **db_datawriter** fixed database roles, and the table owner. Members of the **sysadmin**, **db_owner** role, **db_securityadmin** role and the table owner can grant permissions to other users.

SELECT permissions are also required for the table being updated if the UPDATE statement contains a WHERE clause or if *expression* in the SET clause uses a column in the table.

4.2.2.1 Examples of UPDATE Using the FROM Clause

The FROM clause allows data to be read from one or more tables to determine the value to be set in the target table. It also permits specifying a table alias for the updated table. It is not ANSI SQL compliant.

The target table may appear in the FROM clause or not. Table aliases may be used in the FROM clause as in the example below. A view with INSTEAD OF UPDATE trigger cannot be in both UPDATE and FROM clauses.

Example: The FROM clause includes a table alias t, which is available in the subquery.

SQL

```
UPDATE titles
SET ytd_sales = ( SELECT t.ytd_sales + SUM(s.qty) FROM sales s
        WHERE s.title_id = t.title_id  )
FROM titles t
```

Result

(18 row(s) affected)

Example: Not ANSI SQL Compliant

A FROM clause may be used to obtain data from another table to update target table. First display the current **shippers** table data.

SQL

```
USE mydb
```

SQL

```
SELECT  *  FROM shippers
```

Result

ShipperID	CompanyName	Phone
1	NewCompanyName	(503) 555-9831
2	AAA	(101) 111-1111
3	Federal Shipping	(503) 555-9931

Then use UPDATE to copy the values from the original table in **northwind** back into our **shippers** table in **mydb**. This statement does not replace deleted rows.

SQL

```
UPDATE shippers
SET companyname = orig.companyname , phone = orig.phone
FROM northwind.dbo.shippers orig
WHERE shippers.shipperid = orig.shipperid
```

SQL (cont.)

Result

```
(3 row(s) affected)
```

Display the data after restoring the original values.

SQL

```
SELECT  *  FROM shippers
```

Result

```
ShipperID     CompanyName          Phone
-----------   --------------------  --------------------
1             Speedy Express        (503) 555-9831
2             United Package        (503) 555-3199
3             Federal Shipping      (503) 555-9931
```

ALTERNATIVE SOLUTION: This UPDATE could have been done using a subquery.

SQL

```
UPDATE shippers
SET companyname =
  ( SELECT companyname FROM northwind.dbo.shippers
    WHERE shippers.shipperid = shipperid )
, phone =
  ( SELECT phone FROM northwind.dbo.shippers
    WHERE shippers.shipperid = shipperid )
```

This version is more awkward than using FROM, especially if a large number of columns are involved, but it is ANSI SQL compliant.

Example: Not ANSI SQL Compliant

The FROM clause may be used to specify the rows in the target table that will be updated.

Update only the **first 2 rows of shippers** table **when sorted by CompanyName**.

First do the SELECT to show the rows we want to update.

SQL

```
SELECT TOP 2 * FROM shippers  ORDER BY companyname
```

Result

```
ShipperID      CompanyName            Phone
-----------    --------------------   --------------------
3              Federal Shipping       (503) 555-9931
1              Speedy Express         (503) 555-9831
```

Change the phone to 1111 on these two rows. Use the above query as the FROM clause subquery.

SQL

```
UPDATE  shippers
SET phone = '1111'
FROM (SELECT TOP 2 * FROM shippers
ORDER BY companyname) AS top2
WHERE  shippers.shipperid  =  top2.shipperid
```

Result

```
(2 row(s) affected)
```

SQL

```
SELECT  *  FROM shippers
```

Result

```
ShipperID      CompanyName            Phone
-----------    --------------------   --------------------
1              Speedy Express         1111
2              United Package         (503) 555-3199
3              Federal Shipping       1111
```

This update could have been made ANSI compliant with a subquery as above.

4.3 DELETE

The DELETE command removes rows from a table.

4.3.1 DELETE Syntax

The following code shows the basics of the DELETE syntax and the parameters of its use.

Syntax

```
DELETE   [ FROM ]
{
   table_name WITH ( < table_hint_limited > [ ...n ] )
   | view_name -- view must be updatable, delete may affect only one base
                    table in the view
   | rowset_function_limited
}
[ FROM { < table_source > } [ ,...n ] ]
[ WHERE
   {
     < search_condition >
   |  CURRENT OF  {    [ GLOBAL ] cursor_name |  cursor_variable_name    }
   }
]
[ OPTION ( < query_hint > [ ,...n ] ) ]

< table_source > ::=
   table_name [ [ AS ] table_alias ] [ WITH ( < table_hint > [ ,...n ] ) ]
   | view_name [ [ AS ] table_alias ]
   | rowset_function [ [ AS ] table_alias ]
   | subquery [ AS ] table_alias [ ( column_alias [ ,...n ] ) ]
   | < joined_table >


< joined_table > ::=
   < table_source > < join_type > < table_source > ON < search_condition >
   | < table_source > CROSS JOIN < table_source >
   | < joined_table >


< join_type > ::=   [ INNER | { { LEFT | RIGHT | FULL } [OUTER] } ]
  [ < join_hint > ]  JOIN


< table_hint_limited >   See page 528.


< table_hint >   See page 528.
```

```
< join_hint >   See page 527.

< query_hint > ::=       -- See query_hint descriptions page 526
{
     { HASH | ORDER } GROUP      | { CONCAT | HASH | MERGE } UNION
     | FAST number_rows          | FORCE ORDER
     | MAXDOP                    | ROBUST PLAN
     | KEEP PLAN
}
```

Arguments

DELETE [FROM]

Begin the DELETE statement with DELETE [FROM]. The FROM keyword is optional, but many people prefer to include it.

table_name | view_name

table_name | view_name is the name of the target table, table variable, (updatable) view or rowset function to be modified. It may also be the four-part table or view name using the OPENDATASOURCE function as the server name.table_name | view_name. A view must be updatable and must affect only one base table in the view.

Remember that if the table or view exists in another database or has an owner other than the current user, you should use a four-part qualified name in the format *server_name.database.*[*owner*]*.object_name*.

WITH < table_hint_limited > See page 528.

rowset_function_limited

The rowset_function_limited position specifies either the OPENQUERY or OPENROWSET function. See page 148 and Books Online.

FROM <table_source>

This FROM clause allows other tables to be used to indicate which rows of the target table should be deleted. It is not ANSI SQL compliant. This FROM <table_source> list may do the following things:

- It may include base tables, views, rowset functions and/or subqueries, each of which may have a table alias.
- It may or may not include the target table.
- It may include subquery(ies) identified by a table alias. Each column of a subquery may have a column alias to identify a column in the subquery result set.

See examples in the previous section with the UPDATE statement.

WHERE <search_condition>

This WHERE clause specifies a Boolean predicate to determine the rows of the target table to be deleted. It is ANSI SQL compliant. The rows for which the predicate evaluate to TRUE will be deleted. This is called a **SEARCHED UPDATE** and may modify multiple rows depending on the search condition.

See page 53 for a discussion and examples of Boolean predicates and logic in SQL.See WHERE clause syntax, page 478.

WHERE CURRENT OF

WHERE CURRENT OF specifies that the update or delete is performed at the current position of the specified cursor. It is ANSI SQL compliant. This is a **POSITIONED UPDATE** using a WHERE CURRENT OF *cursor* clause to update the single row at the current cursor position. The positioned update is contrasted with a **searched update** described above.

[GLOBAL] *cursor_name* | *cursor_variable_name*

The name of an open, updatable cursor or cursor variable requires this code. See "Cursors," page 638.

OPTION (<query_hint> [,...*n*])

These keywords indicate that optimizer hints are used to customize SQL Server's processing of the statement.

See query_hint descriptions page 526.

Simplified UPDATE and DELETE Syntax using "WHERE CURRENT OF" clause:

This syntax is appropriate where the cursor specifies a single row in the base table to update or delete.

UPDATE *table*
SET *column_name* = *expression* [,...*n*]
WHERE CURRENT OF *cursor*
DELETE [FROM] *table*
WHERE CURRENT OF *cursor*

where the cursor specifies a single row in the base table to update or delete.

See UPDATE/DELETE Using a Cursor (positioned update), page 648.

Comments

DELETE may be used in the body of a user-defined function if the object modified is a **table** variable.

A four-part table name (or view name) using the OPENDATASOURCE function as the server name may be used as a table source in all places a table name can appear.

The DELETE statement will fail if it causes a trigger to ROLLBACK or if it attempts to remove a row causing a referential integrity violation. If the DELETE is to remove multiple rows and if deleting any one of the rows would violate a trigger or constraint, the statement will be canceled, an error will be returned and no rows will be deleted.

When an INSTEAD-OF trigger on DELETE is defined for a table or view, the trigger executes *instead of* the DELETE statement.

When a DELETE statement encounters an arithmetic error (overflow, divide by zero, or a domain error) occurring during expression evaluation, SQL Server handles these errors as if SET ARITHABORT is ON, that is, the remainder of the batch will be canceled, and an error message will be returned.

The setting of the SET ROWCOUNT option is ignored for DELETE statements against remote tables and local and remote partitioned views. (SET ROWCOUNT on local tables stops processing after the specified number of rows.)

TRUNCATE TABLE *table* is faster than DELETE FROM *table* in removing all rows in a table. It also requires less transaction log space than DELETE. This is true because DELETE physically removes one row at a time and records each deleted row in the transaction log. TRUNCATE TABLE deallocates all pages associated with the table. (It also resets IDENTITY columns to seed.) TRUNCATE TABLE is functionally equivalent to DELETE with no WHERE clause, but TRUNCATE TABLE cannot be used with tables referenced by foreign keys. Also see page 464.

Permissions

DELETE permissions default to members of the **sysadmin** fixed server role, the **db_owner** and **db_datawriter** fixed database roles and the table owner. Members of the **sysadmin**, the **db_owner** role, the **db_securityadmin** role and the table owner can transfer permissions to other users.

SELECT permissions are also required if the statement contains a WHERE clause.

Examples of DELETE

Let's first create a sample database with some sample data to play with. (Execute each "SQL:" section separately or add "go" after each to make it a separate batch.)

SQL

```
CREATE DATABASE mydb
   -- Create a test database to play in.
   -- Omit if you already have one.

USE mydb

SELECT  TOP 8  *  INTO suppliers  FROM northwind.dbo.suppliers
```

Display the data before making changes.

SQL

```
SELECT  supplierid , companyname , contactname
FROM  suppliers
```

Result

supplierid	companyname	contactname
1	Exotic Liquids	Charlotte Cooper
2	New Orleans Cajun Delights	Shelley Burke
3	Grandma Kelly's Homestead	Regina Murphy
4	Tokyo Traders	Yoshi Nagase
5	Cooperativa de Quesos 'Las Cabras'	Antonio del Valle Saavedra
6	Mayumi's	Mayumi Ohno
7	Pavlova, Ltd.	Ian Devling
8	Specialty Biscuits, Ltd.	Peter Wilson

Example: Simple Deletes — ANSI SQL-92 and SQL-99 Compliant

Remove one or more specified rows.

Change the first row company name.

SQL

```
DELETE FROM suppliers
WHERE supplierid =  2
```

Change the second row company name and phone.

SQL

```
DELETE FROM suppliers
WHERE supplierid  BETWEEN 4 AND 7
```

Display the data after making changes.

SQL

```
SELECT  supplierid , companyname , contactname
FROM  suppliers
```

Result

supplierid	companyname	contactname
1	Exotic Liquids	Charlotte Cooper
3	Grandma Kelly's Homestead	Regina Murphy
8	Specialty Biscuits, Ltd.	Peter Wilson

Example: ANSI SQL-92 and SQL-99 Compliant

Omitting the WHERE clause deletes every row in the table.

See comparison with TRUNCATE TABLE on page 464.

SQL

```
DELETE FROM   suppliers
```

Example: ANSI SQL-92 and SQL-99 Compliant

Delete the current (single) row of the cursor named **mycursor**.

SQL

```
DELETE FROM   suppliers
WHERE CURRENT OF   mycursor
```

Example: To set up the next DELETE examples, copy the **products** and **categories** tables from Northwind database into **mydb**.

SQL

```
USE mydb

SELECT  *  INTO products
FROM northwind.dbo.products

SELECT  *  INTO categories
FROM northwind.dbo.categories
```

For reference, show how many rows are in the products table and how many of these products are in a food category which relates to "fish."

SQL

```
SELECT  COUNT(*) NumProducts  FROM products
```

Result

```
NumProducts
-----------
77
```

SQL

```
SELECT  COUNT(*) NumFishProducts
FROM   products p INNER JOIN categories c
   ON p.categoryid =  c.categoryid
WHERE  c.description  LIKE  '%fish%'
```

Result

```
NumFishProducts
-----------
12
```

Example: The boss just told us to delete all of the products that fit in the food category "fish." The FROM clause of the extended DELETE statement lets us do the same inner join. Delete just these 12 "fish" rows. Use the above query as the subquery in the FROM clause.

SQL

```
DELETE FROM   products
          -- Not ANSI SQL compliant
FROM   products p INNER JOIN categories c
       ON p.categoryid =  c.categoryid
WHERE  c.description  LIKE   '%fish%'
```

Result

(12 row(s) affected)

SQL

```
SELECT  COUNT(*) NumProducts  FROM products
```

Result

```
NumProducts
-----------
65
```

An ANSI SQL compliant version of this DELETE statement can be formed using a subquery in the WHERE clause.

SQL

```
DELETE FROM   products
           -- ANSI SQL-92 and SQL-99 compliant
WHERE  categoryid  IN
  ( SELECT  categoryid  FROM categories
    WHERE description  LIKE  '%fish%'  )
```

Result

(12 row(s) affected)

4.4 TRUNCATE TABLE

The TRUNCATE TABLE command removes all rows from a table without logging each row deleted. No logging means it runs faster than DELETE FROM *tablename*. It also resets IDENTITY column to its initial (seed) value. TRUNCATE TABLE cannot be used on parent table of Foreign Key constraint.

4.4.1 TRUNCATE TABLE Syntax

The syntax of TRUNCATE TABLE and some examples of its use are shown here. In addition, Table 4-3 offers a comparison between **DELETE FROM** table and **TRUNCATE TABLE** table.

Syntax

```
TRUNCATE TABLE tablename
```

Example:

SQL

```
SELECT COUNT(*) NumRows FROM products
```

Result

```
NumRows
-----------
65
```

SQL

```
TRUNCATE TABLE  products
  -- Similar effect to:    DELETE  FROM  products
  -- But not logged and resets IDENTITY.
```

Result

The command(s) completed successfully.

SQL
`SELECT COUNT(*) NumRows FROM products`

Result
NumRows ----------- 0

Table 4-3 Comparison of **DELETE FROM** Table and **TRUNCATE TABLE** Table

	DELETE FROM *table*	**TRUNCATE TABLE** *table*
How data is removed	One row at a time	One data page (8 KB) at a time
Logs each row deleted?	Yes—slow, lots of disk, can be recovered to point in time.	No—faster, less disk. No point in time recovery.
Resets IDENTITY column to seed value?	No	Yes
Can be used if target table is parent of Foreign Key constraint?	Yes—referential integrity constraints can be checked since each row is checked. Violations will cause DELETE to fail.	No— Since deletion is done by page, referential integrity of each row cannot be checked. So the statement will not be allowed even if it would not cause a referential integrity violation
Can activate a trigger?	Yes	No
Leaves an empty table with table structure, indexes and permissions intact?	Yes	Yes

4.5 SELECT

The SELECT command retrieves data from the database allowing the selection of rows, columns and tables.

4.5.1 SELECT Statement Syntax

The complete SELECT statement syntax is shown below. Following this material the SELECT statement parameters will be described for each clause in turn.

Syntax

```
SELECT [ DISTINCT | ALL ] [ TOP n [ PERCENT ] [ WITH TIES ] ]   < select_list >
[ INTO new_table ]
[ FROM { < table_source > } [ ,...n ] ]
[ WHERE < search_condition > | < old_outer_join > ]
[ GROUP BY [ ALL ] group_by_expression [ ,...n ] [ WITH { CUBE | ROLLUP } ]  ]
[ HAVING < search_condition > ]
[ ORDER BY { column_name_or_alias [ ASC | DESC ] | column_position [ ASC | DESC ]
    } [ ,...n] ]

[ COMPUTE { { AVG | COUNT | MAX | MIN | STDEV | STDEVP | VAR | VARP | SUM }
     ( expression ) } [ ,...n ]  [ BY expression [ ,...n ] ]  ]

[   FOR BROWSE -- Used with DB-Library browse mode cursor to allow updates.
     |  FOR XML RAW          [ , XMLDATA ]    [ , BINARY base64 ]
     |  FOR XML AUTO         [ , XMLDATA ]    [ , BINARY base64 ] [ , ELEMENTS ]
     |  FOR XML EXPLICIT     [ , XMLDATA ]    [ , BINARY base64 ]
-- See restrictions below
]

[ OPTION ( < query_hint > [ ,...n ]) ]


SELECT statements may be combined using Set operators  UNION, UNION ALL
(page  522)


< select_list >  ::=
   {
        *
      | { table_name | view_name | table_alias }.*
      | { column_name | expression | IDENTITYCOL | ROWGUIDCOL } [ [ AS ]
column_alias ]
      |  column_alias = expression
   } [ ,...n ]


< table_source > ::=
   table_name [ [ AS ] table_alias ] [ WITH ( < table_hint > [ ,...n ] ) ]
```

```
   | view_name [ [ AS ] table_alias ]
   | rowset_function [ [ AS ] table_alias ]
   | derived_table [ AS ] table_alias [ ( column_alias [ ,...n ] ) ]
   | < joined_table >
   | OPENXML


< table_hint >   See page 528.


< joined_table > ::=
   < table_source > < join_type > < table_source > ON < search_condition >
   | < table_source > CROSS JOIN < table_source >
   | < joined_table >


< join_type > ::= [ INNER | { { LEFT | RIGHT | FULL } [ OUTER ] } ]
  [ < join_hint > ]  JOIN


< join_hint >   See page 527.


< query_hint > ::=      -- See query_hint descriptions page 527
   {
       { HASH | ORDER } GROUP
     | { CONCAT | HASH | MERGE } UNION
     | { LOOP | MERGE | HASH } JOIN
     | FAST number_rows
     | FORCE ORDER
     | MAXDOP number
     | ROBUST PLAN
     | KEEP PLAN
     | KEEPFIXED PLAN
     | EXPAND VIEWS
   }
```

Each of the following clauses is individually described in detail with examples given.

SELECT Clause	WHERE Clause	ORDER BY Clause
INTO Clause	GROUP BY Clause	COMPUTE Clause
FROM Clause	HAVING Clause	FOR Clause
		OPTION Clause

4.5.1.1 SELECT Clause

Syntax

```
SELECT [ DISTIN\CT | ALL ] [ TOP n [ PERCENT ] [ WITH TIES ] ] < select_list >
```

Arguments

DISTINCT | ALL

DISTINCT specifies that only unique rows appear in the result set. ALL (default) includes duplicate rows.

TOP *n* [PERCENT] [WITH TIES]

TOP *n* specifies that only the first *n* rows are to be output from the query result set. *n* is an **int** in [0, 4294967295]. TOP n PERCENT specifies that first n percent of the rows are output from the result set. n is an **int** in [0, 100]. If the query contains ORDER BY, the ordering is done first, then the first n rows (or n percent) are listed.

WITH TIES can be used only with TOP n or TOP n PERCENT and ORDER BY.

WITH TIES specifies that if the last row (n^{th} row or n^{th} percent row) in the original result set has more duplicates in the ORDER BY columns, they will all be contained in the final result set. See the examples below.

Examples: Use "TOP *n*", "TOP *n* PERCENT" and "WITH TIES" in SELECT statements.

SQL

```
SELECT *
FROM table1
```

Result

```
a       b       c
---     ---     ---
1       1       1
2       2       2
3       3       3
4       4       4

(5 row(s) affected)
```

SQL

```
SELECT TOP 2    *
FROM table1
```

SQL (cont.)

Result

a	b	c
---	---	---
1	1	1
2	2	2

(2 row(s) affected)

SQL

```
SELECT TOP 50 PERCENT  *
FROM table1
```

Result

a	b	c
---	---	---
1	1	1
2	2	2

(2 row(s) affected)

SQL

```
SELECT TOP 2
    WITH TIES   *
FROM table1
ORDER BY b
```

Result

a	b	c
---	---	---
1	1	1
2	2	2
3	2	3

(3 row(s) affected)

SQL

```
SELECT TOP 50 PERCENT
    WITH TIES    *
FROM table1
ORDER BY b
```

Result

```
a        b        c
---      ---      ---
1        1        1
2        2        2
3        2        3
(3 row(s) affected)
```

4.5.1.2 SELECT List

The select list is a comma-separated series of expressions and columns to be included in the result set.

Syntax

```
< select_list >  ::=
{
   *
   | { table_name | view_name | table_alias }.*
   | { column_name | expression | IDENTITYCOL | ROWGUIDCOL }
     [ [ AS ] column_alias ]
   |  column_alias = expression
} [ ,...n ]
```

Arguments

*

Asterisk, *, specifies that all columns from all tables and views in the FROM clause should be returned.

table_name | view_name | table_alias.*

This phrase limits the scope of the * to the specified table or view.

column_name | expression | IDENTITYCOL | ROWGUIDCOL } [[AS] column_alias]

column_name is the name of a column to return.

If the same *column_name* occurs in more than one table listed in the FROM clause then it must be "qualified" to precisely identify the desired table.column. See page 48 for qualified column names discussion.

expression

expression is any valid expression involving column names constants, variables, functions and subqueries. See page 48 for a discussion and examples of expressions in SQL statements.

IDENTITYCOL

IDENTITYCOL returns the identity column.

ROWGUIDCOL

ROWGUIDCOL returns the row global unique identifier column. If more than one table in the FROM clause has a column with IDENTITY or ROWGUIDCOL property, the column must be qualified with the specific table name, e.g., **T1.IDENTITYCOL** or **T1.ROWGUIDCOL**.

column_alias

column_alias is an alternative name to replace the column name in the query result set. See column aliases, page 516.

Example:

SQL

```
USE mydb
  -- On page 371 we created database mydb and
  -- table emps3 used in the next example.
go
```

SQL

```
SELECT  *  FROM  emps3
    -- Show contents of emps3 for reference
```

Result

ename	empid	deptno	telnum	salary	hiredate	sales_amt
Suzy Smith	1111	102	NULL	20	2003-01-01	NULL
Sammy Sosa	2222	102	2345	30	1992-01-01	200
Bill Johnson	4444	101	NULL	40	1994-01-01	NULL
Mary Smith	5555	100	5678	50	1990-01-01	NULL
Mary Smith	7777	101	7890	60	1996-01-01	400

Example: Select list with column names and an expression with a column alias.

SQL

```
SELECT empid, salary, sales_amt
    , (salary + .05 * sales_amt) "Total Pay"
FROM employees
WHERE empid = 2222;
```

Result

empid	salary	sales_amt	Total Pay
------	------	---------	----------
2222	30	200	40.00

4.5.1.3 INTO Clause

The INTO Clause creates a new table *new_table* and inserts the resulting rows from the query into it.

Syntax

```
INTO new_table
```

Comments

Table *new_table* must not already exist.

Each column in *new_table* has the same name, data type and value as the corresponding expression in the select list.

The INTO clause cannot be used with COMPUTE.

The INTO clause may be used in this version of SQL Server regardless of the setting of **select into/bulkcopy** database option (available only for backward compatibility), but the amount of logging depends on the database recovery model setting. See page 520.

Example: Create a new table **CAauthors** as a copy of part of the authors table.

SQL

```
USE mydb
SELECT  *
INTO  CAauthors
FROM   pubs.dbo.authors
WHERE  state = 'CA'
```

See other SELECT ... INTO examples on page 443.

4.5.1.4 FROM Clause

The FROM clause specifies the table(s) and/or view(s) from which to retrieve rows. ANSI SQL requires the FROM clause always, but MSS allows its omission if the select list contains only constants, variables, functions and expressions with no column names.

Example: SELECT statement with no FROM clause

SQL

```
SELECT  'Today is: ' , CAST( GETDATE() as CHAR(11) )
```

Result

```
----------- ---------------
Today is:   Jun  9 2003
(1 row(s) affected)
```

Syntax

```
FROM { < table_source > } [ ,...n ]

< table_source > ::=
    table_name [ [ AS ] table_alias ] [ WITH ( < table_hint > [ ,...n ] ) ]
  | view_name [ [ AS ] table_alias ]
  | rowset_function [ [ AS ] table_alias ]    --  See page 148
  | OPENXML -- New rowset function in SQL Server 2000.  See page 150.
  | derived_table [ AS ] table_alias [ ( column_alias [ ,...n ] ) ]
  | < joined_table >     -- Combines data from two or more tables.
                            See Joins below.
```

Arguments

table_name | view_name

table_name | *view_name* specifies the table or view name from which to retrieve data.

table_alias

table_alias or correlation name is an optional user defined identifier, usually much shorter than the table name, that is used in place of the table name to qualify column names from the table. The lifetime of a column alias is the statement in which it is defined. If a table alias is specified in a statement, the alias must be used in place of the table name for all references.

rowset_function | OPENXML

Rowset functions return an object that can be used like a table reference in a Transact-SQL statement. See page 148. OPENXML reads an XML document and returns the data as a rowset. It is often used with **sp_xml_preparedocument**. See OPENXML description and example page 149.

derived_table

derived_table is a subquery, a SELECT statement enclosed in parentheses. The amount of logging depends on the database recovery model. See page 560.

Example: SELECT statement with FROM clause using table aliases.

SQL

```
USE pubs
go
```

SQL

```
SELECT  TOP 2   p.pub_name
    , e.lname + ', ' + e.fname EmpName
FROM  publishers p , CAT2_Link.pubs.dbo.employee  e
-- See Qualified Object Names, page 67.
WHERE       p.pub_id  =  e.pub_id
```

Result

```
pub_name                        EmpName
--------------------------      ----------------------------
Algodata Infosystems            Afonso, Pedro
Binnet & Hardley                Accorti, Paolo
```

See "Using Identifiers as Qualified Object Names," page 46.

Example: Use a **derived_table** or subquery in FROM clause. See page 560. The following two queries are equivalent.

SQL

```
SELECT TOP 2    *           -- May use jobs1.*
FROM
 (SELECT max_lvl-min_lvl AS Diff FROM jobs) AS jobs1
```

SQL
Result
Diff ---- 0 50

SQL
SELECT TOP 2 * -- May use jobs1.* or jobs1.Diff **FROM (SELECT max_lvl-min_lvl FROM jobs) AS jobs1 (Diff)**
Result
Same as previous

4.5.1.5 JOIN Clause

A join is a SELECT statement from two or more tables. The various types of join are summarized in Table 4-4.

Syntax

```
< joined_table > ::=
  < table_source > < join_type > < table_source > ON < search_condition >
  | < table_source > CROSS JOIN < table_source >
  | < joined_table >


< join_type > ::= [ INNER | { { LEFT | RIGHT | FULL } [ OUTER ] } ]
    [ < join_hint > ]  JOIN

  < join_hint >   See page 527.
```

Table 4-4 Types of Join

Join Type	Description
INNER	All matching pairs of rows are returned. Discards unmatched rows from both tables. This is the default if no join type is specified.
LEFT OUTER	Returns the INNER JOIN plus all rows from the left table not meeting the specified condition, the latter having NULL returned for the right table columns.

Table 4-4 Types of Join (cont.)

Join Type	Description

RIGHT OUTER	Returns the INNER JOIN plus all rows from the right table not meeting the specified condition, the latter having NULL returned for the left table columns.
	RIGHT OUTER JOIN is the mirror image of the LEFT OUTER JOIN; that is, these two queries contain the same result set data (though the order differs)
	`SELECT * FROM t1 LEFT OUTER JOIN t2 ON t1.id = t2.id`
	`SELECT * FROM t2 RIGHT OUTER JOIN t1 ON t1.id = t2.id`

FULL OUTER	Returns the INNER JOIN plus all rows from the left table not meeting the specified condition, the latter having NULL returned for the right table columns plus all rows from the right table not meeting the specified condition, the latter having NULL returned for the left table columns. FULL OUTER JOIN is equal to LEFT OUTER JOIN UNION RIGHT OUTER JOIN

CROSS JOIN or CARTESIAN PRODUCT CROSS JOIN is an INNER JOIN with no matching criteria so that every row of the first table is matched with every row of the second table. CROSS JOIN is also known as CROSS PRODUCT and CARTESIAN PRODUCT. These three forms are equivalent:

```
SELECT *   FROM  table1 CROSS JOIN table2
SELECT *   FROM  table1 , table2
SELECT *   FROM  table1 INNER JOIN table2  ON   1 = 1
```

Join Examples: Tables 4-5 and Table 4-6 are used for the two Join examples.

Table 4-5 custs

custid	cname	telnum
1	Carey Cust	1234
2	Joe Brown	5678
3	Tina Toons	6789

Table 4-6 accts

acctnum	custid	bal
11	1	100
12	1	150
21	2	300

Example: INNER JOIN displays matching rows from the joined tables based on the ON clause.

SQL

```
SELECT   *
FROM custs c   INNER JOIN  accts a
ON c.custid = a.custid;
```

Result

```
custid   cname            telnum     acctnum   custid   bal
-------  ---------------  ---------  -------   -------  --------
1        Carey Cust       1234       11        1        100
1        Carey Cust       1234       12        1        150
2        Joe Brown        5678       21        2        300
```

Tina Toons, custid 3, has no matching row in accts and so does not appear in the inner join.

Example: Old Style INNER JOIN

It should be noted that this query gives an identical result to the form sometimes called an "old style inner join" shown here. Notice that the join predicate from the ON clause above is now in the WHERE clause.

SQL

```
SELECT   *
FROM custs c , accts a
WHERE c.custid = a.custid;
```

Although the first form (containing the INNER JOIN keywords) is ANSI standard, it is actually less portable than the old style inner join. Not every

RDBMS recognizes the INNER JOIN keywords, Oracle for example, but the old style form works on every RDBMS.

Example: **LEFT OUTER JOIN** displays INNER JOIN plus nonmatching rows of first (left) table.

SQL

```
SELECT    *
FROM custs c   LEFT OUTER JOIN   accts a
ON c.custid = a.custid;
```

Result

custid	cname	telnum	acctnum	custid	bal
	Carey Cust	1234	11	1	100
1	Carey Cust	1234	12	1	150
2	Joe Brown	5678	21	2	300
3	Tina Toons	6789	NULL	NULL	NULL

Tina Toons, custid 3, has no matching row in accts but does appear in the left outer join with NULL values placed in the right table columns of the result set.

4.5.1.6 WHERE Clause

The WHERE clause specifies a search condition to restrict the rows returned.

Syntax

```
WHERE < search_condition > | < old_outer_join >


< search_condition > ::=
{
   { [NOT] <predicate> | ( <search_condition> ) }  [ { AND|OR } [NOT]
       { <predicate> | ( <search_condition> ) } ]
} [ ,...n ]


< predicate > ::=
{
   expression { = | < > | ! = | > | > = | ! > | < | < = | ! < } expression
   | string_expression [ NOT ] LIKE string_expression [ ESCAPE
       'escape_character' ]
   | expression [ NOT ] BETWEEN expression AND expression
   | expression IS [ NOT ] NULL
```

```
   | CONTAINS  ( { column | * } , '< contains_search_condition >' )
   | FREETEXT ( { column | * } , 'freetext_string' )
   | expression [ NOT ] IN ( subquery | expression [ ,...n ] )
   | expression { = | < > | ! = | > | > = | ! > | < | < = | ! < }  { ALL | SOME
      | ANY} ( subquery )
   | EXISTS ( subquery )
}
```

Arguments

WHERE <search_condition>

This WHERE clause specifies a Boolean predicate to determine the rows of the target table to be returned in the result set. The rows for which the predicate evaluate to TRUE will be returned in the result set. It is ANSI SQL compliant. See page 53 for a discussion and examples of Boolean predicates and logic in SQL.

< old_outer_join > ::= column_name { * = | = * } column_name

This is used for backward compatibility only; it is not recommended for new programming. Implement all joins using the FROM clause as described in the previous section.

expression

See page 48.

CONTAINS and FREETEXT

CONTAINS and FREETEXT are full-text search extensions, not ANSI SQL. These can only be used with SELECT statements and on string columns registered for full-text search.

Example: WHERE clauses

SQL

```
USE Northwind
go

SELECT  EmployeeID, LastName , FirstName
FROM  Employees
-- add a WHERE clause from below
```

Other examples of WHERE clauses are shown here:

WHERE EmployeeID = 2

WHERE EmployeeID >= 2 AND EmployeeID <= 9

WHERE EmployeeID BETWEEN 2 AND 9 -- identical result as the previous form

```
WHERE EmployeeID IN ( 1 , 3 , 9 )
WHERE FirstName = 'Nancy'
WHERE FirstName LIKE 'Nan%'
WHERE EXISTS
   (SELECT 1 FROM orders o
    WHERE o.EmployeeID = Employees.EmployeeID)
```

4.5.1.7 GROUP BY Clause

The GROUP BY clause specifies the groups into which output rows are to be placed and, if aggregate functions are included in the SELECT clause <select list>, it calculates a summary value for each group.

When a GROUP BY clause is present, the SELECT List may only contain GROUP BY columns, aggregate functions of any column and Constant values

GROUP BY is often used with ORDER BY of the GROUP BY columns to facilitate readability.

Syntax

```
GROUP BY [ ALL ]  column_list  [ ,...n ] [ WITH { ROLLUP | CUBE } ]
```

Arguments

ALL

ALL includes all grouping values from the underlying table even if some do not meet the WHERE clause criteria. NULL is returned for the summary columns of any such grouping values. See example. You cannot specify ALL with the CUBE or ROLLUP operators.

column_list

column_list is a comma-separated list of column names and/or nonaggregate expressions that reference a column (e.g., col1 + 3). This specifies the columns to be grouped in the result set.

It cannot contain columns of type **text**, **ntext** and **image**.

A maximum of ten column names is permitted when CUBE or ROLLUP is specified.

ROLLUP

ROLLUP does a regular GROUP BY and then adds summary rows for each GROUP BY column. Groups are summarized in hierarchical order from lowest to highest (right = lowest to left = highest). Changing the order of GROUP BY columns usually changes the number of rows produced.

CUBE

CUBE does a regular GROUP BY and then adds summary rows for each GROUP BY column in every combination. See example below.

CUBE specifies that in addition to the usual rows provided by GROUP BY, summary rows are introduced into the result set. A GROUP BY summary row is returned for every possible combination of group and subgroup in the result set. A GROUP BY summary row is displayed as NULL in the result, but it is used to indicate all values. Use the GROUPING function to determine whether null values in the result set are GROUP BY summary values.

The number of summary rows in the result set is determined by the number of columns included in the GROUP BY clause. Each operand (column) in the GROUP BY clause is bound under the grouping NULL and grouping is applied to all other operands (columns). Because CUBE returns every possible combination of group and subgroup, the number of rows is the same, regardless of the order in which the grouping columns are specified.

See more examples of ROLLUP and CUBE in Appendix B.

Example: Use GROUP BY to summarize average price by product category.

First query for the average price of all items in the Products table of Northwind. Second find the average price by each category.

SQL

```
USE Northwind
go
```

SQL

```
SELECT AVG(UnitPrice) AvgPrice
FROM   Northwind..Products
```

Result

```
AvgPrice
------------
28.8663
```

SQL

```
SELECT CategoryID ,
    AVG(UnitPrice) AvgPrice
FROM   Northwind..Products
GROUP BY CategoryID
```

Result

CategoryID	AvgPrice
1	37.9791
2	23.0625
3	25.1600
4	28.7300
5	20.2500
6	54.0066
7	32.3700
8	20.6825

Example: Use GROUP BY with ROLLUP.

ROLLUP can combine these two queries by adding the average of all categories. The overall average is marked by NULL in the CategoryID column.

SQL

```
SELECT CategoryID , AVG(UnitPrice) AvgPrice
FROM   Northwind..Products
GROUP BY CategoryID  WITH ROLLUP
```

Result

CategoryID	AvgPrice
1	37.9791
2	23.0625
3	25.1600
4	28.7300
5	20.2500
6	54.0066
7	32.3700
8	20.6825
NULL	28.8663

Example: Use GROUP BY with ALL and a WHERE clause.
First query for the average price of only certain categories.
Second add ALL to indicate which categories were not included.

SQL

```
SELECT CategoryID , AVG(UnitPrice) Avg
FROM   Northwind..Products
WHERE CategoryID  BETWEEN 2 AND 4
GROUP BY CategoryID
```

Result

```
CategoryID      Avg
-----------     -----------
2               23.0625
3               25.1600
4               28.7300
```

SQL

```
SELECT CategoryID , AVG(UnitPrice) Avg
FROM   Northwind..Products
WHERE CategoryID  BETWEEN 2 AND 4
GROUP BY  ALL  CategoryID
```

Result

```
CategoryID      Avg
-----------     -----------
1               NULL
2               23.0625
3               25.1600
4               28.7300
5               NULL
6               NULL
7               NULL
8               NULL
```

Example: Compare GROUP BY with **ROLLUP** to GROUP BY with **CUBE**.

Consider the following parts table showing quantity on hand (qoh) from each supplier.

SQL

```
CREATE TABLE parts (
     part          VARCHAR(10)
,    supplier      VARCHAR(10)
,    qoh           INT );

INSERT INTO parts VALUES ( 'Item 1' , 'Co A' , 10 )
INSERT INTO parts VALUES ( 'Item 1' , 'Co B' ,  4 )
INSERT INTO parts VALUES ( 'Item 2' , 'Co A' , 20 )
INSERT INTO parts VALUES ( 'Item 2' , 'Co B' ,  8 )
```

Example: Compare ROLLUP to CUBE. (CUBE contains all data in ROLLUP and adds more.)

First display the table contents.

SQL

```
SELECT *  FROM parts
```

Result

part	supplier	qoh
Item 1	Co A	10
Item 1	Co B	4
Item 2	Co A	20
Item 2	Co B	8

Then do a normal GROUP BY.

SQL

```
SELECT part, SUM(qoh) Sum
FROM parts
GROUP BY part
```

Result

part	Sum
Item 1	14
Item 2	28

Now see the result of using ROLLUP on parts and suppliers.

SQL

```
SELECT part, supplier,
               SUM(qoh) Sum
FROM parts
GROUP BY part, supplier
  WITH ROLLUP
```

Result

part	supplier	Sum
Item 1	Co A	10
Item 1	Co B	4
Item 1	NULL	14
Item 2	Co A	20
Item 2	Co B	8
Item 2	NULL	28
NULL	NULL	42

And compare with the result of using CUBE on parts and suppliers.

SQL

```
SELECT part, supplier ,
              SUM(qoh) Sum
FROM parts
GROUP BY part, supplier
  WITH CUBE
```

Result

part	supplier	Sum	
Item 1	Co A	10	
Item 1	Co B	4	
Item 1	NULL	14	◄—Total Item 1
Item 2	Co A	20	
Item 2	Co B	8	
Item 2	NULL	28	◄—Total Item 2
NULL	NULL	42	◄—Total All Items

part	supplier	Sum	
Item 1	Co A	10	
Item 1	Co B	4	
Item 1	NULL	14	◄—Total Item 1
Item 2	Co A	20	
Item 2	Co B	8	
Item 2	NULL	28	◄—Total Item 2
NULL	NULL	42	◄—Total All Items
NULL	Co A	30	◄—Total Co A
NULL	Co B	12	◄—Total Co B

ROLLUP lists each part from each supplier and the totals for each part.

CUBE lists each part from each supplier **and** the totals for each part and the totals for each supplier. CUBE, in general, summarizes each aggregate for each GROUP BY column name.

4.5.1.8 HAVING Clause

HAVING Clause specifies a search condition (predicate) for a group or an aggregate to choose which rows are retained in the result set. It is usually used with GROUP BY clause.

HAVING is similar to WHERE in determining which rows are retained in the result set.

HAVING with no GROUP BY behaves like a WHERE clause. This is not recommended since it is generally more readable to put all normal filtering conditions in the WHERE.

Syntax

```
[ HAVING < search_condition > ]
```

Arguments

< search_condition >

< search_condition > specifies the Boolean search condition for the group or the aggregate to meet that will be included in the result set.

The **text**, **image** and **ntext** data types cannot be used in a HAVING clause.

Example: Use HAVING with GROUP BY to retain only certain rows.

First, repeat the previous query finding the average price for every product category. Second, use HAVING to limit which rows are retained.

SQL

```
SELECT CategoryID , AVG(UnitPrice) AvgPrice
FROM   Northwind..Products
GROUP BY CategoryID  WITH ROLLUP
```

Result

```
CategoryID      AvgPrice
-----------     -----------
1               37.9791
2               23.0625
3               25.1600
4               28.7300
5               20.2500
6               54.0066
7               32.3700
8               20.6825
```

SQL

```
SELECT CategoryID ,
  AVG(UnitPrice) AvgPrice
FROM  Northwind..Products
GROUP BY CategoryID
HAVING AVG(UnitPrice) >= 30
```

Result

```
CategoryID      AvgPrice
-----------     -----------
1               37.9791
6               54.0066
7               32.3700
```

Note that the column alias **AvgPrice** cannot be used in the HAVING clause:
AvgPrice >= 30 -- is not legal

4.5.1.9 ORDER BY Clause

The ORDER BY clause specifies a sort order for the result set. ORDER BY clause is permitted in views, inline functions, derived tables and subqueries only if TOP is specified.

Syntax

```
ORDER BY { column_name_or_alias [ ASC | DESC ] |
column_position [ ASC | DESC ]  } [ ,...n]
```

Arguments

column_name_or_alias | column_position

column_name_or_alias specifies a column, column alias or expression on which to sort.

column_position specifies the ordinal position of an expression in the SELECT list on which to sort.

Multiple sort columns can be specified.

If the SELECT statement contains SELECT DISTINCT or UNION, the sort columns must appear in the select list.

Ntext, text or **image** columns cannot be used in an ORDER BY clause.

ASC

ASC (Default) specifies that the values in the specified column should be sorted in ascending order.

DESC

DESC specifies that the values in the specified column should be sorted in descending order.

Null values are treated as the lowest possible values.

There is no limit to the number of items in the ORDER BY clause.

Example: List the rows of pubs.. jobs table sorted by min_lvl ascending and max_lvl desc.

SQL

```
SELECT * FROM pubs..jobs  WHERE  min_lvl <= 120
ORDER BY  min_lvl ,  max_lvl DESC
   -- DESC applies only to max_lvl sort,
   -- min_lvl will be ASC
```

SQL (cont.)

Result

job_id	job_desc	min_lvl	max_lvl
------	----------------------------------	------	------
1	New Hire - Job not specified	10	10
12	Editor	25	100
13	Sales Representative	25	100
14	Designer	25	100
9	Acquisitions Manager	75	175
10	Productions Manager	75	165
8	Public Relations Manager	100	175
7	Marketing Manager	120	200

Example: Use the column position to sort by an expression in the SELECT list.

SQL

```
SELECT job_id, (min_lvl/2 + max_lvl/2) As AvgLevel
FROM pubs..jobs
ORDER BY  2
  -- Could also specify sorting by
  -- column alias:  ORDER BY AvgLevel
```

Result

job_id	AvgLevel
------	-----------
1	10
12	62
13	62
...	... -- indicates that many lines are missing
4	212
2	225

4.5.1.10 COMPUTE Clause

The COMPUTE clause, including COMPUTE and COMPUTE BY, uses an aggregate function on a column in the SELECT list to generate an additional summary row at the end of the result set that contains the calculated aggregate value The clause generates totals that appear as additional summary rows at the end of the result set. COMPUTE BY (requires ORDER BY) also adds subtotals after each ORDER BY column value. COMPUTE and COMPUTE BY can be used in the same query as separate clauses. An example of the syntax is as follows.

```
SELECT id , a , b  FROM table1   COMPUTE AVG(b)
COMPUTE SUM(c) BY id
```

You may demonstrate this fact by appending the following clause to either example below.

COMPUTE SUM(ProductID)

Syntax

```
COMPUTE
     { { AVG | COUNT | MAX | MIN | STDEV | STDEVP | VAR | VARP | SUM }
        (expression) } [ ,...n ]
[ BY expression [ ,...n ] ]     -- using BY requires ORDER BY
```

Arguments

AVG | COUNT | MAX | MIN | STDEV | STDEVP | VAR | VARP | SUM

This long phrase specifies aggregation to be performed on the *expression* when used with the COMPUTE clause.

AVG: average; COUNT: count of selected rows; MAX: maximum; MIN: minimum; STDEV: standard deviation; STDEVP: standard deviation for the population; VAR: variance; VARP: variance for the population; SUM: total.

(expression)

This is a column name or other expression which appears in the SELECT list just as it originally appears. It has no column alias. **Ntext**, **text** or **image** data types cannot be specified in a COMPUTE or COMPUTE BY clause.

BY expression

COMPUTE BY, which requires ORDER BY, additionally adds subtotals after each ORDER BY column value. One or more column name, column alias or expression may be used.

An ORDER BY clause is required. The COMPUTE BY expression(s) must be identical to the ORDER BY expressions.

E.g. ORDER BY a , b , c

may have any or all of the following

COMPUTE BY a
COMPUTE BY a , b
COMPUTE BY a , b , c

Restrictions

- There is no equivalent to COUNT(*). To find summary information produced by GROUP BY and COUNT(*), use COMPUTE clause without BY.
- These aggregate functions ignore null values.
- The DISTINCT keyword is not allowed with the COMPUTE clause.
- When you add or average integer data, SQL Server treats the result as an **int** value, even if the data type of the column is **smallint** or **tinyint**.
- COMPUTE and COMPUTE BY may not be used with SELECT INTO or with DECLARE CURSOR.

Example: COMPUTE

List Category 7 products with UnitPrice (showing min and avg) and UnitsOn Order (showing max).

SQL

```
SELECT ProductID , ProductName , SupplierID ,
            UnitPrice , UnitsOnOrder
FROM  Northwind..Products
WHERE CategoryID = 5  AND  SupplierID IN ( 9 , 26 )
COMPUTE  MIN(UnitPrice) , AVG(UnitPrice) ,
             MAX(UnitsOnOrder)
```

Result

```
ProductID   ProductName                  SupplierID   UnitPrice     UnitsOnOrder
----------- ---------------------------- -----------  ------------- ------------
22          Gustaf's Knäckebröd           9           21.0000        0
23          Tunnbröd                      9           9.0000         0
56          Gnocchi di nonna Alice       26           38.0000       10
57          Ravioli Angelo               26           19.5000       0

                                                      min
                                                      =====
                                                      9.0000

                                                      avg
                                                      ======
                                                      21.8750

                                                                    max
                                                                    ======
                                                                    10
```

Example: COMPUTE BY

`Add subtotals by SupplierID` by using ORDER BY and COMPUTE BY SupplierID.

SQL

```
SELECT ProductID , ProductName , SupplierID ,
       UnitPrice , UnitsOnOrder
FROM  Northwind..Products
WHERE CategoryID = 5  AND  SupplierID IN ( 9 , 26 )
ORDER BY SupplierID
COMPUTE  MIN(UnitPrice) , AVG(UnitPrice) ,
         MAX(UnitsOnOrder) BY SupplierID
```

Result

```
ProductID   ProductName                 SupplierID  UnitPrice    UnitsOnOrder
----------- --------------------------  ----------- ------------ ------------
22          Gustaf's Knäckebröd         9           21.0000      0
23          Tunnbröd                    9           9.0000       0
                                                    min
                                                    =====
                                                    9.0000

                                                    avg
                                                    ======
                                                    15.0000

                                                                 max
                                                                 ======
                                                                 0
ProductID   ProductName                 SupplierID  UnitPrice    UnitsOnOrder
----------- --------------------------- ----------- ------------ ------------
56          Gnocchi di nonna Alice      26          38.0000      10
57          Ravioli Angelo              26          19.5000      0

                                                    min
                                                    ======
                                                    19.5000

                                                    avg
                                                    ======
                                                    28.7500
```

Result (cont.)

```
max
======
10
```

4.5.1.11 FOR Clause

The FOR clause may specify either FOR BROWSE or FOR XML. These are two unrelated options.

Syntax

```
FOR BROWSE    -- Used with DB-Library browse mode cursor to allow updates.
      | FOR XML RAW        [ , XMLDATA ]  [ , BINARY base64 ]
      | FOR XML AUTO       [ , XMLDATA ]  [ , BINARY base64 ] [ , ELEMENTS ]
      | FOR XML EXPLICIT   [ , XMLDATA ]  [ , BINARY base64 ]  -- See p. 501
```

Arguments

FOR BROWSE

FOR BROWSE causes updates to be allowed in a DB-Library browse mode cursor. This clause will not be discussed further here.

FOR XML {RAW|AUTO|EXPLICIT}

FOR XML specifies that the results of a query are to be returned as an XML fragment in a well-formed XML document except that it has no root element. You must specify {RAW|AUTO|EXPLICIT}.

For displaying a FOR XML result in an XML aware browser see p. 511. See also OPENXML description and example page 149. For more detail on XML with SQL Server see *Programming Microsoft SQL Server 2000 with XML* and *The Guru's Guide to SQL Server Stored Procedures, XML, and HTML.*

Note that the Query Analyzer defaults to 256-character maximum per column which must be increased to show all of the FOR XML output. Use the following directions to do this.

> Open **Query Analyzer: Tools-Options**, click on **Results** tab, by **Maximum characters per column**, enter 2048 or number of your choice.

See p. 496 for details.

RAW

RAW transforms each row in the query result set into an XML element with element tag of **<row />**.

Example: SELECT list columns are mapped to XML attributes.

SQL

```
SELECT TOP 1  au_id , au_lname  FROM pubs..authors  FOR XML  RAW
```

Result

```
<row   au_id="409-56-7008"   au_lname="Bennet"/>
```

AUTO

AUTO returns query results as a nested XML tree. See more detail below.

Each table name in the FROM clause with a column listed in the SELECT clause is represented as an XML element.

Example: SELECT list columns are mapped to XML attributes unless the ELEMENTS keyword is used.

SQL

```
SELECT TOP 1  au_id , au_lname  FROM  pubs..authors  FOR XML  AUTO
```

Result

```
<authors  au_id="409-56-7008"  au_lname="Bennet"/>
```

EXPLICIT

Specifies that the shape of the resulting XML tree is defined explicitly. See more detail below.

Example:

SQL

```
SELECT TOP 1  au_id , au_lname
FROM  pubs..authors
FOR XML  EXPLICIT -- Error
```

Result

```
Error:  FOR XML EXPLICIT requires at least three columns, including the tag column, ....
```

This is to demonstrate that EXPLICIT, which gives the most flexibility, is very picky about format. Correct versions are given below in detail.

XMLDATA

XMLDATA returns in-line XML-Data Reduced (XDR) schema description (in XML form as the <Schema> element) followed by the xml data.

Example: We're using the same schema as for RAW, EXPLICIT.

SQL

```
SELECT TOP 1  au_id , au_lname  FROM  pubs..authors  FOR XML  AUTO , XMLDATA
```

Result

```
<Schema name="Schema14"   xmlns="urn:schemas-microsoft-com:xml-data"
                          xmlns:dt="urn:schemas-microsoft-com:datatypes">
    <ElementType name="authors" content="empty" model="closed">
      <AttributeType name="au_id" dt:type="string"/>
      <AttributeType name="au_lname" dt:type="string"/>
      <attribute type="au_id"/>
      <attribute type="au_lname"/>
    </ElementType>
  </Schema>
  <authors xmlns="x-schema:#Schema14" au_id="409-56-7008" au_lname="Bennet"/>
```

BINARY BASE64

BINARY BASE64 specifies that the query return the binary data in binary base64-encoded format. IT must be specified when retrieving binary data using RAW and EXPLICIT mode. It is the default in AUTO mode.

ELEMENTS

ELEMENTS specifies that the columns are returned as subelements. This is supported in AUTO mode only.

Example:

SQL

```
SELECT TOP 1  au_id , au_lname  FROM  pubs..authors
FOR XML  AUTO , ELEMENTS
```

Result

```
<authors><au_id>409-56-7008</au_id><au_lname>Bennet</au_lname></authors>
```

FOR XML RAW—Details FOR XML RAW transforms each query result set row into an XML element with tag of **<row />**. In addition, SELECT list columns are mapped to XML attributes. For displaying a FOR XML result in an XML-aware browser see p. 511.

Example: FOR XML RAW Mode with a Simple query

SQL

```
SELECT TOP 2  au_id , au_lname , au_fname
FROM  pubs..authors              -- Original data
```

Result

```
au_id          au_lname          au_fname
-----------    ------------      ------------
409-56-7008    Bennet            Abraham
648-92-1872    Blotchet-Halls    Reginald
```

SQL

```
SELECT TOP 2  au_id , au_lname , au_fname
FROM  pubs..authors
FOR XML RAW
  -- The output here is as it appears
  -- in Query Ana.yzer - one long string
```

Result

```
<row au_id="409-56-7008" au_lname="Bennet" au_fname="Abraham"/
><row au_id="648-92-1872" au_lname="Blotchet-Halls" au_fname="Reginald"/>
```

Note: If the XML portion does not end with .".. />" then the Query Analyzer truncated the output at 256 characters. To fix this, follow these directions.

> Open **Query Analyzer: Tools-Options**, click on **Results** tab, by **Maximum characters per column** enter 2048.

To make it easier to see the data, we'll usually format the FOR XML results as shown.

SQL

```
SELECT TOP 2  au_id , au_lname , au_fname
FROM  pubs..authors          -- Identical query
FOR XML RAW
  -- The content is identical, but I have inserted
  -- carriage returns to make it easier to read
```

Result

```
<row au_id="409-56-7008"  au_lname="Bennet"  au_fname="Abraham"/>
<row au_id="648-92-1872"  au_lname="Blotchet-Halls"  au_fname="Reginald"/>
```

Notice that FOR XML output does not have a root element but is otherwise well formed. See the section below on adding a root element and displaying the output in an XML aware browser.

Note: If the XML portion does not end with .".. />" then the Query Analyzer truncated the output at 256 characters.[1]

Example: FOR XML RAW Mode with a Join

SQL

```
-- First display the original data as a normal join
SELECT  TOP 2  a.au_id , a.au_lname , t.title_id
FROM   pubs..authors a , pubs..titleauthor ta ,
                                        pubs..titles t
WHERE a.au_id = ta.au_id
  AND t.title_id = ta.title_id
```

Result

```
au_id          au_lname         title_id
-----------    --------------   ---------
238-95-7766    Carson           PC1035
724-80-9391    MacFeather       PS1372
```

1. **Note:** The Query Analyzer defaults to 256 character maximum per column which must be increased to show all of the FOR XML output. Open QA: **Tools-Options**, click on **Results** tab, by **Maximum characters per column** enter 2048 or number of your choice.

SQL

```
/* Display the same join using FOR XML RAW */
SELECT  TOP 2  a.au_id , a.au_lname , t.title_id
FROM   pubs..authors a , pubs..titleauthor ta ,
                                      pubs..titles t
WHERE a.au_id = ta.au_id
  AND t.title_id = ta.title_id
FOR XML RAW
  --  This output was formatted to ease reading
```

Result

```
<row  au_id="238-95-7766"  au_lname="Carson"  title_id="PC1035"/>
<row  au_id="724-80-9391"  au_lname="MacFeather"  title_id="PS1372"/>
```

FOR XML AUTO—Details FOR XML AUTO returns query results as a nested XML tree. Each table in the FROM clause with a column listed in the SELECT clause is represented as a nested XML element. Nesting is done left to right as each table name or alias first occurs in the SELECT list.

By default, SELECT list columns are mapped to XML attributes. Using **FOR XML AUTO , ELEMENTS** maps them to XML elements. For displaying a FOR XML result in an XML aware-browser see page %10.

Example: FOR XML AUTO with a Simple query

SQL

```
SELECT TOP 2  au_id , au_lname , state
FROM  pubs..authors
FOR XML AUTO
  --  Output was formatted to ease reading
```

Result

```
<authors  au_id="172-32-1176"  au_lname="White"  state="CA"/>
<authors  au_id="213-46-8915"  au_lname="Green"  state="CA"/>
```

Example: FOR XML AUTO , ELEMENTS with a Simple query

SQL

```
SELECT TOP 2  au_id , au_lname , state
FROM   pubs..authors
FOR XML AUTO , ELEMENTS
  --  Output was formatted to ease reading
```

Result

```
XML_F52E2B61-18A1-11d1-B105-00805F49916B
-------------------------------------------------------------------
<authors>
  <au_id>172-32-1176</au_id>
  <au_lname>White</au_lname>
  <state>CA</state>
</authors>
<authors>
  <au_id>213-46-8915</au_id>
  <au_lname>Green</au_lname>
  <state>CA</state>
</authors>
```

Example: FOR XML AUTO with a Join

SQL

```
SELECT   TOP 2  a.au_id , a.au_lname , t.title_id
FROM  pubs..authors a, pubs..titleauthor ta ,
                                             pubs..titles t
WHERE  a.au_id = ta.au_id
  AND t.title_id = ta.title_id
FOR XML AUTO
  --  Output was formatted to ease reading
```

Result

```
<a  au_id="238-95-7766" au_lname="Carson">
   <t  title_id="PC1035"/>
</a>
<a  au_id="724-80-9391" au_lname="MacFeather">
   <t  title_id="PS1372"/>
</a>
```

Example: FOR XML AUTO , ELEMENTS with a Join

SQL

```
USE pubs
```

SQL

```
SELECT  TOP 2  authors.au_id , authors.au_lname ,
                                  titles.title_id
FROM   authors , titleauthor , titles
WHERE authors.au_id = titleauthor.au_id
  AND titles.title_id = titleauthor.title_id
FOR XML AUTO , ELEMENTS
  --  Output was formatted to ease reading
```

Result

```
<authors>  -- Note: If a titles column were before authors in SELECT list it would be the
outer element
   <au_id>238-95-7766</au_id>
   <au_lname>Carson</au_lname>
   <titles>
      <title_id>PC1035</title_id>
   </titles>
</authors>
<authors>
   <au_id>724-80-9391</au_id>
   <au_lname>MacFeather</au_lname>
   <titles>
      <title_id>PS1372</title_id>
   </titles>
</authors>
```

FOR XML EXPLICIT—Details FOR XML EXPLICIT gives the user complete control over formatting of the XML document result set created with a FOR XML query. This fact also makes it the most complex form of FOR XML. With it, you may specify which SELECT list columns become elements and which become attributes and how nesting of subelements is done.

- FOR XML EXPLICIT includes an optional *directive* for each SELECT list column which specifies whether the column becomes an XML attribute or an XML element.
- For displaying a FOR XML result in an XML aware browser see p. 511.

Syntax and basic examples are provided here to demonstrate flexibility. There are many fine examples in Books Online - Index: EXPLICIT Mode. Also see Malcolm's *Programming Microsoft SQL Server 2000 with XML* and Henderson's *The Guru's Guide to SQL Server Stored Procedures, XML, and HTML.*

The suggested approach for building an EXPLICIT mode query is as follows:

1. Do a normal SELECT to see the data you want, perhaps using TOP 3 to limit the quantity of data in the result set.
2. Determine the XML document layout of the data you want to get.
3. Work backward to build a FOR XML query that will produce the desired format.

Example: Even this simple example cannot be done with RAW or AUTO mode. It contains the same data as previous queries but with a mixture of attributes and elements.

Syntax

FOR XML EXPLICIT requires a special SELECT statement syntax::

```
SELECT
 integer AS Tag ,
 {0 | NULL | ParentTagNumber } as Parent ,
 { column_or_expr  AS [EltTag!EltTagNumber!AttrOrSubEltTag!Directive ] }
    [ , .. n ]
FROM clause  [ other usual SELECT statement clauses ]
FOR XML EXPLICIT    [ , XMLDATA ]  [ , BINARY base64 ]
```

SQL

```
USE pubs

SELECT 1 AS Tag ,  0 as Parent ,
 --  Tag and Parent are XML tree formatting, not data.

 -- The next line specifies authors as top level
 -- element and author_id as its attribute
  a.au_id AS [authors!1!author_id],
```

SQL (cont.)

```
 -- au_lname is a subelement of authors
  a.au_lname AS [authors!1!au_lname!element],

  -- titles.title_id is subelement of authors
  t.title_id AS [authors!1!title_id!element]
FROM authors a , titleauthor ta , titles t
WHERE a.au_id = ta.au_id
  AND t.title_id = ta.title_id
FOR XML EXPLICIT
```

SQL

```
/* Same query without comments and showing result*/
SELECT 1 AS Tag ,  0 as Parent ,
  a.au_id AS [authors!1!author_id],
  a.au_lname AS [authors!1!au_lname!element],
  t.title_id AS [authors!1!title_id!element]
FROM authors a , titleauthor ta , titles t
WHERE a.au_id = ta.au_id
  AND t.title_id = ta.title_id
FOR XML EXPLICIT
  --  Output was formatted to ease reading
```

Result

```
<authors   author_id="238-95-7766">
   <au_lname>Carson</au_lname>
   <title_id>PC1035</title_id>
</authors>
<authors   author_id="724-80-9391">
   <au_lname>MacFeather</au_lname>
   <title_id>PS1372</title_id>
</authors>
   ...
```

Arguments

integer AS Tag

The **Tag** and **Parent** columns specify the parent-child hierarchy in the XML tree.

The first column in the SELECT clause must be a tag number that is named "**AS Tag**." The tag number is any unique integer that will identify the current element. The tag number is used with **Parent** column to specify tree structure.

{0 | NULL | ParentTagNumber } as Parent

The **Parent** column stores the **Tag** number of the current element's parent. NULL and 0 have the same effect; if **Parent** column is 0 or NULL, the row is placed on the top level of the XML hierarchy in the XML fragment. Since the fragments do not include their own root element, multiple rows may be returned at the top of the fragment's hierarchy.

{ column_or_expr AS **[** EltTag!EltTagNumber!AttrOrSubEltTag!Directive **]** } [, .. n]

Each one of these entries maps one SELECT list column (expression) to either an XML attribute or an element.

column_or_expr

This is usually a SELECT list item, a column name or an expression providing the data.

The bold **[ ]** brackets are literal and not part of the syntax statement. They are required to hide the exclamation points ! in the statement.

EltTag

This specifies the element tag name in resulting XML output. So foo becomes <foo>.

EltTagNumber

EltTagNumber is any unique integer that will identify EltTag in the statement.

EltTagNumber and Parent name determine the nesting of elements in the XML output tree. For example:

au_lname AS [author!1] becomes <author>Smith</author>

where **au_lname** provides the data—Smith—and **author** is the tag name at level l.

AttrOrSubEltTag

This is either the name of the XML attribute (if *Directive* is not specified) or

the name of the subelement (if *Directive* is either **element**, **xml** or **cdata**).

If *Directive* is specified, *AttrOrSubEltTag* can be empty. In this case, the column data value is directly contained by the element with the specified *EltTag*. For example:

au_lname AS [author!1!LastName] ==> <author LastName="Smith">
where **LastName** is an XML attribute name, since there is no directive for level 1 element author and the attribute value comes from the **au_lname** column.

au_lname AS [author!1!LastName!element] ==> <author><LastName>Smith</LastName></author>
where **LastName** is an XML subelement name of level **1** element **author** and its value comes from the **au_lname** column.

au_lname AS [author!1!!element] ==> <author>Smith</author>
where the XML element name of level **1** element is **author** and its value comes from the **au_lname** column.

This present form and the shortcut form
au_lname AS [author!1]both yield <author>Smith</author>
but the longer form may have the directive changed from "element" to change the effect.

Directive

Directive is optional. If neither *AttrOrSubEltTag* nor *Directive* is specified (for example, **author!1**), an element directive is implied. So **author!1** is the same as **author!1!!element**, which results in <author>Smith</author> as seen above.
Directive has two purposes:

1. to indicate how to map the string data to XML using the keywords **hide**, **element**, **xml**, **xmltext** and **cdata**.
2. to encode ID, IDREF and IDREFS by using the keywords **ID**, **IDREF** and **IDREFS**.

Table 4-7 Directives and Their Meanings.

Directive	Description
element	Represent this column as entity encoded[a] XML element (< becomes **<**)
xml	Represent this column as unencoded XML element (< remains <)
xmltext	Append data from an overflow column, such as OPENXML column
cdata	Represent this column's data as a CDATA section
hide	Hide this universal table column from XML result
id, idref, idrefs	Establish relationship between elements of different XML fragments (only effective with XMLDATA).

a. Entity encoding means that characters with special meaning in XML are encoded as XML entities, e.g., < character becomes the < entity.

The **Tag** and **Parent** columns specify the parent-child hierarchy in the XML tree as is discussed in the next section on nesting elements.

Nesting XML Elements Using FOR XML EXPLICIT FOR XML EXPLICIT queries can create XML fragments with nested subelements in 2 ways.

1. FOR XML EXPLICIT Form 1—simple nesting

Using the SELECT list form

au_lname AS [author!1!LastName!element]

==> <author><LastName>Smith</LastName></author>

where **LastName** is an XML subelement name of level **1** element **author** and the subelement value comes from the **au_lname** column.

In this form, if there are multiple children for an element, the element must be repeated for each child. That is, each element may have only one child element of a given tag.

For example, if an author has more than one book, the author must be repeated with each book as the nested subelement. See details below.

2. FOR XML EXPLICIT Form 2—multiple nesting

Using UNION ALL of two SELECT statements in which the first SELECT statement provides the output XML formatting and the second SELECT provides the data. This form allows you to have multiple subelements of the same element. So you may format it to have the author element appear only once with all of his or her books nested underneath. See the examples below.

To create form 2, the UNION ALL form, recall that in a normal UNION or UNION ALL query there must be the same number of items in the SELECT list and of the same or compatible data types of the two SELECT statements. For example,

```
SELECT itemA1 , itemA2 , itemA3   FROM ...
UNION ALL
SELECT itemB1 , itemB2 , itemB3   FROM ...
```

So there is a logical correspondence of itemA1 with itemB1, itemA2 with itemB2, etc.

First SELECT statement—the first two tags determine the nesting:

1 AS Tag , 0 AS Parent—makes the first SELECT statement the top-level parent

The remaining SELECT list items in the first SELECT statement determine the formatting in the XML output document using the EltTag, EltTagNumber, AttrOr-SubEltTag and Directive rules given above. These combinations are in fact column aliases that are used elsewhere in the statements, such as the ORDER BY clause.

Second SELECT statement—the first two tags determine the nesting:

2 AS Tag , 1 AS Parent —makes the second SELECT the child of the first

Some of the data values come from these items in the first (a.au_lname) and some from the second SELECT statement (t.title_id, but a.au_lname must be provided again for correlation to the first statement items).

Each of these forms is used on the same data to demonstrate the difference.

Example: Form 1—simple nesting with FOR XML EXPLICIT

For each author in the **authors** table, create an element <Author> with an attribute "LastName" from **au_lname** column and a nested element <TitleId> from the title_id column of the **titles** table. Display the this data only for Locksley and O'Leary.

With simple nesting, if an author has more than one title, there will be a separate <Author> element for each <TitleId>.

First, to see the values of interest, display the data in the usual table form.

SQL

```
USE pubs
```

SQL

```
SELECT a.au_lname ,  t.title_id
FROM   authors a,  titleauthor ta ,  titles t
WHERE  a.au_id = ta.au_id
   AND   t.title_id = ta.title_id
   AND
(a.au_lname = 'O''Leary' OR
  a.au_lname = 'Locksley')
ORDER BY a.au_lname ,  t.title_id
```

Result

```
au_lname        title_id
------------    ------------
Locksley        PC9999
Locksley        PS7777
O'Leary         BU1111
O'Leary         TC7777
```

Now use nesting form 1 to create an XML document showing an <author> element for each author with LastName as its attribute and a nested subelement of <title_id>.

SQL

```
SELECT  1 AS Tag ,  0 AS Parent ,
    a.au_lname  AS  [Author!1!LastName] ,
     t.title_id  AS [Author!1!TitleId!element]
FROM      authors a,  titleauthor ta ,  titles t
WHERE  a.au_id = ta.au_id
  AND   t.title_id = ta.title_id
  AND
(a.au_lname = 'O''Leary' OR

     a.au_lname = 'Locksley')
ORDER BY [Author!1!LastName]
                          ,[Author!1!TitleId!element]
FOR XML EXPLICIT -- Output formatted for readability
```

Result

```
<author  LastName="Locksley">
  <title_id>PC9999</title_id>
</author>
<author  LastName="Locksley">
  <title_id>PS7777</title_id>
</author>
<author  LastName="O&apos;Leary">
  <title_id>BU1111</title_id>
</author>
<author  LastName="O&apos;Leary">
  <title_id>TC7777</title_id>
</author>
```

Since this form allows only one <title_id> subelement per <author>, Locksley and O'Leary must be repeated for each title.

Note that in the second author LastName value, O'Leary, the apostrophe has been encoded to the XML entity ' the result is O'Leary. This is usual XML practice, but it can be overridden.

Example: Form 2—multiple nesting with FOR XML EXPLICIT

Using the same example with multiple nesting, each author will have only one <Author> element and nested underneath it will be a <TitleId> for each title.

Form 2 consists of the UNION ALL of two SELECT statements in which the first specifies the XML formatting of each item and the second SELECT provides the data for each corresponding item. The WHERE clause that chooses the result set rows is also required in the first SELECT, or all authors' names will be listed but only these two will have title_id information provided.

SQL

```
-- This SELECT provides the formatting
SELECT  1 AS Tag ,  0 AS Parent ,
    a.au_lname  AS  [Author!1!LastName] ,
                    -- author is Level 1
    NULL  AS  [TitleId!2]
                    -- title_id is Level 2
FROM authors a
WHERE a.au_lname = 'O''Leary'
   OR a.au_lname = 'Locksley'

UNION ALL

-- This SELECT provides the data
SELECT 2 AS Tag, 1 AS Parent, a.au_lname, t.title_id
FROM     authors a, titleauthor ta , titles t
WHERE  a.au_id = ta.au_id
  AND t.title_id = ta.title_id
   AND
(a.au_lname = 'O''Leary' OR a.au_lname = 'Locksley')
ORDER BY [Author!1!LastName] ,[TitleId!2]
FOR XML EXPLICIT -- Output formatted for readability
```

Result

```
<Author LastName="Locksley">
    <TitleId>PC9999</TitleId>
    <TitleId>PS7777</TitleId>
</Author>
<Author LastName="O&apos;Leary">
    <TitleId>BU1111</TitleId>
    <TitleId>TC7777</TitleId>
</Author>
```

Example: We use the same example using Form 2 but call the nested element Title and show its TitleId as an attribute.

SQL

```
SELECT  1 AS Tag ,  0 AS Parent ,
    a.au_lname  AS  [Author!1!LastName], --  Level 1
    NULL  AS  [Title!2!TitleId] -- Level 2
FROM authors a
WHERE a.au_lname = 'O''Leary'
   OR a.au_lname = 'Locksley'

UNION ALL

SELECT 2 AS Tag, 1 AS Parent, a.au_lname, t.title_id
FROM     authors a, titleauthor ta , titles t
WHERE  a.au_id = ta.au_id
  AND t.title_id = ta.title_id
   AND
(a.au_lname = 'O''Leary' OR a.au_lname = 'Locksley')
ORDER BY [Author!1!LastName] ,[Title!2!TitleId]
FOR XML EXPLICIT -- Output formatted for readability
```

Result

```
<Author LastName="Locksley">
    <Title  TitleId="PC9999"/>
    <Title  TitleId="PS7777"/>
</Author>
<Author LastName="O&apos;Leary">
    <Title  TitleId="BU1111"/>
    <Title  TitleId="TC7777"/>
</Author>
```

Example: Again, we use the same example but add the title name as the value of the Title element.

SQL

```
SELECT  1 AS Tag ,  0 AS Parent ,
    a.au_lname  AS  [Author!1!LastName], -- Level 1
    NULL  AS  [Title!2] ,                -- Level 2
    NULL  AS  [Title!2!TitleId]          -- Level 2
FROM authors a
WHERE a.au_lname = 'O''Leary'
   OR a.au_lname = 'Locksley'

UNION ALL

SELECT 2 AS Tag, 1 AS Parent, a.au_lname,
                         t.title, t.title_id
FROM     authors a, titleauthor ta , titles t
WHERE  a.au_id = ta.au_id
  AND t.title_id = ta.title_id
   AND
(a.au_lname = 'O''Leary' OR

   a.au_lname = 'Locksley')
ORDER BY [Author!1!LastName] ,[Title!2!TitleId]
FOR XML EXPLICIT -- Output formatted for readability
```

Result

```
<Author LastName="Locksley">
   <Title  TitleId="PC9999">Net Etiquette</Title>
   <Title  TitleId="PS7777">Emotional Security: A New Algorithm</Title>
</Author>
<Author LastName="O&apos;Leary">
   <Title  TitleId="BU1111">Cooking with Computers</Title>
   <Title  TitleId="TC7777">Sushi, Anyone?</Title>
</Author>
```

Universal Table

The XML formatting specifications may be observed in what Microsoft calls the "Universal Table" for your query. Your Universal Table may be seen by executing your SELECT statement without including the FOR XML EXPLICIT clause; the ensuing result set shows the data and the formatting you will apply to create the actual XML document when you do include that clause. See Books

Online, Malcolm and Henderson for more on the Universal Table and programming with FOR XML EXPLICIT.

Displaying FOR XML Result in XML Aware Browser

The output of a SELECT ... FOR XML statement will be well formed if you provide a root element. Also, the FOR XML output is a single long string with no line breaks, not attractive but inconsequential to an XML parser.

A simple way to observe the output in a well-formatted display and to ensure that it is proper XML is to display the output with root element added in an XML aware browser. The following steps show how this can be done.

1. Open a text editor and create a pair of root element tags with blank lines between, e.g.

```
<myroot>

</myroot>
```

2. Copy the result set output of the **SELECT ... FOR XML** statement and paste it into the text editor between the begin and end root tags. Remember that the Query Analyzer defaults to the 256 character maximum per column, which must be increased as follows.

Open QA: **Tools-Options**, click on **Results** tab, by **Maximum characters per column** enter 2048 or larger for big result sets.

If the FOR XML output starts with <authors> but does not end with </authors>, it has probably been truncated.

3. Save the file with a **.xml** extension.

4. Start an XML aware browser such as Internet Explorer and open the .xml file in it.

Example: Display first two rows of pubs..authors table as XML in a browser.

First let's look at the original data.

SQL

```
SELECT TOP 2  au_id , au_lname , au_fname
FROM pubs..authors
```

Result

```
au_id          au_lname          au_fname
-----------    ------------      ------------
409-56-7008    Bennet            Abraham
648-92-1872    Blotchet-Halls    Reginald
```

Now show the unformatted Query Analyzer output for XML RAW.

SQL

```
SELECT TOP 2  au_id , au_lname , au_fname
FROM pubs..authors
FOR XML RAW
```

Result

```
XML_F52E2B61-18A1-11d1-B105-00805F49916B
----------------------------------------------------------------------
<row au_id="409-56-7008" au_lname="Bennet" au_fname="Abraham"/>
<row au_id="648-92- 1872" au_lname="Blotchet-Halls" au_fname="Reginald"/>
2 row(s) affected)
```

Note: If the XML portion does not end with "</row >" then the Query Analyzer truncated the output. See the directions with item 2 above to increase the column size.

Steps 1, 2, 3 above. Copy the result set output (just the XML text) into the text editor between our begin and end root element tags. Save the file with a .xml extension.

We save it as C:\authors.xml.

```
authors.xml - Notepad
File  Edit  Format  View  Help
<myroot>
<row au_id="409-56-7008" au_lname="Bennet" au_fname="Abraham"/><row au_id="648-92-187
</myroot>
```

Figure 4-1 C:\authors.xml saved.

Step 4 above. Open **C:\authors.xml** in Internet Explorer 5.5 or later.

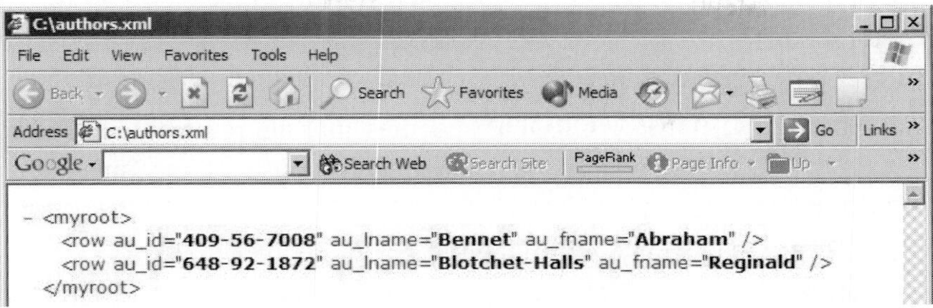

Figure 4-2 C:\authors.xml opened.

4.5.1.12 OPTION Clause

The OPTION clause specifies that the indicated query hint should be used throughout the entire query. Each query hint can be specified only once, although multiple query hints are permitted. Only one OPTION clause may be specified with the statement. The query hint affects all operators in the statement. If a UNION is involved in the main query, only the last query involving a UNION operator can have the OPTION clause.

Caution: Because the query optimizer usually selects the best execution plan for a query, it is recommended that <join_hint>, <query_hint>, and <table_hint> be used only as a last resort by experienced database administrators.

Syntax

```
[ OPTION ( < query_hint > [ ,...n ] ) ]


< query_hint > ::=
-- See query_hint descriptions page 527
{
  { HASH | ORDER } GROUP
  | { CONCAT | HASH | MERGE } UNION
  | { LOOP | MERGE | HASH } JOIN
  | FAST number_rows
  | FORCE ORDER
  | MAXDOP number
  | ROBUST PLAN
  | KEEP PLAN
  | KEEPFIXED PLAN
```

```
    | EXPAND VIEWS
}
```

Arguments

{ HASH | ORDER } GROUP

{ HASH | ORDER } GROUP specifies that aggregations described in the GROUP BY, DISTINCT, or COMPUTE clause of the query should use hashing or ordering.

{ MERGE | HASH | CONCAT } UNION

{ MERGE | HASH | CONCAT } UNION specifies that all UNION operations are performed by merging, hashing, or concatenating UNION sets. If more than one UNION hint is specified, the query optimizer selects the least expensive strategy from those hints specified.

{ LOOP | MERGE | HASH } JOIN

{ LOOP | MERGE | HASH } JOIN specifies that all join operations are performed by loop join, merge join, or hash join in the whole query. If more than one join hint is specified, the optimizer selects the least expensive join strategy from the allowed ones.

FAST number_rows

FAST *number_rows* specifies that the query is optimized for fast retrieval of the first *number_rows* (a nonnegative integer). After the first *number_rows* are returned, the query continues execution and produces its full result set.

FORCE ORDER

FORCE ORDER specifies that the join order indicated by the query syntax is preserved during query optimization.

MAXDOP *number*

MAXDOP *number* overrides the **max degree of parallelism** configuration option (of **sp_configure**) only for the query specifying this option. All semantic rules used with **max degree of parallelism** configuration option are applicable when using the MAXDOP query hint.

ROBUST PLAN

ROBUST PLAN forces the query optimizer to attempt a plan that works for the maximum potential row size, possibly at the expense of performance. When the query is processed, intermediate tables and operators may need to store and process rows that are wider than any of the input rows. The rows may be so wide that, in some cases, the particular operator cannot process the row. If this happens, SQL Server produces an error during query execution. By using ROBUST PLAN, you instruct the query optimizer not to consider any query plans that may encounter this problem.

KEEP PLAN

KEEP PLAN forces the query optimizer to relax the estimated recompile threshold for a query. The estimated recompile threshold is the point at which a query is automatically recompiled when the estimated number of indexed column changes (update, delete, or insert) have been made to a table. Specifying KEEP PLAN ensures that a query will not be recompiled as frequently when there are multiple updates to a table.

KEEPFIXED PLAN

KEEPFIXED PLAN forces the query optimizer not to recompile a query due to changes in statistics or to the indexed column (update, delete, or insert). Specifying KEEPFIXED PLAN ensures that a query will be recompiled only if the schema of the underlying tables is changed or **sp_recompile** is executed against those tables.

EXPAND VIEWS

EXPAND VIEWS specifies that the indexed views are expanded, and the query optimizer will not consider any indexed view as a substitute for any part of the query. (A view is expanded when the view name is replaced by the view definition in the query text.) This query hint virtually disallows direct use of indexed views and indexes on indexed views in the query plan.

The indexed view is not expanded only if the view is directly referenced in the SELECT part of the query and if WITH (NOEXPAND) or WITH (NOEXPAND, INDEX(index_val [,...*n*])) is specified.

Only the views in the SELECT portion of statements, including those in INSERT, UPDATE, and DELETE statements, are affected by the hint.

Example: Use OPTION (FAST 5) to do fast retreival of first five rows and then remainder.

SQL

```
SELECT   au_id , au_lname , au_fname
FROM pubs..authors
OPTION ( FAST 5 )
 -- Very useful for a large result set.
 -- First n rows are returned asap
```

Comment

SELECT statements are allowed in user-defined functions only if the select lists of these statements contain expressions that assign values to variables that are local to the functions.

4.5.2 Column Aliases

ANSI SQL specifies that you can create a ***column alias*** or ***column label*** in the SELECT list, which becomes the column heading in the output. A column alias may also be used in an ORDER BY clause to specify sort order.

Microsoft SQL Server has two methods of creating a column alias.

```
SELECT { column_name | expression } [AS] column_alias
  [ , ..n ] -- ANSI standard

SELECT column_alias = { column_name | expression }
  [ , ..n ] -- MSS only
```

Example:

ANSI Standard form of column alias

SQL

```
SELECT job_desc  Job_Title
FROM jobs
WHERE job_id = 2
```

Result

```
Job_Title
----------------------------
Chief Executive Officer
```

MSS only form of column alias, not ANSI

SQL

```
SELECT Job_Title  = job_desc
FROM jobs
WHERE job_id = 2
```

SQL (cont.)

Result

```
Job_Title
----------------------------
Chief Executive Officer
```

The two methods may be mixed in a single query.

MSS is the only form of column alias, not ANSI.

SQL

```
SELECT job_desc  Job_Title   ,  Job_Title2  = job_desc
FROM jobs
WHERE job_id = 2
```

Result

```
Job_Title                      Job_Title2
----------------------------   ----------------------------
Chief Executive Officer        Chief Executive Officer
```

Use a column alias to improve output readability.

An expression in the SELECT list has no heading in the output (third column).

SQL

```
SELECT job_desc  Job_Title   ,  Job_Title2  = job_desc
FROM jobs
WHERE job_id = 2
```

Result

```
job_desc                     min_lvl                  max_lvl
---------------------------  ------      ----------   ----------
Chief Executive Officer      200         202          250
```

We can label the third output column by adding a column alias.

SQL

```
SELECT job_desc  Job_Title   ,  Job_Title2  = job_desc
FROM jobs
WHERE job_id = 2
```

Result

job_desc	min_lvl	MinPlus2	max_lvl
Chief Executive Officer	200	202	250

Spaces in Column Alias: spaces must be enclosed in quotes or brackets [ ] .
Double Quotes " " to enclose column alias with embedded space is ANSI-92.
Brackets [ ] to enclose column alias with embedded space is MSS only.

Example: If the column alias does not have embedded spaces, delimiters may be omitted.

SQL

```
SELECT job_desc  "Job Title" , job_id  [Job Id]
  -- Double Quotes is ANSI Standard, not Brackets
FROM jobs
WHERE job_id = 2
```

Result

Job Title	Job Id
Chief Executive Officer	2

Example: Using an expression with a column alias

SQL

```
USE mydb
   -- On page 419 we created database mydb and
   -- table emps3 used in the next example.
```

SQL

```
SELECT   *   FROM   emps3
        -- Show contents of emps3 for reference
```

Result

ename	empid	deptno	telnum	salary	hiredate	sales_amt
Suzy Smith	1111	102	NULL	20	2003-01-01	NULL
Sammy Sosa	2222	102	2345	30	1992-01-01	200
Bill Johnson	4444	101	NULL	40	1994-01-01	NULL
Mary Smith	5555	100	5678	50	1990-01-01	NULL
Mary Smith	7777	101	7890	60		1996-01-
01			400			

SQL

```
SELECT empid, salary, sales_amt,
        (salary + .05 * sales_amt) "Total Pay"
FROM emps3
WHERE empid = 2222;
```

Result

empid	salary	sales_amt	Total Pay
2222	30	200	40.00

SQL

```
SELECT TOP 1 'Hello' "My Label", 'Hi There' My_Label
FROM emps3;
    -- Quotes are req'd if have spaces embedded, "AS" is optional
```

Result

My Label	My_Label
Hello	Hi There

(1 row(s) affected)

4.5.2.1 Column Aliases in ORDER BY Clause

Example: Column aliases may be used in an ORDER BY clause (but NOT elsewhere, such as a WHERE, GROUP BY, or HAVING clause).

SQL

```
SELECT empid, salary, (salary * 1.2 ) Total_Pay
FROM emps3
WHERE  (salary * 1.2) >= 40
 -- May NOT use:   Total_Pay  >=  40
ORDER BY Total_Pay
```

Result

```
empid      salary      Total_Pay
------     ------      ---------
4444       40          48.0
5555       50          60.0
7777       60          72.0
```

4.6 SET OPERATIONS

4.6.1 SET Operations — UNION, UNION ALL

4.6.1.1 UNION Operator

UNION Operator combines the results of two or more queries into a single result set consisting of all the rows belonging to all queries in the union. This is different from using joins that combine columns from two tables.

Two basic rules for combining the result sets of two queries with UNION are as follows.

The number and the order of the columns must be identical in all queries.

The data types must be compatible. See Table 4-8.

Syntax

```
{ < query specification > | ( < query expression > ) }
UNION [ ALL ]
< query specification | ( < query expression > )
[ UNION [ ALL ] < query specification | ( < query expression > )
[ ...n ] ]
```

Arguments

< query_specification > | (< query_expression >)

< query_specification > | (< query_expression >) is a query specification or query expression that returns data to be combined with the data from another query specification or query expression. The definitions of the columns that are part of a UNION operation do not have to be identical, but they must be compatible through implicit conversion.

Rules for comparing data types of the *ith* columns of two SELECT lists for UNION compatibility are shown in Table 4-8.

Table 4-8 UNION Compatibility

Data Type of *ith* Column	Data Type of *ith* Column of Results Table
Both fixed-length **char** with lengths L1 and L2.	Fixed-length **char** with length equal to the greater of L1 and L2.
Both fixed-length **binary** with lengths L1 and L2.	Fixed-length **binary** with length equal to the greater of L1 and L2.
Either or both variable-length **char**.	Variable-length **char** with length equal to the maximum of the lengths specified for the *ith* columns.
Either or both variable-length **binary**.	Variable-length **binary** with length equal to the maximum of the lengths specified for the *ith* columns.
Both numeric data types (for example, **smallint**, **int**, **float**, **money**).	Data type equal to the maximum precision of the two columns. For example, if the *ith* column of table A is of type **int** and the *ith* column of table B is of type **float**, then the data type of the *ith* column of the results table is **float** because **float** is more precise than **int**.
Both columns' descriptions specify NOT NULL.	Specifies NOT NULL.
Not data type–compatible (data conversion not handled implicitly by SQL Server).	Error returned by SQL Server.

UNION

UNION specifies that multiple result sets are to be combined and returned as a single result set.

UNION ALL

UNION ALL incorporates all rows into the results, including duplicates. If ALL is not specified, duplicate rows are removed.

Example: List all Customers and Suppliers in Northwind database from Oregon.

SQL

```
SELECT  'Customer    ' AS Type ,CompanyName , Region
FROM Northwind..Customers
WHERE Region = 'OR'
    UNION
SELECT  'Supplier    ' ,  CompanyName , Region
FROM Northwind..Suppliers
WHERE Region = 'OR'
```

Result

Type	CompanyName	Region
Customer	Great Lakes Food Market	OR
Customer	Hungry Coyote Import Store	OR
Customer	Lonesome Pine Restaurant	OR
Customer	The Big Cheese	OR
Supplier	Bigfoot Breweries	OR

UNION vs UNION ALL

UNION removes duplicate rows (if any) and UNION ALL retains them. Since there are no duplicate rows in the previous example, UNION and UNION ALL yield the same result.

Example: Use the previous example but with only the first and last items in the SELECT list so that the row Customer OR would be duplicated.

SQL

```
SELECT  'Customer' AS Type
                 , Region
FROM Northwind..Customers
WHERE Region = 'OR'
    UNION
SELECT  'Supplier', Region
FROM Northwind..Suppliers
WHERE Region = 'OR'
```

SQL (cont.)

Result

```
Type          Region
-----------   ---------------
Customer      OR
Supplier      OR
```

SQL

```
SELECT  'Customer ' AS Type
                   ,Region
FROM Northwind..Customers
WHERE Region = 'OR'
    UNION ALL
SELECT  'Supplier ', Region
FROM Northwind..Suppliers
WHERE Region = 'OR'
```

Result

```
Type          Region
-----------   ---------------
Customer      OR
Customer      OR
Customer      OR
Customer      OR
Supplier      OR
```

4.6.2 SET Operations — INTERSECTION

Microsoft SQL Server does not have a direct implementation of set INTERSECTION, but the operation can be accomplished using EXISTS predicate.

Set INTERSECTION (called "INTERSECT" in ANSI SQL) lists all rows that are identical in the result sets of two SELECT statements.

INTERSECT (ANSI)

```
SELECT a, b, c FROM table1
    INTERSECT
SELECT a2, b2, c2 FROM table2
```

MSS Implementation using EXISTS

```
SELECT DISTINCT a, b, c
FROM table1
WHERE  EXISTS
    (  SELECT 1 FROM table2
    WHERE
        table1.a = table2.a2
        table1.b = table2.b2
        table1.c = table2.c2      )
```

Example: List all cities and their region for which there are both a customer and a supplier.

SQL

```
SELECT  City , Region FROM Northwind..Customers c
WHERE   EXISTS
    ( SELECT 1 FROM Northwind..Suppliers  s
  WHERE s.City = c.City AND s.Region = c.Region )
```

Result

```
City          Region
-----------   --------------
Montréal      Québec
```

Montreal is the only city that occurs in both tables.

4.6.3 SET Operations — SET DIFFERENCE

Microsoft SQL Server does not have a direct implementation of SET DIFFERENCE (EXCEPT / MINUS), but the operation can be accomplished using NOT EXISTS predicate.

Set DIFFERENCE (called "EXCEPT" in ANSI SQL and "MINUS" in Oracle) lists all rows of the first result set that are not in the second result set of two SELECT statements.

MSS Implementation using NOT EXISTS

```
SELECT DISTINCT a, b, c
FROM table1
```

```
WHERE  NOT EXISTS
  (  SELECT 1 FROM table2
    WHERE
      table1.a = table2.a2
      table1.b = table2.b2
      table1.c = table2.c2     )
```

EXCEPT (ANSI)

```
SELECT a, b, c FROM table1
  EXCEPT
SELECT a2, b2, c2 FROM table2
```

Example: List all cities and their region for which there are both a customer and a supplier.

SQL

```
SELECT  City , Region FROM Northwind..Customers c
WHERE  NOT EXISTS
    ( SELECT 1 FROM Northwind..Suppliers  s
  WHERE s.City = c.City AND s.Region = c.Region )
```

Result

```
City            Region
-----------     --------------
Berlin          NULL
México D.F.     NULL
México D.F.     NULL
London          NULL
...
Campinas        SP
Eugene          OR
...

(90 row(s) affected)
```

All cities in the Custormers table other than Montreal have no suppliers in the same city. So SET DIFFERENCE is the complement of INTERSECTION. The UNION of the two results gives all 91 cities in the Customers table.

4.6.4 Hints—Join Hints, Query Hints and Table Hints

Table 4-9 summarizes various hints, including join hints, query hints and table hints.

Table 4-9 Hints Summary

Hint Type	Option	Description	Default Setting
Join	LOOP | HASH | MERGE | REMOTE	Specifies the strategy to use when joining the rows of two tables The first three specify that all join operations are performed by loop join, merge join or hash join in the whole query. REMOTE, only with INNER JOINs, specifies that the join operation is performed on the site of the right table. It should be used only when the left table has fewer rows than the right table.	Chosen by SQL Server
Query	{ HASH | ORDER } GROUP	Specifies whether hashing or ordering is used to compute GROUP BY and COMPUTE aggregations	Chosen by SQL Server
Query	{ MERGE | HASH | CONCAT } UNION	Specifies that all UNION operations should be performed by merging, hashing or concatenating UNION sets	Chosen by SQL Server
Query	FAST *number_rows*	Optimizes the query for retrieval of the specified number of rows After the first *number_rows* are returned, the query continues execution normally and produces its full result set.	No such optimization
Query	FORCE ORDER	Performs joins in the order in which the tables appear in the query	Chosen by SQL Server
Query	MAXDOP *number*	Overrides the **max degree of parallelism** configuration option (of **sp_configure**) for the query specifying this option	sp_configure setting
Query	ROBUST PLAN	Creates a plan that accommodates maximum potential row size	Chosen by SQL Server
Query	KEEP PLAN	Forces the query optimizer to relax the estimated recompile threshold for a query Specifying KEEP PLAN ensures that a query will not be recompiled as frequently when there are multiple updates to a table.	Chosen by SQL Server

Table 4-9 Hints Summary

Hint Type	Option	Description	Default Setting
Query	KEEPFIXED PLAN	Ensures that a query will be recompiled only if the schema of the underlying tables is changed or **sp_recompile** is executed against those tables	Chosen by SQL Server
Query	EXPAND VIEWS	Specifies that the indexed views are expanded; the view SELECT statement is executed rather than using the stored indexed view data. The WITH (NO-EXPAND) clause will override.	Chosen by SQL Server
Table	FASTFIRSTROW	Has the same effect as specifying the FAST 1 query hint	No such optimi-zation
Table	INDEX =	Instructs SQL Server to use the specified indexes for a table	Chosen by SQL Server
Table	HOLDLOCK | SERIAL-IZABLE | REPEAT-ABLEREAD | READCOMMITTED | READUNCOMMITTED| NOLOCK	Specifies the isolation level for a table	Defaults to a transaction iso-lation level
Table	ROWLOCK|PAGLOCK| TABLOCK|TABLOCKX | NOLOCK	Specifies locking granularity for a table	Chosen by SQL Server
Table	READPAST	Skips locked rows altogether	Wait for locked rows.
Table	UPDLOCK	Takes update locks instead of shared locks. Cannot be used with NOLOCK or XLOCK	Take shared locks.
Table	XLOCK	Takes an exclusive lock that will be held until the end of the transaction. Cannot be used with NOLOCK or UPDLOCK.	Chosen by SQL Server

Syntax

```
< join_hint > ::=  { LOOP | HASH | MERGE | REMOTE }


< query_hint > ::=   -- This is the complete list.  DELETE and UPDATE support a
subset of this list.
{
     { HASH | ORDER } GROUP
```

```
    | { CONCAT | HASH | MERGE } UNION
    | { LOOP | MERGE | HASH } JOIN
    | FAST number_rows
    | FORCE ORDER
    | MAXDOP number
    | ROBUST PLAN
    | KEEP PLAN
    | KEEPFIXED PLAN
    | EXPAND VIEWS
}


< table_hint > ::=
{
      INDEX ( index_val [ ,...n ] )
    | FASTFIRSTROW
        -- For backward compatibility to SS 6.x , replace with OPTION(FAST n)
    | HOLDLOCK -- Hold a shared lock until completion of transaction
    | NOLOCK
        -- Do not issue shared locks and do not honor exclusive locks.

        -- Dirty reads are possible. Applies only to the SELECT statement.
    | PAGLOCK  -- Use page locks in place of table lock
    | READCOMMITTED
        -- Use the locking semantics of READ COMMITTED isolation level
        -- READ COMMITTED is the default SQL Server 2000 isolation level.
    | READPAST -- Skip locked rows rather than block this transaction.
               -- Applies only to transactions using at READ COMMITTED isolation
                  and
               -- will only pass row-level locks. Applies only to the SELECT
                  statement.
    | READUNCOMMITTED -- Equivalent to NOLOCK.
    | REPEATABLEREAD
        -- Use the locking semantics of REPEATABLEREAD isolation level
    | ROWLOCK  -- Use row locks
    | SERIALIZABLE
        -- Use the locking semantics of SERIALIZABLE isolation level
    | TABLOCK  -- Use table locks
    | TABLOCKX -- Use exclusive table locks
    | UPDLOCK
        -- Use update locks and hold locks until the end of the transaction.
}


< table_hint_limited > ::=      -- See descriptions above with <table_hint>
{
      FASTFIRSTROW | HOLDLOCK | PAGLOCK | READCOMMITTED | REPEATABLEREAD
    | ROWLOCK | SERIALIZABLE | TABLOCK | TABLOCKX | UPDLOCK
}
```

Note: This <table_hint_limited> list is called *limited* because INDEX, NOLOCK, READPAST and READUNCOMMITTED are not allowed.

CHAPTER 5

Transaction Control, Backup and Restore and Transact-SQL Programming

This chapter covers Transaction Control and Transact-SQL Programming, including the third-generation language (3GL) features of the Transact-SQL language.

5.1 TRANSACTION CONTROL—ANSI SQL AND MSS

5.1.1 Transaction Concepts

A *transaction* is a sequence of one or more SQL statements that together form a logical unit of work that must be either applied to the database in their entirety (COMMIT) or discarded completely (ROLLBACK). A transaction is ALL OR NONE; either all parts are recorded to the database or none are. This is known as the *Atomic* property.

The following is a classic example of a transaction.

Mary goes to the ATM to transfer $1000 from her savings account to her checking account. Her inputs become the following SQL statements.

```
UPDATE savings          SET Balance = Balance - 1000
WHERE customerid   =  444;

UPDATE checking         SET Balance = Balance + 1000
WHERE customerid   =  444;
```

If these were done as independent actions, we would have a problem if the first one completed and the second did not complete, as might occur if the power went out. The solution is to bundle the operations into one piece of work called a transaction.

SQL

```
BEGIN TRANSACTION -- ANSI is "SET TRANSACTION"
    UPDATE savings        SET Balance = Balance - 1000
        WHERE customerid  =  444;
    UPDATE checking       SET Balance = Balance + 1000
        WHERE customerid  =  444;
COMMIT
```

5.1.1.1 ACID Properties

Each transaction is guaranteed to have the **ACID properties**:

- **Atomic—All** statements in the transaction go to the database **or none** do.
- **Consistent—**When completed, all data and metadata in the database are consistent, including constraints, such as Referential Integrity, and internal data structures, such as Indexes.
- **Isolated—**Concurrent transactions do not interfere with each other's changes.
- **Durable**—All changes to the database endure including software and hardware failures.

A Transaction is a sequence of SQL statements bundled together that are certain to have the ACID properties.

Example: Consider two transactions, T1 and T2: (MSS uses BEGIN TRANSACTION to start transaction)

T1

```
BEGIN TRANSACTION -- You want to transfer $1000 from savings to checking
   UPDATE savings SET  Balance = Balance - 1000   WHERE  customerid  =  444;
   UPDATE checking SET  Balance = Balance + 1000  WHERE customerid  =  444;
COMMIT  -- or ROLLBACK
```

T2

```
BEGIN TRAN -- You put $300 into savings and take $100 from checking
   UPDATE savings SET  Balance = Balance + 300   WHERE  customerid  =  444;
```

```
  UPDATE checking SET  Balance = Balance - 100   WHERE  customerid  =  444;
COMMIT  -- or ROLLBACK
```

Although the two transactions may have had some operations interleaved in time, the **Isolated** property, as shown in Figure 5-1, means that the end result will be the same as if one started and completed and then the other started and completed: T1 then T2 or T2 then T1.

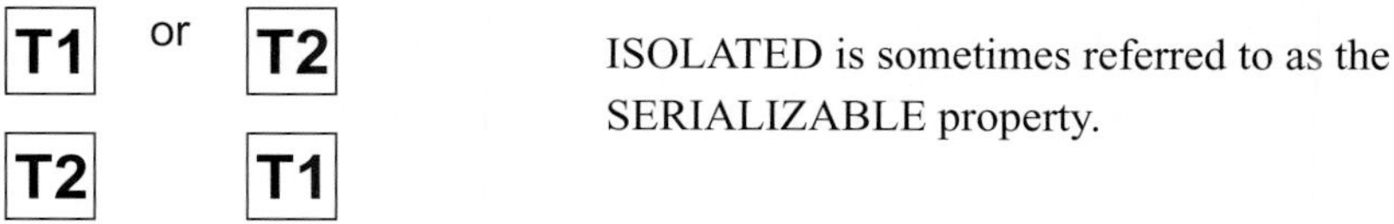
T1
or
T2
T2
T1
ISOLATED is sometimes referred to as the SERIALIZABLE property.

Figure 5-1 The Isolated property keeps the end result the same.

5.1.2 Starting and Ending a Transaction

Every DDL and DML statement executed by SQL Server is done within a transaction. A transaction may be created either explicitly with BEGIN TRANSACTION, or automatically in one of two modes. The two automatic modes are *Autocommit Mode* and *Implicit Transactions Mode*, which are introduced here and further described on page 539.

5.1.2.1 Explicit Transactions

Explicit transactions open with BEGIN TRAN[SACTION] and close with COMMIT. See additional details, page 539.

BEGIN TRANSACTION explicitly starts a new transaction (if one is not already open). The transaction may contain as many statements as desired. See "Nested Transactions" below for the behavior in case a transaction is already open.

COMMIT commits all statements in the transaction.

ROLLBACK aborts all statements in the transaction.

Example: The transaction opens with BEGIN TRAN and closes with COMMIT.

SQL

```
BEGIN TRAN
UPDATE savings SET Balance = Balance - 1000 WHERE customerid  =  444;
UPDATE checking SET Balance = Balance + 1000 WHERE customerid  =  444;
COMMIT     -- or ROLLBACK
```

A transaction is terminated by executing COMMIT or ROLLBACK.

5.1.2.2 Automatic (Implicit) Transactions

If a transaction is not already open when a statement is presented for execution, SQL Server will automatically (implicitly) start a new transaction. When this automatic transaction is committed is determined by which of the two modes described here is set in the current session. See details for setting the mode on page 537.

The AUTOCOMMIT MODE (default) means that if there is not an open transaction, an SQL statement presented to SQL Server starts a new transaction and commits it immediately upon completion of execution.

Example: Each statement is a complete transaction in autocommit mode.

SQL

```
UPDATE savings SET Balance = Balance - 1000 WHERE customerid  =  444;

UPDATE checking SET Balance = Balance + 1000 WHERE customerid  =  444;
```

The IMPLICIT TRANSACTIONS MODE means that if there is not an open transaction, an SQL statement presented to SQL Server starts a new transaction that remains open until there is an explicit COMMIT or ROLLBACK.

MSS may be set to explicit commit with:

SET IMPLICIT_TRANSACTIONS ON

It seems that IMPLICIT TRANSACTIONS mode would be clearer if called EXPLICIT COMMIT mode since autocommit mode also implicitly starts a new transaction.

Example: The transaction opens with the first UPDATE and closes with COMMIT.

SQL

```
UPDATE savings SET Balance = Balance - 1000 WHERE customerid  =  444;
UPDATE checking SET Balance = Balance + 1000 WHERE customerid  =  444;
COMMIT      -- or ROLLBACK
```

5.1.3 ISOLATION Is Obtained through Locking

SQL Server uses locking to permit concurrent operations while ensuring transactional integrity and database consistency. Locking prevents users from reading data being changed by other users and prevents multiple users from changing the same data at the same time. In short, locking maintains data integrity but allows concurrency.

5.1.3.1 Lock Modes

- **S = SHARED LOCK or Read Lock**
  Shared lock permits multiple readers (as for SELECT) but no writers.
- **X = EXCLUSIVE LOCK or Write Lock**
  Exclusive lock permits exclusive access, no other users. It is required to change the data value as for INSERT, UPDATE or DELETE.
- **U = UPDATE LOCK**
  Update lock is used on resources that can be updated to prevent a form of deadlock. Only one update lock may be outstanding for a resource. The update lock is converted to an exclusive lock if the transaction modifies the resource; otherwise it is converted to a shared lock.
- **I = INTENT LOCK**
  Intent lock is used to establish a lock hierarchy corresponding to the data structure hierarchy such as table, extent, page and row. There are three levels of intent lock: intent shared (IS), intent exclusive (IX) and shared with intent exclusive (SIX).
- **Sch-M, Sch-S = SCHEMA LOCK**
  Schema lock is used when an operation dependent on the schema of a table is executing. The types of schema locks are as follows: schema modification (Sch-M) for DDL statements and schema stability (Sch-S) for query compilation.
- **BU = BULK UPDATE LOCK**
  Bulk update lock is used for bulk-copying data into a table when the TABLOCK hint is specified.

5.1.3.2 Locks Example

The first reader requests and is granted a shared lock S for the data row (Figure 5-2). The next two readers also request and are granted shared locks for the same row.

The first writer arrives and requests an exclusive lock X. She is blocked until all shared locks are released.

The second writer arrives and is also put in the queue and blocked waiting for his lock which will be granted after the preceding X lock is released.

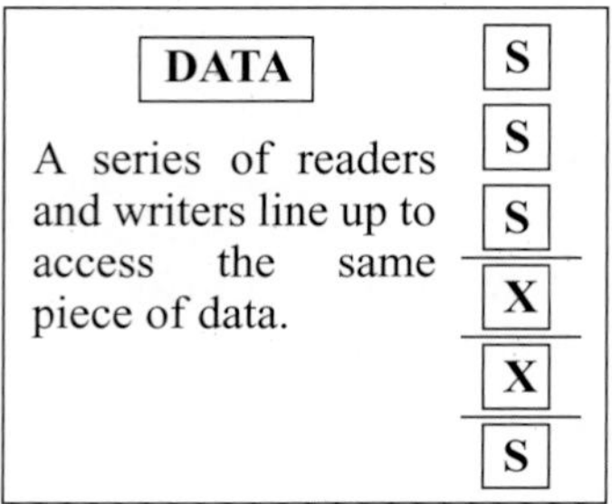

Figure 5-2 A locking hierarchy.

The next reader arrives and requests a shared lock and, for the sake of fairness, is put in the queue in her turn. If this lock is granted before the writers' there is a possibility for "starving" the writers indefinitely.

Locking decreases concurrency, so programmers must COMMIT to release locks as soon as possible.

Lock Types (level or hierarchy) Lock is on a row (RID), page (PG), extent (EXT), table (TAB), database (DB), file (FIL), etc.

Lock Duration The following rules apply if Isolation is READ COMMITTED (the default):

- S — Shared locks are released when the read completes.
- X — Exclusive locks are held until the end of the transaction.[1]

Viewing Locks Use **sp_lock** to see locks on the system and who holds the locks.

The following code allows you to view locks in Query Analyzer.

```
EXEC sp_lock
```

In Enterprise Manager, use the following process to view locks.

ServerName – Management – Current Activity – **Locks / Process ID** or **Locks / Object**

1. Shapiro 2000, pp. 717–718.

QA 1 - Query Analyzer session 1 - Normal User1 - spid 52

SQL

```
EXEC sp_lock
```

Result

spid	dbid	ObjId	IndId	Type	Resource	Mode	Status
------	------	-----------	------	----	--------------	--------	------
51	10	0	0	DB	<blank>	S	GRANT
51	1	85575343	0	TAB	I	S	GRANT
52	10	0	0	DB		S	GRANT
53	5	0	0	DB		S	GRANT

SQL

```
SELECT   @@spid        /* to show my spid = server process
identifier  (really "session" process id)*/
```

Result

```
------
52
```

SQL

```
BEGIN TRAN

UPDATE jobs SET job_desc = 'FOO'
WHERE job_id = 1;
```

Result

job_id	job_desc	min_lvl	max_lvl
------	--------------------------	-------	-------
1	FOO	30	10

QA 2 - Query Analyzer session 2 - Normal User2 - spid 53

SQL

```
SELECT * FROM jobs ;
```

Result

Blocks until QA 1 releases the lock

QA 3 - Query Analyzer session 3 - sa

SQL

```
EXEC sp_lock
```

Result

spid	dbid	ObjId	IndId	Type	Resource	Mode	Status
------	------	-----------	------	----	----------------	--------	------
51	10	0	0	DB		S	GRANT
52	11	0	0	DB		S	GRANT
52	11	1977058079	0	TAB		IX	GRANT
52	11	1977058079	0	RID	1:75:0	X	GRANT
52	11	1977058079	0	PAG	1:75	IX	GRANT
52	1	85575343	0	TAB		IS	GRANT
53	11	1977058079	0	RID	1:75:0	S	WAIT
53	11	1977058079	0	PAG	1:75	IS	GRANT
53	11	1977058079	0	TAB		IS	GRANT
53	11	0	0	DB		S	GRANT

SQL

```
kill 52
```

The command(s) completed successfully.

QA 1 is rolled back. QA 2 now completes.

5.1.4 Automatic (Implicit) Transaction Mechanisms

If a transaction is not already open when a statement is presented for execution, SQL Server will automatically (implicitly) start a new transaction. Each session (connection) has a setting to one of two modes that determines when an automatic transaction is committed. How these two modes behave and how to change the session setting is described here. You may also refer to the section on Session Settings, page 202.

1. AUTOCOMMIT MODE (default behavior). Each statement is a transaction—not ANSI SQL.
   - Automatically starts a new transaction for each SQL statement.
     Note: BOL says "each statement is a transaction" including SELECT statements."
   - Automatically commits each statement.
2. IMPLICIT TRANSACTION MODE (think: explicit COMMIT). ANSI SQL-92 / 99.
   - Automatically starts a new transaction for each SQL statement
   - Requires an explicit COMMIT or ROLLBACK

In Implicit Transaction mode if a transaction is not already open, a statement opens a new transaction and leaves it open until the user does an explicit COMMIT or ROLLBACK. This behavior is ANSI SQL compliant. This mode seems poorly named in my opinion since Autocommit Mode also will start a transaction implicitly if one is not open. But this mode requires an explicit termination (commit or rollback), so I think a better name would have been "Explicit Commit." Again, they didn't ask my opinion. This mode does not seem to be often used in my experience.

SETTING IMPLICIT_TRANSACTIONS ON turns "implicit transaction" on, autocommit off.

SETTING IMPLICIT_TRANSACTIONS OFF turns on autocommit (txn still starts implicitly).

According to BOL, in implicit transaction mode, if there is currently no open transaction, SQL Server automatically starts a new transaction when it first executes any of these statements:

```
ALTER TABLE        FETCH          REVOKE
CREATE             GRANT          SELECT
DELETE             INSERT         TRUNCATE TABLE
DROP               OPEN           UPDATE
```

The transaction remains open for all SQL statements until you issue a COMMIT or ROLLBACK.

Example of Transaction Mechanics: You can do the exercise in Figure 5-3 as a lab exercise.

Query Analyzer 1 - QA1

```
SQL: USE pubs
  -- or  pubs_copy to
  -- preserve pubs data
go

SQL: SELECT min_lvl FROM jobs
     WHERE job_id = 1;
```

Result: 10

Query Analyzer 2 - QA2

```
SQL: USE pubs -- or  pubs_copy to
               -- preserve pubs data
go
```

Same results show in both Query Analyzers.

```
SQL: SELECT min_lvl FROM jobs
     WHERE job_id = 1;
```

Result: 10

-- AUTOCOMMIT TRANSACTION

QA1:

```
SQL: UPDATE jobs SET min_lvl =
min_lvl + 10
     WHERE job_id = 1;
SQL: SELECT min_lvl FROM jobs
     WHERE job_id = 1;
```

Result: 20

QA2:

```
SQL: SELECT min_lvl FROM jobs
     WHERE job_id = 1;
```

Result: 20 -- Default behavior is autocommit
-- so we see the change immediately

SET IMPLICIT_TRANSACTIONS ON
-- Means set explicit COMMIT for this session.

QA1:

```
SQL: UPDATE jobs SET min_lvl =
min_lvl + 10
     WHERE job_id = 1;

SQL: SELECT min_lvl FROM jobs
     WHERE job_id = 1;
```

Result: 30 -- QA1 will see changes immediately

QA2:

```
SQL: SELECT min_lvl FROM jobs
     WHERE job_id = 1;
```

-- QA2 will wait until COMMIT in QA1

QA1:

```
SQL: COMMIT                 ------
EXPLICIT COMMIT !!  ---
 ------ Now QA2 will complete  --->
-- Done, Set back to default
SQL: SET IMPLICIT_TRANSACTIONS OFF
```

QA2:

Result: 30 -- QA2 select statement completes

Figure 5-3 Open two Query Analyzers and execute these commands.

5.1.5 Explicit Transaction Mechanisms

Explicit Transactions use BEGIN TRANSACTION ... COMMIT / ROLLBACK statements and a function @@TRANCOUNT.

SQL

```
BEGIN TRANSACTION
UPDATE savings SET Balance = Balance - 1000
                WHERE customerid  =  444;
UPDATE checking SET Balance = Balance + 1000
                WHERE customerid  =  444;
COMMIT      -- or ROLLBACK
```

- BEGIN TRANSACTION
  BEGIN TRAN[SACTION]
  `BEGIN TRAN` increments @@TRANCOUNT and begins a transaction if there is not one open. It marks the starting point of an explicit, local transaction. Although you can give a transaction a name, it is of no value.
- COMMIT
  COMMIT [TRAN[SACTION] [*transaction_name*] or COMMIT [WORK]
  `COMMIT` decrements @@TRANCOUNT and, if it reaches 0, commits to the database. It marks the end of a successful explicit or implicit transaction. All data modifications performed since the start of the transaction become a permanent part of the database and free the resources held by the connection.
- ROLLBACK
  ROLLBACK [TRAN[SACTION] [**savepoint_name**]
  `ROLLBACK` rolls back to the beginning of the current txn, then proceeds with next stmt.
  `ROLLBACK TRAN <savepoint>` rolls back to named savepoint, then proceeds with next stmt.
- @@TRANCOUNT
  This system function returns the current transaction nesting level.

SQL

```
PRINT @@TRANCOUNT
```

Result

```
0
```

SQL Server has the idea of **nested transactions** in which COMMIT and ROLLBACK behave differently. ROLLBACK rolls back an entire transaction (unless there is a SAVEPOINT), reducing @@trancount to 0. COMMIT commits only the current nested transaction and decrements @@trancount by 1. The upshot is that there can be **partial rollbacks** but **no partial commits**. The authors of Books Online make the following statements:

> When used in nested transactions, commits of the inner transactions do not free resources or make their modifications permanent. The data modifications are made permanent and resources freed only when the outer transaction is committed.

Example of Transaction Mechanics: Do the exercise in Figure 5-4 as a lab exercise.

Query Analyzer 1 - QA1	***Query Analyzer 2 - QA2***
`SQL: USE pubs_copy` `go`	`SQL: USE pubs_copy` `go`
-- AUTOCOMMIT TRANSACTION	-- See same results show in both Query Analyzers -- since QA1 update autocommits

`SQL: UPDATE jobs SET min_lvl = 10`
`WHERE job_id = 1;`
`SQL: SELECT min_lvl FROM jobs`
`WHERE job_id = 1;`
	`SQL: SELECT min_lvl FROM jobs`
	`WHERE job_id = 1;`

Result: 10	Result: 10
-- EXPLICIT TRANSACTION BEGIN TRAN	

`SQL: UPDATE jobs SET min_lvl =`
`min_lvl + 10`
`WHERE job_id = 1;`
`SQL: SELECT min_lvl FROM jobs`
`WHERE job_id = 1;`
	`SQL: SELECT min_lvl FROM jobs`
	`WHERE job_id = 1;`
	—QA2 blocks (waits) since
	—QA1 has lock on data until it commits

Result: 20 -- Also try in QA2 --->	Result: 20
-- MORAL: Always do COMMIT ASAP	

Figure 5-4 Open two Query Analyzers and execute these commands.

5.1.5.1 Nested Transactions in MSS

Nesting transactions are primarily to support transactions in stored procedures that can be called from a process either with or without a current open transaction. Each nested transaction increments and decrements the nesting level value. The current nesting level can be read with the system function `@@TRANCOUNT`. Observe the following code.

Example: Demonstrate nested transactions and the use of @@TRANCOUNT.

```
CREATE TABLE junk  (col DEC(1) DEFAULT 1); -- Autocommits

PRINT @@TRANCOUNT          -- @@TRANCOUNT is 0
BEGIN TRAN -- one -- Increments @@TRANCOUNT to 1
PRINT @@TRANCOUNT          -- @@TRANCOUNT is 1
INSERT INTO junk DEFAULT VALUES;  -- inserts 1 row
  BEGIN TRAN -- two  -- Increments @@TRANCOUNT to 2
  INSERT INTO junk DEFAULT VALUES;  -- inserts 1 row
  PRINT @@TRANCOUNT        -- @@TRANCOUNT is 2
  COMMIT TRAN -- two -- Decrements @@TRANCOUNT to 1
PRINT @@TRANCOUNT          -- @@TRANCOUNT is 1
INSERT INTO junk DEFAULT VALUES;  -- inserts 1 row
COMMIT TRAN -- one -- Decrements @@TRANCOUNT to 0 and commits
SELECT COUNT(*) Rows FROM junk
```

Notes about Nested Transactions and this Example

- The names of inner transactions are ignored by the system and are available only for readability in making it easier to match up BEGIN and COMMIT. You can make this more clear by making them a comment, "BEGIN TRAN -- two" which might avoid giving the impression that they do something.
- Each COMMIT decrements @@TRANCOUNT and actually does the commit when @@TRANCOUNT becomes 0. So "COMMIT two" does nothing but decrement @@TRANCOUNT.
  There is NO partial COMMIT.

Result

```
Rows
-----------
3
```

Example: Observe the values of @@TRANCOUNT when you use "ROLLBACK – two" in place of "COMMIT TRAN -- two"

```
TRUNCATE TABLE junk -- Deletes all rows, not logged

PRINT @@TRANCOUNT   -- @@TRANCOUNT is 0
BEGIN TRAN -- one   -- Increments @@TRANCOUNT to 1
PRINT @@TRANCOUNT   -- @@TRANCOUNT is 1
INSERT INTO junk DEFAULT VALUES;  -- inserts 1 row
 BEGIN TRAN -- two  -- Increments @@TRANCOUNT to 2
 PRINT @@TRANCOUNT  -- @@TRANCOUNT is 2
 INSERT INTO junk DEFAULT VALUES;  -- inserts 1 row
 ROLLBACK -- two    -- Rolls back txn, TC = 0, continues next
PRINT @@TRANCOUNT   -- @@TRANCOUNT is 0
INSERT INTO junk DEFAULT VALUES;  -- inserts 1 row
COMMIT TRAN -- one  -- Decrements @@TRANCOUNT
PRINT @@TRANCOUNT   -- @@TRANCOUNT is 0
SELECT COUNT(*) Rows FROM junk
```

Notes about this Example

- "ROLLBACK -- two" rolls back an entire transaction, sets @@TRANCOUNT to 0 and continues execution at the statement following ROLLBACK.
- **Caution:** ROLLBACK must have either no name or the name of the outermost transaction. If "ROLLBACK -- two" is replaced by "ROLLBACK TRAN two" then a non-fatal error occurs but no rollback. Execution continues giving the same result as the previous page but leaves @@TRANCOUNT at 1. The **Final result is not** what you expect.
- "COMMIT TRAN -- one" is a non-fatal error since @@TRANCOUNT is already 0. The **Final result may be** what you expect. If you want the nested txn to succeed or fail separately from the outer transaction, the inner txn should use a SAVEPOINT.

Result

```
Rows
-----------
1
```

5.1.5.2 Savepoints—Allow for a Partial ROLLBACK

A savepoint is a named point in the transaction to which you can roll back. You create a savepoint by using the following syntax.

```
SAVE TRANSACTION <savepoint-name>

ROLLBACK TRAN[SACTION] <savepoint-name>
-- Note: BOL says "[TRAN]", not true
```

Example: The following script rolls back the inner transaction but keeps the outer.

```
TRUNCATE TABLE junk
SELECT COUNT(*) Rows FROM junk
BEGIN TRAN -- one  -- Works the same with "one" and "-- one"
PRINT 'A: ' + CAST(@@TRANCOUNT AS CHAR)  -- @@TRANCOUNT is 1
INSERT INTO junk DEFAULT VALUES;  -- inserts 1 row
  SAVE TRAN sp_two -- Does not change @@TRANCOUNT
  PRINT 'B: ' + CAST(@@TRANCOUNT AS CHAR)  -- @@TRANCOUNT is 1
  INSERT INTO junk DEFAULT VALUES;  -- inserts 1 row
  ROLLBACK TRAN sp_two -- Rolls back to SAVE TRAN sp_two then
proceeds
PRINT 'C: ' + CAST(@@TRANCOUNT AS CHAR)  -- @@TRANCOUNT is 1
INSERT INTO junk DEFAULT VALUES;  -- inserts 1 row
COMMIT TRAN -- one                       -- Non-fatal error
PRINT 'D: ' + CAST(@@TRANCOUNT AS CHAR)-- @@TRANCOUNT is 0
SELECT COUNT(*) Rows FROM junk           -- @@TRANCOUNT is 0
```

Note

Only use ROLLBACK in nested transactions to roll back the entire transaction or to roll back to a savepoint. In the preceding script, the text says that the ROLLBACK to the savepoint reduces @@TRANCOUNT by 1, but the above exercise shows that ROLLBACK two doesn't change @@TRANCOUNT. The COMMIT at the end matches up with the BEGIN TRAN, and the single row is committed to the table.

Result
Rows ----------- 2

5.1.5.3 Cleanup @@TRANCOUNT

Using "ROLLBACK two" as in the example in 5.1.5.1 will leave @@TRANCOUNT with a value of 1 at the end. This means that the operations in the transaction have not been committed to the database and that all locks taken on the data are still held, thereby shutting others out.

This situation was caused by an illegal but non-fatal ROLLBACK label statement. If you suspect this situation might occur in your code, you may want to follow the transaction by cleanup code, which ensures completion of the proper number of COMMITs.

```
WHILE @@TRANCOUNT > 0
    BEGIN
        COMMIT
    END
```

Suggestions

USE NO NAME FOR "BEGIN TRAN" UNLESS COMMENTED OFF:

BEGIN TRAN -- one

USE NO NAME FOR "COMMIT TRAN" UNLESS COMMENTED OFF:

COMMIT TRAN -- one

USE NO NAME FOR ROLLBACK EXCEPT FOR "ROLLBACK TRAN -- <savepoint>".

ROLLBACK TRAN sp_two

Summary

- `BEGIN TRAN` increments @@TRANCOUNT and begins a transaction if there is not one open.
- `COMMIT` decrements @@TRANCOUNT and when it reaches 0, commits to the database.
- `ROLLBACK` rolls back to the beginning of the current transaction and proceeds with next stmt.
- `ROLLBACK TRAN <savepoint>` rolls back to named savepoint and proceeds with next stmt.

5.2 TRANSACTION CONTROL: ISOLATION LEVELS

5.2.1 Defining Isolation Levels

Four isolation levels are defined by ANSI SQL to permit you to choose the level of data protection you need for a given transaction. Isolation Levels let you balance acceptable correctness with performance (concurrency). Isolation Levels are implemented through locking of data. The four isolation levels are as follows.

- READ UNCOMMITTED—least strict, data inconsistency possible
- READ COMMITTED—default for Oracle and MSS
- REPEATABLE READ—fewer errors possible
- SERIALIZABLE—most strict, result will be correct

Three inconsistency problems that you may experience due to lack of isolation are listed below.

- Dirty Read = read data which is not committed (and might be rolled back later)
- Nonrepeatable read = Same query may return different value if done later in same txn
- Phantom phenomenon = Same query may return newly inserted rows later in same txn

Examples will show how these may cause incorrect results depending on the actions. The least strict level is READ UNCOMMITTED which allows all three inconsistency problems but gives the best performance. We'll show when it is an appropriate choice. The strictest level is SERIALIZABLE which will always provide the correct result but does so at a cost of slower performance. Sometimes speed is more important than absolute accuracy, as we'll explain below. The default isolation level for both Oracle and MSS is read committed. Table 5-1 shows which Isolation Level allows which inconsistency problem.

Table 5-1 Comparing Isolation Levels

Isolation level	Dirty read	Nonrepeatable read	Phantom
READ UNCOMMITTED	Yes	Yes	Yes
READ COMMITTED	No	Yes	Yes
REPEATABLE READ	No	No	Yes
SERIALIZABLE	No	No	No

5.2.2 Implementation of the Isolation Levels Using Locks (MSS)

The four isolation levels just described are actually implemented using locks as summarized here.

READ UNCOMMITTED — No locks are taken nor observed.

Example use: SELECT AVG(price) FROM stocks;

- Maximum concurrency as it observes no locks and takes no locks
- Reads dirty data, but often close enough for statistics such as determining table average

READ COMMITTED — Shared lock is taken during a read and then released

Example use: SELECT ename , salary FROM emps WHERE deptno = 100;

- Reads the last committed value, but the same query later in same transaction will return a different value if another txn has changed the value
- Will also allow phantom reads, which means that new inserts done by another user after our first query will be returned from a query later in same txn

REPEATABLE READ — Shared lock is taken for a read and held until end of transaction.

Example use: Read a value, calculate a value used to update the same record

- Reads last committed value and holds shared lock, so same query later in same transaction will return the same values for previous emps. Until we commit, other users are prevented from changing a value we have read in our transaction.
- However, permits phantoms which means that new emps inserted after the first query will appear if we execute the same query again in the same transaction.

SERIALIZABLE — Range shared lock is taken for the duration of the transaction.

Example use: Two reads of data for the same department in one transaction

- Reads last committed value and holds shared lock on range, perhaps entire table to preclude not only changes in existing records but also precludes new inserts. Least concurrency since large lock is kept until end of transaction.

The **default isolation level** for both Oracle and MSS is **READ COMMITTED**. See Figure 5-5.

Query Analyzer 1 - QA1

```
SQL: CREATE TABLE t (a INT , b INT );
INSERT INTO t  ( a , b ) VALUES ( 1 , 1 );
```

```
SQL: SELECT * FROM  t ;
```

```
Result:   a       b
          ---     ---
          1       1
```

--- SETUP is finished. Ready for test

```
SQL: BEGIN TRAN
```

```
SQL: SELECT * FROM  t ;
```

```
Result:   a       b
          ---     ---
          1       1
```

-- QA2 has changed and committed b to 2
QA1 will see this new value

```
SQL: SELECT * FROM  t ;
```

```
Result:   a       b
          ---     ---
          1       2
```

```
SQL: COMMIT
```

Query Analyzer 2 - QA2

```
SQL: SELECT * FROM  t ;
```

```
Result:   a       b
          ---     ---
          1       1
```

--- SETUP is finished. Ready for test

```
SQL: BEGIN TRAN
UPDATE t  SET  b = b + 1 WHERE a = 1 ;
COMMIT
```

```
SQL: SELECT * FROM  t ;
```

```
Result:   a       b
          ---     ---
          1       2
```

Figure 5-5 Demonstration that the default isolation level is READ COMMITTED.

5.2.3 Setting Isolation Level

To change the isolation level, use a SET TRANSACTION statement. For MSS, you only need to change from the default of READ COMMITTED.

5.2.3.1 MSS SET TRANSACTION

Syntax

```
SET TRANSACTION ISOLATION LEVEL
        { READ UNCOMMITTED   |  READ COMMITTED   |
          REPEATABLE READ    | SERIALIZABLE
        }
```

All subsequent transactions in the connection will have the specified isolation level.

MSS Example:

SQL

```
SET TRANSACTION ISOLATION LEVEL SERIALIZABLE
go

BEGIN TRANSACTION
UPDATE savings SET Balance = Balance - 1000
               WHERE customerid  =  444;
UPDATE checking SET Balance = Balance + 1000
               WHERE customerid  =  444;
COMMIT

SET TRANSACTION ISOLATION LEVEL READ COMMITTED
  -- To return to default
go
```

Question: Is it necessary to set the isolation level in this example?

Answer: Apparently not, since setting the isolation level applies only to how SELECT statements take shared locks and observe exclusive locks. Exclusive locks, once taken, are held until the end of the transaction. So the transaction is necessary for both isolation and atomicity, but the default isolation level of READ COMMITTED seems to be sufficient to ensure correctness. So, can you think of a good example where setting isolation level is appropriate?

5.2.3.2 Locking Hints

Table-level locking hints used in SELECT, INSERT, UPDATE, and DELETE statements override the current transaction isolation level for the session.

Locking Hints are the <table_hint> in FROM clause of SELECT, UPDATE & DELETE.

```
SELECT ... FROM tablename  [ WITH ( <table_hint> , ... n ) ]
<table_hint>

  NOLOCk -- Do not issue shared locks and do not honor exclusive locks.
  READPAST -- Skip locked rows.
  HOLDLOCK --  Hold a shared lock until completion of the transaction
  SERIALIZABLE -- Hold range lock on data set to prevent phantom reads.
  ...  See BOL for others
```

```
UPDATE tablename  [ WITH ( <table_hint_limited> , ... n ) ]
SET colname = expr [ WHERE <search_condition>]

DELETE FROM tablename  [ WITH ( <table_hint_limited> , ... n ) ]
[ WHERE <search_condition>]
<table_hint_limited>
  HOLDLOCK    --  Hold a shared lock until completion of the transaction
  SERIALIZABLE  -- Hold range lock on data set to prevent phantom reads.
  ...  See BOL for others
```

5.2.3.3 NOLOCK

Do not issue shared locks and do not honor exclusive locks. When this option is in effect, it is possible to read an uncommitted transaction or a set of pages that are rolled back in the middle of a read. Dirty reads are possible. NOLOCK only applies to the SELECT statement.

Example: Take no locks and observe no one else's locks.

```
SELECT AVG(stock_price)
FROM stocks
WITH (NOLOCK)
```

The average stock price of a very large number of stocks is a steadily changing value. It is useful only if it can be obtained quickly and does not slow down other transactions.

5.2.3.4 READPAST

READPAST skips locked rows. This option causes a transaction to skip over rows locked by other transactions that would ordinarily appear in the result set, rather than block the transaction waiting for the other transactions to release their locks on these rows. The READPAST lock hint applies only to transactions operating at READ COMMITTED isolation and will read only past row-level locks. It applies only to the SELECT statement.

5.2.3.5 HOLDLOCK

HOLDLOCK holds a shared lock until completion of the transaction instead of releasing the lock as soon as the required table, row or data page is no longer required.

Example:

```
SELECT *
FROM authors
HOLDLOCK
```

Example: This form also works.

```
SELECT *
FROM authors
WITH (HOLDLOCK)
```

5.3 SERVER SHUTDOWN

5.3.1 MSS 2000

Use the following steps to gracefully shut down an SQL Server in MSS 2000.

1. Broadcast a shutdown message. (See BOL: Broadcasting a Shutdown Message). Execute the following in a Windows Command Window (DOS window).

```
C:\> net send  /users  "SQL Server AMY is going down for maintenance in
20 minutes.
  Please finish work and disconnect asap."
```

Note: net send **/user msg** -- sends **msg** to all users connected to the sending host. net send **/domain msg** -- sends **msg** to all users in the domain.

2. Open an Enterprise Manager and Query Analyzer as sa. This must be done before pausing the server since you can't connect after pausing.

3. PAUSE the SQL Server.
   You can use Enterprise Manager or Service Manager.
   According to Books Online, when you pause Microsoft SQL Server, users who are connected to the server can continue, but new connections are not allowed.

4. Broadcast a Final Shutdown Message when the allotted time has expired.

   ```
   net send /users "SQL Server is going down
   immediately."
   ```

5. Set each user database you want to work on to RESTRICTED_USER mode (dbo and sa), probably by a script. For example:

SQL

```
ALTER DATABASE  pubs
    SET RESTRICTED_USER  WITH ROLLBACK IMMEDIATE
ALTER DATABASE  northwind
    SET RESTRICTED_USER  WITH ROLLBACK AFTER 60
...
```

   "IMMEDIATE" causes open connections to be terminated immediately, "AFTER 60" or "AFTER 60 SECONDS" terminates open connections after 60 seconds.

6. **STOP** the SQL Server.
   You can use Enterprise Manager or Service Manager.

7. **START** the SQL Server.
   It is now in RESTRICTED_USER mode allowing you to do maintenance.

8. Do your work on the server.

9. When finished, set each user database back to multiuser mode, possibly via an sql script.

SQL

```
ALTER DATABASE  pubs        SET MULTI_USER
ALTER DATABASE  northwind   SET MULTI_USER
...
```

10. Broadcast a message that SQL Server is back up.

```
C:\>  net send   /domain   "SQL Server AMY is operational."
```

5.3.2 MSS 7

Use the following steps to gracefully shut down an SQL Server in MSS 7.

1. Broadcast a shutdown message. (See BOL: Broadcasting a Shutdown Message). Execute the following in a Windows Command Window (DOS window).

```
C:\> net send /users SQL Server AMY is going down for maintenance in 20 minutes.
   Please finish work and disconnect asap."
```

Note: Using net send /user msg sends msg to all users connected the sending host and using net send /domain msg sends msg to all users in the domain.

2. Open an Enterprise Manager and Query Analyzer as sa. This must be done before pausing the server since you can't connect after pausing.

3. PAUSE the SQL Server.
You can use Enterprise Manager or Service Manager. According to Books Online, when you pause Microsoft SQL Server, users who are connected to the server can continue, but new connections are not allowed.

4. Broadcast a Final Shutdown Message when the allotted time has expired.

```
net send /users "SQL Server is going down
immediately."
```

5. Set each user database you want to work on to 'dbo use only', probably by script. For example:

SQL

```
EXEC sp_dboption 'pubs', 'dbo use only' , 'TRUE'
EXEC sp_dboption 'northwind', 'dbo use only', 'TRUE'
....
```

This statement will fail if anyone is using the database, so rerun the script after restarting the server.

You can see who is connected to each database in Query Analyzer with "EXEC **sp_who**" or in Enterprise Manager with
EM: *ServerName* – Management – Current Activity – Process Info

6. **STOP** the SQL Server.
   You can use Enterprise Manager or Service Manager.
7. **START** the SQL Server.
   Rerun the 'dbo use only' script to catch any remaining databases.
   It is now in 'dbo use only' mode allowing you to do maintenance.
8. Do your work on the server.
9. When finished, set each user database to multiuser mode, possibly via an sql script.

SQL

```
EXEC sp_dboption pubs, 'dbo use only' , 'FALSE'
EXEC sp_dboption  northwind, 'dbo use only', 'FALSE'
...
```

10. Broadcast a message that SQL Server is back up.

```
C:\>  net send   /domain   "SQL Server AMY is operational."
```

5.4 @@VERSION

5.4.1 Identifying Version and Service Pack

Run SELECT @@version.

SQL

```
SELECT @@version
```

Result

```
---------------------------------------------------------------
Microsoft SQL Server  2000 - 8.00.534 (Intel X86)
May 23 2001 00:02:52
Copyright (c) 1988-2000 Microsoft Corporation
Personal Edition on Windows NT 5.0 (Build 2195: Service Pack 1)
```

8.00.***532*** on the first line contains "8.00" which indicates you have MSS 2000 (8.0). The numbers "***532***" are the three digits specifying which Service Pack level is installed:

MSS 2000 Version and Service Pack Information

- MSS 2000 with no SP: 8.00.**194**
- MSS 2000 with SP 1: 8.00.**384**
- MSS 2000 with SP 2: 8.00.**532** or **534**
- MSS 2000 with SP 3 or 3a: 8.00.**760**

MSS 7.0 Version and Service Pack Information

SQL

```
SELECT @@version
```

Result

```
--------------------------------------------------------------
Microsoft SQL Server  7.00 - 7.00.961 (Intel X86)
Mar  2 2000 06:49:37
Copyright (c) 1988-1998 Microsoft Corporation
Desktop Edition on Windows NT 5.0 (Build 2195: Service Pack 1)
```

- MSS 7.0 with no SP: 7.00.**623**
- MSS 7.0 with SP 1: 7.00.**699**
- MSS 7.0 with SP 2: 7.00.**842**
- MSS 7.0 with SP 3: 7.00.**961**

Other useful functions to show system and user information are as follows.

SQL

```
SELECT @@servername
```

Result

```
--------------------------------------------------------------
AMY
```

SQL

```
SELECT SUSER_SNAME()
```

Result

```
----------------------------------------------------------------
sa
```

SQL

```
SELECT CURRENT_USER
```

Result

```
----------------------------------------------------------------
dbo
```

5.5 BACKUP AND RESTORE

5.5.1 File System Backup vs. Database Backup

Both File System Backups by the computer system administrator and Database Backups by the Database Administrator are required to ensure recoverability of a database server machine from failure.

A **File System Backup** copies all files on a computer to tape or other disk from the machine being backed up. This is usually the responsibility of the computer system administrator. A file system backup is necessary in order to account for all files on the computer.

A **Database Backup** is a specially formatted copy of one database's data and metadata in one or more files **sufficient to completely recreate the database**. This is usually the responsibility of the Database Administrator (DBA). If the backup resides on the same machine as the database, it must be copied to a physically separate disk. A copy is often kept in a separate facility to recover in the event of major disaster such as flood, fire, etc. A database backup ensures that all parts of the backup for a database are consistent. It is also the DBA's responsibility to ensure database durability. For this reason, he or she cannot rely on the computer system administrator.

Be sure to test your database backup to ensure that it is functioning!

5.5.2 Database Backup

The following terminology describes database backup operations.

- Backup—A set of one or more files that enable complete restoration of a database. Backups are composed of Transaction Log backup files and data backup files.
- Transaction Log—A record of all changes made in a database.
- Transaction—An atomic unit of database work (see detail starting on page 529).

Example:

```
BEGIN TRANSACTION
  UPDATE savings   SET balance = balance -  1000 WHERE ownerid = 15;
  UPDATE checking SET balance = balance + 1000 WHERE ownerid = 15;
COMMIT ( or ROLLBACK)
```

- A streaming disk image of every change made to the database.
- Stored in .LDF file.
- Writes complete to tran log before to data file.
- Transaction completed with either COMMIT or ROLLBACK.
- Every DDL statement does a commit (it has no rollback capability once executed).

- Data Backup File—A file containing the current image or differential image of the data.
- Restore and Recovery—These processes use the transaction log and data backup file(s) as shown in Figure 5-6.

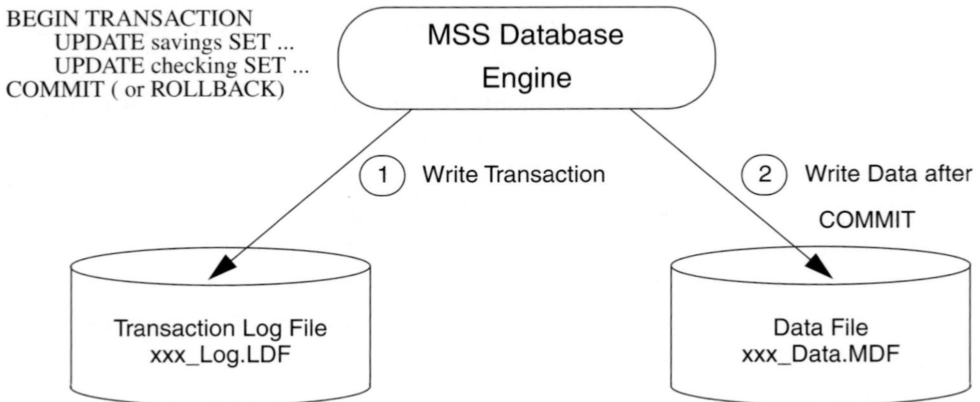

Figure 5-6 Recording a Transaction to Transaction Log File and Data File.

5.5.3 Types of SQL Server Database Backup

There are four kinds of database backups:

- **FBU (Full Database Backup)**—Complete copy of the database in one file, fuzzy. All db data and metadata pages are copied as well as the transaction log of all changes occurring from begin to end of backup. It contains an accurate snapshot of the db as of the completion time of the backup.
- **DBU (Differential Database Backup)**— All changes since last FBU, fuzzy, cumulative. DBU contains all data and metadata pages changed since the last FBU. DBU is cumulative since the last FBU, so only the FBU and most recent DBU are needed. DBU is also a fuzzy backup including the transaction log of all changes made during the backup
- **TLBU (Transaction Log Backup)**—Transaction log since last FBU, DBU or TLBU, incremental. TLBU backs up just transaction log contents since the last FBU or DBU or TLBU. It is incremental, so you need every TLBU since the last FBU or DBU.
- **F/FGBU (File or File Group Backup)**— Just specified files or file groups. FGBU backs up specified file(s) or file group(s). It is useful for very large databases but requires very careful planning for the database to be recoverable. This is quite advanced DBA work.

Books Online advises caution. Backups created with Microsoft SQL Server version 7.0 and later cannot be restored in SQL Server 6.5 and earlier.

Restrictions: In MSS 7 and later, FBUs and DBUs are fuzzy backups that can be done with the db in operation but are restricted to DML operations (INSERT, UPDATE, DELETE, SELECT). **DDL operations are not allowed during backup on the database being backed up.**

Deac's Example Backup Strategy (Backup Schedule): Use this schedule for OLTP database, which includes important data but does not require super high reliability such as banking, which would need clustering, mirroring, etc.

- Saturday night: Full Database Backup
- Nightly: Differential Database Backup
- 10 am, 2 pm, 6 pm: Transaction Log Backup

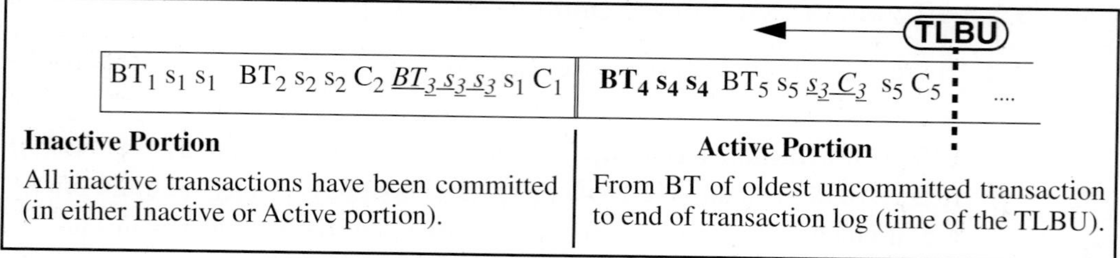

Figure 5-7 A TLBU example.

5.5.4 Transaction Log Backup (TLBU)

The transaction log is a *stream of log records* of transactions for a given database. The transaction log records *every change to the db*, including Inserts, Updates, Deletes and DDL. The log records for each transaction contain a *before image* and *after image* of the row. The transaction log backup (TLBU) backs up the entire transaction log, both active and inactive portions. Then truncates (deletes) the inactive portion. (See Figure 5-7.)

Definitions

- **Active Portion of the Transaction Log**—The portion of the transaction log from the BEGIN TRAN of the oldest uncommited transaction to end of the transaction log.
- **Inactive Portion of the Transaction Log**—The portion of the transaction log from the beginning of the transaction log to the beginning of the active portion of the log.
- **Truncating the Transaction Log**—Delete all log records in the inactive portion of the log.
- **Checkpoint**—The database engine periodically does a "checkpoint" where it writes all data changes from memory to the data file.
- **Recovery**—The *recovery* process occurs at SQL Server system startup to make the database "operational" or ready for user access. Recovery is required at server startup to ensure that the database data is in a consistent state before allowing users to access and change the data. For example, if the server crashed, then some transactions may have been committed and logged to the transaction log file but not yet written to the data file. These transactions need to be *rolled forward* (see below) during recovery to gain consis-

tency. Other transactions may have dirty data in the data file for a transaction that was not committed and must thus be *rolled back* (described below).

- **Roll Back**—Writes the before image from the transaction log to the data file. This occurs during system recovery for each uncommited transaction in the log file.
- **Roll Forward**—Writes the after image from the transaction log to the data file. This occurs during system recovery for each commited transaction in the log file.

To minimize the amount of time required to complete the recovery process, the server periodically executes a Checkpoint (described above). Only that portion of the transaction log after the latest checkpoint must be checked during recovery.

Three Approaches to Database Backup

FBU/DBU/TLBU — Production OLTP database.

FBU/DBU — Read-only database (maybe just FBU).

No BU — Test or Development database which does not need up to date production data.

(Do back up your development code, of course.)

5.5.5 MSS 2000 Recovery Models

SQL Server 2000 management of transaction logging is incorporated in the three different Recovery Models described in this section.

- The Simple Recovery Model enables "truncate log on checkpoint" (see p. 570).
- Intensive Operations, a term invented here to describe the statements listed in Table 5-2, are logged differently in each of the three recovery models.

Table 5-2 Intensive Operations

SELECT List INTO (p. 441)	bcp (bcp/Bulk Copy), p. 561	Bulk Insert (p. 561)
CREATE INDEX (p. 267)	**text** and **image** operations (WRITETEXT, UPDATETEXT, p. 109)	

The main features of the three recovery models in MSS 2000 are summarized in Table 5-3.

Table 5-3 Summary of SQL Server 2000 Recovery Models

Recovery Model	Characteristics	Recover to What Point?
1 **Simple**	**Intensive Operations** are allowed but not logged. Truncate Log on Checkpoint is enabled. Keeps used transaction log space small. Transaction log backups are of no use.	Can recover to the end of any database backup (FBU or DBU). May be used for test databases and possibly for read-only databases.
2 **Bulk-Logged**	**Intensive Operations** are allowed but minimally logged (BOL calls this both minimally logged and nonlogged). Minimal logging of these operations uses less transaction log space and performs them more quickly than full logging. They can be rolled back but not rolled for ward. If the data file is lost, all intensive operations must be redone.	Can recover to the end of any backup (FBU, DBU or TLBU). Point-In-Time Recovery is not supported. I would do a DBU as soon as is convenient.
3 **Full**	**Intensive Operations** are allowed and fully logged (slow), which means that they may be rolled back or rolled forward. Can recover to an arbitrary point in time (for example, prior to application or user error). No work is lost due to a lost or damaged data file.	Can recover to the end of any backup (FBU, DBU or TLBU). Point-In-Time Recovery from the transaction log *is* supported. Use for production OLTP databases.

5.5.5.1 Change Recovery Models

Use the following guides to change the current recovery model for a database (EM or QA).

- **Enterprise Manager (EM):** Open console tree to Servername – Databases – databasename; right click on databasename; select properties: Choose Recovery Model from the menu.
- **Query Analyzer (QA):** Use ALTER DATABASE command as shown.

Syntax

```
ALTER DATABASE database   SET RECOVERY {FULL | BULK_LOGGED | SIMPLE}
```

Example: Set **mydb** database to Full Recovery model.

```
SQL
ALTER DATABASE mydb SET RECOVERY FULL
```

5.5.5.2 Deac's Suggested Recovery Model Strategies

For a **production database,** use the Full Recovery model. If you must do an intensive operation, do it during nonpeak load times. Start with a TLBU, switch to Bulk-Logged model, do the intensive operation, switch back to Full Recovery model and do either FBU or DBU.

For a **read-only, test or development database,** use the Simple Recovery model. For development, you must still remember to back up your development code and objects. If you must do an intensive operation, do it during nonpeak load times. Start with a TLBU, switch to Bulk-Logged model, do the intensive operation, switch back to Full Recovery model and do either FBU or DBU.

IMPORTANT: Loss of a transaction log is nonrecoverable. If the active transaction log is lost (for example, the transaction log disk crashes), all transactions in that log are lost and may not be recovered, even if written to the data disk, which now becomes unusable. To prevent loss of the active transaction log, place the transaction log files on mirrored disks.

5.5.5.3 Other Minimally Logged Operation

```
TRUNCATE TABLE tablename
```

- removes all rows from a table without logging each row deleted
- resets IDENTITY column to its initial (seed) value
- is faster than **DELETE FROM** *tablename* with no WHERE clause

5.5.5.4 Bulk Data Operation Settings in SQL Server 7.0

The operations "SELECT list INTO" and "BULK COPY" are not logged on MSS 7.0 before and must be enabled through database properties to be able to execute either. For a production OLTP database the 'select into/bulk copy' option normally should be set to FALSE and turned on only when one of the two operations is required. The operation should be followed by setting the option back to FALSE and doing either FBU or DBU.

5.5.6 BACKUP DATABASE, BACKUP LOG

There are separate statements to backup a database (including data and metadata) and to backup the transaction log.

5.5.6.1 Backup Database

The statement to backup a database (including data and metadata) is given here.

Simplified Syntax

```
BACKUP DATABASE <db> TO <backup-device>WITH <options>
```

Example: Full backup of the pubs database.

SQL

```
BACKUP DATABASE pubs
  TO DISK = 'F:\MSSQL\BACKUP\pubs.BAK'
  WITH INIT, NAME = 'Pubs FULL backup'
     -- INIT causes overwrite
```

Example: Differential backup of the pubs database.

SQL

```
BACKUP DATABASE pubs
  TO DISK = 'F:\MSSQL\BACKUP\pubs.BAK'
  WITH DIFFERENTIAL,
    NOINIT
 -- Use NOINIT if you use the same file as
 -- for full backup
```

You've just done a differential database backup. Test the backup!

5.5.6.2 Backup Log—SQL Command to Back Up the Tran Log

The statement to back up a transaction log for a given database is given here.

Syntax

```
BACKUP LOG <db> TO <backup-device> [WITH <options>]


<options> ::= INIT | NOINIT | NO_TRUNCATE | ....
```

Example: Use the backup command to back up the pubs database:

```
SQL
BACKUP LOG pubs
  TO DISK = 'F:\MSSQL\BACKUP\pubs.BAK'
  WITH NOINIT
 -- append, as when you use the same file as
 -- for full backup
```

BACKUP LOG performs two steps:

1. Copies the active and inactive portion of Tran Log to specified disk file
2. Truncates the Tran Log which means it deletes the inactive portion just copied. The Tran Log retains the active portion.

Note: Log files should be put on separate physical disks from Data and Index files.

5.5.7 BACKUP DATABASE

This code backs up an entire database or one or more files or filegroups.

Syntax

```
BACKUP DATABASE {database_name | @database_name_var}
   [< file_or_filegroup > [ ,...n ]  ]  -- Use this to back up only specific
files or filegroups
TO < backup_device > [ ,...n ]
[ WITH
   [ BLOCKSIZE = { blocksize | @blocksize_variable } ]
   [ [ , ] DESCRIPTION = { 'text' | @text_variable } ]
   [ [ , ] DIFFERENTIAL ]
   [ [ , ] EXPIREDATE = { date | @date_var } | RETAINDAYS = { days | @days_var } ]
   [ [ , ] PASSWORD = { password | @password_variable } ]
   [ [ , ] { FORMAT | NOFORMAT } ]
   [ [ , ] { INIT | NOINIT } ]
   [ [ , ] MEDIADESCRIPTION = { 'text' | @text_variable } ]
   [ [ , ] MEDIANAME = { media_name | @media_name_variable } ]
   [ [ , ] MEDIAPASSWORD = { mediapassword | @mediapassword_variable } ]
   [ [ , ] NAME = { backup_set_name | @backup_set_name_var } ]
   [ [ , ] { NOSKIP | SKIP } ]
   [ [ , ] { NOREWIND | REWIND } ]
   [ [ , ] { NOUNLOAD | UNLOAD } ]
   [ [ , ] RESTART ]
   [ [ , ] STATS [ = percentage ] ]
]
```

```
 < file_or_filegroup > ::=

   {
     FILE = { logical_file_name | @logical_file_name_var }
   | FILEGROUP = { logical_filegroup_name | @logical_filegroup_name_var }
   }


< backup_device > ::=

   {
     { logical_backup_device_name | @logical_backup_device_name_var }
  | {DISK | TAPE} = { 'physical_backup_device_name' |
-- @physical_backup_device_name_var }
   }
```

Arguments

{ database_name | @database_name_var }

This is the database to be backed up.

< file_or_filegroup >

If the < file_or_filegroup > clause is **missing**, then a full or differential database backup of the entire database is specified.

If the < file_or_filegroup > clause is specified, only those files and filegroups of that database are backed up.

Note: During a full database or differential backup, MSS backs up enough of the transaction log to produce a consistent database for when the database is restored. Only a full database backup can be performed on the **master** database.

... n

Following this marker indicates that multiple files and filegroups may be specified. There is no maximum number of files or filegroups.

FILE = { logical_file_name | @logical_file_name_var }

This names one or more files to include in the database backup.

FILEGROUP = { logical_filegroup_name | @logical_filegroup_name_var }

This names one or more filegroups to include in the database backup.

File and filegroup backups are not allowed if the recovery model is simple.

Note: Use file and filegroup backup when the database size and performance requirements make a full database backup impractical. To restore a database from file and filegroup backups, a separate transaction log backup must be provided by using BACKUP LOG. For more information about file and filegroup backups, see "Using File Backups" in Books Online.

< backup_device >

This specifies the logical or physical backup device to use for the backup operation. Can be one or more of the following:

... n

Following this marker indicates that multiple backup devices may be specified. The maximum number of backup devices is 64.

{ logical_backup_device_name } | { @logical_backup_device_name_var }

This is the logical name of the backup device(s) (created by **sp_addumpdevice**) to which the database is backed up.

{ DISK | TAPE } = 'physical_backup_device_name' | @phys_backup_dev_name_var

This string allows backups to be created on the specified disk or tape device.

Backup to tape is not supported on Windows 98.

BLOCKSIZE = { blocksize | @blocksize_variable }

This specifies the physical block size, in bytes. On Windows NT systems, the default is the default block size of the device. Usually this parameter is not required because SQL Server will choose a block size that is appropriate to the device. On Windows 2000–based computers, the default is 65,536 (64 KB, which is the maximum size SQL Server supports).

For DISK backup, SQL Server determines the appropriate block size for disk devices.

Note: To transfer the resulting backup set to a CD-ROM and then restore from that CD-ROM, set BLOCKSIZE to 2048. The default BLOCKSIZE for tape is 65,536 (64 KB). Explicitly stating a block size overrides SQL Server's selection of a block size.

DESCRIPTION = { '*text*' | @*text_variable* }

You may provide comments, up to 255 characters, describing the backup set.

DIFFERENTIAL

This specifies that the database or file backup will consist only of the portions of the database or file changed since the last full backup. See BOL: on "Differential Database Backups."

Note: During a full database or differential backup, SQL Server backs up enough of the transaction log to produce a consistent database when the database is restored.

EXPIREDATE = { date | @date_var }

This declares the date when the backup set expires and can be overwritten.

RETAINDAYS = { days | @days_var }

This string specifies the number of days that must elapse before this backup media set can be overwritten. If supplied as a variable (@days_var), it must be specified as an integer.

Note: If EXPIREDATE or RETAINDAYS is not specified, expiration is determined by the **media retention** configuration setting of **sp_configure**. These options only prevent SQL Server from overwriting a file.

PASSWORD = { password | @password_variable }

This sets the password for the backup set. PASSWORD is a character string. If a password is defined for the backup set, the password must be supplied to perform any restore operation from the backup set.

FORMAT | NOFORMAT

FORMAT specifies that the media header should be written on all volumes used for this backup operation. Any existing media header is overwritten. The FORMAT option invalidates the entire media contents, ignoring any existing content.

Note: Use FORMAT carefully. Formatting one backup device or medium renders the entire media set unusable. For example, if a single tape belonging to an existing striped media set is initialized, the entire media set is rendered useless.

The FORMAT keyword includes SKIP and INIT whether or not explicitly stated.

NOFORMAT, the default, specifies the media header not be written on all volumes for this backup operation and does not rewrite the backup device unless INIT is specified.

INIT | NOINIT

INIT specifies that all backup sets should be overwritten, but the header is preserved.

The backup medium is not overwritten if any one of the following conditions is met:

- All backup sets on the media have not yet expired. See the EXPIREDATE and RETAINDAYS options.
- The backup set name given in the BACKUP statement, if provided, does not match the name on the backup medium. See the NAME clause.

- Use the SKIP option to override these checks. For more information about interactions when using SKIP, NOSKIP, INIT and NOINIT, see the "Remarks" section of the BACKUP statement in Books Online.

NOINIT, the default, indicates that the backup set is appended to the specified disk or tape device, preserving existing backup sets.

MEDIADESCRIPTION = { text | @text_variable }

You may provide comments, up to 255 characters, describing the media set.

MEDIANAME = { media_name | @media_name_variable }

This string specifies the media name, a maximum of 128 characters, for the entire backup media set. If MEDIANAME is specified, it must match the previously specified media name already existing on the backup volume(s). If not specified or if the SKIP option is specified, there is no verification check of the media name.

MEDIAPASSWORD = { mediapassword | @mediapassword_variable }

This sets the password for the media set. MEDIAPASSWORD is a character string. If a password is defined for the media set, the password must be supplied to create a backup set on that media set and to perform any restore operation from the media set. Password-protected media may be overwritten only by reformatting with the FORMAT option.

NAME = { backup_set_name | @backup_set_var }

This specifies the name of the backup set. Names can have a maximum of 128 characters. If NAME is not specified, it is blank.

NOREWIND | REWIND -- Used only for tape devices

NOREWIND specifies that SQL Server will keep the tape open after the backup operation. NOREWIND implies NOUNLOAD. SQL Server will retain ownership of the tape drive until a BACKUP or RESTORE command is used WITH REWIND.

REWIND, the default, specifies that SQL Server will rewind and release the tape. If neither NOREWIND nor REWIND is specified, REWIND is the default.

NOSKIP | SKIP

NOSKIP instructs the BACKUP statement to check the expiration date of all backup sets on the medium before allowing them to be overwritten.

SKIP disables the backup set expiration and name checking.

NOUNLOAD | UNLOAD

This is used only for tape devices.

NOUNLOAD specifies the tape is not unloaded automatically from the tape drive after a backup. NOUNLOAD remains set until UNLOAD is specified.

UNLOAD specifies that the tape is automatically rewound and unloaded when the backup is finished. UNLOAD remains in effect until NOUNLOAD is specified.

UNLOAD is set by default when a new user session is started. The last one specified remains in effect until the next BACKUP statement with a different value.

RESTART

This is used only for tape devices. It specifies that SQL Server restarts an interrupted backup operation.

The RESTART option restarts the backup operation at the point it was interrupted. To RESTART a specific backup operation, repeat the entire BACKUP statement and add the RESTART option. Using the RESTART option is not required but it can save you time.

Note: This option can only be used for backups directed to tape media and for backups that span multiple tape volumes. A restart operation never occurs on the first backup volume.

STATS [= *percentage*]

Displays a message each time another *percentage* completes, and is used to gauge progress. If *percentage* is omitted, SQL Server displays a message after each 10 percent is completed.

Example: Simple backup and restore example. To back up database **mydb**:

SQL

```
BACKUP DATABASE mydb
  --  Backup may be done while database is
  -- in MULTI_USER operation
  TO DISK = 'F:\MSSQL\BACKUP\mydb.BAK'
  WITH INIT
```

To obtain exclusive access, put database **mydb** in SINGLE_USER (rudely) and make sure your connection is not in that database. (See page 550 for a more graceful shutdown.)

SQL

```
USE master
go
ALTER DATABASE  mydb
     SET SINGLE_USER  WITH ROLLBACK IMMEDIATE
RESTORE DATABASE mydb
      FROM DISK = 'F:\MSSQL\BACKUP\mydb.BAK'
ALTER DATABASE  mydb     SET MULTI_USER
```

For further information, see “Database Layout for Performance and Restorability,” page 588, and examples “Backup/Restore Damaged .MDF,” page 592 and “Production Datebase,” page 598.

5.5.8 BACKUP LOG

5.5.8.1 Backing up a Transaction Log

This code backs up (and truncates) the transaction log of the specified database; see page 558. The log is backed up from the last successfully executed LOG backup to the current end of the log. Once the log is backed up, the space may be truncated when no longer required by replication or active transactions.

Note: If backing up the log does not appear to truncate most of the log, an old open transaction may exist in the log. Log space can be monitored with

```
DBCC SQLPERF (LOGSPACE)
```

Syntax

```
BACKUP LOG { database_name | @database_name_var }
TO < backup_device > [ ,...n ]
[ WITH
   [ BLOCKSIZE = { blocksize | @blocksize_variable } ]
   [ [ , ] DESCRIPTION = { 'text' | @text_variable } ]
   [ [ ,] EXPIREDATE = { date | @date_var }| RETAINDAYS = { days | @days_var } ]
   [ [ , ] PASSWORD = { password | @password_variable } ]
   [ [ , ] { FORMAT | NOFORMAT } ]
   [ [ , ] { INIT | NOINIT } ]
   [ [ , ] MEDIADESCRIPTION = { 'text' | @text_variable } ]
   [ [ , ] MEDIANAME = { media_name | @media_name_variable } ]
   [ [ , ] MEDIAPASSWORD = { mediapassword | @mediapassword_variable } ]
   [ [ , ] NAME = { backup_set_name | @backup_set_name_var } ]
   [ [ , ] NO_TRUNCATE ]
   [ [ , ] { NORECOVERY | STANDBY = undo_file_name } ]
   [ [ , ] { NOREWIND | REWIND } ]
```

```
    [ [ , ] { NOSKIP | SKIP } ]
    [ [ , ] { NOUNLOAD | UNLOAD } ]
    [ [ , ] RESTART ]
    [ [ , ] STATS [ = percentage ] ]
]
```

5.5.8.2 Truncating the Transaction Log

This code truncates the transaction log of the specified database without backing it up. Truncating the log means to delete the inactive portion of the log, see page 558.

Syntax

```
BACKUP LOG { database_name | @database_name_var }
 WITH  { NO_LOG | TRUNCATE_ONLY }
```

Arguments

The parameters for BACKUP LOG are the same as for BACKUP DATABASE given in the previous section except for the following.

NO_TRUNCATE

This allows backing up the log in situations where the database is damaged. Example, p. 592.

NO_LOG | TRUNCATE_ONLY

This removes the inactive part of the log without making a backup copy of it and truncates the log. This option frees space. Specifying a backup device is unnecessary because the log backup is not saved. NO_LOG and TRUNCATE_ONLY are synonyms.

After using NO_LOG or TRUNCATE_ONLY to back up the log, the changes recorded in the log are not recoverable. For recovery purposes, immediately execute BACKUP DATABASE.

NORECOVERY

NORECOVERY is used only with BACKUP LOG. It backs up the tail of the log and leaves the database in the Restoring state. NORECOVERY is useful when failing over to a secondary database or when saving the tail of the log prior to a RESTORE operation.

STANDBY = *undo_file_name*

This is used only with BACKUP LOG. It backs up the tail of the log and leaves the database in read-only and standby mode. The undo file name specifies storage to hold rollback changes, which must be undone if RESTORE LOG operations are to be subsequently applied.

Example: Simple backup and restore example. To back up database **mydb** with FULL backup and LOG backup:

SQL

```
ALTER DATABASE  mydb  SET  RECOVERY FULL
 -- To log transactions and allow log backups
BACKUP DATABASE mydb
      -- Backup may be done while database
      -- is in MULTI_USER operation
      TO DISK = 'F:\MSSQL\BACKUP\mydb.BAK'
      WITH INIT
-- Some time later
BACKUP LOG  mydb
      TO DISK = 'F:\MSSQL\BACKUP\mydb.BAK'
      WITH  NOINIT
```

Example: Restore database **mydb** with FULL backup and LOG backup.

To obtain exclusive access, put database **mydb** in SINGLE_USER (rudely) and make sure your connection is not in that database. (See page 550 for a more graceful shutdown.)

SQL

```
USE master
go
ALTER DATABASE  mydb
     SET SINGLE_USER  WITH ROLLBACK IMMEDIATE
RESTORE DATABASE mydb
      FROM DISK = 'F:\MSSQL\BACKUP\mydb.BAK'
      WITH FILE = 1, NORECOVERY
RESTORE LOG     mydb
      FROM DISK = 'F:\MSSQL\BACKUP\mydb.BAK'
      WITH FILE = 2, RECOVERY
      -- RECOVERY is the default, but I prefer
      -- to state it for clarity
ALTER DATABASE  mydb     SET MULTI_USER
```

5.5.9 Truncate Log—Emptying the Transaction Log

Truncating the log means deleting all Inactive log records. Log truncation reduces the current Transaction Log to a minimum. (It leaves only the Active portion.)

5.5.9.1 When Is the Log Truncated?

BACKUP LOG statement (and only BACKUP LOG) always truncates the tran log file.

Two Uses of BACKUP LOG

1. **TLBU (LOG BACKUP MODE):** a Real Tran Log Backup—this mode saves the Tran Log and then truncates the log.

   ```
   BACKUP LOG pubs TO DISK 'F:\MSS_BAK\pubs.bak' WITH NOINIT
   ```

2. **TRUNCATE LOG ONLY (LOG TRUNCATE MODE):** this truncates the log but does *not* back up the inactive portion—this mode renders prior TLBUs useless.

   ```
   BACKUP LOG pubs WITH TRUNCATE_ONLY

   BACKUP LOG pubs WITH  NO_LOG
   ```

   These two statements have identical results for MSS 7.0 and later. Consider them to be advanced DBA tools for use in emergency only because they leave the transaction log unusable for a restore.

   If tran log (or tran log disk) fills up, no changes may be made to the database. You may use TRUNCATE_ONLY to make the database operational but should immediately do a database backup (FBU or DBU) and then add a disk to solve your disk problem.

   Consider a given database to be in either of the following modes defined for MSS 7.

   - **LOG BACKUP MODE**—You maintain FBU/DBUs plus a sequence of TLBUs. Do a version of Statement 1 above.
     Uses: for **production OLTP databases**

     or

   - **LOG TRUNCATE MODE**—Log truncate mode allows no TLBUs, making current tran logs useless for a restore although the Active portion of the log is maintained because it is still required for Recovery. Use either of the commands in Statement 2 above.
     Uses: For no backup desired (**read-only** or **test databases**) OR FBU/DBU-only databases

The following guidelines apply for MSS 2000.

- *Simple* recovery model is in LOG TRUNCATE MODE.
  NO_LOG and TRUNCATE ONLY are the only BACKUP LOG options allowed.
- *Bulk Logged* and *Full* recovery models are in LOG BACKUP MODE.
  NO_LOG and TRUNCATE ONLY are not allowed BACKUP LOG options.

5.5.10 BACKUP—1. Backup Dialog

This is first of two ways to do database backups: full, differential, transaction log or file/file group.

In this demonstration, we'll back up the pubs database in EM:

- select **Databases – pubs**
- right click on **pubs** and
- select **All Tasks** – **Backup Database** ...

You'll see the dialog shown in Figure 5-8.

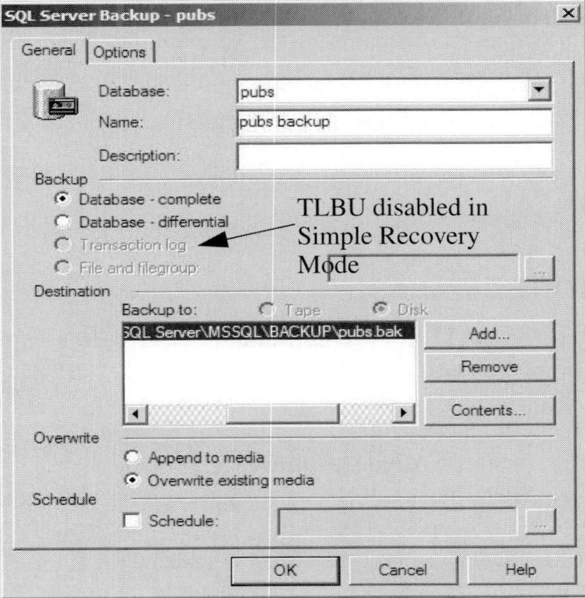

Figure 5-8 The Backup Database General Dialog box.

Confirm the choices or, if you wish, change them.
For a full database backup choose:

- General tab
  - Database: **pubs**
  - Name: **pubs FULL backup**
  - Backup: Database — **complete**
  - Destination: File of your choice (I use "pubs.bak")
  - Overwrite: **Overwrite existing media** (you may use "Append" for DBU and TLBU).
- Options tab
  - You may leave the options.
  - The choice "Verify backup upon completion" does basic disk consistency check.
- Click OK

You've just done a FULL DATABASE BACKUP of the pubs database. After it's finished, open your Windows Explorer to look at the backup file created. If you wish, view the file details and compare the size of backup to the size of the data file.

Note: If the **Transaction Log** option is unavailable, ensure that:

- For MSS 7, the **trunc. log on chkpt.** database option is not set
- For MSS 2K, the **Recovery Model** database option is not set to "simple"

Test the backup to ensure that it's functioning!
Test the backup to ensure it's good!

5.5.11 RESTORE DATABASE

The RESTORE DATABASE command restores backups taken using the BACKUP command. Unlike BACKUP DATABASE, RESTORE DATABASE requires exclusive database access.

5.5.11.1 Restore an Entire Database

Syntax

```
RESTORE DATABASE { database_name | @database_var }
[FROM < backup_device > [ ,...n ] ]  -- If omitted, must specify
[NO]RECOVERY or STANDBY
[WITH
```

```
    [ < remaining_with_clause > ]
    [ [ , ] KEEP_REPLICATION ]
    [ [ , ] { NORECOVERY | RECOVERY | STANDBY = undo_file_name } ]
]
```

5.5.11.2 Restore Part of a Database

See "Partial Database Restore Operations" in Books Online for more detail.

Syntax

```
RESTORE DATABASE { database_name | @database_var } < file_or_filegroup >
  --[ ,...n ]
  [FROM < backup_device > [ ,...n ] ]
  -- If omitted, must specify NORECOVERY
  WITH   PARTIAL
     [ < remaining_with_clause > ]
     [ [ , ] NORECOVERY ]
```

5.5.11.3 Restore Specific Files or Filegroups

Syntax

```
RESTORE DATABASE { database_name | @database_var } < file_or_filegroup > [ ,...n ]
   [FROM < backup_device > [ ,...n ] ] -- If omitted, must specify NORECOVERY
   [ WITH
      [ < remaining_with_clause > ]
      [ [ , ] NORECOVERY ]
   ]


< remaining_with_clause > ::=
   [ RESTRICTED_USER ]
   [ [ , ] FILE = { file_number | @file_number } ]
   [ [ , ] PASSWORD = { password | @password_variable } ]
   [ [ , ] MEDIANAME = { media_name | @media_name_variable } ]
   [ [ , ] MEDIAPASSWORD = { mediapassword | @mediapassword_variable } ]
   [ [ , ] MOVE 'logical_file_name' TO 'operating_system_file_name' ] [ ,...n ]
   [ [ , ] { NOREWIND | REWIND } ]
   [ [ , ] { NOUNLOAD | UNLOAD } ]
   [ [ , ] REPLACE ]
   [ [ , ] RESTART ]
   [ [ , ] STATS [ = percentage ] ]


< file_or_filegroup > ::=
{
     FILE = { logical_file_name | @logical_file_name_var }
   | FILEGROUP = { logical_filegroup_name | @logical_filegroup_name_var }
}
```

```
   < backup_device > ::=
{
     { logical_backup_device_name | @logical_backup_device_name_var }
  | {DISK | TAPE} = { 'physical_backup_device_name' |
@physical_backup_device_name_var }
}
```

Arguments

{database_name | @database_name_var}

This is the database that the database backup is to be restored into. It is also the database that the log is to be restored into.

FROM

This specifies the backup devices from which to restore the backup. If the FROM clause is not specified, the restore of a backup does not take place but instead, the database is recovered. This can be used to attempt recovery of a database that has been restored with the NORECOVERY option, or to switch over to a standby server. If the FROM clause is omitted, NORECOVERY, RECOVERY or STANDBY must be specified.

< file_or_filegroup >

This specifies the names of the logical files or filegroups to be restored.

... n

Following this marker indicates that multiple files and filegroups may be specified. There is no maximum number of files or filegroups.

FILE = { logical_file_name | @logical_file_name_var }

FILE names one or more files to include in the database restore.

FILEGROUP = { logical_filegroup_name | @logical_filegroup_name_var }

FILEGROUP names one or more filegroups to include in the database restore.

If any of the files being restored when < file_or_filegroup > is used, the transaction log must be applied to the database files after the last file or file-group restore operation to roll the files forward to be consistent with the rest of the database. If none of the files being restored have been modified since they were last backed up, a transaction log does not have to be applied. The RESTORE statement informs the user of the situation.

< backup_device >

This string specifies the logical or physical backup device to use for the restore operation. Can be one or more of the following:

- ... *n*
- Following this marker indicates that indicates multiple backup devices may be specified. The maximum number of backup devices is 64.
- { *logical_backup_device_name* } | { *@logical_backup_device_name_var* }
- This is the logical name of the backup device(s) (created by **sp_addumpdevice**) from which the database is restored.
- { DISK | TAPE } = '*physical_backup_device_name*' | *@phys_backup_dev_name_var*

This allows backups to be restored from the named disk or tape device. Backup to tape is not supported on Windows 98.

PARTIAL

PARTIAL specifies a partial restore operation. Application or user errors often affect an isolated portion of the database, such as a table. Examples of this type of error include an invalid update or a table dropped by mistake. To support recovery from these events, SQL Server provides a mechanism to restore part of the database to another location so that the damaged or missing data can be copied back to the original database.

The granularity of the partial restore operation is the database filegroup. The primary file and filegroup are always restored, along with the files that you specify and their corresponding filegroups. The result is a subset of the database. Filegroups that are not restored are marked as offline and are not accessible.

For more information, see “Partial Database Restore Operations” in Books Online.

Note: If you want to recover a specific table (or part of the table), you can restore the database to a new database name, perhaps on the test server. Then you can copy the table of interest to the production database using Data Transformation Services (DTS).

RESTRICTED_USER

This restricts access for the newly restored database to members of the **db_owner**, **dbcreator** or **sysadmin** roles. In SQL Server 2000, RESTRICTED_USER replaces the DBO_ONLY option. DBO_ONLY is available only for backward compatibility.

Use with the RECOVERY option.

FILE = { file_number | @file_number }

FILE identifies the backup set to be restored. For example, a *file_number* of 1 indicates the first backup set on the backup medium and a *file_number* of 2 indicates the second backup set.

PASSWORD = { password | @password_variable }

This provides the password for the backup set. PASSWORD is a character string. If a password was provided when the backup set was created, the password must be supplied to perform any restore operation from the backup set.

MEDIANAME = {media_name | @media_name_variable}

This specifies the name for the media. If provided, the media name must match the media name on the backup volume(s); otherwise, the restore operation terminates. If no media name is given in the RESTORE statement, the check for a matching media name on the backup volume(s) is not performed.

Note: Consistently using media names in backup and restore operations provides an extra safety check for the media selected during the restore operation.

MEDIAPASSWORD = { mediapassword | @mediapassword_variable }

This supplies the password for the media set. MEDIAPASSWORD is a character string.

If a password was provided when the media set was formatted, that password must be supplied to access any backup set on that media set.

MOVE 'logical_file_name' TO 'operating_system_file_name'

This string specifies that the given logical_file_name should be moved to operating_system_file_name. By default, the logical_file_name is restored to its original location. If the RESTORE statement is used to copy a database to the same or different server, the MOVE option may be needed to relocate the database files and to avoid collisions with existing files. Each logical file in the database can be specified in different MOVE statements.

Note: Use **RESTORE FILELISTONLY** to obtain a list of the files from the backup set.

... n

Following this marker indicates that multiple logical files can be moved by specifying multiple MOVE statements.

NORECOVERY | RECOVERY | STANDBY = undo_file_name

NORECOVERY instructs the restore operation not to roll back any uncommitted transactions. Either the NORECOVERY or STANDBY option must be specified if another transaction log has to be applied.

SQL Server requires that the WITH NORECOVERY option be used on all but the final RESTORE statement when restoring a database backup and multiple transaction logs, or when multiple RESTORE statements are needed (for example, a full database backup followed by a differential database backup).

Note: When specifying the NORECOVERY option, the database is not usable in this intermediate, nonrecovered state.

When used with a file or filegroup restore operation, NORECOVERY forces the database to remain in the restoring state after the restore operation. This is useful in either of these situations:

- A restore script is being run and the log is always being applied.
- A sequence of file restores is used and the database is not intended to be usable between two of the restore operations.

RECOVERY, the default, instructs the restore operation to roll back any uncommitted transactions. After the recovery process, the database is ready for use. If subsequent RESTORE operations (RESTORE LOG, or RESTORE DATABASE from differential) are planned, NORECOVERY or STANDBY should be specified.

When restoring backup sets from an earlier version of SQL Server, a database upgrade may be required. This upgrade is performed automatically when WITH RECOVERY is specified.

STANDBY specifies the undo file name so the recovery effects can be undone. The size required for the undo file depends on the volume of undo actions resulting from uncommitted transactions.

STANDBY allows a database to be brought up for read-only access between transaction log restores, and it can be used with either warm standby server situations or special recovery situations in which it is useful to inspect the database between log restores. If the specified undo file name does not exist, SQL Server creates it. If the file does exist, SQL Server overwrites it.

STANDBY is not allowed when a database upgrade is necessary.

KEEP_REPLICATION

This is used with log shipping. It instructs the restore operation to preserve replication settings when restoring a published database to a server other than that on which it was created. KEEP_REPLICATION is to be used when setting up replication to work with log shipping. It prevents replication settings from being removed when a database or log backup is restored on a warm standby server and the database is recovered. Specifying this option when restoring a backup with the NORECOVERY option is not permitted.

NOREWIND | REWIND

NOREWIND is used only for tape devices. It specifies that SQL Server will keep the tape open after the restore operation. Keeping the tape open prevents other processes from accessing the tape. The tape will not be released until a REWIND or UNLOAD statement is issued, or the server is shut down. A list of currently open tapes can be found by querying the sysopentapes table in the master database.

NOREWIND implies NOUNLOAD.

SQL Server will retain ownership of the tape drive until a BACKUP or RESTORE command is used WITH REWIND.

REWIND, the default, specifies that SQL Server will rewind and release the tape.

If neither NOREWIND nor REWIND is specified, REWIND is the default.

NOUNLOAD | UNLOAD

This is used only for tape devices. **NOUNLOAD** specifies the tape is not unloaded automatically from the tape drive after a restore. NOUNLOAD remains set until UNLOAD is specified.

UNLOAD specifies that the tape is automatically rewound and unloaded when the backup is finished. UNLOAD remains in effect until NOUNLOAD is specified.

UNLOAD is set by default when a new user session is started. The last one specified remains in effect until the next BACKUP statement with a different value.

REPLACE

REPLACE Specifies that SQL Server should create the specified database and its related files even if another database already exists with the same name. In such a case, the existing database is deleted.

REPLACE also allows RESTORE to overwrite an existing file which cannot be verified as belonging to the database being restored. Normally, RESTORE will refuse to overwrite pre-existing files.

RESTART

This specifies that SQL Server should restart a restore operation that has been interrupted at the point it was interrupted.

Note: This option can only be used for restores directed from tape media and for restores that span multiple tape volumes.

STATS [= percentage]

This displays a message each time another percentage completes and is used to gauge progress. If *percentage* is omitted, SQL Server displays a message after every 10 percent completed.

Example: Simple backup and restore example. To back up database **mydb**:

SQL

```
BACKUP DATABASE mydb
      -- Backup may be done while database is
      -- in MULTI_USER operation
      TO DISK = 'F:\MSSQL\BACKUP\mydb.BAK'
      WITH INIT:\MSSQL\BACKUP\mydb.BAK'
      WITH  NOINIT
```

To obtain exclusive access, put database **mydb** in SINGLE_USER (rudely) and make sure your connection is not in that database. (See page 550 for a more graceful shutdown.)

SQL

```
USE master
go
ALTER DATABASE  mydb
     SET SINGLE_USER  WITH ROLLBACK IMMEDIATE

RESTORE DATABASE mydb
      FROM DISK = 'F:\MSSQL\BACKUP\mydb.BAK'

ALTER DATABASE  mydb     SET MULTI_USER
```

For further information, see "Database Layout for Performance and Restorability," page 588, and examples "Backup/Restore Damaged .MDF," page 592 and "Production Datebase," page 598.

5.5.12 RESTORE LOG

RESTORELOG restores a transaction log backup to the specified database. Transaction logs must be applied in sequential order. SQL Server checks the backed-up transaction log to ensure that the transactions are being loaded into the correct database and in the correct sequence. To apply multiple transaction logs, use the NORECOVERY option on each restore operation except the last which is done with RECOVERY.

For more information, see "Transaction Log Backups" in Books Online.

5.5.12.1 Restore a Transaction Log

Syntax

```
RESTORE LOG { database_name | @database_name_var }
[ FROM < backup_device > [ ,...n ] ]
[ WITH
   [ RESTRICTED_USER ]
   [ [ , ] FILE = { file_number | @file_number } ]
   [ [ , ] PASSWORD = { password | @password_variable } ]
   [ [ , ] MOVE 'logical_file_name' TO 'operating_system_file_name' ]  [ ,...n ]
   [ [ , ] MEDIANAME = { media_name | @media_name_variable } ]
   [ [ , ] MEDIAPASSWORD = { mediapassword | @mediapassword_variable } ]
   [ [ , ] KEEP_REPLICATION ]
   [ [ , ] { NORECOVERY | RECOVERY | STANDBY = undo_file_name } ]
   [ [ , ] { NOREWIND | REWIND } ]
   [ [ , ] { NOUNLOAD | UNLOAD } ]
   [ [ , ] RESTART ]
   [ [ , ] STATS [= percentage ] ]
   [
         [ , ] STOPAT = { date_time | @date_time_var }
       | [ , ] STOPATMARK = 'mark_name' [ AFTER datetime ]
       | [ , ] STOPBEFOREMARK = 'mark_name' [ AFTER datetime ]
   ]
]
```

Arguments

The parameters for BACKUP LOG are the same as for BACKUP DATABASE given in the previous section except for the following.

STOPAT = date_time | @date_time_var

This specifies that the database be restored to the state it was in as of the specified date and time. Only transaction log records written before the specified date and time are applied to the database. If a variable is used for STOPAT, it must be **varchar**, **char**, **smalldatetime**, or **datetime** data type.

Note: If you specify a STOPAT time that is beyond the end of the RESTORE LOG operation, the database is left in an unrecovered state, just as if RESTORE LOG had been run with NORECOVERY.

STOPATMARK = 'mark_name' [AFTER datetime]

This specifies recovery to the specified mark, including the transaction that contains the mark. If AFTER *datetime* is omitted, recovery stops at the first mark with the specified name. If AFTER *datetime* is specified, recovery stops at the first mark having the specified name exactly at or after *datetime*.

You may create a marked transaction using BEGIN TRAN WITH MARK '*mark_name*'.

STOPBEFOREMARK = 'mark_name' [AFTER datetime]

This string specifies recovery to the specified mark but does not include the transaction that contains the mark. If AFTER *datetime* is omitted, recovery stops at the first mark with the specified name. If AFTER *datetime* is specified, recovery stops at the first mark having the specified name exactly at or after *datetime*.

You may create a marked transaction using BEGIN TRAN WITH MARK '*mark_name*'.

Example: Backup database **mydb** with FULL backup and LOG backup.

SQL

```
ALTER DATABASE  mydb  SET  RECOVERY FULL
 -- To log transactions and allow log backups
BACKUP DATABASE mydb
      -- Backup may be done while database is
      -- in MULTI_USER operation
      TO DISK = 'F:\MSSQL\BACKUP\mydb.BAK'
      WITH INIT
-- Some time later
BACKUP LOG  mydb
      TO DISK = 'F:\MSSQL\BACKUP\mydb.BAK'
      WITH  NOINIT
```

Example: Restore database **mydb** with FULL backup and LOG backup.

To obtain exclusive access, put database **mydb** in SINGLE_USER (rudely) and make sure your connection is not in that database. (See page 550 for a more graceful shutdown.)

SQL

```
USE master
go
ALTER DATABASE  mydb
     SET SINGLE_USER  WITH ROLLBACK IMMEDIATE

RESTORE DATABASE mydb
      FROM DISK = 'F:\MSSQL\BACKUP\mydb.BAK'
      WITH FILE = 1, NORECOVERY

RESTORE LOG     mydb
      FROM DISK = 'F:\MSSQL\BACKUP\mydb.BAK'
      WITH FILE = 2, RECOVERY
      -- RECOVERY is the default, but I prefer
      -- to state it for clarity

ALTER DATABASE  mydb     SET MULTI_USER
```

5.5.13 Restore Dialog

To restore pubs database in Enterprise Manager.

1. Select: Databases – pubs
2. Right click on pubs, Select: All Tasks – Restore Database ...
   You'll see a dialog like the one shown in Figure 5-9.
3. To do a full database restore up to the most recent TLBU, you may take the defaults and click OK, though you should check to make sure the choices are correct. They should be:

- General tab
  - Restore as database: pubs
  - Restore: Database
  - Show backups of database: pubs
  - Under "Restore," the green check marks should be present for the most recent FBU, most recent DBU and each subsequent TLBU

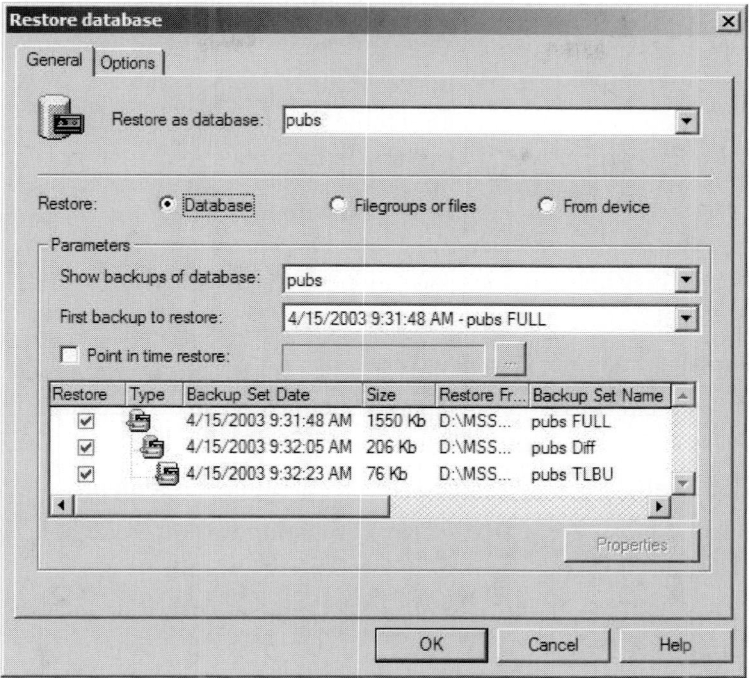

Figure 5-9 Restore Database Dialog.

- Options tab
  Recovery completion state: Leave database operational. No additional ....
- Click OK

You've just done a FULL DATABASE RESTORE of the pubs database to the time that the most recent TLBU was made.

5.5.14 RESTORE Command

Syntax

```
RESTORE DATABASE <mydb>
TO <backup-device>
WITH <options>
```

Example:

```
RESTORE DATABASE pubs
    FROM DISK = 'D:\MSSSQL7\BACKUP\pubs.BAK'
    WITH RECOVERY
```

5.5.15 Restore Using Example Backup Strategy

Here's a sample backup strategy:

Sat night:	Full Database Backup (FBU)
Nightly:	Differential Database Backup (DBU)
10 am, 2 pm, 6 pm:	Transaction Log Backup (TLBU)

5.5.15.1 Restore Procedure (assume disk crashed on Tuesday at 3 pm)

- If Data disk crashed, the transaction log disk is still operational. Immediately do TLBU.
- Replace (and reformat) new Data disk.
- Restore latest **FBU** onto the new Data disk. Leave db **nonoperational** and able to restore additional Txn logs.
- The database is now restored to last Sat night at midnight.
- Restore most recent **DBU**. Leave db **nonoperational** and able to restore additional TLBUs.
- This would be only Mon night's DBU since they hold everything since last FBU.
- Restore each intervening **TLBU**. Leave db **nonoperational** and able to restore additional TLBUs.
- Restore both Tue 10 am and Tue 2 pm TLBUs since they are incremental.
- Restore the TLBU done at 3 pm right after the disk crash. This is the last restore. Restore **last TLBU** just made. Leave db **operational**.

The last restore operation leaves the database operational.

5.5.16 Comments about Backup and Restore

Here are some suggestions to improve your work with backup and restore.

1. Test your backup, probably on a test machine, to make sure your media and methods are valid. Don't wait until you need to restore to discover something's wrong with your backup.
2. The default location for your data files, xxx.MDF, your log files, xxx.LDF, and the backup files, xxx.bak, are on the same physical disk. To be safe and improve performance you must put data, log and backup on three separate drives. See "Database Layout for Performance and Restorability" on page 588.

5.5.16.1 Recovery and Checkpoint

Recovery, which is automatic at server startup, is an internal mechanism to ensure that the data in each database is consistent.

The recovery process is necessary because the database engine when starting up doesn't know whether the server crashed or was taken down gracefully. So it goes through the recovery process to ensure that the data in the database is consistent before declaring it as operational and allows users to access it. Every transaction in the log contains a *before image* and an *after image* consisting of each modified data row before and after the change.

The following events occur during recovery:

- SQL Server examines the transaction log from the last checkpoint and rolls forward all committed transactions by writing the after image to the data file.
- Uncommitted transactions in the log are *rolled back* by writing the before image from the transaction log to the data file.
- After successful recovery the database is *operational*, so it's in a consistent state ready for new work in the database. Let new transactions begin.

If a database has been taken down gracefully, the transaction log is clean and recovery is minimal. If the server crashes, more work must be done to recover in order to make the database consistent and ready to run.

Note: There is a very important recovery startup option. This will be discussed later, but you need to understand now what recovery is.

A checkpoint is done by SQL Server periodically (usually every minute or so). At a checkpoint, SQL Server ensures all modified data pages are flushed from memory to disk. (Uncommitted modified data written to the data pages is dirty until the commit occurs. Access to dirty data is usually prohibited by locks.)

According to Books Online:

> Recovery interval controls when SQL Server issues a checkpoint in each database. Checkpoints are done on a per database basis. At a checkpoint, SQL Server ensures all log information and all modified pages are flushed from memory to disk. This limits the time needed for recovery by limiting the number of transactions rolled forward to ensure they are on disk. No modifications done before the checkpoint need to be rolled forward because they have been flushed to disk at the checkpoint.

The DBA sets recovery interval from which the database engine determines when to do checkpoints. I recommend a recovery interval set at 0 (self-configuring).

Recovery interval is a rough estimate of how long it will take SQL Server to recover. Setting it to 0 (self-configuring) causes it to try to make recovery take about 1 minute per database and so sets the checkpoint frequency accordingly.

The more frequent the checkpoints, the less work and time are needed for recovery. But setting it too small may slow performance during production time.

5.6 DATABASE LAYOUT FOR PERFORMANCE AND RESTORABILITY

This section explains how to improve disk layout for performance and restorability.

When CREATE DATABASE is executed with no location specified, the default is to place all database files (data files, xxx.MDF, log files, xxx.LDF, and backup files, xxx.bak) on the same physical disk. That's because SQL Server doesn't know anything about your disk configuration or your preferences. But such a configuration gives poor performance, especially for an OLTP database, and it precludes complete recovery from data disk failure. Poor performance and poor restorability are very bad for a production database.

Placing data, index, log and backup files on the same disk, as in the default layout, has the following disadvantages:

- Having index and data tables on the same disk causes the interleaved index and data lookups, requiring that a great deal of time be spent in a lot of movement of disk heads—an extremely slow operation.
- Having the transaction log on the same disk as index or data tables slows all data, index and log operations for the same reasons and, worse, renders the transaction log useless if the data disk crashes. If the data disk crashes with the transaction log on the same disk, then the recent transaction log activity is also lost. Backing up a database to the same disk as other database files clearly does not protect those files from a disk crash.

So all of these database components should be placed on separate physical disks, not separate partitions on the same disk. Separate disks is a starting point for laying out a database on disk to enhance performance and reliability. The next two sections provide two layouts that accomplish this goal with an example showing a simulated data disk crash and backup and restore operations to recover the data.

RAID

Once the database is laid out conceptually to put data, indexes, log and backups on separate disks, performance can be enhanced even more by using RAID for the various components instead of a single disk. Here are some initial ideas on how RAID might be used.

- .LDF—Put on RAID 1, mirrored disks. This is important since loss of log files cannot be recovered.
- .MDF and .NDF—Put on RAID 0 to obtain better performance of striping.

More detailed performance tuning information can be found in these references, among others:

- Edward Whalen (Editor), *Microsoft SQL Server 2000 Performance Tuning Technical Reference*. Microsoft Press, 2001.
- Ken England, *Microsoft SQL Server 2000 Performance Optimization and Tuning Handbook*. Digital Press, 2001.

Two disk layouts for performance and restorability are provided here. Our starting point for both disk layouts includes

- placing all database files on disks other than that used by the Operating System (C:)
- placing data tables, indexes and transaction logs on separate disks from each other.

Layout 1 would be appropriate when

- database is read-only or read-mostly, for which the most recent scheduled backup would suffice for restore in case of disk failure (do not need time of failure restore)
- time-of-failure restorability is needed but other databases can be unavailable while restoring the lost database; you cannot afford to buy mirrored disks (as is suggested in Layout 2)

Layout 2 would be appropriate when

- production OLTP database contains critical data; you can afford to buy mirrored disks

5.6.1 Production Database—Suggested Disk Layout 1

Database disk layout 1 is valid for SQL Server 2000, gives good performance and supports restoring a lost .MDF file using **rebuildm**. But **rebuildm** affects the other databases, so I prefer Layout 2, described in Section 5.6.2, which also supports SQL Server 7.0.

Before you choose this or any disk layout, you should test it exhaustively for performance and for restorability. The restorability test with a damaged or lost .MDF file is given here in an example. For performance tests, see the performance references on page 589.

In Layout 1, as depicted in Figure 5-10, user data tables are placed in the .MDF file with the system tables, indexes are placed in a separate filegroup on a different disk and the transaction log is placed on yet another disk. This layout does not work with SQL Server 7.0 for restoring a lost .MDF file; for that, use Layout 2.

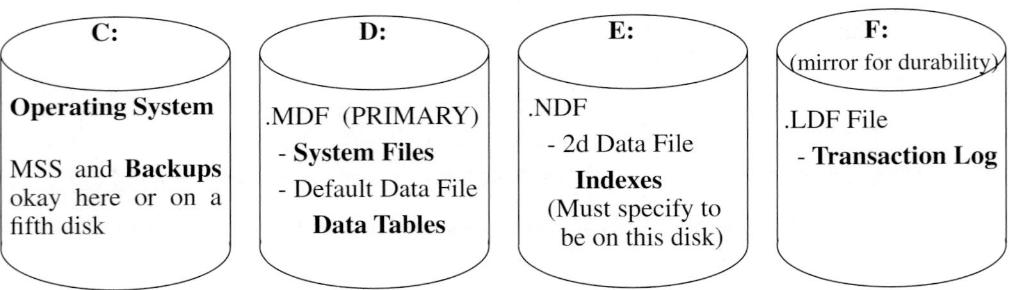

Figure 5-10 Disk Layout 1.

1. C: Operating System (Windows NT) is usually here. It's okay to put SQL Server and backups here or on a fifth separate disk.
2. D: Place System Tables (.MDF) here, which contains system files and is the default for data tables.
3. E: Create a separate filegroup *fg_databasename_Indexes* in an .NDF on a separate disk to contain all indexes to improve performance. Specify this filegroup name in every CREATE INDEX statement.
4. F: Place the Transaction Log (.LDF) on a separate disk for both performance and restorability. Mirror it for durability.

In Figure 5-10:

- The **D:**, **E:** and **F:** drive letters were chosen arbitrarily for this example.
- What are shown as individual drive letters may in fact be complete RAID arrays of several disks to further improve performance. See performance references, page 589.
- SQL Server 7 had a bug that requires a different disk layout to permit backing up the transaction log when the data file is damaged. The .MDF file must be available. See Microsoft Knowledge Base, *http://support.microsoft.com/*, search for Q253817.

5.6.1.1 Layout 1 Sample Statements

The next statements implement Layout 1 for an example critical database, bankdb. See the complete example on p. 592 to create Layout 1, and then lose .MDF and do a full restore.

SQL

```
USE master --  Layout 1 CREATE DATABASE statements
go

CREATE DATABASE bankdb
ON
PRIMARY (NAME = bankdb_Primary ,
                -- D:  PRIMARY on D: has system files
FILENAME='D:\MSSQL\bankdb_Data.MDF' ,
  SIZE = 1 MB) ,

FILEGROUP fg_bankdb_indexes
                -- E:  Separate Filegroup for indexes
( NAME = bankdb_Indexes ,
  FILENAME= 'E:\MSSQL\bankdb_indexes.NDF' ,
    SIZE = 1 MB)

LOG ON
( NAME = bankdb_Log ,
  FILENAME='F:\MSSQL\bankdb_Log.LDF')
                -- F: Specify log to be put on F:

ALTER DATABASE bankdb  SET RECOVERY FULL
```

Layout 1—CREATE TABLE and CREATE INDEX Sample Statements

With the **bankdb** database created with the layout just shown, indexes should be created to explicitly place them on the separate disks and tables created to go on the default disk.

SQL

```
CREATE TABLE persons (
  id               DEC(4) ,
  name             VARCHAR(10) ,
  CONSTRAINT pk_persons PRIMARY KEY
    CLUSTERED ( id )
        -- We may add the specification of
        -- fillfactor, etc.
    WITH FILLFACTOR = 80
        -- Leave clustered PK index on MDF,
        -- it's the data table
);

CREATE INDEX ind_persons_name  ON persons ( name )
                -- Add secondary index
WITH FILLFACTOR = 80
ON fg_bankdb_indexes;
        -- Specify disk when manually
        -- add a secondary index
```

Exercise: Backup/Restore Damaged .MDF with Layout 1 This section demonstrates disk Layout 1 and the ability to recover from an .MDF data disk crash. For easy disk crash simulation, we place the .MDF file on removable flash memory drive G: (instead of the D: drive above) and then simulate the disk crash by removing the drive and deleting the .MDF file.

This procedure is a bit of a hassle and requires running **rebuildm** (which is a bit drastic), so I actually prefer Layout 2 presented in Section 5.6.2. I suggest you look over both and decide which you prefer.

Procedure KB Q253817 Enhanced—Steps to Recover from Lost .MDF file

The procedure followed here is based on *KB Q253817* (Microsoft Knowledge Base article Q253817) with some modifications and additions which allow me to implement a complete working example. For SQL Server 2000, if the .MDF data file of a user database is damaged or lost, but the transaction log file of the database is still accessible, you can still back up the last active transaction log of the database to reduce the loss of data by following these steps:

1. Detach any healthy user databases before running **rebuildm** and reattach afterward.
2. Stop SQL Server. You may replace and format the damaged disk at this time.
3. Rename (or copy) the transaction log files.
4. Manually remove any remaining database files used in the create database statement (see the batch file in the example).
5. Rebuild the **master** database with the **rebuildm** utility (run rebuildm.exe in Tools\BINN).
6. Start SQL Server. Attach other databases from step 1.
7. Use the original SQL script to create the database of the same name with the same disk and file structure layout. The new database does not have to be the same size or contain any user data tables; however, it must contain the same number of data and log files.
8. Stop SQL Server.
9. Delete all the data files of the newly created database so it will fail recovery (use the batch file from step 4). Rename the saved log file back to the original name so it can be backed up.
10. Restart SQL Server. (If you look in EM you will see the database marked as suspect.)
11. Run this command to back the tail of the log:

    ```
    BACKUP LOG  database_name  TO DISK =  device_name
    WITH NO_TRUNCATE
    ```

12. Either DROP DATABASE or use the **sp_dbremove** to remove the database.
13. Restore the database from the last FBU up to and including the TLBU just made. In restoring the last FBU, you need to use “Force” in EM or “with REPLACE” in SQL.

Example: This example creates a new database and a table with some data, then simulates a disk crash and follows the previous steps to recover the lost .MDF file. The example follows this sequence:

1. Create a database with disk layout 1 using G: for the MDF file.
2. Create a table, enter some data and do FBU.
3. Add another row of data and then simulate the disk crash.
4. Follow the "KB Q253817 enhanced" steps above to recover the lost .MDF file.
5. Query the restored database to check that data entered after the FBU is present.

Here is the detailed implementation.

1. Create a database with disk layout as in the previous section using G: for the MDF file.

SQL

```
/*
   Script to create bankdb:      Create_bankdb_0.sql
*/
USE master -- Layout 1 CREATE DATABASE  - Example
go

CREATE DATABASE bankdb
ON
PRIMARY (NAME = bankdb_Primary , -- G:  PRIMARY has system and data files
FILENAME='G:\MSSQL\bankdb_Data.MDF' , -- For test we put .MDF on Flash Memory
G: drive
   SIZE = 1 MB) ,

FILEGROUP fg_bankdb_indexes -- E:  Separate Filegroup for indexes
(  NAME = bankdb_Indexes ,
   FILENAME= 'E:\MSSQL\bankdb_indexes.NDF' ,
      SIZE = 1 MB)

LOG ON
(  NAME = bankdb_Log ,
   FILENAME='F:\MSSQL\bankdb_Log.LDF') -- F: Specify log to be put on F:

ALTER DATABASE bankdb  SET RECOVERY FULL
go
```

2. Create a table, enter some data and do FBU.

SQL

```
/*
  Script to create and populate tables:     Create_bankdb_1.sql
*/
-- CREATE TABLE statement for database layout 1
USE bankdb
go

CREATE TABLE t (  id  INT  IDENTITY , dt DATETIME  DEFAULT GETDATE()  )

INSERT INTO t VALUES (DEFAULT)  -- id = 1

SELECT id , CAST(dt AS VARCHAR) AS Date FROM t
EC sp_lock
```

Result

```
id      Date
----    ----------------------------
1       Apr 21 2003  8:10PM     -- This row will be saved in the FBU

-- ##########################################################################
-- Do FBU                           -- FULL BACKUP --
BACKUP DATABASE bankdb
TO DISK = 'C:\MSSQL\bankdb.BAK'
WITH INIT, NAME = 'bankdb FULL backup'  -- INIT causes overwrite
-- ##########################################################################
```

3. Add another row of data and then simulate the disk crash.

SQL

```
-- Insert another row after FBU
INSERT INTO t VALUES (DEFAULT)  -- id = 2

SELECT id , CAST(dt AS VARCHAR) AS Date FROM t   -- Show after FBU row values.
```

SQL (cont.)
Result

```
id      Date
----    ---------------------------
1       Apr 21 2003  8:10PM      -- This row was saved in the FBU
2       Apr 21 2003  8:11PM

-- ##########################################################################
-- DISK CRASH    SIMULATION - REMOVE FLASH MEMORY FROM G: DRIVE
--       OR      Stop SQL Server, Delete bankdb_Data.MDF, Start Server
-- ##########################################################################
```

4. Follow the "KB Q253817 enhanced" steps above to recover the lost .MDF file.

```
--   ##################### Implement KB Q253817 enhanced" steps
  ################
```

a. Detach any healthy user databases before running **rebuildm** and reattach afterward.

b. *Stop SQL Server*. Replace and format the damaged disk at this time if possible: Replace disk simulation—insert empty Flash Memory G:

c. Rename (or copy) the transaction log files (you may use Command Prompt window or Windows Explorer).

```
<<C:\>    rename    F:\MSSQL\bankdb_Log.LDF bankdb_Log_orig.LDF
```

d. Manually remove any remaining database files used in the create database statement (you c an use batch file like bankdb_file_remove.bat).

e. At this point, there will be errors for missing files (bankdb_Log.LDF), but that's okay.

f. Rebuild the **master** database with **rebuildm** utility (run rebuildm.exe in Tools\BINN):

```
C:\>     "C:\Program Files\Microsoft SQL Server\80\Tools\Binn\rebuildm.exe"
```

Read the notes. If you've preserved your other databases, click "Rebuild." You may get an error message, but it doesn't seem to hurt anything.

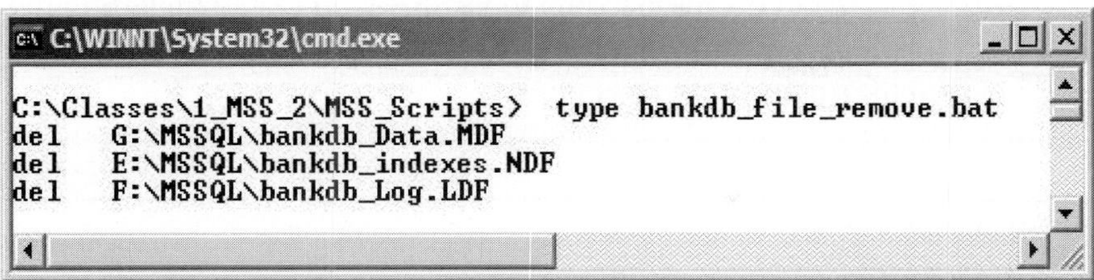
```
C:\Classes\1_MSS_2\MSS_Scripts>  type bankdb_file_remove.bat
del    G:\MSSQL\bankdb_Data.MDF
del    E:\MSSQL\bankdb_indexes.NDF
del    F:\MSSQL\bankdb_Log.LDF
```

Figure 5-11 Removing new db files.

g. START SQL Server. Use **sp_attach_db** to attach other databases from step 1.

h. Use the original SQL script to create the database of the same name with the same disk and file structure layout. The new database does not have to be the same size or contain any user data tables. Run above script “create_bankdb_0.sql” from Query Analyzer.

i. *Stop SQL Server.*

j. Delete all files of the newly created database so it will fail recovery. Remove new database files.. Again, you can use *bankdb_file_remove*.bat. See Figure 5-11.

k. Rename the transaction log to its original name—bankdb_Log.LDF—so it can be backed up (you can use either Windows Explorer or Command Prompt window).

```
-- C:\>  rename   F:\MSSQL\bankdb_Log_orig.LDF    bankdb_Log.LDF
```

l. START SQL Server. If you look in EM, you will see the database marked as suspect, but you'll be able to back up the transaction log.

m. Do TLBU with NO_TRUNCATE to back up the tail of the log:

SQL

```
USE master
go
BACKUP LOG bankdb
   TO DISK = 'C:\MSSQL\bankdb_log.BAK' -- This creates a TLBU that can be used
   WITH INIT , NO_TRUNCATE -- to restore the data since the last backup.
```

n. Either DROP DATABASE or use the **sp_dbremove** to remove the database.

```
DROP DATABASE bankdb
```

o. Restore the database from the last FBU up to and including the TLBU just made. In restoring the last FBU, you need to use "Force" in EM or "with REPLACE" in SQL.

SQL

```
RESTORE DATABASE bankdb
 FROM DISK = 'C:\MSSQL\bankdb.BAK'
   -- If restore with EM, click Options tab and check "Force restore ..."
  WITH NORECOVERY , REPLACE
   -- Leaves database NON-operational, needs final WITH RECOVERY


RESTORE LOG bankdb
 FROM DISK = 'C:\MSSQL\bankdb_log.BAK'
  WITH RECOVERY        -- Leaves database operational, ready to use
--  #################### End KB Q253817 enhanced" steps ##################
```

5. Query the restored database to check that data entered after the FBU is present. *Check that the restore was successful.*

SQL

```
USE bankdb
go

SELECT id , CAST(dt AS VARCHAR) AS Date FROM t  -- Shows all rows!   Yay!!!!!
```

Result

```
id       Date
----     ----------------------------
1        Apr 21 2003  8:10PM       -- This row was saved in the FBU
2        Apr 21 2003  8:11PM
```

5.6.2 Production Database—Suggested Disk Layout 2

Database disk Layout 2 is valid for both SQL Server 2000 and 7.0 and is the one that gives the simplest recovery from a damaged data file as well as good performance. It places both .MDF (containing only system files) and .LDF files on mirrored disks and assumes neither will be lost in case of a disk crash. But a mirroring system does make it more expensive.

Consider the following as a starting point for disk layout for good performance and restorability even with a damaged data file.

- Place all database files on disks other than that used by the Operating System (C:).
- Place data tables, indexes and transaction logs on separate disks.
- The .MDF file, which always contains the database's system files, can be mirrored to protect it and a separate .NDF file created and specified as the default for data files. (With mirroring, .MDF and .LDF can be on the same mirrored set; without mirroring, they must be on separate disks.)

The layout shown in Figure 5-12 achieves these goals. The SQL statements implement the configuration.

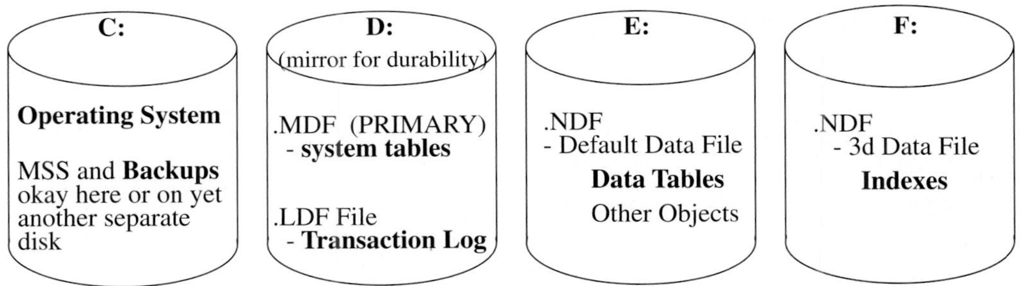

Figure 5-12 Disk Layout 2.

1. **C:** Operating System (Windows NT) is usually here. It's okay to put SQL Server and backups here or on yet another separate disk.
2. **D:** Place both System Tables (.MDF) and Transaction Log (.LDF) on the same disk and mirror it for durability.
3. **E:** Create a separate filegroup *fg_databasename_Default* in a .NDF file on a separate disk and run ALTER DATABASE to make it the default data file. All database objects created without filegroup specification will reside in this filegroup.
4. **F:** Create a separate filegroup *fg_databasename_Indexes* in a .NDF on a third separate disk to contain all indexes to improve performance. Specify this filegroup name in every CREATE INDEX statement.

In Layout 2:

- The **D:**, **E:** and **F:** drive letters were chosen arbitrarily for this example.
- What are shown here as individual disk drive letters may in fact be complete RAID arrays of several disks to further improve performance and recoverability.

5.6.2.1 Layout 2 Sample Statements

The next statements implement Layout 2 for an example critical database, bankdb. See the complete example on pages 601–2 to create Layout 2, then lose .MDF and do full restore.

Layout 2—CREATE DATABASE Sample Statements

SQL

```
USE master                                    --  Layout 2 CREATE
DATABASE statements
go
CREATE DATABASE bankdb
ON
  PRIMARY ( NAME = bankdb_Primary
        -- D:  PRIMARY has .MDF system tables
  , FILENAME='D:\MSSQL\bankdb_Main.MDF'
  , SIZE = 1 MB)
,  FILEGROUP fg_bankdb_Default
        -- E:  DEFAULT .NDF Filegroup for user tables
    (  NAME = bankdb_Default
  , FILENAME= 'E:\MSSQL\bankdb_Data.NDF'
  , SIZE = 1 MB)
,  FILEGROUP fg_bankdb_indexes
        -- F:  Separate .NDF Filegroup for indexes
    ( NAME = bankdb_Indexes
  , FILENAME= 'F:\MSSQL\bankdb_indexes.NDF'
  , SIZE = 1 MB)
  LOG ON
    (NAME = bankdb_Log ,
  FILENAME='D:\MSSQL\bankdb_Log.LDF')
        -- D: Specify log .LDF to be put on D:
```

For SQL Server 2000:

SQL

```
ALTER DATABASE bankdb  SET RECOVERY FULL
```

For SQL Server 7.0:

SQL

```
EXEC sp_dboption bankdb,
                     'select into/bulkcopy' , FALSE

EXEC sp_dboption  bankdb,
                     'trunc. log on chkpt.' , FALSE
```

For SQL Server 2000 and 7.0:

SQL

```
ALTER DATABASE bankdb
MODIFY FILEGROUP fg_bankdb_Default DEFAULT
```

5.6.2.2 Layout 2 CREATE TABLE and CREATE INDEX Sample Statements

SQL

```
USE bankdb
go

CREATE TABLE customers (
  id              DEC(4) ,
  name            VARCHAR(10) ,
  CONSTRAINT pk_customers PRIMARY KEY
    CLUSTERED ( id )
       -- Leave clustered PK index on Primary NDF,
       -- it's the data table
    WITH FILLFACTOR = 80
       -- We could also specify fillfactor, etc.
);

CREATE INDEX ind_customers_name
                         -- Add secondary index
ON customers ( name )
WITH FILLFACTOR = 80
ON fg_bankdb_indexes;
 -- Specify disk when manually add a secondary index
```

Exercise: Backup/Restore Damaged .NDF Data File with Layout 2

This section demonstrates disk Layout 2 and the ability to recover from .NDF data disk crash. For easy disk crash simulation, we will put the Data File on removable Flash Memory drive G:. Removing the drive and deleting the .NDF file will simulate the disk crash.

Example: This example creates a new database and a table with some data, then simulates a disk crash and lists the steps to recover the lost .NDF file. The example follows these steps:

1. Create a database with disk Layout 2.
2. Create a table, enter some data, and do FBU.
3. Add another row of data.
4. Simulate the disk crash and replace the disk with the .NDF file removed.
5. Do TLBU to save the row inserted after the FBU. Use "WITH NO_TRUNCATE."
6. Do complete restore recreating the .NDF file and check that all rows were restored. Use "WITH REPLACE."

Here is the detailed implementation.

1. Create a database with disk Layout 2 using G: for the MDF file.

SQL

```
USE master -- Layout 2 CREATE DATABASE - Example
go

CREATE DATABASE bankdb
ON
  PRIMARY ( NAME = bankdb_Primary -- D:  PRIMARY has .MDF system tables
   , FILENAME='D:\MSSQL\bankdb_Main.MDF'
   , SIZE = 1 MB)
, FILEGROUP fg_bankdb_Default -- G: DEFAULT .NDF Filegroup for user tables
    (  NAME = bankdb_Default
   , FILENAME= 'G:\MSSQL\bankdb_Data.NDF'
   , SIZE = 1 MB)
,  FILEGROUP fg_bankdb_indexes -- F:  Separate .NDF Filegroup for indexes
    ( NAME = bankdb_Indexes
   , FILENAME= 'F:\MSSQL\bankdb_indexes.NDF'
   , SIZE = 1 MB)
  LOG ON
    (NAME = bankdb_Log ,
   FILENAME='D:\MSSQL\bankdb_Log.LDF') -- D: Specify log .LDF to be put on D:
```

For SQL Server 2000

SQL

```
ALTER DATABASE bankdb  SET RECOVERY FULL
```

For SQL Server 7.0

SQL

```
EXEC sp_dboption  bankdb , 'select into/bulkcopy' , FALSE
EXEC sp_dboption  bankdb , 'trunc. log on chkpt.' , FALSE
```

For SQL Server 2000 and 7.0

SQL

```
ALTER DATABASE bankdb MODIFY FILEGROUP fg_bankdb_Default DEFAULT
```

2. Create a table for Layout 2, enter some data, and do FBU.

SQL

```
USE bankdb
go
CREATE TABLE t ( id  INT  IDENTITY , dt DATETIME  DEFAULT GETDATE()  )
INSERT INTO t VALUES (DEFAULT)  -- id = 1
```

SQL

```
SELECT id , CAST(dt AS VARCHAR) AS Date FROM
```

Result

```
id      Date
----    ----------------------------
1       Apr 26 2003  2:18PM

-- Do FULL BACKUP                  -- FBU --
BACKUP DATABASE bankdb
TO DISK = 'C:\MSSQL\bankdb.BAK'
WITH INIT, NAME = 'bankdb FULL backup'  -- INIT causes overwrite
```

3. Insert another row after FBU.

SQL

```
INSERT INTO t VALUES (DEFAULT)   -- id = 2
```

SQL

```
SELECT id , CAST(dt AS VARCHAR) AS Date FROM t -- Show after FBU row values.
```

Result

```
id      Date
----    -----------------------------
1       Apr 26 2003  2:18PM
2       Apr 26 2003  2:24PM

--
#################################################################################
```

4. Simulate the disk crash and replace the disk with the .NDF file removed.

SQL

```
-- DISK CRASH      - SIMULATION - REMOVE FLASH MEMORY FROM G: DRIVE
--                              OR  Stop SQL Server, Delete
bankdb_Data.ndf, Start Server
-- REPAIR DISK      - SIMULATION - INSERT EMPTY Flash Memory G:
-- You must put the correct directory structure on the new disk,
-- though there is no .NDF file
--
#################################################################################
```

5. Do TLBU to save the row inserted after the FBU. Use "WITH NO_TRUNCATE."

SQL

```
USE master   -- IF FAILS, KEEP TRYING or disconnect and open new Query
-- Analyzer connection
go
BACKUP LOG bankdb -- This often gives an error message and reports
-- "Connection Broken".
  TO DISK = 'C:\MSSQL\bankdb_log.BAK' -- But it does create a backup that
-- can be used
  WITH INIT , NO_TRUNCATE -- to restore the data since the
-- previous TLBU
```

6. Do complete restore using Query Analyzer with SQL

SQL

```
USE master
go

ALTER DATABASE bankdb SET SINGLE_USER WITH ROLLBACK IMMEDIATE
-- Need exclusive access

RESTORE DATABASE bankdb -- Probably have to run this statement twice to get
                        -- to run error-free
 FROM DISK = 'C:\MSSQL\bankdb.BAK'
  WITH NORECOVERY , REPLACE   -- Leaves database NON-operational, needs final
                              -- WITH RECOVERY
go

RESTORE LOG bankdb
 FROM DISK = 'C:\MSSQL\bankdb_log.BAK'
  WITH RECOVERY -- Leaves database operational, ready to use go
ALTER DATABASE bankdb SET MULTI_USER

-- These statements in Query Analyzer seem to only work if the RESTORE
-- DATABASE is run twice.
```

SQL (cont.)

```
-- If restoring with EM, click Options tab and check "Force restore ...".
-- You may run it 3 times to get it error free.
-- Skip the following RESTORE DATABASE commands since EM issues them for you.

--   ############################################

---------- CHECK THAT THE RESTORE WAS EFFECTIVE -----------
```

SQL

```
USE bankdb
go
```

SQL

```
SELECT id , CAST(dt AS VARCHAR) AS Date FROM t  -- Shows all rows!   Yay!!!!!
```

Result

```
id    Date
----  ----------------------------
1     Apr 26 2003  2:18PM
2     Apr 26 2003  2:24PM
```

5.7 INTRODUCTION TO TRANSACT-SQL PROGRAMMING

Transact-SQL (T-SQL) is the programming language by which all applications communicate with SQL Server. Users may issue interactive T-SQL programs via applications such as Query Analyzer and osql.

Transact-SQL consists of

- Fourth Generation Language (4GL) SQL composed of the DDL and DML statements discussed elsewhere throughout this book
- 3GL programming constructs described here including local variables, IF-ELSE, and looping. There is great value in having 3GL features available in T-SQL in that when these powerful 3GL constructs are needed, the data does not have to be transferred from the database engine to an external 3GL program written in a language such as C / C++, Visual Basic, Perl, etc. The execution of all T-SQL statements is done by the SQL Server database engine.

Note: The 4GL portion of T-SQL complies with ANSI SQL like other RDBMSs. Each RDBMS has 3GL extensions, but they are not standardized and not portable.

T-SQL 3GL and 4GL constructs may be intermixed as shown in the following example.

Example:

SQL

```
USE pubs
go
```

SQL (cont.)

```
DECLARE  @v_integer_variable   INT

SELECT  @v_integer_variable = COUNT(*)
FROM  pubs..authors

PRINT  'Authors table has:  '  +
CAST(  @v_integer_variable as CHAR(3)  ) + ' rows'
```

Result

```
Authors table has:  23  rows
```

Transact-SQL programs may be stored and executed in three ways:

- As text files usually called SQL scripts and ending in .sql
- As stored procedures and functions in a database
- As triggers attached to a table of a database

The next sections introduce Transact-SQL programming constructs.

5.7.1 Batches

A batch is a sequence of SQL statements that is parsed, optimized, compiled and executed as a group. A parse error (syntax error) in any statement immediately fails the entire batch.

Parse—Each statement is checked for syntax. Any parse error fails the entire batch.

Optimize and Compile—Each statement has a query plan built and is compiled.

Execute—Execution begins.

A fatal run-time error in any statement of the batch usually fails the rest of the batch.

Constraint violations and a few other run-time errors are nonfatal to the batch and fail only the current statement allowing the following statements to be executed.

If a nonfatal run-time error occurs in a statement, the previously executed statements are committed unless they are part of a transaction containing the run-time error, in which case the entire transaction will be rolled back.

Batches cannot be nested.

The **go** keyword following any statement explicitly terminates a batch. Without the **go** keyword, a batch is made up of all statements presented for execution.

Example: A syntax error in any statement in a batch will abort the entire batch. Inserting go divides the statements into separate batches that can proceed independently.

One batch (containing two statements)

SQL

```
SELECT TOP 2 *
FROM  pubs..authorsxxxx

SELECT TOP 2 job_id, min_lvl
FROM pubs..jobs
```

Result

```
Server: Msg 208, Level 16, State 1, Line 2
Invalid object name 'pubs..authorsxxxx'.
```

Two batches (One statement in each batch)

SQL

```
SELECT TOP 2 *
FROM  pubs..authorsxxxx
go

SELECT TOP 2 job_id, min_lvl
FROM pubs..jobs
go
```

SQL (cont.)

Result

```
Server: Msg 208, Level 16, State 1, Line 3
Invalid object name 'pubs..authorsxxxx'.

job_id          min_lvl
------          -------
1               10
2               200

(2 row(s) affected)
```

5.7.2 EXEC[UTE]

The EXEC[UTE] keyword used to invoke a stored procedure is optional as the first word of a batch, but it is required elsewhere.

SQL

```
sp_helpdb   pubs -- "EXEC" may be omitted if this begins a batch
```

Some considerations about batches are as follows:

- The following types of statements must execute alone in their own batch: CREATE VIEW, CREATE PROCEDURE, CREATE TRIGGER, CREATE RULE and CREATE DEFAULT.
- You cannot do ALTER TABLE to add new column(s) and then reference them in the same batch.
- When using OSQL and ISQL you must issue the go keyword to initiate execution.

Example: EXEC[UTE] keyword is required to execute a stored procedure unless it's the beginning of its own batch.

SQL

```
sp_helpdb pubs
  -- 1st in batch,
  -- EXEC optional
```

SQL (cont.)

Result

```
name     db_size    owner   created        ...
-------  ---------  ------  -----------    ...
pubs     2.31 MB    sa      Aug  6 2000    ...
....
```

SQL

```
SELECT GETDATE()
  -- Start of batch

EXEC sp_helpdb pubs
  -- EXEC required
```

Result

```
name     db_size    owner   created        ...
-------  ---------  ------  -----------    ...
pubs     2.31 MB    sa      Aug  6 2000    ...
....
```

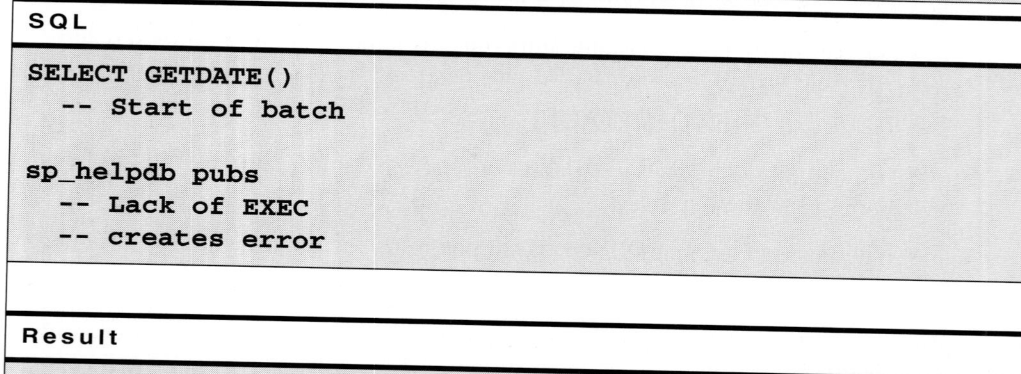

SQL

```
SELECT GETDATE()
  -- Start of batch

sp_helpdb pubs
  -- Lack of EXEC
  -- creates error
```

Result

```
Server: Msg 170, Level 15, State 1, Line 3
Line 3: Incorrect syntax near 'pubs'.
```

5.7.3 Two forms of SQL Comments

A comment is text ignored by the database engine. It is usually added for documentation. In SQL, comments can be introduced in two forms: -- and /* to */

Examples:

```
-- This is a comment to the end of the line

SELECT au_lname       -- the rest of this line is a comment
    FROM    /* This is a comment */  authors


/* This is a multi-line
    comment block */

SELECT  au_lname  FROM  authors;
```

5.7.4 PRINT

The PRINT command outputs a message to the user without any action on the data. It is similar to the Visual Basic PRINT command.

```
PRINT 'Hi there'
PRINT 4 + 5                   -- + here is arithmetic addition
PRINT 'Hello ' + 'There'      -- + here is string concatenation
PRINT GETDATE()
```

Conversions must be made if the message contains different data types.

```
    PRINT 'Today is ' + CAST( GETDATE() AS CHAR(20) )
or  PRINT 'Today is ' + CONVERT(VARCHAR(20), GETDATE() )
```

SQL

```
PRINT GETDATE()
  -- The DATETIME data type output is
  -- implicitly converted to string.
```

Result

Jun 25 2002 1:47PM

But mixing a DATETIME and a string is not allowed without explicit data conversion.

SQL

```
PRINT 'Today is:  ' + CAST( GETDATE() AS CHAR(20) )
  -- Requires conversion
```

SQL (cont.)

Result

```
Today is:  Jun 25 2002  1:47PM
```

SELECT often gives similar results to PRINT but has additional output lines.

SQL

```sql
SELECT 'Today is:   ' + CAST( GETDATE() AS CHAR(20) )
```

Result

```
------------------------------
Today is:  Jun 25 2002  1:47PM

(1 row(s) affected)
```

Printing a NULL

Check out the difference between PRINT and SELECT when an argument is NULL.

SQL

```sql
PRINT 'hi' + NULL
  -- PRINT gives no output at all if
  -- the expression evaluates to NULL
```

No output at all results from a PRINT which has a NULL.

SQL

```sql
SELECT 'hi' + NULL
 -- SELECT displays the word "NULL" if
 -- the expression evaluates to NULL
```

Result

```
----
NULL

(1 row(s) affected)
```

Only SELECT lets you know anything happened. This has faked me out from time to time.

5.7.5 Variables

There are two kinds of variables: local and built-in functions.

5.7.5.1 Local Variables

Local variables are user-created variables local to the batch where they were created.

Syntax

```
DECLARE @variable_name   datatype

@variable_name  - @ sign followed by any legal identifier (no space after @)

datatype        - Any system or user defined type except text, ntext or image
                May also be CURSOR or TABLE types which have special rules.
```

Example: Create a variable, assign it a value and print it with PRINT and SELECT.

SQL

```
DECLARE       @ctr       INT
SELECT @ctr = 1    -- ASSIGN IT A VALUE
SET @ctr = 1       -- ASSIGN IT A VALUE
  -- SET is new with MSS 7, now preferred over SELECT
PRINT @ctr
PRINT '--- separator line in output ----'
SELECT @ctr 'Ctr Value'
```

Result

```
1
--- separator line ----
Ctr Value
-----------
1

(1 row(s) affected)
```

Example: Get a value from the database with SELECT and assign it to a variable.

I use "**v_ename**" to emphasize it's a variable, though the @ might suffice.

SQL

```
DECLARE      @v_ename      VARCHAR(255)
SELECT @v_ename = ename
FROM emps WHERE empid = 1111

PRINT @v_ename
PRINT '--- separator line ----'
SELECT @v_ename 'v_ename Value'
```

Result

```
Suzy Smith
--- separator line ----
v_ename Value
-------------------
Suzy Smith

(1 row(s) affected)
```

There are no user-defined variables that can span batches.

Example: Create a variable, assign it a value and print it with PRINT and SELECT.

5.7.5.2 Built-in Functions Are Predefined Read-only Functions

Built-in functions return system values. They were (incorrectly) called "System Global Variables" prior to MSS 7.0. They all start with @@ followed by the function name and are visible to any user with permission.

The following is a partial list of built-in functions. See complete list page 136.

@@error	The error number resulting from the last SQL command
@@identity	The last identity value used in an INSERT
@@rowcount	The number of rows processed by the preceding command.
@@nestlevel	The nesting level of a stored procedure or trigger
@@spid	The current process id
@@servername	The name of current server
@@version	The SQL Server version
@@fetch_status	The status of previous fetch statement

Example:

SQL

```
SELECT  @@servername
```

Result

```
---------------------
AMY
```

SQL

```
SELECT  @@version
             -- display version of SQL Server we're running
```

Result

```
Microsoft SQL Server  2000 - 8.00.384 (Intel X86)
May 23 2001 00:02:52
Copyright (c) 1988-2000 Microsoft Corporation
Personal Edition on Windows NT 5.1 (Build 2600: )
```

@@ERROR System Function This holds the status code for the last executed T-SQL statement. It is used in noninteractive T-SQL programs and stored procedures for error checking.

SQL

```
SELECT TOP 2   *    FROM  pubs..authorsxxxx
```

Result

```
Server: Msg 208, Level 16, State 1, Line 2
Invalid object name 'pubs..authorsxxxx'.
```

SQL

```
SELECT  @@error AS ErrorNo
--  non-zero value means last SQL statement failed
```

SQL (cont.)

Result

```
ErrorNo
-----------
208
```

SQL

```
SELECT  @@error AS ErrorNo
-- 0 means last SQL statement was successful
```

Result

```
ErrorNo
-----------
0
```

5.7.6 Program Flow Control

T-SQL provides the following program flow control constructs described in ensuing pages.

BEGIN - END	RETURN	IF...ELSE	WHILE, BREAK, CONTINUE	GOTO	WAITFOR

Transact-SQL has no multiway branching construct other than IF-ELSE, but the CASE expression can return a single value based on multiple choices of input value. See CASE, p. 164.

5.7.7 BEGIN - END

BEGIN-END is an SQL Statement Block, a group of Transact-SQL statements grouped between BEGIN and END into a logical block.

BEGIN and END must appear in pairs; every BEGIN must have a matching END. BEGIN-END blocks may be nested but may not overlap. Blocks are often used in conditional statements using IF - ELSE and in looping.

Syntax

statement_block

```
BEGIN
    { sql_statement  } [  [ ; ] ... n ]
END
```

Example:

SQL

```
BEGIN
    PRINT 'Starting a block'
    UPDATE pubs..jobs SET min_lvl = min_lvl;
             -- This is test update that changes nothing.
    PRINT 'At the end of the block'
END
```

Result

Starting a block

(14 row(s) affected)

At the end of the block

5.7.8 RETURN

RETURN exits unconditionally from a batch, procedure (page 272), or function (page 255).

Syntax

```
RETURN [integer] -- See procedure syntax page 273 for use of
  integer with RETURN.
```

Example:

SQL

```
DECLARE  @x  INT
SET @x  =  0
 -- To test run with: SET @x = 0, 1, 2, 3
 -- Then,    Change "int" to "real" and SET @x  = 1.2
IF @x  <  1
    PRINT 'Answer is:  x  <  1 '
ELSE IF @x  =  1
    PRINT 'Answer is:  x  =  1'
ELSE IF @x  =  2
    PRINT 'Answer is:  x  =  2'
ELSE IF @x  >  2
    PRINT 'Answer is:  x  >  2'
ELSE
     PRINT '@x is not = 1 or 2. It''s value is: ' +
                              CAST( @x AS VARCHAR(4) )
```

5.7.9 IF-ELSE

IF-ELSE Syntax

```
IF <condition>
      <SQL Statement | SQL Statement block>
ELSE
      <SQL Statement | SQL Statement block>
```

Example:

SQL

```
DECLARE  @x   INT
  SET @x = -2          -- Lab, Also use: SET @x =  +2

  IF @x > 0
   PRINT 'Answer is:  x > 0'
  ELSE
   PRINT 'Answer is:  x <= 0'
```

Result

Answer is: x < 0.

Note that <condition> can contain a query:

Example:

SQL

```
IF (SELECT COUNT(*) FROM authors) > 1
  PRINT 'We have data!'
```

Result

We have data!

In this example we use BEGIN-END to form a block of statements.

Example:

SQL

```
DECLARE  @x  INT
    SET @x = 2          -- In Lab, Change to: SET @x = -2

    IF @x > 0
        BEGIN
            PRINT 'Answer is:  x > 0'
            PRINT 'Second line in IF block'
        END
    ELSE
        PRINT 'Answer is:  x <= 0'
```

Result

```
Answer is:  x > 0
Second line in IF block
```

IF..ELSE statements can be chained.

SQL

```
DECLARE  @x  INT
     SET @x  =  0 -- In Lab,  Use: SET @x = 0, then = 1, then = 2, then = 3
      -- Then,    Change "int" to "real" and SET @x  = 1.2
     IF @x  <  1
         PRINT 'Answer is:  x  <  1 '
     ELSE IF @x  =  1
         PRINT 'Answer is:  x  =  1'
     ELSE IF @x  =  2
         PRINT 'Answer is:  x  =  2'
     ELSE IF @x  >  2
         PRINT 'Answer is:  x  >  2'
     ELSE
          PRINT '@x is not an int = 1 or 2.  It''s value is: ' + CAST( @x AS
VARCHAR(4) )
```

5.7.10 WHILE, BREAK, CONTINUE

The WHILE Loop is the only real looping construct in Transact-SQL. The WHILE Loop does the following things:

- It executes a loop of commands that repeats as long as the Boolean_expression is true.
- It jumps back to the beginning with CONTINUE.

- It exits immediately with BREAK.

Syntax

```
WHILE Boolean_expression
    { sql_statement | statement_block }


statement_block

    BEGIN
        { sql_statement  } [  [ ; ] ... n ]
    END
```

[CONTINUE]	Causes return to the beginning of the innermost WHILE loop.
[BREAK]	Causes an exit from the innermost WHILE loop.

WHILE Example 1: A simple loop.

SQL

```
DECLARE         @Ctr     INTEGER
SET   @Ctr = 1

WHILE   @Ctr <= 5
    BEGIN
        PRINT @Ctr
        SET @Ctr = @Ctr + 1
           -- Could use SELECT to increment  Ctr
    END
PRINT 'After the loop'
```

Result

```
1
2
3
4
5
After the loop
```

WHILE Example 2: Get 1111's ename with SELECT and reverse the spelling.

SQL

```
DECLARE @vs_ename varchar(100) ,  -- string to be reversed
        @vs_result varchar(100),    -- result string after reversal
        @vi_ctr int    -- counter variable for while loop

     SELECT @vs_ename = ename  FROM emps WHERE empid = 1111
     PRINT 'Original ename is:   '  +  @vs_ename

     SET @vi_ctr = LEN(@vs_ename)
     PRINT 'LEN is:   '  +   CAST(  @vi_ctr  AS CHAR)
     SET @vs_result = ''

     WHILE @vi_ctr >= 1
          BEGIN
          SET @vs_result =
              @vs_result + SUBSTRING(@vs_ename,@vi_ctr,1)

       SET  @vi_ctr  =  @vi_ctr  -  1 -- decrement the counter
            -- PRINT @vi_ctr ; PRINT @vs_result -- Uncomment to troubleshoot
        END
     -- Display the result
     PRINT 'Reversed ename is:   ' + @vs_result
```

Result

Original ename is: Suzy Smith
LEN is: 10
Reversed ename is: htimS yzuS

Example: Using BREAK. Print all values up to 3 and then exit loop.

SQL

```
DECLARE         @Ctr     INT
     SET  @Ctr = 1
     WHILE @Ctr <= 5
         BEGIN
           PRINT @Ctr
           If @Ctr = 3
               BREAK
           SELECT @Ctr = @Ctr + 1  -- Could use SET @Ctr = @Ctr + 1
         END
```

SQL (cont.)

Result

```
1
2
3
```

Example: Using CONTINUE, print all values except 3.

SQL

```
DECLARE         @Ctr     INT
SET  @Ctr = 0
WHILE @Ctr < 5
    BEGIN
      SET @Ctr = @Ctr + 1
            -- Could use SELECT @Ctr = @Ctr + 1
      If @Ctr = 3
        CONTINUE
      PRINT @Ctr
    END
```

Result

```
1
2
4
5
```

5.7.11 GOTO and Labels

GOTO causes an unconditional branch of execution to the first executable statement following the label labelname, which must appear within the same batch.

Syntax

GOTO *labelname*

Argument

labelname

An identifier followed by a colon (:) is called a **label**, which serves as the destination of a GOTO statement.

Example: Use GOTO to implement the simple WHILE loop in example 1 above.

SQL

```
DECLARE        @Ctr     INTEGER
SET   @Ctr = 1

loop1:              -- This label and the following block do
                    -- the same work as the WHILE loop
                    -- in example1.
    BEGIN
    PRINT @Ctr
    SET @Ctr = @Ctr + 1
```

SQL

```
DECLARE        @Ctr     INTEGER
    SET   @Ctr = 1

    loop1:    -- This label and the following block do the
  -- same work as the WHILE loop in example1.
        BEGIN
         PRINT @Ctr
         SET @Ctr = @Ctr + 1  -- Could use SELECT to
  -- increment  Ctr
         IF  @Ctr  <=  5     GOTO  loop1 -- Label  "loop1"
  -- is before the BEGIN for this block
        END
    PRINT 'After the loop'
```

Result

```
1
2
3
4
5
After the loopServer: Msg 208, Level 16, State 1, Line 2
Invalid object name 'pubs..authorsxxxx'.
```

Using GOTO statements is generally discouraged because it makes program code more difficult to read than programming without it, such as using a WHILE loop. The least the programmer can do is to document the location of the label that serves as the GOTO destination.

5.7.12 WAITFOR

WAITFOR command suspends execution until a specified time interval or datetime value.

Syntax

```
WAITFOR { DELAY 'time' | TIME 'time' }
```

Arguments

DELAY 'time'

DELAY '*time*' specifies the duration of the suspension up to 24 hours.

TIME 'time'

TIME '*time*' }specifies a TIME value when the suspension is to end. See TIME formats, page 92 (include TIME only, not a DATE part).

Example: Use WAITFOR DELAY.

SQL

```
SELECT  GETDATE()  AS  BEFORE
WAITFOR DELAY '0:0:02'
      --  Wait 2 seconds before continuing execution
SELECT  GETDATE()  AS  AFTER
```

Result

```
BEFORE
------------------------------
2002-06-26 15:39:22.323

AFTER
-------------------------------
2002-06-26 15:39:24.340
```

Example: Use WAITFOR TIME.

SQL

```
PRINT GETDATE()
go

WAITFOR TIME '3:20 PM'
  --  Wait until 3:20 PM before continuing execution
PRINT GETDATE()
```

SQL (cont.)

Result

```
Jun 26 2002  3:18PM
Jun 26 2002  3:20PM
```

After executing the WAITFOR statement, the connection to SQL Server is not usable until the time or event that you specified occurs.

If *go* is omitted from the above statement the final display would be the same, showing that statements before WAITFOR execute as soon as they are reached. But without *go* the display does not appear until after the WAITFOR has completed.

5.7.13 Example TRANSACT-SQL Stored Procedure

5.7.13.1 Example 1: Insert IP Address and Trap Data into the Database

In this example, we have a program that can capture Simple Network Management Protocol (SNMP)[2] traps, events that occur whenever an error or other specified event occurs on the network. The two pieces of data that we want to store in the database are as follows:

- **ipaddr**—IP Address where the trap occurred
- **trapinfo**—Descriptive information about the event that was trapped

We create two tables: ippaddrs to store IP Addresses and their unique id value, and traps to store the trap information for each trap event, IP Address id and trapinfo.

SQL

```
CREATE TABLE ipaddrs (
   id       INT IDENTITY PRIMARY KEY
,  ipaddr   VARCHAR(15) UNIQUE
);
```

SQL

```
CREATE TABLE traps (
   id         INT
,  trapinfo VARCHAR(15)
, CONSTRAINT fk_trap_addr
    FOREIGN KEY (id)
   REFERENCES ipaddrs (id)
);
```

2. SNMP is the standard protocol used to manage network nodes (servers, workstations, routers, etc.) on an IP (Internet Protocol) network for performance and problem resolution. A trap is a monitored network event, such as occurrence of an error, exceeding a threshold, etc., about which data is collected and analyzed to assist in network management.

Create the two tables and populate them with the sample data shown above.

SQL

```
INSERT INTO ipaddrs
VALUES ('111.111.1.1')
```

SQL

```
INSERT INTO traps VALUES ( 1 ,
  'Info11')
INSERT INTO traps VALUES ( 1 ,
  'Info12')
```

SQL

```
SELECT  *  FROM ipaddrs
```

Result

```
d          ipaddr
-------    --------------
1          111.111.1.1
```

SQL

```
SELECT  *  FROM traps
```

Result

```
id         trapinfo
-------    --------------
1          Info11
1          Info12
```

5.7.13.2 Example 2: Create a Stored Procedure to Contain the ipaddr Solution

Here we implement the previous solution as a stored procedure to encapsulate the code. This makes it much cleaner for an application to execute the operation.

We'll call the procedure **uspIpaddrTraps** where "usp" is my way of identifying it as a user stored procedure. In any case, we shouldn't call it sp_xxxx because it would be confusing.

SQL

```
CREATE PROCEDURE  usp_InsertIpTrap
  @p_ipaddr   VARCHAR(15)
, @p_trapinfo VARCHAR(15)
AS
BEGIN
  DECLARE @v_id     INT

  SELECT @v_id  = id
  FROM ipaddrs WHERE  ipaddr = @p_ipaddr
  IF  @v_id  IS NULL
    BEGIN
      INSERT INTO ipaddrs  (ipaddr)
      VALUES  ( @p_ipaddr )
      SET  @v_id   =  SCOPE_IDENTITY()
                 -- Might use @@IDENTITY
    END
  INSERT INTO  traps ( id , trapinfo ) VALUES ( @v_id , @p_trapinfo )
END
```

Now let's execute the stored procedure twice, once with an existing **ipaddr** and then with a new **ipaddr**. The two SELECT statements above show the contents of the tables before.

SQL

```
EXEC usp_InsertIpTrap  '111.111.1.1' , 'Info13'
-- Trap on an EXISTING IP Addr
```

These two SELECT statements show that the procedure did what we wanted it to.

SQL

```
SELECT  *  FROM ipaddrs
```

Result

```
id       ipaddr
-------  --------------
1        111.111.1.1
2        222.222.2.2
```

SQL

```
SELECT  *  FROM traps
```

Result

```
id       trapinfo
-------  --------------
1        Info11
1        Info12
1        Info13
2        Info21
```

The stored procedure version has a definite advantage for the application program that is monitoring the traps. It detects the new trap and inserts the data in one call to this stored procedure instead of the several lines of explicit code. It also executes faster on the server.

5.8 ERROR HANDLING

Robust programming in any language requires the program to be able to take reasonable action when things don't go as intended. Table 5-4 lists typical error messages.

Table 5-4 Typical Error Messages

Managing Error Messages	**Error Log** Files—record of SQL Server error occurrences and **sysmessages** Table—table of SQL Server error definitions
sp_addmessage, sp_altermessage, sp_dropmessage	Users may add their own error messages.

Table 5-4 Typical Error Messages (cont.)

@@ERROR	The error status of most recently executed statement returns.
RAISERROR	User may invoke a system- or user-defined error condition.

5.8.1 Managing Error Messages

5.8.1.1 Error Log Files—SQL Server Error Logs, Windows NT Application Log

The occurrence of an error by SQL Server is recorded in SQL Server error log files and usually in the Windows NT application log.

The SQL Server Error Log includes seven text files where SQL Server records database errors. The MSS error logs may be read with Enterprise Manager by opening the console tree to Servername—Management—Error Logs. The actual Text Files may be seen in any text editor. Their default location is C:\Program Files\Microsoft SQL Server\MSSQL\LOG Table 5-5 includes equivalent error and file names and their meanings.

Table 5-5 Error Messages

MSS Error Log Names	Text File Names	Meaning
Current	ERRORLOG	current log file
Archive #1	ERRORLOG.1	previous log file
Archive #2-5	ERRORLOG.2-5	even earlier log files
Archive #6	ERRORLOG.6	oldest log file — it is next to be discarded as space is required

Within Windows NT application log, the errors from all applications on the system including SQL Server are kept and may be read with the system Event Viewer. For Windows NT 4.0, Windows 2000 and Windows XP: Start—Programs—Administrative Tools—Event Viewer.

Any SQL Server error that is recorded in the application log is also recorded in the SQL Server error log. You may find the latter more convenient to examine just database errors.

5.8.1.2 sysmessages Table

SQL Server records the definition of all errors regardless of database in a single table called sysmessages in the master database.

The sysmessages table contains the following columns:

- **error:** Unique error number. User errors must be 50001 and greater.
- **Severity:** Severity level of the error in the range 0–25.
- **dlevel:** For internal use only. (0 seems to mean no log, 128 with log.)
- **description:** Explanation of the error with placeholders for parameters.
- **Msglangid:** System message group ID.

Example:

SQL
`SELECT * FROM pubs.dbo.xxx`
Result
Server: Msg 208, Level 16, State 1, Line 1 Invalid object name 'pubs.dbo.xxx'.

5.8.2 sp_addmessage, sp_altermessage, sp_dropmessage

5.8.2.1 sp_addmessage

These system-stored procedures add a new error message to the **sysmessages** table.

Syntax

```
sp_addmessage [ @msgnum = ] msg_id ,  [ @severity = ]
severity ,  [ @msgtext = ] 'msg'
    [ , [ @lang = ] 'language' ]
    [ , [ @with_log = ]  { TRUE | FALSE } ]
    [ , [ @replace = ]   REPLACE  ]
```

Arguments

[**@msgnum** =] *msg_id*

[**@msgnum** =] *msg_id* is a user-defined error message number >= 50,001.

The combination of *msg_id* and *language* must be unique.

[@**severity** =] severity

0–18: Severity levels from 0 through 18 can be used by any user.

19–25: Severity levels from 19 through 25 can be added only by members of the **sysadmin** fixed server role and the WITH LOG option is required.

Severity levels 20 through 25 are considered fatal resulting in the client connection being closed and the error logged in both SQL Server error log and NT application log.

[@**msgtext** =] 'msg'

The message text allows up to 255 characters.

Message strings may be formatted (similar to printf in C) to allow passing of arguments into the message string at run time. See Books Online for the *msg* format.

[@**lang** =] 'language'

To list the language choices for this message, use sp_helplanguage.

When *language* is omitted, the language is the default language for the session.

[@**with_log** =] **{ TRUE | FALSE }**

This string sets default logging behavior.

TRUE means that when this error is raised it will always be written to the Windows NT application log and to the MSS error log file for every RAISERROR call.

FALSE or missing means when this error is raised it will not by default be written to the logs. Logging may still be explicitly specified if raised by RAISERROR WITH LOG.

Only members of the **sysadmin** server role can specify this option.

[@**replace** =] **REPLACE**

REPLACE is used to replace message text and severity of an existing message. If a U.S. English message is replaced, the severity level is replaced for all messages in all other languages that have the same *msg_id*.

5.8.2.2 sp_altermessage

This is only used to change the default logging behavior.

Note: Change text or severity of the error using **sp_addmessage** with REPLACE.

Syntax

```
sp_altermessage [ @message_id = ] msg_id  , [ @parameter = ]
WITH_LOG
                 [ @parameter_value = ] { TRUE | FALSE }
```

Arguments

[@**parameter_value** =] '*value*'

If **TRUE**, the error is always written to the Windows NT application log and SQL Server error log file.

If **FALSE**, the error is not written to the logs unless raised by RAISERROR WITH LOG.

5.8.2.3 sp_dropmessage

This is a system-stored procedure that drops an existing error message from the **sysmessages** table.

Syntax

```
sp_dropmessage [ @msgnum = ] message_number  [ , [ @lang = ] 'language' ]
```

Arguments

[@**msgnum** =] message_number

message_number is the message number to drop. *message_number* must be a user-defined message with a message number greater than 50000.

[@**lang** =] 'language'

This is the language of the message to drop. If all is specified, all language versions of *message_number* are dropped.

Examples: sp_addmessage, sp_altermessage, sp_dropmessage

Example:

SQL

```
EXEC sp_addmessage 50001, 1,
   N' Original 50001 message text.' ,
   @with_log =  FALSE
```

SQL

```
SELECT * FROM master..sysmessages
WHERE error >= 50000
```

SQL (cont.)

Result

```
error    severity     dlevel    description                           msglangid
-------  -----------  --------  ------------------------------------  -------------
50001    1            0         Original 50001 message text.          1033
```

Use **sp_addmessage** with REPLACE to change severity level to 2 and modify message text.

SQL

```
-- Replace message text and change severity level
EXEC sp_addmessage 50001, 2,
  N New 50001 message text,' @replace = REPLACE
```

Use sp_altermessage to change default logging to TRUE.

SQL

```
-- Turns on logging for this message
EXEC sp_altermessage 50001, 'WITH_LOG',  TRUE
```

SQL

```
SELECT * FROM master..sysmessages
WHERE error >= 50000
```

Result

```
error    severity     dlevel    description                           msglangid
-------  -----------  --------  ------------------------------------  -------------
50001    2            128       New 50001 message text.               1033
```

SQL

```
EXEC sp_dropmessage 50001
```

5.8.3 @@ERROR

@@ERROR returns the error number for the last Transact-SQL statement executed. A value of zero means the last statement was successful, non-zero means it failed. User-defined errors raised with RAISERROR will also be returned. See next section.

@@ERROR Examples

Example: Attempt UPDATE statement that causes MSS error — violates FOREIGN KEY.

SQL

```
UPDATE pubs..titles
SET pub_id = '1'
```

Result

```
Server: Msg 547, Level 16, State 1, Line 0
UPDATE statement conflicted with COLUMN FOREIGN KEY constraint
'FK__titles__pub_id__1273C1CD'. The conflict occurred in database 'pubs', table 'publishers',
column 'pub_id'.
The statement has been terminated.
```

Example: Use @@ERROR to print the error number of the update statement.

SQL

```
PRINT 'Error is: ' + CAST(@@ERROR AS VARCHAR)
```

Result

```
Error is: 547
```

SQL

```
PRINT 'Error is: ' + CAST(@@ERROR AS VARCHAR)
--print 0, last statement was "PRINT" which had no error.
```

Result

```
Error is: 0
```

5.8.4 RAISERROR

RAISERROR causes the user-defined error to occur (raises the error) and returns its error message. RAISERROR may raise and retrieve either a predefined error using *msg_id* >= 50,001 which was created using **sp_addmessage**, or an ad hoc error message by using *msg_str* that will have error number 50,000.

Syntax

```
RAISERROR ( { msg_id | msg_str } { , severity , state }
    [ , argument [ ,...n ] ]   )
  [ WITH { LOG | NOWAIT | SETERROR } [ ,...n ] ]
```

Arguments

msg_id

This is the predefined user-defined error message number >= 50,001. Use **sp_addmessage** to add and **sp_dropmessage** to delete user-defined error messages.

msg_st

This is an ad hoc message text of up to 400 characters and a message ID of 50,000. They allow formatting similar to the C printf format style; see Books Online for the *msg_str* format.

severity

The user-defined severity level for this message (0–25).

0–18: Severity levels from 0 through 18 can be used by any user.

19–25: Severity levels from 19 through 25 can be added only by members of the **sysadmin** fixed server role and the WITH LOG option is required.

Severity levels 20 through 25 are considered fatal and result in the client connection being closed and the error logged in both SQL Server error log and NT application log.

State

The user-defined int (1–127) to give information about the error's state at invocation.

argument

You may specify in the msg_str format that arguments may be passed to the string at run time. Formatting is similar to a printf in the C language. See Books Online for formatting.

LOG | NOWAIT | SETERROR

These values are custom options for the error. *option* can be one of these values. See Table 5-6. (Also see Ben-Gan 2000, page 242.)

Table 5-6 Error Values

Value	Description
LOG	Logs the error in the server error log (400 bytes max) and the NT application log even if not specified in **sp_addmessage** definition.
NOWAIT	Sends messages immediately to the client.
SETERROR	Sets @@ERROR value to *msg_id* or 50000, regardless of the severity level.

Summary: RAISERROR sends a message, optionally logging it in the error log, but it does not affect batch execution unless the severity is 20 or more, in which case the connection is closed.

5.8.4.1 *Example 1: sp_addmessage, sp_altermessage, sp_dropmessage, and RAISERROR*

Create error 50002 with severity 12 and no default logging.

SQL

```
EXEC sp_addmessage 50002, 12,
    N' Original 50002 message text.' ,
    @with_log =  FALSE
```

SQL

```
SELECT * FROM master..sysmessages
WHERE error >= 50000
```

Result

```
error       severity     dlevel     description                        msglangid
--------    ----------   -------    ---------------------------------  -----------
50001       1            128        Original 50001 message text.       1033
50002       12           0          Original 50002 message text.       1033
```

Use RAISERROR to cause error 50002 with severity 16, state of 1 to occur with logging.

SQL

```
RAISERROR( 50002 , 16 , 1 )  WITH LOG
                -- Raises error 50002 and enters into logs
```

Result

```
Server: Msg 50002, Level 16, State 1, Line 1      <-- This is the system error message
Original 50002 message text.                     <-- followed by your error message.
```

SQL

```
PRINT  @@ERROR
```

Result

```
50002
```

This error occurrence may now be viewed in Enterprise Manager at Servername—Management—Error Logs (you may need to right click to Refresh).

Now raise error 50002 with severity 0, state of 0 to occur with logging.

SQL

```
RAISERROR( 50002 , 11 , 12 )
                -- Raises error 50002 with no logging
```

Result

```
Server: Msg 50002, Level 11, State 12, Line 1
Original 50002 message text.
```

Refreshing the Enterprise Manager error log doesn't display this error because it wasn't logged.

Use **sp_addmessage** with **REPLACE** to change severity level to 2 and modify message text.

SQL

```
EXEC sp_addmessage 50002, 2,
   N' New 50002 message text.' , @replace = REPLACE
```

Use **sp_altermessage** to change default logging to TRUE.

SQL

```
EXEC sp_altermessage 50002, 'WITH_LOG',  TRUE
                   -- Turns on logging for this message
```

SQL

```
SELECT * FROM master..sysmessages
WHERE error >= 50000
```

Result

error	severity	dlevel	description	msglangid
--------	----------	-------	----------------------------------	-----------
50001	1	128	Original 50001 message text.	1033
50002	2	128	New 50002 message text.	1033

SQL

```
EXEC sp_dropmessage 50002
```

5.8.4.2 *Example 2: RAISERROR to send an ad hoc error message*

SQL

```
RAISERROR ( 'Your ad hoc message goes here' , 16, 1 )
WITH LOG
```

Result

```
Server: Msg 50000, Level 16, State 1, Line 5
Your ad hoc message goes here
```

5.9 CURSORS

A *cursor* is a named SELECT statement in which the result set is accessed one row at time. The cursor may be moved, often in a loop, to a different row in the result set using the fetch statement as follows.

```
FETCH [ NEXT | PREV | FIRST | LAST ]
```

Cursors may be specified as read only or updateable as well as forward only or scrollable (can move forward and backward) and may be specified to have other features.

> **Note:** Cursors are often considered to be inefficient and best avoided if possible. The interested reader is referred to Ben-Gan and Moreau[3] on best use of cursors. They open with the following advice.
>
> In most cases where cursors are being used, they are not really necessary. You should look upon cursors as SQL of last resort, and it had better be the last resort. Sometimes, though, there is no escaping cursors.
>
> They also include a section "SQL Alternatives to Cursors."

SQL Server 2000 has two kinds of cursors. (See DECLARE CURSOR in Books Online.) SQL-92 Cursors are the simplest and most portable. Transact-SQL Extended Cursors include more features, and they may specify to be more efficient.

5.9.1 SQL-92 Cursor

DECLARE CURSOR Syntax

```
DECLARE cursor_name [ INSENSITIVE ] [ SCROLL ] CURSOR
FOR select_statement
  [ FOR { READ ONLY | UPDATE [ OF column_name [ ,...n ] ] } ]
```

DECLARE c1 CURSOR FOR SELECT * FROM pubs..authors

-- SQL-92 cursor defaults to sensitive, forward only, updatable as well as global, optimistic and dynamic.

3. Ben-Gan 2000, p. 553.

Arguments

INSENSITIVE

INSENSITIVE makes the cursor insensitive to data changes by other users (even committed changes) by creating a read only snapshot of the result set into **tempdb** when the cursor is opened and doing all reads from this snapshot.

INSENSITIVE implies read only and may not be used with FOR UPDATE.

If absent, then all committed updates and deletes by any user will be visible in the cursor on the next fetch.

It is the same as T-SQL STATIC cursor.

SCROLL

SCROLL makes all fetch options available for moving within the cursor, FETCH [NEXT | PRIOR | FIRST | LAST | RELATIVE | ABSOLUTE].

If SCROLL is missing then FETCH NEXT is the only option available.

select_statement

select_statement may not include COMPUTE, COMPUTE BY, FOR BROWSE or INTO.

[FOR { READ ONLY | UPDATE [OF column_name [,...*n*]] }]

FOR READ ONLY prevents updates from being made through the cursor.

FOR UPDATE allows updates of all columns in the cursor SELECT list. It is the default.

FOR UPDATE OF *column_name* allows updates of columns specified.

5.9.2 Transact-SQL Extended Cursor (T-SQL Cursor)

DECLARE CURSOR Syntax

```
DECLARE cursor_name CURSOR
        [ LOCAL | GLOBAL ]
        [ FORWARD_ONLY | SCROLL ]
        [ STATIC | KEYSET | DYNAMIC | FAST_FORWARD ]
        [ READ_ONLY | SCROLL_LOCKS | OPTIMISTIC ]
        [ TYPE_WARNING ]
FOR select_statement
        [ FOR UPDATE [ OF column_name [ ,...n ] ] ]
```

DECLARE c2 CURSOR FOR SELECT * FROM pubs..authors

-- T-SQL cursor defaults to global, forward only, dynamic, optimistic, updatable.

Arguments

[LOCAL | GLOBAL]

For LOCAL, The cursor is local to the batch, stored procedure or trigger in which the cursor was created. The cursor is implicitly deallocated when the batch, stored procedure or trigger terminates, unless the cursor was passed back in an OUTPUT parameter. If the cursor is passed back in an OUTPUT parameter, then it is deallocated when the last variable referencing it is deallocated or goes out of scope.

For GLOBAL, the cursor is global to the connection. The cursor name can be referenced in any stored procedure or batch executed by the connection. The cursor is only implicitly deallocated at disconnect.

GLOBAL is the default if neither is specified. If neither GLOBAL or LOCAL is specified, the default is controlled by the setting of the **default to local cursor** database option. In SQL Server 2000 and before, this option defaults to FALSE for local to match earlier versions of SQL Server, in which all cursors were global. The default of this option may change in future versions of SQL Server.

SQL

```
SELECT DATABASEPROPERTYEX( 'pubs' , 'IsLocalCursorsDefault' )
```

Result

```
-----
0
```

0 shows LOCAL is FALSE so the default is GLOBAL.

See p. 187 on setting and changing database options.

[FORWARD_ONLY | SCROLL]

FORWARD_ONLY specifies that the cursor can only be fetched from the first to the last row, so FETCH NEXT is the only supported fetch option.

If FORWARD_ONLY is specified without the STATIC, KEYSET or DYNAMIC keyword, the cursor operates as a DYNAMIC cursor.

SCROLL Makes all fetch options available for moving within the cursor,

```
FETCH [ NEXT | PRIOR | FIRST | LAST | RELATIVE | ABSOLUTE].
```

If SCROLL is missing then FETCH NEXT is the only FETCH option available. SCROLL may not be used with FAST_FORWARD.

SCROLL is the default if neither FORWARD_ONLY nor SCROLL is specified.

FORWARD_ONLY is the default, unless the keyword STATIC, KEYSET or DYNAMIC is specified, all of which default to SCROLL.

Unlike ODBC and ADO cursors, FORWARD_ONLY may be specified with STATIC, KEYSET and DYNAMIC Transact-SQL cursors.

FAST_FORWARD and FORWARD_ONLY are mutually exclusive.

[STATIC | KEYSET | DYNAMIC | FAST_FORWARD]

STATIC makes the cursor insensitive to data changes by other users (even committed changes) by creating a read only snapshot of the result set into **tempdb** when the cursor is opened and doing all reads from this snapshot.

STATIC implies read-only and may not be used with FOR UPDATE.

If absent, all committed updates or deletes by any user will be visible on subsequent fetches.

STATIC is the same as SQL-92 INSENSITIVE cursor.

For KEYSET, when the cursor is opened, a table of keys for each row in the result set is created in **tempdb**. Row membership and order remain fixed.

Committed updates to nonkey columns from any user will be visible.

Inserts from other users will not be visible.

Deletes from other users or changing key column values gives @@FETCH_STATUS = –2.

DYNAMIC is the most sensitive to data changes. It specifies a cursor that shows all committed data changes made by all users to the data as you scroll through the cursor. Data values and membership of the rows can change (due to updates or deletes) on each fetch as well as order.

You can't use the ABSOLUTE fetch option with dynamic cursors.

FAST_FORWARD specifies a FORWARD_ONLY, READ_ONLY cursor optimized for performance. You can not specify FAST_FORWARD with FORWARD_ONLY, SCROLL or FOR_UPDATE.

FAST_FORWARD is the default if neither STATIC, KEYSET, DYNAMIC, nor FAST_FORWARD is specified.

[READ_ONLY | SCROLL_LOCKS | OPTIMISTIC]

READ_ONLY prevents updates made through this cursor. The cursor cannot be referenced in a WHERE CURRENT OF clause in an UPDATE or DELETE statement. This option overrides the default capability of a cursor to be updated.

SCROLL_LOCKS are used for updatable cursors, MSS will place an exclusive lock on a row as it is fetched to guarantee that your data change will succeed.

SCROLL_LOCKS and FAST_FORWARD cannot both be specified.

The OPTIMISTIC command uses optimistic locking in that no lock is taken when the row is read, but if you update or delete the row, SQL Server will check to see if the row has been updated by another user. If so, you will receive error 16934 after which you may try again until you succeed.

OPTIMISTIC and FAST_FORWARD can not both be specified.

The following defaults apply if none of these three is specified.

The cursor will be READ_ONLY if the SELECT does not support updates (e.g., it lacks change permissions or has aggregates) or if STATIC or FAST_FORWARD is specified.

The cursor will be OPTIMISTIC if DYNAMIC or KEYSET is specified.

Hint: Specify every option you desire and then test thoroughly that it works correctly.

[TYPE_WARNING]

TYPE_WARNING causes a warning message to be sent to the client if the cursor is implicitly converted from one requested type to another. (See Books Online "Implicit Cursor Conversions.")

select_statement

select_statement may not include COMPUTE, COMPUTE BY, FOR BROWSE or INTO.

[FOR UPDATE [OF column_name [,...*n*]]

FOR UPDATE allows updates of all columns in the cursor SELECT list.

FOR UPDATE OF *column_name* allows updates of columns specified.

If missing or if READ_ONLY is specified above, the cursor does not allow updates

5.9.3 Commands Used with Cursors

Both SQL-92 and T-SQL Cursors use the following commands, in the order given.

1. **DECLARE:** To declare the cursor or cursor variable. This is described above.
2. **OPEN:** To execute the SELECT statement to populate the cursor.

3. **FETCH:** To move the cursor to a new row and retrieve the row's column values.

4. **UPDATE / DELETE:** To modify the data on an updatable cursor.

5. **CLOSE:** To close the cursor and release the result set but retain the cursor name.

6. **DEALLOCATE:** To remove the cursor name and some other resources.

Each command is explained below, but first we'll look at a simple example demonstrating cursors.

Example: Simple cursor programs—using the SQL-92 Cursor

Use all cursor commands but UPDATE and output cursor data to the screen.

SQL

```
DECLARE  c1   INSENSITIVE  CURSOR
FOR SELECT au_id , au_lname
    FROM pubs..authors
    OPEN  c1 -- Runs SELECT and fills cursor
    FETCH c1 -- Outputs next (1st) row to screen
    FETCH c1 -- Outputs next (2d) row to screen
    CLOSE  c1 -- Releases result set and locks
    DEALLOCATE  c1 -- Drops cursor reference
```

Result

```
au_id            au_lname
---------------  ---------------
409-56-7008      Bennet

au_id            au_lname
---------------  ---------------
648-92-1872      Blotchet-Halls
```

Now use all cursor commands but UPDATE and output cursor data to the local variables.

SQL

```
DECLARE   @v_au_id              VARCHAR(11)
DECLARE   @v_au_lname    VARCHAR(40)
DECLARE   c1   INSENSITIVE   CURSOR
FOR SELECT au_id , au_lname
FROM pubs..authors
OPEN c1
FETCH  c1    INTO   @v_au_id  , @v_au_lname
PRINT '1. ' +  @v_au_id  + '    ' +  @v_au_lname
FETCH  c1    INTO   @v_au_id  , @v_au_lname
CLOSE c1
DEALLOCATE c1
PRINT '2. ' + @v_au_id   + '    ' +  @v_au_lname
```

Result

```
1. au_id: 409-56-7008        au_lname: Bennet
2. au_id: 648-92-1872        au_lname: Blotchet-Halls
```

For T-SQL Cursor (page 639), replace the DECLARE CURSOR statement above with:

```
DECLARE   c1   CURSOR    FORWARD_ONLY     STATIC
FOR SELECT  au_id , au_lname   FROM pubs..authors
```

It is common to use the version on the right side above which declares local variables to hold the data for further processing. The one on the left outputs each row to the screen, which can be done more easily and more attractively using SELECT without a cursor.

The following commands may be used interchangeably to fetch the next row:

```
FETCH  c1    or    FETCH FROM  c1    or    FETCH NEXT
FROM  c1
```

5.9.3.1 OPEN CURSOR

OPEN CURSOR executes the cursor's SELECT statement and populates the cursor with the result set.

Syntax

OPEN { { [GLOBAL] *cursor_name* } | *cursor_variable_name* }

Argument

GLOBAL

GLOBAL refers to a T-SQL cursor which was declared as global to the connection. You may declare both of the following at the same time.
DECLARE c1 CURSOR LOCAL FOR SELECT ....
DECLARE c1 CURSOR GLOBAL FOR SELECT ....

The first may be called as **OPEN c1** or **OPEN LOCAL c1**.

The second must use **OPEN GLOBAL c1** since there is a LOCAL one of the same name.

The keyword GLOBAL is optional if there is no local cursor with the same name.

5.9.3.2 FETCH CURSOR

FETCH CURSOR retrieves a row of data from the cursor.

Syntax

```
FETCH
   [
     [ NEXT | PRIOR | FIRST | LAST | ABSOLUTE { n | @nvar } | RELATIVE
  { n | @nvar } ]
     FROM
   ]
{ { [ GLOBAL ] cursor_name } | @cursor_variable_name }  [ INTO @variable_name
  [ ,...n ] ]
```

Arguments

NEXT

NEXT returns the result row immediately following the current row. For the first fetch against the cursor, FETCH NEXT returns the first row in the result set. NEXT is the default cursor fetch option (but if NEXT is used, FROM must also be used).

The following commands may be used interchangeably to fetch the next row: FETCH c1 or FETCH FROM c1 or FETCH NEXT FROM cl.

NEXT is the only valid direction keyword unless the cursor was declared with SCROLL.

PRIOR

PRIOR returns the result row immediately preceding the current row.

For the first fetch against the cursor, FETCH PRIOR returns no row and the cursor is left positioned before the first row.

FIRST

FIRST returns the first row in the cursor and makes it the current row.

LAST

LAST returns the last row in the cursor and makes it the current row.

ABSOLUTE {*n* | @*nvar*}

If positive, ABSOLUTE returns the row *n* or @*nvar* rows from the front of the cursor.

If negative, ABSOLUTE returns the row *n* or @*nvar* rows before the end of the cursor.

If *n* or @*nvar* is 0, no row is returned.

Notes: +1 is the first row, –1 is the last row. For a cursor with 4 rows, +7 and –7 return no rows and place the cursor one before first or one after the last row.

n must be an integer constant and @*nvar* must be **smallint**, **tinyint** or **int**.

RELATIVE {*n* | @*nvar*}

If positive, RELATIVE returns the row *n* or @*nvar* rows after the current row; or before if negative.

If *n* or @*nvar* is 0, RELATIVE returns the current row.

If the first fetch against the cursor and FETCH RELATIVE is specified with *n* or @*nvar* set to 0 or a negative number, no row is returned.

Notes: If +n or –n is beyond the first or last row of the cursor, no row is returned and the cursor is positioned one before the first or one after the last row.

n must be an integer constant and @*nvar* must be **smallint**, **tinyint**, or **int**.

Notes about the Direction Keywords:

PRIOR, FIRST, LAST, ABSOLUTE and RELATIVE are valid only with a SCROLL cursor.

For a T-SQL Cursor these additional rules apply:

- FORWARD-ONLY or FAST_FORWARD cursors support only FETCH NEXT.
- KEYSET, STATIC, and SCROLL cursors support all FETCH if all of DYNAMIC, FORWARD_ONLY and FAST_FORWARD are not specified.
- DYNAMIC SCROLL cursors support all the FETCH options except ABSOLUTE.

GLOBAL

Global means the same as for OPEN.

INTO @variable_name[,...n]

INTO allows data from the columns of a fetch to be placed into local variables.

Each variable in the list, from left to right, is associated with the corresponding column in the cursor result set. The data type of each variable must either match or support implicit conversion of the data type of the corresponding result set column.

The number of variables must match the number of columns in the cursor select list.

The @@FETCH_STATUS function reports the status of the last FETCH statement. The same information is recorded in the **fetch_status** column in the cursor returned by **sp_describe_cursor**. This status information should be used to determine the validity of the data returned by a FETCH statement prior to attempting any operation against that data. See @@FETCH_STATUS below.

Example: Demonstrate several FETCH options.

SQL

```
SELECT TOP 4 * FROM pubs..jobs
        -- Display the data for reference
```

Result

```
job_id    job_desc                              min_lvl     max_lvl
------    -----------------------------------   ---------   ------ ---
1         New Hire - Job not specified          10          10
2         Chief Executive Officer               200         250
3         Business Operations Manager           175         225
4         Chief Financial Officier              175         250
```

SQL

```
DECLARE  @result  INT
   --  Variable to capture cursor job_id value

DECLARE c1 CURSOR SCROLL FOR SELECT TOP 4  job_id FROM
pubs..jobs
OPEN c1
```

SQL (cont.)

```
FETCH RELATIVE 7 FROM c1 INTO @result
       --  Returns no row, places 1 beyond last row
PRINT ISNULL( @result , -99 )

FETCH PRIOR FROM c1 INTO @result
                  --  Returns last row =  4
PRINT ISNULL( @result , -99 )

FETCH ABSOLUTE 1  FROM c1 INTO @result
    --  Returns first row =  1
PRINT ISNULL( @result , -99 )

FETCH ABSOLUTE 2  FROM c1 INTO @result
    --  Returns second row =  2
PRINT ISNULL( @result , -99 )

FETCH NEXT FROM c1 INTO @result
                   --  Returns third row =  3
PRINT ISNULL( @result , -99 )

CLOSE c1

DEALLOCATE c1
```

Result

```
—99
4
1
2
3
```

UPDATF/DELETE Using a Cursor (positioned update)

A **POSITIONED UPDATE** uses a WHERE CURRENT OF cursor clause to update or delete the single base table row corresponding to the current cursor position.

Simplified UPDATE and DELETE Syntax

This applies where the cursor specifies a single row in the base table to update or delete.

UPDATE *table* SET *column_name* = *expression* [,...*n*] WHERE CURRENT OF *cursor*	DELETE [FROM] *table* WHERE CURRENT OF *cursor*

See complete UPDATE syntax on page 448 and DELETE syntax on page 456.

Note: The positioned update is contrasted with a **SEARCHED UPDATE** that uses a WHERE search_condition clause and may modify multiple rows.

WHERE CURRENT OF cursor clause is ANSI SQL-92 compliant.

Example: Demonstrate UPDATE *table* WHERE CURRENT OF cursor.

SQL

```
DECLARE jobs_csr SCROLL CURSOR
FOR SELECT * FROM pubs2..jobs
       --  pubs2 is a copy of pubs

OPEN jobs_csr

FETCH ABSOLUTE 2 FROM jobs_csr
          -- In reality the cursor requires more
          -- exotic logic to find the row to update.
          -- This one could be done without a cursor.

UPDATE jobs
SET job_desc = 'New job desc'
WHERE CURRENT OF jobs_csr
          -- In real life the cursor would use more
          -- exotic logic than shown here.

CLOSE jobs_csr

DEALLOCATE jobs_csr

SELECT * FROM pubs2..jobs
  --  pubs2 is a copy of pubs
WHERE job_id = 2
```

SQL (cont.)

Result

```
-- This is from the FETCH
job_id    job_desc                      min_lvl     max_lvl
------    ---------------------------   ---------   ----------
2         Chief Executive Officer       200         250

job_id    job_desc                      min_lvl     max_lvl

-- This is from the SELECT
------    ----------------------------  ---------   ----------
2         New job desc                  200         250
```

Note: This example is just to show the mechanics. It is not a good use for a cursor.

5.9.3.3 CLOSE CURSOR

CLOSE CURSOR releases the cursor result set and frees locks. It must be issued on an open cursor. The cursor may be reopened, at which time fetches and updates may again be issued.

Syntax

```
CLOSE { { [ GLOBAL ] cursor_name } | cursor_variable_name }
```

GLOBAL - Means the same as for OPEN.

SQL

```
DECLARE  @result  INT
   --  Variable to capture cursor job_id value

DECLARE c1 CURSOR SCROLL FOR SELECT TOP 4  job_id FROM
pubs..jobs

OPEN c1
           FETCH FIRST FROM c1 INTO @result
               --  Returns first row =  1
           PRINT ISNULL( @result , -99 )
CLOSE c1
```

Example: Play with OPEN and CLOSE.

SQL

```
          FETCH FIRST FROM c1 INTO @result
             --  Fails, cursor not open

OPEN c1
          FETCH LAST FROM c1 INTO @result
             --  Returns last row =  4
          PRINT ISNULL( @result , -99 )
CLOSE c1

DEALLOCATE c1
```

Result

```
1
Server: Msg 16917, Level 16, State 2, Line 12
Cursor is not open.
4
```

5.9.3.4 DEALLOCATE CURSOR

DEALLOCATE CURSOR removes a cursor reference. When the last cursor reference is deallocated, the cursor data structures are released.

Syntax

```
DEALLOCATE { { [ GLOBAL ] cursor_name } | @cursor_variable_name }
```

5.9.4 Cursor Functions and Stored Procedures

5.9.4.1 Cursor Functions

Cursor Functions return cursor status information. All are nondeterministic (see page 163). They are summarized in Table 5-7 and detailed below.

Table 5-7 Descriptions of Cursor Functions

Function Name	Description and Syntax
@@CURSOR_ROWS	Returns the number of rows in the last cursor opened on the connection

Table 5-7 Descriptions of Cursor Functions (cont.)

Function Name	Description and Syntax
@@FETCH_STATUS	Returns the status of the last cursor FETCH statement issued against any cursor currently opened by the connection. Global function to all cursors in the connection, so use it immediately after the FETCH whose status you're interested in.
CURSOR_STATUS	A scalar function that allows the caller of a stored procedure to determine whether or not the procedure has returned a cursor and result set.

@@CURSOR_ROWS

Syntax

```
@@CURSOR_ROWS
```

@@CURSOR_ROWS returns the number of rows in the last cursor opened on the connection.

The command returns an integer whose value has the following meaning:

0 No cursor is opened on the connection or no rows are in the last opened cursor.

–1 The cursor is dynamic, which has possibly varying number of rows.

–n The cursor is being populated asynchronously, currently n rows loaded.

+n A positive number means the cursor is fully populated and has n rows.

@@FETCH_STATUS

Syntax

```
@@FETCH_STATUS
```

@@FETCH_STATUS returns the status of the last cursor FETCH statement issued against any cursor currently opened by the connection.

It is a global function to all cursors in the connection, so use it immediately after the FETCH whose status you're interested in.

It returns an integer whose value has the following meaning:

0 Last FETCH statement was successful.

–1 Last FETCH statement failed or the row was beyond the result set.

–2 Row fetched is missing (like KEYSET row deleted by another user).

CURSOR_STATUS

Syntax

```
CURSOR_STATUS      (    { 'local' , 'cursor_name' }
                   | { 'global' , 'cursor_name' }
                   | { 'variable' , 'cursor_variable' }
                      )
```

CURSOR_STATUS is a scalar function that allows the caller of a stored procedure to determine whether or not the procedure has returned a cursor and result set.

The word *local*, *global* or *variable* is required even if there is only one cursor of the specified name. The CURSOR_STATUS returns a **smallint** value with the meanings described in Table 5-8.

Table 5-8 CURSOR_STATUS Return Values

Return Value	Cursor Name	Cursor Variable
1	For dynamic cursor, the result set has 0, 1 or more rows. For other cursors, the result set has at least one row	The cursor allocated to this variable is open and: For dynamic cursor, the result set has 0, 1 or more rows. For insensitive and keyset cursors, the result set has at least one row.
0	The result set of the cursor is empty.	The cursor allocated to this variable is open, but the result set is empty. (Dynamic cursors cannot return this value.)
–1	The cursor is closed.	The cursor allocated to this variable is closed.
–2	Not applicable.	Can be any of these three possibilities: 1. No cursor was assigned to this OUTPUT variable by the previously called procedure. 2. A cursor was assigned to this OUTPUT variable by the previously called procedure but closed there and thus not returned to the calling environment. 3. There is no cursor assigned to a declared cursor variable.
–3	A cursor with this name does not exist.	A cursor variable with this name does not exist or it exists but is not yet assigned to a cursor.

5.9.4.2 Cursor Stored Procedures

Cursor Stored Procedures can be used to determine the characteristics of the cursor after a cursor has been declared. The procedures are described in Table 5-9 and detailed below.

Table 5-9 Description of Cursor Stored Procedures

System Stored Procedure	Description
sp_cursor_list	List of cursors and their attributes currently on the connection
sp_describe_cursor	Describes the attributes of a cursor, such as whether it is forward-only or scrolling, read only or for update
sp_describe_cursor_columns	Describes the attributes of the columns in the cursor result set
sp_describe_cursor_tables	Describes the base tables accessed by the cursor

Variables may be used as part of the *select_statement* that declares a cursor. Cursor variable values do not change after a cursor is declared.

sp_cursor_list This reports a list of cursors currently open on this connection and their attributes. The report list is itself returned as an output cursor, which you must declare before calling the procedure.

Syntax

```
sp_cursor_list      [ @cursor_return = ] cursor_variable_name   OUTPUT
                  , [ @cursor_scope = ] cursor_scope
```

Arguments

[@cursor_return =] cursor_variable_name OUTPUT

This is the name of a cursor variable that you have declared as a scrollable, dynamic, read-only cursor to hold the results of the report.

[@cursor_scope =] cursor_scope

This integer value specifies the level of cursors to report.

Values: 1 Report all Local cursors
2 Report all Global cursors
3 Report all Local and Global cursors

The format of the cursor returned by **sp_cursor_list** is the same as **sp_describe_cursor**. The cursor columns returned by sp_cursor_list and sp_describe_cursor are shown in Table 5-10.

Table 5-10 Cursor Columns Returned by **sp_cursor_list** and **sp_describe_cursor**

Column Name	Data Type	Description
reference_name	***sysname***	Reference name of the cursor or cursor variable. Often same as cursor or cursor variable name.
cursor_name	***sysname***	Name of the cursor or cursor variable
cursor_scope	***smallint***	1 = LOCAL; 2 = GLOBAL
status	***smallint***	Same values as reported by CURSOR_STATUS system function: 1 = The cursor referenced by the cursor name or variable is open. If the cursor is insensitive, static or keyset, it has at least one row. If the cursor is dynamic, the result set has zero or more rows. 0 = The cursor referenced by the cursor name or variable is open but has no rows. Dynamic cursors never return this value. –1 = The cursor referenced by the cursor name or variable is closed. For example, before first FETCH or after CLOSE. –2 = Cursor variables only: there is no cursor assigned to the variable. –3 = A cursor or cursor variable with the specified name does not exist, or the cursor variable has not had a cursor allocated to it.
model	***smallint***	1 = Insensitive (or static); 2 = Keyset; 3 = Dynamic; 4 = Fast Forward
concurrency	***smallint***	1 = Read-only; 2 = Scroll locks; 3 = Optimistic
scrollable	***smallint***	0 = Forward-only; 1 = Scrollable
open_status	***smallint***	0 = Closed; 1 = Open
cursor_rows	***int***	Number of qualifying rows in the result set See **@@CURSOR_ROWS**.
fetch_status	***smallint***	Status of the last fetch on this cursor See **@@FETCH_STATUS**. 0 = Fetch successful; –1 = Fetch failed or is beyond the bounds of the cursor; –2 = The requested row is missing; –9 = There has been no fetch on the cursor
column_count	***smallint***	Number of columns in the cursor result set.
row_count	***smallint***	Number of rows affected by the last operation on the cursor See **@@ROWCOUNT**.
last_operation	***smallint***	Integer indicating the last operation performed on the cursor 0 = No operations have been performed; 1 = OPEN; 4 = UPDATE; 2 = FETCH; 5 = DELETE; 7 = DEALLOCATE; 3 = INSERT; 6 = CLOSE
cursor_handle	***int***	A unique integer that identifies the cursor.

Example 1

Using **sp_cursor_list** can be a bit clumsy, so we'll create a user-stored procedure to serve as a utility to display the results of **sp_cursor_list**.

SQL

```
/*  CREATE PROC   uspShowGlobalCursorList  AS PRINT 'stub' go   */
--  I like to start with a stub CREATE PROC
--  statement which I highlight and execute in
--  Query Analyzer followed by an ALTER PROC
--  statement used to make all changes and still
--  preserve permissions.
--  This is better than DROP PROC x; CREATE PROC x
--  which loses permissions granted on the proc.

ALTER PROC uspShowGlobalCursorList
  @p_scope    SMALLINT   -- 1 for Local cursors, 2 for Global
AS
BEGIN

  SET NOCOUNT ON
  DECLARE @List   CURSOR

    -- Execute the system stored procedure to fill
    -- the List cursor
  EXEC master.dbo.sp_cursor_list
    @cursor_return = @List  OUTPUT,
    @cursor_scope = @p_scope

  FETCH NEXT from @List
            -- Fetch the first row from the List
            -- cursor and display it

  IF @@FETCH_STATUS = -1
    PRINT 'No current cursors'
      ELSE
    WHILE (@@FETCH_STATUS <> -1)
            -- Fetch and display the rest of the rows
    BEGIN
       FETCH NEXT from @List
    END  -- WHILE
  -- END IF

  CLOSE @List
  DEALLOCATE @List

  SET NOCOUNT OFF
END
```

Example 2

Use the stored procedure to list current cursors in the connection (session).

SQL

```
DECLARE c1 INSENSITIVE CURSOR
FOR SELECT au_id , au_lname FROM pubs..authors

OPEN c1

          EXEC uspShowGlobalCursorList  2
                -- Shows 1 open cursor (status = 1)
CLOSE c1

          EXEC uspShowGlobalCursorList  2
                -- Shows 1 closed cursor (status = -1)
DEALLOCATE c1

          EXEC uspShowGlobalCursorList  2
                -- Shows no cursor in the connection (session)
```

Result

reference_name	cursor_name	cursor_scope	status	model	concurrency
c1	c1	2	1	1	1

reference_name	cursor_name	cursor_scope	status	model	concurrency
c1	c1	2	-1		1 1

reference_name	cursor_name	cursor_scope	status	model	concurrency

No current cursors

I should note that while writing and using this stored procedure was fun, it will not list LOCAL cursors because they will not be passed in to our user-stored procedure. To show local cursors, you have to embed our stored procedure code into the code being checked

SQL

```
DECLARE c1 CURSOR   LOCAL
FOR SELECT au_id , au_lname FROM pubs..authors
OPEN c1
  DECLARE @List   CURSOR


    -- Execute the system stored procedure to
    -- fill the List cursor
  EXEC master.dbo.sp_cursor_list
      @cursor_return = @List   OUTPUT, @cursor_scope = 1


  FETCH NEXT from @List
    -- Fetch the first row from the List cursor and display it


  IF @@FETCH_STATUS = -1
    PRINT 'No current cursors'
  ELSE
    WHILE (@@FETCH_STATUS <> -1)
    -- Fetch and display the rest of the rows
    BEGIN
      FETCH NEXT from @List
    END  -- WHILE
  -- END IF


  CLOSE @List
  DEALLOCATE @List
CLOSE c1
DEALLOCATE c1
```

Result

```
reference_name  cursor_name     cursor_scope    status    model    concurrency    ...
--------------  --------------  --------------  --------  -------  -------------- ...
c1              c1              1               1         3        3              ...

reference_name  cursor_name     cursor_scope    status    model    concurrency    ...
--------------  --------------  --------------  --------  -------  -------------- ...
```

This is the format of the cursor returned by **sp_cursor_list**. The format of the cursor is the same as the format returned by **sp_describe_cursor**.

sp_describe_cursor This reports the attributes of a specified local or global cursor or of a cursor variable associated with an open cursor in the current connection.

The attributes reported and the format of the result (output cursor) are the same for **sp_describe_cursor** and **sp_cursor_list**. See **sp_cursor_list** for format details.

Syntax

```
sp_describe_cursor
        [ @cursor_return = ]    output_cursor_variable     OUTPUT
    ,   [ @cursor_source = ] { N'local' | N'global'   |   N'variable' }
    ,   [ @cursor_identity = ] N'cursor_or_cursor_variable_name'
```

Arguments

[@cursor_return =] output_cursor_variable OUTPUT

@cursor_return is the name of a cursor variable that you have declared as a scrollable, dynamic, read-only cursor to hold the results of the report. The variable must not be associated with any cursors.

[@cursor_source =] { N'local' | N'global' | N'variable' }

@cursor_source specifies whether the cursor being reported on is specified using the name of a local cursor, a global cursor or a cursor variable.

[@cursor_identity =] N'cursor_or_cursor_variable_name

@cursor_identity is the name of the cursor or cursor variable being reported on.

Example:

SQL

```
DECLARE c1 CURSOR   FOR SELECT au_id , au_lname
        FROM pubs..authors
OPEN c1
  DECLARE @Report   CURSOR

    -- Execute the system stored procedure to
    -- fill the Report cursor
  EXEC master.dbo.sp_describe_cursor    @cursor_return = @Report   OUTPUT
        ,  @cursor_source = 'global' ,@cursor_identity = 'c1'
```

SQL (cont.)

```
   FETCH NEXT from @Report
      -- Fetch the first row from the Report cursor and display it

   IF @@FETCH_STATUS = -1
        PRINT 'No current cursors'
     ELSE
        WHILE (@@FETCH_STATUS <> -1)
     -- Fetch and display the rest of the rows
     BEGIN
        FETCH NEXT from @Report
     END  -- WHILE
   -- END IF

   CLOSE @Report
   DEALLOCATE @Report
CLOSE c1
DEALLOCATE c1
```

Result

```
reference_name  cursor_name  cursor_scope  status  model  concurrency ...
--------------  -----------  ------------  ------  -----  ----------- ...
c1              c1           2             1       3      3           ...

reference_name  cursor_name  cursor_scope  status  model  concurrency ...
--------------  -----------  ------------  ------  -----  ----------- ...
```

sp_describe_cursor_columns This reports the attributes of the result set columns of a specified local or global cursor or of a cursor variable associated with an open cursor in the current connection.

The attributes reported and the format of the result (output cursor) may be found in Books Online, but you can get a good idea of the output from the example below.

Syntax

```
sp_describe_cursor_columns
        [ @cursor_return = ]  output_cursor_variable   OUTPUT

    ,   [ @cursor_source = ] { N'local' | N'global'  |  N'variable' }

    ,   [ @cursor_identity = ] N'cursor_or_cursor_variable_name'
```

Arguments

[@cursor_return =] output_cursor_variable OUTPUT

@cursor_return is the name of a cursor variable that you have declared as a scrollable, dynamic, read-only cursor to hold the results of the report. The variable must not be associated with any cursors.

[@cursor_source =] { N'local' | N'global' | N'variable' }

@cursor_source specifies whether the cursor being reported on is specified using the name of a local cursor, a global cursor or a cursor variable.

[@cursor_identity =] N'cursor_or_cursor_variable_name

@cursor_identity is the name of the cursor or cursor variable being reported on.

Example:

SQL

```
DECLARE c1 CURSOR   FOR SELECT au_id , au_lname
                        FROM pubs..authors
OPEN c1
  DECLARE @Report   CURSOR

    -- Execute the system stored procedure to
    -- fill the Report cursor
  EXEC master.dbo.sp_describe_cursor_columns @cursor_return
    -- = @Report   OUTPUT
         ,  @cursor_source = 'global' , @cursor_identity = 'c1'

  FETCH NEXT from @Report
    -- Fetch the first row from the
    -- Report cursor and display it

  IF @@FETCH_STATUS = -1
         PRINT 'No current cursors'
    ELSE
         WHILE (@@FETCH_STATUS <> -1)
      -- Fetch and display the rest of the rows
    BEGIN
      FETCH NEXT from @Report
    END  -- WHILE
  -- END IF

  CLOSE @Report
  DEALLOCATE @Report
CLOSE c1
DEALLOCATE c1
```

SQL (cont.)

Result

```
column_name    ordinal_position   column_characteristics_flags   column_size   data_type_sql
-------------  -----------------  -----------------------------  ------------  -------------
au_id          0                  0                              11            257

column_name    ordinal_position   column_characteristics_flags   column_size   data_type_sql
-------------  -----------------  -----------------------------  ------------  -------------
au_lname       1                  0                              40            167

column_name    ordinal_position   column_characteristics_flags   column_size   data_type_sql
-------------  -----------------  -----------------------------  ------------  -------------
```

This result shows that the two columns in the cursor SELECT list have, among others, the following characteristics: au_id is position 0 (first) in the result set, 0 means NOT NULL and variable length, max size of 11 bytes and data type 257, which is a user-defined type "id" in **pubs** database mapping to VARCHAR(11) (see SELECT below).

au_lame is position 1 (second) in the result set, NOT NULL and variable length, max size of 40 bytes and data type 167 which is shown.

SQL

```
SELECT   *   FROM      pubs..SYSTYPES
WHERE xusertype = 167 OR xusertype = 257
```

Result

```
name     xtype   status   xusertype   length   xprec   xscale   tdefault   domain   uid
-------  ------  -------  ----------  -------  ------  -------  ---------  -------  ---
varchar  167     2        167         8000     0       0        0          0        1
id       167     3        257         11       0       0        0          0        1
```

sp_describe_cursor_tables This reports the base tables referenced by a specified local or global cursor or by a cursor variable associated with an open cursor in the current connection.

The attributes reported and format of the result (output cursor) may be found in Books Online, but you can get a good idea of the output from the example below.

Syntax

```
sp_describe_cursor_tables
        [ @cursor_return = ]   output_cursor_variable    OUTPUT

      , [ @cursor_source = ] { N'local' | N'global'  |  N'variable' }

      , [ @cursor_identity = ] N'cursor_or_cursor_variable_name'
```

Arguments

[@cursor_return =] output_cursor_variable OUTPUT

@cursor_return is the name of a cursor variable which you have declared as a scrollable, dynamic, read-only cursor to hold the results of the report. The variable must not be associated with any cursors.

[@cursor_source =] { N'local' | N'global' | N'variable' }

@cursor_source specifies whether the cursor being reported on is specified using the name of a local cursor, a global cursor or a cursor variable.

[@cursor_identity =] N'cursor_or_cursor_variable_name

@cursor_identity is the name of the cursor or cursor variable being reported on.

Example:

SQL

```
DECLARE c1 CURSOR   FOR SELECT au_id , au_lname FROM
pubs..authors
OPEN c1
  DECLARE @Report   CURSOR

    -- Execute the system stored procedure to
    -- fill the Report cursor
  EXEC master.dbo.sp_describe_cursor_tables @cursor_return =
@Report  OUTPUT
       ,  @cursor_source = 'global' ,  @cursor_identity
= 'c1'

  FETCH NEXT from @Report
      -- Fetch the first row from the
      -- Report cursor and display it
```

SQL (cont.)

```
   IF @@FETCH_STATUS = -1
         PRINT 'No current cursors'
      ELSE
    WHILE (@@FETCH_STATUS <> -1)
            -- Fetch and display the rest of the rows
    BEGIN
            FETCH NEXT from @Report
    END  -- WHILE
   -- END IF

   CLOSE @Report
   DEALLOCATE @Report
CLOSE c1
DEALLOCATE c1
```

Result

table_owner	table_name	optimizer_hint	server_name	dbname
-------	-----	------------------	------------	--------
dbo	authors	0	AMY	pubs

5.9.5 Dynamic SQL

For dynamic SQL, use either **sp_executesql** string statement where string contains an SQL statement or **EXEC**(string) statement where string contains an SQL statement. Remember that the latter always requires ()'s and it executes in its own context, so it cannot change a caller's variables.

This rule solves an important problem about how to pass in parts of an SQL statement as variables, e.g., table name.

Examples: This is the wrong way to attempt to contruct and execute a SQL statement as a string.

SQL

```
DECLARE @table CHAR(10)
SET @table = 'Authors'

SELECT  TOP 2   * FROM @table
-- FAILS - can't do this
```

Result

Line 4: Incorrect syntax near '@table'.

Correct, using **sp_executesql**

SQL

```
DECLARE @table VARCHAR(10) , @sql  NVARCHAR(255)
                               -- SUCCEEDS
SET @table = 'Authors'
SET @sql = 'SELECT * FROM ' + @table
        -- var must be NCHAR or NVARCHAR
EXEC sp_executesql @sql                                   -
- Works
```

Result

au_id	au_lname	au_fname	phone	....
172-32-1176	White	Johnson	408 496-7223	
213-46-8915	Green	Marjorie	415 986-7020	

Correct, using EXEC()

SQL

```
DECLARE @table CHAR(10)
SET @table = 'Authors'

EXEC ('SELECT  TOP 2   * FROM ' + @table)
                                -- SUCCEEDS
```

Result

```
au_id            au_lname      au_fname       phone          ....
---------------- ------------- -------------- ---------------
172-32-1176      White         Johnson        408 496-7223
213-46-8915      Green         Marjorie       415 986-7020
...              ...           ...            ...
```

The EXEC() statement may also be used with embedded C host variables. See PREPARE statement in Books Online.

APPENDIX A

Transact-SQL Keywords and System Stored Procedures

This appendix contains Microsoft SQL Server 2000 keywords and system stored procedures.

A.1 RESERVED KEYWORDS

Microsoft SQL Server 2000 has the reserved keywords that are listed in the following table.These keywords may not be used as identifiers unless they are done as delimited identifiers. In general, this practice is discouraged. Both uppercase and lowercase versions are reserved.

ADD	DELETE	IS	RETURN
ALL	DENY	JOIN	REVOKE
ALTER	DESC	KEY	RIGHT
AND	DISK	KILL	ROLLBACK
ANY	DISTINCT	LEFT	ROWCOUNT
AS	DISTRIBUTED	LIKE	ROWGUIDCOL
ASC	DOUBLE	LINENO	RULE
AUTHORIZATION	DROP	LOAD	SAVE
BACKUP	DUMMY	NATIONAL	SCHEMA
BEGIN	DUMP	NOCHECK	SELECT
BETWEEN	ELSE	NONCLUSTERED	SESSION_USER
BREAK	END	NOT	SET
BROWSE	ERRLVL	NULL	SETUSER
BULK	ESCAPE	NULLIF	SHUTDOWN
BY	EXCEPT	OF	SOME
CASCADE	EXEC	OFF	STATISTICS
CASE	EXECUTE	OFFSETS	SYSTEM_USER
CHECK	EXISTS	ON	TABLE
CHECKPOINT	EXIT	OPEN	TEXTSIZE
CLOSE	FETCH	OPENDATASOURCE	THEN
CLUSTERED	FILE	OPENQUERY	TO
COALESCE	FILLFACTOR	OPENROWSET	TOP
COLLATE	FOR	OPENXML	TRAN
COLUMN	FOREIGN	OPTION	TRANSACTION
COMMIT	FREETEXT	OR	TRIGGER

COMPUTE	FREETEXTTABLE	ORDER	TRUNCATE
CONSTRAINT	FROM	OUTER	TSEQUAL
CONTAINS	FULL	OVER	UNION
CONTAINSTABLE	FUNCTION	PERCENT	UNIQUE
CONTINUE	GOTO	PLAN	UPDATE
CONVERT	GRANT	PRECISION	UPDATETEXT
CREATE	GROUP	PRIMARY	USE
CROSS	HAVING	PRINT	USER
CURRENT	HOLDLOCK	PROC	VALUES
CURRENT_DATE	IDENTITY	PROCEDURE	VARYING
CURRENT_TIME	IDENTITY_INSERT	PUBLIC	VIEW
CURRENT_TIMESTAMP	IDENTITYCOL	RAISERROR	WAITFOR
CURRENT_USER	IF	READ	WHEN
CURSOR	IN	READTEXT	WHERE
DATABASE	INDEX	RECONFIGURE	WHILE
DBCC	INNER	REFERENCES	WITH
DEALLOCATE	INSERT	REPLICATION	WRITETEXT
DECLARE	INTERSECT	RESTORE	
DEFAULT	INTO	RESTRICT	

A.2 SYSTEM STORED PROCEDURES

The following is a list of system stored procedures by category. For details look up the stored procedure by name in Books Online.

Unless specifically documented otherwise, all system stored procedures return a value of zero, which indicates success. To indicate failure, a nonzero value is returned.

Active Directory Procedures	
sp_ActiveDirectory_Obj	sp_ActiveDirectory_SCP\eop

Catalog Procedures	
sp_column_privileges	sp_special_columns
sp_columns	sp_sproc_columns
sp_databases	sp_statistics
sp_fkeys	sp_stored_procedures
sp_pkeys	sp_table_privileges
sp_server_info	sp_tables

Cursor Procedures	
sp_cursor_list	sp_describe_cursor_columns
sp_describe_cursor	sp_describe_cursor_tables

Database Maintenance Plan Procedures	
sp_add_maintenance_plan	sp_delete_maintenance_plan_db
sp_add_maintenance_plan_db	sp_delete_maintenance_plan_job
sp_add_maintenance_plan_job	sp_help_maintenance_plan
sp_delete_maintenance_plan	

Distributed Queries Procedures	
sp_addlinkedserver	sp_indexes
sp_addlinkedsrvlogin	sp_linkedservers
sp_catalogs	sp_primarykeys
sp_column_privileges_ex	sp_serveroption
sp_columns_ex	sp_table_privileges_ex
sp_droplinkedsrvlogin	sp_tables_ex
sp_foreignkeys	

Full-Text Search Procedures	
sp_fulltext_catalog	sp_help_fulltext_catalogs_cursor
sp_fulltext_column	sp_help_fulltext_columns
sp_fulltext_database	sp_help_fulltext_columns_cursor
sp_fulltext_service	sp_help_fulltext_tables
sp_fulltext_table	sp_help_fulltext_tables_cursor
sp_help_fulltext_catalogs	

Log Shipping Procedures	
sp_add_log_shipping_database	sp_delete_log_shipping_database
sp_add_log_shipping_plan	sp_delete_log_shipping_plan
sp_add_log_shipping_plan_database	sp_delete_log_shipping_plan_database
sp_add_log_shipping_primary	sp_delete_log_shipping_primary
sp_add_log_shipping_secondary	sp_delete_log_shipping_secondary
sp_can_tlog_be_applied	sp_get_log_shipping_monitor_info
sp_change_monitor_role	sp_remove_log_shipping_monitor
sp_change_primary_role	sp_resolve_logins
sp_change_secondary_role	sp_update_log_shipping_monitor_info
sp_create_log_shipping_monitor_account	sp_update_log_shipping_plan
sp_define_log_shipping_monitor	sp_update_log_shipping_plan_database

OLE Automation Extended Stored Procedures	
sp_OACreate	sp_OAMethod
sp_OADestroy	sp_OASetProperty
sp_OAGetErrorInfo	sp_OAStop
sp_OAGetProperty	Object Hierarchy Syntax

Replication Procedures	
sp_add_agent_parameter	sp_enableagentoffload
sp_add_agent_profile	sp_enumcustomresolvers
sp_addarticle	sp_enumdsn
sp_adddistpublisher	sp_enumfullsubscribers
sp_adddistributiondb	sp_expired_subscription_cleanup
sp_adddistributor	sp_generatefilters
sp_addmergealternatepublisher	sp_getagentoffloadinfo
sp_addmergearticle	sp_getmergedeletetype
sp_addmergefilter	sp_get_distributor
sp_addmergepublication	sp_getqueuedrows
sp_addmergepullsubscription	sp_getsubscriptiondtspackagename
sp_addmergepullsubscription_agent	sp_grant_publication_access
sp_addmergesubscription	sp_help_agent_default
sp_addpublication	sp_help_agent_parameter
sp_addpublication_snapshot	sp_help_agent_profile
sp_addpublisher70	sp_helparticle
sp_addpullsubscription	sp_helparticlecolumns
sp_addpullsubscription_agent	sp_helparticledts
sp_addscriptexec	sp_helpdistpublisher
sp_addsubscriber	sp_helpdistributiondb
sp_addsubscriber_schedule	sp_helpdistributor
sp_addsubscription	sp_helpmergealternatepublisher
sp_addsynctriggers	sp_helpmergearticle
sp_addtabletocontents	sp_helpmergearticlecolumn
sp_adjustpublisheridentityrange	sp_helpmergearticleconflicts
sp_article_validation	sp_helpmergeconflictrows
sp_articlecolumn	sp_helpmergedeleteconflictrows
sp_articlefilter	sp_helpmergefilter
sp_articlesynctranprocs	sp_helpmergepublication
sp_articleview	sp_helpmergepullsubscription

Replication Procedures (cont.)	
sp_attachsubscription	sp_helpmergesubscription
sp_browsesnapshotfolder	sp_helppublication
sp_browsemergesnapshotfolder	sp_help_publication_access
sp_browsereplcmds	sp_helppullsubscription
sp_change_agent_parameter	sp_helpreplfailovermode
sp_change_agent_profile	sp_helpreplicationdboption
sp_changearticle	sp_helpreplicationoption
sp_changedistpublisher	sp_helpsubscriberinfo
sp_changedistributiondb	sp_helpsubscription
sp_changedistributor_password	sp_ivindexhasnullcols
sp_changedistributor_property	sp_helpsubscription_properties
sp_changemergearticle	sp_link_publication
sp_changemergefilter	sp_marksubscriptionvalidation
sp_changemergepublication	sp_mergearticlecolumn
sp_changemergepullsubscription	sp_mergecleanupmetadata
sp_changemergesubscription	sp_mergedummyupdate
sp_changepublication	sp_mergesubscription_cleanup
sp_changesubscriber	sp_publication_validation
sp_changesubscriber_schedule	sp_refreshsubscriptions
sp_changesubscriptiondtsinfo	sp_reinitmergepullsubscription
sp_changesubstatus	sp_reinitmergesubscription
sp_change_subscription_properties	sp_reinitpullsubscription
sp_check_for_sync_trigger	sp_reinitsubscription
sp_copymergesnapshot	sp_removedbreplication
sp_copysnapshot	sp_repladdcolumn
sp_copysubscription	sp_replcmds
sp_deletemergeconflictrow	sp_replcounters
sp_disableagentoffload	sp_repldone
sp_drop_agent_parameter	sp_repldropcolumn
sp_drop_agent_profile	sp_replflush

Replication Procedures (cont.)	
sp_droparticle	sp_replicationdboption
sp_dropanonymouseagent	sp_replication_agent_checkup
sp_dropdistpublisher	sp_replqueuemonitor
sp_dropdistributiondb	sp_replsetoriginator
sp_dropmergealternatepublisher	sp_replshowcmds
sp_dropdistributor	sp_repltrans
sp_dropmergearticle	sp_restoredbreplication
sp_dropmergefilter	sp_revoke_publication_access
	sp_scriptsubconflicttable
sp_dropmergepublication	sp_script_synctran_commands
sp_dropmergepullsubscription	sp_setreplfailovermode
	sp_showrowreplicainfo
sp_dropmergesubscription	sp_subscription_cleanup
sp_droppublication	sp_table_validation
sp_droppullsubscription	sp_update_agent_profile
sp_dropsubscriber	sp_validatemergepublication
sp_dropsubscription	sp_validatemergesubscription
sp_dsninfo	sp_vupgrade_replication
sp_dumpparamcmd	

Security Procedures	
sp_addalias	sp_droprolemember
sp_addapprole	sp_dropserver
sp_addgroup	sp_dropsrvrolemember
sp_addlinkedsrvlogin	sp_dropuser
sp_addlogin	sp_grantdbaccess
sp_addremotelogin	sp_grantlogin
sp_addrole	sp_helpdbfixedrole
sp_addrolemember	sp_helpgroup

Security Procedures (cont.)	
sp_addserver	sp_helplinkedsrvlogin
sp_addsrvrolemember	sp_helplogins
sp_adduser	sp_helpntgroup
sp_approlepassword	sp_helpremotelogin
sp_changedbowner	sp_helprole
sp_changegroup	sp_helprolemember
sp_changeobjectowner	sp_helprotect
sp_change_users_login	sp_helpsrvrole
sp_dbfixedrolepermission	sp_helpsrvrolemember
sp_defaultdb	sp_helpuser
sp_defaultlanguage	sp_MShasdbaccess
sp_denylogin	sp_password
sp_dropalias	sp_remoteoption
sp_dropapprole	sp_revokedbaccess
sp_dropgroup	sp_revokelogin
sp_droplinkedsrvlogin	sp_setapprole
sp_droplogin	sp_srvrolepermission
sp_dropremotelogin	sp_validatelogins
sp_droprole	

SQL Mail Procedures	
sp_processmail	xp_sendmail
xp_deletemail	xp_startmail
xp_findnextmsg	xp_stopmail
xp_readmail	

SQL Profiler Procedures	
sp_trace_create	sp_trace_setfilter
sp_trace_generateevent	sp_trace_setstatus
sp_trace_setevent	

SQL Server Agent Procedures	
sp_add_alert	sp_help_jobhistory
sp_add_category	sp_help_jobschedule
sp_add_job	sp_help_jobserver
sp_add_jobschedule	sp_help_jobstep
sp_add_jobserver	sp_help_notification
sp_add_jobstep	sp_help_operator
sp_add_notification	sp_help_targetserver
sp_add_operator	sp_help_targetservergroup
sp_add_targetservergroup	sp_helptask
sp_add_targetsvrgrp_member	sp_manage_jobs_by_login
sp_addtask	sp_msx_defect
sp_apply_job_to_targets	sp_msx_enlist
sp_delete_alert	sp_post_msx_operation
sp_delete_category	sp_purgehistory
sp_delete_job	sp_purge_jobhistory
sp_delete_jobschedule	sp_reassigntask
sp_delete_jobserver	sp_remove_job_from_targets
sp_delete_jobstep	sp_resync_targetserver
sp_delete_notification	sp_start_job
sp_delete_operator	sp_stop_job
sp_delete_targetserver	sp_update_alert
sp_delete_targetservergroup	sp_update_category
sp_delete_targetsvrgrp_member	sp_update_job
sp_droptask	sp_update_jobschedule

SQL Server Agent Procedures (cont.)	
sp_help_alert	sp_update_jobstep
sp_help_category	sp_update_notification
sp_help_downloadlist	sp_update_operator
sp_helphistory	sp_update_targetservergroup
sp_help_job	sp_updatetask
	xp_sqlagent_proxy_account

System Procedures	
sp_add_data_file_recover_suspect_db	sp_helpconstraint
sp_addextendedproc	sp_helpdb
sp_addextendedproperty	sp_helpdevice
sp_add_log_file_recover_suspect_db	sp_helpextendedproc
sp_addmessage	sp_helpfile
sp_addtype	sp_helpfilegroup
sp_addumpdevice	sp_helpindex
sp_altermessage	sp_helplanguage
sp_autostats	sp_helpserver
sp_attach_db	sp_helpsort
sp_attach_single_file_db	sp_helpstats
sp_bindefault	sp_helptext
sp_bindrule	sp_helptrigger
sp_bindsession	sp_indexoption
sp_certify_removable	sp_invalidate_textptr
sp_configure	sp_lock
sp_create_removable	sp_monitor
sp_createstats	sp_procoption
sp_cycle_errorlog	sp_recompile
sp_datatype_info	sp_refreshview
sp_dbcmptlevel	sp_releaseapplock

System Procedures (cont.)	
sp_dboption	sp_rename
sp_dbremove	sp_renamedb
sp_delete_backuphistory	sp_resetstatus
sp_depends	sp_serveroption
sp_detach_db	sp_setnetname
sp_dropdevice	sp_settriggerorder
sp_dropextendedproc	sp_spaceused
sp_dropextendedproperty	sp_tableoption
sp_dropmessage	sp_unbindefault
sp_droptype	sp_unbindrule
sp_executesql	sp_updateextendedproperty
sp_getapplock	sp_updatestats
sp_getbindtoken	sp_validname
sp_help	sp_who

Web Assistant Procedures	
sp_dropwebtask	sp_makewebtask
sp_enumcodepages	sp_runwebtask

XML Procedures	
sp_xml_preparedocument	sp_xml_removedocument

General Extended Procedures	
xp_cmdshell	xp_logininfo
xp_enumgroups	xp_msver
xp_findnextmsg	xp_revokelogin
xp_grantlogin	xp_sprintf
xp_logevent	xp_sqlmaint
xp_loginconfig	xp_sscanf

A.2.1 API System Stored Procedures

Users running SQL Profiler against ADO, OLE DB, ODBC and DB-Library applications may notice the use of system stored procedures that are not covered in the Transact-SQL Reference. These stored procedures are used by the Microsoft OLE DB Provider for SQL Server, the SQL Server ODBC driver and the DB-Library dynamic-link library (DLL) to implement the functionality of a database API. These stored procedures are simply the mechanism the provider or drivers use to communicate user requests to SQL Server. They are intended only for the internal use of the OLE DB Provider for SQL Server, the SQL Server ODBC driver, and the DB-Library DLL. Calling them explicitly from an SQL Server application is not supported.

The complete functionality from these stored procedures is made available to SQL Server applications through the API functions they support. For example, the cursor functionality of the **sp_cursor** system stored procedures is made available to OLE DB applications through the OLE DB API cursor properties and methods, to ODBC applications through the ODBC cursor attributes and functions, and to DB-Library applications through the DB-Library Cursor Library.

The following system stored procedures support the cursor functionality of ADO, OLE DB, ODBC and the DB-Library Cursor Library:

sp_cursor	sp_cursorclose	sp_cursorexecute
sp_cursorfetch	sp_cursoropen	sp_cursoroption
sp_cursorprepare	sp_cursorunprepare	

These system stored procedures below support the prepare/execute model of executing Transact-SQL statements in ADO, OLE DB and ODBC:

sp_execute	sp_prepare	sp_unprepare

APPENDIX B

Select—Advanced Queries

The advanced queries include subqueries, pivot, rollup and cube.

Most examples in this section indicate whether the Microsoft SQL Server being shown does or does not comply with SQL-92, the ANSI Standard. Sometimes there are two ways of correctly getting the same result with the same performance, in which case it is useful to know if one way is portable to other RDBMS systems. Sometimes one has to write nonportable code to get the job done, but striving for portability is desirable.

Some of the examples later in the appendix are presented as exercises with the solutions provided later in the text. Unlike the body of the book, which is primarily intended as a reference, the tutorial approach used here is to give the reader a chance to try to solve the problem before seeing my way of doing it. Your solution may be better than mine.

The following intermediate and advanced queries will be addressed in this appendix.

- Review ORDER BY, Aggregate Functions, GROUP BY, HAVING
- Arithmetic Operations in SELECT
- CASE, COALESCE
- Subqueries
    - BETWEEN, IN, EXISTS, SOME/ANY, ALL
- Pivots, ROLLUP, CUBE

B.1 INTRODUCTION

On page 419 we created database playdb and tables emps3 and depts3 for examples. See Figure B-1 and Tables B-1 and B-2.

SQL

```
USE mydb
go
```

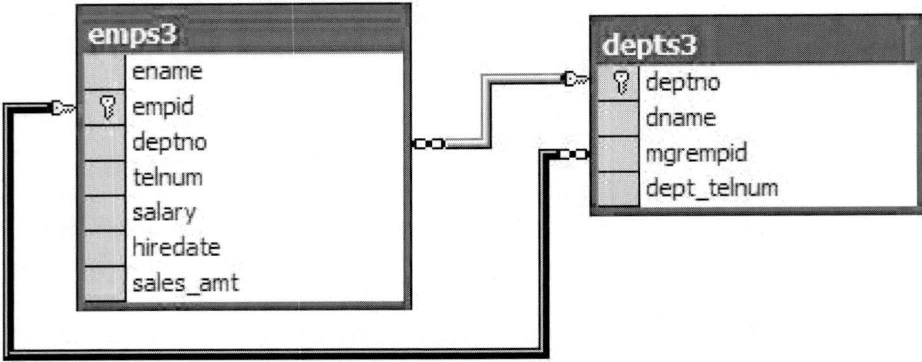

Figure B-1 Tables emps3 and depts3 are interconnected.

B.1.1 Test Machine and Production Machine

For the design and development of new tables and new database application software,do all work on test machine until it's exhaustively tested and ready to deploy.Then deploy it onto production machine during off-production hours with time to back it out.

For performance tuning, practice tuning the test machine loaded with the same tables and the same amount of data.

Do initial tuning of production machine during off-peak hours, then gather tuning data during peak production. Wait until off-peak hours before doing big jobs such as creating a new index.

These tables are populated with sample data.

Table B-1 emps3

ename	empid	deptno	telnum	salary	hiredate	sales_amt
Suzy Smith	1111	102	NULL	20	1/1/98	NULL
Sammy Sosa	2222	102	2345	30	1/1/92	200
Bill Johnson	4444	101	NULL	40	1/1/94	NULL
Mary Smith	5555	100	5678	50	1/1/90	NULL
Mary Smith	7777	101	7890	60	1/1/96	400

Table B-2 depts3

dname	deptno	dept_telnum	mgrempid
Accounting	100	9100	1111
Engineering	101	9101	7777
Sales	102	9102	2222

B.2 SELECT GENERAL FORM

Before looking at GROUP BY, let's recall the general form of the SELECT statement:

```
SELECT [ DISTINCT ]{ select-item-list | * }
    FROM table-or-view-list
    [ WHERE search-condition  ]
    [ GROUP BY column-reference-list ]
    [ HAVING search-condition ]
    [ ORDER BY sort-item-list ]
```

Consider the flow, shown in Figure B-2, from base tables to a series of virtual tables involved in a SELECT statement.

The **FROM clause** picks which tables and views will be worked on, ultimately going down to all base tables where the actual data is located.

These tables are input to the **WHERE clause** that then works to find only the rows that satisfy the WHERE clause *search-condition*. The output of the WHERE clause is the set of all rows that can ultimately appear in the output result set (though HAVING may filter out a few more).

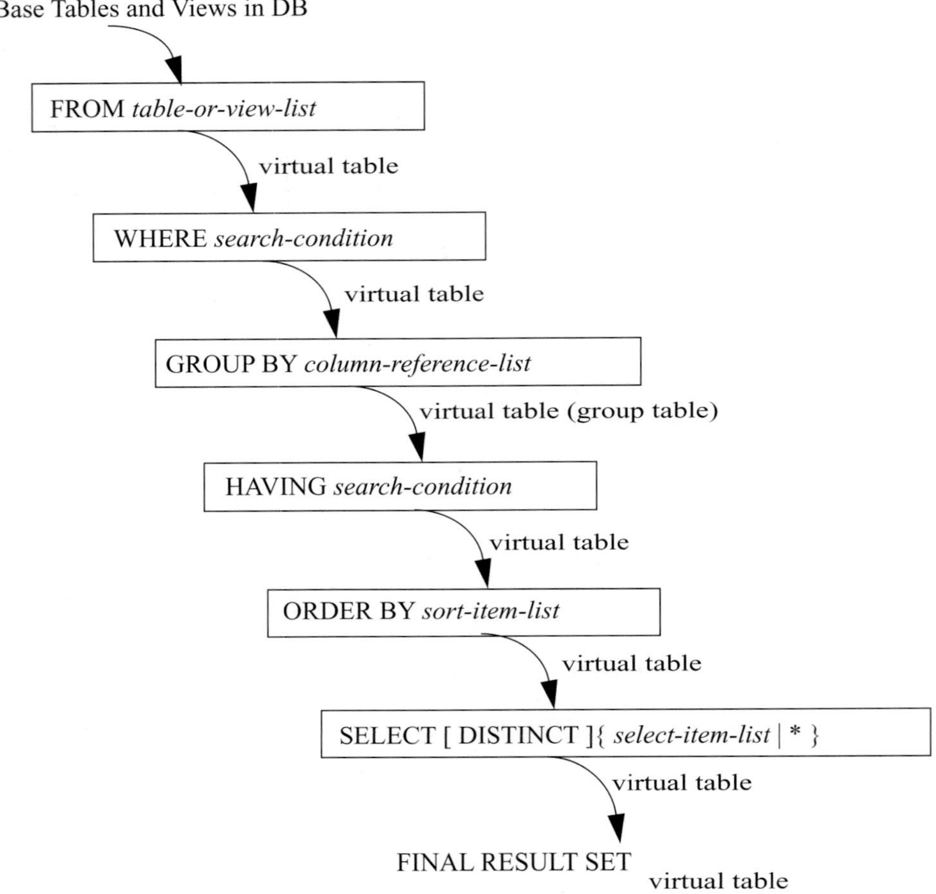

Figure B-2 The flow in a SELECT statement

The **GROUP BY clause** then takes these rows and rearranges them into groups of the same value in the column specified in the GROUP BY column-list as we will see next. The output from the GROUP BY operation is called the *group table*.

The **HAVING clause** acts very much like a WHERE clause because it has a search-condition which specifies only certain rows to move on. HAVING can only reference grouping columns, that is, columns grouped by the GROUP BY clause.

The rows are then sorted according to the **ORDER BY clause** if present. Finally, the **SELECT clause** reports only its specified columns to the final result set, optionally eliminating duplicate rows if the **DISTINCT** keyword is present.

This discussion is not intended to imply that any RDBMS does operations in any specified order or manner, but at least conceptually it is useful to look at it in the way described.

B.2.1 Review of ORDER BY

Without ORDER BY, the RDBMS displays the rows in whatever order the Database Engine finds most efficient to produce the result set.

Using the ORDER BY clause allows the user to require that the listing be in a certain order by specifying a primary sort order and optionally a secondary, tertiary, etc.

Performance Note

Omitting ORDER BY gives better performance, especially if the result set is large (100,000's of rows or more). Figure B-3 compares code without ORDER BY and with ORDER BY.

Syntax:

```
ORDER BY { column-name | ordinal_number } [ ASC | DESC ]
```

Arguments

Column Name

The *column-name* may be any column name in the table.

Note: if programming with cursors, the *column-name* must be one of the names in the select list.

Ordinal Number

Instead of column name, you may use its ordinal_number, an integer that specifies the position of the column in the select list.

Example: Both of these examples comply with both MSS and ANSI SQL. The first has no ORDER BY clause and the second does have an ORDER BY clause.

Without ORDER BY - RDBMS picks order

SQL

```
SELECT ename
FROM emps3;
```

Result

```
ENAME
---------------
Mary Smith
Sammy Sosa
Bill Johnson
Mary Smith
Suzy Smith
5 rows selected.
```

With ORDER BY ename, ascending

SQL

```
SELECT ename
FROM emps3
ORDER BY ename;
```

Result

```
ENAME
---------------
Bill Johnson
Mary Smith
Mary Smith
Sammy Sosa
Suzy Smith
5 rows selected.
```

Figure B-3 Code Comparison.

ASC and DESC

ASC: Specifies ascending order (default)

DESC: Specifies descending order for the column where it is placed

MSS and ANSI SQL:

SQL

```
SELECT ename      -- Using ORDER BY ename, descending
FROM emps3
ORDER BY ename DESC;
```

Result

```
ENAME
---------------
Suzy Smith
Sammy Sosa
Mary Smith
Mary Smith
Bill Johnson
5 rows selected.
```

ASC and DESC apply individually only to the column where they appear. The sort order (ASC or DESC) of each column is independent of each other and must be specified for each column. If not specified, ASC is the default sort order.

MSS and ANSI SQL:

SQL

```
SELECT ename, deptno
FROM emps3
ORDER BY ename, deptno DESC;
   -- Same as ORDER BY ename ASC, deptno DESC
```

Result

```
ENAME                DEPTNO
-------------------- ----------
Bill Johnson         101
Mary Smith           101
Mary Smith           100
Sammy Sosa           102
Suzy Smith           102
5 rows selected.
```

B.2.1.1 Using Ordinal Number with ORDER BY

The integer indicating the position of the column in the select list may be used to specify the column in an ORDER BY. Using the ordinal number may be appropriate in cases where there is no column name as in an unlabeled calculated column.

MSS and ANSI SQL:

SQL

```
SELECT empid,   telnum,   (telnum + 1000)
      -- Using ordinal number to specify
      -- the ORDER BY column
FROM emps3
ORDER BY 3;
```

SQL (cont.)

Result

empid	telnum	
---------	-------	-----------
1111	NULL	NULL
4444	NULL	NULL
2222	2345	3345
5555	5678	6678
7777	7890	8890

(5 row(s) affected)

The same result could be obtained by specifying a column name in the select list, e.g., "col name," in which case "col name" could be used in the ORDER BY clause. So the previous query could be made as follows.

MSS and ANSI SQL:

SQL

```
SELECT empid, telnum, (telnum + 1000) "Tel + 1000"
-- Using a column label
FROM emps3
-- in ORDER BY in place
ORDER BY "Tel + 1000";
-- of an ordinal number
```

Result

empid	telnum	Tel + 1000
---------	-------	-----------
1111	NULL	NULL
4444	NULL	NULL
2222	2345	3345
5555	5678	6678
7777	7890	8890

(5 row(s) affected)

B.2.1.2 NULL in output of a SELECT with DISTINCT

If you use DISTINCT, NULL will be listed as one of the DISTINCT values if present in the data.When you use ORDER BY, NULL appears before or after the domain values depending on the RDBMS.

In MSS, NULL values are listed as the word NULL **before** domain values are listed.

MSS: NULL in output without and then with DISTINCT

MSS and ANSI SQL:

SQL

```
SELECT telnum
FROM emps3;
    --  telnum without DISTINCT, each NULL appears
```

Result

```
telnum
------
NULL
2345
NULL
5678
7890

(5 row(s) affected)
```

MSS and ANSI SQL:

SQL

```
SELECT DISTINCT telnum
FROM emps3;
  --  telnum with DISTINCT, a single NULL appears
```

Result

```
telnum
-------
NULL
2345
7890
5678

(4 row(s) affected)
```

B.2.1.3 NULL in output of a SELECT with ORDER BY

The following queries are with NULL and ORDER BY.

MSS: Lists NULL before the domain values

SQL

```
SELECT empid, telnum
        -- MSS lists NULL before domain values
FROM emps3
ORDER BY telnum;
```

Result

```
empid       telnum
------      ------
1111        NULL
4444        NULL
2222        2345
5555        5678
7777        7890

(5 row(s) affected)
```

B.2.2 Review of Aggregate Functions—Count, SUM, AVG, MIN, MAX

SQL has aggregate functions that summarize data values in numeric columns.

The five aggregates in ANSI SQL are as follows:

- Count: count(*) = number of rows in the result set,
  -- count(columnName) = number of non-NULLs for named column in result set
- SUM: SUM(numericColumn)
- AVG: AVG(numericColumn)
- MIN: MIN(numericColumn)
- MAX: MAX(numericColumn)

B.2.2.1 Rules for Using Aggregate Functions

1. Aggregate functions other than count() must have a numeric argument.
2. Aggregate functions ignore NULL values (except that count(*) counts all rows).

3. If a SELECT list contains an aggregate function, then the SELECT list may only contain the following:

   - Aggregate functions
   - GROUP BY columns (aggregate functions are often used with GROUP BY)
   - Constants

SQL

```
USE mydb
    --  On page 371 we created database mydb and
    --  table emps3 used in the next example.
go
```

SQL

```
SELECT  *  FROM  emps3
-- Show contents of emps3 for reference
```

Result

ename	empid	deptno	telnum	salary	hiredate	sales_amt
Suzy Smith	1111	102	NULL	20	2003-01-01	NULL
Sammy Sosa	2222	102	2345	30	1992-01-01	200
Bill Johnson	4444	101	NULL	40	1994-01-01	NULL
Mary Smith	5555	100	5678	50	1990-01-01	NULL
Mary Smith	7777	101	7890	60	1996-01-01	400

SQL

```
SELECT empid, salary, sales_amt from emps3;
```

Result

empid	salary	sales_amt
1111	20	NULL
2222	30	200
4444	40	NULL
5555	50	NULL
7777	60	400

Example:

SQL

```
SELECT count(*)  NumRows ,   count(salary) NumSals ,
  AVG(salary) AvgSals,count(sales_amt) "Num SA's",
  AVG(sales_amt) "Avg SA's"
FROM emps3;
```

Result

NumRows	NumSals	AvgSals	Num SA's	Avg SA's
5	5	40.00	2	300.00

Notice that there are two non-NULL values for sales_amt.

Example violation of aggregate rule 3: MSS: Cannot mix regular column name with Aggregate function.

SQL

```
SELECT empid , count(*)
FROM emps3;
```

Result

Server: Msg 8118, Level 16, State 1, Line 1
Column 'emps3.empid' is invalid in the select list because it is not contained in an aggregate function and there is no GROUP BY clause.

Performance Note:

Would the following two queries give the same result (empid is the primary key)?

Which, if either, would have better performance?

```
a. SELECT count(*)
   FROM emps3;
```

or

b.
```
SELECT count(empid)
FROM emps3;
```

The answers are that they would always give the same result, but the second form would give faster performance. The reason is that we know that the primary key always has an index defined, and that this index has exactly as many entries as does the data table. So counting the number of entries in the index requires fewer disk page reads and is therefore faster. (This ability to completely satisfy a query from an index, without accessing the base data table, is called "index covering.")

Some modern cost-based query optimizers would recognize that the first query can also be satisfied from the primary key index. If so, the queries would take the same amount of time. But using the form of the second query improves your chances for efficiency.

B.2.3 Review of GROUP BY and HAVING

SELECT Statement Syntax: Form 3

```
SELECT [ DISTINCT ]{ select_item_list | * }
    FROM table-or-view-list
    [ WHERE search_condition  ]
    [GROUP BY column_list ]
    [HAVING having_predicate]
    [ ORDER BY sort_item_list ]
```

SQL

```
SELECT empid, salary, deptno FROM emps3;
  -- Show data for reference
```

Result

EMPID	SALARY	DEPTNO
1111	20	102
2222	30	102
4444	40	101
5555	50	100
7777	60	101

5 rows selected.

SQL

```
SELECT AVG(salary) FROM emps3; -- AVG(salary),  no GROUP BY
```

Result

```
AVG(SALARY)                -- List AVG(salary) for all employees in the table
----------
40
1 row selected.
```

B.2.3.1 GROUP BY Clause

The GROUP BY clause specifies the groups into which output rows are to be placed and,
if aggregate functions are included in the SELECT list,
it calculates the aggregate summary value for each group.

SQL

```
SELECT deptno,  AVG(salary)
           -- AVG(salary) with GROUP BY deptno
FROM emps3
GROUP BY deptno;
            -- List  AVG(salary) by deptno
```

Result

```
DEPTNO        AVG(SALARY)
----------    ----------
100           50
101           50
102           25
3 rows selected.
```

Notes:

The column names in the GROUP BY column_list are called GROUP BY columns.

When a GROUP BY clause is used, each item in the select list must produce a single value for each group. Null values in one item are placed in one group.

Restrictions on SELECT columns with GROUP BY are as follows:

When a GROUP BY clause is present, the select_item_list items are restricted to:

- GROUP BY columns
- Aggregate functions of any column
- Constant values

B.2.3.2 HAVING Clause

HAVING clause specifies a search condition for a group or an aggregate.

HAVING is usually used with the GROUP BY clause.

Notes:

HAVING is like a WHERE clause because it filters which rows stay in the result set.

When GROUP BY is not used, HAVING behaves like a WHERE clause.

Example: HAVING

SQL

```
SELECT deptno,  AVG(salary)
    -- AVG(salary) with GROUP BY and HAVING
FROM emps3
GROUP BY deptno
HAVING AVG(salary) > 30;
            -- List only deptno's with AVG(salary) over 30
```

Result

```
DEPTNO          AVG(SALARY
----------      ----------
100             50
101             50
2 rows selected.
```

The only columns allowable in the *select-item-list* when GROUP BY is used are:

- grouping column names
- aggregate functions
- constants

When this restriction in choosing SELECT list columns is violated, an error message is shown and the statement fails as shown in the following example.

Example: Put **ename** column in the SELECT list but not the GROUP BY list to show the resulting error message.

SQL

```
SELECT  ename, AVG(Salary) "Avg_Sal", deptno FROM emps3
GROUP BY deptno;
```

Result

```
Server: Msg 8120, Level 16, State 1, Line 1
Column 'emps3.ename' is invalid in the select list because it is not contained in either
an aggregate function or the GROUP BY clause.
```

These errors can be fixed as follows (though it may not be what you had in mind).

It is often useful to just add an extra group by column so you can display it, but not in this case.

SQL

```
SELECT  ename, AVG(Salary) "Avg_Sal", deptno FROM emps3
GROUP BY deptno, ename;
```

Result

```
ename              Avg Sal            deptno
-----------------  ----------------   -----
Bill Johnson       40.000000          101
Mary Smith         50.000000          100
Mary Smith         60.000000          101
Sammy Sosa         30.000000          102
Suzy Smith         20.000000          102
```

B.2.4 ARITHMETIC OPERATIONS in SELECTs

The *select-item-list* in a query may include arithmetic operations on numeric fields and/or numeric constants.

Syntax

```
SELECT [ DISTINCT ]{ select-item-list | * }
    FROM table-or-view-list
    [ WHERE search-condition  ]
```

This is a good place to define a column alias or label to be shown in the output as we have done previously with Label.

SQL

```
SELECT (telnum * 2 ) "2 * Tel" FROM emps3;
```

Result

```
2 * Tel
-----------
NULL
4690
NULL
11356
15780

(5 row(s) affected)
```

(I never said that doubling one's telephone number made sense. Ha!)

Notice that the two **emps3** for whom telnum is NULL are empty, meaning that the result is NULL (UNKNOWN * 2 -> UNKNOWN).

Note: Recall that telnum data type is CHAR(4) though it contains only numeric characters. So for the above operations to succeed, the RDBMS must automatically do some data type conversion to a numeric type. Most RDBMSs will convert data types when possible.

If the word "hi" had been entered for a telnum value, then the above SELECT would fail completely in MSS (and probably every other RDBMS).

It is much safer to explicitly use CAST or other data type conversion functions than to rely on implicit data type conversion by the RDBMS.

Arithmetic expressions may also be put into the WHERE clause.

SQL

```
SELECT ename, empid, telnum
FROM emps3
WHERE telnum > empid + 20;
```

SQL (cont.)

Result

```
-ENAME          EMPID       TELNUM
--------------- ----------  --------
Mary Smith      5555        5678
Sammy Sosa      2222        2345
Mary Smith      7777        7890
3 rows selected.
```

B.2.4.1 Arithmetic and DATE values

In some RDBMSs including MSS, adding or subtracting a number from a DATE (DATETIME in MSS) value represents a change in days.

MSS:

SQL

```
SELECT hiredate, hiredate + 3  "Hire_+_3"
FROM emps3;
```

Result

```
HIREDATE                    Hire_+_3
-------------------------   --------------------------
2003-01-01 00:00:00.000     2003-01-04 00:00:00.000
2000-10-13 00:00:00.000     2000-10-16 00:00:00.000
1994-01-01 00:00:00.000     1994-01-04 00:00:00.000
1990-01-01 00:00:00.000     1990-01-04 00:00:00.000
1996-01-01 00:00:00.000     1996-01-04 00:00:00.000

(5 row(s) affected)
```

Query: Display the names of all emps3 hired within the past 90 days.

MSS:

SQL

```
SELECT ename, hiredate
FROM emps3
WHERE  hiredate >= GETDATE() - 90;
```

PERFORMANCE NOTE:

Sometimes a field that has an index appears in the WHERE predicate in an arithmetic expression.

I suggest that the field with the index be isolated to one side of the relational operator. This is to allow the index to speed the query.

If there is an **index on hiredate**, it **can not be used** with the following form,

WHERE hiredate + 90 >= SYSDATE; -- Disables use of index

But isolating the indexed field, hiredate, on one side of the relational operator allows the index on hiredate to be used.

WHERE hiredate >= SYSDATE - 90; -- Preferred, enables index

The query logic and thus the result set are the same, but the second form will respond more quickly, greatly so on a very large table.

B.3 CASE AND COALESCE

The CASE and COALESCE expressions give capabilities for decision-making similar to multi-way branching statements in some 3GLs. They each return a single value based on the input(s).

B.3.1 CASE—ANSI and MSS

There are two forms of syntax for the CASE expression.

Syntax: Form 1—Simple CASE, exact match

```
CASE input-expression  WHEN match-expression THEN result
                      [ WHEN match-expression THEN result ]
                      ...
                      [ELSE result]
```

Syntax: Form 2—Searched CASE, inequality and general Boolean condition

```
CASE              WHEN Boolean-condition THEN result
                      [ WHEN Boolean-condition THEN result ]
                      ...
                      [ELSE result2]
```

Note: An expression written using the first form could be rewritten using the second form by explicitly stating the WHEN condition for each value:

```
CASE      WHEN input-expression  = match-expression THEN result
          [ WHEN input-expression = match-expression THEN result ]
```

```
...
[ ELSE else-result]
```

B.3.1.1 CASE—Form 1—ANSI and MSS

In the first form, the CASE expression can be useful for converting the values stored in the database with slightly cryptic wording into more easily readable text for the user.

Example of **first form of CASE** expression.

Suppose there is a table, Table B-3, about automobiles.

Table B-3 Autos

Make	Manufacturer	...	...
Buick	GM		
Quattro	Au		
Jeep	DC		
Sebring	DC		
	...		

It might not be obvious to the user that Au means Audi and DC means Daimler-Chrysler, etc. The correlation of abbreviated name to full name could easily be done using a lookup table. But it would be faster to use a CASE statement.

```
SELECT Make, CASE Manufacturer
               WHEN 'GM' THEN 'General Motors'
               WHEN 'Au'THEN 'Audi'
               WHEN 'DC'THEN 'Daimler-Chrysler'
               ...
               ELSE 'Manufacturer not found'
FROM Autos;
```

B.3.1.2 CASE—Form 2—ANSI and MSS

The first form of CASE must be an exact match of a single input value. If there is more than one input value or if the choice is based on an inequality, then the second form is called for.

Example: of **second form of CASE** expression.

Suppose you want to assign letter grades from Table B-4.

Table B-4 Grades

Student	Grade	...	...
Torie	87		
James	76		
Amy	93		
Tim	82		

SQL

```
SELECT Student, CASE    WHEN Grade > 90 THEN 'A'
                        WHEN Grade > 80 THEN 'B'
                        WHEN Grade > 70 THEN 'C'
                        WHEN Grade > 60 THEN 'D'
                        ELSE 'F'    LetterGrade
FROM Grades
ORDER BY Student;
```

Result

```
Student     LetterGrade
----------  --------------
Amy         A
James       C
Tim         B
Torie       B
```

B.3.2 COALESCE—ANSI, MSS

COALESCE returns the first non-NULL value from a list of values.

Syntax

COALESCE(*value* [, *value* ...])

One or more *values* may be specified, but all must be of the same or compatible type.

Example: The simplest and most commonly used example uses COALESCE with two arguments, the first is a column name and the second is a literal to be used in case the column value is NULL.

MSS:

SQL
`SELECT ename, COALESCE(telnum, 'No Telephone listed') TelNum FROM emps3;`

Result

```
ename            TelNum
---------------  -------------------
Suzy Smith       No Telephone listed
Sammy Sosa         2345
Bill Johnson     No Telephone listed
Mary Smith       5678
Mary Smith       7890

(5 row(s) affected)
```

Multiple arguments to COALESCE

ANSI and MSS:

```
SELECT COALESE( a, b, c, d)
FROM table.
```

B.4 SUBQUERIES

A subquery is a SELECT statement inside parentheses within another DML statement. It can be in **INSERT**, **UPDATE**, **DELETE** or **SELECT** statement. It is always enclosed in parentheses (). The ability to use a query within a query was the original reason for the word *structured* in the name Structured Query Language.[1]

The result of a SELECT is a virtual table called a result set.

As shown in Table B-5, there are four result set sizes which are useful when discussing subqueries.

1. Groff 1999, p. 218.

1. INSERT INTO table SELECT ...   -- target table must exist

Table B-5 Result Set Sizes

Subquery Result Set Dimensions	Result Set Name	Example
1 X 1	Scalar	(SELECT AVG(salary) FROM emps3) (SELECT SUM(order_amt) FROM orders WHERE custid = 11)
N X 1	List	(SELECT pub_id FROM titles)
N X M	Regular table	(SELECT pub_name , pub_id FROM titles)
0 x M	Empty table	(SELECT * FROM titles WHERE 1 = 0)

A subquery can be used in an SQL statement virtually anywhere the subquery returns a result set of the appropriate size.

```
SELECT  scalar -list
  FROM    regular table-list
  WHERE   column = (scalar)        -- WHERE clause comments also
    OR    column IN (list)         --  apply to UPDATE and DELETE
    OR    EXISTS (non-empty table  OR NOT EXISTS (empty table)
UPDATE table SET column = (scalar)     WHERE <see above>
INSERT INTO table (column) VALUES (scalar)
```

Example of a subquery: List all emps3 in the Engineering department.

SQL

```
SELECT empid , ename , telnum  FROM emps3 e
WHERE e.deptno = (SELECT d.deptno
        FROM depts3 d WHERE dname = 'Engineering');
```

Result

```
empid       ename             telnum
--------    ---------------   ------
4444        Bill Johnson      NULL
7777        Mary Smith        7890

(2 row(s) affected)
```

Question: What should we do to ensure that this subquery returns only one deptno value?

Answer: Put a unique index on dname in the depts3 table, probably a good idea anyway since most companies don't want two departments with identical names.

Example: Find all employees whose salary is equal to or above average.

SQL

```
SELECT empid, Salary FROM emps3
WHERE
    Salary >= (SELECT AVG(Salary) "Avg Sal" FROM emps3)
```

Result

```
EMPID          SALARY
----------     ----------
5555           50
4444           40
7777             60
```

Example: List all employees whose salary is at least 50% above the average.

SQL

```
SELECT empid, Salary FROM emps3
WHERE
    Salary >= 1.5 * (SELECT AVG(Salary) "Avg Sal" FROM emps3)
```

Result

```
EMPID          SALARY
----------     -----------
7777           60
```

B.4.1 Subqueries in an INSERT Statement

A subquery may be used to provide input data for an INSERT statement.

Example: Subquery in an INSERT statement—insert average salary and date.

Suppose we want to keep a weekly or monthly log with the date and average company salary for that date. We could make a table called salhist and periodically run the INSERT statement, which would do a subquery to obtain the data.

SQL

```
USE mydb        -  For MSS
CREATE TABLE  salhist (
        avgsal      FLOAT
,       saldateDATETIME
);
```

MSS: SQL Server has two forms for using a SELECT to provide data for an INSERT, see page 440.

1. **INSERT INTO** *table* SELECT . . . *--target table must exist*

2. **SELECT** *list* **INTO** *table* FROM …*--target table must NOT exist*

SQL

```
INSERT INTO salhist ( avgsal , saldate )
        SELECT  AVG(Salary)     , GETDATE()  FROM emps3;
```

SQL

```
SELECT *  FROM  salhist
```

Result

```
avgsal          saldate
--------        ------------------------------
37.0            2002-06-28 22:04:10.283
40.0            2002-07-28 22:04:46.690

(2 row(s) affected)
```

B.4.2 Subqueries in an UPDATE Statement

A subquery may be used to provide input data for an UPDATE statement.

Example: Set everyone's salary equal to the average current salary.

SQL

```
UPDATE emps3
SET salary =
    (SELECT AVG(salary) FROM emps3 )
```

This is a silly example, but it works.

B.4.3 Subqueries in the WHERE clause.

Subqueries can be used to provide values in the WHERE clause of an UPDATE, DELETE or SELECT statement.

You may do further nesting of queries to several levels, the limit of nesting turns out to be one of practicality and performance rather than syntactic limits.

Subqueries most often appear in the WHERE or HAVING clause where they help in the row selection process as will be demonstrated shortly.

We will later discuss subqueries in the WHERE clause used with the following commands:

- IN: WHERE *identifier* IN (*subquery*)
- EXISTS: WHERE EXISTS (*subquery*)
- UNIQUE: WHERE UNIQUE (*subquery*)
- MATCH: WHERE MATCH (*subquery*)

Although different, there is some similarity between subqueries and joins because both work on two or more tables (or instances of one table). We will also see that in some cases the same information may be obtained using either a subquery or a join.

Recall that queries occur within SELECT, UPDATE and DELETE statements either in the WHERE clause to pick which rows are chosen or by the absence of a WHERE clause which chooses every row.

The following UPDATE statement gives a 10% raise (salary * 1.1) to each person returned by a query that finds the salespersons whose sales amounts exceed the sales target for their branches.

```
UPDATE employees  e
    SET salary = salary * 1.1
    WHERE e.sales_amt >
```

```
( SELECT b.sales_target
  FROM branches b
  WHERE  b.branchid  =  e.branchid );
```

(The tables in this query don't match any sample data tables we've constructed, so you won't be able to test it without creating employees and branches tables with appropriate columns.)

B.4.3.1 Subquery Example in WHERE Clause

Often a query can be done by either a join or a subquery, as in the following example.

Query: What are the name and telephone number of Bill Johnson's (4444) dept mgr?

You can see from the tables below that Bill is in Engineering, which is managed by empid 7777, Mary Smith. Next we'll form the query that produces this result. The tables used for this Example are shown below.

Result

```
ENAME              TEL_
------------------ ---------
Mary Smith         7890
1 row selected.
```

Table B-6 Employee

ename	empid	deptno	telnum	salary	hiredate
Mary Smith	5555	100	5678	20	1/1/90
Sammy Sosa	2222	102	2345	30	1/1/92
Bill Johnson	4444	101		40	1/1/94
Mary Smith	7777	101	7890	50	1/1/96
Suzy Smith	1111	102		60	1/1/98

Table B-7 depts3

dname	deptno	dept_telnum	mgrempid
Accounting	100	9100	1111
Engineering	101	9101	7777
Sales	102	9102	2222

Query: What are the name and telephone number of Bill Johnson's (4444) dept mgr?

Solution using a three-way inner join (emps3, emps3 and depts3)

SQL

```
SELECT E2.ename Bills_Mgr, E2.telnum Mgr_telnum
FROM     emps3 E1, emps3 E2, depts3 D
WHERE  E1.empid = 4444
      AND D.deptno = E1.deptno
   AND E2.empid = D.mgrempid;
```

Result

Same result as next.

Solution using a two-way join (emps3, depts3) **and subquery** (emps3).

SQL

```
SELECT emps3.ename Bills_Mgr, emps3.telnum Mgr_telnum
FROM     emps3, depts3
WHERE  emps3.empid = depts3.mgrempid
       AND depts3.deptno =
      (SELECT emps3.deptno
       FROM emps3
       WHERE emps3.empid = 4444);
```

Result

Same result as next.

Solution using a subquery (on depts3) **containing a subquery** (emps3).

SQL

```
SELECT emps3.ename Bills_Mgr, emps3.telnum Mgr_telnum
FROM     emps3
WHERE  emps3.empid =
```

SQL (cont.)

```
    (SELECT depts3.mgrempid
    FROM depts3
    WHERE depts3.deptno =
      (SELECT emps3.deptno
       FROM emps3
       WHERE emps3.empid = 4444) );
```

Result

```
Bills_Mgr         Mgr_telnum
---------------   ----------
Mary Smith        7890
```

B.4.4 Subqueries in the SELECT column-list

A subquery may occur as a single column in a SELECT column-list if it's assured to return one value for every row of the main (outer) query. Here's an example.

Example: Use the two tables, custs and accts, constructed in Tables B-8 and B-9.

SQL

```
USE mydb
CREATE TABLE custs (
      custidINT   PRIMARY KEY
,     cnameVARCHAR(15)
,     telnumDEC(6)
);
CREATE TABLE accts (
      acctnumINT
,     custidINT
,     bal INT ,
);
INSERT INTO custs (custid,cname , telnum)
VALUES (1, 'Carey Cust', 1234);

INSERT INTO custs (custid,cname , telnum)
VALUES (2, 'Joe Brown', 5678);

INSERT INTO custs (custid,cname , telnum)
VALUES (3, 'Tina Toons', 6789);
```

SQL (cont.)

```
INSERT INTO accts ( acctnum,custid,bal) VALUES (11, 1, 100);
INSERT INTO accts ( acctnum,custid,bal) VALUES (12, 1, 150);
INSERT INTO accts ( acctnum,custid,bal) VALUES (21, 2, 300);
```

Table B-8 custs

custid	cname	telnum
1	Carey Cust	1234
2	Joe Brown	5678
3	Tina Toons	6789

Table B-9 accts

acctnum	custid	bal
11	1	100
12	1	150
21	2	300

Query: Display each customer id, name and total of all his or her balances.

SQL

```
SELECT c.custid, c.cname,
    ( SELECT SUM(bal)
      FROM accts a
      WHERE a.custid = c.custid)  Sum_Bal
FROM custs c;
```

Result

```
custid          cname              Sum_Bal
--------        ---------------    -----------
1               Carey Cust         250
2               Joe Brown          300
3               Tina Toons         NULL
```

Since the subquery is in the SELECT list, there needs to be assurance that the subquery returns exactly one value, Sum_Bal, for each row of the outer query. This assurance is accomplished here by using a *correlated subquery*, discussed in the next section.

B.4.5 Correlated Subquery

In a normal, or uncorrelated, subquery, the subquery does not reference any column in the table of the outer query. A normal subquery is evaluated once for the execution of the outer query.

SQL

```
SELECT empid, Salary
FROM emps3
WHERE
    Salary >= (SELECT AVG(Salary) "Avg Sal" FROM emps3)
```

Result

```
empid          Salary
--------       ----------
4444           40
5555           50
7777           60

(3 row(s) affected)
```

A **correlated subquery** is a subquery that references column(s) of an outer query table.

SQL

```
SELECT c.custid, c.cname, --  Same as query on the previous page
   ( SELECT SUM(bal)
      FROM accts a
      WHERE a.custid = c.custid)  Sum_Bal
FROM custs c;
```

A **correlated subquery** gives great power with significant performance cost. However, a correlated subquery has a significant performance cost due to running the subquery once for each row of the outer query.

There are other approaches to get the same query result with similar performance.

Original query: Display each customer id, name and total of all his or her balances.

SQL

```
SELECT c.custid, c.cname,
    ( SELECT SUM(bal)
      FROM accts a
      WHERE a.custid = c.custid)  Sum_Bal
FROM custs c;
```

Result

```
custid      cname             Sum_Bal
--------    ---------------   -----------
1           Carey Cust        250
2           Joe Brown         300
3           Tina Toons        NULL
```

Switch the tables in the main query and subquery. Is it still a correlated subquery?

SQL

```
SELECT a.custid,
   ( SELECT c.cname
     FROM custs c
     WHERE c.custid = a.custid) cname,
SUM(a.bal) Sum_Bal
FROM accts a
GROUP BY custid;
```

Result

```
custid      cname             Sum_Bal
--------    ---------------   -----------
1           Carey Cust        250
2           Joe Brown         300
```

Notice that this form does not give a result for Tina Toons since she does not have an account, and the outer query is on the accts table.

Another approach to the same problem is to use a VIEW to obtain the SUM(bal).

SQL

```
CREATE VIEW custSumBal
AS
SELECT custid, SUM(bal) Sum_Bal FROM accts
GROUP BY custid
```

SQL

```
SELECT c.custid, c.cname, v.Sum_Bal
FROM custs c, custsumbal v
WHERE c.custid = v.custid;
```

Result

custid	cname	Sum_Bal
--------	---------------	-----------
1	Carey Cust	250
2	Joe Brown	300

This INNER JOIN form works also.

SQL

```
SELECT c.custid, c.cname, SUM(a.bal) "Sum_Bal"
FROM custs c, accts a
WHERE c.custid = a.custid   -- Note that you need to group
by both cols
GROUP BY c.custid, c.cname   -- in order to put both in the
SELECT list.
```

Result

Same result as previous.

To include Tina Toons, use the LEFT OUTER JOIN.

SQL

```
SELECT c.custid, c.cname, SUM(a.bal) "Sum_Bal"
FROM custs c   LEFT OUTER JOIN  accts a
     ON c.custid = a.custid   -- Note that you need to group
by both cols
GROUP BY c.custid, c.cname   -- in order to put both in the
SELECT list.
```

Result

```
custid      cname            Sum_Bal
--------    ---------------  -----------
1           Carey Cust       250
2           Joe Brown        300
3           Tina Toons       NULL
```

B.4.6 Subquery as Alternative to Inner Join

Refer to Tables B-10 and B-11 for the examples in this section.

Table B-10 emps3

ename	empid	deptno	telnum	salary	hiredate	sales_amt
Suzy Smith	1111	102	NULL	20	1/1/98	NULL
Sammy Sosa	2222	102	2345	30	1/1/92	200
Bill Johnson	4444	101	NULL	40	1/1/94	NULL
Mary Smith	5555	100	5678	50	1/1/90	NULL
Mary Smith	7777	101	7890	60	1/1/96	400

Table B-11 depts3

dname	deptno	dept_telnum	mgrempid
Accounting	100	9100	1111
Engineering	101	9101	7777
Sales	102	9102	2222

The following two queries are equivalent in terms of result sets and performance. Notice that the query requires values from only one table (emps3). **Sales-Persons**

Query 1: List **employee number and name** of each person in the Sales department.

SQL

```
SELECT   e.empid , e.ename                                    -
- INNER JOIN
FROM       emps3  e , depts3  d
WHERE    e.deptno  =  d.deptno
  AND          d.dname = 'Sales';
```

Result

Same result as next.

SQL

```
SELECT   e.empid , e.ename                                    -
- Subquery
FROM       emps3  e
WHERE    e.deptno  =
               ( SELECT d.deptno FROM depts3  d    WHERE
d.dname = 'Sales' );
```

Result

empid	ename
------	---------------
1111	Suzy Smith
2222	Sammy Sosa

The next query seems clearer as an INNER JOIN since it requests values from both tables, but performance is still probably about the same as INNER JOIN or subquery.

Query 2: List the employee number, name **and department name** of each employee.

SQL

```
SELECT  e.empid , e.ename , d.dname
-- INNER JOIN
FROM      emps3  e , depts3  d
WHERE    e.deptno  =  d.deptno ;
```

Result

Same result as next.

SQL

```
SELECT  e.empid , e.ename ,
-- Subquery
 ( SELECT d.dname FROM depts3  d WHERE d.deptno =
e.deptno ) dname
FROM      emps3  e ;
```

Result

empid	ename	dname
1111	Suzy Smith	Sales
2222	Sammy Sosa	Sales
4444	Bill Johnson	Engineering
5555	Mary Smith	Accounting
7777	Mary Smith	Engineering

With more than one column required from each table, an INNER JOIN is more efficient since the subquery form requires a correlated subquery for each second table column.

Query 3: List each employee's number, name, department name and dept_telnum.

SQL

```
SELECT     e.empid  ,  e.ename  ,  d.dname  ,  d.dept_telnum
-- INNER JOIN
FROM      emps3  e , depts3  d
WHERE    e.deptno  =  d.deptno ;
```

SQL (cont.)

Result

Same result as next.

SQL

```
SELECT   e.empid , e.ename ,
-- Subquery
    ( SELECT dname FROM depts3  WHERE deptno = e.deptno )
dname ,
    ( SELECT dept_telnum FROM depts3 WHERE deptno =
e.deptno ) dtelno
FROM      emps3  e ;
```

Result

empid	ename	dname	dtelno
1111	Suzy Smith	Sales	9102
2222	Sammy Sosa	Sales	9102
4444	Bill Johnson	Engineering	9101
5555	Mary Smith	Accounting	9100
7777	Mary Smith	Engineering	9101

B.4.7 Subqueries in the FROM Clause

Subqueries may be used to provide a virtual table which can be used in the table list of a FROM clause. It is usually given a table alias to identify it in other parts of the SELECT statement.

B.4.7.1 INNER JOIN of Two Subqueries to Count Matches

Example: List each salesperson and find the number of their active customer accounts and the number of their inactive customer accounts from the tables in Tables B-12 and B-13.

SalesPersons (empid, ename, telnum, OffCity, deptno)

CustAccts (custid, empid, status, acctid, orderdate)

Note: status: "A" is Active, "I" is Inactive, "N" is New account—never been Active.

Table B-12 SalesPersons

empid	ename	...
1	Amy	...
2	Betty	...
3	Carl	...
4	Dave	...

Table B-13 CustAccts

empid	ename	...
1	Amy	...
2	Betty	...
3	Carl	...
4	Dave	...

Complete the following form, Table B-14, for each empid. This will be the information we want to have returned by our final query solution.

Table B-14 Contents of Final Query Solution

empid	ename	NumActive	NumInactive
1	Amy		
2	Betty		
3	Carl		
4	Dave		

First let's do a simple join to count the number of Active customer accounts each salesperson has.

SQL

```
SELECT  s.empid , s.ename ,  count(*) NumActive
FROM salespersons s , custaccts c
WHERE s.empid  =  c.empid
  AND c.status = 'A'
GROUP BY s.empid , s.ename;
```

SQL (cont.)

Result

```
empid    ename           NumActive
------   --------------  -----------
1        Amy             1
2        Betty           2      -- Absence of Carl and Dave => no Active accounts
```

Now let's check the number of Inactive accounts. Change 'A' to 'I' and change the column alias to "NumInActive."

Result

```
empid    ename            NumInActive
------   ---------------  -----------
1        Amy              1
3        Carl             1 -- Absence of Amy and Dave => no InActive accounts
```

Now let's try to combine this into a single report by making each inner join a subquery and doing an inner join of the subqueries based on empid.

SQL

```
SELECT  a.empid , a.ename ,  a.NumActive , b.NumInActive
FROM
   (SELECT s.empid , s.ename ,  count(*) NumActive
    FROM salespersons s , custaccts c
    WHERE s.empid  =  c.empid
      AND c.status = 'A'
    GROUP BY s.empid , s.ename )   a  ,
   (SELECT s.empid , s.ename ,   count(*) NumInActive
    FROM salespersons s , custaccts c
    WHERE s.empid  =  c.empid
      AND c.status = 'I'
    GROUP BY s.empid , s.ename )   b
WHERE a.empid = b.empid
```

Result

```
empid  ename            NumActive  NumInActive
------ ---------------  ---------- -----------
1      Amy              1          1     -- Amy is only one with both Active and Inactive
```

This shows that we can do an INNER JOIN of two subqueries.

To get the complete report we need the two subqueries to list ALL empids including those with zero for NumActive or NumInActive. These are shown on the next page.

Query to List empid and Number of Matches Including Zero Matches

MSS (and ANSI):

First, do a subquery in the SELECT list showing the count of the number of Active accounts. Since Carl and Dave have none, they get count(NULL) which is NULL.

SQL

```
SELECT  sp.empid , sp.ename ,
     (SELECT ( count( ca.status ) )
    FROM custaccts ca
    WHERE   status  =  'A'
    AND   ca.empid  =  sp.empid
    GROUP BY empid )   NumActive
FROM  salespersons sp
```

Result

empid	ename	NumActive
1	Amy	1
2	Betty	2
3	Carl	NULL
4	Dave	NULL

Now do a subquery in the SELECT list showing the count of the number of Inactive accounts. Since Betty and Dave have none, they get count(NULL) which is NULL.

SQL

```
SELECT  sp.empid , sp.ename ,
     (SELECT ( count( ca.status ) )
    FROM custaccts ca
    WHERE   status  =  'I'
    AND   ca.empid  =  sp.empid
    GROUP BY empid )   NumInActive
FROM  salespersons sp
```

SQL (cont.)

Result

```
empid        ename             NumInActive
------       ---------------   -----------
1            Amy               1
2            Betty             NULL
3            Carl              1
4            Dave              NULL
```

We next do an INNER JOIN on these two as subqueries and add the code to convert NULL to a count of 0. In MSS we'll use CASE ... END.

MSS (and ANSI):

SQL

```
SELECT a.empid , a.ename ,
       CASE WHEN a.Active IS NULL THEN 0 ELSE a.Active END
NumActive ,
      CASE WHEN b.InActive IS NULL THEN 0 ELSE b.InActive END
NumInActive

FROM
-- INNER JOIN of 2 subqueries a and b in FROM clause
   (SELECT  sp.empid , sp.ename ,
         (SELECT ( count( ca.status ) )
        FROM custaccts ca
        WHERE   status  =  'A'
        AND   ca.empid  =  sp.empid
        GROUP BY empid )   Active
    FROM  salespersons sp )  a    ,      --   a  INNER JOIN  b

   (SELECT  sp.empid , sp.ename ,
         (SELECT ( count( ca.status ) )
      FROM custaccts ca
      WHERE   status  =  'I'
      AND   ca.empid  =  sp.empid
      GROUP BY empid )   InActive
      FROM  salespersons sp   )   b
WHERE   a.empid  =  b.empid;
```

SQL (cont.)

Result

empid	ename	NumActive	NumInActive
1	Amy	1	1
2	Betty	2	0
3	Carl	0	1
4	Dave	0	0

B.4.8 BETWEEN—Range Queries

The BETWEEN predicate is one way to form a range query.

`WHERE` *`identifier`* `BETWEEN` *`value1`* `AND` *`value2`*

is equivalent to

`WHERE (`*`identifier`* `>=`*`value1`*`) AND (`*`identifier`* `<=`*`value2`*`)`

Query: Find all emps3 with empid's between 2222 and 4444.
ANSI SQL and MSS:

SQL

```
SELECT ename, empid
FROM emps3
WHERE  empid BETWEEN 2222 AND 4444;
```

—or

SQL

```
SELECT ename, empid
FROM emps3
WHERE  empid >= 2222 AND empid <= 4444;
```

Result

ENAME	EMPID
Sammy Sosa	2222
Bill Johnson	4444

2 rows selected.

NOT BETWEEN

Query: Find all emps3 with empids NOT between 2222 and 4444.

ANSI SQL and MSS:

SQL

```
SELECT ename, empid
FROM emps3
WHERE  empid NOT BETWEEN 2222 AND 4444;
```

—or

SQL

```
SELECT ename, empid
FROM emps3
WHERE  NOT (empid BETWEEN 2222 AND 4444);
```

—or

SQL

```
SELECT ename, empid
FROM emps3
WHERE  NOT (empid >= 2222 AND empid <= 4444);
```

—or (careful on this one!)

SQL

```
SELECT ename, empid
FROM emps3
WHERE  empid < 2222 OR empid > 4444;
```

Result

```
ENAME            EMPID
---------------- -----------
Mary Smith       5555
Mary Smith       7777
Suzy Smith       1111
3 rows selected.
```

B.4.9 IN and NOT IN

The **IN predicate tests set membership** in a list of specific acceptable values. It returns TRUE if the test value (often a column value) matches one of the values in the list.

Example: Here are two example IN predicates. Usually it would compare an expression such as a column name on the left side.

`2 IN ( 1 , 2 , 3 , 4 )` is TRUE

`7 IN ( 1 , 2 , 3 , 4 )` is FALSE

Syntax

```
WHERE identifier IN ( value1, value2, .... )
-- Explicit (hard coded) list
```

or

```
WHERE identifier IN (subquery)
-- Subquery (data driven) list, more flexible
```

Query: Using tables B-15 and B-16, find all employees with empids in the list 2222, 3333, 7777.

```
SELECT ename, empid, telnum
       FROM emps3
       WHERE empid   IN
              (SELECT mgrempid FROM depts3);
```

Tables B-15 and B-16 are Employee and Department Tables (3).

Table B-15 emps3

ename	empid	deptno	telnum
Mary Smith	5555	100	5678
Sammy Sosa	2222	102	2345
Bill Johnson	4444	101	
Mary Smith	7777	101	7890
Suzy Smith	1111	102	

Table B-16 depts3

dname	deptno	mgrempid
Accounting	100	1111
Engineering	101	7777
Sales	102	2222

ANSI SQL and MSS:

SQL

```
SELECT ename, empid
FROM emps3
WHERE  empid IN ( 2222, 3333, 7777);
```

Result

```
ENAME            EMPID
-----------------  -------
Mary Smith       7777
Sammy Sosa       2222
2 rows selected.
```

Notice that since there is no 3333, there is no error, just no 3333 in the result.

B.4.9.1 The IN Predicate with a Subquery

The subquery used with the IN predicate needs to be a SELECT statement that returns a single column, that is, a list.

Query: List all employees (names and telephone numbers) who are managers.

First write the query that lists the `mgrempids` for all managers…

SQL

```
SELECT mgrempid FROM depts3;
```

SQL (cont.)

Result

```
mgrempid
--------
5555
7777
2222
```

…and use that as a subquery.

SQL

```
SELECT ename, empid, telnum
FROM emps3
WHERE empid   IN
       (SELECT mgrempid FROM depts3);
```

Result

```
ename            empid        telnum
---------------  ------       ---------
Suzy Smith       1111         NULL
Sammy Sosa       2222         2345
Mary Smith       7777         7890
```

NOT IN

Query: List all employees (names and telephone numbers) who are **NOT managers**.

SQL

```
SELECT ename, empid, telnum
FROM emps3
WHERE empid  NOT IN
       (SELECT mgrempid FROM depts3);
```

SQL (cont.)

Result

```
ename            empid     telnum
---------------  ------    ---------
Bill Johnson     4444      NULL
Mary Smith       5555      5678
```

Caution: NOT IN always returns zero rows if the (*list*) contains NULL. Use NOT EXISTS.

B.4.10 EXISTS and NOT EXISTS

The EXISTS subquery is TRUE if the subquery returns any rows (nonempty result set). It is used only with subqueries.

Syntax:

```
WHERE  EXISTS subquery -- TRUE only if subquery returns non-empty result set
WHERE  NOT EXISTS subquery -- TRUE only if subquery returns empty result set
```

EXISTS is most commonly used with a correlated subquery to report whether there is a match between two tables.

```
SELECT T1.col1 FROM Table1  T1
    WHERE EXISTS
        ( SELECT   1   FROM Table2  T2
          WHERE  T2. column2 = T1.column2)
```

For each row in Table1, there will be a subquery into Table2 whose result will either be a nonempty set of values of T2.anycolumn or NULL (an empty set). If nonempty, then the EXISTS predicate is TRUE, if NULL then it is FALSE.

Example: Same query, list all employees who are managers.

SQL

```
SELECT e.ename, e.empid , e.telnum
FROM emps3  e
WHERE   EXISTS
  ( SELECT  1  FROM depts3 d  WHERE d.mgrempid = e.empid );
```

SQL (cont.)			
Result			
ename	empid	telnum	-- same result as with IN and JOIN
---------------	------	---------	
Suzy Smith	1111	NULL	
Sammy Sos	2222	2345	
Mary Smith	7777	7890	

Question: Which method is most efficient for this query: IN, EXISTS or JOIN?

Answer: IN is more efficient: IN is Order(n), EXISTS and JOIN are Order(n^2).

Example: A Video Retail Store which sells and rents tapes has the Tables B-17 and B-18 shown.

Schema: Video_Store

Table B-17 Movies

title	cost	vhs_onhand
The Way We Were	29.95	5
Butch Cassidy	19.95	9
The Sting	24.95	7
...		

Table B-18 Stars

title	cost	vhs_onhand
The Way We Were	29.95	5
Butch Cassidy	19.95	9
The Sting	24.95	7
...		

Query: List all movie names starring Paul Newman and the number of tapes in stock.emps3.

ANSI SQL and MSS:

SQL

```
SELECT M.title, M.vhs_onhand          -- EXISTS Solution
FROM Movies M
WHERE EXISTS
    ( SELECT 1 FROM Stars S WHERE M.title = S.title
                                                   AND
S.star_name = 'Paul Newman');
```

Result

```
title               vhs_onhand
-----------------   ---------------
Butch Cassidy       9
The Sting           7
```

SQL

```
SELECT DISTINCT M.title, M.vhs_onhand      -- JOIN Solution
FROM Movies M, Stars S
WHERE S.star_name = 'Paul Newman' AND M.title = S.title;
```

SQL

```
SELECT DISTINCT M.title, M.vhs_onhand   -- IN Solution
FROM Movies M
WHERE M.title  IN
       ( SELECT title FROM Stars WHERE star_name  =
'Paul Newman' );
```

Result

Same result as with EXISTS

B.4.11 NOT IN versus NOT EXISTS

If (*list*) contains no NULL values, then IN (*list*) and NOT IN (*list*) are complements.

Tables B-19 and B-20 show the data in the emps3 and depts3 tables, which is used in the next examples.

Table B-19 emps3

ename	empid	deptno	telnum
Mary Smith	5555	100	5678
Sammy Sosa	2222	102	2345
Bill Johnson	4444	101	
Mary Smith	7777	101	7890
Suzy Smith	1111	102	

Table B-20 depts3

dname	deptno	mgrempid
Accounting	100	1111
Engineering	101	7777
Sales	102	2222

SQL

```
SELECT mgrempid FROM depts3;    -- Contains no NULL values.
```

Result

```
mgrempid
--------
1111
7777
2222
```

So the UNION of the next two queries contains all employees.

Example: IN List all employees who are department managers.

SQL

```
SELECT ename, empid
FROM emps3
WHERE empid IN
    (SELECT mgrempid FROM depts3);  -- ( 5555, 7777, 2222 )
```

Result

```
ename           empid
--------------- ------
Suzy Smith      1111
Sammy Sos       2222
Mary Smith      7777
```

Example: NOT IN List all employees who are NOT department managers.

Result

```
ename           empid      -- Replace "IN" with "NOT IN" in above query
--------------- ------
Bill Johnson    4444
Mary Smith      5555
```

Caution When Using NOT IN

The NOT IN predicate always returns zero rows if there is a NULL in the (*list*). NOT EXISTS is safer.

SQL

```
BEGIN TRANSACTION    -- We put this work into a Transaction
and ROLL it back so it's not saved
```

SQL

```
INSERT INTO  depts3 (dname,deptno,mgrempid) VALUES
( 'Newdept' , 999 , NULL );
```

After this insert, the **emps3** and **depts3** tables appear as shown here.

Table B-21 emps3

ename	empid	deptno	telnum
Mary Smith	5555	100	5678
Sammy Sosa	2222	102	2345
Bill Johnson	4444	101	
Mary Smith	7777	101	7890
Suzy Smith	1111	102	

Table B-22 depts3

dname	deptno	mgrempid
Accounting	100	1111
Engineering	101	7777
Sales	102	2222

SQL

```
SELECT mgrempid FROM depts3;      -- Now contains NULL.
```

Result

```
--------
5555
7777
2222
NULL
```

Notes:

¥ NOT IN is more efficient that NOT EXISTS

¥ NOT IN is only safe with a subquery whose return column has a NOT NULL constraint.

SQL

```
SELECT ename, empid       -- List all employees who are NOT
managers, ERROR
FROM emps3 e
WHERE e.empid NOT IN --   ( 5555 , 7777 , 2222 , NULL )
     ( SELECT mgrempid FROM depts3 );
-- NOT IN with NULL => 0 rows
```

Result

```
ename              empid
---------------    ---------
0 rows selected.
```

SQL

```
SELECT ename, empid      -- List all employees who are NOT
managers
FROM emps3 e
WHERE   NOT EXISTS
       ( SELECT  1  FROM depts3 WHERE mgrempid = e.empid );
```

Result

```
ename              empid                -- NOT EXISTS with NULL =>
Correct Result anyway
---------------    ------
Bill Johnson       4444
```

> Note:
> In predicate is safe even with NULL in (*list*)

SQL

```
ROLLBACK      -- This throws away the INSERT so our depts3
table is unchanged.
```

B.4.12 (SOME/ANY) and ALL

The SOME/ANY and ALL predicates may be used with any relational operator of equality or inequality (recall that the IN predicate only matches equality). The SOME and ANY predicates mean exactly the same thing. Their syntax and meanings are given below.

Syntax

MSS documentation shows the syntax for SOME/ANY and ALL as follows:

```
scalar_expression { = | <> | != | > | >= | !> | < | <= | !< }
{SOME | ANY} (subquery)
```

```
scalar_expression { = | <> | != | > | >= | !> | < | <= | !< }
ALL (subquery)
```

SOME/ANY compares the test value, *scalar_expression*, to each value in the subquery result, one at a time. If **any** return TRUE then the predicate returns TRUE.

ALL compares the test value, *scalar_expression*, to each value in the subquery result, one at a time. If **all** return TRUE then the predicate returns TRUE.

Example using SOME/ANY: This query can be done using INNER JOIN or IN or SOME/ANY predicate.

Query: List all employees in the Sales or Accounting department.

SQL

```
SELECT empid, deptno
FROM emps3
WHERE deptno = ANY   -- ANY or SOME give the same result
      (SELECT deptno FROM depts3
      WHERE  dname = 'Sales'  OR  dname = 'Accounting' );
```

Result

empid	deptno
1111	102
2222	102
5555	100

SOME/ANY and ALL predicates work well with numeric values

Example using ALL:

Query: Find the employee(s) Minimum salary without using the MIN() function.

SQL

```
SELECT empid, salary
FROM emps3
WHERE  salary  <=  ALL ( SELECT salary FROM emps3 )
```

Result

```
empid          salary
-----------    -------
1111           20
```

SOME/ANY have greater flexibility than IN by being able to specify an inequality as well as equality.

Use caution when using brackets, <>, with SOME/ANY. Brackets reverse the way we usually use the words ANY and ALL. Tables B-23 and B-24 are used for the next examples.

Table B-23 emps3

ename	empid	deptno	telnum
Mary Smith	5555	100	5678
Sammy Sosa	2222	102	2345
Bill Johnson	4444	101	
Mary Smith	7777	101	7890
Suzy Smith	1111	102	

Table B-24 depts3

dname	deptno	mgrempid
Accounting	100	1111
Engineering	101	7777
Sales	102	2222

Here is a query from a previous exercise and the correct solution using NOT EXISTS.

Example: For the table above, display summaries of `Amount by Year` and `Quarter`.

Query: Display all employees who are not department managers.

SQL

```
SELECT ename, empid FROM emps3 e WHERE NOT EXISTS
   ( SELECT 1 FROM depts3 d WHERE  e.empid = d.mgrempid );
```

Result

ename	empid
Bill Johnson	4444
Mary Smith	5555

Writing this to use ANY or ALL takes some thought because "<> ANY" doesn't mean "not any" in the sense of "none." It returns TRUE if there **are any** for which it is <>.

So, if we do the following "<> ANY" query, we do not get the result desired by the previous example.

Incorrect Result

SQL

```
SELECT ename, empid
FROM emps3
WHERE empid <> ANY
  (SELECT mgrempid FROM depts3);
-- This is incorrect, every empid has some
-- mgrempid that is not equal
```

Result

ename	empid
Suzy Smith	1111
Sammy Sosa	2222
Bill Johnson	4444
Mary Smith	5555
Mary Smith	7777

To see why this doesn't work, we need to return to the definition:

If the current empid <> **any** one value in mgrempid list, then the predicate returns TRUE. If the current empid <> any one value in mgrempid list, then the predicate returns TRUE. So if there are two or more values in the list on the right side, then the single value on the left side will be unequal to at least one of them and the predicate will be TRUE.

The correct version, then, must use "<> ALL."

SQL

```
SELECT ename, empid
FROM emps3
WHERE empid <> ALL
    (SELECT mgrempid FROM depts3);
```

Result

```
ename            empid
---------------  ------
Bill Johnson     4444
Mary Smith       5555
```

Note: This version is also not safe. It returns zero rows if there is a NULL value for any mgrempid in the depts3 table. So the NOT EXISTS version earlier is the only one to give all of the correct rows that do have a current match in depts3 table even though there may be some NULL mgrempid values in the table.

B.5 PIVOTS (OR ROTATING DATA OR CROSS TABULATIONS)

Pivoting, also called **rotating** or **cross-tabulating** a table, is similar to creating a spreadsheet Pivot Table. It roughly "pivots" a table to rotate some row values into columns to show summary information. Pivoting allows you to summarize a data column by primary and secondary columns.

Primary source column **heading** becomes **first column heading** in the output.

Secondary source column **values** become **output column headings 2 through N**.

The *data column* **of the source table is presented as summary values** under output columns 2 through N. It is often summarized using `SUM()`.

First pivot example—

Consider the following table, `SalesByQtr`:

SQL

```
SELECT * FROM SalesByQtr;
```

Result

Year	Quarter	Amount
2000	1	100
2000	2	200
2000	3	300
2000	4	400
2001	1	110
2001	2	210
2001	3	310
2001	4	410

Example: For the table above, display summaries of `Amount` by `Year` and `Quarter`.

That is, **pivot the SalesByQtr table to summarize for each Year, Amount for each Quarter.**

Desired Result:

Year	Q1	Q2	Q3	Q4
2000	100	200	300	400
2001	110	210	310	410

Step 1 for Solution 1: Solution 2: Pivot using a Correlated Subquery (ANSI and MSS).

First, try to use `CASE` to pivot by `Quarter` to display the `Amount` for each `Quarter`.

Now add `SUM()` and `GROUP BY Year` to get the desired output.

SQL

```
SELECT Year
    ,CASE WHEN Quarter = 1 THEN Amount ELSE 0 END  Q1
    ,CASE WHEN Quarter = 2 THEN Amount ELSE 0 END  Q2
    ,CASE WHEN Quarter = 3 THEN Amount ELSE 0 END  Q3
    ,CASE WHEN Quarter = 4 THEN Amount ELSE 0 END  Q4
FROM SalesByQtr
```

Result

Year	Q1	Q2	Q3	Q4
2000	100	0	0	0
2000	0	200	0	0
2000	0	0	300	0
2000	0	0	0	400
2001	10	0	0	0
2001	0	210	0	0
2001	0	0	310	0
2001	0	0	0	410

Solution 1: Pivot using SUM of CASE (ANSI and MSS).

SQL

```
SELECT Year
   ,  SUM( CASE  WHEN Quarter = 1 THEN Amount ELSE 0 END )  Q1
   ,  SUM( CASE  WHEN Quarter = 2 THEN Amount ELSE 0 END )  Q2
   ,  SUM( CASE  WHEN Quarter = 3 THEN Amount ELSE 0 END )  Q3
   ,  SUM( CASE  WHEN Quarter = 4 THEN Amount ELSE 0 END )  Q4
FROM SalesByQtr
GROUP BY Year;
```

Result

Year	Q1	Q2	Q3	Q4
2000	100	200	300	400
2001	110	210	310	410

Solution 2: Pivot using a Correlated Subquery (ANSI and MSS).

SQL

```
SELECT Year            -- "SELECT DISTINCT Year" may replace
"GROUP BY Year"
   ,  ( SELECT SUM( Amount )  FROM SalesByQtr s1
          WHERE s1.Year = s.Year  AND s1.Quarter = 1 )  Q1
   ,  ( SELECT SUM( Amount )  FROM SalesByQtr s1
          WHERE s1.Year = s.Year  AND s1.Quarter = 2 )  Q2
   ,  ( SELECT SUM( Amount )  FROM SalesByQtr s1
          WHERE s1.Year = s.Year  AND s1.Quarter = 3 )  Q3
   ,  ( SELECT SUM( Amount )  FROM SalesByQtr s1
          WHERE s1.Year = s.Year  AND s1.Quarter = 4 )  Q4
FROM SalesByQtr s
GROUP BY Year ;
```

Result

Same Output as Solution 1

Question: Which is more efficient, Solution 1 or Solution 2? Use the previous query as a subquery in the FROM clause to add YearTotal in output.

Answer: Solution 1 appears to be more efficient since each CASE is evaluated just once per row of the original table and then SUMmed. But Solution 2 contains a correlated subquery, which means a new query must be executed for each row of the original table. So Solution 1 is Order(n), Solution 2 is Order(n^2).

Add Total Sales for the Year

We may treat either Solution 1 or Solution 2 as a source table by making it a subquery in the FROM clause.

It then becomes easy to add a final column which is the Total Sales for the year.

SQL

```
SELECT Year --  Repeat solution 1 code for reference
    , SUM( CASE Quarter WHEN 1 THEN Amount ELSE 0 END ) Q1
    , SUM( CASE Quarter WHEN 2 THEN Amount ELSE 0 END ) Q2
    , SUM( CASE Quarter WHEN 3 THEN Amount ELSE 0 END ) Q3
    , SUM( CASE Quarter WHEN 4 THEN Amount ELSE 0 END ) Q4
FROM SalesByQtr
GROUP BY Year;
```

Result

Year	Q1	Q2	Q3	Q4
2000	100	200	300	400
2001	110	210	310	410

Use the previous query as a subquery in the FROM clause to add YearTotal in output.

SQL

```
SELECT *, (Q1 + Q2 + Q3 + Q4) YearTotal
FROM (SELECT Year
  , SUM(CASE Quarter WHEN 1 THEN Amount ELSE 0 END) AS Q1
  , SUM(CASE Quarter WHEN 2 THEN Amount ELSE 0 END) AS Q2
  , SUM(CASE Quarter WHEN 3 THEN Amount ELSE 0 END) AS Q3
  , SUM(CASE Quarter WHEN 4 THEN Amount ELSE 0 END) AS Q4
      FROM SalesByQtr
      GROUP BY Year) s
```

Result

Year	Q1	Q2	Q3	Q4	YearTotal
2000	100	200	300	400	1000
2001	110	210	310	410	1040

Pivot Exercise: Consider the following data from the `titles` table.

SQL

```
SELECT   title_id , pub_id , type    , ytd_sales , price
FROM   titles;
```

Result

title_id	pub_id	type	ytd_sales	price
BU2075	0736	business	18722	2.9900
BU1032	1389	business	4000	19.9900
BU1111	1389	business	2000	11.9500
PS1372	0877	psychology	375	21.5900
PS2091	0736	psychology	2000	10.9500
PS2106	0736	psychology	111	7.0000
PS3333	0736	psychology	3000	19.9900

Example: For the *titles* table above, display summaries of the *ytd_sales* by *pub_id* based on the *type* of title. (Uses only three middle columns above.)

That is,

pivot the `titles` table to summarize `ytd_sales` for each `pub_id` **and title `type`.**

Result

pub_id	business	psychology
0736	18722	5111
0877	0	375
1389	6000	0

Write your solution using either CASE or Correlated Subquery.
A solution follows.

Solution 1: Using CASE

SQL

```
SELECT  pub_id  -- Uses ANSI SQL form of column alias
   , SUM( CASE WHEN type = 'business' THEN ytd_sales ELSE 0
END ) business
   , SUM( CASE WHEN type = 'psychology' THEN ytd_sales ELSE
0 END ) psych
FROM Titles t
GROUP BY  pub_id
```

Result

pub_id	business	psych
0736	18722	9564
0877	0	375
1389	12066	0

Solution 2: Correlated subqueries can be used to produce pivots.

SQL

```
SELECT  t.pub_id, -- ANSI SQL form of column alias
     (SELECT SUM(ytd_sales) FROM Titles t1
        WHERE t1.pub_id = t.pub_id AND t1.type =
  'business')     business,
     (SELECT SUM(ytd_sales) FROM Titles t1
     WHERE t1.pub_id = t.pub_id  AND t1.type =
  'psychology')  psychology
FROM Titles t
GROUP BY t.pub_id;
```

Alternatively, instead of GROUP BY, you may use SELECT DISTINCT and get the same result.

SQL

```
SELECT DISTINCT t.pub_id, -- ANSI SQL form of alias
    (SELECT SUM(ytd_sales) FROM Titles t1
       WHERE t1.pub_id = t.pub_id
       AND t1.type =  'business')      business,
    (SELECT SUM(ytd_sales) FROM Titles t1
      WHERE t1.pub_id = t.pub_id
        AND t1.type = 'psychology')  psychology
FROM Titles t ;
```

Result

```
pub_id          business            psychology
------          -----------         -----------
0736            18722               9564
0877            NULL                375
1389            12066               NULL
```

Notice that Solution 1 shows 0 (from the SUM) whereas Solution 2 shows NULLs since there some subqueries return no rows.

Both GROUP BY with CUBE and GROUP BY with ROLLUP compute the same sort of information as shown in the example but in a slightly different format.

Other pivot examples follow.

B.5.1 Subquery Examples

These subquery examples came from a company wanting to analyze their sales history. The desired results are shown for each query. Solutions are given at the end of this chapter. For the first example, use Table B-25.

For code examples, this table is called **t1**.

Table B-25 t1

c1	c2	c3	c4
a	5	1	10
a	2	4	6
a	7	7	8

Table B-25 t1 (cont.)

b	4	20	50
b	4	15	20
b	2	0	0
c	1	1	1
c	NULL	NULL	NULL

SQL

```
USE mydb
```

SQL

```
CREATE TABLE t1 (
   id    DEC(4),
   c1    VARCHAR(2),
   c2    DEC(2),
   c3    DEC(2),
   c4    DEC(2)
);
```

SQL

```
INSERT INTO t1 VALUES ( 1 ,
'a' , 5 , 1 , 10 );
INSERT INTO t1 VALUES ( 2 ,
'a' ,2 ,4 ,6 );
INSERT INTO t1 VALUES ( 3 ,
'a' ,7 ,7 ,8 );
INSERT INTO t1 VALUES ( 4 ,
'b' ,4 ,20 ,50 );
INSERT INTO t1 VALUES ( 5 ,
'b' ,4 ,15 ,20 );
INSERT INTO t1 VALUES ( 6 ,
'b' ,2 ,0 ,0 );
INSERT INTO t1 VALUES ( 7 ,
'c' ,1 ,1 ,1 );
INSERT INTO t1 VALUES ( 8 ,
'c' ,NULL ,NULL ,NULL );
```

ROLLUP operator provides summary rows above those from GROUP BY

Query 1: Create a histogram summing c2 for each c1 value.

Desired Result

```
c1          c2_SumBy_c1
----        -------------------
a           14
b           10
c            1
```

Fill in your answer here.

Query 2: Create a cumulative histogram over time, showing c1 and accumulating c2.

Desired Result

```
c1      c2_Cum
----    -------------------
a       14
b       24
c       25
```

Fill in your answer here.

Query 3: Do the modified Pivot on c1 as shown. (This does not require a subquery.)

Desired Result

```
C2      C3      C4      a       b       c
----    ----    ----    -----   -----   ------
5       1       10      1       0       0
2       4       6       1       0       0
7       7       8       1       0       0
4       20      50      0       1       0
4       15      20      0       1       0
2       0       0       0       1       0
1       1       1       0       0       1
NULL    NULL    NULL    0       0       1

(8 row(s) affected)
```

Fill in your answer here.

Pivot Exercise 2

Query 4: Pivot table t1 on c1 to summarize the values of each of the other columns.

SQL
`SELECT * FROM t1 -- Data Table, for reference`

Result

c1	c2	c3	c4
a	5	1	10
a	2	4	6
a	7	7	8
b	4	20	50
b	4	15	20
b	2	0	0
c	1	1	1
c	NULL	NULL	NULL

Desired Result:

c1	c2_Sum	c3_Sum	c4_Sum
a	14	12	24
b	10	35	70
c	1	1	1

Fill in your answer here.

Query 5: Write a query to retrieve the top two c2 values for each c1.

Modified Table **t1** -- Has `id` column as Primary Key.

id	c1	c2	c3	c4
----	----	----	----	----
1	a	5	1	10
2	a	2	4	6
3	a	7	7	8
4	b	4	20	50
5	b	4	15	20
6	b	2	0	0
7	c	1	1	1
8	c	NULL	NULL	NULL

Desired Result for this data:

c1	c2_Max	c2_MaxNext	-- MaxNext is next value <= Max
----	------	----------	
a	7	5	
b	4	4	
c	1	NULL	

Either the preceding or the following format is acceptable for the output.

ID	C1	C2
-------	---	----
3	a	7
1	a	5
4	b	4
5	b	4
8	c	Null
7	c	1

Fill in your answer here.

Query 6: Write a query to retrieve the top 2 c2 values for each c1. Same problem as Query 5, BUT NO PRIMARY KEY.

SQL
`SELECT * FROM t1 -- Data Table, for reference`

Result

c1	c2	c3	c4
a	5	1	10
a	2	4	6
a	7	7	8
b	4	2	50
b	4	1	20
b	2	0	0
c	1	1	1
c	NULL	NULL	NULL

Final Desired Result:

c1	c2_Max	c2_MaxNext	
a	7	5	
b	4	4	
c	1	NULL	

-- MaxNext is next value <= Max

First Try, easier to program. Try to obtain this result:

c1	c2_Max	c2_MaxLess	-- MaxLess is next value < Max
a	7	5	
b	4	2	-- Incorrect solution, doesn't notice that top two values are same
c	1	NULL	

Fill in your answer here.

Note: This could be the correct solution if that's what the customer wanted. In this case, they wanted a duplicate of the max value to show up as top and top next.

B.5.1.1 Problem from MI Company

Create the data for the ***MI Company*** example.

SQL

```
Use mydb

CREATE  TABLE   tests (
   testidINT    PRIMARY KEY,
   tnameVARCHAR(10)
);

CREATE TABLE runs (
   runidINT     PRIMARY KEY,
   testidINT,
   rundateDATETIME,
);

CREATE TABLE steps (
   runidINT ,
   stepidINT ,
   statusVARCHAR(10),
   CONSTRAINT pk_steps PRIMARY KEY (runid,stepid)
);

INSERT INTO tests VALUES ( 1, 'test1' );
INSERT INTO tests VALUES ( 2, 'test2' );
INSERT INTO tests VALUES ( 3, 'test3' );

INSERT INTO runs  VALUES ( 11, 1 , '2001-01-01' );
INSERT INTO runs  VALUES ( 12, 1 , '2001-02-02' );

INSERT INTO steps VALUES ( 11, 1 , 'Passed' );
INSERT INTO steps VALUES ( 11, 2 , 'Failed' );
INSERT INTO steps VALUES ( 11, 3 , 'Failed' );
INSERT INTO steps VALUES ( 21, 1 , 'Passed' );
INSERT INTO steps VALUES ( 21, 2 , 'Passed' );
INSERT INTO steps VALUES ( 21, 3 , 'Passed' );
```

Data is shown below.

Query 7: List every test in the `tests` table and show the `runs` and `steps` for each test that has them. Display: testid, test name, runid, rundate, stepid, status. (Note: there is another table test_steps that defines each step for each test. It is not needed for this query.)

Data

SQL

```
SELECT  *  FROM tests;
```

Result

testid	tname
1	test1
2	test2
3	test3

SQL

```
SELECT * FROM runs;
```

Result

runid	testid	rundate
11	1	2001 0101
12	1	2001 0202

SQL

```
SELECT * FROM steps;
```

SQL (cont.)

Result

```
runid        stepid       status
-----------  ----------   ----------
11           1            Passed
11           2            Failed
11           3            Failed
21           1            Passed
21           2            Passed
21           3            Passed
```

The desired output for the data shown in the tables is given here.

Result

```
testid   tname    runid    rundate         stepid    status
-------  ------   ------   ---- --------   -------   ----------
1        test1    11       2001 0101       1         Passed
1        test1    11       2001 0101       2         Failed
1        test1    11       2001 0101       3         Failed
1        test1    12       2001 0202       NULL      NULL
2        test2    NULL     NULL            NULL      NULL
3        test3    NULL     NULL            NULL      NULL
```

B.5.1.2 Some Solutions to the MI Company Problem

Some MSS Solutions:

SQL

```
SELECT t.testid, t.tname , r.runid , r.rundate ,
       s.status
FROM ( tests  t  LEFT OUTER JOIN  runs  r
  ON  t.testid = r.testid  )  -- ()'s optional
       LEFT OUTER JOIN   steps  s
    ON  r.runid = s.runid
ORDER BY t.testid
```

Result

Same as above.

SQL

```
SELECT t.testid, t.tname , r.runid , r.rundate ,
       s.status
FROM  tests t LEFT OUTER JOIN
       ( runs r  LEFT OUTER JOIN  steps s
          -- Why does INNER  miss some?
   ON  r.runid = s.runid )
    ON  t.testid = r.testid
ORDER BY t.testid
```

Result

Same as above.

SQL

```
SELECT t.testid , t.tname , b.runid , b.rundate , b.status
FROM  tests t LEFT OUTER JOIN
    ( SELECT r.runid , r.rundate , s.status , r.testid
      FROM  runs r  LEFT OUTER JOIN steps s
      ON  r.runid = s.runid ) b
ON  t.testid = b.testid
ORDER BY t.testid
```

Result

Same as above.

Question: Why doesn't this work?

SQL

```
SELECT t.TS_TEST_ID, t.TS_NAME , r.RN_RUN_NAME, s.ST_DESCRIPTION
FROM  Atest t LEFT OUTER JOIN Arun r LEFT OUTER JOIN Astep s
  ON  t.TS_TEST_ID = r.RN_TEST_ID
  ON  s.ST_RUN_ID = r.RN_RUN_ID
ORDER BY t.TS_TEST_ID
```

Answer: It's the wrong syntax. ;-) It must be: t1 LOJ t2 ON c1=c2 LOJ t3 ON c3=c4

B.6 MORE SUBQUERY EXAMPLES—SALES REPS AND QUOTAS

For this example, consider these tables:

Reps(SRName, SRid, OffCity, Quota) -- Reps contains sales reps
Sales(RepSSAN, Custid, Amount) -- Sales custs and amounts for each rep
Offices(OffName, Target) -- Sales offices and their sales ta gets

Consider this sample data:

SQL

```
SELECT * FROM Reps;
```

Result

SRName	SRid	OffCity	Quota
Amy	111	San Jose	30
Sue	333	San Jose	50
Zeb	555	San Jose	70
Bob	777	Boston	50
Bab	888	Boston	55

SQL

```
SELECT * FROM Sales;
```

Result

RepSSAN	Custid	Amount
111	10	10
111	20	20
333	30	30
333	30	50
555	60	60
777	70	40
888	70	60

SQL

```
SELECT * FROM Offices;
```

SQL (cont.)

Result

```
OffName      Target
----------   ------
San Jose     40
Boston       50
```

Query 1: For each sales rep whose total sales have exceeded his or her office's target, list the sales rep's (name), OffCity and the office target.

Solution:

SQL

```
SELECT R.SRName,  R.OffCity,  O.Target "Office Target"
FROM Reps R, Offices O
WHERE R.OffCity = O.OffName
    AND O.Target <
        (SELECT Sum(S.Amount)
         FROM Sales S
          WHERE S.RepSSAN = R.SRid); --Total_Sales
```

Result

```
SRName         OffCity      Office Target
-------------  ----------   ----------------
Sue            San Jose     40
Zeb            San Jose     40
Bab            Boston       50

(3 row(s) affected)
```

This result is correct, but it would be nice to show it by displaying the sales reps' total sales to demonstrate that it exceeds the office target. This is done below.

Query2: For the same query, also display the sales reps' total sales.

Notice that it requires executing the subquery twice.

SQL

```
SELECT R.SRName,  R.OffCity,
       O.Target "Office Target",
    (SELECT Sum(S.Amount)
     FROM Sales S
     WHERE S.RepSSAN = R.SRid) Total_Sales
FROM Reps R, Offices O
WHERE R.OffCity = O.OffName
    AND O.Target <
        (SELECT Sum(S.Amount)
      FROM Sales S
      WHERE S.RepSSAN = R.SRid);
```

Result

SRName	OffCity	Office Target	Total_Sales
Sue	San Jose	40	80
Zeb	San Jose	40	60
Bab	Boston	50	60

(3 row(s) affected)

Let's try the same query by creating a view using GROUP BY to do the totalling.

SQL

```
CREATE VIEW TotalSRSales
AS
    SELECT S.RepSSAN, Sum(S.Amount) Total_Sales
    FROM Sales S
    GROUP BY S.RepSSAN
```

SQL

```
SELECT * FROM TotalSRSales;
```

SQL (cont.)

Result

```
RepSSAN          Total_Sales
---------------  ----------------------------------
111              30
333              80
555              60
777              40
888              60

(5 row(s) affected)
```

Then our new solution is as follows:

Query 2: Using View TotalSRSales

SQL

```
SELECT R.SRName,  R.OffCity,
       O.Target "Office Target", T.Total_Sales
FROM Reps R, Offices O, TotalSRSales T
WHERE R.OffCity = O.OffName
    AND R.SRid    = T.RepSSAN
    AND O.Target < T.Total_Sales;
```

Result

```
SRName        OffCity      Office Target   Total_Sales
------------  ---------    ------------    -----------------------
Sue           San Jose     40              80
Zeb           San Jose     40              60
Bab           Boston       50              60
(3 row(s) affected)
```

This is a more satisfying solution.

The same tables are repeated for reference.

SQL

```
SELECT * FROM Reps;
```

SQL (cont.)

Result

SRName	SRid	OffCity	Quota
Amy	111	San Jose	30
Sue	333	San Jose	50
Zeb	555	San Jose	70
Bob	777	Boston	50
Bab	888	Boston	55

SQL

```
SELECT * FROM Sales;
```

Result

RepSSAN	Custid	Amount
111	10	10
111	20	20
333	30	30
333	30	50
555	60	60
777	70	40
888	70	60

Example: Display each Sales Rep's name and the total she or he sold to each customer.

Solution, Step 1: To get the amount each rep sold each customer, pivot `Sales` table on `RepSSAN` to SUM the `Amount` for each `Custid`.

SQL

```
SELECT DISTINCT RepSSAN ,
   ( SELECT SUM(Amount)  FROM Sales s2
         WHERE s2.RepSSAN = s1.RepSSAN
       AND s2.Custid = 10)  Cust_10 ,
   ( SELECT SUM(Amount)  FROM Sales s2
         WHERE s2.RepSSAN = s1.RepSSAN
       AND s2.Custid = 20)  Cust_20 ,
   ' ... etc. for each Custid ... '
FROM Sales s1;
```

SQL (cont.)

Result

RepSSAN	Cust_10	Cust_20	
111	10	20	... etc. for each Custid ...
333	NULL	NULL	... etc. for each Custid ...
55	NULL	NULL	... etc. for each Custid ...
777	NULL	NULL	... etc. for each Custid ...
888	NULL	NULL	... etc. for each Custid ...

Solution, Step 2: Combine this result as a join with the `Reps` table to get `SRName`.

SQL

```
SELECT DISTINCT r.SRName ,
     ( SELECT SUM(Amount) FROM Sales s1
      WHERE s1.RepSSAN = s.RepSSAN
        AND s1.Custid = 10)  Cust_10 ,
     ( SELECT SUM(Amount) FROM Sales s1
      WHERE s1.RepSSAN = s.RepSSAN
        AND s1.Custid = 20)  Cust_20 ,
     ( SELECT SUM(Amount) FROM Sales s1
      WHERE s1.RepSSAN = s.RepSSAN
        AND s1.Custid = 30)  Cust_30 ,
     ( SELECT SUM(Amount) FROM Sales s1
      WHERE s1.RepSSAN = s.RepSSAN
        AND s1.Custid = 60)  Cust_60 ,
     ( SELECT SUM(Amount) FROM Sales s1
      WHERE s1.RepSSAN = s.RepSSAN
        AND s1.Custid = 70)  Cust_70
FROM Sales s,  Reps r
WHERE s.RepSSAN = r.SRid;
```

Result

SRName	Cust_10	Cust_20	Cust_30	Cust_60	Cust_70
Amy	10	20	NULL	NULL	NULL
Bab	NULL	NULL	NULL	NULL	60
Bob	NULL	NULL	NULL	NULL	40
Sue	NULL	NULL	80	NULL	NULL
Zeb	NULL	NULL	NULL	60	NULL

Alternative Solution: Join the Reps table with Step 1 as a subquery.

SQL

```
SELECT r.SRName , Cust_10 , Cust_20 , Cust_30 , Cust_60 ,
Cust_70
FROM    Reps r ,
      ( SELECT DISTINCT RepSSAN ,
            ( SELECT SUM(Amount) FROM Sales s2
                  WHERE s2.RepSSAN = s1.RepSSAN
                  AND s2.Custid = 10)  Cust_10 ,
            ( SELECT SUM(Amount) FROM Sales s2
                  WHERE s2.RepSSAN = s1.RepSSAN
                  AND s2.Custid = 20)  Cust_20 ,
            ( SELECT SUM(Amount) FROM Sales s2
                  WHERE s2.RepSSAN = s1.RepSSAN
                  AND s2.Custid = 30)  Cust_30 ,
            ( SELECT SUM(Amount) FROM Sales s2
                  WHERE s2.RepSSAN = s1.RepSSAN
                  AND s2.Custid = 60)  Cust_60 ,
            ( SELECT SUM(Amount) FROM Sales s2
                  WHERE s2.RepSSAN = s1.RepSSAN
                  AND s2.Custid = 70)  Cust_70
        FROM Sales s1    ) s
WHERE s.RepSSAN = r.SRid;          -- Same Result as above
```

B.7 ROLLUP AND CUBE

ROLLUP and CUBE are used with GROUP BY to find additional sums or aggregates. ROLLUP adds summary rows from right to left on the GROUP BY list. For example,

GROUP BY a , b , c WITH ROLLUP

yields summaries for: (a , b) and (c) values.

B.7.1 ROLLUP

Note: Distinct aggregates, for example, AVG(DISTINCT *column_name*) and COUNT(DISTINCT *column_name*), are not supported when using CUBE or ROLLUP. GROUP BY a , b with ROLLUP

ROLLUP operator

provides summary rows above those from GROUP BY

The GROUP BY column order specifies a ROLLUP hierarchical order, from hi (left) to lo (right).

Groups are summarized in this hierarchical order, from the lowest level to the highest.

Example: GROUP BY a , b , c WITH ROLLUP

Lists values for a , b , c,

lists a , b and summarizes (SUM/AVG/...) all values for that a and b

lists a and summarizes (SUM/AVG/...) all values for that a

See the examples to make more sense of this

Note: Changing the order of grouping columns can affect the number of rows produced.

Each GROUP BY summary row shows the values for the columns being summarized and NULL in the other GROUP BY columns. This is easier to see by looking at the examples.

Note: Distinct aggregates, for example, AVG(DISTINCT *column_name*) and COUNT(DISTINCT *column_name*), are not supported when using CUBE or ROLLUP.

Create sample data to work with.

SQL

```
USE mydb

CREATE TABLE  data (
  a     VARCHAR(5)
, b     VARCHAR(5)
, c     VARCHAR(5)
, d     DEC(4,2)
);
INSERT INTO  data ( a , b , c , d )
  VALUES ( 'a1' , 'b1' , 'c1' , 1 ) ;
INSERT INTO  data ( a , b , c , d )
  VALUES ( 'a1' , 'b1' , 'c2' , 2 ) ;
```

SQL (cont.)

```
INSERT INTO  data ( a , b , c , d )
  VALUES ( 'a1' , 'b2' , 'c1' ,  3);
INSERT INTO  data ( a , b , c , d )
  VALUES ( 'a1' , 'b2' , 'c2' , 4) ;
INSERT INTO  data ( a , b , c , d )
  VALUES ( 'a2' , 'b1' , 'c1' , 5 ) ;
INSERT INTO  data ( a , b , c , d )
  VALUES ( 'a2' , 'b1' , 'c2' , 6 ) ;
INSERT INTO  data ( a , b , c , d )
  VALUES ( 'a2' , 'b2' , 'c1' , 7 ) ;
INSERT INTO  data ( a , b , c , d )
  VALUES ( 'a2' , 'b2' , 'c2' , 8 ) ;
```

SQL

```
SELECT  *  FROM  data
```

Result

a	b	c	d
-----	---	---	-----
a1	b1	c1	1.00
a1	b1	c2	2.00
a1	b2	c1	3.00
a1	b2	c2	4.00
a2	b1	c1	5.00
a2	b1	c2	6.00
a2	b2	c1	7.00
a2	b2	c2	8.00

(8 row(s) affected)

B.7.1.1 Basic ROLLUP Example

We know how to use GROUP BY with aggregate functions to summarize data as in the example below on the left. By adding ROLLUP, shown on the right, the totals are also given for each unique combination of values higher in the GROUP BY hierarchy; that is, totals are added for all a1 and a2.

Notice that when the a column is being summarized (a1 totals and a2 totals), the b column is NULL. So three rows are added to the output: summary for a1, summary for a2 and overall summary.

The CUBE operator provides summary rows above those from GROUP BY and ROLLUP.

SQL

```
SELECT a , b , SUM(d) Sum_d
, AVG(d) Avg_d
FROM data
GROUP BY a, b
ORDER BY a;
```

Result

a	b	Sum_d	Avg_d
a1	b1	3.00	1.500000
a1	b2	7.00	3.500000
a2	b1	11.00	5.500000
a2	b2	15.00	7.500000

(4 row(s) affected)

SQL

```
SELECT a , b , SUM(d) Sum_d ,
      AVG(d) Avg_d
FROM data
GROUP BY a, b   WITH ROLLUP;
```

Result

a	b	Sum_d	Avg_d
a1	b1	3.00	1.500000
a1	b2	7.00	3.500000
a1	NULL	10.00	2.500000
a2	b1	11.00	5.500000
a2	b2	15.00	7.500000
a2	NULL	26.00	6.500000
NULL	NULL	36.00	4.500000

(7 row(s) affected)

By adding the c column we essentially just add each of the eight rows of the underlying table. This may be useful to show everything in one result.

GROUP BY a , b , c with ROLLUP

SQL

```
SELECT   *   FROM   datSELECT a , b , c , SUM(d) Sum_d ,
AVG(d) Avg_d
FROM data
GROUP BY a, b , c    WITH ROLLUP;
```

Result

a	b	c	Sum_d	Avg_d
a1	b1	c1	1.00	1.00
a1	b1	c2	2.00	2.00
a1	b1	NULL	3.00	1.500000 -- Summary Row: a1 b1

Result (cont.)

```
a1      b2      c1      3.00    3.00
a1      b2      c2      4.00    4.00
a1      b2      NULL    7.00    3.500000 -- Summary Row:  a1  b2
a1      NULL    NULL    10.00   2.500000 -- Summary Row:  a1
a2      b1      c1      5.00    5.00
a2      b1      c2      6.00    6.00
a2      b1      NULL    11.00   5.500000 -- Summary Row:  a2  b1
a2      b2      c1      7.00    7.00
a2      b2      c2      8.00    8.00
a2      b2      NULL    15.00   7.500000 -- Summary Row:  a2  b2
a2      NULL    NULL    26.00   6.500000 -- Summary Row:  a2
NULL    NULL    NULL    36.00   4.500000 -- Summary Row:  All

(15 row(s) affected)
```

B.7.2 CUBE

CUBE is used with GROUP BY to find additional sums or aggregates beyond ROLLUP. ROLLUP adds summary rows from right to left on the GROUP BY list. GROUP BY a , b , c WITH ROLLUP yields summaries for (a , b) and (a) values.

CUBE adds summary rows for every combination of the GROUP BY columns. GROUP BY a , b , c WITH CUBE yields summaries for (a , b), (a , c) , (b , c), (a), (b) and (c)

Knowing ROLLUP will be very helpful in understanding CUBE.

GROUP BY without ROLLUP

Note: Distinct aggregates, for example, AVG(DISTINCT *column_name*) and COUNT(DISTINCT *column_name*), are not supported when using CUBE or ROLLUP.

Below are the basic data table and GROUP BY query for reference.

CUBE operator

provides summary rows above those from GROUP BY and ROLLUP

- Groups are summarized by **every combination** of GROUP BY columns

  Note: Order of grouping columns has no effect on the number of rows since a summary row is produced for every combination of GROUP BY column values.

  Example: GROUP BY a , b , c WITH CUBE

  Understanding ROLLUP is very helpful toward understanding CUBE.

  Includes the ROLLUP results: (a , b , c) and (a , b , total c's) and (a, total b's)
  plus every other combination taken 1, 2 and 3 at a time.

  See the examples to make more sense of this

Each GROUP BY summary row is indicated by displaying NULL in the other GROUP BY columns See Examples.

Data table contests.

SQL

```
SELECT  *  FROM  data
```

Result

a	b	c	d
a1	b1	c1	1.00
a1	b1	c2	2.00
a1	b2	c1	3.00
a1	b2	c2	4.00
a2	b1	c1	5.00
a2	b1	c2	6.00
a2	b2	c1	7.00
a2	b2	c2	8.00

(8 row(s) affected)

GROUP BY a , b with ROLLUP

SQL

```
SELECT a , b , SUM(d) Sum_d
, AVG(d) Avg_d
FROM data
GROUP BY a, b
ORDER BY a;
```

Result

a	b	Sum_d	Avg_d
a1	b1	3.00	1.500000
a1	b2	7.00	3.500000
a2	b1	11.00	5.500000
a2	b2	15.00	7.500000

(4 row(s) affected)

B.7.2.1 Basic CUBE Example

ROLLUP using GROUPING

SQL

```
SELECT a , b , SUM(d) Sum_d ,
        AVG(d) Avg_d
FROM data
GROUP BY a, b   WITH ROLLUP;
```

Result

a	b	Sum_d	Avg_d
a1	b1	3.00	1.500000
a1	b2	7.00	3.500000
a1	NULL	10.00	2.500000
a2	b1	11.00	5.500000
a2	b2	15.00	7.500000
a2	NULL	26.00	6.500000
NULL	NULL	36.00	4.500000

(7 row(s) affected)

GROUP BY a , b with CUBE

SQL

```
SELECT a , b , SUM(d) Sum_d ,
AVG(d) Avg_d
FROM data
GROUP BY a, b   WITH CUBE;
```

Result

a	b	Sum_d	Avg_d
a1	b1	3.00	1.500000
a1	b2	7.00	3.500000
a1	NULL	10.00	2.500000
a2	b1	11.00	5.500000
a2	b2	15.00	7.500000
a2	NULL	26.00	6.500000
NULL	NULL	36.00	4.500000
NULL	b1	14.00	3.500000
NULL	b2	22.00	5.500000

(9 row(s) affected)

GROUP BY a , b , c with CUBE

When column c is added, more data rows and summary rows result.

SQL

```
SELECT a , b , c , SUM(d) Sum_d , AVG(d) Avg_d
FROM data
GROUP BY a, b , c   WITH CUBE;
```

SQL (cont.)

Result

```
a       b       c       Sum_d     Avg_d
-----   ----    -----   --------- -----------
a1      b1      c1      1.00      1.000000
a1      b1      c2      2.00      2.000000
a1      b1      NULL    3.00      1.500000 -- Summary Row:  a1  b1
a1      b2      c1      3.00      3.000000
a1      b2      c2      4.00      4.000000
a1      b2      NULL    7.00      3.500000  -- Summary Row:  a1  b2
a1      NULL    NULL    10.00     2.500000  -- Summary Row:  a1
a2      b1      c1      5.00      5.000000
a2      b1      c2      6.00      6.000000
a2      b1      NULL    11.00     5.500000  -- Summary Row:  a2  b1
a2      b2      c1      7.00      7.000000
a2      b2      c2      8.00      8.000000
a2      b2      NULL    15.00     7.500000  -- Summary Row:  a2  b2
a2      NULL    NULL    26.00     6.500000  -- Summary Row:  a2
NULL    NULL    NULL    36.00     4.500000  -- Summary Row:  All
NULL    b1      c1      6.00      3.000000  -- Summary Row:      b1  c1
NULL    b1      c2      8.00      4.000000  -- Summary Row:      b1  c2
NULL    b1      NULL    14.00     3.500000  -- Summary Row:      b1
NULL    b2      c1      10.00     5.000000  -- Summary Row:      b2  c1
NULL    b2      c2      12.00     6.000000  -- Summary Row:      b2  c2
NULL    b2      NULL    22.00     5.500000  -- Summary Row:      b2
a1      NULL    c1      4.00      2.000000  -- Summary Row:  a1      c1
a2      NULL    c1      12.00     6.000000  -- Summary Row:  a2      c1
NULL    NULL    c1      16.00     4.000000  -- Summary Row:          c1
a1      NULL    c2      6.00      3.000000  -- Summary Row:  a1      c2
a2      NULL    c2      14.00     7.000000  -- Summary Row:  a2      c2
NULL    NULL    c2      20.00     5.000000  -- Summary Row:          c2

(27 row(s) affected)
```

B.7.2.2 ROLLUP and CUBE Example with Meaningful Data

Example: Census Data summarized by state and county

Consider the following hierarchically organized data table called `census`.

SQL

```
/* Represents population data by state and county
   "u" means urban, "r" means rural, u + r = total pop */
SELECT  *
FROM census;
```

Result

state	county	urban	pop
CA	Lake	u	13
CA	Lake	r	14
CA	Napa	u	11
CA	Napa	r	12
OR	Grant	u	1
OR	Grant	r	2
OR	Lake	u	3
OR	Lake	r	4

Example: GROUP BY—MSS and ANSI

SQL

```
SELECT state , county , SUM(pop) Population   FROM census
GROUP BY state, county
```

Result

state	county	Population
CA	Lake	27
CA	Napa	23
OR	Grant	3
OR	Lake	7

Example: ROLLUP—MSS and ANSI

SQL

```
SELECT state , county , SUM(pop) Population
FROM census
GROUP BY state, county WITH ROLLUP
    -- ANSI code:  GROUP BY ROLLUP (state, county)
```

Result

```
state    county      Population
-----    ---------   -----------
CA       Lake        27  -- MSS output shown so "NULL" will appear instead of blanks
CA       Napa        23
CA       NULL        50      -- Summary row inserted by ROLLUP, Total of CA
OR       Grant       3
OR       Lake        7
OR       NULL        10      -- Summary row inserted by ROLLUP, Total of OR
NULL     NULL        60      -- Summary row inserted by ROLLUP, Grand Total
```

Example: CUBE—ANSI

SQL

```
SELECT state , county , SUM(pop) Population
FROM census
GROUP BY state, county WITH CUBE
        -- ANSI code: GROUP BY CUBE (state, county);
```

Result

```
state    county      Population
-----    ---------   -----------
CA       Lake        27
CA       Napa        23
CA       NULL        50            -- Total of CA  (same as ROLLUP)
OR       Grant       3
OR       Lake        7
OR       NULL        10            -- Total of OR  (same as ROLLUP)
NULL     NULL        60            -- Grand Total  (same as ROLLUP)
NULL     Grant       3       -- CUBE Summary of all "Grant" values
NULL     Lake        34      -- CUBE Summary of all "Lake" values
NULL     Napa        23      -- CUBE Summary of all "Napa" values
```

CUBE would be useful for analyzing a chain store sales, such as Walmart, by store and by item category and by individual items.

B.7.3 GROUPING Function

With both ROLLUP and CUBE, each GROUP BY summary row is indicated by displaying NULL in the GROUP BY column being summarized.

The `GROUPING` function can be used to determine whether null values in the result set are GROUP BY or are generated by ROLLUP or CUBE to indicate a summary row or NULL values in the actual underlying data.

GROUPING(*columnname*)

returns 1 if a NULL under *columnname* is generated by ROLLUP or CUBE

returns 0 if a NULL under *columnname* is from the underlying data

Here are the same examples with GROUPING: using GROUPING to improve readability.

Example `census` **Table—Repeated for reference**

SQL

```
 /* Displays population data by state and county
   "u" means urban,  "r" means rural,   u */
SELECT *
FROM census;
```

Result

state	county	urban	pop
-----	---------	-----	-----------
CA	Lake	u	13
CA	Lake	r	14
CA	Napa	u	11
CA	Napa	r	12
OR	Grant	u	1
OR	Grant	r	2
OR	Lake	u	3
OR	Lake	r	4

GROUP BY Repeated for Reference

SQL

```
SELECT state , county , SUM(pop) Population   FROM census
GROUP BY state, county
```

Result

```
state      county       Population
-----      ----------   -----------
CA         Lake         27
CA         Napa         23
OR         Grant        3
OR         Lake         7
```

ROLLUP using GROUPING

SQL

```
SELECT
  CASE WHEN GROUPING(state) = 1
    THEN 'All States'
    ELSE ISNULL(county, 'Unknown')  END As state
, CASE WHEN GROUPING(county) = 1
    THEN 'All Counties'
    ELSE ISNULL(county, 'Unknown')  END As county
, SUM(pop) Population
FROM census
GROUP BY state, county WITH ROLLUP;
```

Result

```
state        county         Population
----------   -----------    -----------
CA           Lake           27
CA           Napa           23
CA           All Counties   50
OR           Grant          3
OR           Lake           7
OR           All Counties   10
All States   All Counties   60

(7 row(s) affected)
```

CUBE using GROUPING

SQL

```
SELECT
   CASE WHEN GROUPING(state) = 1
     THEN 'All States'
     ELSE ISNULL(state, 'Unknown')  END As state
,  CASE WHEN GROUPING(county) = 1
     THEN 'All Counties'
     ELSE COALESCE(county, 'Unknown')  END As county
,  SUM(pop) Population
FROM census
GROUP BY state, county WITH CUBE;
```

Result

```
state          county          Population
----------     ------------    -----------
CA             Lake            27
CA             Napa            23
CA             All Counties    50
OR             Grant           3
OR             Lake            7
OR             All Counties    10
All States     All Counties    60
All States     Grant           3
All States     Lake            34
All States     Napa            23

(10 row(s) affected)
```

Another Example: CUBE and ROLLUP
MSS:

SQL

```
SELECT pub_id, type, sum(ytd_sales)
FROM titles
GROUP BY pub_id, type
WITH ROLLUP
```

SQL (cont.)

Result

```
pub_id     type
------     ------------    -----------
0736       business        18722
0736       psychology      9564
0736       NULL            28286        -- Sum for pub_id 0736
0877       mod_cook        24278
0877       psychology      375
0877       trad_cook       19566
0877       UNDECIDED       NULL
0877       NULL            44219        -- Sum for pub_id  0877
1389       business        12066
1389       popular_comp    12875
1389       NULL            24941        -- Sum for pub_id  1389
NULL       NULL            97446        -- Sum for pub_id  NULL

(12 row(s) affected)

Warning: Null value is eliminated from aggregate.
```

Compare and contrast with the following query.
MSS:

SQL

```
SELECT pub_id, type, sum(ytd_sales)
FROM titles
GROUP BY pub_id, type
WITH CUBE
```

Result

```
pub_id     type
------     ------------    -----------
0736       business        18722
0736       psychology       9564
0736       NULL            28286        -- Sum for pub_id 0736
0877       mod_cook        24278
0877       psychology       375
0877       trad_cook       19566
```

Result (cont.)

```
0877      UNDECIDED      NULL0
0877      NULL           44219       -- Sum for pub_id  0877
1389      business       12066
1389      popular_comp   12875
1389      NULL           24941       -- Sum for pub_id  1389
NULL      NULL           97446       -- Sum for pub_id  NULL
NULL      business       3078        -- Sum for type business
NULL      mod_cook       24278       -- Sum for type mod_cook
NULL      popular_comp   12875       -- Sum for type popular_comp
NULL      psychology      9939       -- Sum for type psychology
NULL      trad_cook      19566       -- Sum for type trad_cook
NULL      UNDECIDED   NULL           -- Sum for type NULL

(18 row(s) affected)
```

B.7.4 Subquery Exercises—Solutions

Use Table B-26 for reference in these exercises.

Table B-26

c1	c2	c3	c4
a	5	1	10
a	2	4	6
a	7	7	8
b	4	20	50
b	4	15	20
b	2	0	0
c	1	1	1
c	NULL	NULL	NULL

Do some queries for sales history analysis.

Query 1 Solution: Create a histogram summing c2 for each c1 value.

SQL

```
SELECT DISTINCT C1 , -- Query 1 ,  A Correct Solution for MSS
   ( SELECT SUM(c2) FROM t1 b WHERE b.c1 = a.c1 ) C2_SumByC1
FROM t1 a;
```

Result

```
C1          C2_SumByC1
----        -------------------
a           14
b           10
c            1
```

Query 2 Solution:

Create a cumulative histogram over time, showing c1 and accumulating c2.

SQL

```
SELECT DISTINCT C1 , -- Query 2 ,  A Correct Solution for MSS
   ( SELECT SUM(c2) FROM t1 b WHERE b.c1 <= a.c1 ) C2_Cum
FROM t1 a;
```

Result

```
C1          C2_Cum
----        -------------------
a           14
b           24
c           25
```

Query 3 Solution:

Do the modified Pivot on c1 as shown. (This does not require a subquery.)

SQL

```
SELECT C2 , C3 , C4
   , CASE WHEN C1 = 'a' THEN 1 ELSE 0 END a
   , CASE WHEN C1 = 'b' THEN 1 ELSE 0 END b
   , CASE WHEN C1 = 'c' THEN 1 ELSE 0 END c
FROM t1
```

SQL (cont.)

Result

```
C2    C3    C4    a     b     c
----  ----  ----  ----- ----- ------
5     1     10    1     0     0
2     4     6     1     0     0
7     7     8     1     0     0
4     20    50    0     1     0
4     15    20    0     1     0
2     0     0     0     1     0
1     1     1     0     0     1
NULL  NULL  NULL  0     0     1

(8 row(s) affected)
```

Note: This could be the correct solution if that's what the customer wanted. In this case, the customer wanted a duplicate of the maximum value to show up as top and top next.

Pivot Exercise: Query 4 Solution:

Pivot table t1 on c1 to summarize the values of each of the other columns.

SQL

```
SELECT c1 ,
  ( SELECT SUM(c2) FROM t1 y WHERE y.c1 = x.c1   ) c2,
  ( SELECT SUM(c3) FROM t1 y WHERE y.c1 = x.c1 ) c3 ,
  ( SELECT SUM(c4) FROM t1 y WHERE y.c1 = x.c1   ) c4
FROM t1 x
GROUP BY x.c1
```

Result

```
c1    c2      c3     c4
----  ------  -----  -----
a     14      12     24
b     10      35     70
c      1       1      1
```

Query 5 Solutions: Write a query to retrieve the top two c2 values for each c1.

Modified Table **t**1: Has `id` column as Primary Key.

Result

id	c1	c2	c3	c4
----	----	----	----	----
1	a	5	1	10
2	a	2	4	6
3	a	7	7	8
4	b	4	20	50
5	b	4	15	20
6	b	2	0	0
7	c	1	1	1
8	c	NULL	NULL	NULL

Desired Result for this data:

```
c1     c2_Max c2_MaxNext    -- MaxNext is next value <= Max
----   ------ ----------
a      7      5
b      4      4
c      1      NULL
```

MSS solution to Query 5: Most correct but not portable approach.

A subquery to find the MAX(c2) for a given c1 is straightforward.

The subquery to find c2_MaxNext takes some work as described here.

- Subquery with ORDER BY c2 DESC lists largest to smallest values of c2 for each c1.
- Used with MSSs Top 2 feature, it returns only the first two result set rows.
- Then ORDER BY c2 ASC with Top 1 fetches the second largest value of c2.

SQL

```
SELECT DISTINCT c1
-- Query 5 - a correct, non-portable solution
-- for MSS
   , (  SELECT MAX(c2) FROM t1 WHERE c1 = t.c1 ) C2_Max
   , (  SELECT top 1 c2
      FROM ( SELECT TOP 2 c2 FROM t1 x
```

SQL (cont.)

```
    WHERE x.c1 = t.c1
    ORDER BY c2 DESC )   y
      ORDER BY c2
    ) C2_MaxNext
FROM t1 t
ORDER BY c1;
```

Result

Same as desired result above.

Query 6 Solutions: Write a query to retrieve the top two C2 values for each C1.

Same problem as Query 5, BUT NO PRIMARY KEY.

Table t1 (for reference)

c1	c2	c3	c4
a	5	1	10
a	2	4	6
a	7	7	8
b	4	20	50
b	4	15	20
b	2	0	0
c	1	1	1
c	NULL	NULL	NULL

Desired Result for this data:

c1	C2_Max	C2_MaxNext
a	7	5
b	4	4
c	1	NULL

MSS solution 1 to Query 6: Most correct but not portable approach.

A subquery to find the MAX(c2) for a given c1 is straightforward.

The subquery to find c2_MaxNext takes some work as described here.

- The subquery with ORDER BY c2 DESC lists largest to smallest values of c2 for each c1.

- It is used with MSSs Top 2 feature, it returns only the first two result set rows.
- Then ORDER BY c2 ASC with Top 1 fetches the second largest value of c2.

SQL

```
/* Query 6 - a correct non-portable MSS solution */
SELECT DISTINCT  c1
   , (  SELECT MAX(c2) FROM t1 WHERE c1 = t.c1 ) C2_Max
   , (  SELECT top 1 c2
      FROM ( SELECT TOP 2 c2 FROM t1 x
             WHERE x.c1 = t.c1 ORDER BY c2 DESC )  y
      ORDER BY c2
     ) C2_MaxNext
FROM t1 t
ORDER BY c1;
```

Result

Same as desired result above.

Query 6 Solution 2: Perhaps a less desirable approach.

SQL

```
SELECT DISTINCT C1 ,       -- Query 6 Solution 2 ,   Step 1
   ( SELECT MAX (c2) FROM t1 x  WHERE x.c1=t.c1) C2_Max ,
   ( SELECT MAX(c2)  FROM t1 y  WHERE y.c1 = t.c1
      AND  y.c2 < ( SELECT MAX (c2) FROM t1 x WHERE x.c1=t.c1)
    ) C2_MaxLess
FROM t1 t;
```

Result

```
C1     C2_Max    C2_MaxLess
----   ------    ----------
a      7         5
b      4         2  -- Incorrect solution, doesn t notice that top two values are same
c      1         NULL
```

Note: This could be the correct solution if that's what the customer wanted.

In this case, the customer wanted a duplicate of the maximum value to show up as top and top next.

SQL

```
SELECT DISTINCT c1 ,      -- Query 6 MSS Solution 2 ,   Step 2
   ( SELECT MAX(c2) FROM t1 x WHERE x.c1 = t.c1) C2_Max ,
   ( SELECT MAX(c2) FROM t1 y WHERE y.c1 = t.c1
      AND y.c2  < ( SELECT MAX(c2)
                    FROM t1 z
                    WHERE z.c1 =  t.c1 ) )  C2_MaxLess ,
   ( SELECT count(*)
     FROM ( SELECT c2 FROM t1 f
            WHERE f.c1 =  t.c1
            AND f.c2 = ( SELECT MAX(c2) FROM t1 g WHERE g.c1 =  t.c1 )
           ) h
    ) Num_at_Max
FROM t1 t;
```

Result

c1	C2_Max	C2_MaxLess	Num_at_Max
----	------	----------	-----------
a	7	5	1
b	4	2	2
c	1	NULL	1

SQL

```
SELECT c1 , C2_Max ,       -- Query 6 MSS Solution 2 ,   Final Version
     (CASE WHEN Num_at_Max > 1 THEN C2_Max ELSE C2_MaxLess END) C2_MaxNext
FROM
    ( SELECT DISTINCT c1 ,
      ( SELECT MAX(c2) FROM t1 x WHERE x.c1 = t.c1) C2_Max,
      ( SELECT MAX(c2) FROM t1 y WHERE y.c1 = t.c1
                AND y.c2  < ( SELECT MAX(c2)
                        FROM t1 z
                        WHERE z.c1 =  t.c1 ) )  C2_MaxLess ,
      ( SELECT count(*)
         FROM ( SELECT c2 FROM t1 f
         WHERE f.c1 =  t.c1
         AND f.c2 = ( SELECT MAX(c2) FROM t1 g WHERE g.c1 =  t.c1 )  ) h
         ) Num_at_Max
    FROM t1 t   ) g
```

Result

c1	C2_Max	C2_MaxNext
----	------	----------
a	7	5
b	4	4
c	1	NULL

Bibliography

ANSI/ISO/IEC 9075-1-1999 through ANSI/ISO/IEC 9075-5-1999. New York: American National Standards Institute, Inc., 1999.

Ben-Gan, Itzik, et al. *Advanced Transact-SQL for SQL Server* 2000. Berkeley, CA: APress, 2000. ISBN: 1-893115-82-8.

Celko, Joe. *SQL For Smarties: Advanced SQL Programming,* 2d ed. San Francisco: Morgan Kaufmann, 2000. ISBN: 1-55860-576-2.

Groff, James R. and Paul N. Weinberg. *SQL: The Complete Reference.* Berkeley, CA: Osborne/ McGraw-Hill, 1999. ISBN: 0-07-211845-8

Gulutzan, Peter and Trudy Pelzer. *SQL-99 Complete, Really.* San Francisco: Miller Freeman, 1999. ISBN: 0-87930-568-1.

Harrison, Guy. *Oracle Desk Reference.* Upper Saddle River, NJ: Prentice Hall, 2000. ISBN 0-13-013294-2.

Henderson, Ken. *The Guru's Guide to SQL Server Stored Procedures, XML, and HTML.* Boston: Addison-Wesley, 2002. ISBN: 0-201-70046-8

Malcolm, Graeme. *Programming Microsoft SQL Server 2000 with XML,* 2d ed., Redmond, WA: Microsoft Press, 2002. ISBN: 0-7356-1774-0.

Melton, Jim and Alan Simon. *Understanding the New SQL: A Complete Guide.* San Francisco, CA: Morgan Kaufmann Publishers, 1993. ISBN: 1-55860-245-3.

Microsoft Corporation, Microsoft SQL Server 2000 Books Online, 1988–2002. Online documentation included with SQL Server 2000, updated to 2002.

Patrick, John. *SQL Fundamentals.* Upper Saddle River, NJ: Prentice Hall, 1999. ISBN: 0-13-096016-0.

Reilly, Michael, et al. *SQL Server 2000 Design & T-SQL Programming.* New York: McGraw-Hill, 2000. ISBN: 0-07-212375-3.

Shapiro, Jeffrey *SQL Server 2000: The Complete Reference with SQL Server 2000 Developer's Guide.* New York: McGraw-Hill, 2000. ISBN: 0-07-212588-8.

Vieira, Robert. *Professional SQL Server 2000 Programming.* Chicago: Wrox Press Inc., 2000. ISBN: 1-861004-48-6.

INDEX

Symbols

A

E

G

H

I

J

K

L

N

O

S

U

V

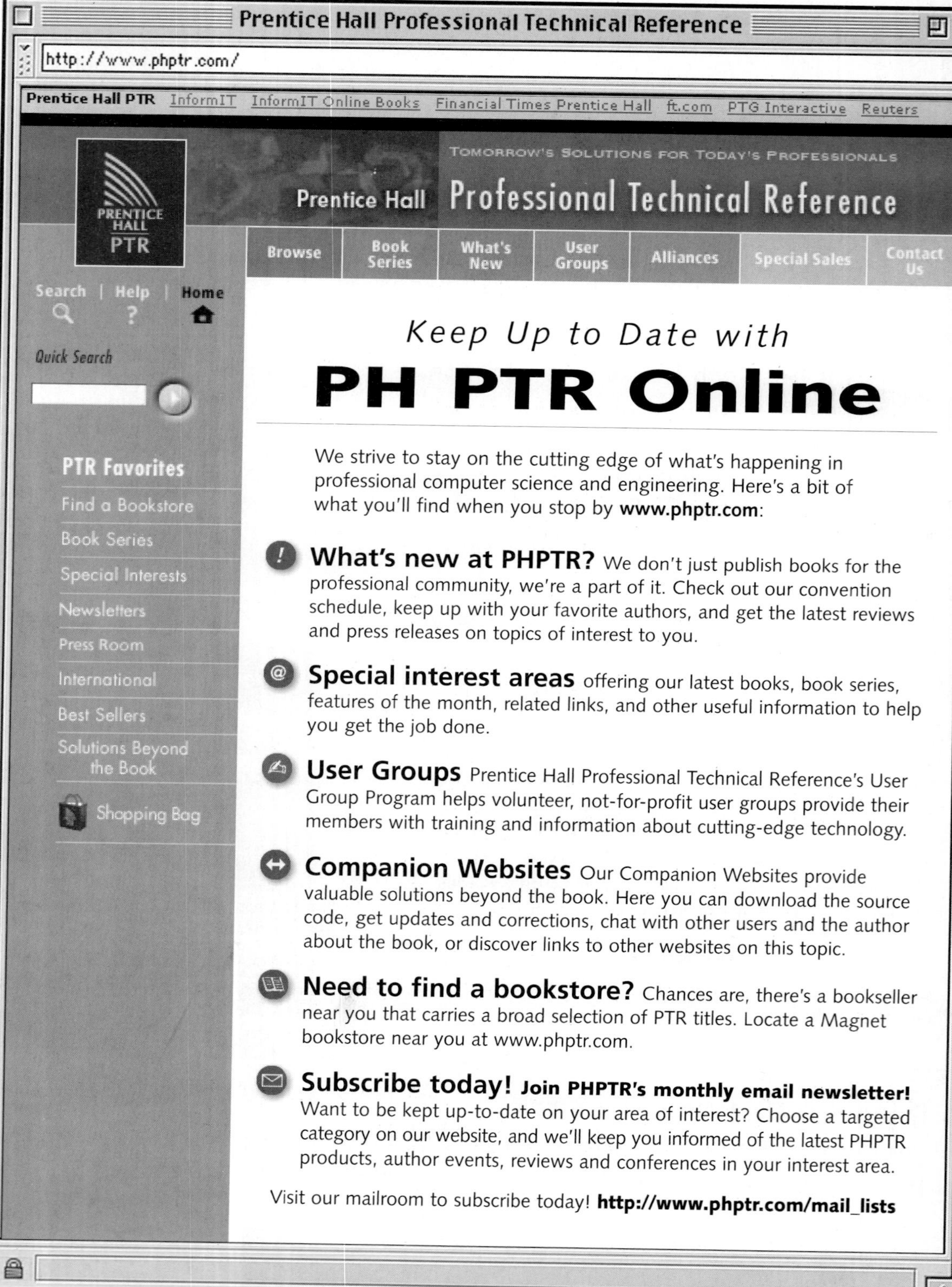
Prentice Hall Professional Technical Reference
http://www.phptr.com/
Prentice Hall PTR
InformIT
InformIT Online Books
Financial Times Prentice Hall
ft.com
PTG Interactive
Reuters
PRENTICE HALL PTR
TOMORROW'S SOLUTIONS FOR TODAY'S PROFESSIONALS
Prentice Hall Professional Technical Reference
Browse
Book Series
What's New
User Groups
Alliances
Special Sales
Contact Us
Search | Help | Home
Quick Search
PTR Favorites
Find a Bookstore
Book Series
Special Interests
Newsletters
Press Room
International
Best Sellers
Solutions Beyond the Book
Shopping Bag
Keep Up to Date with
PH PTR Online
We strive to stay on the cutting edge of what's happening in professional computer science and engineering. Here's a bit of what you'll find when you stop by www.phptr.com:
What's new at PHPTR? We don't just publish books for the professional community, we're a part of it. Check out our convention schedule, keep up with your favorite authors, and get the latest reviews and press releases on topics of interest to you.
Special interest areas offering our latest books, book series, features of the month, related links, and other useful information to help you get the job done.
User Groups Prentice Hall Professional Technical Reference's User Group Program helps volunteer, not-for-profit user groups provide their members with training and information about cutting-edge technology.
Companion Websites Our Companion Websites provide valuable solutions beyond the book. Here you can download the source code, get updates and corrections, chat with other users and the author about the book, or discover links to other websites on this topic.
Need to find a bookstore? Chances are, there's a bookseller near you that carries a broad selection of PTR titles. Locate a Magnet bookstore near you at www.phptr.com.
Subscribe today! Join PHPTR's monthly email newsletter! Want to be kept up-to-date on your area of interest? Choose a targeted category on our website, and we'll keep you informed of the latest PHPTR products, author events, reviews and conferences in your interest area.
Visit our mailroom to subscribe today! http://www.phptr.com/mail_lists